STUDIES IN CHRISTIAN HISTORY AND THOUGHT

Infant Baptism in Historical Perspective

Collected Studies

STUDIES IN CHRISTIAN HISTORY AND THOUGHT

Commendations

'Professor David Wright has done a tremendous service to both the academy and the Church with this truly impressive volume of essays probing the history and theology of infant baptism from the New Testament to the present day. In its erudition, independence of judgment, and challenging relevance for today, this is an indispensable resource.'
Timothy Bradshaw, Senior Tutor, Regent's Park College, and a member of the Oxford Faculty of Theology

'In these essays, Professor Wright brings his prodigious knowledge of Church history and historical theology to bear on a vital theme for the Christian faith. He traces, with clarity and insight, both the Church's understanding of baptism through the centuries and the continuing debates.'
Stewart J. Brown, Professor of Ecclesiastical History, University of Edinburgh

'Karl Barth once compared infant baptism to the Cathedral of Cologne, an ecclesiastical landmark that has survived many battles and is still standing. Despite its perdurance across the centuries, the practice of infant baptism remains both ecumenically sensitive and theologically controversial. I know of no scholar who has pursued this issue with greater depth or care than David F. Wright. This well-developed volume of essays contains the fruit of his many labours on this topic and will, I predict, become a standard resource for scholarly work on the history and meaning of infant baptism in the future.'
Timothy George, Dean of Beeson Divinity School of Samford University, and executive editor of Christianity Today

'This is an outstanding and eminently coherent collection of studies on aspects of baptismal theologies and practices spanning the Christian era. They help restore the topic to a high place on the theological agenda—all with a characteristic spirit of catholicity, evangelical concern, scholarly expertise, and literary finesse.'
Ian Hazlett, Professor of Ecclesiastical History, University of Glasgow

'Over the last twenty-plus years David Wright has produced a series of important studies on baptism in general and infant baptism in particular. These have been scattered around many different publications and this collected volume performs a valuable task in bringing them together. There is much learned historical scholarship here illuminating the history of the practice. There is also much wise reflection on the pastoral implications of the practice for the church then and now. No one with a serious interest in the doctrine of baptism can afford to neglect this volume.'
Anthony N.S. Lane, Director of Research and Professor of Historical Theology, London School of Theology

STUDIES IN CHRISTIAN HISTORY AND THOUGHT

'The sub-title for David Wright's book—*Collected Studies*—is altogether too modest for the wealth of scriptural, historical, and pastoral material contained in these pages. Wright's penetrating historical vision is combined with persuasive arguments for the unduly neglected, but critical importance of baptism for the whole church. The result is a book that challenges both received traditions and current practices, but in the most edifying way imaginable.'
Mark A. Noll, McAnaney Professor of History, University of Notre Dame

'An invaluable resource for the history and understanding of infant baptism in the Church from the New Testament to the present day.'
David M. Thompson, Fellow of Fitzwilliam College, and Reader in Modern Church History, University of Cambridge

'In a collection of his essays that spans twenty years of research and twenty centuries of history, David Wright guides readers through the convoluted story of how the Christian church has interpreted and reinterpreted the sacrament of baptism, particularly as applied to infants and children. The overlap among these essays is very small, and their serial effect is a steady accumulation of curiosity, as a chain of mysteries and inconsistencies in the theology and practice of baptism is investigated one link at a time. Wright's expertise in patristic, reformation, and ecumenical theology comes to full fruition here, yielding an invaluable resource for reflection among historians, theologians, exegetes, and church leaders. *Infant Baptism in Historical Perspective* will awaken and reinvigorate our consideration of crucial questions of faith, mission, and Christian self-understanding in a post-Christendom world—and do so by addressing matters of substance and consequence in a discussion more marked by tiresome polemics and a superficial grasp of the past. The essays thus bring belated but welcome nuance to a controversial topic. David Wright has bequeathed a sterling example of how historical theology can and must inform systematics and practical theology today.'
John L. Thompson, Professor of Historical Theology and Gaylen and Susan Byker Professor of Reformed Theology, Fuller Theological Seminary

STUDIES IN CHRISTIAN HISTORY AND THOUGHT

A full listing of all titles in this series
appears at the close of this book

STUDIES IN CHRISTIAN HISTORY AND THOUGHT

Infant Baptism in Historical Perspective

Collected Studies

David F. Wright

MILTON KEYNES · COLORADO SPRINGS · HYDERABAD

Copyright © David F. Wright 2007

First published 2007 by Paternoster

Paternoster is an imprint of Authentic Media
9 Holdom Avenue, Bletchley, Milton Keynes, Bucks, MK1 1QR
1820 Jet Stream Drive, Colorado Springs, CO 80921, USA
OM Authentic Media, Medchal Road, Jeedimetla Village,
Secunderabad 500 055, A.P., India
www.authenticmedia.co.uk
Authentic Media is a division of IBS-STL UK, a company limited by guarantee
(registered charity no. 270162)

13 12 11 10 09 08 07   7 6 5 4 3 2 1

The right of David F. Wright to be identified as the Author of this Work
has been asserted by him in accordance with the Copyright, Designs
and Patents Act 1988

All rights reserved. No part of this publication may be reproduced, stored in a retrieval system, or transmitted in any form by any means, electronic, mechanical, photocopying, recording or otherwise, without the prior permission of the publisher or a license permitting restricted copying. In the UK such licenses are issued by the Copyright Licensing Agency, 90 Tottenham Court Road, London W1P 9HE.

British Library Cataloguing in Publication Data
A catalogue record for this book is available from the British Library

ISBN 978-1-84227-464-4

Typeset by A.R. Cross
Printed and bound in Great Britain
for Paternoster
by Nottingham Alphagraphics

STUDIES IN CHRISTIAN HISTORY AND THOUGHT

Series Preface

This series complements the specialist series of *Studies in Evangelical History and Thought* and *Studies in Baptist History and Thought* for which Paternoster is becoming increasingly well known by offering works that cover the wider field of Christian history and thought. It encompasses accounts of Christian witness at various periods, studies of individual Christians and movements, and works which concern the relations of church and society through history, and the history of Christian thought.

The series includes monographs, revised dissertations and theses, and collections of papers by individuals and groups. As well as 'free standing' volumes, works on particular running themes are being commissioned; authors will be engaged for these from around the world and from a variety of Christian traditions.

A high academic standard combined with lively writing will commend the volumes in this series both to scholars and to a wider readership.

Series Editors

Alan P.F. Sell, Visiting Professor at Acadia University Divinity College, Nova Scotia, Canada

David Bebbington, Professor of History, University of Stirling, Stirling, Scotland, UK

Clyde Binfield, Professor Associate in History, University of Sheffield, UK

Gerald Bray, Anglican Professor of Divinity, Beeson Divinity School, Samford University, Birmingham, Alabama, USA

Grayson Carter, Associate Professor of Church History, Fuller Theological Seminary SW, Phoenix, Arizona, USA

*To
Anne-Marie
uxori meae fidelissimae, iamiam complementi
annum quadragesimum coniugii nostri—Deo gratias*

Contents

Acknowledgements xv

Preface xix

Abbreviations xxi

Introduction: The Strange History of Infant Baptism,
Not Least in Scotland xxiii

PART A: THE EARLY CENTURIES: SLOW DEVELOPMENT 1

Chapter 1
The Origins of Infant Baptism—Child Believers' Baptism? 3

Chapter 2
How Controversial Was the Development of Infant Baptism
in the Early Church? 22

Chapter 3
The Apostolic Fathers and Infant Baptism: Any Advance
on the Obscurity of the New Testament? 44

Chapter 4
The Meaning and Reference of 'One Baptism for the Remission
of Sins' in the Niceno-Constantinopolitan Creed 55

Chapter 5
At What Ages Were People Baptized in the Early Centuries? 61

Chapter 6
Augustine and the Transformation of Baptism 68

Chapter 7
Monnica's Baptism, Augustine's Deferred Baptism, and
Patricius 89

Chapter 8
Donatist Theologoumena in Augustine? Baptism, Reviviscence
of Sins, and Unworthy Ministers 105

Chapter 9
Infant Dedication in the Early Church 116

Chapter 10
The Baptism(s) of Julian the Apostate Revisited 139

PART B: THE REFORMATION ERA: SCRIPTURE AND THE APPEAL TO THE FATHERS 147

Chapter 11
Out, In, Out: Jesus' Blessing of the Children and
Infant Baptism 149

Chapter 12
Infant Baptism and the Christian Community in Bucer 166

Chapter 13
George Cassander and the Appeal to the Fathers in
Sixteenth-Century Debates about Infant Baptism 179

Chapter 14
1 Corinthians 7:14 in Fathers and Reformers 192

Chapter 15
The Donatists in the Sixteenth Century 212

Chapter 16
Development and Coherence in Calvin's *Institutes*: The Case
of Baptism (*Institutes* 4:15–4:16) 226

Chapter 17
Baptism at the Westminster Assembly 238

PART C: TOWARDS A MODERN CONSENSUS 257

Chapter 18
The Baptismal Community 259

Chapter 19
One Baptism or Two? Reflections on the History of
Christian Baptism 268

Chapter 20
Scripture and Evangelical Diversity with Special Reference to
the Baptismal Divide 285

Chapter 21
Baptism in Scotland 301

Chapter 22
Baptism, Eucharist and Ministry (the 'Lima Report'):
An Evangelical Assessment 308

Chapter 23
The Lima Report: *Baptism* and *Eucharist* Compared 327

Chapter 24
Habitats of Infant Baptism 334

Chapter 25
Children, Covenant and the Church 344

Chapter 26
Recovering Baptism for a New Age of Mission 362

Chapter 27
Christian Baptism: Where Do We Go From Here? 377

Scripture Index 385

Name Index 387

Subject Index 397

Acknowledgements

The author and publisher are grateful to those named for permission to reprint the following papers:

Chapter 1, 'The Origins of Infant Baptism—Child Believers' Baptism?', *Scottish Journal of Theology* 40 (1987), pp. 1-23: Dr Iain Torrance, Editor of the *Scottish Journal of Theology*.

Chapter 2, 'How Controversial Was the Development of Infant Baptism in the Early Church?', in James E. Bradley and Richard A. Muller (eds), *Church, Word and Spirit: Historical and Theological Essays in Honor of Geoffrey W. Bromiley* (Grand Rapids, MI: Eerdmans, 1987), pp. 45-63; chapter 20, 'Scripture and Evangelical Diversity with Special Reference to the Baptismal Divide', Philip E. Satterthwaite and David F. Wright (eds), *A Pathway into the Holy Scripture* (Grand Rapids, MI: Eerdmans, 1994), pp. 257-75; and chapter 24, 'Habitats of Infant Baptism', in Wallace M. Alston (ed.), *Theology in the Service of the Church: Essays in Honor of Thomas W. Gillespie* (Grand Rapids, MI: Eerdmans, 2000), pp. 254-265: Wm. B. Eerdmans Publishing Co., Grand Rapids, MI.

Chapter 3, 'The Apostolic Fathers and Infant Baptism: Any Advance on the Obscurity of the New Testament?', in A.F. Gregory and C.M. Tuckett (eds), *Trajectories through the New Testament and the Apostolic Fathers* (Oxford: Oxford University Press, 2005), pp. 123-33: Oxford University Press.

Chapter 4, 'The Meaning and Reference of "One Baptism for the Remission of Sins" in the Niceno-Constantinopolitan Creed', *Studia Patristica* 19 (1989), pp. 281-85; chapter 5, 'At What Ages Were People Baptized in the Early Centuries?', *Studia Patristica* 30 (1997), pp. 389-94; chapter 10, 'The Baptism(s) of Julian the Apostate Revisited' (Fourteenth International Conference on Patristic Studies), *Studia Patristica* (2007), forthcoming: Peeters Publishers, Leuven.

Chapter 6, 'Augustine and the Transformation of Baptism', in A. Kreider (ed.), *The Origins of Christendom in the West* (Edinburgh: T&T Clark, 2001), pp. 287-310: Dr Alan Kreider, Editor of *The Origins of Christendom*.

Chapter 7, 'Monnica's Baptism, Augustine's Deferred Baptism, and Patricius', *Augustinian Studies* 29.2 (1998), pp. 1-17: Dr Allan Fitzgerald, Editor of *Augustinian Studies*.

Chapter 8, 'Donatist Theologoumena in Augustine? Baptism, Reviviscence of Sins and Unworthy Ministers', in *Congresso Internationale su S. Agostino nel XVI Centenario della Conversione. Atti II* (Studia Ephemerides 'Augustinianum', 25; Rome: Institutum Patristicum 'Augustinianum', 1987), pp. 213-24: Dr Angelo Di Berardino, Augustinianum Istituto Patristico, Rome.

Chapter 9, 'Infant Dedication in the Early Church', in S.E. Porter and A.R. Cross (eds), *Baptism, the New Testament and the Church: Historical and Contemporary Studies in Honour of R.E.O. White* (*Journal of the Study of the New Testament*, Supplement Series, 171; Sheffield: Sheffield Academic Press, 1999), pp. 352-78; and chapter 11, 'Out, In, Out: Jesus' Blessing of the Children and Infant Baptism', in S.E. Porter and A.R. Cross (eds), *Dimensions of Baptism: Biblical and Theological Studies* (*Journal for the Study of the New Testament*, Supplement Series, 234; Sheffield: Sheffield Academic Press, 2002), pp. 188-206: Continuum International Publishing Group Ltd, London.

Chapter 12, 'Infant Baptism and the Christian Community in Bucer', in David F. Wright (ed.), *Martin Bucer: Reforming Church and Community* (Cambridge: Cambridge University Press, 1994), pp. 95-106: Cambridge University Press.

Chapter 13, 'George Cassander and the Appeal to the Fathers in Sixteenth-Century Debates about Infant Baptism', in L. Grane, A. Schindler and M. Wriedt (eds), *Auctoritas Patrum. Contributions on the Reception of the Church Fathers in the 15th and 16th Century* (Veröffentlichungen des Instituts für Europäische Geschichte Mainz, Abteilung Religionsgeschichte, 37; Mainz: Philipp von Zabern, 1993), pp. 259-269; and chapter 15, 'The Donatists in the Sixteenth Century', in L. Grane, A. Schindler and M. Wriedt (eds), *Auctoritas Patrum II. New Contributions on the Reception of the Church Fathers in the 15th and 16th Centuries* (Veröffentlichungen des Instituts für Europäische Geschichte Mainz, Abteilung abendländische Religionsgeschichte 44; Mainz: Philipp von Zabern, 1998), pp. 281-293: Institut für Europäische Geschichte Mainz, and Verlag Philipp von Zabern, Mainz.

Chapter 14, '1 Corinthians 7:14 in Fathers and Reformers', in D.C. Steinmetz (ed.), *Die Patristik in der Bibelexegese des 16. Jahrhunderts* (Wolfenbütteler Forschungen, Band 85; Wiesbaden: Harrasowitz, 1999), pp. 93-113: Herzog August Bibliothek, Wolfenbüttel.

Chapter 16, 'Development and Coherence in Calvin's *Institutes*: The Case of Baptism (*Institutes* 4:15-4:16)', in M. Holt (ed.), *Adaptations of Calvinism in Reformation Europe: Essays in Honour of Brian G. Armstrong* (Aldershot: Ashgate, 2007), forthcoming: Ashgate Publishing Ltd, Aldershot.

Chapter 17, 'Baptism at the Westminster Assembly', in J.H. Leith (ed.), *The Westminster Confession in Current Thought* (Calvin Studies, 8; Davidson, NC: Davidson College, 1996), pp. 76-90. Reprinted in J. Ligon Duncan (ed.), *The Westminster Confession into the 21st Century*, Vol. 1 (Fearn, Ross-shire: Christian Focus Publications, 2003), pp. 161-85: The late Revd Professor John H. Leith, Richmond, VA.

Introduction

Chapter 18, 'The Baptismal Community', *Bibliotheca Sacra* 160 (2003), pp. 3-12: Dr Roy B. Zuck, Editor of *Bibliotheca Sacra*, Dallas, TX.

Chapter 19, 'One Baptism or Two? Reflections on the History of Christian Baptism', *Vox Evangelica* 18 (1988), pp. 7-23: London School of Theology (formerly London Bible College).

Chapter 21, 'Baptism in Scotland', in Nigel de S. Cameron *et al.* (eds), *Dictionary of Scottish Church History and Theology* (Edinburgh: T&T Clark, 1993), pp. 57-58: T&T Clark, Edinburgh.

Chapter 22, *Baptism, Eucharist & Ministry (the 'Lima Report'): An Evangelical Assessment* (Rutherford Forum Papers, 3; Edinburgh: Rutherford House, 1984): Rutherford House, Edinburgh.

Chapter 23, 'The Lima Report: *Baptism* and *Eucharist* Compared', *Theology* 87 (1984), pp. 330-36.

Chapter 25, 'Children, Covenant and the Church', *Themelios* 29.2 (Spring, 2004), pp. 26-39: The Editors of *Themelios*, Religious and Theological Studies Fellowship, Leicester.

Chapter 26, 'Recovering Baptism for a New Age of Mission', in Donald Lewis and Alister McGrath (eds), *Doing Theology for the People of God: Studies in Honor of J.I. Packer* (Downers Grove, IL: Inter-Varsity Press, 1996), pp. 51-66: Inter-Varsity Press, Leicester, and InterVarsity Press, Downers Grove, IL.

Chapter 27, 'Christian Baptism: Where Do We Go From Here?', *Evangelical Quarterly* 78 (2006), pp. 163-69: The Editors of the *Evangelical Quarterly*, and Paternoster, Milton Keynes.

Preface

The standard disclaimer, that as author of this book I have contracted so many debts of gratitude that any attempt to name them all would inevitably fall some way short of exhaustiveness and so were honourably best avoided, seems inescapable for a collection of essays spanning a quarter of a century. For each was originally separately conceived and executed, and behind each severally stands its own particular nexus of collaboration and mutual stimulus. Yet it would be churlish in the extreme to fail to pay tribute to the many collegial relationships, conferences, study circles and special occasions through which most of these pieces first saw the light of day. The four-yearly International Patristic Conferences at Oxford, the annual Christian Doctrine Study Group (at Cambridge) and triennial plenary conference (at Nantwich) of the Tyndale Fellowship for Biblical and Theological Research, the biennial Colloquium on Calvin Studies at Davidson College, North Carolina, presided over by the late John Leith, the privileged sabbatical resort of the Center of Theological Inquiry at Princeton and the series of workshops on the reception of the Church Fathers in the fifteenth and sixteenth centuries initiated by the late Leif Grane and by Alfred Schindler at Rolighed near Copenhagen all witnessed the origin of one or more of these papers. Others emanated from one-off occasions—a conference at Rome, marking the 1600th anniversary of Augustine's conversion, a round-table meeting of minds on the origins of Christendom convened by Alan Kreider at Paris as part of the Missiology of Western Culture Project, a conference organized at my old college, Lincoln College, Oxford, by Andrew Gregory to commemorate the 1905 publication of *The New Testament in the Apostolic Fathers*, and an Arbeitsgespräch on the patristic contribution to sixteenth-century biblical exegesis led by David Steinmetz in the handsome Herzog August Bibliothek in Wolfenbüttel. Some of these chapters were written to honour senior colleagues—Tom Gillespie of Princeton, Jim Packer of Vancouver, Geoffrey Bromiley of Pasadena, Brian Armstrong of Atlanta and R.E.O White of Glasgow. One marked the quincentenary of the birth of Martin Bucer, another was delivered at the London School of Theology (then London Bible College) to preserve the name of John Laing, outstanding Christian layman and benefactor. Behind all of them lie invaluable interactions with colleagues, fellow-researchers and hearers, indubitably too many to remember and name.

I owe a special word of thanks to my fellow Ecclesiastical Historians over nearly forty years in New College, University of Edinburgh—the late Alec Cheyne, Andrew Ross, Peter Matheson, Jay Brown and Jane Dawson—and indeed to colleagues in other disciplines within and beyond the Faculty of Divinity and in other institutions who likewise in various ways have enlarged my horizons, enriched my knowledge and corrected and sharpened my understanding. I salute the noble army of librarians, innumerous libraries but especially New College, Library, Edinburgh, where their service is always cheerful, and sometimes well beyond the call of duty. No one has been a more diligent fellow traveller with me in the quest for a fuller and truer history of baptism than Tony Lane. It is a huge pleasure to acknowledge all I owe to his stimulus and encouragement over many years. Finally, for his enormous and ever-cheerful labours in bringing this volume to completion, I remain deeply indebted to Anthony R. Cross.

Abbreviations

ANCL	*Ante-Nicene Christian Library* (25 vols; Edinburgh, 1864–97)
ARCIC	Anglican-Roman Catholic International Commission
AugLex	C. Mayer (ed.), *Augustinus-Lexikon* (Basel, 1986–)
BA	*Bibliothèque Augustinienne* (Oeuvres de Saint Augustin; Paris, 1949–)
BDS	*Martini Buceri Opera Omnia*, series I: *Deutsche Schriften* (Gütersloh and Paris, 1960–)
BOL	*Martini Buceri Opera Omnia*, series II: *Opera Latina* (Paris, Gütersloh, Leiden, 1955–)
BCor	*Martini Buceri Opera Omnia*, series III: *Correspondence* (Leiden, 1979–)
BEM	*Baptism, Eucharist and Ministry* (Faith and Order Paper, 111; Geneva, 1982)
CD	Karl Barth, *Church Dogmatics* (4 vols in 14; Edinburgh, 1956–75)
CCSL	*Corpus Christianorum, Series Latina* (Turnhout, 1953–)
CO	*Joannis Calvini Opera quae extant Omnia*, eds. G. Baum, E. Cunitz, E. Reuss (59 vols [= *CR* vols 29-87]; Brunswick, 1863–1900)
CPL	E. Dekkers (ed.), *Clavis Patrum Latinorum* (Steenbrugis, 3rd edn, 1995)
CR	*Corpus Reformatorum* (Halle, Berlin, Brunswick, Leipzig and Zurich, 1834–)
CSEL	*Corpus Scriptorum Ecclesiasticorum Latinorum* (Vienna, 1866–)
DACL	*Dictionnaire d'Archèologie Chrétienne et de Liturgie* (15 vols; Paris, 1907–53)
DTC	*Dictionnaire de Théologie Catholique* (18 vols; Paris, 1903–72)
GCS	*Die Griechische Christliche Schriftsteller der ersten [drei] Jahrhunderte* (Leipzig and Berlin, 1897–)
LB	Erasmus, *Opera Omnia*, ed. J. Le Clerc (10 vols; [Lugduni Batavorum =] Leiden, 1703–06)
LW	*Luther's Works*, eds. J. Pelikan and H.T. Lehmann ['American Edition'] (55 vols; Philadelphia and St Louis, 1955–86)
NPNF 1	P. Schaff *et al.* (eds), *Nicene and Post-Nicene Fathers of the Christian Church*, Series 1 (14 vols; Edinburgh, 1887–94/Grand Rapids, MI, 1991–98)
NPNF 2	P. Schaff *et al.* (eds), *Nicene and Post-Nicene Fathers of the Christian Church*, Series 2 (14 vols; Edinburgh, 1887–94/Grand Rapids, MI, 1994–98)
OS	*Joannis Calvini Opera Selecta*, eds. P. Barth and W. Niesel (5 vols; Munich, 1926–36)

PG	J.-P. Migne (ed.), *Patrologia cursus completus... Series graeca* (166 vols; Paris, 1857–83)
PL	J.-P. Migne (ed.), *Patrologia cursus completus... Series prima [latina]* (221 vols; Paris, 1844–65)
QBI	Martin Bucer, *Quid de Baptismate Infantium...Sentiendum* (Strasbourg, 1533)
SC	*Sources Chrétiennes* (Paris, 1942–)
TA	*Martini Buceri Scripta Anglicana [Tomus Anglicanus]* (Basel, 1577)
TU	*Texte und Untersuchungen zur Geschichte der altchristlichen Literatur* (Leipzig and Berlin, 1882–)
WA	*D. Martin Luthers Werke: Kritische Gesamtausgabe* [Weimarer Ausgabe] (65 vols; Weimar, 1883–1993)
WABr	*D. Martin Luthers Werke: Kritische Gesamtausgabe, Briefwechsel* (18 vols; Weimar, 1930–85)
WADB	*D. Martin Luthers Werke: Kritische Gesamtausgabe, Deutsche Bibel* (12 vols; Weimar, 1906–61)
WATR	*D. Martin Luthers Werke: Kritische Gesamtausgabe, Tischreden* (6 vols; Weimar, 1912–21)

Introduction:
The Strange History of Infant Baptism, Not Least in Scotland

When a collection of writings originally issued quite separately from each other over more than twenty years is published as a single volume, the reader is entitled to an initial explanation of how they have been treated. In brief, they appear here almost exactly in their original form. No attempt has been made to synthesise them into a single argument or narrative. As a result, a minor degree of duplication is inescapable—but a little repetition may serve to reinforce the point in question and draw attention to issues of particular importance.

A few factual corrections have been entered where an obviously erroneous name or date or statement has been identified in the original, but this has for the most part not extended as far as revising any of the subject-matter to take account of subsequent research. A few exceptions to this general rule, however, have been allowed where it was judged significant enough to warrant doing so. Thus note has been taken of the revised dating (c. 400) of the Asterius who was the author of homilies on the Psalms and had previously been identified with the early-fourth-century Arian known as Asterius the Sophist, and similarly of the more precise dates recently assigned to some of Augustine's works. Given the importance for the development of primitive infant baptism of the treatise known for most of the twentieth century as the *Apostolic Tradition* of Hippolytus, it would have been unthinkable to omit mention of the highly significant reconsiderations gathered up in the new commentary in the Hermeneia series by Paul Bradshaw and colleagues (2002).

But such cases are rare, and this is to all intents and purposes an assemblage of unrevised essays (a condition of permission being granted for reprinting some of them). So, for example, references to George H. Williams' large-scale summa on *The Radical Reformation* remain as first given, despite the extensive revision and expansion in the even more massive third edition (1992). This also means that where I have changed my opinion, I have not changed what I had earlier written, although I must immediately state that the number of pages which might have merited corrective treatment for this reason would have been few indeed. (The first chapter, which was among the earliest of the whole collection, preceded only by two evaluations of *Baptism, Eucharist and Ministry*, now chapters 22 and 23, would probably have contained more of them than any other, but would still have survived largely unscathed.) This circumstance, so I reckoned, justified me in arranging the contents of the volume according to not their dates of publication but the time-line of baptismal history.

This explanation of the shape of the book does not mean that my thinking about baptism, especially baby baptism, has not undergone significant development during the more than two decades since I first put pen to paper (*sic*!) on the subject. At the outset I was not driven by the passion that has since taken hold of me for the recovery of the prime importance of baptism as portrayed in the New Testament. Integral to this rediscovery, nowhere more needed, I dare to claim, than in the church evangelical, where my own roots are still firmly planted, is the espousal of what I find it simplest to call a realist understanding of the significance of New Testament baptism—and therefore of all Christian baptism as properly professed and practised. This realist sense must be contrasted with a solely symbolical or representational or even designatory view of the role of baptism. To risk a shorthand explication of what this realist understanding amounts to, it holds that baptism is the normal means by which God through the Holy Spirit confers the gifts of the gospel of Christ—forgiveness of sins, eternal life, new birth and adoption as the children of God, as well as incorporation into the body of Christ the church. Appropriate weight attaches to the word 'normal' in this statement: it entails nothing automatic, for God has not so bound himself to the ordinance of baptism that he cannot bestow these blessings apart from baptism or that he necessarily imparts them through every act of baptism.

I came to this enlarged appreciation of the import of Christian baptism from revisiting the New Testament in the best evangelical fashion, but this return to the apostolic testimony was itself prompted by historical investigations, especially of the foundations of the Reformed evangelical heritage which I own. Of these studies none was so influential on me as the paper I did on the baptismal teaching of the divines of the Westminster Assembly, principally in the Westminster Confession itself, which is still the qualified subordinate doctrinal standard of the Church of Scotland. It appears here as chapter 17. Its conclusion, that the Confession teaches baptismal regeneration (hedged around with the requisite qualifications), may have shocked many a Reformed adherent of the Confession, just as it surprised me. To the best of my knowledge, no-one has seriously attempted to refute directly my interpretation of Westminster's baptismal theology, which I have subsequently come to appreciate as an index of the divines' highly conscientious fidelity to scripture.

The point to be emphasised is that the route by which I have reached my present position on baptism has been irreducibly historical. It has been a wide range of historical enquiries that have both compelled and liberated me to read the New Testament afresh. Yet my quest (for what a witty friend has characterized as *The Historical Reflections of an Intrepid Scottish Patrologist, Being a Survey of the Entire History of the Development of Baptism*—to which I plead not guilty) as an historian of Christianity has not itself been confessionally driven, although I have no wish to deny the fact, evident enough to any reader of this book, that as a Christian, and not least as an elder in the Church of Scotland, my interest in baptism is much more than that of a professional scholar. But again the balance must be kept, for it has been largely the burden of historical research that has intensified my concern for baptism's contemporary fortunes among the churches. The conviction has been increasingly borne in upon me that baptism's present weal and woe are wonderfully illuminated by an understanding of its past, and perhaps more truly so than of any comparable issue for the simple reason that its past has been only patchily exposed by historians. It is a past replete with surprise and fascination, as I hope at least some of the chapters in this corpus will reveal to investigators.

The previous two or three paragraphs also explain the variation in levels between the component chapters of this collection. Some of them had their first impression in the proceedings of international conferences when translations of Greek and Latin quotations would have been superfluous (and probably subject to an editorial exclusion order). At the other end of the spectrum, and chiefly in the third section, will be found several pieces that belong more to the genre of practical divinity in the service of the churches, with one even totally uncluttered by footnotes. From another angle the differences between essays will strike some readers as marking off the intensively research-driven from the reflections of an unapologetic believer. Yet I claim only one authorial identity, and would spurn any implication denying the value of the former for the churches' renewal of baptism no less firmly than any suggestion that in the latter I have written without the benefit of my historian's persona.

Underlying many of the disparate articles in this collection lurks the growing conviction that it is not only the issue of scripture that poses sharp questions to contemporary practices of baptism—most searchingly whether its teaching warrants the baptizing of helpless babies—but also the strange history of infant baptism, which I suppose is the issue of tradition. Protestants cannot duck the challenge by taking a principled stand on the former to the exclusion or demotion of the latter, because one question this strange history raises in an acute form is that of the use of scripture in the defence, doctrine and liturgy of infant baptism. What surfaces here is a raft of problems extending far beyond the interminably debated New Testament evidences for its dominical or apostolic origins—household baptisms, 1 Corinthians 7.14, and Colossians 2.11-12 and Acts 2.39 and the like, Jesus' blessing of children, and this or that eloquent silence.

Karl Barth brought some of these problems into provocative focus when he asserted that 'There is a genuine doctrine of infant baptism only from the time of the Reformation. For it was only then that there was any serious questioning or disputing of what had become the venerable institution of infant baptism.' He went on to argue that 'the presupposition of the [Reformers'] proofs' of the practice 'was a recognition of the validity of the powerful fact of Church history whereby infant baptism had long since become the rule in Christendom. Even the churches of the Reformation thought they must yield to the fact of Church history and accept its claim to validity.' This church-historical account by the eminent theologian is not, of course, incontestable. After all, it is grist to his mill in exposing what he indicts as the incoherent and *post factum* character of their doctrinal efforts to justify 'something alien, a foreign body, which they were not prepared to reject, and which, for good or evil, they thus had to live with, trying to assimilate it into the rest of their teaching'.[1]

In fact, Barth was, I believe, mistaken in claiming that infant baptism became the general rule 'only in the course of the greatest historical transformation which Christianity had thus far undergone', namely, the Constantinian revolution which, from the fourth century onwards, issued in the unitary world of Christendom.[2] Since this was patently for Barth more a matter of causation than mere chronological simultaneity, it flies in the face of the commonplace that the new Christian emperors' chief contribution to baptismal development—which is scarcely *le mot juste* for historians like Joachim Jeremias!—was the postponement of baptism until their death-bed. In reality, there is little evidence either to justify burdening Constantine and his successors with responsibility for such momentous changes (whether a general tendency to defer baptism until the end of life or infant baptism's becoming standard practice, as in Barth's book) or to pinpoint the fourth century as the time when baptizing babies first became more or less the customary norm in the Roman world in the West.

If there is one lacuna I regret in this volume it is the lack of a focused examination of the fourth century as a key phase in the strange history of infant baptism. Interested readers will be able to stitch together at least the outlines of this missing chapter from threads major and minor in chapters 4–7 and 9–10. The century fascinates because almost for the first time in the story we reach *terra firma*—hard, factual evidence of the baptismal biographies of known and named individuals who were the children of

---

[1] Karl Barth, *CD* IV/4, pp. 166-67.
[2] Barth, *CD* IV/4, p. 168.

Christian parents. And—surprise, surprise—paedobaptism is scarcely discernible at all. Had I set out to revise these collected studies in line with my present understanding, I would have challenged the vocabulary of deferment which patristic scholars of the later twentieth century, and I among them, too facilely applied to fourth-century baptismal phenomena, on the insecure assumption that, during the third century if not earlier, infant baptism had been the practical norm.

Barth would have done better to look not to socio-political changes primarily but to theological forces at work, and crucially the epochal influence of Augustine of Hippo's development of the doctrine of original sin and the necessity of baptism *quam primum* (at the first opportunity) to deliver the otherwise hell-bound newborn from its guilt. More than any other factor, Augustine's anti-Pelagian theology universalised infant baptism in the West. Although the full severity of this Augustinian teaching was never wholly canonized in medieval Catholicism, the Council of Trent found it imperative to reaffirm in its decrees on original sin and on baptism, against the Reformers' denial that infants dying unbaptized were condemned eternally, a position which preserved Augustinianism's dogmatic core on the issue, republishing in full the critical canon of the decisive anti-Pelagian Council of Carthage of AD 418.[3]

The texts need not be set out here, for the important point is this: the leaders of the Protestant Reformations in the sixteenth century perpetuated a rite which had first come into its own (in the post-Augustinian era) and was sustained for virtually all its centuries-long medieval life by doctrinal stipulations which they could no longer endorse. There is much more to be said, but my present purpose is strictly limited. Barth was largely right: the Protestant churches have been indebted almost entirely for their doctrines of infant baptism to the fresh constructions of the early-modern Reformers. (Note carefully that this statement refers to theological justification, not to biblical-historical apologetic.) A remarkable feature of this new-generation paedobaptist theology is the range of scriptural material recruited for the purpose: the Gospels' pericope of Jesus' blessing of children (embarking for the first

---

[3] Council of Trent, 'Decree concerning Original Sin', esp. 4-5, *Canons and Decrees of the Council of Trent* (trans. H.J. Schroeder; Rockford, IL, 1978 [1941]), pp. 22-23. Cf. N.P. Williams, *The Ideas of the Fall and of Original Sin* (London, 1929), pp. 395-423. The *Catechism of the Catholic Church* (London, 1994), in its section on 'The Necessity of Baptism', having affirmed that 'The Church does not know of any means other than Baptism that assures entry into eternal beatitude', goes on to provide for adults and children who die without it: 'As regards *children who have died without Baptism*, the Church can only entrust them to the mercy of God'. God's mercy and Jesus' tenderness to children 'allow us to hope that there is a way of salvation for children who have died without Baptism' (pp. 285-86, italics original).

time on its long career as a leading—sometimes the leading—biblical warrant for baptizing babies), and heavy use of Old Testament texts coupled with neglect of many of the obvious New Testament presentations of Christian baptism. The facts can be verified by scrutinizing Anglican *Books of Common Prayer* and Reformed/Presbyterian *Books of Common Order* between the Reformation and the later twentieth century. This is another bewildering aspect of the strange history of infant baptism.

Or take the provision of baptisteries. Why were Italian churches in the central Middle Ages still constructing baptisteries big enough to accommodate the immersion (or at least affusion, that is, the pouring of water on the head while a person stands in water) of adult candidates for baptism? First a brief comment on vocabulary is called for, since usage varies. Many writers use the word 'font' of any receptacle for the water of baptism, from a small metal bowl, perhaps mounted in a movable wooden stand, or a larger stone basin, often with a lid or cover and quite immovable, to a sunken tank or pool of varying shape into which candidates would descend for immersion or affusion (Greek, κολυμβήθρα; Latin, *piscina*). Baptists and others who practise immersion generally call such a pool a baptistery, a term which in the more specialized literature is normally reserved for the part of a church building or the separate edifice or structure which houses the baptismal font or pool. Churches which have a baptistery in the former sense rarely have a baptistery in the latter sense. On visiting Tunis a few years back I was proudly shown in the churchyard of St George's Anglican Church a sunken baptistery open to the sky recently constructed on the model of a much-photographed one famous for its mosaic decoration from the fifth or sixth century in Sbeitla (ancient Sufetula) in central Tunisia. Access to the church itself was prevented by building work, but I assume it also possessed, or had possessed, a typically small Anglican font.

I prefer to distinguish between a receptacle incapable of accommodating immersion or affusion, except perhaps, in the manner of the Orthodox, for babies, and one capable of expressing a wider range of New Testament and primitive Christian imagery for baptism, such as burial, death and rising, and unclothing and reclothing. Eliding the distinction between font and baptistery risks contributing to the endemic simplification of baptismal history, as though baptism was always administered using a vessel of similar shape and size to the typical modern font. Karl Barth's words, once read, are not easily forgotten:

> One can hardly deny that baptism carried out as immersion—as it was in the West until well on into the Middle Ages—showed what was represented in far more expressive fashion than did the affusion which later became customary, especially

when this affusion was reduced to a sprinkling and eventually in practice to a mere moistening.[4]

He almost certainly exaggerated the currency of immersion, to the exclusion of affusion—it has been argued with impressive erudition that 'no other method [than affusion] was adopted till the general introduction of infant baptism in the early middle ages made submersion possible',[5] which strikes me as the opposite exaggeration—but the point was well made. Its force became obvious when the production of a common baptismal certificate for use among the Scottish churches was held up after a Roman Catholic participant in the discussions watched a Church of Scotland infant baptism on television and was less than satisfied that water actually flowed from the minister's hand to the baby's brow. Moistening was not enough.

But whether complete immersion of the whole body beneath the water, or the partial immersion which submerged at least the head below the surface of the water in which the candidate stood, or affusion was commonest or commoner in the early centuries, it is beyond doubt that the early Christians constructed their baptismal pools of a size in most cases to accommodate these forms of baptism. Moreover, in parts of the Christian world, especially Italy, they continued to do so into the medieval centuries long after infant baptism had more or less completely superseded the baptism of responsible adults. An obvious adaptation was the fitting of a small basin (or font) inside the inner edge of a commodious baptistery, or the latter might have permanently suspended over it and occupying most of its surface area an elaborate canopy, somewhat like an altar baldachin. J.G. Davies has drawn attention to other changes consequent upon the switch to infant baptizands, which together made the provision of a separate baptistery building unnecessary.[6] These ranged from dispensing with the need to cater for baptism of the sexes unclothed and hence separately,[7] to the lapsing of the 'discipline of

---

[4] Karl Barth, *The Teaching of the Church regarding Baptism* (trans. Ernest A. Payne; London, 1948), pp. 9-10.

[5] Clement F. Rogers, *Baptism and Christian Archaeology* (Oxford, 1903), p. iii (reprinted from *Studia Ecclesiastica* 5 [1903]).

[6] J.G. Davies, *The Architectural Setting of Baptism* (London, 1962), pp. 51-53, 63-64. See also W.N. Cote, *The Archaeology of Baptism* (London, 1876); H. Leclercq, 'Baptistère', *DACL* 2.1, cols. 382-469.

[7] I owe to Professor Clyde Curry Smith of River Falls, WI, a delightful extract from the annals of the monastery of St Gallen in Switzerland concerning the baptism of Viking converts in the age of Louis the Pious in the ninth century: 'The real reason [the Northmen came in such numbers] was that they wanted to get the white baptismal clothes the Franks offered to the baptized. So once there arrived about half a hundred at one time who asked to be baptized. When there were not so many baptizing garments ready, [the Franks] were forced in haste to cut each garment in two pieces and make do with these. A

secrecy' (*disciplina arcani*) governing aspects of the candidates' weeks-long pre-baptismal schooling. But the stubborn persistence of large baptistery pools long after normal practice required them was but one example of the perpetuation of the dominant model of Christian baptism, that of respondent believers, despite their replacement by infants.

The practice of baptizing helpless babies who have to be, and can be, brought to baptism by others has often raised an acute question of which babies should be so privileged. In eighteenth-century Nepal Capuchin missionaries gathered a church of about eighty converts, but baptized thousands of children.[8] By contrast the distinguished Scottish pioneer, Robert Moffat, after years of service in Kuruman in modern Botswana, in 1829 baptized the first six converts with five of their children.[9] Behind such divergent statistics lie, of course, divergent baptismal theologies, but it should not be assumed that within a single confessional tradition, even one with a fairly coherent and unified theological outlook such as Scottish Presbyterianism, consensus always reigned on which infants should be baptized.

Already in 1559 John Knox had sent an enquiry to John Calvin in Geneva: should the illegitimate children of idolaters and excommunicated persons be admitted to baptism before either their parents had through repentance submitted themselves to the church or their offspring were able to seek baptism for themselves?[10] Calvin replied at some length after consulting his pastoral colleagues. After applauding the proper caution implicit in Knox's question, Calvin directs his attention to the key issue of the divine promise on which baptism is founded.

> The promise not only comprehends the offspring of each of the faithful in the first degree, but is extended to a thousand generations. Hence it is the case that the interruption of true religion which prevailed under the papacy did not remove the force and efficacy of baptism. Therefore we have not the least doubt that the descendants of holy and godly ancestors belong to the body of the church, even though their own grandparents and parents have been apostates… So wherever the profession of Christianity has not entirely perished or become extinct, infants are

---

fragmentary garment of this sort was put on one of the oldest among them. Very surprised he looked at it, and then he said: "Now I have been baptized more than twenty times, and I have always been given nice clothes, but this time I have been given a sack that fits a cowherd and not a warrior, and if I were not ashamed of being naked, you could immediately give it back to your Christ'" (cited from Tre Tryckare, *The Viking*, [Gothenburg, 1972], p. 141).

[8] Cf. Jonathan Lindell, *Nepal and the Gospel of God* (New Delhi, 1979), pp. 8, 16, 24, 27.

[9] Cited without source reference by Iain H. Murray, *A Scottish Christian Heritage* (Edinburgh, 2006), p. 252.

[10] David Laing (ed.), *The Works of John Knox* (6 vols; Edinburgh, 1846–64), VI, p. 76; *apud* Calvin's letters, *CO* 17, col. 619.

deprived of their rights if they are debarred from the common symbol... In essence, just as each person is accepted for baptism not out of regard for or favour to simply a single forebear (*patris*), but because of God's unceasing covenant, so it is rationally intolerable that infants be forbidden entry to the church through one parent's reprobation.

An immediate concession prevents Calvin's argument undermining the defence of infant baptism he gives elsewhere (cf. chapter 16 below).

At the same time we grant that sponsorship is essential. Nothing is more absurd than engrafting into Christ's body those whom we do not expect (*speramus*) to be his disciples. Hence if no relative appears to pledge his own faith to the church and undertake the responsibility of instructing the child, the action is a farce and baptism is profaned.

The unsettled situation of the church, undergoing reassembly after fearful dissolution, means that baptism must be retained while discipline is restored in course of time, and then parents must be compelled (*cogendi*) to present their children themselves and be their main sponsors.[11] Calvin's rather fraught reasoning reveals how utterly determined he was that infant baptism be not only preserved but also administered as universally as possible.

No trace survives of any response from Knox, nor can the influence of Calvin's position be discerned in the brief treatment of infant baptism in the Scots Confession produced the following year. Yet the order of baptism in *The Forme of Prayers*, the earliest version of the Church of Scotland's *Book of Common Order*, approved by the General Assembly in 1562, contains in the minister's exposition and exhortation phrases which might appear to have been derived direct from Calvin's reply to Knox. In fact, the whole book came from Geneva, having first been published there in 1556 and used by the English-speaking congregation which Knox pastored in the city during 1556–59 before his return to Scotland. Therefore it is probably unwarranted to attribute to Knox himself without further evidence the view which formed his question and which Calvin rejected.[12]

The central argument which Calvin dispatched to Knox found fuller expression in Samuel Rutherford (1600–61), best known today as the

---

[11] Calvin, *Letter* 3128, *CO* 17, cols. 666-67; Laing, *Works of Knox*, VI, pp. 95-97 (altered).

[12] Cf. Richard G. Kyle, *The Mind of John Knox* (Lawrence, KS, 1984), p. 166: 'Knox denied baptism to the children of idolaters and the excommunicated until both parents repented and submitted to the church.' For the text, cf. Laing, *Works of Knox*, IV, pp. 187-88; William D. Maxwell, *The Liturgical Portions of the Genevan Service Book* (London, 1965 [1931]), pp. 105-106 (this book carries as an additional title *John Knox's Genevan Service Book 1556*).

author of a collection of letters which is one of the classics of Scottish spirituality, in a Reformed or Covenanting-Puritan but altogether idiosyncratic mode. In his time he earned another second-to-none reputation, as a master of scholastic controversy. In *The Due Right of Presbyteries or, a Peaceable Plea for the Government of the Church of Scotland* (London, 1644),[13] Rutherford decked out Calvin's case (but without naming him; he prefers Beza to Zwingli and Oecolampadius) with extensive scriptural support, to the effect that the covenant God made with Abraham extends to the whole Gentile race (cf. Galatians 3.8), and hence children are within the covenant on the ground of 'the faith of their fathers', not of their nearest parents. Thus the offspring of all papists, Anabaptists and other heretics are in a totally different case from those of Turks and pagans because the parents of the former were once dedicated to Christ in baptism, and the bairns have interest only in that part of the covenant which is 'sound and Catholike', not in their parents' personal contribution—of heresy. Rutherford has assembled an impressive armoury of biblical texts illustrating the truth of Romans 11.28, 'As concerning the Gospell they are enemies for your sake, but as touching the election they are beloved for the fathers' sake', including even Acts 2.39, 'the promise is to...your children', despite their fathers having killed the prophets (cf. Matthew 23.30-35, 37). Truly 'fathers' was a chronologically mobile generation!

Rutherford's demonstration is also cluttered with theological arguments of which Calvin's reply was wholly innocent, including the following gem:

> Then the seed and infants of no Parents, but of such only as are members of the *invisible Church of the first borne*, are to be baptized, the contrary whereof you [his opponent] teach, while you say, *The Sacraments are not given to the invisible Church, and the members thereof, but to the visible particular Churches.*

This seems to me to be as good an example as one needs for manifesting the detrimental effect on theological commonsense of the distinction between the invisible church and the visible church. So then 'The Infants of the unbeleeving parents, though members of the visible Church, have no right to baptisme, and the Covenant, though they be the elect of God, and borne within the visible Church'—but the same children qualify for it as members of the invisible church.

Only further research will uncover what future lay ahead for this particular apologia. It would not wholly surprise me if it has been

---

[13] See Samuel Rutherford, *The Due Right of Presbyteries or, a Peaceable Plea for the Government of the Church of Scotland* (London, 1644), pp. 255-266 ['267'] in the second part of the book. In fact, the book is not divided into parts with separate pagination, but after p. 484 the numbering jumps back to 185.

Introduction xxxiii

recruited by advocates of universal infant baptism (a former colleague of mine in New College, Edinburgh, was of their number). It has a curiously contemporary relevance in post-Christendom societies like Scotland, where it is often grandparents rather than parents who press for the new baby's baptism. Family pressure of this kind, which by its very nature will last at most another generation, was responsible for the Church of Scotland's General Assembly, on the advice of its Panel of Doctrine, making provision in 2003 for an 'other family member (with parental consent)' supplying a parent's role in presenting the child and undertaking the child's Christian upbringing.[14] But this careful and qualified extension is a good deal more than three and a half centuries distant from Rutherford's *Due Right*.

Thomas Boston's 'celebrated treatise on Baptism....almost reads like a polemic against *The Due Right of Presbytery*',[15] but it never mentions Rutherford, although Calvin is among Boston's sources.[16] One of the 'Miscellaneous Questions' addressed by Boston (1676–1732) and first published after his death (1753) was 'Who have right to baptism, and are to be baptised?' At nearly a hundred pages it was quite possibly the fullest treatment of baptism yet produced in Scotland. The main point of his enquiry Boston sets out as follows:

> Whether or no all infants born of Christian parents, so called in opposition to Jews, Turks, and pagans, have a right before the church to baptism? or, whether the open wickedness, profanity, or gross ignorance of the parents, should hinder the infants to be baptized, till either the parents reform, or the child come to mature age, and by his personal walk satisfy the church as to his right to that ordinance?[17]

Boston is aware of 'many godly and learned' who have answered his first question in the affirmative, including the eminent Italian Reformed theologian, Girolamo Zanchi, the little-known Oliver Bowles (c.1577–c.1646), minister of Sutton in Bedfordshire, one of the oldest members of the Westminster Assembly and author of *De pastore evangelico tractatus* (1649), as well as of a sermon preached before the Assembly, *Zeale for Gods house quickned* (1643), and Richard Baxter. Though their arguments vary, they all entail that, solely by virtue of their birth privilege, children have a right to baptism without either parent

---

[14] Church of Scotland, *General Assembly 2003* (Edinburgh, 2003), sect. 13, p. 17.
[15] James Walker, *The Theology and Theologians of Scotland 1560–1750* (Edinburgh, 2nd edn, 1982 [1888]), p. 122.
[16] Samuel M'Millan (ed.), *The Whole Works of the Late Reverend Thomas Boston of Ettrick* (12 vols; Aberdeen, 1848–52), VI: *Sermons and Discourses on Several Important Subjects in Divinity*, pp. 125-220.
[17] Boston, *Sermons and Discourses on Several Important Subjects in Divinity*, in *Works*, VI, p. 139.

being any kind of visible or credible believer, 'laying aside the case of such sponsors from whom the infants wholly derive their right to the ordinance'.[18] By restating the core issue in these terms, Boston has almost effected a *reductio ad absurdum* of the affirmative answer. He will go further, claiming that this answer dispenses with the need for the parents to have been baptized themselves.[19]

Boston seems to my reading to dispose most effectively of the main supports of the position we have examined in Rutherford. He draws the proper implications from 1 Corinthians 7.14, Acts 2.38-39 and Galatians 3.29 (we become Abraham's seed by becoming Christ's, not vice-versa), and in general constructs his arguments from the New Testament and not least its baptismal texts to a greater extent than the opposing case.[20] He affirms that 'Christ hath not two churches, one invisible, and another visible; but one church, that in one respect is visible, in another respect invisible', with the consequence that 'visible church members are none other but such as apparently are true members of the church of Christ; so that if none be true members but real believers, none can be visible members but such as appear to be true believers'.[21]

Skill in drawing out insupportable conclusions from the contrary standpoint is well deployed by Boston. If godly ancestry is what counts, then the children of some pagans (he means unevangelized heathen) and Muslims have a right to baptism. Indeed, 'I think it will be hard to find any in the world that are a thousand generations removed from godly parents.'[22] If this last comment reveals the limitations of Boston's world history and geography, he is unafraid to accept the implications of making the faith of immediate not remote parents determinative for baptism. Why, if none but the infants of visible believers have a right to baptism, then families, parishes and whole countries might be paganized in a short time. Boston's defiant riposte, *Fiat justitia, et ruat mundus* ('Let right prevail, and the world go hang') is tempered by his judgement that the reverse would probably follow, 'that this would be a mean to

---

[18] Boston, *Sermons and Discourses on Several Important Subjects in Divinity*, in *Works*, VI, pp. 139-40. At p. 140 Boston gives Bowles's opinion on the necessity of sponsors without any indication that either knew that it was an almost verbatim quotation from Calvin, as given above. Elsewhere Boston cites Calvin a few times in support of his case.

[19] Boston, *Sermons and Discourses on Several Important Subjects in Divinity*, in *Works*, VI, p. 145.

[20] Boston, *Sermons and Discourses on Several Important Subjects in Divinity*, in *Works*, VI, pp. 160, 153-54, 147.

[21] Boston, *Sermons and Discourses on Several Important Subjects in Divinity*, in *Works*, VI, p. 200.

[22] Boston, *Sermons and Discourses on Several Important Subjects in Divinity*, in *Works*, VI, pp. 146, 152.

Introduction xxxv

bring them to be visibly christianised... It is truly a sad matter that people have nothing but their baptism to discern them from pagans.'[23]

Most readers will sense that with Boston they are on recognizably modern, even contemporary, ground. Yet he is quite capable of reasoning syllogistically, nor does he end up with a strictness of paedobaptismal discipline which alone some would make a condition of countenancing infant baptism today. Facing finally the objection that 'the children of many openly scandalous and wicked parents, are the children of baptized church members', he first distinguishes the openly scandalous from the openly wicked. 'David and Peter in the hour of temptation were openly scandalous, but not openly wicked persons.' So he yields on the baptism of the children of the many openly scandalous. Furthermore, so long as the parents are *de jure*, not merely *de facto*, baptized church members, then their offspring also ought to be baptized, which means the children of some who are openly wicked.[24]

Boston's treatise deserves to be better known, but its obscurity seems almost par for the course in baptismal history. So many research investigations await pursuit, and perhaps they will have to wait until this Cinderella of evangelical church life and of pukka theology is promoted to royal status. The Great Commission alone demands no less (Matthew 28.18-20). Meanwhile, surprises continually light up the strange history of infant baptism, and none more so for this researcher than one last phase of Scottish theology.

William Cunningham (1805–61), the Free Church of Scotland's first Professor of Theology in 1844 and soon Thomas Chalmers' successor as second Principal of New College, Edinburgh (1847–61), has been claimed to be Scotland's greatest theologian—a bold assertion indeed but made by one who knows the story of Scottish theology more profoundly than any of his contemporaries.[25] Well, even Homer nods, so Cunningham may. My first surprise came when I read his insistence that what the Westminster Confession and Catechisms had to say about the efficacy of baptism did not apply, could not apply and was not intended by the Assembly divines to apply to infants. (Let me declare my interest, set forth in chapter 17 below.) First affirming something to be almost presuppositionally a metaphysical impossibility ('It is very certain that the Westminster divines did not intend, in this deliverance [in the Shorter Catechism], or in any other which they put forth, to teach baptismal regeneration'), secondly advancing as equally *a principio*

---

[23] Boston, *Sermons and Discourses on Several Important Subjects in Divinity*, in *Works*, VI, pp. 144, 217.

[24] Boston, *Sermons and Discourses on Several Important Subjects in Divinity*, in *Works*, VI, pp. 219-20.

[25] Donald Macleod, in Nigel M. de S. Cameron, David F. Wright *et al.* (eds), *Dictionary of Scottish Church History and Theology* (Edinburgh, 1993), p. 231.

incontrovertible what is certainly not beyond challenge ('The doctrine of baptismal regeneration, whatever else it may include, is always understood to imply, that all baptized infants are regenerated.'), Cunningham proceeds to an interpretation of the Westminster documents which is aprioristic in the extreme. Truly he has dug a pit for himself.

> The difficulty is, not that the catechism appears to teach, that infants are all regenerated in baptism; but that it appears to teach, that believers are the only proper recipients of baptism, as well as of the Lord's Supper; while yet at the same time it also explicitly teaches, that the infants of such as are members of the visible church are to be baptized.

'This will require some explanation.'[26] In due course we will give his explanation, which is again surprising, in more ways than one, and suggest our own.

One remarkable aspect of this exposition is its appearance in an essay on 'Zwingle, and the Doctrine of the Sacraments' in a volume on the theology of the Reformers, an assemblage of disparate essays by colleagues after Cunningham's death. It abounds in insightful one-sidedness and seems driven by the bogeymen of baptismal regeneration and its patron, the Church of Rome. Its key argument hinges largely on the one and only occurrence of the possessive adjective 'our' in Shorter Catechism 94, which is without parallel in the baptismal chapters in the Confession and the Larger Catechism. I defy anyone to read the sections on baptism in the three texts (Confession 28.1-7, Larger Catechism 165–67, Shorter Catechism 94–95) and to emerge with Cunningham's bizarre interpretation. He does not set out to work with scripture, but he is no more than selective in his engagement with the actual Westminster documents. '[N]o Protestants, except some of the Lutherans, have ever held that infants are capable of exercising faith.'[27] Well, Calvin did, in the first edition of the *Institutes*, nor did he rule it out in the final edition. 'It has always been a fundamental principle in the theology of Protestants, that the sacraments were instituted and intended for believers, and produce their appropriate beneficial effects, only through the faith which must have previously existed.'[28] I am left wondering how much of Luther on baptism Cunningham read, to say nothing of that vast acreage of magisterial Reformation writings devoted to the scriptural evidences and theology of infant baptism. But the main gravamen against Cunningham's case must be that the plain sequence of exposition in the three texts, section by section, paragraph by paragraph and sentence by

---

[26] William Cunningham, *The Reformers and the Theology of the Reformation* (Edinburgh, 1967 [1862]), pp. 241, 242, 244-45.

[27] Cunningham, *The Reformers and the Theology of the Reformation*, p. 249.

[28] Cunningham, *The Reformers and the Theology of the Reformation*, p. 244.

Introduction xxxvii

sentence, simply cannot accommodate a reading which ends up leaving, as he himself admits, as we have seen, infant baptism affirmed but strictly meaningless, that is, given no meaning in the three documents. Since Cunningham served a Church which in practice knew baptism almost entirely in the baptizing of infants, it would be one of the strangest windows into the strange history of infant baptism if its confessional cupboard on infant baptism were almost bare.

Attack is the best form of defence, and Cunningham makes a virtue out of departing from all ecclesial reality. Here I find his explanation unbelievable textually, i.e., in terms of the Westminster documents, but astonishingly modern and audacious.

> [W]e fear it is a very common thing for men, just because they ordinarily see infant, and very seldom see adult, baptism, to take the baptism of infants, with all the difficulties attaching to giving a precise and definite statement as to its design and effect in their case, and to allow this to regulate their whole conceptions with respect to this ordinance... This is a very common process; and we could easily produce abundant evidence, both of its actual prevalence, and of its injurious bearing upon men's whole opinions on this subject. The right and reasonable course is plainly just the reverse of this,—viz., to regard adult baptism as affording the proper fundamental type of the ordinance,—to derive our great leading conceptions about baptism from the case, not of infant, but of adult, baptism...; and then, since infant baptism is also fully warranted in Scripture, to examine what modifications the leading general views of the ordinance may or must undergo, when applied to the special and peculiar case of the baptism of infants.[29]

I am almost tempted to cry 'Alleluia!' Cunningham's analysis is sound in its fundamental instinct, but fails to recognise that it indicts most Protestant theology from the Reformers on and that the genius of the Westminster divines was indeed to start with the baptism of believers but not leave infant baptism out in unilluminated darkness. They could not have taken the whole of Cunningham's ultimate step.

> [I[nfant baptism is to be regarded as a peculiar, subordinate, supplemental, exceptional thing, which stands, indeed, firmly based on its own distinct and special grounds, but which cannot well be brought within the line of the general abstract definition or description of a sacrament, as applicable to adult baptism and the Lord's Supper.[30]

Well, perhaps we should not accord such weight to 'general abstract definitions' of matter-heavy actions like baptism and the supper. This point apart, it takes the breath away to read the much-lauded theologian-

---

[29] Cunningham, *The Reformers and the Theology of the Reformation*, p. 247.
[30] Cunningham, *The Reformers and the Theology of the Reformation*, p. 250.

in-chief of the heroic Free Church of Scotland writing so diminishingly of virtually the only baptism experienced by Presbyterian Scotland for centuries before and after—'peculiar, subordinate, supplemental, exceptional'. His explanation left his Church with a confessionally rich baptism to which it was largely a stranger and another, confessionally naked, baptism which they witnessed and took part in all the time. His explanation helps to explain, of course, a good deal more than Cunningham suspected. It set him and all who espoused it free, except in negative terms, from confessional guidance in constructing a theology of infant baptism, free to quarry from other sources of their choice. It exempted them from bothering with the New Testament's presentations of baptism, for these dealt only with adult baptism, on Cunningham's own admission. (Infant baptism can scarcely have fallen within the scope of even the Great Commission, which prefaces making disciples to baptizing.) It helps historians like me understand why low views of baptism and of the Lord's supper are so prevalent in Presbyterian evangelicalism in Scotland. May it even help to explain, I am bold enough to surmise, why in 1892 the Free Church adopted a Declaratory Act which gave subscribing ministers and elders diversity of opinion 'on such points in the [Westminster] Confession as do not enter into the substance of the Reformed Faith'? Did baptism belong to the substance of the faith? It would be an easy task today to recruit an evangelical majority for an answer in the negative. Better to have liberty of opinion than to have to wriggle like Cunningham, one might reason.

Unfortunately Cunningham was not alone. The Professor of Apologetics and Pastoral Theology at New College, Edinburgh, from 1849 until his death was James Bannerman (1807–68). He was one of the editors of Cunningham's collected essays on the Reformers and their theology. His best-known work, still in print like Cunningham's, is *The Church of Christ* (2 vols, Edinburgh, 1868). Its lengthy discussion of baptism sets an unbridgeable gulf between adult baptism and infant baptism. The lawfulness of the latter is demonstrated from the essential sameness between former and later times (i.e., the Old and New Testament eras) in respect of the covenant of grace, the church of God, the ordinance of outward admission into the church, the principle on which the initiatory ordinance of admission has been administered and the practice of that administration.[31] Whereas the efficacy of adult believers' baptism is easily stated, that of infant baptism is a 'delicate and difficult subject'. Some preliminary principles must be laid down.

> The proper and true type of Baptism, as a Sacrament in the Church of Christ, is the Baptism of adults, and not the Baptism of infants... The growth and prevalence of the visible Church, and the comparative fewness of the instances of adult

---

[31] James Bannerman, *The Church of Christ* (2 vols, Edinburgh, 1868), II, p. 68.

Introduction xxxix

> conversion to an outward profession of Christianity amongst us, have led to the Baptism of infants being almost the only Baptism with which we are familiar. The very opposite of this was witnessed in the Church of Christ at first. And the true type of Baptism, from examining which we are to gather our notions of its nature and efficacy, is to be found in the adult Baptisms of the early days of Christianity, and not in the only Baptism commonly practised now in the professing Church, the Baptism of infants.[32]

Failure to recognise this has even led some to reverse 'the legitimate order of the argument' and to reason from the case of infants to that of adults, whereas 'It is abundantly obvious that adult Baptism is the rule, and infant Baptism the exceptional case... The Bible model of Baptism is adult Baptism, and not infant.'[33] I am thinking of opening a book on attempts by churchmen sympathetic to Free Church theology to identify the author of that last sentence.

The Westminster Assembly's documents play a minimal role in Bannerman's exposition of baptism, with a few references to the Shorter Catechism and no engagement with the substantive paragraphs of the Confession. Whether he judged Cunningham's treatment adequate, or too embarrassingly risqué to stand beside we can only guess. All in all, if we make allowance for the damage wrought by so sharply demarcating two baptisms—and it is an absolutely huge allowance (for he does not in fact argue from his adult baptism to infant baptism, but establishes the latter on independent premises)—Bannerman's account is more balanced and rounded than Cunningham's. Although of his three heads on the efficacy of infant baptism two merely give the child a promissory note to be cashed in later ('Now, what the Word of God addressed to the intelligent and responsible adult is, that Baptism is when administered to the unconscious and irresponsible infant'[34]), the third endorses the inference that, in baptized infants dying very young and presumed to be saved, their baptism was the moment of their regeneration. But of course that presumption does not attach to all the instances of infant mortality in the baptized.[35]

Only further enquiry will disclose the extent and duration of the influence enjoyed by this strange baptismal theology among the early Free Church of Scotland fathers, at a time when its New College in Edinburgh rose rapidly from its foundation in the 1840s to become one of the leading schools of divinity in the English-speaking world. But one thing at least I now understand with fresh clarity—how evangelical circles in my adoptive land which still set high store by the Westminster

---

[32] Bannerman, *The Church of Christ*, II, pp. 108-109.
[33] Bannerman, *The Church of Christ*, II, p. 109.
[34] Bannerman, *The Church of Christ*, II, p. 115.
[35] Bannerman, *The Church of Christ*, II, pp. 117-21.

Confession come to profess such a base estimate of baptism. (To be strictly accurate, I should write 'of infant baptism', but since that is the only baptism they are familiar with, the qualification is otiose. If they cherish in their bosom a more elevated view of faith-baptism, it must count as a secret indulgence.) The history of the interpretation of the Confession's paragraphs on baptism might well make a fascinating doctoral thesis. But then there are dozens of good PhD topics to be found once one ventures into the strange history of infant baptism.

To conclude on a personal note, I also now see with sharper vision why I was led by a higher providence to devote my Didsbury Lectures in 2003 to the question *What has Infant Baptism done to Baptism?*[36] Cunningham and Bannerman were right, insofar as believers' baptism is in an appropriate sense the norm of Christian baptism. They were ahead of their time, but they spoiled their case by exaggeration, and by bifurcating the baptismal waters like the Red Sea at the exodus. One could have confidently forecast that by so doing they would fail in their endeavour to give a high profile to the New Testament's picture of baptism—a form of baptism which by their own admission lay behind the ken of the church of their day. The mission to recover New Testament baptism must go on, with sounder historical exegesis of both scripture and confession, and without relegating infant baptism to simply a Christian version of circumcision.

---

[36] Published by Paternoster Press, Milton Keynes, 2005, with the subtitle *An Enquiry at the End of Christendom*.

PART A

THE EARLY CENTURIES: SLOW DEVELOPMENT

CHAPTER 1

The Origins of Infant Baptism— Child Believers' Baptism?

Baptism has been placed firmly on the agenda of ecumenical theology by the Lima report, *Baptism, Eucharist and Ministry*. It makes no attempt to resolve the question of baptismal origins, but judiciously summarizes the state of the debate: 'While the possibility that infant baptism was practised in the apostolic age cannot be excluded, baptism upon personal profession of faith is the most clearly attested pattern in the New Testament documents.'[1] The paucity of recent discussion of the beginnings of infant baptism may suggest that they are deemed insoluble, short of the discovery of new evidence. Theology, at any rate, may neither be able nor need to wait until historians of primitive Christianity reach a consensus. The possibility that infant baptism was practised relatively early, perhaps even in the New Testament churches themselves, was no deterrent to Karl Barth's regarding it as theologically indefensible. Nevertheless, he could not ignore what he called 'the brute fact of a baptismal practice which has become the rule in churches in all countries and in almost all confessions', and he ventured his own explanation of the triumph of infant baptism and of the New Testament passages to which its advocates customarily appeal.[2] His sharp critique of the tradition provoked a greater stir on the continent of Europe than in the English-speaking world.[3] A fresh look at the historical question is

---

[1] *Baptism, Eucharist and Ministry* (Faith and Order Paper, 111; Geneva, 1982), p. 4 para. 11. This article is itself based on a paper prepared in April 1985 for the conversations between representatives of the Church of Scotland and the Baptist Union of Scotland. The 1984 report of the Multilateral Conversation in Scotland has subtly altered the judgment in *Baptism, Eucharist and Ministry* into 'While baptism on profession of faith is the most commonly attested practice in the New Testament, there is some evidence that infant baptism also took place' (para. 14).

[2] Karl Barth, *CD* IV/4, pp. 164-94 (cf. pp. 168, 165).

[3] Cf., e.g., W. Kasper (ed.), *Christsein ohne Entscheidung, oder Soll die Kirche Kinder Taufen* (Mainz, 1970); H. Hubert, *Der Streit um die Kindertaufe* (Berne, 1972); several essays in H.J. Auf der Maur and B. Kleinheyer (eds), *Zeichen des Glaubens. Studien zu Taufe und Firmung Balthasar Fischer zum 60. Geburtstag* (Cologne, Freiburg, 1972); W. Molinski (ed.), *Diskussion um die Taufe mit Arbeitshilfen für eine erneuerte Praxis der Kindertaufe* (Munich, 1971); and the bibliography given by L. Ligier in *Gregorianum* 57

certainly overdue, although its starting-point is bound to be the celebrated exchange between Joachim Jeremias and Kurt Aland of two decades ago.[4] Ecumenical discussion, and in some churches ecumenical reality, call on both paedobaptists and credobaptists to examine the others' practice with a new seriousness. In such a context the beginnings of the dominant tradition cannot healthily be left unscrutinized or treated as inscrutable.

Three preliminary points must be made. First, the word 'infant' may foster ambiguity, and we would be wiser to distinguish between 'children' and 'babies'. This is in effect the distinction that Aland insisted on (between Kindertaufe and Säuglingstaufe) but the English translations ignored. Some important early sources differentiate between those who can answer for themselves, from the age of perhaps three onwards, and those who cannot. It is here that the divide falls between believers' baptism and what has traditionally been called infant baptism. Not only is this not equivalent to an adult/infant distinction, but believers' baptism may be the baptism of children whose ages would classify them as infants, e.g., in the British school system. In what follows, except where greater precision is explicit, infant baptism will be used of the baptism of those who cannot answer for themselves.

Secondly, we must beware of the assumption that child or baby baptism emerged at the same time or developed at a uniform pace throughout the early church. Much recent study of primitive Christianity has emphasized its diversity; monepiscopacy is a prominent development varying considerably in timescale from region to region. Recognition of the variables of time and place may help in making consistent sense of apparently conflicting evidence.

Thirdly, it may be the case that in one and the same church at any one time only some infants were baptized. That is to say, infants may conceivably be divided into different categories, quite apart from the

---

(1976), pp. 614-16. Barth's comment that, even today, the national Church may stand or fall with the practice of baptism (*CD* IV/4, p. 168), is not irrelevant to Scotland.

[4] Joachim Jeremias, *Infant Baptism in the First Four Centuries* (London, 1960; a revised translation of *Die Kindertaufe in den ersten vier Jahrhunderten* [Göttingen, 1958]); Kurt Aland, *Did the Early Church Baptize Infants?* (London, 1963; translation of *Die Säuglingstaufe im Neuen Testament und in der Alten Kirche* [Munich, 1961]); Jeremias, *The Origins of Infant Baptism* (London, 1963; translation of *Nochmals: Die Anfänge der Kindertaufe* [Munich, 1962]); Aland's revision of *Die Säuglingstaufe* (Munich, 2nd edn, 1963) included a response to Jeremias' *Origins*; he has also written *Die Stellung der Kinder in der frühen christlichen Gemeinden und ihre Taufe* (Munich, 1967), and *Taufe und Kindertaufe. 40 Sätze zur Aussage des Neuen Testaments und dem historischen Befund, zur modernen Debatte darüber...* (Gütersloh, 1971), which also takes in the discussion provoked by Barth. The Jeremias–Aland encounter is reviewed by A. Strobel, 'Säuglings- und Kindertaufe in der ältesten Kirche. Eine kritische Untersuchung der Standpunkte von J. Jeremias und K. Aland', in O. Perels (ed.), *Begründung und Gebrauch der heiligen Taufe* (Berlin, Hamburg, 1963), pp. 7-69.

issue of age. This study will in fact consider three possible classes of infants as subjects for baptism.

The Jeremias–Aland debate issued in no consensus, although among New Testament scholars the view is increasingly widespread that infant baptism was not practised in the New Testament churches. The study of the New Testament might conceivably justify a range of conclusions. It may be held that its evidence does not enable us to decide whether infant baptism was practised in apostolic Christianity.[5] Or a distinction may be made between historical and theological evidence, leading possibly to the conviction that, although historical evidence is lacking, the theological evidence shows or implies that infants were baptized. Less likely is the view that the theological evidence gives us no ground for supposing the practice but the historical suggests the opposite. Some will hold that both kinds of evidence rule out the baptizing of infants, or again that both demonstrate its observance in the New Testament churches. It is perhaps an unlikely verdict that the historical and theological evidence conflict, with one leaving no room for paedobaptism and the other requiring us to believe the opposite, although this study will suggest that the practice may have been current in the face of apparently conclusive evidence to the contrary.

The distinction between historical and theological evidence may be open to challenge, if only because all theological material in the New Testament is *ipso facto* historical, even if it cannot he assumed that all historical evidence is of obvious theological import. By 'historical evidence' I have in mind such matters as household baptisms and proselyte baptism, and by 'theological evidence' material about the significance of baptism or the place of children or the continuity and discontinuity between old and new Israel. The distinction is broadly between what was done and what was believed and taught. Advocates of infant baptism may be too indifferent to the quest for historical evidence in their readiness to take a stand on theological foundations alone. They conclude that the apostolic generation must have baptized infants because of what it believed about, say, the covenant people of God, or taught, say, about Jesus' blessing of children. On the other hand, those who claim that the New Testament allows only believers' baptism may be presuming to know too much about primitive Christian practice if they infer that infant baptism did not happen from the undoubted fact that only faith-baptism is incontrovertibly attested in the New Testament. This is in effect Barth's position. Advocates of infant baptism are justified in insisting that the New Testament nowhere explicitly excludes the practice.[6] It is possible

---

[5] So recently Gerhard Barth, *Die Taufe in frühchristlicher Zeit* (Biblisch-Theologische Studien, 4; Neukirchen-Vluyn, 1981), p. 144.

[6] Cf. Church of Scotland Special Commission on Baptism, *Interim Report* (Edinburgh, 1955), p. 19. The claim that 'if the New Testament had meant to exclude

that baptism was given to infants without leaving any historical trace and without entailing any special rationale in baptismal theology.

This is very nearly what confronts us in the earliest unmistakable evidence for the practice of baptizing both children and babies, in Hippolytus' *Apostolic Tradition*. The order it lays down for baptism may confidently be held to reflect Roman practice not only when it was compiled, c.AD 215, but a generation or so earlier, back to c.180. But its claim to prescribe *apostolic* tradition is not to be taken seriously; there is much in the work which can by no stretch of the imagination be regarded as apostolic practice. The Greek for the chapter in question is not extant, but the Latin and the oriental versions agree in speaking of the baptism of 'the little ones' (*parvulos*), first those who can answer the baptismal interrogations for themselves and then those who cannot.[7] How was this ability to speak for oneself measured—in maturity of comprehension or in speaking competence expressive of only basic levels of understanding? Hippolytus is commonly regarded as describing a Christian proselyte baptism, and it is quite conceivable that, in the conversion-baptism of a family, children of infant age, perhaps of four or five, were told by their parents to answer for themselves and instructed how to do so. Thus in our earliest explicit text, the sharp lines between paedobaptism and credobaptism are blurred, for Hippolytus' *parvuli* who answer for themselves are receiving child believers' baptism.

By this time baptism was probably given only once a year, at Easter, except during outbreaks of persecution. Unless Hippolytus' account deals only with Christian proselyte baptism (in which case it would tell us nothing about babies born to parents already baptized), those receiving baptism must have included some babies born since the last baptismal service a year ago. If so, baby baptism would not take place at intervals throughout the year, but only once, for babies whose ages might range up to virtually twelve months. There is thus a liturgical delay built into church practice, which is markedly different from Jewish circumcision on the eighth day after birth.

---

infants from Christ's Baptism, it would have used language...to make this quite clear', is quite untenable. Cf. Barth, *CD* IV/4, p. 179, and Aland, *Die Stellung*, p. 21 (there is solid evidence of the presence of children of all ages in the earliest congregations, but nothing is said about their baptism).

[7] Cf. Jeremias, *Infant Baptism*, pp. 73-75; Aland, *Did the Early Church*, pp. 49-52; Jeremias, *Origins*, pp. 28-32. Jeremias is probably right that the fact that children, males and females, were baptized separately and that parents answered for their little ones before they were themselves baptized does not count decisively against our seeing here the baptism of adult converts (proselytes) along with their children. Hippolytus' text (*Apost. Trad.* 21) may be found in H. Kraft, *Texte zur Geschichte der Taufe, besonders der Kindertaufe in der Alten Kirche* (Kleine Texte, 174; Berlin, 2nd edn, 1969), p. 20.

Among the issues left unclear by Hippolytus is the form of words in which parents or relatives answer for 'the little ones'. All the available evidence indicates that the early baptismal rites were originally established to cater solely for those able to speak for themselves, and were only slowly and sometimes awkwardly adapted to infant (baby) subjects.[8] Although Hippolytus could not be plainer in revealing the contemporary Roman practice of baptizing babies and children, all that the rest of the work says about baptism, its preparation and its sequel, makes sense only of persons of responsible years. The point can be made another way. If one were to remove three brief sentences about *parvuli*, everything else in the work would require one to conclude that only professing believers were baptized.[9] Infant baptism nestles wholly under the mantle of believers' baptism, although it is quite visible. This might suggest that infant baptism is of recent origin, but the slow adaptation of liturgical procedure to infants evident in later sources cautions against overconfident deductions.[10] As late as, and later than, Augustine, the baptismal questions were still being addressed about the baby to the parent or sponsor in the third person, 'Does he believe in God?' etc., with the reply, 'He believes'. Already in Hippolytus the special provision made for those who cannot answer for themselves marks babies out as abnormal subjects for baptism, and we must assume, in default of contrary evidence, that at this time the third person was used in question and answer about them, thus drawing attention to their abnormal, even if by now routine, inclusion.

The almost contemporary evidence of Tertullian from Roman North Africa plainly reveals that infants (*parvuli*) had been or were now being baptized there, but does not tell us how well and long established the practice was. Is his preference for the deferment of baptism ('let them be made Christians when they have become competent to know Christ')[11] a protest against an innovation, or his dissent from common observance? Jeremias has no doubt: 'Tertullian's reservations...are directed against an established usage... Thus right at the beginning of the North African

---

[8] Cf. J.C. Didier, 'Une adaptation de la liturgie baptismale au baptême des enfants dans l'Église ancienne', *Mélanges de science religieuse* 22 (1965), pp. 79-90.

[9] Cf. Aland, *Did the Early Church*, p. 50: 'all the needful material is present for a plausible interpolation hypothesis'! Even Jeremias, *Origins*, p. 40, says that infants appear 'quite unexpectedly'. Cf. too B. Neunhauser, 'Die Liturgie der Kindertaufe. Ihre Problematik in der Geschichte', in Auf der Maur and Kleinheyer (eds), *Zeichen des Glaubens*, pp. 319-34, at p. 321.

[10] Theological factors could retard the development. When Augustine argued that infants were baptized for the same reason as others, Pelagius countered by insisting that they should be baptized by exactly the same ritual. Cf. Augustine, *The Grace of Christ and Original Sin* 1:32:35, 2:1:1, 2:21:24.

[11] Tertullian, *Baptism* 18:5 (Kraft, *Texte zur Geschichte*, p. 13).

Church we find infant baptism as a universally observed practice.' This is coupled with an interpretation of Tertullian's *De Baptismo* that restricts the reference to *parvuli* to 'the children of pagans joining the Church', and of other works of Tertullian that makes him both 'emphatically oppose' 'the tendency to postpone joining the Church' and 'not only presuppose the practice of infant baptism' but even 'advocate it'.[12] Aland's analysis of these texts gives a far more satisfying and consistent account of Tertullian's thought, but he goes too far in asserting that 'In Tertullian's tract *De baptismo*...we catch a glimpse of the very beginnings of infant baptism in Carthage and Africa... Tertullian's polemic is directed against something new.'[13] But novelty is one argument that Tertullian does *not* level against infant baptism — presumably because he knew he could not convincingly do so. Moreover, Aland takes no note of Tertullian's acceptance of emergency baptism for infants, or of the apparently established role of the *sponsores*. Above all, Aland underestimates the idiosyncratic character of Tertullian's case for delaying baptism, which he also urges upon unmarried women, especially widows and virgins. This has been impressively spelt out by Eduard Nagel, who also points to the possible influences making for delay exerted by the risk of persecution, the experience of difficulties in daily life and the church's penitential discipline.[14] We conclude that Tertullian's objections were directed against a practice already prominent in the Carthaginian church.

So infant baptism is first inescapably attested early in the third century both in Rome (baby as well as child baptism) and in Carthage, in texts which require us to believe that it had been observed in both centres for a generation or more. Can we move any further back towards the New Testament?

All the earlier evidence is vulnerable to some element of uncertainty or qualification. For example, Justin Martyr, who had experience of Christianity in Asia Minor as well as Rome, declares that he knows of 'many men and women of the age of sixty and seventy years who have

---

[12] Jeremias, *Infant Baptism*, pp. 81, 83-85. For a similar view cf. the Church of Scotland's Special Commission *Interim Report* (Edinburgh, 1956), p. 18.

[13] Aland, *Die Säuglingstaufe*, pp. 61-69. Jeremias, *Origins*, pp. 66-68, accepts the force of only some of Aland's criticisms. Aland's interpretation is generally sustained against Jeremias' in E. Nagel, *Kindertaufe und Taufaufschub. Die Praxis vom 3.-5. Jahrhundert in Nordafrika und ihre theologische Einordnung bei Tertullian, Cyprian und Augustinus* (Europäische Hochschulschriften, 23:144; Frankfurt am Main, 1980), pp. 41-48, 73-74.

[14] Nagel, *Kindertaufe*, pp. 55-76. Although he does not directly address the question how well established infant baptism was, it is clearly his view that in the late second century it was the standard practice (cf. p. 166).

been disciples of Christ from childhood (ἐκ παίδων)'.[15] Jeremias argues that this last phrase and the verb used (μαθητεύειν) must mean that these persons were baptized as infants 'in the time between A.D. 80 and 95'.[16] But ἐκ παίδων may well denote 'from childhood' rather than 'from babyhood' or 'from birth', and this would accord better with the force of μαθητεύειν. Aland, for whom the sentence means 'they had been instructed in Christian faith from childhood, and grown up as members of a Christian family', succeeded in eliciting a more precise analysis from Jeremias, although the latter still insists that it was 'in early childhood' that they 'had become disciples of Christ' and that we have here a definite allusion to baptism.[17]

Nothing more definite can be deduced from two other first-person testimonies to long Christian lives in the later second century—Polycarp's 'Eighty-six years have I served [Christ]' and Polycrates' 'I have now lived in the Lord sixty-five years'.[18] The latter belongs to AD 190–91, which enables Jeremias to conclude that Polycrates 'was baptized as a child about A.D. 125'. Polycarp's martyrdom is variously dated between 153 and 177, which would give an infant, perhaps baby, baptism for Polycarp in the first century. The discussion of such statements between Jeremias and Aland is inconclusive, although in his later book Jeremias concedes that some of them show only that the persons concerned 'were not first converted as adults, but were Christians already from their youth up'. He makes no mention of a reference introduced into the discussion by Aland from *1 Clement* (c.AD 96) to certain Christians who 'have walked among us from youth to old age unblameably', where on no reasonable chronology can ἀπο νεότητος specify the years of babyhood.[19] Such testimonies can more confidently be held to reflect the baptism of teenagers or children as believers (cf. Hippolytus' *parvuli* who can speak for themselves), than baby baptism.

Irenaeus' *Against Heresies* was written c.180. His knowledge of Christianity embraced Asia Minor and Rome as well as Gaul. In a familiar passage, extant only in Latin, he includes *infantes*, *parvuli* and *pueri*

---

[15] Justin, *1 Apol.* 15:6.

[16] Jeremias, *Infant Baptism*, p. 72.

[17] Aland, *Did the Early Church*, pp. 73-74; Jeremias, *Origins*, pp. 55-58. Jeremias, *Infant Baptism*, pp. 68-69, argues that the *Grundschrift* of the Pseudo-Clementines, compiled perhaps in the early third century, presupposes the baptism of children on the conversion of their parents. Although this may follow from certain general considerations, the children in question are obviously young adults (*Recog.* 7:21ff). Celsus, writing c.170, shows that young children were taught and converted (Origen, *Contra Celsum* 3:56; Strobel, 'Säuglings- und Kindertaufe', pp. 33-34).

[18] Jeremias, *Infant Baptism*, pp. 59-63; Aland, *Did the Early Church*, pp. 71-73; Jeremias, *Origins*, pp. 58-62.

[19] *1 Clement* 63:3 (cf. 65:1); Aland, *Did the Early Church*, pp. 71-72.

among all 'the ages of man' which Christ came to save by passing through himself and thereby sanctifying, and which 'are reborn (*renascuntur*) through him to God'.[20] Everything hinges on the verb. Jeremias has the better of this argument with Aland, and rightly stresses that the reference *presupposes* the practice of infant baptism (including baby baptism[21]), which must therefore go back at least a couple of decades before Irenaeus wrote, i.e., to c.150. This is roughly the date of Justin's description of baptism as administered in Rome and perhaps also Asia Minor, which presupposes only confessing believers as subjects.[22] If Irenaeus' evidence holds good for Rome as well as Gaul (and Asia Minor?), how are we to reconcile his testimony with Justin's? Perhaps in Justin's rite infants (or babies) nestled under the wing of older (parental) candidates, but invisibly rather than visibly as in Hippolytus. Aland mentions also Hermas' references to baptismal practice, which likewise relate to Rome around the mid-second century and *prima facie* envisage only responsible recipients.[23]

The significance of the silence of such sources is an important question, because to the texts referring to baptismal procedure in terms relevant solely to candidates capable of speaking for themselves or otherwise acting responsibly (e.g., in undergoing instruction or fasting), belongs also the *Didache,* which most scholars date c.100. Aland regards it as automatically ruling out infants and little children.[24] It is among the negative evidence omitted by Jeremias in his first work, but incorporated into a broader argument in the second.[25] First, Jewish ritual arrangements are often framed entirely to suit adults, even in cases, such as proselyte baptism, in which it is otherwise known that infants took part. Secondly, Tertullian and Hippolytus seem almost invariably to have in view the baptism of persons of mature years, and yet we know by their own testimony that infants too were included in baptism. Jeremias then combines these two points in support of his larger thesis of the

---

[20] Irenaeus, *Adv. Haer.* 2:22:4 (2:33:2 in some editions); Kraft, *Texte zur Geschichte*, p. 10. Cf. Jeremias, *Infant Baptism*, pp. 72-73; Aland, *Did the Early Church*, pp. 58-59; Jeremias, *Origins*, pp. 62-63. Irenaeus' allusion scarcely warrants talk of his 'doctrine of infant baptism' (Church of Scotland Special Commission, *Interim Report* (1956), pp. 14-15). Cf. Barth, *CD* IV/4, p. 166: 'There is a genuine doctrine of infant baptism only from the time of the Reformation'.

[21] The retroversion by A. Rousseau and I. Doutreleau in the edition in *SC* 293 (1982), p. 286, suggests the Greek terms were βρέφος (or νήπιος), νήπιος (or παιδίον), and παῖς. The critical clause becomes τοὺς δι' αὐτοῦ ἀναγεννωμένους εἰς τὸν θεόν.

[22] Justin, *1 Apol.* 61; cf. Aland, *Did the Early Church*, pp. 54-55. Jeremias omits this evidence.

[23] Aland, *Did the Early Church*, p. 54.

[24] Aland, *Did the Early Church*, pp. 53-54.

[25] Jeremias, *Origins*, pp. 38-41.

correspondence between Jewish proselyte baptism and primitive Christian baptism.

There is, however, one demurrer to be entered against this reasoning. As far as the Jewish observances are concerned, we have explicit evidence for the inclusion of infants when the ritual regulations fail to mention them. This is precisely what we lack for baptism in the era of the *Didache*. Nevertheless, Jeremias' argument may be held to have shown a prejudice in favour of preferring explicit incidental evidence over the silence of accounts of ritual when the two appear to conflict, as we suggest they do for Rome in the mid-second century. But we cannot do this with the silence of the *Didache*. Also left unexplained is why the ritual silence is broken early in the third century in Hippolytus. The question is the more acute the longer one supposes it to have lasted—over a century, on Jeremias' supposition.

The *Apology* of Aristides probably belongs to the reign of Hadrian (117–38). Its most pertinent passage (not discussed by Jeremias until Aland adduced it) describes Christians as persuading (πείθουσιν) any male or female slaves they may have, 'or children (τέκνα)', to become Christians.[26] To Aland the text expressly places the baptism of the children of Christians 'only after they have attained the needful insight, hence not before they have become several years old'. Jeremias interprets them as the children of the slaves, in yet another case of a house baptism. Then 'persuade them to become Christians' applies only to the slaves; it is scarcely appropriate to any but adults. While one or two features in this deceptively simple text count in Jeremias' favour, such as the mention of children after the slaves, Aland's explanation is more natural. For Jeremias' version to carry conviction, '*and* children' would be required, not '*or* children' as given by both Greek and Syriac versions. Aristides is therefore another witness to a form of young believers' baptism.

There is one further area of evidence to investigate before we come to the New Testament, and that is epitaph inscriptions of Christians dying in childhood. They have evoked one of the very few fresh contributions to the whole debate in the last few years. Jeremias distinguished two main groups of inscriptions. In the first only the child's age at death is given, together with some indication that the child was a Christian and occasionally that its parents were Christians. All these Jeremias takes to reflect the baptism as infants of the offspring of Christian parents. In the second group the date of baptism is mentioned along with the child's age

---

[26] Aristides, *Apology* 15:6 (Kraft, *Texte zur Geschichte*, pp. 2-3). Cf. Aland, *Did the Early Church*, pp. 57-58; Jeremias, *Origins*, pp. 43-48. Strobel, 'Säuglings- und Kindertaufe', p. 40, largely agrees with Aland. Jeremias' earlier argument from Aristides' *Apology* 15:11 is not persuasive; cf. Jeremias, *Infant Baptism*, pp. 70-71; Aland, *Did the Early Church*, pp. 55-56; Jeremias, *Origins*, p. 48 n. 2.

at death, showing that baptism was administered *in extremis.* 'In all probability in these cases the parents were pagan.'[27]

Aland knocks some sizeable holes in this construction.[28] The inscriptions in question date from the third century. In order to avoid irrefutable evidence of the non-observance of infant baptism so soon after it is first unambiguously attested, Jeremias advances the anachronistic notion of pagan parents requesting, and succeeding in securing, the baptism of their dying children, ranging in age from eleven months to twelve years, in the century *before* the Peace of the Church. If these inscriptions belonged to the fourth century, they would be further evidence of the well-attested deliberate postponement of baptism. Jeremias is no more convincing in his response to Aland, with a hypothesis that, in the emergency baptism of a twelve-year-old in AD 268, the parents were catechumens, which would explain why the child had not been baptized earlier.[29]

It remains possible that some of the inscriptions which do not give the date of baptism but disclose that the child died a Christian refer to children baptized as babies, but no firm conclusions can be drawn without clear indication. Incidentally, it is noteworthy that in inscriptions even children of a few months or years are called *fidelis* or πιστός to attest their baptized status, which is further evidence that the πιστός of infants has been accommodated to an observance designed for faith-professing candidates.

An American scholar, Everett Ferguson, in an article in the *Journal of Theological Studies* in 1979, used the evidence of the inscriptions to argue that infant baptism developed by the regularising of emergency procedures. 'Tertullian stood at the point where there was pressure from some to extend the emergency measure to other circumstances.'[30] Ferguson linked the emergency baptism of children observed in the inscriptions to the influence of John 3.5, 'the favourite baptismal text of the second century', which was thought to deny heaven to the unbaptized. 'The high mortality rate of infants in the ancient world, to which the Christian inscriptions are a powerful if mournful witness, would encourage the practice of giving baptism soon after birth as insurance no matter what might happen.'[31]

This thesis is not inconsistent with the evidence surveyed so far. It offers an alternative explanation to Jeremias' of Justin's failure to

---

[27] Jeremias, *Infant Baptism*, pp. 41-42, 55-56, 75-80, 85, at p. 80; cf. Kraft, *Texte zur Geschichte*, pp. 79-85, for relevant inscriptions.

[28] Aland, *Did the Early Church*, pp. 75-79.

[29] Jeremias, *Origins*, pp. 49-53.

[30] Everett Ferguson, 'Inscriptions and the Origin of Infant Baptism', *Journal of Theological Studies* n.s. 30 (1979), pp. 34-46, at p. 45.

[31] Ferguson, 'Inscriptions', pp. 45, 46.

mention infants in his account of baptismal practice at Rome at a time when, from Irenaeus' assertion, we inferred that baby and infant baptism were already being observed there. Justin's silence would show that the emergency baptism of infants had not by then become the regular baptism of all infants, while Irenaeus might be alluding to the regular practice of emergency baptism of children. Ferguson's account also has the advantage of smoothing out the course of the early history of paedobaptism, at least if it did not begin until well into the second century and did not become common until the third century, and then in the fourth century became less common. To Ferguson the fourth-century delay of baptism arose from the same association of baptism with death evident in the emergency baptism of infants.[32]

Ferguson's hypothetical account does not comprehensively answer the question when infant baptism began, for it does not tell us when the emergency baptism of infants began. Worth quoting at this point is Beasley-Murray's comment on 1 Corinthians 15.29: 'The attitude that could adapt the baptism of believers to baptism for dead people, that they might gain the benefits believed to attach to the rite, would find it a short step to baptize infants, that they too might receive its blessings.'[33] It is not clear whether he implies that the baptism of infants might have begun as early as 1 Corinthians, but the link between baptism for the dead and emergency baptism is a suggestive one. Both, in Beasley-Murray's view, find their roots in a sacramental-magical perversion of Paul's teaching.

But does baptism *in extremis* necessarily entail regarding baptism as essential in order to avoid hell after death? It is possible to view it, in the case of at least some of the children in these inscriptions, as an appropriate mark or seal for those brought up in the nurture of the Lord, perhaps regarded as 'holy' by virtue of their Christian parentage (see the following discussion of 1 Corinthians 7.14), and thereby marked out for baptism as and when they become able and ready to answer the baptismal questions for themselves.[34] Their baptism prior to their premature death would be a fitting, rather than an indispensable, act, to which their

---

[32] Ferguson, 'Inscriptions', p. 46. Cf. Aland, *Did the Early Church*, pp. 108-109.

[33] G.R. Beasley-Murray, *Baptism in the New Testament* (London, 1962), p. 354. According to J.C. O'Neill, 'I Corinthians 15^{29}', *Expository Times* 91 (1979–80), pp. 310-11, baptism for the dead *was* emergency baptism.

[34] This pattern would avoid standard objections levelled at each others' practices by paedobaptists and credobaptists, in that it postulates a baptism as (young) believers of those *whose previous standing from birth has* not *been a matter of uncertainty*. Babies and younger infants, being 'holy' from birth, would be unambiguously members of the Christian community, and would receive baptism not to effect entry into membership but as its seal, when they were in a position to respond in their own person to the baptismal questions. See further at n. 43 below.

'holiness' and perhaps also their innocence or sinlessness[35] would impart a quite different meaning than, say, Constantine's death-bed baptism.

The most intriguing New Testament text is 1 Corinthians 7.14, which is popularly viewed as one of its clearer warrants for infant baptism. The structure of Paul's reasoning is widely misunderstood. When Paul asserts 'Otherwise your children would be unclean, but as it is, they are holy' (RSV, NIV), he is not basing the children's holiness on their having *two* holy parents, one a believer and the other sanctified through the believer. Rather he is adducing the same principle both in what he says about the unbelieving partner in a mixed marriage and in what he says about the children of a mixed marriage. The holiness of the believing spouse covers both the unbelieving partner and their children. Paul is not interested in the relation between the children and the unbelieving parent. A parallel obtains between the unbelieving partner and the children, in their relations to the believing wife/mother or husband/father.

Furthermore Paul's argument moves from the children to the unbelieving spouse. The holiness of the children of a single Christian parent is the acknowledged assumption upon which Paul bases his substantive assertion about this parent's unbelieving spouse, an assertion which clearly does not possess the self-evident validity of what he says about the children.

The next step is to note that the argument holds water only if the children, like the unbelieving partner, are unbaptized. It is inconceivable that, if they had been baptized, their holiness should have been grounded not on the fact of their baptism but on their relationship to a Christian parent—which it must be if the analogy is to retain its force. Furthermore, it follows that if the children of a single Christian parent in a mixed marriage are holy, so *a fortiori* are the children of two Christian parents, and in both cases without baptism, on the basis of their Christian parentage. This exegesis has the broad support of the Fathers, as well as generally of exegetes today, including both Jeremias and Aland.[36] It

---

[35] Most sources prior to the third century presuppose the sinlessness of young children. Cf. Aland, *Die Stellung*, pp. 17-21, *Taufe und Kindertaufe*, pp. 33-34; B. Klaus, 'Die Erbsündenlehre als Motiv des kirchlichen Handelns in der Taufe', *Kerygma und Dogma* 15 (1969), pp. 50-70, at pp. 54-58; J.C. Didier, 'Un cas typique de développement du dogme à propos du baptême des enfants', *Mélanges de science religieuse* 9 (1952), pp. 191-213, at pp. 194-200; Strobel, 'Säuglings- und Kindertaufe', pp. 34-39.

[36] Jeremias, *Infant Baptism*, pp. 45-46; Aland, *Did the Early Church*, pp. 80-84. On Tertullian's use of the text in *De Anima* 39 see J.H. Waszink's edition, *De Anima, Edited with Commentary* (Amsterdam, 1947), pp. 440-47. See ch. 14 in this volume.

suggests a parallel with Jewish proselyte baptism, which was not given to children born after the conversion-baptism of their parent(s).[37]

We must not obscure possibly important distinctions. Paul says nothing directly about baptism, although it is unquestioned that the unbelieving husband or wife was unbaptized. Exegesis can establish only that the presupposition (the holiness of the children) of the main argument (the holiness of the unbelieving spouse) is not grounded in the children's baptism. There exists, however, the strongest presumption that the children had not in fact been baptized. Moreover, Paul is obviously alluding to a matter of common practice rather than to a specific instance. The verse is therefore of unique relevance to this enquiry, for *no other material in the New Testament enables us to be so confident that any child or children were or were not baptized.*

Can we deduce anything further—in particular, whether the children were subsequently baptized, and if so, at what age? The Greek itself can give us little clue as to their age.[38] Whether, in addition to being 'holy' by birth, they were also baptized, already or subsequently, is an issue on which Jeremias changed his mind. In the German edition of his first work, he endorsed the view that, according to this text, the Pauline churches did not baptize children born to Christian parents. By the time of the English translation he had 'begun to doubt the validity of this reasoning', for it ignored 'the important fact that in Judaism all boys, whether their birth was "in holiness" or not, were circumcised on the eighth day'. Since baptism replaced circumcision, the holiness from birth of the children of 1 Corinthians 7.14 did not preclude the possibility that they were already baptized. The holiness of the unbelieving spouse did not make it unnecessary that he or she be subsequently converted and baptized. But Jeremias affirms only that 'the baptism of children on the eighth day [*sic!*], in place of circumcision' is *no more excluded* by the verse than is the later baptism of the unbelieving spouse. In emphatic italics he

---

[37] The relation of Jewish proselyte baptism to primitive Christian baptism remains disputed. G. Barth, *Die Taufe*, pp. 30-31, 141, denies any significant influence on Christian practice until the later second century. Cf. similarly Strobel, 'Säuglings- und Kindertaufe', pp. 11-12.

[38] Beasley-Murray, *Baptism*, pp. 119, 331, argues from the fact that the church at Corinth was only about four years old when 1 Corinthians was written that most of the children in it must have been born before their parents' conversion, and were either baptized with their parents (in which case Paul's argument here falls) or still unclean (because born before their parents' conversion but not baptized). But this argument holds only if 'your children' denotes *all* the children of the Corinthian Christians. It is more naturally taken only of those parallel to unbelieving parents, viz., those unbaptized and perhaps also unbelieving.

declares: '*We must accordingly be content with the conclusion that 1 Cor. 7.14c bears no reference to baptism*'.[39]

This revision of opinion significantly alters the thrust of Jeremias' case, which separates the baptism of children of parents joining the church from the baptism of children born to Christian parents. On the former he is never in any doubt. As in Jewish proselyte baptism, the children were baptized together with their converted parents. But in the German edition he argued that, to start with, both the Pauline churches and the church in Jerusalem did not baptize the children of baptized parents, and this practice changed in the Pauline churches some time after 1 Corinthians, and in the Jerusalem church around the same time, say, between 60 and 70. His main evidence for holding that in Jerusalem the children of Christians were not at first baptized is his inference from Acts 21.21, that c.55 the male children of the Christian Jews were still being circumcised.

In the English version of 1960, scarcely more than a hint is given of a change in practice from non-baptism to baptism of the children of Christian parents. The shift in Jeremias' reading of 1 Corinthians 7.14 is the chief factor behind this revised account. On Acts 21.21 he has very little to say. He maintains his inference that 'in AD 55 new-born male infants of the Jerusalem Church were circumcised', and merely poses the question whether they were also baptized. He is altogether more confident in drawing another twofold conclusion from Acts 21.21 combined with Colossians 2.11, namely that in Pauline territory the children even of Jewish parents were not circumcised but were baptized.[40]

Aland exposes the weakness of Jeremias' argument that Jewish proselyte baptism provides the background to 1 Corinthians 7.14 when he points to the totally non-Jewish character of the notion that the unbelieving partner in a marriage may continue in his or her unbelief and yet be regarded as holy.[41] Jeremias' response does not attempt to counter this objection. Furthermore, the parallel Jeremias draws between the non-exclusion of the subsequent baptism of the unbelieving spouse and of the prior baptism of the children is not the most obvious one to draw. A truer parallel would be between the non-exclusion of the *subsequent* baptism of both unbelieving spouse *and children*. We must remember that the weight-bearing element in Paul's argument is the holiness of the children, which is already self-evident in a way that does not hold for the holiness of unbelieving spouses.

It is generally held that the children of 1 Corinthians 7.14 were born after their parent's baptism, which for Jeremias rests on the parallel with

---

[39] Jeremias, *Infant Baptism*, pp. 47-48; Aland, *Did the Early Church*, pp. 19, 33-36, 80, on the differences between Jeremias' editions. Jeremias, *Origins*, pp. 37-38, maintains his revised position.

[40] Jeremias, *Infant Baptism*, p. 48.

[41] Aland, *Did the Early Church*, pp. 81-82; Beasley-Murray, *Baptism*, p. 331.

Jewish proselyte baptism. Although Aland rejects this parallel, he does not develop another possible line of reasoning suggested by this verse. The mixed marriages resulted from the marriage of two pagans, one of whom was subsequently converted. Why then should the statement about children not apply to children born *before* the parent's conversion and baptism? This would make the parallel between the two cases even closer. It is too readily assumed that, when only one spouse was baptized on becoming a believer, the children were also baptized at the same time.[42] This would presumably be less likely if the wife and not the husband were converted. Variation might be expected according to the unbeliever's strength of opinion. It is quite possible that the children envisaged by Paul included some born before the parental conversion but not baptized with the parent. Only children in this position offer a *precise* parallel to the unbelieving partner. Whether all the children so born were in this position can be determined only by extraneous factors.

We have got this far without broaching the meaning in this verse of ἡγίασται (of the unbelieving partner) and ἅγια (of the children), nor is a detailed enquiry called for at this stage. The words seem to indicate status or relation, presumably both to God and to the Christian community, rather than religious influence *(pace* Barth) or ritual cleansing. Their meaning is important for the question before us: is the holiness predicated of the children such as to be likely to preclude or promote their baptism as babies? (Their later baptism as children able to answer for themselves would simply put their case on a par with that of the unbelieving spouse.) If they already 'belong to God' (NEB) by virtue of their Christian parentage, would this exclude any need for speedy baptism, or would it, in the words of the Church of Scotland Special Commission, 'demand' it?[43]

Jewish proselyte baptism provides no model for the baptism of children born to baptized Christians. Nevertheless, we should not rule out the possibility that the baptism of infants as part of household baptisms may, in due time, alone or in concert with other factors, have fostered the separate baptism of infants born after their parents' entry into the Christian community. There would thus be two kinds of infant baptism, one of them starting perhaps considerably earlier than the other. On any

---

[42] Perpetua was baptized in prison prior to martyrdom in AD 203 apparently without her child who at the time was not allowed to be with her in prison (*Passion of Perpetua* 3:5, 9). The narrative nowhere mentions Perpetua's husband.

[43] *Interim Report* (1955), p. 27. The commission lands itself in self-contradiction. It argues that ἅγια implies *either* that they were already baptized *or* that they participated in their parent's baptismal incorporation. But since primitive Christianity knows nothing of unbaptized Christians, their being already within the Holy People demands that they were subsequently baptized. But how could they require to be baptized if they already partook of their parent's baptism?

construction *some* interval is required between the two, in so far as, before one had any babies born to Christian converts to baptize, one had to have adult Christian converts. At the very least two different bases for infant baptism must have been involved. If Jewish proselyte baptism was a catalyst for the separate Christian baptism of infants, via the intermediary of Christian household baptism, then the interval may have been considerably longer than the nature of the case itself demanded, for the Jewish practice did not imply any special treatment for the newborn.

A second possible factor predisposing to the baptism of both categories of infants in Christianity is circumcision. On the dependence of Christian baptism on Jewish circumcision Jeremias could scarcely be more emphatic. In Colossians 2.11 Paul 'names baptism " the Christian circumcision" ...and describes it thereby as the Christian sacrament which corresponds to Jewish circumcision and replaces it'.[44] But if in Jerusalem male babies of Jewish Christian parents continued to be circumcised for two decades or more, as Acts 21.21 implies, would they also have been baptized—and on the same eighth day? Is it not much more likely that communities which continued to practise circumcision would *for that very reason* not have baptized their male babies? And by what logic would female babies who could not be circumcised be baptized? (Did baby baptism begin solely as a female rite, as a counterpart to male circumcision?) In the Pauline world, circumcision was so closely identified with the Jewish law that not only was it not countenanced for male Gentile converts (and presumably also their male children; cf. Galatians 5.2), but its continuance by Christians of Jewish origin may also have been actively discouraged, as Acts 21.21 indicates. The polemic against circumcision must have militated against its exercising a significant influence on Christian observance. Nor is there an obvious formal carry-over from circumcision to baptism, such as obtains in the relationship between the Jewish Passover and the Christian Pascha and Lord's supper. Nor can we point to any significant moment or focus of transition from one to the other comparable to the role of the Last Supper. Much more plausible is the hypothesis that the parallel between circumcision and baptism became influential at a later date (as it plainly was by Cyprian's time),[45] when the controversies over the Christians' non-observance of the Jewish law had largely receded. No writer in the first two centuries used Colossians 2.11-12 to relate circumcision positively to baptism. It is not until Cyprian that we have any grounds for viewing infant baptism as a rite for the newborn, as might have been expected if circumcision had influenced Christian practice. A closely

---

[44] Jeremias, *Infant Baptism*, pp. 39-40, cf. 47, 48. Cf. Aland, *Did the Early Church*, pp. 82-84.

[45] Cyprian, *Epistle* 64 (Kraft, *Texte zur Geschichte*, pp. 27-29).

parallel development can be seen in Christian attitudes to the sabbath. Until the fourth century, it was either part of the jettisoned law of Moses or spiritualized. Early Christian writers frequently discuss circumcision and sabbath in similar terms in the same context.[46]

There remains Colossians 2.11-12, which starts with a spiritualizing of circumcision as a way of describing the Christian experience of Christ's redemption, and then refers to the baptismal incorporation of Christians into Christ's spiritually circumcising atonement. The correspondence is not between two rites, of circumcision and baptism, but between the Jewish rite and the divine work of spiritual circumcision accomplished by Christ. 'The circumcision of Christ' is the atoning death of Christ.

A third possible stimulus for the baptism of babies or children in the apostolic churches might be sought in the example or teaching of Jesus himself, which brings us to the blessing of the children (Mark 10.13-16 par.). The issue here is not the intention of Jesus as such, which can scarcely have related directly to the baptism of infants, but how the pericope was understood, and why it received the form it did in the developing Gospel tradition. Tertullian reveals that 'Let the children come to me...' was in his day adduced by the defenders of infant baptism,[47] but Jeremias believes that the command to give the children to Jesus through baptism was inferred from the passage much earlier than Tertullian. The evidence for this he finds in its interrelationship with other Gospel texts, especially Matthew 18.3 and John 3.5, both within the Gospels and in second-century tradition. The use of κωλύειν shows, according to Oscar Cullmann's thesis picked up by Jeremias, that 'in the period in which the Gospel tradition took shape the question of infant baptism was a live one, and that the passage about the blessing of the children was used as an argument against doubts about it.' The laying on of hands must also be seen in connexion with baptism.[48]

It is not clear whether Jeremias would argue that the command to baptize infants would have been inferred from this passage alone, in the absence of other factors precipitating its development. Once infant baptism had begun, the passage would of course be used in its defence against critics, but is its import clear enough, with or without Jeremias' accompanying evidence, for it to have been responsible for initiating the baptism of children born to Christians in a situation like Corinth? Was it a

---

[46] Cf. Justin, *Dialogue with Trypho* 19. This work contains the fullest Christian discussion of circumcision to date. It speaks of circumcision and baptism in close proximity, but falls short of suggesting any positive correspondence. Justin takes a pejorative view of circumcision, which was given only for Israel's hardness of heart and to mark her out for condign punishment at the hands of Rome. Cf. M. Simon, *Verus Israel* (Paris, 2nd edn, 1964), pp. 198ff.

[47] Tertullian, *Baptism* 18:5 (Kraft, *Texte zur Geschichte*, p. 13).

[48] Jeremias, *Infant Baptism*, pp. 48-55; Aland, *Did the Early Church*, pp. 95-99.

decisive factor in the extension of infant baptism to the children of baptized Christians which Jeremias originally posited for the very decade, AD 60–70, during which Mark's Gospel was probably produced? In any case, does it refer with any clarity to babies rather than, or as well as, to young children?

If, however, the final form of the passage reflects an established practice or controversy about an incipient practice, we would have to look elsewhere for a precipitating factor or factors, unless we could attribute that role to the blessing of the children in its pre-Marcan existence. It is difficult to identify such an initiating cause elsewhere in the ministry of Jesus.

This review has yielded regrettably few certainties. The evidence will sustain the confidence neither of a Jeremias nor of an Aland. The former's is even less warranted than the latter's. Before 200 in Rome, and possibly in North Africa too, the baptism of babies had become routine, but in a form of service devised for professing believers. Irenaeus implies that by about the mid-second century babies were being baptized in Southern Gaul and probably Rome and Asia Minor, but Justin's account of baptism at Rome c.150 suggests that they were not routinely baptized there. We noted two different ways of resolving this conflict, one based on the nature of ritual regulations and the other finding Irenaeus' allusion consistent with the solely emergency (albeit regular) baptism of infants. Some evidence is best interpreted of the believers' baptism of quite young children, which is provided for by Hippolytus. Many inscriptions do not allow us to determine whether the Christian children had been baptized as babies or later, but some reveal in the third century the emergency baptism of both babies and older children.

The New Testament seems to show that in the Pauline churches until at least c.55 the offspring of baptized Christians were not themselves baptized. It is not impossible that, on the model of Jewish proselyte baptism, converts were baptized in families on their accession to the church (solely Gentile converts, i.e., quite strictly on the model of the Jewish practice?), but the influence of proselyte baptism on Christian practice before the second century is increasingly doubted.[49] Nevertheless, Aland's attempt to demonstrate, from other things that are said about the members of baptized households, that infants could not have been included, ultimately fails to carry conviction. We have no right to expect such precision of these texts, as even Barth came near to seeing.[50] There is, of course, a close parallel in the silence of the baptismal liturgies of the *Didache* and Justin, on one interpretation of it, and in the

---

[49] The so-called '*oikos*–formula' has not survived critical scrutiny; cf. e.g., Strobel, 'Säuglings- und Kindertaufe', pp. 43-45.

[50] Barth, *CD* IV/4, p. 180.

near silence of Hippolytus. The point is relevant to Barth's objection[51] that the possibility that baptism might have embraced infants simply does not rear its head in the biblical discussion.

The analogy of circumcision is unlikely to have played a significant role until the later second century. The blessing of the children may reflect debates c.AD 60 about whether infants or young children were fit subjects for baptism. If it does, it clearly supports their baptism. But it is only in such a conjectural context that the passage is directly relevant to the question of infant baptismal origins. It is most unlikely, without other and weightier causes, to have led the early Christians to believe that they should baptize baby infants.

So the baptism of babies in families converted to Christianity may have begun early in the apostolic age, although the baptism of babies born to Christian parents probably did not. The latter may have developed out of the emergency baptism of infants sometime in the second century, or out of the inclusion of infants in household conversion-baptisms, or out of the practice of baptizing very young children who could answer for themselves. In so far as more of the evidence points to young children belonging to the Christian community alongside their elders and hence presumably on the same basis of faith-baptism, the extension of children's baptism to baby baptism is becoming an increasingly attractive hypothesis.[52]

In the year 381 Gregory Nazianzen advised that children should normally be baptized at about the age of three 'when they can take in something of the mystery, and answer (the questions), and even if they do not yet understand fully, can nevertheless retain some impression'.[53] In the whole debate the place of *parvuli* who can answer for themselves has not been given the consideration it deserves. Texts such as Acts 2.39 and Mark 10.14 should he read in the light of the portrayal of children in the apostolic churches of the Epistles, where they are addressed as responsive and responsible Christian like their parents.[54] These pictures, viewed against the background of synagogue practice, are fully consistent with the children's incorporation into congregational life according to their developing capacities. Child believers' baptism fits very well into this scenario.

---

[51] Barth, *CD* IV/4, pp. 165-66.

[52] Cf. Strobel, 'Säuglings- und Kindertaufe', pp. 63-68.

[53] Gregory Nazianzen, *Oratio* 40:28 (Kraft, *Texte zur Geschichte*, p. 53). Cf. Jeremias, *Infant Baptism*, p. 96.

[54] Strobel, 'Säuglings- und Kindertaufe', pp. 46-56. Cf. Barth's reflection on Mt. 21.14-17 (*CD* IV/4, p. 183). Overall he exaggerates the independent responsibility of the reception of baptism in the New Testament, and hence could not entertain child believers' baptism.

CHAPTER 2

How Controversial Was the Development of Infant Baptism in the Early Church?[1]

Baptism remains one of the most sensitive points of disagreement among the churches. Although the level of theological and historical debate has subsided since the stir excited by Karl Barth's celebrated rejection of infant baptism[2] and by the exchanges between Joachim Jeremias and Kurt Aland,[3] baptism has come increasingly to the fore in ecumenical discussion, largely as a result of *Baptism, Eucharist and Ministry*.[4]

But if paedobaptism has been a major topic of inter-confessional controversy intermittently since the sixteenth century, how controversial a subject was it in the early centuries of the church? This question is different from the modern historical one whether babies were baptized in primitive Christianity, and also from that of the biblical and theological rationale for baptizing them today—to which Geoffrey Bromiley has made an invaluable contribution from the perspective of Reformed theology.[5] The precise question before us in this essay is the extent to which the baptizing of babies was attended by argument and debate within the early church itself. But although it does not set out to confront the fundamental historical and theological issues, it will scarcely be able to avoid touching upon them here and there.

---

[1] This is a revised and expanded version of a paper contributed to a Joint Study Group between representatives of the Church of Scotland and the Baptist Union of Scotland. An earlier contribution, similarly revised, appeared in the *Scottish Journal of Theology* as 'The Origins of Infant Baptism—Child Believers' Baptism?' (see ch. 1 above).

[2] K. Barth, *The Teaching of the Church Regarding Baptism* (London, 1948); and *CD* IV/4, pp. 164-94.

[3] Joachim Jeremias, *Infant Baptism in the First Four Centuries* (London, 1960); Kurt Aland, *Did the Early Church Baptize Infants?* (London, 1963); Jeremias, *The Origins of Infant Baptism* (London, 1963); Aland, *Die Stellung der Kinder in der frühen christlichen Gemeinden und ihre Taufe* (Munich, 1967), and *Taufe und Kindertaufe. 40 Sätze zur Aussage des Neuen Testaments und dem historischen Befund, zur modernen Debatte darüber...* (Gütersloh, 1971).

[4] *Baptism, Eucharist and Ministry* (Faith and Order Paper, 111; Geneva, 1982). See my evaluations printed as chs 22 and 23 below.

[5] G.W. Bromiley, *Children of Promise: The Case for Baptizing Infants* (Edinburgh, 1979).

Although Christian baptism was often surrounded by contention in the patristic centuries, especially in the western church, the period saw no significant disagreement about the acceptability of baptizing babies. There is no precedent in the era of the Fathers for the baptismal divide of the sixteenth and subsequent centuries. The magisterial Reformation equated the error of the Anabaptists with that of the Donatists of Roman North Africa[6] (and Anabaptists were punished under the provisions of anti-Donatist legislation enacted by the emperors of Christian Rome), but the Donatists' baptismal dispute with the Catholic Church had nothing to do with the propriety of baptizing infants.

Nevertheless, the development of infant baptism in the early church was far from uncontroversial. The fourth century witnessed the widespread deferment of baptism, and the evidence of the inscriptions strongly suggests that this had happened in the third century also, albeit for different reasons.[7] Furthermore, the Pelagian conflict raised in an acute form the question why babies were baptized, and discussion of baptismal issues often exposed uncertainties relating to infant baptism. Solely in the idiosyncratic person of Tertullian did it appear to challenge the practice altogether, although this is not the whole truth.

New Testament Echoes of a Primitive Controversy?

Do the Gospel accounts of Jesus' blessing of the children (Mark 10.13-16, par.) preserve traces of a debate within the primitive Christian communities on whether babies should be baptized? New Testament scholarship yields no agreed answer to this question (nor indeed to the related question, which is not our concern here, whether the pericope reflects the uncontroverted practice of baptizing babies). The case for a *Sitz im Leben* in which the question of infant baptism was a live issue has been made chiefly by Oscar Cullmann and Joachim Jeremias.[8] They lean in particular on the use of the Greek verb κωλύειν, whose occurrence in baptismal contexts in New Testament writings and other early Christian literature they take to reflect a standard inquiry in primitive Christian baptismal procedure whether any hindrance existed to a candidate's baptism. The inclusion of this technical term shows, in Cullmann's words, 'that those who transmitted this story of the blessing of children wished to

---

[6] L. Verduin, *The Reformers and Their Stepchildren* (Exeter, 1964), ch. 1. See also ch. 15 below.

[7] See E. Ferguson's suggestive study, 'Inscriptions and the Origin of Infant Baptism', *Journal of Theological Studies* n.s. 30 (1979), pp. 36-46.

[8] O. Cullmann, *Baptism in the New Testament* (Studies in Biblical Theology, 1; London, 1950), pp. 71-80; Jeremias, *Infant Baptism*, pp. 48-55.

recall to the remembrance of Christians of their time an occurrence by which they might be led to a solution of the question of infant baptism'.[9]

The κωλύειν hypothesis has not gone uncontested. A.W. Argyle, for example, has objected that a technical liturgical verb would be unlikely to show such variation in the objects it governs as κωλύειν does—the candidate (Mark 10.14, par.; Acts 8.36; Ps-Clementines); water (Acts 10.47); the baptizer (Matthew 3.14; Epiphanius); and God (Acts 11.17).[10] Other considerations must incline us toward a verdict of uncertainty on the special role of κωλύειν. Although the claims that the Synoptic narrative must be read against a context in which the baptizing of infants was disputed is not wholly dependent upon the κωλύειν hypothesis, the claim itself enjoys no more than some degree of plausibility. The conclusion must be that, if there are grounds for holding that the baptizing of babies began or was extended around the time Mark's Gospel was compiled,[11] we can do no more than conjecture that this development ran into controversy which the incident of the blessing of the children was invoked to resolve. It may be speculated that, if the practice of paedobaptism was hotly contested in these early decades, the dispute would have been expected to leave early discernible traces in early Christian writings, within or without the New Testament. Apart from the debatable κωλύειν, nobody claims that it has.

Tertullian's Controversy

Tertullian's well-known objections to baptizing infants, spelled out in his homily on *Baptism* (c.200), should be interpreted not as opposition to a novel practice (his failure to state his objection in these terms being undoubtedly significant) but as a corollary of his broader approach to baptism. Although he expresses this in a highly characteristic fashion, it is not far removed from a remarkably common patristic understanding of baptism which should perhaps be regarded as the single most serious weakness of early baptismal thought. Tertullian's plea for delayed baptism therefore merits more extended treatment than his idiosyncratic presentations might suggest.

---

[9] Cullmann, *Baptism*, p. 78. Neither Cullmann nor Jeremias notes that Cyprian uses *prohibere* thrice and *inpedire* four times in discussing the baptism of the newborn in *Ep.* 64:5-6 (discussed below).

[10] A.W. Argyle, 'O. Cullmann's Theory concerning κωλύειν', *Expository Times* 67 (1955–56), p. 17. Cf. the guarded reserve of G.R. Beasley-Murray, *Baptism in the New Testament* (London, 1962), pp. 324-25. The English translator of Cullmann has not helped his case by using four different English verbs to tanslate κωλύειν. Cullmann's German and French each use only one—*hindern* and *empêcher* respectively.

[11] As Jeremias believed, prior to the English version of his *Infant Baptism*. See Aland, *Did the Early Church*, pp. 33-36, and ch. 1 above, for his change of mind.

Tertullian is concerned with the profitability of baptismal reception. Deferment is advocated because it is 'more profitable' (*utilior*), in accordance with the candidate's character, attitude, and age (*Baptism* 18:4). Therefore, postponement is particularly appropriate in the case of young children. Tertullian gives no suggestion that he views baby baptism as invalid, as not true baptism at all, as though the person baptized as a baby could subsequently receive a proper (second) baptism. His quarrel with the baptizing of babies is not that of a latter-day credobaptist but seems to be twofold: it is needless, and it is attended with very great risk. On both counts it is unprofitable, or at least highly likely to prove so.

First, it is needless because baptism imparts the remission of sins and infancy is the age of innocence (*innocens aetas*; *Baptism* 18:5). The implication is clear: because of their innocence babies have nothing or little to gain from baptism. Tertullian does not unpack for his readers the implications of *innocens* in this celebrated phrase, but its primary reference must be to a baby's lack of sins of his own commission. We should not deduce from it that Tertullian held no belief in original sin, nor is it altogether safe to assert that 'he could hardly have taken this attitude [to infant baptism] unless he had held lightly to the doctrine of original sin.[12] Although his doctrine has occasioned considerable debate, he is not reticent in speaking about the effects upon all mankind of Adam's fall. In particular, 'he is more explicit and outspoken about this sinful bias [of a vitiated nature] than previous theologians',[13] and in his treatise on *The Soul*, in a difficult passage, he declares every soul to be impure (*immunda*) until it is reborn in Christ.[14] This impurity is more than the soul's 'investment by pagan influences before and after birth',[15] although Tertullian makes much of these; it also, or rather primarily, encompasses a transmitted natural infection by sin.

But if *innocens aetas* provides no pointers to Tertullian's view of original sin, its place in the argument seems to suggest either that no close connection had yet been forged by him or the church between original sin and infant baptism or that, in his thought about the benefits of baptism, the sins of responsible free will loomed much larger than the inheritance from Adam, in whatever terms this was defined. The latter is

---

[12] Ernest Evans (ed. and trans.), *Tertullian's Homily on Baptism* (London, 1964), p. 101. See the full discussion in E. Nagel, *Kindertaufe und Taufaufschub. Die Praxis vom 3.-5. Jahrhundert in Nordafrika und ihre theologische Einordnung bei Tertullian, Cyprian und Augustinus* (Europäische Hochschulschriften, 23:144; Frankfurt am Main, 1980).

[13] J.N.D. Kelly, *Early Christian Doctrines* (London, 5th edn, 1977), p. 176.

[14] Tertullian, *De Anima* 40:1. See the helpful analysis in the edition by J.H. Waszink, *De Anima, Edited with Commentary* (Amsterdam, 1947), p. 446.

[15] Evans, *Tertullian's Homily on Baptism*, p. 102. Kelly is a sounder guide, and cf. Norman P. Williams, *The Ideas of the Fall and Original Sin* (London, 1927), pp. 231-45.

the more likely explanation, and brings us in fact to the second reason why Tertullian advocated the postponement of baptism. We will have cause, however, to return to the former possibility.

The second, and weightier, consideration that argues for the utmost circumspection in giving Christian baptism are the risks attendant upon its premature reception. In his homily on baptism, Tertullian has far more to say about these than his one brief, tantalizing mention of *innocens aetas*. For they are not limited to infant candidates:

> With no less reason ought the unmarried also to be delayed until they either marry or are firmly established in continence; until then, temptation lies in wait for them, for virgins because they are ripe for it, and for widows because of their wandering about. (*Baptism* 18:6)

Tertullian ends this chapter with a sentence that takes us to the heart of his concern: 'All who understand what a burden (*pondus*) baptism is will have more fear of obtaining it than of its postponement' (*Baptism* 18:6). It is this awesome *pondus* that should deter *sponsores* from promoting infant candidates, since death may prevent them ensuring the fulfillment of the baptismal promises they take on their behalf, or 'the subsequent development of an evil disposition' in the baptized youngster may frustrate their (the sponsors') purpose (*Baptism* 18:4).

The fearful prospect that governs Tertullian's counsel is that of serious post-baptismal sin. Indeed, the very fact that he argues as he does about the risks of the premature baptism of infants shows conclusively that baby baptism, however unwise, was real baptism, after which there remained no subsequent (second) baptismal washing. What surfaces here in Tertullian, and much more starkly elsewhere in his corpus, especially in his later (Montanist) treatise *De Paenitentia*, is by no means confined to his convictions alone. It was a pervasive belief among the Fathers that the washing of baptism covered only those sins committed up to this point in one's life. Providing for sins committed after baptism, especially for grave offences, was a major problem in the early centuries, and was eventually responsible for the development of a system of ecclesiastical penance. In the literature of the period, a clear parallelism obtains between baptism and any subsequent opportunity for remission of grave sins; the latter could be spoken of as a 'second repentance (penance)', or even as a 'second baptism'. Considerable controversy surrounded the questions whether, for what offences, and whether more than once such post-baptismal remission could be granted. The Montanist Tertullian was of course a strident contributor to these arguments, which constitute the background to the wording of the clause in the Nicene Creed, 'one baptism for the remission of sins'.[16]

The baptizing of babies and infants was bound to appear fraught with the greatest peril so long as such profound anxiety contemplated the possibility of moral lapses after baptism. At the very least, baptism should be given only to the person who asks for it, which in the context of Tertullian's baptismal treatise must mean the person who receives baptism in the full knowledge of, even in spite of, its forbidding *pondus*. It makes no sense to entrust *substantia divina* to one too young to be trusted with *substantia terrena*. What emerges clearly from the battery of arguments Tertullian discharges is that baptism is most wisely received by the person whose preparation for it has been so thorough that his or her maintenance of baptismal purity thereafter is as fully guaranteed as possible. While this assumes in practice the baptism only of believers, it goes far beyond this essential requirement of credobaptist teaching. At the end of this chapter of *De Baptismo* Tertullian declares that 'a person whose faith is entire (*integra*), i.e., who has sufficient faith in God, can be sure (*secura*) that though he defers his baptism God will not let him die unbaptized.'[17] We must remind ourselves that Tertullian's position did not entail his treating the baptism of babies or young children as other than Christian baptism. In fact, in cases of 'necessity', he seems to have regarded it as the proper course of action. 'Necessity' was constituted routinely, it must be assumed, by the likelihood of death, and occasionally by the threat of persecution. Martyrdom in turn was another form of second baptism, a blood baptism which covered all outstanding sin, and was the supreme baptism inasmuch as it cut off every possibility of subsequent sin.

Tertullian's controversy with infant baptism turns out to reflect a framework of reference unlikely to be shared by any of the participants in latter-day baptismal disputes, at least among Protestants. On the other hand, baptism (or its higher surrogate, martyrdom) was essential for salvation (*Baptism* 12:1, quoting John 3.5), and hence had to be administered in emergency even to infants. But on the other hand, because baptism's capacity to deal with sin was limited to the burden of

---

[16] A further study would be needed to show the evidence for this. Briefly, the absence of references to 'one baptism' in western creeds shows that its inclusion is unrelated to the (largely western) controversies over baptism; the specified purpose 'for the remission of sins' indicates the reason for insisting on '*one* baptism'; and the exposition given by Cyril of Jerusalem, one of the earliest witnesses to such a clause in a creed and the first to provide an explanation of it, makes it clear that it excludes the possibility of setting things right a second time if a person fails once after baptism (*Procatechesis* 7). John Chrysostom's comment is very similar (*Baptismal Catechesis* 3:23).

[17] Evans' paraphrase in *Tertullian's Homily on Baptism*, p. 106, of *fides integra secura est de salute* (*Baptism* 18:6).

sin already accumulated by the candidate,[18] it must be sought only with the utmost caution and sense of responsibility, and hence would normally never be granted to, because never requested by, infants. It is fair to say that neither of these two fundamental convictions would command much assent in baptismal debate today. Baptizers on both sides of the 'waters that divide' are likely to place much greater weight on a belief which the calculating prudence of Tertullian's theology inevitably undervalued—namely, that the gift or strengthening of the Spirit associated with baptism is God's provision enabling the baptized to overcome the temptations that continue to assail him or her to the end of life. This conviction led the early church to baptize catechumens when persecution threatened, so that they might be fortified to stand firm in the hour of trial.

A Practice in Search of a Theology?

In Tertullian, it seems, the reality of original sin had scarcely begun to influence the practice of baptism—although it was presumably original sin that created, or contributed to, the 'necessity' of baptism for dying babies. (But only in *dying* babies was the need constituted by original sin allowed by Tertullian to override prudential considerations and necessitate baptism.) Precisely because most of the early references to infant baptism are so brief and allusive, not to say debatable, it is difficult to speak with any confidence of the reasons why baptism was felt to be necessary for babies in the first two centuries or so of the church's history. Hippolytus is the first to report what might be called the routine inclusion of babies in baptism in his *Apostolic Tradition*, written c.215, but he provides no evidence whatsoever about the rationale of baby baptism. Since the whole of the rest of Hippolytus' account of baptism, including its preparation and sequel, assumes responsible believers as its subjects, we are left to draw the conclusion that babies too needed to be saved from what responsible believers were saved from in baptism. But if the plight of those needing baptism was held to lie in the sins they had committed, what could one say about babies or very young children who had committed no such sins? Early Christian writers commonly ascribe to infants innocence or sinlessness,[19] attributes which should be read not so

---

[18] No clearer illustration of this common early Christian conviction could be given that that of Chrysostom: 'The sins committed before baptism are all cancelled by the grace and kindness of the strength of Christ crucified. The sins committed after baptism require great earnestness, that they may again be cancelled. Since there is no second baptism, there is need of our tears, repentance, confession, almsgiving, prayer, and every other kind of devotion' (*De s. Pentecoste hom.* 1:6; *PG* 50, col. 463).

[19] For the evidence see Aland, *Die Stellung*, pp. 17-21; B. Klaus, 'Die Erbsündenlehre als Motiv des Kirchlichen Handelns in der Taufe', *Kerygma und Dogma* 15 (1969), pp. 50-

much as denying original sin as reflecting a stage prior to its conscious articulation as a teaching of the church. What they assert, of course, is that young children have yet to commit the culpable, wilful sins of their elders.

In this context it is not surprising that the practice of infant baptism became a potent factor in the development of the doctrine of original sin. It is now commonplace to refer to confirmation as a rite in search of a theology, but one could apply the same description of infant baptism in the early church. In the West, if not so obviously in the East, it found the theological justification it needed in the dogma of original sin. If there is a persisting controversy about infant baptism in the patristic age, it concerns primarily the question 'why?' rather than 'whether?', although the absence of confident answers to the former must to some extent have diverted pressure onto the latter.

There is no doubt that the custom of infant baptism was the single most powerful catalyst of the formulation of doctrines of original sin, and that the direction of argument moved from the accepted practice of infant baptism to the truth of the doctrine, and not vice-versa.[20] We have here an unmistakable illustration of the axiom *lex orandi lex credendi*. The church baptizes babies who, it is agreed, have not sinned *in propria persona*; therefore, we must believe that they are baptized for the cleaning or remission of original sin. Original sin must be part of the faith of the church; why else does the church baptize babies?

Although the contours of this argument are clearly recognizable from the third century until the Pelagian controversy in the fifth, it is not always possible to discern the backcloth to discussions in ecclesiastical practice or dispute. That they took place in very varied contexts is obvious enough from the contribution of Cyprian.

How Close a Correspondence to Circumcision?

In one of his letters written in the name of a council of African bishops that met in the spring of 253, Cyprian reports the council's unanimous response to a question raised by bishop Fidus (of an unknown see).[21] Fidus believed that the analogy with circumcision decreed that babies should be baptized on the eighth day after birth and not before it. The letter reveals little more than this about Fidus' position. We do not know whether others shared his view, but it is a reasonable inference that

---

70, at pp. 54-58; J.C. Didier, 'Un cas typique de développement du dogme à propos du baptême des enfants', *Mélanges de science religieuse* 9 (1952), pp. 191-213, at pp. 194-200.

[20] Jaroslav Pelikan, *Development of Christian Doctrine: Some Historical Prolegomena* (New Haven, CT/London, 1969), ch. 3.

[21] Cyprian, *Epistle* 64 (numbered 58 in the *ANCL* translation).

disagreement with actual practice, whether established or innovatory, provoked the voicing of his opinion. If we may judge from the terms of Cyprian's refutation, Fidus had made three points in support of his case.

First, and least clear of the three, Fidus may have claimed that a baby of only two or three days old was not yet capable of receiving the divine gift of baptism. We cannot be certain in inferring that Fidus argued along these lines, but Cyprian's first rejoinder is to stress that the newborn baby is a completed creature of God, lacking nothing as a human being, and that age makes no difference at all in the equality of the divine grace (*Epistle* 64:2-3). 'The mercy and grace of God is not to be refused to anyone born of man.'

Second, Fidus had undoubtedly pleaded the impurity of an infant in the first days after its birth, which made people shudder to kiss it. Cyprian has no patience with this kind of almost physical distaste, and seems ready to kiss and baptize even the baby still wet and unwashed from the womb. In embracing the freshly made handiwork of God, we in some sense kiss 'the still recent hands of God themselves' (*Ep.* 64:4). Scripture declares all persons clean.

Third, 'spiritual circumcision ought not to be hindered by carnal circumcision'. Cyprian's response implies the acceptance of the parallel between shadow and substance, but lays its main emphasis on the dissolution of the former once the latter had come in Christ (*Ep.* 64:4-5).

The greatest interest of the letter, however, is found in the way Cyprian combines both original sin and the child's freedom from sin of his or her own in arguing for the earliest administration of baptism. The bishop of Carthage recommends a course of action directly contrary to that advocated by his earlier fellow-citizen, but oddly enough he shared with Tertullian the ingredients out of which the two concocted such totally different recipes. For Cyprian, the fact that the newborn has not sinned on his or her own account but, 'being born after the flesh according to Adam, has contracted the contagion of the ancient death at his earliest birth' (with both of which counts Tertullian would agree) argues for, not against, his or her speedy baptism, even to the extent of not waiting until the eighth day after birth. When the sins to be remitted are not his own but another's, he comes 'the more easily' to the forgiveness of baptism. Arguing *a maiori ad minus*, Cyprian reasons that, if an adult convert's erstwhile flagrant wickedness is no bar to his baptism, nothing can possibly stand in the way of the baptism of the newborn innocent. The contrast with Tertullian's viewpoint could hardly be more marked, and it is difficult not to discern in this part of the letter a response to Tertullian rather than to Fidus. Otherwise Cyprian must appear to be wielding a theological sledgehammer to crack a minor procedural nut. He gives no hint that Fidus needed persuading of the doctrine of original sin, whereas the force of Cyprian's theological reasoning seems specifically designed to counter Tertullian's appeal to *innocens aetas*. The difference between them is attributable in large measure to the conjunction Cyprian makes between infant baptism and original sin. Although the sins needing remission are not the baby's own, they necessitate his baptism. Cyprian fancifully interprets the crying of the newborn as his tearful entreaty for divine grace, which by its very helplessness lays the more powerful claim upon the succor of baptism (*Ep.* 64:5-6). As he repeats three times in the letter (*Ep.* 64:2, 5, 6), since God is merciful toward all, the grace of baptism is to be denied to none.

It was Cyprian's paradoxical contribution, in a writing in which the weight of the reasoning falls on the innocence of babyhood, to have made original sin part of the framework of thought about infant baptism for the first time in the West. The vigor of his episcopate, the prestige of his subsequent martyrdom, and the fact that he wrote with conciliar authority all conspired to exalt his letter as the authentic voice of Catholic tradition. It would prove a priceless weapon in Augustine's armoury against the Pelagians.

An Apostolic Tradition: Origen and Original Sin

Cyprian's older contemporary in the East, Origen of Alexandria and Caesarea, is also a clear witness to the church's baptism of infants. In three passages from the later Caesarean period of his life,[22] he followed through an explicit chain of reasoning which concluded that, since baptism was given for the remission of sins and was administered according to the church's practice to *parvuli* as well as older persons, there must be something in infants requiring the baptismal washing, for otherwise there would be no rationale for their baptism. Since they have at no time committed sin, the answer is found in the uncleanness of which Job 14.4 (LXX) speaks: 'None is pure from uncleanness (*sorde*), not even if his life on earth is but one day old.' This text (which was not unknown to Cyprian)[23] was backed up by Psalm 51.5 (50.7, LXX): 'In iniquities was I conceived, and in sins did my mother give me birth.' In fact, Origen's conception of original sin was hardly mainstream, although it remains disputed whether it developed toward a more orthodox configuration.[24] His belief in the pre-cosmic fall of pre-existent souls

---

[22] Origen, *Homilies on Luke* 14 (on Lk. 2.22); *Homilies on Leviticus* 8.3; *Commentary on Romans* 5.9. It has been argued that Origen's lack of explicit reference to infant baptism in his Alexandrian writings implies that it was not practised in the Alexandrian church.

[23] Cf. Cyprian, *Testimonies* 3:54, where with Ps 51.5 and 1 Jn 1.8 it proves that 'No one is without uncleanness and without sin.'

[24] Cf. Kelly, *Early Christian Doctrines*, pp. 180-82. A rather different account of Origen's thought is given by Williams, *Fall and Original Sin*, pp. 223-30.

required that the sinfulness attested by Job and the Psalmist was the legacy, not of solidarity with Adam's sin, but of each soul's previous transgression. In this knowledge that all human beings were born into this world in impurity, the apostles mandated the church to give baptism to infants also.[25]

Not only does Origen press the practice of infant baptism into the service of his own speculative theory of pre-cosmic sin, but he is also the first Christian writer to claim the apostolic origin of the church's custom. Kurt Aland alleges that all his statements

> stand on the defensive against the belief that infants do not need baptism, on the ground that as infants have not actually committed any sins, they do not require forgiveness of sins... There must have been circles and that not small and uninfluential, whose members held a different opinion as to the necessity of infant baptism and who correspondingly maintained a different practice, in that they abstained from baptizing infants. Hence arises Origen's appeal to the 'tradition of the Church received from the apostles'..., which was the strongest argument that he possessed.[26]

This interpretation of Origen is quite unconvincing, and Jeremias' rejoinder makes much better sense.[27] Origen's argument proceeds not from the fact of the sinfulness of newborn babies to the need for their prompt baptism but in the reverse direction. He does, however, report that 'the brethren' frequently discussed the question how infants could be baptized for the remission of sins (the purpose of all Christian baptism) when they had committed no sin of their own.[28] The debates within the Christian community which Origen refers to concerned not whether but why babies should be baptized.

Again we have found the rite in search of an agreed meaning. That this should be the case towards the middle of the third century in Caesarea may suggest that the practice can scarcely have been regularly observed there for almost two hundred years. If it is true that 'there is no clearer instance of the control exercised by liturgical or devotional practice over the growth of dogma than that provided by the study of the relations between the custom of Infant Baptism and the doctrine of Original Sin',[29] it is an entirely proper question why in this instance the *lex orandi* took such a long time to establish the *lex credendi*—if, that is, infant baptism was, at least in Caesarea, a tradition of apostolic origin. Origen's reference to frequent ecclesiastical discussion of the theoretical justification for

---

[25] Origen, *Commentary on Romans* 5:9.
[26] Aland, *Did the Early Church*, p. 47.
[27] Jeremias, *Origins*, pp. 69-74. He brings out well the context and sequence of thought of Origen's references.
[28] Origen, *Homilies on Luke* 14 (on Lk. 2.22).
[29] Williams, *Fall and Original Sin*, p. 223.

baptizing infants may therefore imply not that the practice was a recent introduction, still resisted by some of the brethren, but that by the 230s and 240s it had not had a sufficiently long history in the church of Caesarea to have evoked a received theological basis in the tradition. Origen's expositions were still needed to provide one. But it remains unambiguously clear from Origen that the practice pre-existed his explanation of it.

The East after Origen: Consensus Elusive

It is not the purpose of this paper to trace the history of infant baptism in the church of the Fathers but to attempt to ascertain how far it remained a subject of controversy. In the eastern church there is little indication that Origen's biblical discussions had much influence on beliefs about why babies needed baptism. There is in fact not much evidence that churchmen were unduly concerned about infant baptism at all, and the considerable body of fourth-century Christian literature in the East yields remarkably few references to it. After Origen the first witness is the Arian Asterius the Sophist, whose homilies on Psalms 1–15 were delivered probably in the second quarter of the fourth century. Three of these homilies[30] assume the baptism of newborn babies as the norm but do not connect it with sin or original sin. But baptism of infants is presented as protection against demons, heresy, and premature death. Indeed, it is difficult to point to a single eastern Father in the fourth century who links infant baptism with sin or original sin.[31] Chrysostom's enormous corpus yields less than a handful of references to infant baptism, one of which asserts that 'we baptize little children, even though they have no sins', in order that they may receive gifts such as righteousness and adoption and become members of Christ and the abode of the Spirit.[32] The

---

[30] Cf. J.C. Didier, 'Le Pédobaptisme au IVe siècle. Documents nouveaux', *Mélanges de science religieuse* 6 (1949), pp. 223-46. The original texts are also given in the two main collections of sources: H. Kraft, *Texte zur Geschichte der Taufe, besonders der Kindertaufe in der Alten Kirche* (Kleine Texte, 174; Berlin, 2nd edn, 1969), pp. 41-43; and Didier, *Le Baptême des enfants dans la tradition de l'Eglise* (Monumenta Christiana Selecta, 7; Tournai, 1959), pp. 28-30. Since this essay was written, these homilies by Asterius have been redated, and are now placed in the early fifth century. See Wolfram Kinzig, *In Search of Asterius: Studies on the Authorship of the Homilies on the Psalms* (Göttingen, 1990).

[31] For references see Didier, *Le Baptême des enfants*, pp. 233-35, and 'Un cas typique de développement du dogme', pp. 204-11.

[32] John Chrysostom, *Baptismal Catecheses* 3:6 (A. Wenger [ed.], *Jean Chrysostome. Huit catéchèses baptismales inédites* [SC 50; Paris, 1957], pp. 153-54); P.W. Harkins, *St. John Chrysostom: Baptismal Instructions* (Ancient Christian Writers, 31; Westminster, MD/London, 1963), p. 57. When Jeremias wrote *Infant Baptism* (1958, 1960), he was aware of Chrysostom's catechetical comment only in the form of Augustine's quotation in *Against Julian the Pelagian* 1:6:21-22 (cf. 94 n. 7). Julian had

Cappadocians, like Chrysostom, pleaded with their congregations not to delay their baptism, but nearly always, it seems, with adult converts in view. Their pleas are hardly ever directed toward parental responsibility for their offspring in the matter of baptism. Several prominent fourth-century Fathers, although of Christian parentage, were not baptized until adult years. In the East these included John Chrysostom, Basil the Great, and Gregory Nazianzen.[33]

The sole writer to address the issue of the delay of infant baptism directly is Gregory Nazianzen in his oration on baptism. His counsel is clear. Babies in danger of death must be baptized without delay, 'for it is better that they should be unconsciously sanctified than depart this life unsealed and uninitiated'. Circumcision is cited as the warrant for so doing. But for others Gregory advises a wait until they are about three years old,

> when they may be able to listen and to answer something about the sacrament, so that, even though they do not perfectly understand it, yet at any rate they know the outlines, and then to sanctify them in soul and body with the great sacrament of our consecration... They begin to be responsible for their lives at the time when reason is matured and they may be instructed in the mystery (for of sins of ignorance owing to their tender years they have no account to give), and it is far more profitable on all accounts to be fortified by the font, because of the sudden assaults of danger that befall us.[34]

That this and similar questions on the timing of baptism were currently matters of discussion among Christian congregations may be implied by the way Gregory responds in his *Oration* to real or imagined objections and queries.

---

cited Chrysostom's text in a Latin form (*non coinquinatos...peccato*, 'not defiled by sin'), which demonstrated to Julian that Chrysostom did not believe in original sin in infants. Augustine was able to correct him by producing Chrysostom's Greek.

[33] Cf. Jeremias, *Infant Baptism*, pp. 88-89, for details. Basil's exhortation (*Homily* 13:1, 5; *PG* 31, cols. 424, 432) illustrates the pastor's dilemma. In urging young and old alike to be baptized without delay, he stresses that the whole of life is the right time (καιρός) for baptism, which must have militated against an insistence on invariable infant baptism.

[34] Gregory Nazianzen, *Oration* 40:28; 40:17, is presumably to be read in terms of this later passage, but the consistency is not obvious: 'Do you have an infant child? Do not allow sin any opportunity. Let him be sanctified from babyhood, and consecrated by the Spirit from his tenderest days.' He goes on to refer to Samuel, who was consecrated to God immediately after birth. See ch. 9 below. Gregory's mention in sect. 23 of those who 'because of infancy' have been unable to receive baptism indicates, not the existence of 'some parts of the church where paedobaptism was unknown' (Williams, *Fall and Original Sin*, p. 290 n. 4), but simply infants' dependence on negligent parents.

We cannot, however, speak of controversy about infant baptism in this period in the East. Much remains obscure. Baptism is generally assumed to be necessary for salvation, but little clarity is forthcoming on what babies are to be saved from. More is said about the positive gifts imparted to them in baptism, which is also viewed as fortifying the baptized against the perils of life. A poem of Gregory Nazianzen in speaking of baptism describes it as the seal of God—for infants only a seal, but for adults a remedy as well as a seal.[35] But overall the evidence is too scanty to allow us to delineate a consensus. Gregory Nazianzen shows that there was scope for considerable variety of teaching, and all that seems agreed is an unwillingness to adopt the standpoint of Origen, the first articulate advocate of infant baptism in the eastern tradition. We must not forget however, that it was in circles strongly influenced by the Cappadocians (among whom Gregory of Nyssa appears to ignore infant baptism altogether)[36] that the phrase 'one baptism for the remission of sins' found its way into the Nicene Creed. When this is set in the context of the teachings of the fourth-century Greek Fathers about infants and baptism, it is difficult to regard it as having any intended reference to paedobaptism. It could be paraphrased in the following terms: insofar as baptism is given for the remission of sins (which, it is agreed, is not the case with the baptism of babies), a person may receive it only once.[37]

The West after Cyprian

It is easy to overlook the overwhelming extent to which the body of early Christian writing about infant baptism is dominated by Augustine's works, very largely against the Pelagians.[38] The critical issue raised early in the fifth century by Pelagius and, more acutely, his associate Caelestius

---

[35] Gregory Nazianzen, *Carmina Dogmatica* 9:91-92 (*PG* 37, cols. 463-64, with note *ad loc.*). Cf. Williams, *Fall and Original Sin*, pp. 289-90. Neither Kraft nor Didier includes this text.

[36] Cf. Williams, *Fall and Original Sin*, pp. 278-80. It is not at all clear from Gregory of Nyssa's treatise *On Infants Who Die Early* whether the problem it tackles arises from their not having received infant baptism or from their dying before reaching the appropriate later age for baptism. Since infant baptism is not mentioned, the latter seems more likely. Gregory's *Against Those Who Defer Baptism* likewise makes no allusion to infant baptism. His sermon *The Baptism of Christ* attributes to the newly baptized old person the innocence of the baby and the newborn infant's freedom from accusations and penalties (*PG* 46, col. 579).

[37] On this issue, see Williams, *Fall and Original Sin*, pp. 553-54, who also concludes that those who framed or included this clause could only have had believers' baptism in mind. See ch. 4 below.

[38] In Didier's collection, *Le Baptême des enfants*, material from the first four centuries occupies forty-four pages (including ten pages of inscriptions), while Augustine is allotted sixty.

was simple enough. Their denial of the transmission of original sin dismantled what Augustine depicted as the traditional theological rationale for the practice of baptizing infants—given that, as was agreed on all sides, infants had no sins of their own commission which required baptismal remission. Augustine and other African bishops not unnaturally feared that the airing of such questions would stiffen parental reluctance to bring their babies to the baptistry, at a time when churchmen in the West no less than in the East were striving to overcome the widespread delay of baptism. Augustine's *Confessions* did not hesitate to criticize even his own mother for refusing to have him baptized during a serious childhood illness, despite his pleas.[39]

But how firmly established in the western tradition was the doctrine of original sin as the strongest theological undergirding for baby baptism? The Pelagians appealed to earlier Fathers, but invariably with reference to the transmission of sin from Adam and never explicitly on the grounds for baptizing infants.[40] In the ascetic circles to which they belonged, the related issue of the origin of the soul remained the subject of lively debate, fired in particular by continuing controversy over the teachings of Origen;[41] but, whereas this was a question to which, as even Augustine was only too aware, scripture and tradition yielded no incontrovertible answer, could the same be claimed for the presence of original sin in infants as the reason why they had to be baptized if they were to be delivered from damnation? Augustine could with some justice lay claim to an identifiable current of western doctrinal reflection on this subject. After Cyprian, whose *Epistle* 64 was, of course, Augustine's star witness for the prosecution, there is a gap in the evidence comparable to that in the East. But toward the end of the fourth century, the convictions of western churchmen emerged into the light of day with a clarity that eludes us in the East. A decretal of Siricius, bishop of Rome, in the year 385 urges the prompt baptism of infants whose age prevents them speaking for themselves, lest, dying unbaptized, they should lose eternal life and the kingdom of heaven—thus neatly excluding in advance the distinction the Pelagians would make between the two.[42] In a letter of AD 400, Jerome, a westerner writing in the East, seems to imply that infants are baptized for 'sin',[43] but the most important catholic contributor prior to Augustine

---

[39] Augustine, *Confessions* 1:11:17-18.

[40] Cf. especially Augustine, *Nature and Grace* 61:71–67:81. Augustine also discusses earlier Fathers' opinions in *Against Two Letters of the Pelagians* 4:8:20–12:34; and *The Grace of Christ and Original Sin* 1:42:46–50:55.

[41] Cf. Robert F. Evans, *Pelagius: Inquiries and Reappraisals* (London, 1968), ch. 2.

[42] Siricius, *Epistle* 1: 3 (Kraft, *Texte zur Geschichte*, p. 67; Didier, *Le Baptême des enfants*, p. 36).

[43] Jerome, *Epistle* 107:6. Jerome is inculcating parental responsibility for children. Until they reach years of discretion, both their *mala* and their *bona* are attributed to their

was Ambrose of Milan. He not only presents a well-developed doctrine of Adamic fall and its effects upon all humanity (described by N.P. Williams as 'Augustinianism before Augustine'),[44] but he also makes no distinction between infants and adults in talking about sin as constituting the need for baptism. Yet even Ambrose falls far short of the decisive sharpness of Augustine's refutation of Pelagian teachings. The bishop of Milan disappoints us if we are looking for an umambiguous declaration that infants are baptized for the forgiveness of original *guilt*, although he certainly taught this doctrine.[45]

Augustine and the Pelagian Controversy

It was, therefore, the peculiar distinction of anti-Pelagian Augustine to make the bonds uniting infant baptism to original sin, in the sense of guilt as well as weakness, disease, or corruption, so firm as to remain virtually unbreakable for over a millennium in the western church. But although it has become commonplace to treat the Pelagian controversy as a western—and typically western—affair, the suggestion has well been made that 'Probably the germ of the controversy was the now undisputed fact that differing explanations of infant baptism were held in the East and in the West.'[46] The teaching of Caelestius, which first significantly disturbed catholic churchmen in Carthage in 411, maintained that infants were baptized not in order to be delivered from the condemnation attendant upon original sin, and hence not to exchange salvation and eternal life for perdition and death, but in order to secure entry to the kingdom of heaven.[47] Although Caelestius could not challenge the use of the formula 'for the remission of sins', he was unable to salvage any real meaning for it in his baptism of infants: 'it is fitting, indeed, to confess

---

parents—'unless you happen to suppose that the children of Christians, if they have not received baptism, are themselves liable for [their] sin (*reos...peccati*) and that guilt (*scelus*) is not ascribed to those who declined to give them baptism...'. Is Jerome implying that infants are baptized for their own 'sin' but that, where baptism is withheld from them, their parents become liable for their sin? Yet *scelus* appears not to be synonymous with *peccati* but to designate the particular offence of parental neglect. In *Ep.* 85:2, 5, Jerome responds to an enquiry from Paulinus of Nola: 'how the children of believing, that is, baptized parents are "holy" [cf. 1 Cor. 7.14], seeing that without the gift of grace afterwards received [in baptism] and kept they cannot be saved.' Jerome's reply does not question Paulinus' assumptions.

[44] Williams, *Fall and Original Sin*, p. 300.

[45] Cf. Didier, 'Un cas typique de développement du dogme', pp. 202-204; Williams, *Fall and Original Sin*, pp. 304-306.

[46] Eugene TeSelle, *Augustine the Theologian* (New York, 1970), p. 280; 'Rufinus the Syrian, Caelestius, Pelagius: Explorations in the Prehistory of the Pelagian Controversy', *Augustinian Studies* 3 (1973), pp. 61-95, esp. pp. 86-87.

[47] Augustine, *Epistle* 157:22; *The Grace of Christ and Original Sin* 2:2:2–6:6.

this lest we should seem to make different kinds of baptism'.[48] Pelagius' position was virtually identical; if anything, he exacerbated its provocativeness by insisting that 'We hold one baptism, which we affirm ought to be administered to infants in the same sacramental formula as to adults'[49]—which was handy grist to Augustine's mill, as we shall see.

The first of Augustine's anti-Pelagian treatises is entitled *The Merits and Remission of Sins and the Baptism of Infants* (411–412). Much of the first and third books are directed against the central Pelagian convictions about Adam's sin and infant baptism, but the precise target of book one is probably the *Liber de Fide* of one Rufinus the Syrian, an obscure figure who is nevertheless credited in one source with being the inspirer at Rome of the whole Pelagian heresy. His *Liber* certainly includes an attack on the transmission of sins and the damnation of infants and an assertion that infants are baptized for admission to the kingdom of God.[50] This Rufinian-Caelestian-Pelagian approach to paedobaptism is formally similar to that of eastern churchmen, such as Gregory Nazianzen[51] and John Chrysostom; and the eastern—in particular the Syrian or Antiochene—affinities of Pelagianism have been explored by scholars.[52] Pelagius and Caelestius found a more sympathetic hearing in the East than in the West, and although each side accused the other of innovation and heresy, the Pelagians in addition threatened their opponents with condemnation by the churches of the East.[53] There are, then, good grounds for discerning, as a significant contributory factor to the controversy, at least the absence of consensus, if not a clear disagreement, between East and West on the significance of infant baptism.

The dispute was not whether infants should be baptized but why.[54] When Caelestius complained to Innocent, bishop of Rome, that he was being defamed for refusing baptism to infants, whereas he had always maintained that they should be baptized, Augustine countered that Caelestius was misrepresenting the charge against him in order to dismiss it more readily.[55] For Augustine the answer to the question 'why?'

---

[48] Augustine, *The Grace of Christ and Original Sin* 2:6:6.

[49] Augustine, *The Grace of Christ and Original Sin* 1:32:35, 2:1:1, 2:21:24.

[50] TeSelle, *Augustine the Theologian*, p. 279, and his 'Rufinus the Syrian'; see also Gerald Bonner, 'Rufinus of Syria and African Pelagianism', *Augustinian Studies* 1 (1970), pp. 31-47, and his *Augustine and Modern Research on Pelagianism* (Villanova, 1972), pp. 9, 19-31.

[51] Cf. Williams, *Fall and Original Sin*, p. 345.

[52] See the studies of Evans, TeSelle, and Bonner noted above, and the literature to which they refer.

[53] Augustine, *The Proceedings of Pelagius* 11:25.

[54] Augustine, *Sermon* 294:2.

[55] Augustine, *The Grace of Christ and Original Sin* 2:4:3, 2:17:19, 2:18:20.

emerged with crystal clarity from a consideration of basic Christian beliefs.

1. By ancient tradition of apostolic authority[56] the church baptizes infants who neither have committed sins of their own nor can answer for themselves in the baptismal ritual. Although the movement of Augustine's argument does not often proceed from the church's traditional practice to the doctrine of original sin as the sole indispensable basis for it, it does so on some occasions: 'What necessity could there be for an infant to be conformed to the death of Christ by baptism, if he were not altogether poisoned by the bite of the serpent?'[57] When accused of Manichaeism for maintaining the transmission of sin, he responds that, long before the time of Mani, infant candidates for baptism were being exorcized with exsufflation, showing that they needed deliverance from the power of darkness.[58] It can, moreover, be plausibly claimed that the whole shape of his defense of original sin takes as its starting point the datum of ecclesiastical practice.

2. The church knows only one baptism, and that 'for the remission of sins'.[59] Augustine resisted, and not only in this particular, the kind of distinction between the baptism of infants and the baptism of adult believers which had, as we have seen, found some currency among the Greek Fathers, and which he regarded the Pelagians as advocating. His consistent principle was to insist at every turn on the application to infants of the church's understanding and practice of baptism.

3. Newborn babies are included in the one humanity of which all sinned in Adam and of which none is saved except in Christ. 'That infants are born under the guilt of [Adam's] offence is believed by the whole Church.'[60] If infants have nothing from which they need to be saved, then Jesus cannot be their saviour, for only the sick need a doctor.[61]

4. None, not excluding baby children, is saved in Christ except through baptism.[62] Punic-speaking Christians in Africa spoke about baptism as 'salvation'. Unless infants pass into the company of believers through the

---

[56] Augustine, *Baptism* 4:24:30.
[57] Augustine, *Merits and Remission of Sins* 1:32:61, cf. 3:4:7.
[58] Augustine, *Marriage and Concupiscence* 2:29:50.
[59] Augustine, *Sermon* 293:11.
[60] Augustine, *Epistle* 166:21. In this letter Augustine pleads with Jerome to demonstrate to him the consistency of the creationist view of the soul's origin (which holds that God creates a soul afresh for each person—Augustine's preferred option on this disputed question) with the fundamentals of the faith, such as those in para. (3) here. Cf. also *Epistle* 166:24-28, and 157:11, 18.
[61] Augustine, *Sermon* 174:7-8.
[62] Augustine, *Sermon* 174:9.

sacrament divinely instituted for this purpose, they will undoubtedly remain in the darkness of sin.[63]

5. Infants are saved through baptism as believers, not as non-believers. Augustine recalls that by ancient custom the church calls baptized infants 'believers' (*fideles*, πιστοί),[64] as the inscriptions bear out. They believe in the hearts of others (parents or other sponsors) and they confess through the tongues of others, thus fulfilling the requirements of Romans 10.10.[65] Just as they were wounded by another's disobedience, so they are healed by another's confession of faith. It must be remembered here that, in baptismal practice at this time, the infant's parent or sponsor responded to the question, 'Does he/she believe?' with the direct affirmative 'He/she believes.'[66]

6. Infants who die unbaptized are lost and condemned, although their punishment will be 'more tolerable' and 'milder' than those who have sinned on their own account.[67] In Augustine's book there is no middle ground for infants dying unbaptized akin to the Pelagians' 'eternal life' outside the kingdom of heaven. Catholic faith provides no warrant for believing that they may attain to forgiveness of their original sin.[68]

In addition to this tireless rehearsal of these basic teachings of the church which confound the errors of the Pelagians, Augustine also deploys some *ad hominem* arguments. Since they grant infants salvation and eternal life without baptism, how would they respond to someone who wanted to grant them the kingdom of heaven as well? They would appeal to John 3.5[69]—a text which since the second century had played a major role in shaping the church's baptismal beliefs. If it were not for this text, the Pelagians would not accept infant baptism at all![70]

More often, however, Augustine has to reply to Pelagian counter-arguments which appeal to the principles of transmission and solidarity that were so important in his own account of catholic doctrine. For example, if Adam harms those who have not themselves sinned, Christ

---

[63] Augustine, *Merits and Remission* 1:24:34-35.

[64] Augustine, *Sermon* 294:14.

[65] Augustine, *Sermon* 176:2; cf. *Epistle* 98:9-10 for a different approach, and 98:2 for a community of souls that avails to the child in baptism through the shared possession of the Spirit by parent and child alike.

[66] Cf. J.C. Didier, 'Une adaptation de la liturgie baptismale au baptême des enfants dans l'Eglise ancienne', *Mélanges de science religieuse* 22 (1965), pp. 79-90.

[67] Augustine, *Epistle* 186:29; *Merits and Remission* 1:16:21; *Enchiridion* 93; *Against Julian* 5:11:44.

[68] Augustine, *The Soul and its Origin* 3:9:12. On this question see the chapter on 'The Salvation of Infants' in Bromiley's *Children of Promise*, pp. 91-104.

[69] Augustine, *Sermon* 294:5-8.

[70] Augustine, *Merits and Remission* 1:30:58.

should benefit those who have not believed.[71] We have already noted, in section (5) above, part of Augustine's rejoinder. He also turns the tables on the objectors by showing that it is they who accept that Christ benefits those who do not believe, for they cannot deny that in baptism Christ benefits infant non-believers.

An objection that Augustine dealt with in one form or another on many occasions claimed that, if sinful parents produced sinful offspring, parents cleansed of original sin through baptism should surely produce offspring no longer subject to original sin. His counter-attack is nothing if not versatile.[72] He contends that the claim is tantamount to assuming that baptized Christian parents should be expected to bear baptized Christian children, but male babies were not begotten already circumcised by circumcised fathers! If 1 Corinthians 7.14 is cited in this connection, then whatever *sanctified* might mean when applied to the unbelieving spouse or children of a Christian, it will prevent no more the child than the spouse from perishing unless they are subsequently baptized. Moreover, the parallelism does not always obtain; whereas all infants contract sin through their parents, some are presented for baptism by other persons.[73] In any case, parents generate, not regenerate their offspring. 'Even renewed parents beget children not out of the first-fruits of their renewed condition, but carnally out of the remains of the old nature';[74] for concupiscence, which is one element of original sin, persists in the baptized. 'The fault of our nature remains in our offspring so deeply impressed as to make it guilty, even when the guilt of the self-same fault has been washed away in the parent.'[75] The true benefit of birth from Christian parents is to be brought by them without delay to the saving waters of baptism.

Augustine was also asked how it is that a child profits from its parents' faith at baptism but is not prejudiced by their later fall from faith when they seek the aid of pagan gods for the healing of the child. He argues that, by virtue of baptism, the child becomes 'a soul having a separate life', so that Ezekiel 18.4 now governs its destiny. The bond of guilt contracted in natural birth, once cancelled in spiritual rebirth, cannot be reimposed by subsequent parental sin.[76]

It did not escape Augustine that to place such a weight on the necessity of baptism for infants provoked the most searching questions about the accidents of baptismal administration. 'The baptized mother bewails her

---

[71] Augustine, *Sermon* 294:17-18.
[72] Augustine, *Merits and Remission* 2:9:11, 2:25:39–27:44. 3:8:16–9:17; *Sermon* 294:16, 18.
[73] Augustine, *Epistle* 98:6.
[74] Augustine, *Merits and Remission* 2:27:44.
[75] Augustine, *The Grace of Christ and Original Sin* 2:39:44.
[76] Augustine, *Epistle* 98:1-2.

own little one who was not baptized [before death], while the chaste virgin gathers in for baptism the offspring of outsiders, exposed by an unchaste mother.'[77] Often when the parents are eager and the ministers prepared for giving baptism, it is still not given because death intervenes.[78] Since the Pelagians acknowledge that baptism confers some good value on babies, even they cannot evade the issue altogether. They refuse to ascribe such discrimination to fate or divine election, and must therefore base it on merit, but no such option is available for Augustine. Even the infants who are successfully brought to baptism come crying and kicking; 'grace cleaves to them even in their resisting struggles'.[79] In this priority of grace, an inscrutable divine providence is at work. The diverse fortunes of infants afford the best illustration known to Augustine of the truth that grace is bestowed according to God's election. 'Must we so attribute it to the negligence of parents that infants die without baptism that heavenly judgments have nothing to do with it?'[80] We must conclude that it was of God's choice that he did not keep this particular child in this life a little while longer in order that it might receive baptism.[81]

At this point we have reached the end of the road in more senses than one. If the tradition of baptizing infants acted as a powerful catalyst in the formulation of the western church's high doctrine of original sin, so too, it seems, the somewhat random reception of it by infants was a contributory factor in the formulation of its doctrine of divine election. This is not to claim that Augustine had no other grounds for developing his theology as he did than the implications of infant baptism and its haphazard administration. It is merely to recognize how his theological understanding took shape under the pressure of controversy and harsh experience.

Few paedobaptists, however, will be able to follow Augustine all the way. The Pelagians were the heirs of the long and widespread uncertainty of earlier Christian generations about why newborn children needed to be baptized. Such lack of clarity bred discussion and even controversy. In a Tertullian and a Gregory Nazianzen, and perhaps in those responsible for the later childhood baptisms attested by third-century inscriptions, as well as in the wider post-Constantinian deferment of baptism, this absence of consensus issued in the avoidance of infant baptism, in theory or in practice. It was Augustine who finally set the necessity of paedobaptism on an impregnable basis. But here lies the rub. For if at last the rite had found its theological rationale, it was one that today's practitioners of

---

[77] Augustine, *Against Two Letters of the Pelagians* 2:6:11.

[78] Augustine, *Gift of Perseverance* 12:31. Cf. Williams, *Fall and Original Sin*, p. 377, for an illustration starkly depicting this division at the font.

[79] Augustine, *Grace and Free Will* 22:44.

[80] Augustine, *Gift of Perseverance* 12:31.

[81] Cf. TeSelle, *Augustine the Theologian*, pp. 323-24.

infant baptism will scarcely be able to endorse, except perhaps to a very minor extent. We are left in the somewhat uncomfortable position of receiving the traditional observance from the early church, while at the same time rejecting the main planks of the theology in which the church of the Fathers found its conclusive justification.

But there is one point on which the voice of Augustine deserves to be seriously heeded. It is a strength of his anti-Pelagian corpus that he endeavors to treat the baptism of infants on all fours with the baptism of adult candidates. We may judge the way he did this to be not very successful, although the rite he knew was obviously framed on the assumption that confessing believers were the normative subjects of baptism with only minimal adjustment made for those who could not answer for themselves. Nevertheless, the challenge to avoid setting up two kinds of baptism has rarely been far distant from the advocacy of infant baptism. Moreover, the subsequent separate development of rites of confirmation and their reformed substitutes has exposed paedobaptists to the associated temptation of treating infant baptism as something less than real and complete Christian baptism. Augustine's theology, however unacceptable as the definitive response to the persistently controversial question 'why?' in the early history of infant baptism, at least counsels us both against distinguishing too sharply between infant and adult baptism and against denying full, unqualified integrity to the baptism given to babies.

CHAPTER 3

The Apostolic Fathers and Infant Baptism: Any Advance on the Obscurity of the New Testament?

The hugely influential Faith and Order Paper on *Baptism, Eucharist and Ministry,* published in 1982, put the issue as follows:

> While the possibility that infant baptism was also practised in the apostolic age cannot be excluded, baptism upon personal profession of faith is the most clearly attested pattern in the New Testament documents.[1]

A dozen years later the massive *Catechism of the Catholic Church* struck a similar note:

> There is explicit testimony to this practice [of infant baptism] from the second century on, and it is quite possible that, from the beginning of the apostolic preaching, when whole 'households' received Baptism, infants may also have been baptized.[2]

The phrases 'cannot be excluded' and 'quite possible' are a far cry from the maximalist certainties of Joachim Jeremias and of the Church of Scotland's Special Commission on Baptism in the 1950s and 1960s.[3] Ever since the sixteenth century, the *onus probandi* has probably rested on those affirming the first-century or apostolic origins of infant baptism, rather than on those who reject this claim. For more than one reason, the position which Jeremias espoused so stalwartly has within the last few

---

[1] *Baptism, Eucharist and Ministry* (Faith and Order Paper, 111; Geneva, 1982), p. 4 ('Baptism', para. 11).

[2] *Catechism of the Catholic Church* (London, 1994), p. 284 (§1252).

[3] Joachim Jeremias, *Infant Baptism in the First First Centuries* (London, 1960). The German original appeared in 1958. The Scottish Special Commission laboured during 1953–63 under the convenership of Thomas F. Torrance, who wrote most of the voluminous reports. It remains probably the most comprehensive investigation of baptism, especially in its theological aspects, ever undertaken. For details, see D.F. Wright, 'Baptism', in Nigel de S. Cameron *et al.* (eds), *Dictionary of Scottish Church History and Theology* (Edinburgh, 1993), pp. 57-58 (ch. 21 below).

decades become more difficult to vindicate.[4] The aim of this paper is to enquire whether the works of the Apostolic Fathers throw any light on the obscurity which envelops the issue in the New Testament writings. It will proceed by asking a series of questions, and, as so often in intellectual enquiry, the validity of the outcome will depend on the appropriateness of the questions.

Are there any Explicit References to Infant Baptism in the Apostolic Fathers?

The first is likely to prove the easiest to answer, since no scholar known to me now answers in the affirmative.

Are there any Indirect References or Implicit Allusions to Infant Baptism in the Apostolic Fathers?

We are immediately into trickier territory, in which Polycarp's declaration to the proconsul of Asia, 'Eighty and six years have I served [Christ]', deserves priority treatment, if only because of the prominence it receives in arguments like that of Jeremias.[5] Is there anything new to be said to resolve what I judge to be an impasse? It may be highly probable, although it falls short of certainty, that the number of years denotes Polycarp's age.[6] The text belongs, of course, to a group of similar statements in early Christian literature attesting Christian identity or service from birth or childhood or lifelong Christian discipleship. Kurt Aland contributed to the debate, with a particular relish, since Jeremias had overlooked it, the only other such assertion in the Apostolic Fathers. *1 Clement* tells the Corinthian church that the letter is being carried to them by men who 'have passed blameless lives among us from youth (ἀπὸ νεότητος) until old age'.[7] Aland is keen to emphasize the indefiniteness of 'youth'.

There is little point in retracing here the lines of a familiar, and perhaps tedious, discussion. This clutch of testimonies may or may not hang together, but one comment is worth making before we move on. Insufficient attention has been given to the possibility of other non-

---

[4] I note that the article 'Baptism 1. *Early Christianity*' by Maxwell E. Johnson in P. Bradshaw (ed.), *The New SCM Dictionary of Liturgy and Worship* (London, 2002), pp. 35-37, mentions infant baptism first in connection with third-century sources.

[5] *Martyrdom of Polycarp* 9:3; Jeremias, *Infant Baptism*, pp. 59-63; K. Aland, *Did the Early Church Baptize Infants?* (London, 1963), pp. 70-73 (German original, 1961); J. Jeremias, *The Origins of Infant Baptism* (London, 1963), p. 58 (German original, 1962).

[6] It is so assumed by H. König in S. Döpp and W. Geerlings (eds), *Dictionary of Early Christian Literature* (New York, 2000), p. 494 (German original, 1998).

[7] Aland, *Did the Early Church*, p. 71, citing *1 Clem.* 63:3.

baptismal markers of Christian belonging in the first three centuries. The fourth and fifth centuries furnish varied evidence of dedication or consecration or enrolment in the catechumenate soon after birth of individuals baptized only in responsible years. The fact that none of the pre-Constantinian texts explicitly identifies baptism as the starting-point of long-lasting or whole-life Christian discipleship at least leaves open the possibility that there may have been at hand some other way, even liturgical in form, of marking a child of Christian parents as intended for Christ. Jeremias and Aland disputed the import of two passages in the *Apology* of Aristides to this effect, but their exchanges focused rather myopically on the presence or absence of infant baptism, with not even Aland entertaining other possibilities.[8]

Statements like Polycarp's when facing martyrdom may not dispel the obscurity of the New Testament, but they do add a new category of evidence to be taken into account, or at least, in instances specifying span of life, evidence of greater precision. The closest parallel in the New Testament must be Timothy, who is declared to have 'known the holy scriptures from infancy (ἀπὸ βρέφους)', within a family in which grandmother and mother were, at least eventually, believers.[9] Jeremias' silence on the case of Timothy no doubt reflects the difficulty of fitting his Christian, rather than Jewish, discipleship from infancy into a credible chronology. In the nature of the case, the New Testament corpus only marginally allows for the elapse of time sufficient to accommodate generational transmission of the faith.

I doubt if any other alleged implicit references to infant baptism in the Apostolic Fathers are clear enough to merit discussion or add anything to the evidence of the New Testament—that is to say, they do not serve to resolve the uncertainties of the New Testament writings. Jeremias cites Ignatius' greeting in *Smyrnaeans* 13:1 'to the families (οἴκους) of my brethren with their wives and children' as showing what—better, who—was or were 'commonly understood' by the word οἶκος in the well-known texts in 1 Corinthians and Acts, 'i.e., father and mother of the household and children of all ages'.[10] Ignatius certainly provides an

---

[8] See my essay 'Infant Dedication in the Early Church', in S.E. Porter and A.R. Cross (eds), *Baptism, the New Testament and the Church: Historical and Contemporary Studies in Honour of R.E.O. White* (*Journal of the Study of the New Testament*, Supplement Series, 171; Sheffield, 1999), pp. 352-78, on pp. 362-64 (see ch. 9 below).

[9] 2 Tim. 3.15; 1.5; cf. Acts 16.1.

[10] Jeremias, *Infant Baptism*, pp. 19-20. On p. 20 n. 1 Jeremias discusses Ignatius, *Pol.* 8:2 where the household(s) of grown-up children seem to be in view, but appears to want both to have his cake and eat it in claiming that even in this case 'οἶκος does not refer to the household without children'. In *Vis.* 3:1:6, Hermas is instructed to 'ask also concerning righteousness, that you may take a part of it to your family (οἶκον)'. Hermas' children (τέκνα) and wife are depicted as sinful and in need of repentance (*Vis.* 1:3:1-2;

element of detail lacking in the New Testament references, but without, I judge, making the so-called οἶκος formula any more persuasive in the case for infant baptism than it is in its own terms in the New Testament. There is no direct evidence of any kind in the Apostolic Fathers of a household baptism. In *Didache* 4:9-11, part of the pre-baptismal instruction is suggestive of household inclusiveness, with children and slaves within the family of Christian nurture, but how this relates to the baptismal order of *Didache* 7 is wholly obscure.

Do References to Baptism in the Apostolic Fathers Throw any Light on the Inclusion of Infants among its Recipients?

The directions for baptism in the *Didache* envisage responsible participants as its subjects. There is no provision for young children, but nor are they explicitly excluded.[11] If we recall that only one small paragraph betrays the place for infants in the lengthy baptismal order in the Hippolytan *Apostolic Tradition*, such that most questions about their inclusion are left unanswered, we should hesitate to regard the *Didache* as debarring them. Its text does contribute, however, to the general picture which emerges from all the patristic sources, that the rite of baptism developed throughout the era as a rite for believing respondents, into which non-responding babies when they came to be baptized were accommodated with adaptation minimal to the point of being often near invisible.

The *Epistle to Barnabas* also furnishes an explicit discussion of baptism, from the perspective of its Old Testament foreshadowing. Not only does the writer with unmistakable purposefulness trace no connection between baptism and circumcision (see section 7 below), but what he does say about baptism clearly has responsible agents in view.

2:2:2-4; 2:3:1), but the children are by now probably adult (so Carolyn Osiek, *The Shepherd of Hermas: A Commentary* [Hermeneia; Minneapolis, MN, 1999], p. 49), and nothing can be inferred concerning the time of their baptism.

[11] *Didache* 7. Willy Rordorf, 'Baptism according to the Didache', in J.A. Draper (ed.), *The* Didache *in Modern Research* (Arbeiten zur Geschichte des antiken Judentums und des Urchristentums, 37; Leiden, 1996), pp. 212-22, mentions infant baptism only in connection with the use of warm water and only to dismiss it summarily from consideration (p. 219). There is no mention of infants in Nathan Mitchell, 'Baptism in the *Didache*', in Clayton N. Jefford (ed.), *The* Didache *in Context* (*Novum Testamentum*, Supplements, 77; Leiden, 1995), pp. 226-55. Neither Rordorf (pp. 221-22) nor Mitchell (pp. 226-27) includes provision for infants among the *Didache*'s notable omissions. In 1949 Jeremias still related warm water to the baptism of children, in *Hat die Urkirche der Kindertaufe geübt* (Göttingen, 2nd edn, 1949), p. 29, but no longer in *Infant Baptism* (1958/60). Cf. André Benoît, *Le Baptême chrétien au second siècle: la théologie des pères* (Études d'histoire et de philosophie religieuses, 43; Paris, 1953), p. 31: 'Rien dans la *Didaché* n'apporte d'argument positif en faveur du baptême des enfants.'

They go down into the water (καταβαίνω, *Barn.* 11:8, 11) 'with their hopes set on the cross' (*Barn.* 11:8), and ascend out of it 'bearing the fruit of fear in [their] hearts and having hope in Jesus in [their] spirits' (*Barn.* 11:11). How instinctively Barnabas avoided envisaging infants as subjects of Christian initiation appears earlier in his work.

> So we are the ones whom [God] brought into the good land. What then do 'milk and honey' mean [in Exod. 33.3]? That a child is brought to life first by honey and then by milk. So accordingly we too are brought to life by faith in the promise and by the word, and will then go on to live possessing the earth. (*Barn.* 6:16-17)

When Ignatius through Polycarp exhorts the Smyrnaean Christians, 'Let your baptism remain as your weapons, your faith as a helmet, your love as a spear, your endurance as your panoply' (Ign. *Pol.* 6:2),[12] is it fair comment that baptism fits better with faith, love, and endurance in this context as a recognizable feature of their conscious Christian experience? The assumption would be similar to that made by Paul in Romans 6.3-4.

2 Clement's interest in baptism is restricted to keeping it 'pure and undefiled' (*2 Clem.* 6:9). Twice 'seal' is used of the baptism to be preserved at all costs (*2 Clem.* 7:6; 8:6). Nothing can be confidently inferred from these references.

Hermas was given the explanation of the stones which fell away from the tower near water, yet could not be rolled into the water: 'These are those who have heard the word and wish to be baptized into the name of the Lord', but subsequently return to their former wickedness (*Vis.* 3:7:3). The author's preoccupation with repentance as the prerequisite for baptism is writ large throughout the work, as is the necessity of baptism ('water') for salvation (*Vis.* 3:3:5; *Sim.* 9:16:2-4). Yet in all of Hermas' elaborate symbolism, no category appears which might specifically accommodate those originally baptized in early infancy.

This survey has not touched on every reference to baptism in the Apostolic Fathers, but only on those which might be pertinent to our enquiry. No baptismal reference is identifiable which envisages other than responding penitents or believers as candidates.

---

[12] The plural τὸ βάπτισμα ὑμῶν makes clear that no specific reference to Polycarp's baptism is intended.

Do Statements about Children in the Apostolic Fathers Throw any Light on the Possibility of their having been Baptized?

The *Didache*, Polycarp, *1 Clement*, and *Barnabas* all instil the Christian duty of bringing up children in the nurture of the Lord.[13] *1 Clement* depicts God's creative love preparing 'his blessing for us before we were born' (*1 Clem.* 38:3). Yet when Ignatius advises Polycarp on the care of the church of Smyrna, he urges attention to widows, slaves, wives and husbands, but not to children (Ign. *Pol.* 4-5). *Barnabas'* version of the sacrifice of a heifer in Numbers 19 includes among its extra-biblical elements boys (παιδια, παῖδες) who sprinkle all the people, whom he interprets as those who preached the gospel of forgiveness of sins to his own generation. There were three boys, standing for Abraham, Isaac, and Jacob (*Barn.* 8:1, 3-4). Again *Barnabas* shows his instinctive lack of interest in Christian children.

Hermas provides the fullest and clearest parallel to the strain in the teaching of Jesus which set forth children as models of discipleship. From the twelfth mountain, the white one, came believers who are

> like innocent babies (βρέφη), and no evil rises in their heart nor have they known what wickedness is, but have remained always in innocence. Such believers shall undoubtedly dwell in the kingdom of God, because in none of their conduct did they defile the commandments of God, but remained in innocence all the days of their life with a single mind. All of you who will persevere and be as babies, having no evil, shall be more glorious than all of those mentioned before, for all babies (βρέφη) are glorious before God and come first with him (*Sim.* 9:29:1-3).[14]

What it means for contemporary church practice that very young children—if 'babies' is not merely symbolic—have primacy of honour before God is not so much as hinted at. The message of Hermas (so the passage continues) is blessing on all who reject evil and assume freedom from wickedness, 'for you will live first of all people with God'. Such an exposition surely creates a presumption that the newborn belong to God's people, but it does nothing to dispel the uncertainty inherent in New Testament parallels. In sum, references of this type in the Apostolic Fathers fall some way short of the picture that may be drawn from the

---

[13] *Did.* 4:9; Poly. *Phil.* 4:2; *1 Clem.* 21:6; *Barn.* 19:5. Hermas, *Vis.* 1:3:2, is told to persevere in correcting his children.

[14] Cf. *Sim.* 9:31:2. For Osiek, *Shepherd*, p. 252, Hermas has in view a 'strictly ideal' group. Cf. *Barn.* 6:11, explaining the bringing of God's people into the land of milk and honey: 'When he made us new people by the remission of sins, he fashioned us into another pattern (τύπον), that we should have the souls of children (παιδίων) as though he were creating us afresh.' At several places in the Apostolic Fathers, Christians are addressed as children: e.g., *1 Clem.* 22:1; *Barn.* 7:1; *Did.* 3:1, 3, 4, 5, 6; 4:1.

New Testament writings on the presence of young children in the church community.

Are there General Theological Statements or Emphases in the Apostolic Fathers which might Suggest that Baptism was given to Infants?

The History of Infant Baptism by the Anglican writer William Wall, published in 1705, retains its value today as an assemblage of patristic sources. 'It has remained the English classic on the subject.'[15] From the Apostolic Fathers he cites *1 Clement*'s quotation of Job 14.4: 'No one is clean from defilement, not even if his life be but one day old', which would become in later Fathers a proof-text for the necessity of baptism to deal with original sin in the newborn.[16] Wall also adduces passages from Hermas which show the necessity of baptism for salvation, passages which bear all the greater authority because Hermas wrote, so Wall believes, before John compiled his Gospel, including the standard proof-text among the Fathers for the necessity of baptism, John 3.5.[17] Such arguments are likely to weigh less heavily with modern students of the Fathers, not least because of the uncertain relationship between baptism and original sin in the Greek patristic tradition.

In an entirely different direction, Ignatius' proto-credal summaries are notable in twice including the baptism of Jesus between his birth and his passion. The anti-Docetic thrust is obvious in the letter to Smyrna. Jesus Christ was 'truly born of a virgin, baptized by John, in order that all righteousness might be fulfilled by him' (*Smyrn.* 1:1: γεγεννημένον... βεβαπτισμένον). The perfect tense of 'baptized' may point to the lasting significance of his submission to John. Writing to the Ephesians, Ignatius' concern is not so patently anti-heretical: 'Jesus Christ our God was conceived by Mary both of the seed of David and of the Holy Spirit. He was born and was baptized, so that τῷ πάθει he might purify the water' (*Eph.* 18:2 ἐγεννήθη καὶ ἐβαπτίσθη).[18] If τῷ πάθει is translated 'by his passion', then lurking here is a suggestively profound yet undeveloped parallel to Jesus' own anticipation of his death as a 'baptism' (cf. Mark 10.38-39; Luke 12.50). Less plausible, however, is a reference to his undergoing baptism at John's hands as an act of submission. Nevertheless, Ignatius' understanding of the baptism of Jesus, and of his

---

[15] F.L. Cross (ed.), *Oxford Dictionary of the Christian Church* (ed. E.A. Livingstone; Oxford, 3rd edn, 1997), p. 1717.

[16] *1 Clem.* 17:4; W. Wall, *The History of Infant Baptism* (3 vols; London, 4th edn, 1819), I, p. 23.

[17] Wall, *History*, I, pp. 24-27.

[18] Cf. W.R. Schoedel, *Ignatius of Antioch: A Commentary on the Letters of Ignatius of Antioch* (Hermeneia; Philadelphia, PA, 1985), pp. 84-86.

death as a baptism, is insufficiently developed to have any bearing on our enquiry concerning paedobaptism.

A theological topic of obvious baptismal reference is that of the church as the body of Christ. Clement's deployment of this imagery is at times less than Pauline, but he maintains the interdependence of small and great, strong and weak, within the one body, yet without indicating how children might fit in (*1 Clem.* 37:4-5).

It is not possible, then, to identify in any of the Apostolic Fathers theological developments of a non-baptismal character which bear on the question of the baptismal inclusion of infants. The emphasis on faith is pervasive enough, but is never spelt out in such a manner, so I judge, as to exclude youngsters not yet of age to believe.

Do the Apostolic Fathers Throw any Light on the Interpretation of Contested New Testament Texts?

We may leave aside all questions of which New Testament writings the Apostolic Fathers severally may have known, and in which form, since our interest is in whether they help us to clear away any of those writings' obscurities about baptism given to infants. To this question only a confident negative can be given. None, I think I am right in saying, of the New Testament verses commonly in contention with reference to the apostolic origins of paedobaptism is quoted or alluded to by any of the Apostolic Fathers. By such disputed texts I mean Acts 2.39; 1 Corinthians 7.14; Colossians 2.11-12; and several mentions of household baptisms, in 1 Corinthians 1.16; Acts 16.15, 33; 18.7, and also 11.14, together with the Synoptic accounts of Jesus' blessing of the children, in Matthew 19.13-15; Mark 10.13-16 (cf. 9.36b); and Luke 18.15-17.[19] On none of these does the corpus of the Apostolic Fathers help to resolve their controverted bearing on the beginnings of infant baptism.

We have already noted Ignatius' greeting to 'the families of my brothers with their wives and children' at Smyrna (13:1), but this cannot be treated as evidence of his, or any other Apostolic Father's, understanding of the supposed 'household baptism' texts listed in the previous paragraph. Remember that establishing how these texts should rightly be read is not part of my remit.

Even if we enlarge the circle of putatively relevant New Testament texts to encompass verses such as Acts 21.21[20] and the occurrences of κωλύειν

---

[19] On the subsequent fortunes of this pericope, see my paper 'Out, In, Out: Jesus' Blessing of the Children and Infant Baptism', in S.E. Porter and A.R. Cross (eds), *Dimensions of Baptism: Biblical and Theological Studies* (*Journal of the Study of the New Testament*, Supplement Series, 234; Sheffield, 2002), pp. 188-206 (see ch. 11 below).

[20] Cf. Jeremias, *Infant Baptism*, p. 48.

in baptismal contexts in Matthew 3.14 and Acts 8.36, 10.47, and 11.17, which helped Oscar Cullmann and others after him read Jesus' blessing of the children baptismally (the Greek verb occurs in all three Synoptics),[21] we still draw a blank among the Apostolic Fathers. This holds also for John 3.3-5, perhaps echoed in the *Shepherd* (*Sim.* 4:15:3),[22] Matthew 18.10,[23] and for that matter the other places where Jesus commends the child as a model for his followers, such as Matthew 18.3.[24]

It is not inappropriate here, although the point might well have been made in section 3 above, to state that none of the other baptismal texts in the New Testament which are not normally cited specifically in support of the primitive status of infant baptism is used or alluded to by any of the Apostolic Fathers in a manner which suggests a link between baptism and infants. Most of them have left no trace at all, including [Mark 16.16]; Acts 1.5; 8.36, 38; 19.3-4, etc.; 1 Corinthians 1.13-16; 10.2; 12.13; and Galatians 3.27. A non-baptismal phrase from Romans 6.3-4 maybe found in Ignatius' *Ephesians* 19:3 (καινότης ζωῆς). In passages of plausible dependence on Ephesians 4.4-6, 'one baptism' is missing from *1 Clement* 46:6, but has become 'the seal' in the *Shepherd* (*Sim.* 9:17:4), while in *Similitude* 9:13:7 'one clothing' may stand proxy for one baptismal identity. Hermas at *Vision* 3:3:5 has probably got 'saved through water' from 1 Peter 3.20-21, but the 'washing' or 'bath' of Titus 3.5 (λουτρόν) has not been preserved in a probable borrowing in *Barnabas* 1:3.[25] The only possible indebtedness of the baptismal section in *Didache* 7 is the threefold name from Matthew 28.19, while *Barnabas* 11 on baptism betrays none at all. This is in sum a meagre harvest, which must be borne in mind in evaluating the absence of any influence of New Testament texts which later generations have judged pertinent to the paedobaptism debate.

---

[21] Cf. O. Cullmann, *Baptism in the New Testament* (Studies in Biblical Theology, 1; London, 1950), pp. 71-80 (German original, 1948); Jeremias, *Infant Baptism*, pp. 48-55.

[22] Cf. Jeremias, *Infant Baptism*, p. 58: 'The Gospel of John could scarcely have formulated in so unqualified a manner the proposition that only those begotten by water and the spirit can enter the kingdom of God (John 3.5), if in its time baptism had been withheld from children of Christian parents.' Cf. the highly cautious comments in *The New Testament in the Apostolic Fathers*, by A Committee of the Oxford Society of Historical Theology (Oxford, 1905), p. 123.

[23] Cf. Jeremias, *Infant Baptism*, p. 65; J. Héring, 'Un texte oublié: Mathieu 18:10. A propos des controverses récentes sur le pédobaptisme', in *Aux sources de la tradition chrétienne: Mélanges offerts à M.M. Goguel* (Neuchâtel and Paris, 1950), pp. 95-102.

[24] On Mt. 18.3, cf. Jeremias, *Infant Baptism*, pp. 49-52. There may be an echo in Hermas, *Sim.* 9:29:1-3; cf. *New Testament in the Apostolic Fathers*, p. 122.

[25] On these texts see *New Testament in the Apostolic Fathers*, pp. 69, 53, 106 (with reference also to *Sim.* 9:13:5; 9:18:4), 115, 14.

Do any of the Apostolic Fathers Support a Parallelism between Circumcision and Baptism?

This larger issue was no more than alluded to in the previous section's reference to Colossians 2.11-12 as a contested text. According to Jeremias, 'Paul here names baptism "the Christian circumcision" (ἡ περιτομὴ τοῦ Χριστοῦ) and describes it thereby as the Christian sacrament which corresponds to Jewish circumcision and replaces it'.[26] This sentence aptly summarizes what had become a common attitude in Cyprian's time in the mid-third century. It is certainly not attested in the Apostolic Fathers. Apart from Ignatius' Delphic utterance to the Philadelphians that 'it is better to hear of Christianity from a man who is circumcised than of Judaism from one who is uncircumcised' (*Phld.* 6:1) and a polemical dismissal of the Jews' 'pride in circumcision' as mere 'mutilation of the flesh' in *Epistle of Diognetus* 4:1, 4, all of the uses of the verb περιτέμνω and the noun, and of ἀκροβυστία, 'uncircumcision; appear in the *Epistle of Barnabas*. None of these is found in section 11 on baptism, and Everett Ferguson is warranted in asserting that 'one thing baptism did not mean to Barnabas: it was not associated with circumcision. The counterpart of circumcision in the flesh is circumcision of the ears and heart by the Holy Spirit (*Barn.* 9:1-9; 10:11)'.[27] Not only did the author devote a full section (*Barn.* 9) to circumcision, in which he apparently denies that it was for the people of Israel a seal of their covenant (*Barn.* 9:6), but his discussion of baptism explicitly sets out at the beginning to ascertain whether the Lord gave any Old Testament foreshadowing of it (*Barn.* 11:1). The deliberateness of his failure to relate circumcision to baptism could scarcely be more unequivocal.

Concluding Reflections: Any Advance on New Testament Obscurity?

To focus an enquiry of this nature on the writings known since at least the seventeenth century as the Apostolic Fathers cannot escape the limitations of this conventional designation. It must not be seen as synonymous with an investigation of a particular span of years, such as 90–170, since I have not pursued other possible sources within the era. The earliest Apostolic Father(s) may pre-date one or more New Testament texts, and the latest, presumably the *Epistle to Diognetus* (if it still deserves to be included), is certainly later than a handful of other patristic texts meriting consideration.

Nevertheless, the enquiry is not pointless—unless it is pointless to perpetuate the category of Apostolic Fathers. In this paper I have not set

---

[26] Jeremias, *Infant Baptism*, pp. 39-40.
[27] E. Ferguson, 'Christian and Jewish Baptism according to the *Epistle of Barnabas*', in Porter and Cross (eds), *Dimensions of Baptism*, pp. 207-23, at pp. 222-23.

myself a task which ignores these limitations, but have modestly asked whether any of these writings helps to dispel the obscurity surrounding the baptism of infants in the New Testament. The answer must be that none of them does so. What has been quite widely regarded as evidence supporting infant baptism—the eighty-six-years-long Christian service of Polycarp—does not take us beyond uncertainty at best. The statement itself has no obvious baptismal connotations, though it has been thought to imply one.

In reality, in contrast to the New Testament, the Apostolic Fathers of themselves barely sustain a picture even of obscurity concerning infant baptism. So far are they from dispersing the shadows of the New Testament that, if one started from the Apostolic Fathers and not the New Testament, one could scarcely claim that the baptizing of infants was even obscurely in view. The Apostolic Fathers do not, therefore, present us with any advance on the indeterminate evidence of the New Testament; nor do they leave us with a similarly uncertain *status quaestionis*. Rather, for those who seek dissipation of the darkness, they mark a move backwards rather than forwards, or perhaps sideways into a more uniform blankness concerning the practice of paedobaptism.

If it is right to continue, with much earlier commentary, to discern among the Apostolic Fathers in general a shared concern with the internal ordering of the life of congregations, with domestic affairs rather than apologetic or doctrinal engagement with the external world, what bearing does this perspective have on our enquiry? Perhaps it allows us to deduce merely that the baptizing of the newborn was not a cause of discord in any of the Apostolic Fathers' churches. On the other hand, the primitive church order in the *Didache* betrays no hint that it was uncontroversial routine practice. Where it might have left some impress, in the chapters in *Barnabas* on baptism and on circumcision, the silence may be more eloquent than in the *Didache*.

The overall conclusion must be that the Apostolic Fathers do not strengthen the case for judging that infant baptism was practised in the New Testament churches. If anything, they weaken the case. A critical question remains as to how we should interpret their silence.

CHAPTER 4

The Meaning and Reference of 'One Baptism for the Remission of Sins' in the Niceno-Constantinopolitan Creed

The creed that most of the Christian world knows as the Nicene Creed, and that patristic scholars commonly refer to by the first letter (C or K) of Constantinople, enjoys unparalleled ecumenical acceptance. The significance of the phrase with which this paper is concerned ('one baptism for the remission of sins') has taken on increased importance in the light of the intensified interest in baptism in recent ecumenical discussion.[1] Yet it is a phrase that very rarely attracts more than passing attention. I have yet to find a single extended examination of it.[2] Students of the Constantinopolitan Creed concentrate on far weightier matters,[3] and students of baptism in the Fathers hardly ever mention it.[4] Perhaps it

---

[1] Cf. P.C. Empie and T.A. Murphy (eds), *Lutherans and Catholics in Dialogue I–III* (Minneapolis, MN, n.d.), Pt. II: *One Baptism for the Remission of Sins*.

[2] I have not seen W. Beinert, *Das Glaubensbekenntnis der Oekumene. Eine Auslegung des Nizänischen Glaubensbekenntnisses* (Freiburg, 1973). There is a brief discussion in older works, e.g., Johann Caspar Suicer's *Symbolum Niceno-Constantinopolitanum Expositum* (Utrecht, 1718), pp. 361ff; A.P. Forbes, *A Short Explanation of the Nicene Creed* (Oxford and London, 2nd edn, 1866), pp. 292ff. See now Susan K. Wood, 'I Acknowledge One Baptism for the Forgiveness of Sins', in Christopher Seitz (ed.), *Nicene Christianity: The Future for a New Ecumenism* (Grand Rapids, MI, 2001), pp. 189-201, but her interest is not historical.

[3] E.g., J.N.D. Kelly, *Early Christian Creeds* (London, 3rd edn, 1972), p. 160; I. Ortiz de Urbina, *Nicée et Constantinople* (Histoire des Conciles Oecuméniques, 1; Paris, 1963), p. 189; A.M. Ritter, *Das Konzil von Konstantinopel und sein Symbol* (Forschungen zur Kirchen- und Dogmengeschichte, 15; Göttingen, 1965); and in C. Andresen *et al.*, *Die Lehrentwicklung im Rahmen der Katholizität* (Handbuch der Dogmen- und Theologiegeschichte, 1; Göttingen, 1982), pp. 206-14; K. Lehmann and W. Pannenberg (eds), *Glaubensbekenntnis und Kirchengemeinschaft. Das Modell des Konzils von Konstantinopel (381)* (Dialog der Kirchen, 1; Freiburg and Göttingen, 1982).

[4] E.g., G. Kretschmar, 'Die Geschichte des Taufgottesdienstes in der alter Kirche', in K.F. Müller and W. Blankenburg (eds), *Leiturgia. Handbuch des evangelischen Gottesdienstes*, volume 5 (Kassel, 1970); B. Neunhauser, *Taufe und Firmung* (Handbuch der Dogmengeschichte IV/2; Freiburg, 2nd edn, 1983); R.F.G. Burnish, *The Meaning of*

is assumed on all sides that the meaning of the clause is self-evident. It is the contention of this paper that it is by no means as straightforward as it might appear or as its free and easy citation by theologians might suggest.

We are faced with at least two main issues: 1. the meaning of 'one' (ἓν βάπτισμα);[5] and 2. the significance of the confession not of 'one baptism' without qualification but of 'one baptism for the remission of sins'. We will begin with this second question, which raises what may be called the 'reference' of this credal statement.

The sharpness of this question is inescapably focused by the interpretation given in the late John Burnaby's *The Belief of Christendom,* which is subtitled *A Commentary on the Nicene Creed.* His concern is more scriptural than historical, but he explains 'one baptism' as '*one* baptism for infants and adults', and insists that baptism's 'mystical washing away of sin' must mean the same thing for infants and adults alike.[6] This explanation takes us to the heart of the issue.

The historical meaning of the clause should presumably be sought in the works of those Greek Fathers of the fourth century who may be judged closest to the circles in which the Creed, or this particular part of it, was formulated and adopted.[7] This requires that we look to Cyril of Jerusalem and the Antiochene theologians, such as Chrysostom and Theodore, as well as to Epiphanius and the Cappadocians. Such evidence as may be gathered from these Fathers makes it clear that newborn infants were not baptized for the remission of sins for the very simple reason that they had no sins requiring remission. John Chrysostom is the most explicit witness. In his *Catechetical Instructions* he enumerates ten gifts of baptism, to correct those who think that the only gift it confers is the remission of sins. 'It is on this account that we baptize even infants, although they have no sins, in order that they may be given the further gifts of sanctification, righteousness, filial adoption...'[8] Nearer to the Council of 381, one of Gregory Nazianzen's poems refers to baptism as a

---

Baptism: A Comparison of the Teaching and Practice of the Fourth Century with the Present Day (Alcuin Club Collections, 67; London, 1985).

[5] For the text see the critical edition of G.L. Dossetti, *Il Simbolo di Nicea e di Constantinopoli* (Rome, 1967), p. 250.

[6] J. Burnaby, *The Belief of Christendom: A Commentary on the Nicene Creed* (London, 1959), pp. 162, 164.

[7] Cf. the studies listed at n. 3 above.

[8] John Chrysostom, *Instr.* 3:6 (A. Wenger [ed.], *Jean Chrysostome. Huit catéchèses baptismales inédites* [SC 50; Paris, 1957], pp. 152, 154; P.W. Harkins, *St. John Chrysostom: Baptismal Instructions* [Ancient Christian Writers, 31; Westminster, MD/London, 1963], p. 57).

seal and a remedy (ἄκος) for adults but only a seal for infants,[9] while his oration on baptism similarly regards the sacrament when administered to infants as strengthening them against sin rather than cleansing them from it.[10] Gregory of Nyssa's treatise *On the Untimely Death of Infants* is written, according to N.P. Williams,[11] 'in the completest apparent unconsciousness of any idea that a newly born babe is as such subject to God's wrath or stained with any kind of sin', and his baptismal sermon *On the Day of Lights* declares that the newly-minted Christian emerging from the baptismal water is as free from accusations and penalties as the newborn baby.[12] Cyril of Jerusalem's *Catecheses* show no awareness of infant baptism, but he teaches that we come into the world sinless and now sin of our free will (*Catech.* 4:19). Moreover, Cyril tells us that the creed of the Church of Jerusalem acknowledged 'one baptism *of repentance* (μετανοίας) for the remission of sins' (*Catech.* 18:22), which rendered the clause more obviously inapplicable to the newborn.[13] The second creed at the end of Epiphanius' *Ancoratus* speaks more briefly of 'one baptism of repentance'.[14]

The conclusion is inescapable. Although the evidence is not abundant (partly because infant baptism was clearly exceptional in the Greek Church for most of the fourth century[15]), enough is available to establish that 'one baptism for the remission of sins' could not have been understood to encompass the baptism of babies. If the Creed's original meaning is allowed to determine its meaning for later centuries, then its confession of 'one baptism' is of very limited direct relevance to subsequent baptismal practice among the churches of both East and West.

---

[9] Gregory Nazianzen, *Carmina* I:1:9, lines 91-92 (*PG* 37, col. 464). In a similar fashion Asterius later depicts baptism as given to a child for its protection against demonic assault and heresy (*Homil. in Pss.* 12:4, M. Richard, *Asterii Sophistae Commentariorum in Psalmos* [Oslo, 1956], p. 82).

[10] Gregory Nazianzen, *Oration* 40:17, 28 (*PG* 36, cols. 380-81, 400).

[11] N.P. Williams, *The Ideas of the Fall and of Original Sin* (London, 1927), p. 279; Gregory of Nyssa, *On the Untimely Death of Infants* (*PG* 46, cols. 161-92).

[12] Ed. E. Gebhardt, in W. Jaeger *et al.*, *Gregorii Nysseni Opera*, vol. 9 (Leiden, 1967), p. 224.

[13] A.A. Stephenson, 'The Text of the Jerusalem Creed', *Studia Patristica* 3 (ed. F.L. Cross; Texte und Untersuchungen, 78; Berlin, 1961), p. 307.

[14] Epiphanius, *Ancor.* 119:11 (K. Holl [ed.], *Ancoratus und Panarion* [*GCS* 25; Leipzig, 1915, p. 149). The creed in *Ancor.* 118:9-13 (Holl, pp. 146-47), which is virtually identical to C, is widely regarded as an interpolation. Cf. B.M. Weischer, 'Die ursprüngliche nikänische Form des ersten Glaubenssymbols in Ankyrōtos des Epiphanios von Salamis', *Theologie und Philosophie* 53 (1978), pp. 407-14.

[15] Note the remarkably infrequent mentions of paedobaptism in Chrysostom's voluminous corpus.

For the meaning of the numeral 'one' there are a number of possibilities, not all mutually exclusive, but the main candidates seem to boil down to two:

1. 'One' in the sense of Ephesians 4.5—'one Lord, one faith, one baptism'. This phrase 'one baptism' is misinterpreted far more often than our credal clause. The context puts the meaning beyond doubt. Paul is talking about the common baptism received by all Christians, the one and the same baptism which unites them in one Lord and one body. A temporal reference, excluding rebaptism, for example, is as inappropriate as it would be for 'one Lord' and 'one faith'.

2. 'One' in a temporal sense, perhaps parallel to, and grounded in, the once-for-all character of the saving work of Christ. The clause is most frequently interpreted in this way, as affirming the unrepeatability of baptism, but a further narrowing of its meaning may be possible, or even required:

A. Does the Creed reflect the consensus, firmly established by now at least in the Latin West, that those who had received baptism in heresy or schism should not be rebaptized on admission to the Catholic Church?

B. Or does it relate instead to the early church's persisting preoccupation with the problem of post-baptismal sin?

The evidence points unmistakably to the second of these possibilities. 'One baptism *for the remission of sins*'—and here again the specification of the purpose or benefit of baptism is important—declares that the washing away of sins in baptism may be received only once. This is how Cyril of Jerusalem explains the words in his *Procatechesis*:

> A person cannot be baptized a second or a third time. Otherwise, he could say: 'I failed once; the second time I shall succeed'. Fail once and there is no putting it right. For [there is] 'one Lord, one faith, one baptism'. It is only heretics who are rebaptized, and then because the first [baptism] was no baptism.

Thus Cyril interprets the phrase in a manner that explicitly denies that it debars the rebaptism of those baptized at the hands of heretics. Speaking to neophytes Chrysostom warns them to 'be alert to prevent any second contract [i.e., of debt from post-baptismal sins]. For there is no second cross, nor a second remission by the bath of regeneration. There is remission, but not a second remission by baptism.'[16] On other occasions also he denies that there is any second baptism to cancel sins committed after baptism.[17] Theodore likewise insists that, 'As we will not receive a

---

[16] John Chrysostom, *Instr.* 3:23 (Wenger [ed.], *Jean Chrysostome*, p. 164; Harkins, *St. John Chrysostom*, p. 63).

[17] Cf. John Chrysostom, *De Pentecoste* 1 (*PG* 50, col. 463); *Homil. in Eph.* 11:1 (*PG* 62, cols. 79-80).

second renewal, so we should not expect a second baptism, just as we hope for but a single resurrection'.[18]

That this is the correct explanation of the clause finds confirmation from other considerations. In the first place, the possibility of western influence, reflecting the recognition of schismatic baptism and hence exclusion of re-baptism established in the controversies of the third and fourth centuries, seems extremely unlikely. Western creeds hardly ever include an explicit mention of 'baptism', let alone 'one baptism', even in North Africa.[19] Secondly, the eastern attitude to heretical and schismatic baptism was much less uniform than the western. We have already cited Cyril of Jerusalem, and one need refer further only to the long discussions in Basil's two letters to Amphilochius on the canons,[20] and to the *Apostolic Constitutions*' ban on recognizing baptism 'conferred by wicked heretics' (6:15). Thirdly, it is a major pastoral concern of the Cappadocians and Chrysostom that baptism should not be indefinitely deferred.[21] At first sight, the credal affirmation that no second baptismal repentance and remission are available to the baptized might seem to militate against this concern, in tending to confirm the procrastinating in their reluctance to take the plunge. From another angle, however, it reinforces the Fathers' emphasis on the seriousness with which baptism must be sought.

It would be misleading to give the impression that none of the Fathers whose testimony is pertinent to ascertaining the original significance of the baptismal clause in the Constantinopolitan Creed, ever understood the oneness of 'one baptism' in ways other than that isolated above. The constraints of this communication allow no consideration of other interpretations.[22] But the paper claims to have identified the fundamental meaning and scope of the phrase for the Fathers in question.

Nor on this occasion can we broach the larger hermeneutical questions about a text like the Creed of 381, which has had a long history, and has

---

[18] Theodore of Mopsuestia, *Catech. Homil.* 14:13 (R. Tonneau and R. Devreesse [eds], *Les homélies catéchétiques de Théodore de Mopsueste* [Rome, 1949], p. 439).

[19] For the evidence cf. A. Hahn, *Bibliothek der Symbole und Glaubensregeln der Alten Kirche* (Breslau, 3rd edn, 1897), pp. 17, 25, 27-28, 40-41, 59, 62, 64, etc.

[20] Basil the Great, *Epp.* 188:1, 199:20, 47. On the so-called canon 7 of Constantinople (381) see W. Bright, *The Canons of the First Four General Councils* (Oxford, 2nd edn, 1892), pp. 119-23. Asterius would later speak of a child who, through a heterodox father or mother, was baptized and yet not baptized but rather plunged (κατεβαπτίσθη) into heresy (*Homil. in Pss.* 12:4, Richard, *Asterii Sophistae*, p. 82).

[21] Cf. Basil the Great's *Homil.* 13 (*PG* 31, cols. 423-44), which is from first to last a dissuasive against the postponement of baptism.

[22] For Theodore of Mopsuestia, for example, 'baptism is one because those who are invoked in it have one will, one power and one action' (*Catech. Homil.* 14:21, Tonneau and Devreesse [eds], *Les homélies catéchétiques*, p. 447).

made history, in the experience of the churches. What recognition should be given to the extended meanings that it has acquired in the course of the centuries? Would we be justified in according to a clause such as 'one baptism for the remission of sins' a far wider reference than could ever have crossed the minds of its fourth-century formulators?

The last word must lie with historical study. Patristic scholars surely fulfill their proper function when they remind dogmatic theologians and ecumenical conversationalists that this Creed did not fall from heaven, expressed in timeless, unconditioned language. It must be interpreted in its historical matrix. When this is done, we conclude that 'one baptism for the remission of sins' has little to say to the major issues of baptismal debate in the late twentieth century, and indeed that its reference solely to the baptism of responsible penitent sinners severely qualifies any application to broader questions about 'one baptism'.

CHAPTER 5

At What Ages Were People Baptized in the Early Centuries?

The quest for statistics of the ages of baptismal candidates must appear attractive to a generation that has witnessed the rise of cliometrics. Yet for the patristic era it is a quest that proves frustratingly elusive. The history of baptism has not greatly engaged the attentions of patristic scholars—a history, that is, going beyond baptismal theologies and baptismal liturgies to encompass also the religious, social and cultural aspects of baptism. Among the questions such a history must answer is the subject of this paper. It is a question that goes beyond paths well-trodden in pursuit of the origins of infant baptism, although it cannot forget that enquiry altogether.

Let us start, in fact, with this question: who was the first Christian we can name to have been baptized as an infant? It is, of course, a different question from the hoary one which asks by what date one can be confident that infants were being baptized. Can we name anyone before the fourth century? We might not expect many candidates for consideration in this era of primary mission, but even in the case of obvious possibilities, such as Origen,[1] we simply do not know. The Athanasian *Vita* records that Antony too was raised as a Christian by Christian parents but makes no mention of his baptism.[2] Few young children star in the story of pre-Nicene Christianity. In the rare appearance of a newborn baby, Perpetua's son did not share in his mother's prison baptism.[3] I deliberately leave on one side the candidacy of long-serving Christians such as Polycarp, Polycrates and the martyr Felix[4] because the time of their baptisms is wholly uncertain.

---

[1] Henri Crouzel, *Origen* (Edinburgh, 1989), p. 5, acknowledges that 'no source tells us anything about the age at which Origen was baptised'. He thinks it 'not unlikely' that Origen was baptized as an infant, on the unconvincing grounds that Origen is an important witness to infant baptism. It must be highly doubtful whether, when Origen was born, any Christian teacher justified infant baptism along the lines Origen would later follow, i.e., presupposing the pre-existence of souls.

[2] Athanasius, *Vita Antonii* 1.

[3] *Passio Perpetuae* 3:5, with 3:9.

[4] *Martyrium Polycarpi* 9:3; Eusebius, *H.E.* 5:24:7; *Passio Felicis Thibiacensis* 30 (*CPL*, no. 2054).

From the vantage-point of this chapter, we may refine the question: what would qualify as 'infant baptism' in this context? At a minimal level one could include any baptisms of children young enough to be called infants—under three, let us say. If this criterion satisfies us, we can probably find some epitaph inscriptions attesting such baptisms prior to the fourth century. The evidence was famously debated by Joachim Jeremias and Kurt Aland a generation ago. More recently, in 1979, Everett Ferguson revisited the bearing of the inscriptions on the origin of infant baptism.[5] He pointed out that all the inscriptions which mention the time of baptism place it near death. Such baptisms might be better described as emergency or clinical baptisms than infant baptisms.[6] To be sure, they show that being a baby was no bar to receiving baptism, but they cannot be counted as satisfying a more principled criterion—that soon after birth, as in circumcision, was the appropriate or right or even obligatory time for children of Christian parents to be baptized. This is the message given by Cyprian and Origen and clearly implied by the Hippolytan *Apostolic Tradition*, but can we cite any named subjects, or even unambiguous particular cases lacking a name, prior to the era of the Christian empire? The most persuasive instances are likely to be identified in those inscriptions which, by the presence of *in pace* or *fidelis* or pertinent symbolism, attest the baptized status of those dying very young but, unlike the category noted above, do not indicate the date of their baptism. However, that these were not clinical baptisms is a question on which confidence is ill-advised.

Two points should be underlined at this stage: first, the elusiveness of information about the ages, or even stages of life, at which individuals were baptized (we shall return to this problem), and second, the importance of drawing distinctions. Working with a single *omnium-gatherum* category of infant baptisms obscures critical differences.[7]

We next ask what guidance the Fathers provide about the right age for baptism. One obvious answer is exemplified by Cyprian, Asterius[8] and the anti-Pelagian Augustine. It is the position canonized by the Council of Carthage in 418, which decreed anathema on all who taught that newborn babies were not to be baptized.[9] Another response to the question is

---

[5] Everett Ferguson, 'Inscriptions and the Origin of Infant Baptism', *Journal of Theological Studies* 30 (1979), pp. 34-46.

[6] Not all, of course, were baptisms of infants; ages range from twenty-four days to fifty-nine years.

[7] See my paper 'The Origins of Infant Baptism—Child Believers' Baptism?', *Scottish Journal of Theology* 39 (1987), pp. 1-23 (ch. 1 above).

[8] Cf. J.C. Didier, 'Le pédobaptisme an IVe siècle. Documents nouveaux', *Mélanges de science religieuse* 6 (1949), pp. 223-46. This Asterius is now dated in the early fifth century.

[9] Canon 2 (*CCSL* 149, pp. 69-70).

supplied by several writers, such as Optatus of Milevis[10] and Zeno of Verona,[11] but especially by bishops inveighing against the interminable deferment of baptism—Basil, the Gregories and John Chrysostom in particular. Every age is ripe for baptism; or to be more specific, your age, whatever it be, is no excuse for your not seeking baptism quickly, i.e. your present age is the best time for you to be baptized. If you are smart enough to appeal to the example of Jesus, who deferred his baptism until he was thirty years old, Gregory Nazianzen will rapidly disarm you: Jesus was divine and wholly pure and could afford to delay his baptism, but you ordinary thirty-somethings cannot.[12]

At this point we must avoid the mistake of assuming that the norm or ideal by which postponement is exposed as wrong-headed (and positively dangerous—for you never know when you might fall under a Caesarean or Antiochene omnibus) is infant baptism. Those homilies which attempt variously to cajole or frighten their listeners into hastening to the font say little about baptism of the newborn. This is scarcely surprising: most of the hearers had lost the chance of being baptized as babies years ago. But nor do the preachers highlight their duties as parents to bring their offspring for baptism without delay.

A monograph by Eduard Nagel entitled *Kindertaufe und Taufaufschub*[13] deals solely with North Africa, where this pairing—of infant baptism and postponement of baptism—seems peculiarly appropriate. But the witnesses from Roman Africa—Tertullian, Cyprian and Augustine, each with sharply pointed testimony to bear—have probably been allowed to influence perspectives on this debate to an exaggerated degree. They have too readily been allowed to give the impression that the two poles of practice were invariably paedobaptism on the one hand and deferred baptism on the other.

In respect of the crowds listening to these late fourth-century Greek bishops, we have no means of telling whether any of them had once been possible candidates for baby baptism, that is, as the children of Christian parents. The burden of the preaching was their irresponsibility in putting off something which has been, and still is, within their own competence to obtain. To put the issue anachronistically, for the most part these sermons could have been delivered to baptism-postponing believers' baptists!

Two or three Fathers furnish more precise answers to our question about the right age for baptism. In his *Oratio* 40, Gregory Nazianzen advised that children be baptized not before the age of three or soon

---

[10] Optatus of Milevis, *Contra Parmenianum Donatistam* 5:10.
[11] Zeno of Verona, *Tractatus* I:13:11, II:43.
[12] Gregory Nazianzen, *Oratio* 40:29.
[13] Eduard Nagel, *Kindertaufe und Taufaufschub. Die Praxis vom 3.-5. Jahrhundert in Nordafrika und ihre theologische Einordnung bei Tertullian, Cyprian und Augustinus* (Europäische Hochschulschriften, 23:144; Frankfurt 1980).

after, 'when they can take in something of the mystery, and answer the questions, and even if they do not yet fully understand, can nevertheless retain some impression'.[14] Not Gregory at his best, one might think (but perhaps three-year-olds are not what they were), especially since a little earlier he apparently recommended the baptism of the newborn.[15] His inconsistency illustrates to a tee the difficulties churchmen got into in encompassing within a rite created for responsible—literally, capable-of-answering—sinners infants who could neither answer for themselves nor had any sins to be forgiven.[16] I do not know of any three-or-four-year-olds in the early centuries baptized in accordance with Nazianzen's guidance.

Less problematic is Augustine's assertion that seven is the age at which children can both lie and tell the truth, both confess and deny; hence when they are baptized, *iam et symbolum reddunt, et ipsi pro se ad interrogata respondunt*.[17] This reflects general Roman assumptions that at the age of seven children emerge from infancy,[18] and is corroborated by a letter of Jerome. Advising Gaudentius on bringing up Pacatula, who is at present 'without teeth and without ideas', Jerome looks forward to her becoming seven, when she can start learning the Psalter and the books of Solomon.[19] Seven was the age of a child's second dentition, and fourteen marked the milestone of puberty.

The only named seven-year-old I know of in these centuries is the one mentioned by Augustine in recording the competence enjoyed by children of this age—Dinocrates, the brother of Perpetua, who was seven when he died. In a vision Perpetua saw Dinocrates in torments and realizes that her prayers can release him—which they do.[20] To Augustine it is unthinkable that Dinocrates can have been delivered from hell, and so he has to believe that he died as a baptized Christian who had backslidden and for that reason was suffering *post mortem*. Augustine knows that Dinocrates' parents—Perpetua's parents—were pagans and hence he

---

[14] Gregory Nazianzen, *Oratio* 40:28.

[15] Gregory Nazianzen, *Oratio* 40:17. Gregory urges that any parent who has an infant (νήπιον) should have him sanctified ἐκ βρέφους, from his tenderest age.

[16] Cf. J.C. Didier, 'Une adaptation de la liturgie baptismale au baptême des enfants dans l'Église ancienne', *Mélanges de science religieuse* 22 (1965), pp. 79-90; D.F. Wright, 'The Meaning and Reference of "One Baptism for the Remission of Sins" in the Niceno-Constantinopolitan Creed', *Studia Patristica* 19 (1989), pp. 281-85 (ch. 4 above).

[17] Augustine, *De anima et eius origine* 1:10:12, 3:9:12.

[18] G. Clark, 'The Fathers and the Children', in D. Wood (ed.), *The Church and Childhood* (Studies in Church History, 31; Oxford, 1994), pp. 1-27 at 12; T. Wiedemann, *Adults and Children in the Roman Empire* (London, 1989), p. 114.

[19] Jerome, *Epistle* 128:3.

[20] *Passio Perpetuae* 7.

cannot assume Dinocrates' baptism as an infant. Fortunately for Augustine Dinocrates was old enough to have been able to seek and be granted baptism in his own cognizance. It is an improbable tale—of precocity in both faith and unfaithfulness—but it is Augustine's.[21] The water-symbolism of Perpetua's vision may imply that he received some baptism-substitute the far side of death.

However, I have not yet found other identifiable children of seven or older who were baptized answering the questions for themselves. It is always possible that some children commemorated by inscriptions fall into this category, but the lack of differentiation between children of widely varying ages leaves this possibility stone dead. The distinction made by the *Apostolic Tradition* between children who can and who cannot answer for themselves may assume the Roman belief noted above.[22]

If we move from precept to practice, we encounter that widespread group of later fourth-century churchmen and churchwomen nurtured in Christian families but not baptized until they were of independent years. It is extensive: Ambrose (and his brother Satyrus and probably also their sister Marcellina), Augustine, Basil the Great, Ephraem Syrus, Gregory Nazianzen (and his brother Caesarius and sister Gorgonia), Gregory of Nyssa (and his sister Macrina, in all likelihood), Jerome (and his friend Heliodorus), John Chrysostom, Paulinus of Nola (and his brother), Rufinus of Aquileia, and quite possibly others, like Ulfilas and Cassian.[23] Some of these instances come very close to death-bed baptism (in which otherwise the Christian emperors were specialists). But although several of these persons later became vocal among the ranks of preachers condemning baptismal delay, only in the case of Augustine is criticism voiced of his own parent's default. Our reading of these famous instances of adult baptism has probably been biased by the exceptional censure uttered by this single North African Father. Far commoner is a picture which is virtually the reverse of Augustine's finding fault with a negligent

---

[21] Augustine, *De anima et eius origine* 1:10:12, 3:9:12.

[22] Hippolytus, *Apostolic Tradition* 21. For some evidence of precocious piety recognizable at, or near, the age of seven, see Clark, 'The Fathers and the Children', pp. 13-16. Ennodius' *Vita Epiphanii* (*CPL*, no. 1494) depicts this child of Christian parents as enlisting in the heavenly militia when 'scarcely eight years old'. Martin of Tours, whose parents were not believers, got himself enrolled as a catechumen when ten. Augustine's son Adeodatus was baptized when fourteen. Despite his penchant for number symbolism, Augustine makes nothing of this being twice seven; he was, says *Confessions* 9:6:14, nearly fifteen.

[23] Cf. J. Jeremias, *Infant Baptism in the First Four Centuries* (London, 1960), pp. 88-89; F.J. Dölger, 'Die Taufe Konstantins und ihre Probleme', in F.J. Dölger (ed.), *Konstantin der Grosse und seine Zeit. Gesammelte Studien* (Römische Quartalschrift Supplem., 19; Freiburg im Breisgau, 1913), pp. 377-447 at pp. 429-37.

Monnica. Gregory Nazianzen is the most impressive witness, describing in glowing terms the godly upbringing he and his siblings enjoyed—without a word about baptism and his parents' dereliction in not securing it.

The ages at which these men and women received baptism are of no great importance for our enquiry, for they were by then all of adult years, they varied with individual circumstances and the dates are in several cases only approximate. But for the record they range from the late teens (Chrysostom eighteen, perhaps younger) to the mid-thirties (Ambrose thirty-four), with most falling in the twenties.

This phenomenon is obviously different from the delay until death's door so influentially exemplified by Constantine. It is so common and widely dispersed that it resists being viewed simply as a fourth-century fashion.[24] Indeed, where is the evidence that it was ever otherwise? When Jeremias asserted, in his own italics, *'that the earliest case known to me in which Christian parents postponed the baptism of their children, is in the year* 329/30 (Gregory of Nazianzus)',[25] his tendentious presuppositions are glaringly exposed. Perhaps the earliest case occurred a generation later when Monnica failed to have Augustine baptized—but our warrant for reading it thus is forthcoming only forty years later, in the *Confessions*.

Here we pick up again the elusiveness of biodata about baptisms. Jerome and Gennadius are of no help at all, and in a number of instances—Athanasius is typical—we simply do not know when baptism was given. It will greatly facilitate future researches if every scholar who contributes a biographical entry to a dictionary or lexicon is required to say what is known of the subject's baptism—even if it is nothing.

The frustrating character of many patristic sources is well illustrated by Gerontius' life of Melania the Younger. A daughter was born to her and Pinian, 'whom they promptly dedicated to God for the virginal estate' (*Vita* 1). With or without baptism? Later, a premature male child was delivered after a difficult labour, 'and after he was baptized, he departed for the Lord' (*Vita* 5—a case of clinical, not infant, baptism). Soon their daughter vowed to virginity also died (*Vita* 6)—with or without baptism?[26] The only normative baptismal practice visible here is clinical baptism.

---

[24] Canon 45 of Elvira (c.305) allowed that someone once admitted to the catechumenate who had not darkened the door of the church *per infinita tempora* was not to be denied baptism if his catechumen status was reliably attested.

[25] Jeremias, *Infant Baptism*, p. 89. Similarly, he reads inscriptions certifying that the dead had been recently baptized as instances of the postponement of baptism (p. 91); more plausibly, they attest its advancement in the hour of death.

[26] *Vita Melaniae Iunioris* (*CPL*, no. 2211), trans. E.A. Clark, *The Life of Melania the Younger* (Studies in Women and Religion, 14; New York and Toronto, 1984), pp. 28, 29, 30.

The silence or apparent disinterest of numerous sources must pose searching questions about the importance assigned to baptism, or at least about the dissonance between theological and biographical writers. The silence has been too readily absorbed into theories of the generality of infant baptism, and the ample vocalness of the fourth century minimized as a regression into the deferment of baptism. Several strands of evidence[27] suggest the conclusion that, when infant baptism finally became the norm in practice (which in the West may well not have happened until a century or more after the decisive contribution of Augustine), the history of Christian baptism started all over again. Although babies—some babies, especially dying babies—were baptized certainly from about the middle of the second century onwards, there is not too much in common between the baptism of the first four centuries or so—basically, a rite of conversion—and the universalized paedobaptism of the post-Augustinian era.[28]

---

[27] E.g., the absence of counsel about baptism in guides to the rearing of Christian children, such as Chrysostom, *On Vainglory*; Jerome *Epistle* 128, and even his *Epistle* 107, to Laeta about Paula, where Jerome is less than directive about the duty of baptism.

[28] Cf. P. Cramer, *Baptism and Change in the Early Middle Ages c.200–c.1150* (Cambridge, 1993), p. 3.

CHAPTER 6

Augustine and the Transformation of Baptism

Summary

Before Augustine of Hippo, baptismal practice and theology assumed the active participation of converts; baptism of infants and children took place, but far from routinely and perhaps primarily in cases of illness. Augustine's early writings show that he, like other Christians of his time, had done little theological thinking about infant baptism. On baptism they are neither passionate nor profound. A new clarity came to his treatment of baptism after c.410 in his anti-Pelagian writings. Theologically he came to believe that infant baptism was the sole cure for the guilt of original sin; practically he came to advocate the universal baptism of infants soon after their birth. The result was a devaluation of baptism in the West which did much to determine the contours of Christendom.

'The atmosphere at their [i.e., Patricius' and Monnica's] home was Christian, yet Augustine was not baptized.'[1] A simple enough sentence, one might think, from a recent distinguished study of Augustine's thought, but it is in fact not wholly unexceptionable. I would amend it to read '...and Augustine was not baptized'. John Rist's 'yet' implies an unfulfilled expectation, whereas in all the best Christian homes in the later fourth century—some of them patently more Christian than the maritally mixed menage at Tagaste—one did not baptize babies, or young children at all, for that matter. Whatever Augustine may later have believed, by these standards there was nothing incongruous in Monnica's not having had him baptized in tender infancy.

I have set out the evidence in outline elsewhere.[2] On the one hand, one can cite a lengthy and impressive list of later-fourth-century churchmen and churchwomen nurtured in Christian families but not baptized until they were adults—normally in their twenties. It embraces not only all in

---

[1] John M. Rist, *Augustine: Ancient Thought Baptized* (Cambridge, 1994), p. 2.
[2] D.F. Wright, 'At What Ages Were People Baptized in the Early Centuries?', *Studia Patristica* 30 (1997), pp. 387-92 (ch. 5 above).

the family circles of the Cappadocian Fathers and similarly those around Jerome and Rufinus, but also Ephraem Syrus, John Chrysostom, Paulinus of Nola and Ambrose. On the other hand, it is difficult, and perhaps impossible, to advance any counter-examples, that is, of named individuals born of Christian parentage in this era and known to have been baptized as infants. This problem in turn may be wrapped up in a larger question: who was the first Christian we can name who was baptized in infancy? Youngsters baptized clinically within sight of death would not qualify, but I forbear to pursue this surprisingly elusive enquiry further on this occasion.[3]

What is at issue here is not simply practice—were they, were they not, baptized as babies? More intriguing are the assumptions at work and the judgements passed, and here we encounter the distorting influence of the case of Augustine. There is no more prominent baptismal history in the whole early church than that of Augustine. It is known and read of all on the face of the *Confessions*, which means that generations of students have got used to perceiving it through Augustine's eyes. What have they learned about Augustine's baptismal story from the author of the *Confessions*?

Baptism in the *Confessions*

In the first place, Augustine passes over in silence the fact that he was not baptized soon after birth. We deduce it both from his being ceremonially registered as a catechumen straight from the womb and from his need to beg for baptism when as a young boy (*puer*) he fell gravely ill (*paene moriturus*). His mother prepared him for baptism but he suddenly recovered, whereupon 'my cleansing was deferred'.[4] Writing perhaps some thirty-five years after the event, Augustine laments the laxity still heard on all sides, 'Let him be, let him do it; he is not yet baptized.' Then the never-to-be-forgotten censure of his mother's negligence:

> How much better for me if I had been quickly healed and if, thanks to the diligent care of my family and my own decision [*meorum meaque diligentia*], action had been

---

[3] See Wright, 'At What Ages...?'.

[4] Augustine, *Confessions* 1:11:17. Henry Chadwick translates *puer* 'a small boy' in his edition of Augustine's *Confessions* (Oxford, 1991), p. 13. The word elicits no comment in J.J. O'Donnell's three-volume edition and commentary, *Confessions* (3 vols; Oxford, 1992), but see II, pp. 52-56 on *pueritia* in Augustine's scheme of the 'ages of man'. See also n. 9 below. In *De Genesi ad litteram* 10:13:23, Augustine rejects the opinion that personal sin should not be attributed to children before puberty at fourteen. But he is sure that this holds for infancy (10:14:23).

taken by which I received the health of my soul and was kept safe under the protection which you would have given me. Certainly much better.[5]

Augustine piously subsumes his mother's fault in the broader responsibility of his parents and himself. Much later, when he again fell perilously ill after arriving in Rome from Carthage (*iam ibam et peribam*), by contrast he had no desire for baptism. 'I did better as a boy when I begged for it from my devout mother, as I have recalled and confessed.'[6]

One of the most moving passages in the *Confessions* records Augustine's desolation at the death of a close, but unnamed, friend, whom he had converted from Catholic Christianity to Manichaeism. While he lay, mortally sick of fever, he was given Catholic baptism all unknowing. On recovering temporarily, he rebuffed Augustine's mockery of his unconscious baptism. Augustine's confusion was further confounded when the friend's condition relapsed and he died in his absence.[7] The episode is almost a reverse image of Augustine's boyhood frustration. Although the tale is told in the *Confessions* chiefly, it seems, to introduce a searching meditation on human love, one might read it as reinforcing the mild, but real, criticism of Monnica. Even when totally unsought, baptism had the power to convert and establish firmly in the truth.

The uniqueness of Augustine's verdict on his failure to be given baptism lies here, that he alone of the sons and daughters of Christian households not baptized until their adult years is known to have found fault with his parent's or parents' omission. In all other cases known to me where biographical or autobiographical accounts are available, none blames parent or parents for not having secured them baptism as infants.

On the contrary, the more normal picture is that painted by Gregory Nazianzen, who depicts in glowing colours the godly nurture he and his siblings received, without a hint of their parents' remissness in not having them baptized. If we read these experiences as instances of the deferral of baptism, we owe that gratuitous insight at least in part to our familiarity with what has been called the most famous mother–son relationship in antiquity. Part of its perennial appeal lies in the dissonance between the two, of which Monnica's refusal to go through with his boyhood baptism

---

[5] Augustine, *Confessions* 1:11:18; Chadwick, *Confessions*, p. 14. 'The story tells us much about the prevailing view of evil: on the one hand, it was felt that there was sin in the child which must be stilled, on the other that, if possible, each postulant to Catholicism should make his or her own, willed, profession through the medium of baptism.' Peter Cramer, *Baptism and Change in the Early Middle Ages, c.200–c.1150* (Cambridge, 1993), p. 118.

[6] Augustine, *Confessions* 5:9:16; Chadwick, *Confessions*, p. 83.

[7] Augustine, *Confessions* 4:4:8.

is a signal example. But why should we privilege this baptismal history and make it the lens through which to view the spiritual life-stories of others?

All the other mentions of baptism in the *Confessions* relate to what I will call, if only by convenient shorthand, believers' baptism or perhaps better conversion-baptism: Monnica's hope for Augustine (*Confess.* 6:13:23), the famously public baptism of Victorinus, 'an infant born at your font' (*Confess.* 8:2:3-5), Verecundus' death-bed conversion and baptism (*Confess.* 9:3:5), that of Nebridius (*Confess.* 9:3:6), of Alypius with Augustine himself and his son Adeodatus (*Confess.* 9:6:14), of Evodius (*Confess.* 9:8:17), of Patricius his father (*Confess.* 9:10:22), and even it seems of Monnica herself (*Confess.* 9:13:34).[8] Together these instances remind us how consistently the *Confessions* bear witness to the baptismal practice of the pre-Augustinian era, when the norm was for it to be deliberately sought by responsible believers. There is no allusion whatever in *the Confessions* to infant baptism. Monnica's advertised omission was not in failing to baptize the baby Augustine but in desisting from carrying through with the baptism he had himself importunately requested.[9]

The religious significance of Augustine's own reception of baptism at the hands of Ambrose is, to be sure, not easily reducible to the model of conversion-baptism *simpliciter*. He had reactivated his status as a catechumen after encountering Ambrose's preaching in Milan,[10] and delicate questions of continuity and discontinuity between his earlier spiritual and intellectual peregrinations and his Milanese experience press for an answer. George Lawless has the narrative of the *Confessions* on his

---

[8] Rist, *Augustine*, p. 4, strangely has Monnica baptized with Augustine in 387. O'Donnell does not comment on her baptism on *Confess.* 9:13:34. Monnica's baptism is relegated to a footnote in A. Mandouze, *Prosopographie de l'Afrique chrétienne (303–533)* (Paris, 1982), pp. 758-62, *s.n.* 'Monnica'. This passing over baptism in silence is not unusual: see Wright, 'At What Ages...?', pp. 389, 392 (pp. 61 and 65 above), and 'Monnica's Baptism, Augustine's Deferred Baptism, and Patricius', *Augustinian Studies* 29.2 (1998), pp. 1-17 (ch. 7 below).

[9] Later, in *The Soul and its Origin*, 1:10:12, 3:9:12, Augustine would identify seven as the age at which children could first answer for themselves in baptism. See my article, 'At What Ages...?', p. 392 (pp. 64-65 above). He is described as having attained the 'age of reason' by the time of this unfulfilled baptism by J.C. Didier, 'Saint Augustin et le baptême des enfants', *Revue des études augustiniennes* 2 (1956), pp. 109-29, at p. 110, and by R. De Latte, 'Saint Augustin et le baptême: Étude liturgico-historique du rituel baptismal des enfants chez Saint Augustin', *Questions liturgiques* 57 (1976), pp. 41-55, at p. 41 n. 2.

[10] Augustine, *Confessions* 5:14:25, 6:11:18.

side in arguing that the complex of conversion and baptism constituted more the choice of a particular religious vocation than anything else.[11]

Nevertheless, Augustine's own baptismal history must stand, by his own design in the *Confessions*, for the decisive transition from an old life to a new that marked early Christian baptism: the abandonment of his profession of rhetoric, and of all expectation of a successful career in the public eye; a final turning away from the pleasures of the flesh, within or without marriage; the divine remission of all his 'horrendous and mortal sins';[12] the ultimate reconciliation with his devoted mother,[13] sealed in the climactic vision of Ostia; the new delights of the Psalms, of the hymns and chants of worship in Milan, and fresh plans for a shared life in the service of God back in Africa.[14]

Comments on Baptism in Early Works

Disentangling the densely interwoven threads of history and theology in the *Confessions* is a daunting—and surely unappealing—task. By the time he wrote them, some dozen years after his baptism, near the turn of the century, Augustine certainly intended his baptismal passage to be received as the dramatic turning-point of his life. But that was before he had got to grips with that nexus of theological challenges that would turn him into the most uncompromising champion of infant baptism—and effectively doom to obsolescence that model of conversion-baptism of which the *Confessions* made him so convincing an icon.

This metamorphosis took something over a decade. The immensity of the change involved is evident from what is probably Augustine's first mention of infant baptism, in *The Size of the Soul* written at Rome in 388. Discussing the stages by which 'true religion' binds the soul by reconciliation to God alone, he comments that 'the question what benefits

---

[11] George Lawless, *Augustine of Hippo and His Monastic Rule* (Oxford, 1987), pp. 11-12.

[12] Augustine, *Confessions* 9:2:4.

[13] Cf. Augustine, *Confessions* 9:13:37 (the sole mention of Monnica's name in Augustine's works). In *Confessions* 9:9:22, O'Donnell's punctuation and reading (*Confessions*, III, p. 121) are to be preferred to Chadwick's (*Confessions*, p. 170), which allow for the misunderstanding found in Rist, *Augustine*, p. 4. Neither *vivebamus* nor *percepta gratia baptismi tui* includes Monnica.

[14] Augustine, *Confessions* 9:4:8, 9:6:14, 9:8:17. On the central significance of Augustine's baptism, even within the text of the *Confessions*, see O'Donnell, *Confessions*, I, pp. xxviii-xxix; III, pp. 72, 106-109; also David C. Alexander, 'The Emergence of Augustine's Early Ecclesiology (386–91)' (PhD thesis, University of Edinburgh, 1995), pp. 47-52, 250-51. The radical character of the rupture with his social and political aspirations is well stressed by C. Lepelley, 'Un aspect de la conversion d'Augustin: la rupture avec ses ambitions sociales et politiques', *Bulletin de littérature ecclésiastique* 88 (1987), pp. 229-46.

the consecrations even of infant children [*etiam puerorum infantium*] may confer is a very obscure one, but we must believe that they have some benefit [*nonnihil...prodesse*]. Reason will find this out, when it falls to be investigated.'[15]

A few years later, in his third book on *Free Will* written at Hippo as a presbyter or perhaps a newly-consecrated bishop, Augustine's understanding has advanced sufficiently to attempt an answer to the puzzling question 'what good the sacrament of Christ's baptism does to infants, since most of them [*plerumque*] die after receiving it before they can have known anything of it.' The 'pious and right belief' is that the infant is benefited by the faith of those who bring him to baptism. This is corroborated by the soundest authority of the church.[16] It is at best half an answer—responding in terms of 'how?' to the question 'what?' Later, of course, almost the whole burden of Augustine's promotion of infants' baptism would rest on their receiving it before they died. That the context of this short discussion in *Free Will* is infant death is noteworthy.

To Simplician on Various Questions was written, so Augustine tells us, at the very beginning of his episcopate, i.e., in 396. His grappling with Simplician's second question, on the interpretation of Romans 9.10-29, by Augustine's own acknowledgement effected a significant advance in his comprehension of grace. 'I had tried hard to maintain the free choice of the human will, but the grace of God prevailed.'[17] His commentators agree on the cruciality of the turning-point. 'The position is now reached in all its essential features which provoked the protest of Pelagius.'[18] Augustine had 'derived from a seemingly unambiguous text, an intricate

---

[15] Augustine, *De quantitate animae* 36:80. Note the assumption of voluntary action in an earlier statement in this book (3:4): 'The injunction is rightly made in the sacraments that whoever wishes to be restored to such as God made him should condemn all things bodily and renounce this whole world, which, as we see, is bodily.' Augustine's difficulties are sketched by E.R. Fairweather, 'St Augustine's Interpretation of Infant Baptism', in *Augustinus Magister: Congrès International Augustinien, Paris 21-24 Septembre 1954* (Paris, 1954), II, pp. 897-903, but his presentation fails to take account of development in Augustine's understanding. An able survey is given by B. Delaroche, *Saint Augustin lecteur et interprète de saint Paul dans le De peccatorum meritis et remissione (hiver 411–412)* (Paris, 1996), pp. 347-56.

[16] Augustine, *De libero arbitrio* 3:23:67: *Ecclesiae...saluberrima auctoritas* is the tradition of baptizing infants (cf. Fairweather, 'St Augustine's Interpretation', pp. 898-900). It is important not to read into such brief phrases questionable assumptions about the frequency or normative character of the traditional practice. Such references are fully compatible, *ex hypothesi*, with an established tradition of the clinical baptism of dying infants. Cramer, *Baptism and Change*, p. 117, comments that 'Infant baptism has no obvious place' in the general argument of *Free Will*.

[17] Augustine, *Retractationes* 2:1.

[18] J.H.S. Burleigh (ed.), *Augustine: Earlier Writings* (Library of Christian Classics, 6; London, 1953), p. 375.

synthesis of grace, free will and predestination. For the first time, Augustine came to see man as utterly dependent on God, even for his first initiative of believing in Him.'[19]

But as John Rist notes, 'His first mature account of man's need for grace, worked out in the reply to Simplicianus, had inevitably focused on the sinfulness of adults, as was only to be expected since Christianity was originally a missionary religion, making adult converts.'[20] It is rather remarkable that, when the nettle to be grasped is the election of Jacob and the rejection of Esau before they were born, no connection is drawn between the priority of grace in election and the salvation of newborn babies through baptism. The whole tenor of the discussion suggests the domination of Augustine's mind by the paradigm of the responsible person coming to faith. In 399 or 400 Augustine would oblige Deogratias, a deacon at Carthage, by composing a short guide to *Catechizing the Uninstructed* with precisely such candidates in mind. In 393, when addressing the African bishops assembled in council in Hippo, this precocious presbyter had commented on the credal phrase 'in the remission of sins' without mentioning baptism at all.[21]

The Literal Meaning of Genesis

In the early years of the fifth century in two further discussions of the value of infant baptism Augustine leans heavily on the authority of church practice. The date of the tenth book of *The Literal Meaning of Genesis* has not yet been fixed with any certainty. He began this neglected *magnum opus* perhaps in 404–05 and completed its twelve books probably in 413. Book 10 may well belong to the early years of the Pelagian controversy, around 412–13. At issue is the origin of the soul, on which Augustine never came down decisively in favour of either of the two main competing theories, traducianism and creationism. Here he evinces a sharp awareness that the practice of parents 'rushing' (*curro*, 'run', is used twice, perhaps implying that clinical baptism is chiefly in mind) with infants to baptism is far easier to square with the derivation of the soul, and not merely the body, from Adam through the immediate parents. The infant in his own person has done neither good nor evil, and his soul is spotless if it has not descended from Adam; what harm, then, would he (i.e., his soul) suffer if it left the body in death without baptism? If baptism benefits only the body, why not baptize dead bodies? It will be

---

[19] Peter Brown, *Augustine of Hippo* (London, 1967), p. 154.
[20] Rist, *Augustine*, p. 17; cf. p. 125.
[21] Augustine, *De fide et symbolo* 22.

a marvel if anyone can show, on a non-traducianist supposition, why the soul of an infant dying unbaptized should be justly condemned.[22]

He proceeds to venture a creationist's response to this conundrum. In a nutshell, the soul that God creates anew for each individual either tames the flesh which is inherited from Adam already tainted by sin, or is tamed by it. 'Even an infant as long as he is alive should be baptized so that union with sinful flesh may not harm his soul.'[23]

Augustine is obviously not satisfied. The infant dying unbaptized is a different matter from the adult dying unbaptized, who will have unforgiven personal sins. Is the newly-created soul's contamination by contact with sinful flesh sufficient of itself to doom it if it fails, through parental unbelief or negligence, to win baptism before death? Perhaps the solution lies in God's foreknowledge, supplying 'the ministry of the saving waters' to each one whom, dying untimely young, he foreknows would have been a godly believer had he lived.[24] (The recourse to divine foreknowledge offers no escape. Towards the end of his life Augustine firmly rejects divine foreknowledge of future merits to explain why some infants receive baptism and others die without it.[25] But by then the framework of discussion had been drastically changed.) God foreknows vices as well as virtues, and if judgement covers not only what one has done while alive but what one would have done had one lived longer, the salvation of those who have died in good standing would become a prey to uncertainty. Augustine pleads again for any who, without resorting to traducianism, can reconcile scripture (he has Romans 5.12, 18-19 in mind) or scripture-informed reason with infant baptism to come forward to help him.[26]

Augustine rounds off his weighing up of the alternative explanations in *The Literal Meaning of Genesis* with the judgement that 'the weight of arguments and scriptural evidences would be equal or nearly equal on each side' did not infant baptism lend greater weight to the opinion that derives souls from parents. For the moment Augustine cannot counter this view; subsequently he will not hesitate if God gives him something to say on it. He then adds a somewhat elusive sentence:

---

[22] Augustine, *De Genesi ad litteram* 10:11:19. For the chronology, see now P.-M. Hombert, *Nouvelles recherches de chronologie augustinienne* (Paris, 2000), pp. 137-88.

[23] Augustine, *De Genesi ad litteram* 10:14:24-25.

[24] Augustine, *De Genesi ad litteram* 10:15:26-27.

[25] Augustine, *De praedestinatione sanctorum* 24.

[26] Augustine, *De Genesi ad litteram* 10:16:28-29.

Now, however, I give notice in advance that the witness of [the baptism of] infants is not to be despised, so that one fails to refute a position [on this ground], if the truth counts against it.[27]

Meantime, persistence in humble searching and knocking is certainly preferable to resting satisfied with present knowledge. In conclusion Augustine repeats himself with added emphasis.

But the custom of mother church in baptizing infants is not in the least to be scorned and in no way to be regarded as irrelevant, nor to be believed at all unless it were an apostolic tradition. That tiny age, which won the distinction of being the first to shed its blood for Christ, bears a witness of great weight.[28]

Surely Augustine is speaking to himself. He would so obviously have loved to believe in God's fresh creation of a soul for each new life. Alas for him, the further deepening of his understanding of the relation between Adam's sin and babies would push this desirable apple even further beyond his grasp.

De baptismo

Augustine's only work to be called *De baptismo* was directed, as its longer title indicates, 'against the Donatists'. It has commonly been dated in 400/401 but has recently been brought forward to 405 at the earliest.[29] It may seem paradoxical in a paper devoted to exposing Augustine's transformation of baptism that this extensive treatise should have so little to contribute. In reality, here too, in the anti-Donatist polemic, Augustine was effecting *another* transformation of baptism (what versatility!)—and

---

[27] Augustine, *De Genesi ad litteram* 10:23:39: '*Nunc tamen non esse contemnendum testimonium parvulorum, ut quasi refelli, si veritas contra est, negligatur, ante denuntio.*' The translation of J.H. Taylor, *St Augustine: The Literal Meaning of Genesis*, II (Ancient Christian Writers, 42; New York and Ramsey, 1982), p. 127, does not make coherent sense in context: 'Now, however, I want to state in advance that the argument from the baptism of infants is not to be so despised that we should neglect to refute it if the truth is against it.' It is difficult to imagine Augustine, even in the early 400s, feeling the need to warn against so low an esteem for infant baptism that one did not even bother to expose its untruth. The final sentences of 10:23:39, cited in the text, will not tolerate Taylor's reading. The French translation by P. Agaësse and A. Solignac in *Bibliothèque Augustinienne* 49, pp. 215-17, is nearer Taylor's than mine: '...n'est pas à mépriser, si bien qu'on ne doit pas négliger de le réfuter en quelque sorte, s'il est contraire à la vérité'. I remain unpersuaded.

[28] Augustine, *De Genesi ad litteram* 10:23:39.

[29] A. Schindler in *AugLex*, I, col. 574; on the title, p. 573; F. Dolbeau, *Augustin d'Hippone: Vingt-six sermons au peuple d'Afrique* (Paris, 1996), p. 359 (= *Recherches augustiniennes* 26 [1992], p. 83). But cf. Hombert, *Nouvelles recherches*, pp. 93-94: later 404.

getting himself here too, in all manner of fixes.[30] The notion of baptismal character, with its corollary of the sundering of baptism from the church, was nevertheless less fateful than the transformation which is my present subject. The fact that *De baptismo* has little specific grist for this mill should remind us that the baptismal divide between Donatists and Catholics had nothing to do with infant baptism as such—which the magisterial Reformers' assimilation of Anabaptists to Donatists still sometimes obscures.[31]

Yet the one discussion of infant baptism in *De baptismo* is revealing. It arises in the sequel to a consideration of instances of persons who lacked baptism itself—e.g. martyred catechumens and the penitent thief—but indubitably received salvation. Likewise when the sacrament is given but faith and repentance are unavoidably absent, as with infants, salvation, according to 'the firm tradition of the universal church', is nevertheless present. Why, babies by screaming and girning even raise their voices in opposition to the words of the sacrament!²

Augustine proceeds to develop for the first time the parallel with circumcision, which, commanded first as a seal of Abraham's faith, was afterward decreed for all males eight days old. There is no problem when baptized infants come later to that 'conversion of heart', whose sacramental sign had gone before. But as with the thief God supplied what was lacking, so too in baptized infants who die young, we must believe that the same grace of the Almighty fulfils what, not by wilful perversity but by poverty of age, they could not—i.e. 'believe in their hearts for righteousness and confess with their mouths for salvation'.

---

[30] See my paper 'Donatist Theologoumena in Augustine? Baptism, Reviviscence of Sins and Unworthy Ministers', in *Congresso Internazionale su S. Agostino...Atti II* (Rome, 1987), pp. 213-24 (ch. 8 below).

[31] Cf. my paper 'The Donatists in the Sixteenth Century', in L. Grane, A. Schindler and M. Wriedt (eds), *Auctoritas Patrum II. Neue Beiträge zur Rezeption der Kirchenväter im 15. und 16. Jahrhundert* (Mainz, 1998), pp. 281-93 (ch. 15 below). In *The Soul and its Origin* 1:9:10–1:11:13, 2:9:13-2:12:16, 3:9:12–3:10:14, Augustine refutes the opinion of one Vincentius Victor that infants dying unbaptized entered the kingdom of heaven, but his error seemed unrelated to his former allegiance to Rogatist Donatism.

[32] Augustine, *De baptismo* 4:23:30. This must be the first appearance of this fatuous argument from the tears of babies at the font, vainly resisting irresistible grace, as it is often characterized. In *Epistle* 187, written in 417, as part of his response to Dardanus' question whether infants truly do not know God, Augustine is careful to absolve infants at baptism of any blame for appearing by crying and wriggling to fight against receiving the grace of Christ. 'They do not know what they are doing and hence are not credited with doing it.' *Epistle* 187:7:25. Dardanus had been praefectus praetorio of the Gauls in 412–13; cf. J.R. Martindale, *The Prosopography of the Later Roman Empire*, II (Cambridge, 1980), pp. 346-47.

Hence the responses made by others on their behalf, since they cannot answer for themselves, unquestionably avail for their consecration to God.[33]

This approach to infant baptism is eloquent enough. Augustine keeps close enough to the New Testament to assume faith- or conversion-baptism as the norm, in the light of which some vindication of infant (literally 'non-speaking') baptism is called for. Augustine's vindication is not wholly coherent; if the parallel with the thief on the cross holds good, God supplies the deficiency, presumably faith and confession, but it breaks down, and sponsors seem to supply it also. As we will see, neither explanation corresponds precisely to the liturgical reality.

The more general point to be made about *De baptismo* follows neatly: the whole of its discussion of baptismal cases, actual and hypothetical, presupposes persons of independent responsibility. It takes quite a leap of imagination to assume that in the congregations of Africa, whether Donatist or Catholic, infant baptism was in any sense normal practice. To be sure, this baptismal controversy, between Africa's two mainstream denominations, directed no attention to infant baptism as such. Nevertheless, when such extended argument with frequent citation of particular instances can be read from first to last—with the exception of two chapters—as though it was dealing with a squabble among African Baptists, we rightly sit up and take note.

It is in *De baptismo* that Augustine develops his theory of the reviviscence of sins.[34] In response to the Donatists' charge that his view of their baptisms left him impaled on the horns of a dilemma, Augustine allowed that through Donatist baptism sins were indeed momentarily remitted (and the Spirit received, etc.)—but immediately returned on the baptized's heads because of their sinful persistence in schism. This is difficult, if not impossible, to apply to the infant-baptized.

---

[33] Augustine, *De baptismo* 4:24:31. Augustine cites John 9.21, 'He is of age, let him speak for himself'. See the comment of J.H. Lynch, *Godparents and Kinship in Early Medieval Europe* (Princeton, MA, 1986), p. 127. The earliest attested mark of differentiation between what so much of the tradition has defined in terms of ages—adult baptism and infant baptism—is the rubric in the Hippolytan *Apostolic Tradition* 21:4, distinguishing those who can speak for themselves from those who cannot. See now Paul F. Bradshaw, Maxwell E. Johnson and L. Edward Phillips, *The Apostolic Tradition: A Commentary* (Hermeneia; Minneapolis, MN, 2002), pp. 112-13.

When Augustine says that *universa tenet ecclesia* the practice of infant baptism (*De baptismo* 4:24:31), he presumably indicates its universal acceptance, not its routine invariability throughout the church.

[34] See my 'Donatist Theologoumena in Augustine?' (ch. 8 below).

Epistle 98

One further text falls to be considered before we reach the critical watershed in Augustine's baptismal understanding. In *Letter* 98 he responds to a series of questions relating to the baptism of infants, or baptized infants, addressed to him by an episcopal colleague named Boniface, probably bishop of Cataquas not far from Hippo.[35] The letter is generally dated 408.[36] It comprises Augustine's most extended treatment of infant baptism so far—despite Boniface's request that Augustine respond briefly, not citing the authority of tradition but furnishing a reasoned explanation.[37] All the questions were grounded in the relationship between the child, baptized or baptizand, and the parent or other sponsor—territory from which Julian in particular would fire off repeated salvos at Augustine's defences. The question that deserves to detain us in this paper is of interest not least because of what it reveals about one of the earliest adaptations of the baptismal liturgy to accommodate infants.

Whereas a candidate capable of answering the baptismal interrogations for himself was asked 'Do you believe...?', the question addressed to the promoter of an infant candidate was 'Does he (she) believe in God...?', and the reply expected was 'He (she) believes.'[38] There is no evidence of a variant practice. Boniface had expressed surprise that a confident answer could be given by parents or other presenters at that age of the

---

[35] The precise location is unknown. On the identity of this Boniface, see S. Lancel in *AugLex*, I, p. 652, and Mandouze, *Prosopographie*, pp. 148-50, *s.n.* 'Boniface'.

[36] But Mandouze, *Prosopographie*, p. 149 n. 10, thinks it probable that it belongs to the years of the Pelagian controversy, on the inadequate ground that it deals with infant baptism. Section 5 certainly has Donatist error in view. In my judgement, the answers of sections 9-10, reviewed in the text, are not redolent of that intense reflection on infant baptism that the Pelagians evoked from him. J.C. Didier places the letter in 411, just before Pelagius' arrival in Africa: 'Observations sur la date de la lettre 98 de S. Augustin', *Mélanges de science religieuse* 27 (1970), pp. 115-17, in reponse to V. Grossi's hazardous argument for a date between 411/12 and 413, in 'Il battesimo e la polemica pelagiana negli anni 411/413 (De peccatorum meritis et remissione—Ep. 98 ad Bonifacium)', *Augustinianum* 9 (1969), pp. 30-61. M.F. Berrouard holds to 408–10 in '*Similitudo* et la définition du réalisme sacramental d'après l'Epître 98, 9-10 de S. Augustin', *Studia Patristica* 6 (1962), pp. 277-93, at p. 277; Delaroche, *S. Augustin lecteur*, pp. 353-56, holds to 408–11, as also does Lynch, *Godparents*, pp. 128-32, but Hombert, *Nouvelles recherches*, p. 161 n. 329, argues for 411–13.

[37] Augustine, *Epistle* 98:7.

[38] Augustine, *Epistle* 98.7. See J.C. Didier, 'Une adaptation de la liturgie baptismale au baptême des enfants dans l'Eglise ancienne', *Mélanges de science religieuse* 22 (1965), pp. 79-90; R. De Latte, 'Saint Augustin et le baptême: Étude liturgico-historique du rituel baptismal des enfants chez S. Augustin', *Questions liturgiques* 57 (1976), pp. 41-55. For Pseudo-Dionysius' handling of this practice, see Lynch, *Godparents*, pp. 138-39.

child when he or she does not so much as know that there is a God. Moreover, they would not presume to answer other questions about the child's future character or conduct.

Augustine's response is less direct and subtler than his response to a not dissimilar problem in *De baptismo*. First he shows by analysis how sacraments take the name of the reality or transaction of which they are sacraments.

> Just as in a certain manner the sacrament of Christ's body is Christ's body..., so the sacrament of faith is faith... When, on behalf of an infant as yet lacking the capacity for faith, the response is given that 'He believes', this response means that he has faith because of the sacrament of faith, and the response that 'He converts to God' is made because of the sacrament of conversion, for the response itself belongs to the celebration of the sacrament.[39]

Not Augustine at his best, we must trust. He seems to have travelled no distance at all towards Boniface's testing ground. He tries a slightly different tack, still not without some unclarity.

Even though an infant as yet lacks 'that faith which rests upon the will of those believing' (does he then, one must interject, possess some other kind of faith?), nevertheless the *sacramentum fidei* makes him a *fidelis*, a believer, one of the faithful. Augustine is on safe ground; as the inscriptional evidence alone makes abundantly plain, very young baptized children were consistently called *fideles*. That Augustine's explanation of this fact is probably not historically secure need not detain us now.

Furthermore, though still lacking faith rooted in understanding, at least the infant does not obstruct it with an inimical understanding, and 'hence receives the sacrament of faith beneficially [*salubriter*]'. As the baptized *fidelis* matures, he or she grows into knowledge and faith. Before he is able to do so, the sacrament protects him against forces of evil, to such effect that if he dies before the age of reason, 'he is freed by Christian help from that condemnation which through one man entered the world, as the love of the church commends him through this very sacrament'.[40]

Augustine reckons that his responses will satisfy peaceable and understanding souls, but not the dull and argumentative. Boniface should obviously have asked for a longer answer. The answer that an historian

---

[39] Augustine, *Epistle* 98.9.

[40] Augustine, *Epistle* 98.10. Augustine would have done better to refer Boniface back to part of his first answer, where he explains that the common possession of the Spirit by parent (or other presenter) and child alike enables the will (and presumably the words) of the parent to benefit the child. 'We are made partakers of grace along with others through the unity of the Holy Spirit' (*Epistle* 98.2). See the discussion of this letter in Cramer, *Baptism and Change*, pp. 125-29, although Cramer fails to acknowledge that *Epistle* 98 by no means expresses Augustine's mature mind on infant baptism.

today would have to give him would only exacerbate his anxiety, namely, that the practice of addressing questions about infants to their presenters in the third person is to be explained simply as a minor adaptation of a rite developed solely for self-respondent believers.[41] At its best we may regard it as a strange device to maintain the unity of the baptismal observance.

The Anti-Pelagian Writings: A *Bouleversement* in Augustine's Thinking

This is a convenient point at which to make the transition to the anti-Pelagian phase of Augustine's reflection on baptism. For one of the tracks along which he chased Caelestius, in particular, led, claimed Augustine, to two kinds of baptism. If infants had no original sin, and no sins of their own commission, how could they be given the church's baptism 'for the remission of sins'? 'Shall we create another kind of baptism for infants, in which remission of sins does not take place?'[42] Eventually Caelestius was prevailed upon to grant that infants should be baptized for the remission of sins according to the church's universal custom. 'It is appropriate to confess this, lest we seem to be making different kinds of baptism.'[43] Pelagius got himself off the same hook by insisting that 'infants ought to be baptized with the same formula of sacramental words as adults'.[44]

Such concessions played into Augustine's hands, for it was a cardinal principle in his vindication of infant baptism against what he perceived to be Pelagian attack that the church's full understanding and practice of baptism applied no less to infants than to responsible adults. What this meant, in effect—and it emerges with crystal clarity at the moment of the baptismal questions—was that a sacrament formed around the active participation of converts was accommodated to passive silent infants, and in the process was transformed.

One route that Augustine did not travel was followed by many of the Greek Fathers of his generation; to distinguish between the two classes of baptismal candidates by recognizing that infants were baptized not for the remission of sins—for they had no sins to be remitted—but for the reception of the gifts of sanctification, adoption, strengthening against future sin, and so on. Such thinking meant that the clause in the Niceno-

---

[41] This is the argument of my Didsbury Lectures, *What has Infant Baptism done to Baptism? An Enquiry at the End of Christendom* (Milton Keynes, 2005).

[42] Cf., e.g., Augustine's *Sermon* 293:11. 'The theology determining Augustine's doctrine of infant baptism is identical with that of his theology of baptism in general', G. Bonner in *AugLex*, I, col. 592.

[43] Augustine, *The Grace of Christ and Original Sin* 2:5:5–6:6.

[44] Augustine, *The Grace of Christ and Original Sin* 2:1:1, etc.

Constantinopolitan Creed 'one baptism for the remission of sins' cannot in its framers' minds have encompassed infant baptism—and in any case the 'one baptism' it affirmed was quite different from the 'one baptism' that Augustine thought the Pelagians threatened.[45] Through Julian of Eclanum, Augustine became aware of John Chrysostom's quintessential enunciation of the Eastern view, and spent most of the first book of *Against Julian* evading the plain sense of his words. What John had written was that infants had no sins; elsewhere in John's works Augustine thought he could demonstrate his belief in original sin.[46]

It was, of course, the doctrine of original sin that served as the springboard for the great leap forward that Augustine's apprehension of infant baptism experienced during the Pelagian contest. Already in his *Homilies on the First Epistle of John* in 407 Augustine could say *en passant*, 'If we are born with no sin, why is it that people rush [*curritur*] with infants to baptism for their release from it?' (We note again the telltale verb *curritur*, which may well echo the fear of early death that counselled speed in the baptism of many babies.) This brief text has often not been accorded its place in Augustine's developing baptismal understanding because for long these *Homilies* were dated later, after the onset of the Pelagian debates.[47] As Gerald Bonner puts it in his sympathetic article on 'Baptismus paruulorum' in the *Augustinus-Lexikon*, 'The problem [how baptism benefited infants] was eventually resolved for Augustine by the doctrine of Original Sin and the *massa damnata*...: infants share in Adam's guilt, from which they must be cleansed by baptism'[48] This is much more familiar territory than Augustine's pre-Pelagian essays in resolving the puzzles of infant baptism, and needs no mapping here.[49] It must suffice to tease out some

---

[45] See my paper 'The Meaning and Reference of "One Baptism for the Remission of Sins" in the Niceno-Constantinopolitan Creed', *Studia Patristica* 19 (1989), pp. 281-85 (ch. 4 above). Cf. E. TeSelle, *Augustine the Theologian* (London, 1970), p. 280: 'Probably the germ of the [Pelagian] controversy was the now undisputed fact that differing explanations of infant baptism were held in the East and in the West.'

[46] Augustine, *Against Julian* 1:6:21–7:35.

[47] Augustine, *Homilies on First Epistle of John* 4:11. Augustine instinctively connects infant baptism with the dread of infant death: e.g., *Homilies on John's Gospel* 38:6: 'Even the baby at the breast is brought in his mother's devout arms to the church, lest he depart this life without baptism and die in the sin with which he was born.' The correct reading is *sugens* (*BA*), not *surgens* (*PL, CCSL*).

[48] Bonner in *AugLex*, I, col. 592.

[49] See Bonner in *AugLex*, I, cols. 592-602, and my brief discussion in 'How Controversial Was the Development of Infant Baptism in the Early Church?', in J.E. Bradley and R.A. Muller (eds), *Church, Word and Spirit: Historical and Theological Essays in Honor of Geoffrey W. Bromiley* (Grand Rapids, MI, 1987), pp. 45-63, at pp. 56-63 (see ch. 2 above). Rist, *Augustine*, p. 17, is wrong in asserting that not until *The Merits and Remission of Sins* 2:20:34, in 411–12, does Augustine raise the question

salient threads of argument to sustain my claim that at Augustine's hands baptism underwent a fateful transformation.

Gerald Bonner has written that 'The Pelagian theology of baptism was constructed on the model of adult baptism; the infant baptizand was, for them, the anomaly. For Augustine the urgency of the need for baptism made him the norm.'[50] But for Augustine it was not always so. We have seen sufficient evidence above to conclude that, until the latter years of the first decade of the fifth century, Augustine too worked with adult baptism (I prefer to characterize it without reference to age, as conversion-baptism or the like) as the norm. Which simply means that he was a man of his time.

I am myself convinced that the baptizing of infants was, until the era of Augustine and beyond, far more minimal and marginal, at least in the West, than is often assumed. It is perhaps easier to demonstrate this in terms of theology than of practice. One has only to look at an anthology of patristic texts on infant baptism to become starkly aware of Augustine's domination of the field. Thus in J.C. Didier's collection, documents from the first four centuries occupy forty-four pages (including ten of inscriptions) while Augustine is allotted sixty pages.[51] And in Augustine himself, discussion prior to the Pelagian dispute is a drop in the bucket compared with the oceans released by the Pelagian challenges. If Augustine became the catalyst for far-reaching change within the church at large, it was as a result of the *bouleversement* in his own understanding. Even Didier himself, who starts with a conviction of 'le fait extremement repandu du pedobaptisme' in Africa, is puzzled that in his ante-Pelagian years Augustine shows himself uninterested in establishing the necessity and even the legitimacy of infant baptism.[52]

As for practice, the evidence advanced at the outset of this paper in my judgement damagingly disrupts the standard graph of developments in the early centuries, plotted influentially by Joachim Jeremias.[53] This shows infant baptism present from very early days and becoming increasingly commonplace until the fourth century, when for the first time postponement becomes a problem for some decades.[54] A far more

---

'what sins had an infant committed, and when, and how?' He later recognizes that *Epistle* 98 does so, in 408 (p. 125), and, we should add, so does *The Literal Meaning of Genesis* 10.

[50] Bonner in *AugLex*, I, col. 596.

[51] J.C. Didier, *Le Baptême des enfants dans la tradition de l'Eglise* (Tournai, 1959).

[52] Didier, 'Saint Augustin', pp. 110, 128.

[53] Joachim Jeremias, *Infant Baptism in the First Four Centuries* (London, 1960), with minor adjustments in his *The Origins of Infant Baptism* (London, 1963) following the challenge of Kurt Aland's *Did the Early Church Baptize Infants?* (London, 1963).

[54] The so-called vogue for 'postponing' baptism in the fourth and fifth centuries has not received the exhaustive investigation it merits. For the North Africans see E. Nagel,

plausible coherence can be discerned in the patchy evidence (I remember C.F.D. Moule commenting on Jeremias' monograph that it contained 'at least all the evidence'!) by something more akin to a single line tracing a fairly low trajectory until after Augustine.[55] Apart from any other considerations, such as the liturgical conservatism considered above,[56] the glaring *lacuna* of any agreed theology of infant baptism defies comprehension if the practice had been common, let alone standard, for centuries. At the very least it has to be acknowledged that the development remains in major respects puzzling, a fact which a loose undifferentiated use of 'postponement' has too often glossed over. No less a cause of the vulnerability of the Jeremias consensus has been the facile transition in its assumptions from the attested occurrence or acceptance of infant baptism to its general prevalence as the norm.

The Necessity of Infant Baptism for Infant Salvation

Undoubtedly one's estimate of Augustine's role in baptismal change will be significantly shaped by one's conception of developments before his time. In this connection greater interest must attach to his own pre-Pelagian ruminations. Collectively they are hardly impressive. They give little hint of the floodgates that would open wide in 411. Not least marked is the contrast between his *Confessions* (apart from the isolated and, as we have seen, unparalleled criticism of his mother for not having had him baptized *in extremis* as a boy—not an infant) and his anti-Pelagian corpus.

So wherein did the Augustinian transformation of baptism consist? First and foremost, of course, in making infant baptism essential for infant salvation. Although to the end Augustine allowed that 'unbaptized

---

Kindertaufe und Taufaufschub: Die Praxis vom 3–5. Jahrhundert in Nordafrika und ihre theologische Einordnung bei Tertullian, Cyprian und Augustinus (Europäische Hochschulschriften, 23:144; Frankfurt am Main, 1980). I have not seen Holger Hammerich, 'Taufe und Askese: Der Taufaufschub in vorkonstantinischer Zeit' (dissertation, University of Hamburg, 1994).

[55] In addition to the articles cited in nn. 2 and 49 above, see my 'The Origins of Infant Baptism—Child Believers' Baptism?', *Scottish Journal of Theology* 40 (1987), pp. 1-23 (ch. 1 above). For the late fifth or sixth century as the age when infant baptism first became the common practice, see Cramer, *Baptism and Change*, pp. 138ff; Didier, 'Adaptation', p. 85; T.M. Finn, *Early Christian Baptism and the Catechumenate: Italy, North Africa, and Egypt* (Message of the Fathers of the Church, 6; Collegeville, MN, 1992), pp. 91-92, 230.

[56] Cf. Cramer, *Baptism and Change*, p. 3: 'Thus one of the great questions posed by the history of baptism is how it was that even after the habit of infant baptism had become widespread in the churches of Latin Christendom, the *form* of adult baptism—of a rite of conversion celebrated either at Easter or Pentecost, and not just of passive or magical exorcism—continued largely to prevail.'

infants, having only original sin and no burden of their own sins, will suffer the lightest condemnation of all',[57] it was still condemnation, not limbo or some middle ground between heaven and hell. In some ways, this placed infants in a harsher position than adults. 'Though unbaptized adults outside the sphere of the people of God may be saved by heeding cryptic admonitions from God, infants can be saved only through baptism.'[58] 'The need to baptise early, the necessity of infant baptism rather than its possibility or desirability, is perhaps the most obvious legacy of Augustine to the Middle Ages.'[59]

Augustine was not blind to the apparently fortuitous circumstances that left one baby dying unbaptized, albeit the child of pious parents, and another baptized in time, although the castaway of a promiscuous mother taken in by virgins.[60] He could not concede the decision to the play of chance. And so what he had come to believe about baptism as the sole cure for the guilt of original sin reinforced his doctrine of predestination. TeSelle appositely quotes Warfield:

> It was not because of his theology of grace, or of his doctrine of predestination, that Augustine taught that comparatively few of the human race are saved. It was because he believed that baptism and incorporation into the visible Church were necessary for salvation.[61]

But Augustine could not stop there. Divine judgement and providence must be involved. This is not to imply that Augustine tightly correlated predestination and the receiving of baptism as an infant. He did not, but the parent grieving the loss not only of a young child but one unbaptized through some unhappy accident should not draw the cold comfort of haphazard change: 'often when the parents are eager and the ministers prepared for giving baptism to the infants, it still is not given, because

---

[57] Augustine, *Against Julian* 5:11:44.

[58] TeSelle, *Augustine the Theologian*, p. 323.

[59] Cramer, *Baptism and Change*, p. 125. Walahfrid Strabo (c.808–49) may have been the first commentator to link the transition from faith-baptism to infant baptism to clarification of the doctrine of original sin: see his *Libellus de exordiis et incrementis quarundam in observationibus ecclesiasticis rerum* (ed. and trans. Alice L. Harting-Corre; Mittellateinische Studien und Texte, 19; Leiden, 1996), pp. 176-79 (ch. 27, 511-12), with p. 306 on Walahfrid's historical interest.

[60] Augustine, *Against Two Letters of the Pelagians* 2:6:11; *The Gift of Perseverance* 12:31. Cf. TeSelle, *Augustine the Theologian*, p. 324; Bonner in *AugLex*, I, cols. 600-601.

[61] TeSelle, *Augustine the Theologian*, p. 323, from B.B. Warfield, *Studies in Tertullian and Augustine* (New York, 1930), p. 411.

God does not choose'.[62] When life expectancy was so precarious, baptism became burdened with a heavy incubus of doom.

The Effects of Augustine's Baptismal Revolution

Such a framework of belief could not tolerate a wait until the paschal season between Easter and Pentecost. Any time was ripe for baptism of a newborn of uncertain viability.[63] Inevitably, baptism, distributed randomly throughout the year, and indeed the days of the week, would become less of a celebration of the whole congregation. Changes such as these might take decades or centuries to unfold, but Augustine's baptismal revolution prescribed them.

By the same token, and for other weightier reasons, with infant baptism increasingly the norm, the baptismal ceremony would itself tend to shrink. The 'awe-inspiring rites of Christian initiation', as E.J. Yarnold has called them, whose dramatic richness can be glimpsed already in the Hippolytan *Apostolic Tradition* and discerned more clearly in the mystagogy of the fourth- and fifth-century Fathers, would become the midwives' routine of the Middle Ages and, on a longer perspective, the innocuous and colourless mini-rite of modern western Protestantism lambasted by Karl Barth.

From another angle, baptism as a normative rite of early childhood lost much of the theological and spiritual creativity it had exercised in the early centuries. We easily lose sight of the success of early Christian baptism as the fruitful mother of many offspring: the catechumenate, and the rich catechetical homiletic harvest of the golden age of the Fathers; the stimulus to the elaboration of the paschal celebration; its provocation of the penitential system (not all of baptism's children turned out too well!); the deep fountain of imagery that bound baptism with martyrdom, that developed the motifs of passover and exodus, that linked up with the symbolism of the transition from seventh-day sabbath to eighth-day, i.e. first-day Sunday, that exploited darkness and light, unclothing to nakedness and then reclothing in a new outfit, and so one could go on.

---

[62] Augustine, *The Gift of Perseverance* 12:31. In a recent essay provoked by one of the newly discovered Mainz sermons of Augustine, Eric Rebillard has argued that the postponement of baptism did not constitute a pastoral challenge to Augustine. He dealt with it in his preaching only during Lent, the period of preparation for baptism. His sermons do not conjure up a picture of crowds of indifferent Christians awaiting until their last days to be baptized. See 'La figure du catéchumène et le problème du delai du baptême dans la pastorale d'Augustin', in G. Madec (ed.), *Augustin prédicateur (395–411): Actes du Colloque International de Chantilly (5–7 septembre 1996)* (Paris, 1998), pp. 285-92. This may be an issue on which his preaching and his controversial treatises speak in discordant tones.

[63] Cf. De Latte, 'Saint Augustin et le baptême', pp. 50-51.

When infant baptism became standard, baptism's productivity began to atrophy, and the consequences lived stubbornly on, through the Reformation into the modern era.

But the chief result of the metamorphosis of baptism of which Augustine was the most significant catalyst is to be found simply in the replacement of the experience of a willing and purposive heart and mind with helpless passivity. (Theologians ever since have not been above making capital out of the baby's physical immobility and bare receptacle-capacity.) The import of this greatest of all transformations of baptism has been suggestively, if not always fully coherently, explored by Peter Cramer's *Baptism and Change*:

> [T]his whole view of sacrament as meeting and dialogue...apparently fades to nothing before Augustine's teaching—developed from *c*.406 onward—that mankind, and thus the child at birth, inherits the sin of Adam. In this perspective, baptism is suddenly exorcism again: it has the exact and negative function of removing the adverse judgement incurred by 'birth in Adam'. The rite loses all its ethical colour: instead of something done by the candidate, it becomes something done to him... The combined effect of original sin and infant baptism thus appears to make the candidate a vessel, an involuntary being, a theatre of good and evil.[64]

Cramer discerns here ground for a conflict in Augustine's mind:

> [O]n the one hand he wants baptism (whether infant or adult) as part of the *cultus*, to be *transitus*, dialogue, meeting, a ritual expression of the soul's capacity for God; on the other hand, partly in response to the Pelagians, he presents it as a substitution of good for evil, with no reference to the personal will of the subject.[65]

As I read Augustine (although I acknowledge the need for further exploration of this front), the conflict was in essence resolved in favour of his anti-Pelagian stance. We are dealing more with successive phases in his thought than with coexisting alternatives. When infant baptism became the norm, as it undoubtedly did in his later theology, it cut baptism *in genere* down to the size of what may and must be believed about the baptism of infants. It has, I suggest, ever been the case: infant baptism,

---

[64] Cramer, *Baptism and Change*, pp. 113-14. Cf. also on the domination of Augustine's late conception of infant baptism by the theme of exorcism, H.A. Kelly, *The Devil at Baptism: Ritual, Theology and Drama* (Ithaca, NY, 1985), esp. pp. 112-13. On the profound change that baptism underwent by the shift to infant baptism, see the contributions by Paul de Clerck and others on the paper by Arnold Angenendt, 'Der Taufritus im frühen Mittelalter', *Segni et riti nella chiesa altomedievale occidentale*, I (Settimane di Studio, 33; Spoleto, 1987), pp. 275-336, at pp. 325ff.

[65] Cramer, *Baptism and Change*, p. 114.

when normative in practice as well as in church doctrine, has effected a massive baptismal reductionism.[66]

I doubt if the Augustine of the 410s and 420s could have felt very comfortable rereading the portrayal of baptism he had scripted in the *Confessions*. We touch here, of course, on the large-scale transitions that Augustine's theological mind underwent from the 390s onwards and from c.410. It was not simply that Augustine's baptismal thinking revolved around infants and Pelagius' around converts. Augustine could no longer endorse what Pelagius believed about the decisiveness of baptism for the convert.[67] He had earlier been much closer to the Pelagian attitude; indeed, he had been a living exemplar of it himself. But the worm had turned, and the devaluation of baptism attendant upon its irreversible turn to the baby must apply to baptism *in toto*. The wider context in Augustine's shifting teaching has been sensitively exposed by Peter Brown.[68] In the process not only Augustine's understanding of baptism changed, but that change set in motion a far broader transformation that determined the contours of the Christianity of Christendom, in large measure to the present day.

---

[66] See my *What has Infant Baptism done to Baptism?*

[67] Cf. my brief review, 'Pelagius the Twice-Born', *Churchman* 86 (1972), pp. 6-15.

[68] In both *Augustine of Hippo* and the essays on Pelagius reprinted in *Religion and Society in the Age of Saint Augustine* (London, 1972).

CHAPTER 7

Monnica's Baptism, Augustine's Deferred Baptism, and Patricius

That Augustine's mother, Monnica, had been baptized is not in doubt. This much we know from Augustine's *Confessions*, a work which displays a persistent, yet sometimes laconic, interest in baptism. In his tearful tribute to his mother after her death, Augustine did not 'dare to say that, since the day you gave her new birth through baptism, no word contrary to your command issued from her mouth'.[1] But of the circumstances of her baptism, her pious son tells his readers nothing, except that it had taken place 'so many years' ago.[2]

Nor is it easy to find serious discussion of Monnica's baptism in the vast secondary literature on Augustine and his mother. It is relegated to a footnote, almost an afterthought, in the entry on Monnica in the *Prosopographie de l'Afrique chrétienne (303–533)*,[3] and it attracts no comment in either the edition of the *Confessions* in the *Bibliothèque Augustinienne* (1962/1992) or the three-volume edition and commentary of J.J. O'Donnell (1992). In the recent extensive Italian edition, the only point that attracts comment is the problem of post-baptismal sin, both in Monnica's case and in the broader context of early Christianity.[4] The lengthy entry on Monnica by Henri Leclercq in the *Dictionnaire d'archéologie chrétienne et de liturgie* omits to mention her baptism.

Nor does Monnica's baptism receive attention in a number of recent studies more closely focused on Augustine's mother. Thus Margaret O'Ferrall can characterize the celebrated wine-bibbing episode in her girlhood as Monnica's 'conversion' without marking or implying any

---

[1] Augustine, *Confessions* 9:13:34 (*BA* 14, p. 132): *ex quo eam per baptismum regenerasti*.
[2] Augustine, *Confessions* 9:13:35 (*BA* 14, p. 134): *dimitte illi et tu debita sua, si qua etiam contraxit per tot annos post aquam salutis*.
[3] A. Mandouze, *Prosopographie de l'Afrique chrétienne (303–533)* (Prosopographie chrétienne du Bas Empire, 1; Paris, 1982), pp. 758-762, *s.n.* 'Monnica', at p. 759 n. 29.
[4] Sant' Agostino, *Confessioni* (ed. M. Simonetti; trans. G. Chiarini; comment. M. Cristiani *et al.*; 5 vols; Milan, 1992–97), III, p. 349. The commentary in vol. III is the work of Goulven Madec and Luigi F. Pizzolato, and of Book IX of the *Confessions* in particular of the latter-named.

connexion with her baptism.⁵ William Frend's essay on Augustine's family, subtitled 'A Microcosm of Religious Change in North Africa', does not investigate the place of baptism in Monnica's Christianity.⁶ A Dutch scholar's presentation of *Augustinus' visie op zijn moeder* reviews the pertinent chapters in Book 9 of the *Confessions* but again without taking any cognizance of Monnica's baptism.⁷ The article on Monnica by Agostino Trapé in the *Bibliotheca Sanctorum* also leaves it unnoticed.⁸

It is hardly surprising, in the light of the reticence of the *Confessions*, that Monnica's baptism has evoked so little scholarly interest. It is more remarkable that some of the more popular and devotional lives of Monnica should fail to mention it. Wilkinson Sherren's *St. Monica* is certain that as a 'girl of devout habits, she was a frequent communicant', but must be taken to assume her earlier baptism.⁹ Similarly Frances Alice Forbes appears to take her baptism as a youngster for granted.¹⁰ Occasionally among this edifying genre the time of her baptism is identified explicitly as soon after birth. So the *Life* by Baroness Herbert of Lea has her receiving at the baptismal font the name of Monnica as a newborn baby.¹¹

---

⁵ Margaret More O'Ferrall, 'Monica, the mother of Augustine. A reconsideration', *Recherches augustiniennes* 10 (1975), pp. 23-43, at pp. 28-30, concerning *Confessions* 9:8:18.

⁶ W.H.C. Frend, 'The Family of Augustine: A Microcosm of Religious Change in North Africa', *Congresso Internazionale su S. Agostino...Roma, 15–20 settembre 1986. Atti* I (Studia Ephemeridis 'Augustinianum', 24; Rome, 1987), pp. 135-51. Nor is Monnica's baptism or spiritual nurture touched on in John J. O'Meara, 'Monica, the Mother of Augustine', *The Furrow* 5 (1954), pp. 555-62, or in Brent D. Shaw, 'The Family in Late Antiquity: The Experience of Augustine', *Past and Present* 115 (1987), pp. 3-51.

⁷ P.M.A. van Kempen-van Dijk, *Monnica...* (Amsterdam, 1978), pp. 76-77. Likewise Heikki Kotila, 'Monica's Death in Augustine's *Confessions* IX.11-13', *Studia Patristica* 27 (1993), pp. 337-41, notes merely that Augustine expresses, in *Confessions* 9:13:34, both appreciation of his mother's exemplary life 'in the communion of the Church and its sacraments' and fear lest she had sinned after baptism.

⁸ Agostino Trapé, 'Monica', *Bibliotheca Sanctorum* (12 vols; Rome, 1960–70), IX (1967), cols. 548-58. A similar silence prevails in the earlier collection of Simon Martin and François Giry, *Les Vies des Saints* (revd. Claude Raffson; 3 vols; Paris, 1719), I, cols. 1317-1320, and in Jules L. Baudot and Leon Chaussin (eds), *Vies des saints et des bienheureux* (13 vols; Paris, 1935–59), V, pp. 87-93.

⁹ W. Sherren, *St. Monica* (London, 1949), p. 18. The *Confessions*, to be sure, says nothing of Monnica's attendance at communion.

¹⁰ F.A. Forbes, *The Life of Saint Monica* (London, 1915).

¹¹ Mary Elizabeth Herbert, *The Life of St Monica, the Mother of St Augustine* (London, 1894), p. 2.

It is rare for such biographies to acknowledge the silence of the evidence: 'On ignore...si la mère d'Augustin reçut très jeune le baptême et les autres sacrements; même chez les chrétiens pieux, ce n'était pas toujours l'usage, surtout il est vrai pour les garçons.'[12] Much more common is the older tradition that links Monnica's baptism, at least chronologically, to that experience in her childhood when a slavegirl in her parents' household administered a salutary rebuke to her as 'a little boozer'.[13] As we have noted, O'Ferrall reads this incident as Monnica's 'conversion', according to the *Confessions*. Without using this vocabulary, the Maurists' *Vita S. Augustini* cites the passage from *Confessions* 9:8:18 as far as '*Quo illa stimulo percussa, respexit foeditatem suam, confestimque damnavit atque exuit*', and follows immediately with the comment:

> Baptismum Christi non in extremis posita, sed multis ante mortem annis percepit Monnica: quo ex tempore sic vitam instituit, ut fidei morumque puritate cuilibet ad laudandum Dei nomen esset incitamento

with a reference to *Confessions* 9:13:34.[14]

The same link was made in Alban Butler's late-eighteenth-century *Lives of the Saints*, where it survives through sundry revisions and abbreviations to the present day. So ashamed was young Monnica of the servant's smarting insult that 'Indeed, from the day of her baptism, which took place soon afterwards, she seems to have lived a life exemplary in every particular.'[15]

On the other hand, the widely popularized French biography of Monnica by Louis-Victor Bougaud places her baptism near the time of the return of the Christian community in her home town of Tagaste from

---

[12] Louise André-Delastre, *Sainte Monique. Mère de Saint Augustin* (Collection Saintes Mères et Mères de Saints; Lyons, 1960), p. 44.

[13] Augustine, *Confessions* 9:8:18 (*BA* 14, pp. 104-108): 'boozer' is Henry Chadwick's translation of *meribibulam*, in *Confessions* (Oxford, 1991), p. 168.

[14] *Vita S. Augustini* II:2, *PL* 32, col. 145. The life *De Sancta Monica Vidua* by Walter, a twelfth-century canon-regular of Arrouaise (*Bibliotheca Hagiographica Latina* [2 vols; Brussels, 1898–1901; 2nd edn, 1949], no. 6000), which is printed in *Acta Sanctorum* Maii I, cols. 473-480, simply reproduces *Confs.* 9:13:34 without comment (480B).

[15] Alban Butler, *Butler's Lives of the Saints* (ed. H. Thurston and D. Attwater; 5 vols; London, 1956), II, p. 226. The edition of 1780 similarly places the two events in close temporal, and by implication causal, proximity: 'She after this received baptism, from which time she lived always in such a manner, that she was an odour of edification to all who knew her' (vol. V, p. 57). The same tradition is found earlier, in Adrien Baillet, *Les Vies des Saints* (4 vols; Paris, 1710), II, p. 211, discerning God's providential design to save Monnica in allowing her to quarrel with the servant-girl. The revised edition (10 vols; Paris, 1729), retains the temporal, but not the providential, link: 'Elle fut baptisée bientôt après...' (vol. IV, p. 80).

Donatism to Catholicism, in AD 348/49, when she was around sixteen years of age.[16] This tradition is not consistent with the one reflected in the Maurist editors' *Vita*, for the recovery of Monnica from incipient bibulousness by the divinely intended *correptio* of a slavegirl happened when she was no more than a *puella*, 'scarcely past her early childhood'.[17] John O'Meara also helps to cut the incident down to size, in remarking on the 'slightly painful rhetoric' in which Augustine elaborates how Monnica 'was *suddenly* (as is usual in the 'conversions' he alludes to in the *Confessions*) converted through the taunt of a mischief-making maidservant'.[18] The point is rarely if ever made that, since it was not Monnica's mother or father whose correction precipitated this 'conversion' but a servant woman, it would presumably have had little bearing on the issue of Monnica's baptism—unless, that is, it provoked Monnica into requesting baptism herself. Several writers observe that Augustine seems to attribute Monnica's piety more to this servant than to her parents.

The lack of any firm consensus about the time of Monnica's baptism may partly account for the careless slip in the recent fine study by John Rist, which has her baptized with Augustine and Adeodatus (three generations at once!) in 387.[19] But this lapse should perhaps also be brought into connexion with a sentence in the *Confessions*, which has not proved wholly straightforward for editors or translators. Speaking of the culmination of his mother's lifetime of service, and immediately before embarking on the vision of Ostia, Augustine states:

---

[16] L.-V.E. Bougaud, *Life of St. Monica* (trans. Mrs Edward A. Hazeland; London, 1886 [from the 2nd French edn, 1866]), pp. 54-55: 'if, as some think, this was also the august moment of her baptism and first communion...' On the untidy mixture of history and legend in Bougaud's work, see L. Brix, 'Bulletin augustinien pour 1979', *Revue des études augustiniennes* 26 (1980), p. 380; Clarissa W. Atkinson, '"Your Servant, my Mother": The Figure of Saint Monica in the Ideology of Christian Motherhood', in Clarissa W. Atkinson et al. (eds), *Immaculate and Powerful: The Female in Sacred Image and Social Reality* (Boston, MA, 1985), pp. 139-72, at pp. 159-162. On the possibilities of Monnica's roots in Donatism see J.J. O'Donnell (ed.), *Augustine Confessions* (3 vols; Oxford, 1992), II, p. 118. H. Leclercq in *DACL* 11:2, col. 2233, is sure that Monnica was born into a catholic home, and so too is John J. Gavigan, 'The Mother of St Augustine', *American Ecclesiastical Review* 119 (1948), pp. 254-80, at p. 255. Leon Cristiani, *The Story of Monica and Her Son Augustine* (Boston, MA, 1977), p. 19, believes that Monnica's family was the only one (in Tagaste, of course) 'that had not succumbed to the Donatist schism'. He reports the conjecture that it was as a result of the town's return from Donatism to Catholicism that Monnica was baptized when she was seventeen or eighteen (qualified by 'probably not...until' on p. 25).

[17] H.C.G. Moule, in W. Smith and H. Wace (eds), *A Dictionary of Christian Biography* (4 vols; London, 1877–87), III, p. 932, *s.n.* 'Monnica'.

[18] O'Meara, 'Monica, the Mother of Augustine', p. 557.

[19] John M. Rist, *Augustine: Ancient Thought Baptized* (Cambridge, 1994), p. 4.

> Postremo nobis, Domine, omnibus, quia ex munere tuo sinis loqui servis tuis, qui ante dormitionem eius in te iam consociati vivebamus percepta gratia baptismi tui, ita curam gessit, quasi omnes genuisset, ita servivit, quasi ab omnibus genita fuisset (*Confs.* 9:9:22).

This is the text of M. Skutella (Teubner, 1934) retained by L. Verheijen (*CCSL* 27, 1981) and by the editors of the *Bibliothèque Augustinienne Confessions* (1962, 1992). But a correction to the French translation in the 1992 *BA* edition implies an adjustment to the punctuation, inserting a comma before *servis tuis*.[20] This is indeed the reading of the first part of the sentence adopted by James O'Donnell, and earlier by Gibb and Montgomery.[21]

But this detail of punctuation does not remove the uncertainties of translation, as the following version of Henry Chadwick illustrates:

> Lastly, Lord—by your gift you allow me to speak for your servants, for before her falling asleep we were bound together in community in you after receiving the grace of baptism—she exercised care for everybody as if they were all her own children.[22]

A rapid and perhaps not unnatural reading of this sentence might easily assume that Monnica was included in the 'we...bound together in community...after receiving the grace of baptism', and that this group was identical with the Lord's servants on behalf of whom Augustine speaks. Certainly, it would in this translation be difficult to discern any distinction between those bound together in community and those who received baptism. It is, I suggest, a translation like this that might have triggered the momentary confusion evinced by John Rist.

A review of other translators' efforts with this tricky Latin sentence shows the importance of maintaining the syntactical connexion between '*nobis...omnibus*' for whom Monnica cared and those '*qui...consociati vivebamus...*' The *Bibliothèque Augustinienne* translators—E. Tréhorel and G. Bouissou—have managed this successfully:

> Nous tous enfin, Seigneur, ...nous qui avant son dernier sommeil vivions déjà associés en toi après avoir reçu la grâce de ton baptême, nous avons été l'objet de ses soins.[23]

---

[20] *BA* 14, p. 115, has the rendering, 'Nous tous enfin, Seigneur, puisque ta bienveillance nous permet de nous dire tes serviteurs, nous qui...', but a corrigendum in the 1992 reimpression (*BA* 14, p. 691) construes it as follows: 'Nous tous enfin, Seigneur, nous, tes serviteurs, puisque ta bienveillance nous permet de nous appeler ainsi, nous qui...'

[21] O'Donnell (ed.), *Confessions*, I, p. 113; III, p. 121; John Gibb and William Montgomery (eds), *The Confessions of Augustine* (Cambridge Patristic Texts; Cambridge, 1908), p. 258.

[22] Chadwick, *Confessions*, p. 170.

A reliable translation must make it clear that Monnica is not here counted among the company of 'all of us...who...already shared common life together after the reception' of the grace of your baptism'—but is depicted as caring for all as if mother of them all and serving all as if daughter of all.

It is remarkable how few of the English translations reproduce the force of the adverb *iam*, which, with *servis tuis* (= *servi Dei*), *consociati* and *vivebamus*, must indicate a link by anticipation between this post-baptismal experience of male Christian community, while Monnica was still alive, and the fuller enjoyment of it back in Africa that would follow her death.[24] Vernon Bourke's rendering helpfully reshapes the sentence in the interest of clarity:

> Finally, O Lord, she took such care of all of us, whom in Thy bounty Thou does permit me to call Thy servants—for, before she went to her rest in Thee we were already living in a group after receiving the grace of Thy baptism...[25]

Before leaving this sentence in the *Confessions*, we must face another issue where translation challenges comprehension. Are most English translators on safe ground in turning Augustine's ablative absolute, *percepta gratia baptismi tui*, into an active participle, 'after receiving', in apposition with *vivebamus*? Had 'all of us' who were sharing life together recently received baptism? With Augustine himself Alypius and Adeodatus had been baptized (*Confs.* 9:6:14). Evodius was also present, having been converted and baptized before Augustine but, by implication, not long before (*Confs.* 9:8:17). Nebridius, although by now possibly baptized, cannot be located with confidence during the months in question.[26] But of no one else can we be certain, although Navigius, Augustine's only known brother, seems a very likely candidate, having shared in the Cassiciacum months and being in attendance at his mother's

---

[23] *BA* 14, p. 115. For this purpose the correction in the 1992 printing noted above is of no relevance.

[24] There is no recognition of *iam* in the translations by A.C. Outler (Library of Christian Classics, 7), Frank J. Sheed, E.B. Pusey, J.G. Pilkington, as well as Chadwick. Only Vernon J. Bourke, *St Augustine: The Confessions* (Fathers of the Church, 21; Washington, DC, 1953), picks it up. Outler's version is further marred by the failure to translate *percepta gratia baptismi tui*.

[25] Bourke, *St Augustine*, p. 250. For the interpretation of this sentence given here, cf. *Confessions* 9:8:17, of the interval between baptism at Milan and the return to Africa: *Qui habitare facis unanimes in domo, consociasti nobis et Evodium... Simul eramus simul habitaturi placito sancto. Quaerebamus, quisnam locus nos utilius haberet servientes tibi: pariter remeabamus in Africam.*

[26] Cf. Mandouze, *Prosopographie*, pp. 774-75, s.n.; M. Marie de Gonzagne, 'Un correspondant de Saint Augustin: Nebridius', in *Augustinus Magister* (3 vols; Paris, 1954–55), I, pp. 93-99, at p. 98.

death-bed in Ostia (*Confs*. 9:11:27). But was Navigius a baptized Christian, yet, if ever?[27] For this inchoate household fellowship of God's servants, baptism may have been a condition of membership. But perhaps we should not envisage it as so restricted—more a cross between an open family ménage and a group of pledged *consociati* in faith.[28] At any rate, caution in translation is advised.[29] The collaborative Italian edition retains the punctuation of the Latin text of Skutella *et al*. (and translates the pertinent clause 'poiché generosamente concedi ai tuoi servi di parlare'), but by its use of the absolute construction avoids the assumption or implication that 'all of us' had 'received the grace of baptism'.

> E infine, Signore, di noi tutti —...— di noi che, ricevuta la grazia del tuo battesimo, già prima che si addormentasse in te, vivevamo in te uniti, si prese cura.[30]

The phrase *percepta gratia baptismi tui*, read in the wider context of Books 8 and 9 of the *Confessions*, unambiguously applies only to Augustine, Alypius and Adeodatus. It was their joint baptism that brought this small community into being and they were the core of the perhaps only slightly larger number indicated by *nobis...omnibus*.

It may not be solely imprecise translations of a sentence in *Confessions* 9:9:22 that have given rise to the misconception that Monnica shared in Augustine's baptism (which I have encountered from time to time in students' essays owing nothing to Rist's book). James O'Donnell's commentary on Book 9 begins as follows:

> Book 9 is the book of death and rebirth. Baptism stands at its centre, and baptism is both death in Christ (Rom. 6:3) and rebirth. Verecundus, Nebridius, Patricius, Adeodatus, and Monnica are all reported to have been baptized and died—though of those deaths only that of Monnica falls within what might be thought the

---

[27] Cf. O'Donnell (ed.), *Confessions*, III, p. 138. Mandouze, *Prosopographie*, p. 772, *s.n*. 'Navigius 1', is not explicit about his Christian identity.

[28] On this post-baptismal temporary Christian community, perhaps first essayed at Milan and then resumed at Rome after Monnica's death, see Peter Brown, *Augustine of Hippo* (London, 1967), pp. 126-27; George Lawless, *Augustine of Hippo and his Monastic Rule* (Oxford, 1987), pp. 38-39, 43-44; Adolar Zumkeller, *Augustine's Ideal of the Religious Life* (New York, 1986), pp. 13-14. *Confessions* 9:8:17 is regularly cited in this context, 9:9:22 rarely.

[29] The *BA* version turns the Latin's passive into active, and hence ambiguous: 'nous qui...vivions déjà associés en toi après avoir reçu...' (*BA* 14, p. 115).

[30] Sant' Agostino, *Confessioni*, III, pp. 138-39. I am grateful to one of my research students, Angus Morrison, for help in elucidating this point.

chronological limits of this book (August 386–late 387). Augustine, Alypius, and Evodius are baptized and go on to a new life.[31]

'Monnica [is] reported to have been baptized and died'! Such foreshortened perspective is sufficient to mislead the unwary, especially when the author proceeds to divide the book into two symmetrical halves, 'The death and rebirth of Augustine', 9:1:1–7:16, and 'The death and rebirth of Monnica', 9:8:17–13:37. The parallelism deploys the different meanings of both 'death' and 'rebirth':

Milan before Cassiciacum	X	Monnica's life before Ostia
Cassiciacum	X	Ostia
Hearing the Word	X	Hearing the Word
Milan after Cassiciacum	X	After Ostia
Baptism	X	Monnica's death

Not surprisingly, O'Donnell shows no interest in the references in Book 9:13:34-35 to Monnica's rebirth in the baptismal waters (*regenerasti*) many years earlier.

Yet the design of the author of the *Confessions* should not be forgotten. Augustine has chosen to include his only explicit mention of his mother's baptism in Book 9, which stresses her intimate association with the baptismal progress of her son and his son and companions. Book 9 is in some ways a book of baptisms—eight in all, as O'Donnell's introduction to it rightly emphasizes. It is almost as if Augustine's own baptism acts as a catalyst in bringing to the surface the baptismal stories of others. Baptisms are recorded elsewhere in the *Confessions*, but Victorinus is the only other named candidate (8:2:3-5).

There is, however, a possible allusion to Monnica's baptism elsewhere in the *Confessions*. When Augustine was fifteen, financial hardship kept him at home. His father observed signs of his emergent sexuality and rejoiced in anticipation of grandchildren. Not so Monnica:

> Sed matris in pectore iam inchoaveras templum tuum et exordium sanctae habitationis tuae: nam ille adhuc catechumenus et hoc recens erat.

Monnica sensed with foreboding what errant behaviour lay ahead for one who had turned his back on God. Vehement were her warnings against

---

[31] O'Donnell (ed.), *Confessions*, III, p. 72. Earlier the same author had noted that the *Confessions*, like Augustine's other works, shows no interest in the 'cult act' of baptism (I, p. xxix). See the discussion in David C. Alexander, 'The Emergence of Augustine's Early Ecclesiology (386–391)' (PhD thesis, University of Edinburgh, 1995), pp. 47ff.

fornication and adultery. Thank goodness Augustine had not yet been baptized (*quamvis mihi nondum fideli*)!³²

One thing is obvious, that Monnica had already been baptized, unlike Patricius (and Augustine).³³ But it would inevitably strain probabilities to draw the inference that her baptism had only recently taken place. Even O'Donnell's comment on *inchoaveras* seems partly unwarranted:

> Nothing here indicates great or long-standing piety on Monnica's part; quite the contrary. In view of the contrast with Patricius in the next line, this may mean only that she had already been baptized. Her actions so far are those of a worldly mother.³⁴

Although shortly hereafter Augustine acknowledges Monnica's mixed motivations towards his development,³⁵ here no criticism is implied—as though no more than the rudiments of piety had taken hold of her heart. Her being a baptized Christian (*fidelis*) is more unambiguously established by the contrasting position of Patricius, than is any temporal pointer indicated by the verb *inchoaveras*.

We must therefore turn back to Book 9 to investigate whether anything further may be determined about the timing of Monnica's own baptism. We may safely deduce from Augustine's silence in his summary of her early nurture *in domo fideli*—both her parents, it seems, were baptized³⁶—that she was not baptized as a baby or infant. Nor should this

---

³² Augustine, *Confessions* 2:3:6-7. But O'Donnell (ed.), *Confessions*, II, p. 121, surely exaggerates: 'If he is not a Christian, then his moral failings are irrelevant.'

³³ So W. Hartke, 'Monica', in *Paulys Real-Encyclopädie der klassischen Altertumswissenschaft*, ed. G. Wissowa *et al.* (Stuttgart, 1893–1972), Supplem. VI (1935), cols. 520-529, at col. 526.

³⁴ O'Donnell (ed.), *Confessions*, II, p. 121. Gavigan, 'The Mother of St Augustine', p. 255, is emphatic that Monnica was baptized many years before her death.

³⁵ Augustine, *Confessions* 2:3:8: *quae iam de medio Babylonis fugerat, sed ibat in ceteris eius tardior*.

³⁶ O'Donnell (ed.), *Confessions*, III, p. 116, on *in domo fideli* (*Confs.* 9:8:17). But again there is an issue of translation: is the immediately following phrase *bono membro ecclesiae tuae* in apposition to *domo fideli* (as in BA 14, p. 103, 'dans une maison de foi qui était un membre sain de ton Église') or an independent instrumental ablative (cf. Chadwick, *Confessions*, p. 166, 'in a believing household through a good member of your Church')? If the latter, who was this 'good member'? The following sentence at first suggests her mother but the following paragraph another candidate: *Nec tantam erga suam disciplinam diligentiam matris praedicabat quantam famulae cuiusdam decrepitae, quae patrem eius infantem portaverat... Cuius rei gratia et propter senectam ac mores optimos in domo christiana satis a dominis honorabatur. Unde etiam curam dominicarum filiarum commissam diligentia gerebat, et erat in eis cohercendis, cum opus esset, sancta severitate vehemens atque in docendis sobria prudentia* (*Confs.* 9:8:17). If we opted for the second translation possibility, then the *sagax anus* (9:8:18) would seem more suited to be the 'good member of your Church'. (Mandouze, *Prosopographie*, p. 758, n. 4,

be deemed remarkable as early as this stage—the mid-fourth century—in the history of infant baptism. The evidence is plentiful, with no instances to the contrary, that the baptizing of their newborn children had no place in the minds of even the most pious Christian parents during this period.[37]

It would be wholly speculative to link Monnica's baptism with Tagaste's turning from Donatist to Catholic allegiance, partly because this event cannot be dated with any precision,[38] partly because we cannot be certain that Tagaste was Monnica's home town,[39] and partly because no evidence suggests such a link. By no means free of hazard is the identification of her 'conversion', as O'Ferrall and other writers call it,[40] from her precocious tippling as the occasion of her baptism. Her age at the time may be immaterial. If Augustine's description of her as *puella* supports Peter Brown's surmise that she was six years old,[41] that would put her in the same bracket as the *puer* Augustine who was refused baptism by his mother—to her fault, as he later believed when writing the *Confessions*.[42] One might have expected him to have mentioned Monnica's baptism if it had occurred at that juncture, not least because it would have implicitly strengthened his criticism of her failure to have him baptized at a similar stage in life. Furthermore, if those interpreters are correct who regard Monnica's 'conversion' from *consuetudo mala* in *Confessions* 9:8:18 as intended 'to correspond to Augustine's own moral renewal in the garden scene',[43] nothing could have highlighted the

---

warns against exaggerating her parents' influence, citing 9:9:19: *Educata itaque pudice ac sobrie potiusque a te subdita parentibus quam a parentibus tibi*. They come off none too commendably in O'Donnell's note on mothers and fathers in the *Confessions*, II, p. 70.) But the appositional reading seems more natural (otherwise one would have expected a preposition, *a* or *per*, with *membrum*), but then the *domus fidelis* should be viewed as including the *sagax anus* rather than indicating the parents alone. Most English translators have *bono membro* as descriptive of *domo fideli*, but Outler confusingly expands 'in the house of one of thy faithful ones who was a good member...' (Library of Christian Classics, 7, p. 189). (I raise for future translators another question from the end of the quotation above from *Confs.* 9:8:17. BA and Chadwick both take *sobria prudentia* as parallel to *sancta severitate*, but where is the parallel to *vehemens*?, or does it govern both phrases?, or should *sobria* be taken as a nominative?)

[37] See my paper 'At What Ages Were People Baptized in the Early Centuries?', *Studia Patristica* 30 (1997), pp. 387-92 (ch. 5 above).

[38] Cf. R. Crespin, *Ministère et sainteté. Pastorale du clergé et solution de la crise Donatiste dans la vie et la doctrine de S. Augustin* (Paris, 1965), p. 140, and W.H.C. Frend, *The Donatist Church* (Oxford, 1951), p. 184, who both suggest a time after the Macarian mission and before Julian, in the late 340s or the 350s.

[39] O'Donnell (ed.), *Confessions*, II, p. 118.

[40] O'Donnell (ed.), *Confessions*, III, p. 117 and elsewhere agrees with O'Ferrall.

[41] Brown, *Augustine of Hippo*, p. 174.

[42] Augustine, *Confessions* 1:11:17-18.

[43] O'Donnell (ed.), *Confessions*, II, p. 117.

parallelism more effectively than an account of her baptism consequent upon her abandonment of corrupting custom. Augustine's silence must again be read as significant.

We are brought back to *Confessions* 9:13:34-35. From the way these chapters speak about Monnica's baptism, the inference is, I believe, a plausible one that it took place after she had attained years of personal responsibility:

> Although after being made alive (*vivificata*) in Christ, even while not yet released from the flesh, she so lived that your name is praised in her faith and practice, nevertheless I dare not claim that from the time you gave her new birth through baptism, no word contrary to your command issued from her mouth...
>
> I know that she acted mercifully and cordially forgave the sins of those who sinned against her; will you also forgive her any sins that she incurred during the many years following the water of salvation.[44]

The implication is clear. Baptism occurred at a point in Monnica's life when she was able so to fashion her Christian profession and conduct as to be held accountable for it. We are justified in assuming that she sought and received baptism at her own discretion. While these conclusions may be drawn with a residual tentativeness, they would accord with what we know of baptismal practice in every other identifiable case during most of the fourth century.[45] Furthermore, they would concur with the understanding of baptism discernible in Augustine's other early writings up to c.400. These expose a range of uncertainties, hesitations and limitations whenever he considers the baptism of infants.[46] The overall impression is the one conveyed by the *Confessions*, that Christian baptism is sought and given on the deliberate decision of the candidate, to which the only attested exception is the crisis of imminent death.

This brings us to the baptism Augustine requested but was not in the end granted, when he fell gravely ill while still a boy (*adhuc puer*).[47] Later Augustine pinpointed seven as the age at which *pueri* could first answer for themselves in baptism.[48] The record in the *Confessions* makes it clear that baptism was pursued on Augustine's initiative: *vidisti, Deus meus, ...quo motu animi et qua fide baptismum...flagitavi a pietate matris*

---

[44] Augustine, *Confessions* 9:13:34, 35.

[45] See my 'At What Ages...?'.

[46] See my essay 'Augustine and the Transformation of Baptism', in Alan Kreider (ed.), *The Origins of Christendom in the West* (Edinburgh and New York, 2001), pp. 287-310 (ch. 6 above).

[47] Augustine, *Confessions* 1:11:17-18. O'Donnell does not comment on *adhuc puer ad loc.*, but see his discussion of *pueritia* in Augustine's scheme of the ages of man in *Confessions*, II, pp. 52-56.

[48] Augustine, *De anima et eius origine* 1:10:12, 3:9:12 (*PL* 44, cols. 481, 516-17).

meae.⁴⁹ Monnica's co-operation was indispensable and she hastily arranged *ut sacramentis salutaribus initiarer et abluerer, te, Domine Jesu, confitens in remissionem peccatorum*. It was to be a baptism in which young Augustine would answer for himself, i.e. the baptism of a believer: *ita iam credebam*, 'So I was already a believer.'⁵⁰

Augustine's non-baptism would not have been a deferred infant baptism (the *Confessions* know nothing of infant baptism, in the sense of the baptism of those too young to answer for themselves), but rather an advanced adult-believer's baptism, advanced because of the prospect of early death. As such it conforms to the frame of reference within which we have surmised that Monnica's own baptism would have taken place. We have no evidence whatsoever that Monnica ever considered having baby Augustine baptized. He faults her not for this neglect but for frustrating his zeal to confess his own faith in baptism for the remission of sins while *adhuc puer*.⁵¹

So the youthful, perhaps pre-teenage Augustine would have been a believing candidate for baptism in his own right. Yet he was not old enough to act independently of his mother. Although the text of the *Confessions* is respectfully phrased, we might think, so as to spare his mother's name (note the passives: *dilata est...mundatio mea; dilatus sum ne tunc baptizarer; quanto ergo melius et cito sanarer et id ageretur mecum meorum meaque diligentia*), eventually Augustine blames the cancellation on his mother, but even then in somewhat opaque imagery.⁵²

Even this was too bitter for the hagiographical tradition of St Monnica to bear. Authors of devotional lives repeatedly shift the responsibility for the change of plan on to Patricius. Unbeliever though he still was (as the

---

⁴⁹ Cf. too Augustine, *Confessions* 5:9:16: *melior eram puer quo illum* [= *baptismum*] *de materna pietate flagitavi, sicut iam recordatus atque confessus sum*.

⁵⁰ Chadwick, *Confessions*, p. 14.

⁵¹ In a brief study of 'St. Monica', in *The Month* 17 (1957), pp. 309-320, Muriel Spark notes that Augustine was not baptized in infancy, 'nor perhaps were his brother and sister'. She thinks it strange that 'Monica should have followed the dubious custom of late baptism', but attributes it to her characteristic attachment to 'popular and local religious customs' (p. 312). L.F. Pizzolato considers the postponement of Augustine's baptism solely in relation to doubts about the remissibility of post-baptismal sins: Sant' Agostino, *Confessioni*, I, p. 151. Agostino Trapé, *Saint Augustine: Man, Pastor, Mystic* (New York, 1986), pp. 25-26, 347 n. 30, cites the example of Alypius to show that deferred baptism was not uncommon in Tagaste. But evidence that Alypius was the child of Christian parents is lacking. The entry on him in Mandouze, *Prosopographie*, pp. 53-65, is singularly unhelpful on this point. Its first mention of anything religious in Alypius' life is his seduction into Manichaeism by Augustine (p. 53).

⁵² Augustine, *Confessions* 1:11:18: *sed quot et quanti fluctus impendere temptationum post pueritiam videbantur, noverat eos iam illa mater et terram per eos, unde postea formarer, quam ipsam iam effigiem committere volebat*. See the discussion in O'Donnell (ed.), *Confessions*, II, pp. 72-73.

Confessions remind us at this very point, 1:11:17: *ille nondum crediderat*), he would have permitted the baptism *in periculo mortis*, but saw no need once Augustine began to recover. Monnica had to resign herself to his change of mind. She said nothing, even though she was familiar with the risks that unbaptized Augustine would face.[53] Another tradition records the aborted baptism without assigning blame.[54] These versions suffer not only from an excess of imagination and *pietas* but also from reading the incident of Augustine's on–off baptism from a post-Augustininian baptismal perspective. Monnica died long before the Pelagian debates brought about that significant shift which would regard paedobaptism as the norm.

A more recent interpretation in effect excuses Monnica by viewing her refusal as serving the true design of God:

> Augustine even suggests that when Monica resisted his youthful desire for baptism she may unknowingly have been acting as God's agent: 'I ask you, my God—for, if it is your will, I long to know—for what purpose was my baptism postponed at that time?' [*Confs.* 1:11:18]. Although even then Monica is laboring to bring forth a new life in faith, God's motherhood knows that the infant Augustine is not yet ready to be weaned or to be reborn.[55]

But this interpretation cannot be sustained, both because its quotation stops selectively short and hence omits the outcome of Augustine's questioning—*quanto ergo melius et cito sanarer...melius vero*—and because it appears to misconstrue what it does quote: *Rogo te, deus meus: vellem scire, si tu etiam velles*. The meaning must be, 'I would wish to know, if you would also wish me to know.' As O'Donnell explains, 'The imperfect of an optative subjunctive [*vellem*] denotes the wish as unaccomplished in present time, but the following clause, "*si tu etiam velles*", creates a present contrary-to-fact condition: Augustine does not know, because God does not will him to know.'[56] We might almost translate, 'I would have wished to know, if you had wanted me to.'

The hagiographical fancies noted above at least serve to focus attention on Patricius' role in Augustine's religious upbringing. Possidius, it will

---

[53] This is the account given with only minor variations by Wilkinson Sherren, *St Monica*, p. 27; Frances Forbes, *Life of St Monica*, pp. 35-36; Mary Herbert, *Life of St Monica*, p. 17; Louis-Victor Bougaud, *Life*, p. 79. But Cristiani, *The Story of Monica*, pp. 44-45, keeps to the story-line of the *Confessions*.

[54] So Alban Butler, *Lives of the Saints*, V, p. 59. It is not even mentioned in Giry, *Vies des Saints*, I, cols. 1317-1320.

[55] Marsha L. Dutton, '"When I Was a Child": Spiritual Infancy and God's Maternity in Augustine's Confessiones', in Joseph C. Schnaubelt and Frederick Van Fleteren (eds), *Collectanea Augustiniana. Augustine: 'Second Founder of the Faith'* (New York, 1990), pp. 113-40, at p. 123.

[56] O'Donnell (ed.), *Confessions*, II, p. 71. *BA* 13, p. 305 n. 1, to similar effect.

be remembered, makes Augustine the offspring of a Christian father as well as a Christian mother,[57] which cannot be squared with the *Confessions*. Yet Augustine, both in the *Confessions* and elsewhere, does not depict the unbelieving Patricius as merely a spectator of Augustine's early religious course. In fact, contrary to a widespread impression, whenever Augustine assigns responsibility for his being registered as a catechumen from birth, he credits both his parents together. Amid bewilderment and uncertainty at Milan, he resolved to 'fix my feet on that step (*gradu*) on which I had been placed by my parents' (*Confs.* 6:11:18). The *gradus* he means is the status of a catechumen, as a closely parallel earlier statement makes clear: 'I therefore decided meantime to be a catechumen in the catholic Church which my parents had entrusted to me [*ecclesia mihi a parentibus commendata*] until some certainty should light up the path I should follow' (*Confs.* 5:14:25).[58] In *De utilitate credendi*, when writing of his Milan sojourn, he recorded, 'I had decided meanwhile to be a catechumen in the Church, to which I had been assigned by my parents...' (8:20; *PL* 42, col. 79).

Perhaps all these three statements should be referred to the last year or so of Patricius' life when he had joined his wife in Christian baptism, and together they had 'commended' the church afresh to their wayward son. But a phrase from Augustine's reflections on his unrealized baptism, cited earlier but not commented on at the time, may also be relevant at this point. 'How much better if I were quickly healed *et id ageretur mecum meorum meaque diligentia, ut recepta salus animae meae tuta esset tutela tua*' (*Confs.* 1:11:18). The issue of Augustine's baptism somehow lay in the discretion not simply of himself and his mother, but who else was included in the *mei*? English translators divide between 'my family' and 'my friends'—although one wonders what the latter's influence can have amounted to in the case of Augustine *adhuc puer*. French can happily use 'la diligence des miens' without further specification.[59]

Most probably *mei* should send us back to the believing household—*omnis domus nisi pater solus*—of the previous paragraph. But it may well allude to the strong likelihood that Patricius would not have gone unconsulted and voiceless in the decision over his young son's

---

[57] Possidius, *Vita* 1 (ed. H.T. Weiskotten [Princeton, NJ, 1919], p. 40): *de numero curialium parentibus honestis et Christianis progenitus erat*. Hartke in *Paulys Real-Encyclopädie Supplem.* VI, col. 526, understands from this that Patricius was already a catechumen, but this is inconsistent with the chronology of *Confs.* 2:3:6. Cf. Pierre Courcelle, *Les Confessions de Saint Augustin dans la tradition littéraire* (Paris, 1963), p. 611 n. 1.

[58] Cf. André Mandouze, *Saint Augustin. L'aventure de la raison et de la grâce* (Paris, 1968), p. 91.

[59] *BA* 13, p. 307.

baptism. A semi-popular but not over-inventive life of Monnica envisages the scene once she has yielded to the boy's demand to be baptized.

> Mais d'abord, en parler au père. Ah! Patricius a trop de chagrin pour contrarier dans une circonstance pareille son épouse et son fils; d'ailleurs auprès de cette épouse le peu de préjugés qu'il nourrissait à l'égard des chrétiens a bien fondu... *'Mon père n'évinça point me mère de son droit de piété sur mois,* attestera plus tard saint Augustin, *car en ce point elle l'emportait sur son mari à qui* (il croit bon de rappeler l'heureuse tactique) *elle se tenait soumise pour le reste.'*[60]

The picture conveys a certain air of plausibility. It carries Patricius' influence on events no further. Monnica is held alone responsible for calling off the baptism, again plausibly enough.[61] Even if she had to secure her husband's consent for the baptism, it is inconceivable that he would insist on going through with it after she had changed her mind. If Monnica was swayed by no conviction that baptism was best administered as early in life as possible, we may be certain that Patricius was a total stranger to such notions.

Yet if, as we have seen evidence to believe, Augustine's father was involved both in his newborn son's enrolment as a catechumen and in the boy's frustrated baptism, we should not view him as hostile to Monnica's faith so much as uncommitted. It is not impossible, to be sure, that he had himself as a baby been admitted as a catechumen. Only many years later, as with Augustine himself, was that formal status activated, as it were, preparatory to his baptism—which was not strictly a death-bed baptism.[62]

The baptismal careers of Monnica, Patricius and Augustine have more in common than is realized, despite their otherwise starkly different religious histories. The timing of baptism in these circles was governed by two salient convictions: first, that it belonged to the self-determining choice of responsible years, when the direction of one's life could be firmly and irrevocably set; and, second, that the only normal exception to

---

[60] André-Delastre, *Sainte Monique*, p. 96, with an abridgement of *Confs.* 1:11:17.

[61] Cf. Pizzolato in Sant' Agostino, *Confessioni*, I, p. 151: 'Agostino rimprovera una scarsa *diligentia*...ai suoi familiari...; ma la figura di Monica ha anche un carattere positivo...' He notes the ambivalence of the *Confessions* on the unconsummated baptism, because the reason for the cancellation was 'interne all fede'.

[62] As Gillian Clark, *Augustine Confessions Books I–IV* (Cambridge, 1996), pp. 101-102. Although Augustine says that Monnica won him over (*lucrata est*) *in extrema vita temporali eius*, he had enough of an active life left—perhaps a year or so—for Augustine to add *nec in eo iam fideli planxit, quod in nondum fideli toleraverat* (*Confs.* 9:9:22). This statement removes any uncertainty about Patricius' baptism (cf. Mandouze, *Prosopographie*, p. 834, *s.n.* 'Patricius 2'). F. van der Meer, *Augustine the Bishop* (London, 1961), p. 149, makes Patricius a catechumen 'for many years' before he was baptized, but the references he gives (p. 613, n. 94, to *Confs.* 2:3:6 and 3:4:7) do not support this reading.

this pattern was imminence of early death. Of the notion that newborn babies should be baptized there is no glimpse at all.

CHAPTER 8

Donatist Theologoumena in Augustine? Baptism, Reviviscence of Sins, and Unworthy Ministers

The chief question with which this paper is concerned is this: What did Augustine believe happened when a person was baptized in the Donatist schism?

To this question some answers are incontrovertibly clear. For example, such a person was truly baptized. He or she received 'the sacrament of grace', a genuine baptism which was, and remained, *sanctus*.[1] In the vocabulary of later theology, the baptism imparted was valid, and indestructibly so.

Other answers to our question are not so self-evident and still provoke discussion. For instance, in what sense did the candidate for baptism in schism receive a baptismal 'character'?[2] Was this anything other than the unrepeatable external rite itself, or the rite's ineffacable designation of the baptized as *fidelis*[3] or *filius*,[4] or was it a *consecratio*[5] or *sanctificatio*[6] which might even encompass a 'spiritual effect' of baptism, 'la présence permanente de la vertu divine à tous baptisé juste ou pécheur'?[7]

---

[1] Augustine, *De baptismo* 3:10:15, etc.

[2] Cf. G. Bavaud, 'Le problème de la réviviscence des péchés', in *BA* 29, pp. 579-82.

[3] Augustine, *De baptismo* 1:8:10: *Illi quos baptizant sanant a vulnere idololatriae vel infidelitatis.*

[4] Augustine, *De baptismo* 1:10:14. G.G. Willis, *Saint Augustine and the Donatist Controversy* (London, 1950), p. 159, is not strictly accurate when he claims that 'Schismatic baptism constitutes a man a member of Christ's Church.'

[5] Augustine, *Epistle* 98:5: *Christiani baptismi sacramentum...etiam apud haereticos valet et sufficit ad consecrationem.*

[6] Augustine, *De baptismo* 4:23:30: *Satis indicat quod et in malis...ipsa* [*sanctificatio sacramenti*] *integra est.*

[7] Bavaud, 'Le problème', in *BA* 29, p. 581, who speaks of 'cette *consécration* qui est toujours le fruit du baptême, même chez les indignes. Le chrétien est enveloppé de la vertu du Seigneur prêt à donner la grâce du salut au moment où l'*obex* sera enlevé'. For Augustine, baptismal 'character' is 'une realité *visible*, le sacrement en tant qu'il produit un effet spirituel qui n'est pas la grâce du salut, mais la présence permanente...' Bavaud appeals in particular to *sacramento suo divina virtus adstitit* (*De baptismo* 3:10:15), but fails to give due weight to the immediately following words *sive ad salutem bene utentium sive ad perniciem male utentium*. The 'character' of baptism would then be twofold, either

Another answer to our initial question which might appear to allow of no qualification is that the schismatic who received the *sacramentum gratiae* did not receive the *gratia sacramenti*.[8] This grace, which brings salvation, is not bestowed outside the fold of the Catholic Church. The terms of Augustine's argument are only too familiar.

There is, however, one issue which threatens to blur Augustine's clarity on even this cardinal point of his teaching. He shows an interest in the hypothesis that the grace of baptism may in truth be imparted to the schismatic, but only momentarily because he is a schismatic and lacks love, his sins, which have been for that instant remitted, return to him forthwith. This is the question normally discussed under the heading of the reviviscence of sins.[9] Some interpreters of Augustine have held not only that Augustine taught this account of what happened in Donatist baptism but that it was a significant factor in enabling him to maintain at one and the same time both the full reality of the baptism given in schism and its total inefficacy for salvation.[10] But in a communication at the Oxford Patristic Conference of 1959, F. Floëri argued that Augustine presented this momentary reception of the remission of sins only as a hypothesis, on the truth of which he always avoided pronouncing.[11] Since the publication of this study, scholars have been more guarded in attributing the theory to Augustine, but G. Bavaud comes very close to regarding it as his decided opinion in his edition of the *De baptismo*.[12] He views it as reconciling, in Augustine's mind, the emphatically positive evaluation he felt led to make of the baptism of the Donatists, who had all,

---

salvific or damnatory, in accordance with Augustine's frequent citation of 2 Cor. 2.15-16 (e.g., *De baptismo* 3:13:18).

[8] Augustine, *De baptismo* 4:14:21, 5:21:29, 7:19:37. Willis, *Donatist Controversy*, pp. 154, 156, 159, is inaccurate in speaking of the grace of baptism as being 'there [in the schismatic], as it were latent and useless... It is impossible to confine the grace of the sacraments within the Church.' This is precisely what Augustine did—except in the theory of reviviscence considered in this paper. Without showing any knowledge of this theory in Augustine, Willis ascribes to him the 'reviviscence' of grace (pp. 156, 159). Nor is it a matter of degrees of grace (cf. Willis, *Donatist Controversy*, p. 156: only in the church is grace received 'in full').

[9] Cf. A. Michel, 'Reviviscence des péchés', in *Dictionnaire de Théologie Catholique* (15 vols; Paris, 1903–50), XIII, cols. 2644-52.

[10] So P. Pourrat and P. Batiffol, discussed by F. Floëri, 'L'Argument de la «Réviviscence des Péchés» dans le *De Baptismo* de saint Augustin', *Studia Patristica* 6 (1962), pp. 384-85.

[11] Floëri, 'L'Argument', pp. 383-89.

[12] G. Bavaud, 'Le problème de la réviviscence des péchés', in *BA* 29, pp. 585-86; cf. p. 582. For Rémi Crespin, however, following Floëri, the theory is no more than an explanatory hypothesis, *Ministère et sainteté. Pastorale du clergé et solution de la crise donatiste dans la vie et la doctrine de saint Augustin* (Paris, 1965), p. 259 n. 3.

for example, 'put on Christ' by their baptism,[13] with his equally emphatic conviction that it produced no effect in the soul of the baptized schismatic—unless, that is, such a person did in truth receive 'une consécration intérieure, celle de la justification, mais…une grâce transitoire'.

The status of this theory in Augustine's writings may not appear a question of great importance. It appears (to my knowledge) only in the *De baptismo*, although in more than twice the three passages identified by Floëri.[14] The question may also be insoluble, for Floëri is undoubtedly correct in arguing that Augustine invariably presents the theory as one of two competing hypotheses (the other being simply that those baptized in schism are not cleansed of their sins at all, but even defiled by receiving baptism in schism), and never adjudicates between them.

The problem is, however, not without implications for major elements in Augustine's anti-Donatist case. It should not be thought, for example, that what is at issue is simply the remission of sins. Two of Augustine's discussions in *De baptismo* show clearly that the gift of the Spirit is also involved,[15] and we must conclude that Augustine is really talking about the fleeting enjoyment of the whole effect of baptism. This immediately touches on the fundamental axiom *extra ecclesiam nulla salus*. Furthermore, if the reviviscence of sins is part of Augustine's teaching, it implies that the sole *obex* to the baptized schismatic's continuing enjoyment of salvation lies in himself, and that the minister of schismatic baptism may be a minister not only of the sacrament of grace but also of the grace of the sacrament, however short-lived that grace may be in the baptized. Such a conclusion would not be inconsistent with Augustine's repeated insistence, in opposition to the Donatists' obsession with the minister of baptism, that the two key agents in baptism are God (or Christ) and the recipient, and that it is the latter's disposition, not the minister's, that determines whether he receives not only the sacrament of grace but also the grace of the sacrament. But while Augustine unambiguously holds that within the Catholic Church the minister's disposition is no insuperable obstacle to the candidate's receiving both the sacrament and its grace, it is not at all clear that the parallel with the minister in schism, which is otherwise so central to Augustine's refutation of the Donatist position, holds in this instance except with reference solely to the sacrament itself.

---

[13] Gal. 3.27. Cf. Augustine, *De baptismo* 1:11:16, etc., and see further below.

[14] Floëri discusses *De baptismo* 1:12:17–13:21, 3:13:18, 5:8:9, to which should be added 4:11:17, 5:21:29, 7:3:5, 7:6:11, and cf. 4:4:5. When Augustine says that baptism does not avail for 'the irrevocable remission of sins' outside Catholic unity, it is unlikely that he implies a distinction between revocable and irrevocable remission (*De baptismo* 3:17:22; cf. 5:8:9, 'remission of irrevocable sins').

[15] Augustine, *De baptismo* 1:12:18-19, 5:21:29.

In order to determine whether the notion of the reviviscence of sins is any more than a hypothesis for Augustine, we must consider it in the broader context of his anti-Donatist theology. The texts in which the theory appears do not provide us with a clear answer.

Augustine certainly believed that the return of sins once forgiven was taught by Christ in the parable of the unmerciful servant (Mt. 18.23-35). 'The fact that he had not forgiven his fellow-servant did not prevent his master from forgiving him all his debts... But what did it profit him, since they all immediately returned (*replicata sunt*) again upon his head because of his persisting hatred?' Augustine deduces therefrom that the grace of baptism is not prevented from giving (momentary) remission of all sins, even to a person of unremitting hatred.[16] He discusses this parable only once in his anti-Donatist treatises, but in three of his sermons draws from it the same warning to the unforgiving, lest God bring back (*replicare*) sins earlier forgiven.[17]

Such cases often occur in the church, comments Augustine.[18] In *De baptismo* he presents two kinds of persons in whom such a return of sins might be hypothesized. The catechumen baptized in some sudden danger of death may show on recovery an unmitigated hostility towards an enemy. A murderer may have secured baptism without any accompanying change of heart. Both of them either experience no baptismal remission of sins, or, if their sins are remitted in baptism, they return to them forthwith.[19] But it is noteworthy that, even here, the fleetingly transient baptismal remission appears as no more than one of two possible explanations, between which Augustine invites his readers to choose. He seems unwilling to affirm it for himself, even in the context of the Catholic Church where predicating such a baptismal forgiveness posed none of the *prima facie* difficulties for his theology that it did in the context of schism.

What of the baptized Catholic who subsequently strays into schism? Does his abandonment of the bonds of peace and love recall upon his head the sins forgiven at his baptism, perhaps years ago? Augustine repeatedly affirms that such a person, while not losing his baptism by seceding, henceforth possesses it unlawfully and unprofitably and is

---

[16] Augustine, *De baptismo* 1:12:20. Cf. Bauvaud's note, 'Le problème', in *BA* 29, pp. 586-87.

[17] Augustine, *Sermon* 5:2 (*non solum deinceps non illis dimittatur sed etiam omnia quae dimissa fuerant replicentur*); *Sermon* 83:7 (*si non dimiseris, revocabo te; et quidquid tibi dimiseram, replicabo tibi*); *Sermon Frangipani* (= *Sermon* 114A) 9:2 (*totum quod relaxaverat in caput eius replicavit*).

[18] Augustine, *De baptismo* 1:12:20 (*et saepe ista contingunt in ecclesia*).

[19] Augustine, *De baptismo* 1:13:21, 5:21:29. Cf. too 7:3:5, where Augustine poses the two possibilities generally of those *fallaciter conversi* who have been baptized.

bereft of the Holy Spirit.[20] But he never suggests that the seceder from the Catholic Church has his sins, remitted earlier in baptism, reimposed in schism. Yet in every other respect he is no different from the schismatic baptized in schism.

A critical question is whether Augustine believed that a schismatic could in any circumstances be the minister of the remission of sins in baptism. He undoubtedly could in one kind of case, that of the Catholic catechumen facing imminent death and able to obtain a prompt baptism only from a Donatist minister. Provided that he receive it with a Catholic mind and heart not alienated from the unity of peace and unimplicated in the schismatic's perversity, he is baptized *salubriter*.[21] This has happened to many Catholics (*plerisque*), comments Augustine. He apparently feels no need to explain the exceptional function of the schismatic minister, other than by emphasizing the correct disposition of the recipient.

Ascertaining Augustine's mind about the normal run of schismatic ministrations of baptism is more difficult, partly because of the parallel he frequently sets up between the unworthy minister within the Catholic Church and the schismatic minister without. Both impart a valid sacrament, but not an efficacious one. Augustine's standard position seems to be that neither unworthy Catholic nor schismatic can fulfil with regard to the grace of the sacrament the ministerial role he fulfils for the sacrament itself, but that in the Catholic Church alone this obstacle is circumvented. The prayers of the spiritual and holy in the church, like the cooing of the dove, by 'a secret dispensation of the mercy of God' avail to secure the remission of sins for those baptized not by the dove but by the hawks, but such a resource is not to be found outside the bounds of Catholic unity.[22]

There is a crucial distinction here which it is easy to miss.[23] Augustine declares that 'God gives the sacrament of grace even *per malos*, but grace itself he bestows only *per se ipsum vel per sanctos suos*'. He proceeds to record his agreement with Cyprian that schismatics cannot give the

---

[20] Augustine, *De baptismo* 6:15:25, 5:23:33.

[21] Augustine, *De baptismo* 6:5:7; cf. 1:2:3, 7:52:100. The same situation may also be implied in 4:12:18.

[22] Augustine, *De baptismo* 3:17:22–18:23; cf. Crespin, *Ministère et sainteté*, pp. 259, 281.

[23] Crespin's account, *Ministère et sainteté*, pp. 237-39, could easily mislead ('le péché des ministres ne compromet pas la sanctification des fidèles... La sainteté—ou l'iniquité—du ministre n'entre donc pas en ligne de compte, quando il s'agit de l'efficacité des sacrements...'). As he later makes plain, the powers that belong alike to the sinful Catholic minister and the schismatic minister belong to 'l'ordre sacramentel et non l'ordre de la grâce' (p. 281).

remission of sins, nor, he adds, can the wicked within the church.[24] This declaration in *De baptismo* appears to conflict with another in *Contra epistulam Parmeniani*:[25] if the minister is a hypocrite, the Spirit flees from his duplicity and denies him salvation, but does not abandon his (the hypocrite's) ministry, whereby he (the Spirit) effects the salvation of others through him.[26] More obviously consistent with the former is a statement in one of the letters: 'If the minister is good, he cleaves to God and works together with God; but if he is evil, God works through him (*per illum*) the visible form of the sacrament, but himself bestows the invisible grace.'[27]

It is clear that, for all Augustine's minimizing of the role of the minister,[28] he assigned a more substantial function to the good minister than to the wicked or hypocritical.[29] If it is true that, 'when the name of Christ is invoked, the sins of one do not obstruct the salvation of another',[30] it is also true that they require God to bypass, as it were, the ministry of the sinful and to grant salvation *per se ipsum*.[31] If this was the case with the corrupt minister within the Catholic Church, was it also the case with the minister of baptism in schism, seeing that Augustine's argument so frequently paralleled the two? The hypothesis of the momentary remission of sins followed by their immediate reviviscence requires something of the sort to be true. It is worth enquiring to what or to whom Augustine ascribes this hypothetical fleeting remission.

In so far as Augustine provides an answer to this question, he speaks in the following terms in the relevant passages in *De baptismo*:

---

[24] Augustine, *De baptismo* 5:21:29–22:30. Jn 20:23 was not addressed to the wicked, who cannot remit sins even though they baptize (6:14:23; cf. 6:16:27).

[25] Crespin, *Ministère et sainteté*, p. 241 n. 1, juxtaposes the two quotations without comment.

[26] Augustine, *Contra epistulam Parmeniani* 2:11:24: *ministerium tamen eius non deserat, quo per eum salutem operatur aliorum.*

[27] Augustine, *Epistle* 105:3:12.

[28] Cf. Crespin, *Ministère et sainteté*, pp. 246-47.

[29] 'When a person preaches God's word or administers God's sacrament, he does not, if he is evil, preach or administer *de suo*' (Augustine, *Contra litteras Petiliani* 2:6:13). The pure preacher is a partner with the word and has his share in begetting (*congenerat*) the believer, but when the unregenerate preaches, faith is born 'not from the barrenness of the minister but from the fruitfulness of the word' (2:5:11; cf. 3:55:67).

[30] Augustine, *Contra litteras Petiliani* 2:54:124.

[31] Yet at the same time there cannot be said to be no association between the wicked's baptizing and God's gift of grace. 'Since "no-one can give what he does not have", how does the murderer give the Holy Spirit? Yet he baptizes even within the Church. Therefore God gives the Holy Spirit even when the murderer baptizes (*etiam ipso baptizante*)' (Augustine, *De baptismo* 5:20:28). Cf. *per eum* in *Contra epistulam Parmeniani* 2:11:24 (n. 26 above).

— once only of the Holy Spirit coming to the baptized;[32]
— three times of the *baptismi sanctitas* clothing the candidate with Christ or remitting his sins;[33]
— once of the 'grace of baptism' not being prevented from forgiving the impenitent;[34]
—twice of the *vis sacramenti* (*sancta vis tanti sacramenti*) remitting sins.[35] On one of these occasions, Augustine parallels the working of this *vis* outside the church with the *vis nominis Christi* casting out demons outside the church.

These phrases of Augustine's take us no farther forward in our attempt to determine whether or not he believed in the return of sins after a moment's remission. We shall reserve further comment until later, except to note that in all these passages Augustine makes no mention of the minister of baptism in schism. The focus is heavily on the recipient of baptism, and, by implication, on the operation of God's grace *per se ipsum*. It is, therefore, no bar to believing that Augustine affirmed this hypothesis *ex animo* that he undoubtedly endorsed Cyprian's dictum, adopted by the Donatists, that no-one can give what he does not have.[36] The Donatist minister's lack of salvation would not prevent its being momentarily imparted by God *per se ipsum* when the Donatist baptized. Indeed, for the theory to be part of Augustine's own teaching, this is what it must be held to entail.

Since on any understanding this transient remission of sins in Donatist baptism is not only here-and-gone in a flash but also a very minor motif in his case against the schismatics, we must not allow the unambiguous and unqualified apparent contradictions of it with which these writings abound to exclude the possibility of his actually believing in it. For example, schismatics, like corrupt Catholics, 'both have and confer baptism without remission of sins'.[37] It is pointless to multiply quotations. Not only is the fruit of baptism—grace, remission of sins, the gift of the

---

[32] Augustine, *De baptismo* 1:12:19.
[33] Augustine, *De baptismo* 1:12:19, 3:13:18.
[34] Augustine, *De baptismo* 1:12:20.
[35] Augustine, *De baptismo* 1:12:19, 4:11:17. With the latter's reference to exorcism outside the church, cf. 5:24:34.
[36] Cf. Augustine, *De baptismo* 5:20:28 (n. 31 above) and for its application in a positive form to baptism itself, 7:29:57. Cf. Cyprian, *Epistle* 70:3, 69:11. Willis, *Donatist Controversy*, p. 160, says Augustine countered Cyprian's catchword with *Deum esse datorem*. But Augustine's acceptance of Cyprian's dictum is reflected in his repeated demonstration that the Donatists do have baptism, which originally they took with them from the church and did not lose by seceding, and therefore can give it. Cf. *De baptismo* 1:1:2, 4:9:13, 4:23:33, 6:29:56, 7:36:71, etc.
[37] Augustine, *De baptismo* 7:44:87.

Spirit, eternal salvation—not to be had in schism, but even what may be had—the church's baptism—is received *perniciose, poenaliter, ad judicium, in mortem*. It would be risky to hold that this solid dogmatic core of Augustine's anti-Donatist theology precludes his genuinely believing in a fleeting remission of sins followed by their return, for this supposition makes a negligible difference to the plight of the baptized schismatic. His interest is undoubtedly in the burden of unforgiven sin carried by the baptized who remains in schism, and hence, as far as this hypothesis is concerned, in the return of sins rather than their very temporary remission. Statements which appear to rule out the possibility of this momentary enjoyment of salvation can easily be viewed as omitting it, by a foreshortened perspective or because of its transience and insignificance, rather than deliberately rejecting it.

This bring us to consider why Augustine should have entertained, even hypothetically, a notion apparently at odds with his basic convictions about Donatist baptism. First and foremost, the theory should be viewed as a minimal concession on Augustine's part, offered only as a hypothesis, enabling him to escape the horns of an awkward dilemma posed by the Donatists. At the same time, the fact that he advances it even as a hypothesis suggests some recognition of a vulnerable spot in his position. I submit that in the territory covered by this paper Augustine appears uncharacteristically insecure and indecisive.

The Donatists objected to his insistence that they had baptism but without the remission of sins. To be consistent he should grant them either both or neither, for baptism could not be Christ's without forgiveness through the Spirit.[38] In the North African church, unlike the Eastern churches, no credal connection between baptism and the remission of sins had yet been forged,[39] but the Pelagian controversy discloses the inseparability of the two in the African tradition. The hypothesis of momentary remission concedes this correlation to the Donatists, but with the most minimal *prima facie* damage to Augustine's position, for the sins are immediately reimposed. As he says in his first discussion of the theory, 'Are this person's sins forgiven or not? Let them [the Donatists] choose as they will. For if they are forgiven, they immediately return. The gospel says so, the truth declares it.'[40] In fact, the very first appearance of the theory takes the form of a conclusion hypothetically adopted *by the Donatists* in the light of their verdict on the experience of Simon Magus: 'But if they should say (*Si autem*

---

[38] Augustine, *De baptismo* 1:11:15-17. Cf. 5:23:33, for the same objection, taken from Cyprian, and 6:12:19.

[39] Cf. Augustine, *De baptismo* 1:18:27: 'on the subject of baptism we should believe what the universal Church maintains'.

[40] Augustine, *De baptismo* 1:13:21.

dixerint)...'[41] Augustine develops the idea, and does not rule out the reception, for one short moment, of the forgiveness of sins in Donatist baptism. He even furnishes dominical warrant for believing in it—but also, and much more importantly, in the return of sins upon the baptized head.[42]

But Augustine's readiness to countenance this explanation, albeit only as an hypothesis, is surely symptomatic not so much of his generosity in debate as of, let us say, a sneaking feeling of unease. It should scarcely surprise us if his doctrine of schismatic baptism from time to time failed to carry his full conviction. It was, so he taught, true baptism, complete (*integer*), holy, God's baptism, Christ's baptism, the church's baptism, a baptism that 'consecrated' and 'sanctified', that gave birth to sons and daughters, even a baptism that clothed you with Christ—but still a baptism that brought no benefit, but only death and condemnation, to its recipients.

Galatians 3.27 was a text that Augustine largely avoided in his anti-Donatist treatises: 'All who have been baptized in Christ have put on Christ.' It had to accommodate the distinctions of his baptismal theology, and so evoked the interpretation, 'Men put on Christ sometimes as far as receiving the sacrament, sometimes so much further as to sanctify their lives.'[43] When making this comment in *De baptismo* Augustine refers to his earlier discussion, 'at sufficient length', of this text. It occurs in the midst of his first presentation of the reviviscence hypothesis, first of all as an ingredient in the dilemma about the relation between baptism and remission of sins (for 'putting on Christ' appears to imply renewal of life and deliverance from sin),[44] and then as a text whose difficulty is resolved by the hypothesis in question, for the *sanctitas baptismi* clothes the baptized with Christ for an instant and the sinfulness of deceit or schism straightway strips him of Christ.[45] This, it seems, is Augustine's sufficient word on a Pauline verse that clearly embarrassed his doctrine of Donatist baptism.

The *sanctitas baptismi* which here momentarily clothes the baptized schismatic with Christ is used elsewhere by Augustine not of the efficacy

---

[41] Augustine, *De baptismo* 1:12:19.

[42] Note the emphasis at the end of Augustine's discussion of the parable of the unmerciful servant: 'Yesterday is forgiven, and all that preceded it is forgiven, even the very hour and moment before baptism and in baptism itself. But then the person immediately begins to be answerable not only for the days, hours and moments which ensue, but also for those that are past, as everything which has been forgiven returns to him' (Augustine, *De baptismo* 1:12:20).

[43] Augustine, *De baptismo* 5:24:34.

[44] Augustine, *De baptismo* 1:11:16.

[45] Augustine, *De baptismo* 1:12:19. For Donatist appeal to the verse, cf. *Contra litteras Petiliani* 2:44:103.

of baptism but of its bare validity.[46] But as we noticed above, Augustine also ascribes the short-lived benefits enjoyed under this theory to the Holy Spirit or to the grace of baptism, both of which in his standard teaching belong solely to the fruit of baptism denied to schismatics. We should probably discern, in the hearing that he gives to our hypothesis, a glimpse of recognition on his part that, if the Donatists have baptism, it may not be entirely without effect—such is the *sancta vis tanti sacramenti*.[47] The phrase *vis sacramenti*, which he twice uses in spelling out this hypothetical momentary remission of sins, does not belong to his technical vocabulary on Donatist baptism. It reflects, I suggest, his sympathy for the view of Cyprian and the Donatists that baptism cannot be convincingly separated from its fruit, as his refutation normally maintained. That Augustine never *ex professo* endorsed this hypothesis, indicates no doubt his awareness of its incompatibility with the main burden of that refutation. That nevertheless he gave it house room in *De baptismo*, instead of unambiguously rejecting it, points to a degree of affinity with Donatist convictions that the reader of his anti-Donatist works rarely suspects.

A similar sympathy with the position of the Donatists is evident when Augustine denies that God gives the grace of the sacrament *per malos*. As we have seen, for Augustine the unworthiness of the minister is a barrier to the efficacy of baptism,[48] but one that God circumvents *per se ipsum* within the Catholic Church. Augustine has not so much abandoned the traditional African standpoint as redefined its field of application. The unworthy minister is no longer debarred from giving the sacrament itself, but he is unable to fulfil the proper ministerial role in imparting the spiritual blessings of the sacrament. Had he been entirely consistent, this element in Augustine's thought should have prevented him entertaining the hypothesis in question, at least as far as Donatist baptism is concerned, for in schism God does not work *per se ipsum* to compensate for the inadequacy of the minister. *De baptismo* shows us at times an Augustine who is more comfortable when he can take his stand on the recipients, rather than the ministers, of Donatist baptism. One revealing chapter deserves to be quoted at length:

> As I seem to be hard pressed (*urgeri*) when the question is put to me, 'Does therefore a heretic remit sins [since Christ's baptism is found among heretics]?, so I in turn

---

[46] Augustine, *Contra epistulam Parmeniani* 2:15:34 (translated by G. Finaert in *BA* 28, p. 363, 'la chose sainte qu'est le baptême'), *De baptismo* 3:14:19.

[47] This blurring of the distinction between the sacrament itself and its effects, normally so sharp in Augustine's anti-Donatist teaching, is relevant to the meaning of 'character' in his thought. See n. 7 above.

[48] Again *contra* Willis, *Donatist Controversy*, pp. 154-55.

press hard when I say, 'Does therefore the person who fails to keep the commands of heaven... [in the Catholic Church], remit sins?' If *per vim sacramenti Dei*, the former does so no less than the latter; if *per meritum suum*, neither the one nor the other does. For this sacrament is recognized as Christ's even in wicked men, but in the body of the one dove...neither one nor the other is found. Just as baptism does not profit the person who renounces the world in word and not in deed, so it does not profit the person baptized in heresy or schism.[49]

The question about the heretical minister of baptism is left unanswered. Firm ground is reached when the focus shifts from the minister to the recipient. The unworthy Catholic and the schismatic are in precisely the same position as subjects of baptism. Apart from the slight doubt imported by the hypothetical reviviscence of sins (which applies equally to both), they cannot receive any benefit from baptism. No such clarity or parity attaches to them as givers of baptism. Hence we observe Augustine more than once elsewhere in *De baptismo* resolving or evading a tricky question about ministers by adopting an unambiguous stance about the recipients of baptism.[50] This manner of argument is consistent with his insistence that the cleansing of baptism depends not on its minister but on *dantis Dei gratia et percipientis bona conscientia*.[51] The unrighteous who confers baptism, may do so *perniciose*, not because of his own character or the character of baptism but because of the character of the recipient. Yet when he confers it on a good person, his *malitia* has to be, and is indeed, overcome (*superatur*).[52] It is not theologically irrelevant. To the extent that the unworthiness of the minister proved troublesome to Augustine in connexion with the efficacy of baptism, we may recognise, as in some other respects, his sympathy with Donatist positions.

---

[49] Augustine, *De baptismo* 4:4:5. This is precisely the kind of controversy in which elsewhere in *De baptismo* Augustine imports the hypothesis of reviviscence.

[50] E.g., Augustine, *De baptismo* 5:21:29, 6:23:41, 6:32:62.

[51] Augustine, *Ad Cresconium grammaticum partis Donati* 4:18:21, and A.C. de Veer's note in *BA* 31, pp. 783-86.

[52] Augustine, *De baptismo* 6:4:6. The translation in *BA* 29, p. 413, wrongly implies that he who has baptism *perniciose*, always confers it *perniciose*.

CHAPTER 9

Infant Dedication in the Early Church

All historians of the development of early Christian baptism are agreed that for a period of several decades in the fourth century the children of most Christian parents were not baptised in infancy. They may not be of one mind in their accounts of baptismal practice before this period or of how long it lasted, nor indeed of how to explain it and hence how to speak about it. For Joachim Jeremias it was a 'crisis' that consisted in the postponement of their children's baptism by Christian parents[1]—but this is no neutral description of what happened. Anyone writing on this subject at the end of the second Christian millennium inherits the weight of decades of earlier debate, whose formulations almost inescapably condition the terms in which he or she has to discuss it, and which to that extent predetermine the discussion.

That the language of postponement has skewed or limited enquiry is evident from the simple fact that no one to my knowledge has addressed the question what if anything was done during at least half a century to the offspring of Christian parents who were not given baptism. It seems a fairly obvious question to raise, but I have found no more than the occasional footnote or paragraph. (The domination of enquiry by a simple 'yes/no' interest in baby baptism may explain why no investigation has been made of the non-baptismal influence of, and non-baptismal counterparts to, Jesus' blessing of babies, on which R.E.O. White passes some eminently wise comments in *The Biblical Doctrine of Initiation*.) The failure to tackle it may not have been entirely accidental, for it has fostered the impression that for two generations and more these children received no ecclesial recognition. They were left in a vacuum caused by the deplorable postponement of the baptism that was properly their due. They suffered from baptismal deprivation. Had they lived in a much later century, lawyers might have queued up to batten on any inclination they showed to sue their parents for neglect.

The surprising thing is that the very opposite seems to have been the case. Almost everyone born in these baptism-deprived generations who has left us his or her story seems to have turned out remarkably well. From their ranks came that distinguished bevy of theologians, bishops,

---

[1] J. Jeremias, *Infant Baptism in the First Four Centuries* (London, 1960), pp. 87-91.

church statesmen, monastic leaders, biblical scholars and preachers who constituted 'the golden age of the church Fathers' as early church historians once had no qualms in calling it.[2] Nor did they find fault with their godly parents for not having had them baptised at birth, nor even evince the awareness that their parents had not done something that they might have done—no awareness, that is, that there had been a baby-baptism available to them at their parents' discretion.

The biographical and autobiographical evidence gives the lie to any implication that the non-baptising of such children (how hard it is to avoid expressions that buy into a prejudiced reading of the situation!) betokened parental dereliction of duty or indifference. Many of these parents gave their children an admirable Christian upbringing, not too different in essence from John Chrysostom's counsel on the Christian nurture of children—which never mentions baptism.[3] This would make it all the more remarkable if their parents had not acknowledged the gift of a child from the hand of God by a religious ceremony of some kind.

The example most likely to spring to readers' minds is that of Augustine, who wrote of himself as follows in the *Confessions*:

> I had heard while still a boy of the eternal life promised to us through the self-humbling of the Lord our God who stooped to confront our pride, and right from my mother's womb, for her confidence in you was strong, I began to be signed with the sign of his cross and seasoned with his salt (1:11:17).[4]

The imperfect tenses of the last two verbs (*signabar, condiebar*) clearly imply that this was no one-off ritual but regularly repeated. Nevertheless the first such occasion would have constituted a kind of dedication of the baby Augustine to Christ and his church. This is indeed how he will talk about its significance in other contexts. It was in 'the one-and-only church, the body of God's one-and-only Son', that 'the name of Christ was bestowed on me as an infant' (*Confs.* 6:4:5). If here the Latin for 'bestowed' (*inditum*) might also possibly mean 'instilled, imparted' with reference to the effect of childhood instruction, an allusion to his initial registration as a catechumen is more probable.[5] Later at Milan, unsettled and yet not unhopeful, Augustine resolved to re-activate his status as a

---

[2] Jean Daniélou and Henri Marrou, *The First Six Hundred Years* (The Christian Centuries, 1; London, 1964), ch. 23, 'The Golden Age of the Church Fathers'.

[3] *On Vainglory and the Right Way for Parents to Bring up their Children*, in M.L.W. Laistner (trans.), *Christianity and Pagan Culture in the Later Roman Empire* (Ithaca, NY, 1951).

[4] See F. van der Meer, *Augustine the Bishop* (London and New York, 1961), pp. 354-56; J.J. O'Donnell, *Augustine: Confessions* (3 vols; Oxford, 1992), II, pp. 67-68; Emilien Lamirande, 'Catechumenus', in *AugLex*, I, cols. 788-94 at 791, but he gives little attention to the distinctiveness of enrolment from birth.

[5] So O'Donnell, *Confessions*, II, p. 349.

catechumen, to 'fix my feet on that step (*gradu*) on which I had been placed by my parents' (*Confs.* 6:11:18). 'I therefore decided meantime to be a catechumen in the catholic church which my parents had committed to me until some certainty should light up the path I should follow' (*Confs.* 5:14:25). The reference to 'the church *commendata* to me by my parents' is slightly puzzling. One might have expected 'to which I had been *commendatus* by my parents', parallel to his comment on his time at Milan in *The Advantage of Believing*: 'I had decided meanwhile to be a catechumen in the church, to which I had been entrusted (*traditus*) by my parents' (8:20). But however we translate *commendata*—commended, urged, assigned, designated?—the point is clear. Even if the very young Augustine received repeated cross-signing and salt-seasoning, the commencement of his catechumenate was equivalent to his infant dedication to the church, and implicitly also to a pledge of intent by his parents (puzzlingly Patricius himself, not yet a catechumen at Augustine's birth, is included in every mention by his son of his own initiation as a catechumen) to his Christian upbringing.[6]

Yet if the *Confessions* furnish a credible account, mother Monnica had no thoughts of having her son baptised early on, and she even avoided going through with the baptismal ceremony that had been hurriedly prepared for him when he fell seriously ill as a six- or seven-year-old (*puer*)—for he suddenly recovered in time (*Confs.* 1:11:17-18). During most of the fourth century, if not longer, most children of Christian parents would have shared Augustine's experience, of infant dedication as catechumens with no parental intention of baptism while they remained under parental responsibility.[7] Identifiable individuals in this position do not surface very often in the documentation, other than by implication from their later situation, but then firm evidence of what happened to named children or the observed children of named parents is hard to come by in any terms. So if we can cite few instances of parallels to baby Augustine's dedication, we are no better placed in pinpointing the first

---

[6] Augustine's early biographer, Possidius, presents him as the child of Christian parents (*Life* 1), which has raised the possibility that Patricius was already a catechumen. This cannot be squared with Augustine's plain statement in *Confessions* 2:3:6, unless, like Augustine, Patricius had been a nominal catechumen all his life until in the last year or so of his life through his wife's persuasion he 'gave in his name' as a committed applicant (*competens*) for baptism next Easter. The conflicting evidence is amenable to resolution in the framework of the two-level catechumenate.

[7] See the discussion in van der Meer, *Augustine the Bishop*, pp. 347-57; 'Innumerable Christians remained catechumens all their lives' (p. 350), 'The catechumenate was the customary status of the nominal Christian' (p. 357), 'Even among the truly believing, parents who had themselves undergone baptism preferred not to have their children baptised' (p. 350).

known child of Christian parents who was baptised routinely, i.e. not clinically, as a newborn.

In one of his sermons Augustine told of a recent miraculous incident in the town of Uzalis, where the bishop was Evodius, a fellow-Thagastan converted and baptised in Italy shortly before Augustine. A young boy still at the breast died in his mother's arms. He was a catechumen and so 'irreparably lost'. She bore his body to the chapel Evodius had built to house relics of St Stephen, where her prayers restored him to life. 'She immediately took him to the presbyters, he was baptised, consecrated, anointed, hands were laid on him, when all the sacraments were completed he was taken up', but now with a transformed countenance his mother deposited him beside Stephen (*Sermon* 324).

At least two other prominent Christian writers of the late fourth and early fifth centuries are known to have been dedicated to Christ at birth without baptism. Jerome declares himself to be 'a Christian born of Christian parents and bearing the banner of the cross on my brow'. 'From the very cradle' he had been 'nourished on catholic milk', but he was baptised only as a young adult.[8] Gregory Nazianzen paid tribute to his mother Nonna for promising him to God even before his birth and presenting (ἀνέθηκε) him immediately after he was born.[9] Again we know for certain that Gregory's baptism took place much later. In a poem on his own life Gregory spoke of his birth as an answer to his mother's special prayers for a male child. A vision of both his likeness and his name was granted her in a dream.

> As soon as I made my appearance, straightway in the noblest of contracts, I became Another's. Like some lamb, some pleasing calf, but a victim of high quality endowed with reason I was offered to God (I hesitate to say it) like a young Samuel.[10]

---

[8] Jerome, *Preface to the Book of Job* (*PL* 28, col. 1082), *Epistle* 82:2 (*PL* 22, col. 757). See J.N.D. Kelly, *Jerome: His Life, Writings, and Controversies* (London, 1975), p. 7; Georg Grützmacher, *Hieronymus: Eine Biographische Studie zur Alten Kirchengeschichte* (Studien zur Geschichte der Theologie und der Kirche 6:3–7:2; 3 vols; Leipzig, 1901–08), I, pp. 129-31.

[9] Gregory Nazianzen, *Oration* 18:11 (*PG* 35, col. 997; L.P. McCauley *et al.* [trans.], *Funeral Orations* [Fathers of the Church, 22; Washington, DC, 1953], p. 127).

[10] *Carmina de seipso* XI: *De vita sua* 68-91 (*PG* 37, cols. 1034-36; D.M. Meehan [trans.], *Three Poems* [Fathers of the Church, 75; Washington, DC, 1987], p. 79). Gregory writes of the same dream and of himself its outcome in *Carmina de seipso* I: *De rebus suis* 425-49 (*PG* 37, cols. 1001-03; Meehan [trans.], *Three Poems*, p. 39)—but cf. other dreams in the two other texts listed by Meehan (trans.), *Three Poems*, p. 79 n. 9.

Gregory's *Epitaphia* three times at least echo this theme of his being offered as another Samuel at birth in fulfilment of his mother's vow when her prayers were answered.[11]

In his eulogy of Basil the Great, Gregory likens him too to Samuel who was given to God before birth and immediately sanctified. 'Was not Basil from infancy and from the very womb consecrated (καθιερωμένος) to God, and presented with a mantle at the altar?'[12]

In the *Life of Porphyry*, supposedly bishop of Gaza 395–420, attributed to his deacon Mark, commonly thought to owe its final form to a redactor in the middle of the fifth century, but probably a seventh-century compilation, the Roman Empress Eudoxia gave birth to a male child who was soon to be proclaimed Emperor Theodosius II.[13] Seven days later she brought her son to the bishops who 'sealed both her and the child with the seal of Christ' (44-45). Eudoxia then revealed her set purpose, now strengthened by bishop Porphyry's disclosure of a vision he had been given, to have the baby baptised. According to this account Theodosius II thus became early in 402, nine months after birth, the first Roman emperor baptised in infancy (46-47). But the text reads as if the routine observance was the sealing, i.e. the marking of the forehead with the sign of the cross, and the exceptional the baptism.

Earlier in the *Life*, a notable woman of Gaza named Aelias was safely delivered of her first child when the lives of both had been despaired of, through the intervention of their nurse who was a believer and bishop Porphyry. The whole extended family to the number of sixty-four presented themselves to the bishop 'seeking the seal in Christ. The blessed man having sealed them and made them catechumens dismissed them in peace'. After a little while he catechised them and baptised them all (28-31). The baby child was included in this unusually large family conversion and baptism.

---

[11] Gregory, *Epitaphia* 27, 79, 80, in W.R. Paton (ed. and trans.), *The Greek Anthology* (Loeb Classical Library; 5 vols; London and New York, 1916–18), II, pp. 412, 434.

[12] *Oration* 43:73 (*PG* 36, col. 596; McCauley *et al.* [trans.], *Funeral Orations*, pp. 91-92).

[13] The *Life of Porphyry* is edited by Henri Grégoire and M.-A. Kugener, *Vie de Porphyre* (Collection Byzantine; Paris, 1930), and translated by G.F. Hill, *Life of Porphyry* (Oxford, 1913). For a date no earlier than the seventh century, see T.D. Barnes, 'The Baptism of Theodosius II', *Studia Patristica* 19 (1989), pp. 8-12, citing a study by Paul Peeters in *Analecta Bollandiana* 59 (1941), pp. 65-216, and similar scepticism expressed by Ramsay MacMullen, *Christianizing the Roman Empire (A.D. 100–400)* (New Haven, CT, and London, 1984), pp. 86-89, and Alan Cameron, 'Earthquake 400', *Chiron* 17 (1987), pp. 344-60 at pp. 355-56 n. 60. On the date of the baptism, see Adolf Lippold, 'Theodosius II', in *Paulys Realencyclopädie der Classischen Altertumswissenschaft*, Supplementband XIII (1973), pp. 961-1044 at pp. 962-63.

John Chrysostom's homilies from time to time rebuked Christians who responded to anxieties about their infant children by resorting to pagan practices. Instead of choosing one of the saints' names, they light lamps and name the child after the one that burns longest as though promising longevity. They deck the child with amulets and bells and scarlet thread instead of girding him or her with the protection of the cross. The womenfolk mark the child's forehead with a special mud to turn away the evil eye, when it should be the cross that is inscribed on the forehead with its provision of invincible security. How can a mud-defiled child be brought to the presbyters? 'How do you presume to have the seal placed on the forehead by the presbyter's hand where you have smeared the mud?' Parents should from the start of life train children to seal their own foreheads, but 'before they are capable of this with their own hands, brand the cross upon them yourselves'.[14] What is remarkable here is the absence of reference to baptism. The common English translation interprets the first mention of the cross in this passage of the baptismal sign of the cross, but subsequent references show this to be untenable.[15]

The absence of mention of baptism in contexts where modern investigators expect it is a repeated feature of early Christian literature. Even in another homily of Chrysostom's, on Colossians, which similarly inveighs against Christians who take refuge in such idolatrous devices but does not refer to the initial sealing of the newborn, again the preacher is silent about baptism. Defence against a child's death is not baptism but the seal of the cross. Is baptism presupposed, and the fear only that parents who seek aid from idols nullify their children's baptism?[16] It remains remarkable that in the whole of John Chrysostom's extensive body of writings there are only three clear statements on infant baptism.[17]

Basil the Great's homily exhorting procrastinators to come to baptism chides them as follows: 'You have been a catechumen of the Word since infancy and have you not yet assented to the truth? You have always been learning and have you not yet arrived at knowledge?'[18] In one of his responses to Simplicianus of Milan, Augustine allows for the growth of faith through grace from the first beginnings of hearing the Word. They

---

[14] Chrysostom, *Homilies on 1 Corinthians* 12:7.

[15] *NPNF* 1 vol. 12, pp. 71-72 n. 3. It is an unsafe assumption that Chrysostom 'takes for granted...that infants would be brought to baptism'. Not even Jeremias cites this text, *Infant Baptism*, p. 16.

[16] Chrysostom, *Homilies on Colossians* 8:5.

[17] They are *Homilies on Genesis* 40:4 (*PG* 53, col. 373), *Homilies on Acts of the Apostles* 23:3 (*PG* 60, col. 182), *Baptismal Catechesis* 3:5-6 (A. Wenger [ed.], Jean Chrysostome, *Huit catéchèses baptismales inédits* [*SC* 50; Paris, 1957], pp. 153-54)—but not *Homilies on Philippians* 3-4 (*PG* 62, col. 203).

[18] Basil, *Homily* 13:1 (*PG* 31, col. 425). The first phrase is, more literally, 'catechised in the Word', τὸν λόγον κατηχούμενος.

may be compared to conception, which must lead on to the birth.[19] One of Augustine's recently discovered Mainz sermons makes the same distinction. Catechumens have not yet been born, but at least they are already conceived. 'But when or in what manner were they conceived in the womb (*visceribus*) of mother church if they were not marked by some sacrament of faith (*aliquo sacramento fidei signarentur*)?'[20]

Franz Dölger's series of studies on the sign of the cross in early Christianity deal separately with its use within the catechumenate, where he seems to have in view only catechumens old enough to respond in their own right to instruction, and what he calls 'The Sealing of Children with the Sign of the Cross as a Devotional Practice in the Home of the Christian Family'.[21] Citing several of the instances discussed above in which signing with the cross is mentioned, he is reluctant to discern anything more than a private action of a Christian mother (Monnica) or both mother and father (Jerome's), even when presbyters or bishops are undeniably involved, as in the *Life of Porphyry* and Chrysostom's twelfth homily on 1 Corinthians. Before us here is no liturgical ceremony, no ecclesiastical reception of the child into the Christian community.

The broader scope of the source material reviewed here, including references in which the sign of the cross is not recorded (and see further below), makes Dölger's sharp differentiation highly questionable. He has not taken into account the strongly ecclesial terms in which Augustine speaks of his dedication as an infant, he places excessive weight on the parallel practices of pagan piety rebuked by Chrysostom—and hence plays down the unparalleled bringing of the child to the presbyter for sealing with the cross—and he fails to consider the evidence that the throngs of cross-sealed catechumens whom fourth-century bishops insistently summoned to baptism included hordes who had thus been sealed from soon after birth. The newly-recovered sermon of Augustine from a manuscript in Mainz points to the imagery of conception for this enrolment of the newborn, which need in its own way be no less ecclesial than the subsequent birth of baptism. Even when Dölger reviews the use of the sign of the cross as a ritual of admission (Aufnahmeritus), with at least one instance including infants, he fails to make connexions with the

---

[19] Augustine, *De diversis quaestionibus ad Simplicianum* 1:2:2 (*PL* 40, cols. 111-12).

[20] Augustine, *Sermo Dolbeau* 14 (*Sermo* 352A): 3 (F. Dolbeau [ed.], 'Sermons inédits de saint Augustin prêchés en 397 [4ème série]', *Revue Bénédictine* 103 [1993], pp. 307-38 at pp. 313-14, reprinted in F. Dolbeau [ed.], *Augustin d' Hippone: Vingt-six sermons au peuple d' Afrique* [Collection des Etudes Augustiniennes, Série Antiquité 147; Paris, 1996], pp. 108-109).

[21] F.J. Dölger, 'Beiträge zur Geschichte des Kreuzzeichens IV', *Jahrbuch für Antike und Christentum* 4 (1961), pp. 5-17 at pp. 5-13 (in catechesis and admission), and 'Beiträge...VIII', *Jahrbuch für Antike und Christentum* 8/9 (1965–66), pp. 7-52 at pp. 42-45 ('...in der häuslichen Frömmigkeitsübung...').

so-called domestic observance on the one hand and registration in the catechumenate on the other. Thus for young children this Aufnahmeritus hovers in limbo.[22]

Although the texts which speak explicitly of admission to the catechumenate soon after birth are not numerous, the practice must have been extremely common.[23] Very many in the crowds of catechumens urged incessantly by bishops in their sermons to overcome their lethargy or reluctance and commit themselves to baptism must have first been registered as catechumens at birth. It is not our concern in this study to assess what the emergence of this lifelong and largely nominal catechumenate meant for the institution of the catechumenate as a whole. On the evidence surveyed here, it seems reasonable to regard such entry into the status of catechumen at birth as a form of infant dedication. It should never have been viewed as other than the initial step on the way to baptism, although our sources reveal little of what bishops and their clergy attempted in instruction of children and youth within the ministry of the congregation. Catechumens requiring urgent stimulus to move forward to baptism surfaced in hordes in the Sunday assemblies for worship, but whether Christian nurture was otherwise provided for younger catechumens, apart from within the family, remains at best highly elusive, and on a realistic judgement highly improbable.[24]

---

[22] Dölger, 'Beiträge...IV', pp. 9-10, citing the *Life of Porphyry* 31 (see above), and also Theodoret, *Church History* 4:18:11. If, as Dölger argues, 'the Lord's seal' here in Theodoret does not denote baptism, then no identifiable children are included in those who receive the sign of the cross, i.e. 'the Lord's seal'. Theodoret is best understood as speaking first about sick children whose healing Protogenes refused to pray for unless the parents first had them baptized, and then separately about healthy persons of responsible age whom he won to the Christian faith. (The translation in the *NPNF* 2 vol. 3, pp. 118-19, partly obscures the distinction.) The account is not yet problem-free: were the parents in view pagan or Christian? They cannot, it seems, have been baptized with their children.

[23] Cf. André Laurentin and Michel Dujarier, *Catéchuménat: Données de l'histoire et perspectives nouvelles* (Vivante Liturgie, 83; Paris, 1969), pp. 63-65, 69; M. Dujarier, *A History of the Catechumenate: The First Six Centuries* (New York, 1979), pp. 81-84, 92.

[24] The same question could be asked, probably with similar results, about those who had received baptism as infants. See briefly Werner Jentsch, *Urchristliches Erziehungsdenken: Die Paideia Kyriou im Rahmen der hellenistisch-jüdischen Umwelt* (Beiträge zur Förderung christlicher Theologie, 45:3; Gütersloh, 1951), pp. 215-16; Kurt Aland, *Die Stellung der Kinder in den frühen christlichen Gemeinden und ihre Taufe* (Theologische Existenz Heute, 138; Munich, 1967). Cf. Suzanne Poque, 'Un souci pastoral d'Augustin: la persévérance des chrétiens baptisés dans leur enfance', *Bulletin de littérature ecclésiastique* 88 (1987), pp. 273-86 at p. 274: 'on s'étonne de ne rien savoir sur les modalités de la formation chrétienne des enfants baptisés en bas age'. But J.A. Jungmann, *Handing on the Faith* (New York, 1959), p. 9, goes too far in asserting that 'There can be found no trace of an ecclesiastical catechesis for baptized children' (he does

In view of this strange lacuna in the church's educational programme, some reassessment of the common disparagement of the long-lasting catechumenate is overdue. Two things at least can be said in its favour. It did lead to considerable numbers of men and women remaining within the orbit of congregational life, attending the pre-eucharistic service of the Word and so placed as to be able to seek baptism when circumstances changed and called for it. These changing circumstances must have ranged from the desire to marry a baptised Christian, or to please a superior or a friend, political ambition under the Christian emperors, imminence of death, other exposure to critical peril (e.g. a risky sea voyage), panic in the face of public calamity (such as the Gothic sack of Rome in 410 when thousands queued up for baptism) right through to genuine conversion of heart and mind.

For in the second place, probably a majority of the distinguished array of later-fourth-century and early-fifth-century Fathers had been catechumens from birth but baptised in early adulthood. In his chapter on 'The Golden Age of the Church Fathers', Henri Marrou tabulated fourteen of them extending in time from Athanasius (b. c.295) to John Cassian (d. c.435).[25] Of these half or more (Basil of Caesarea, Gregory Nazianzen, Gregory of Nyssa, John Chrysostom, Augustine, Jerome, Ambrose, and Theodore of Mopsuestia, and quite possibly John Cassian) were products of the pattern of Christian pilgrimage sketched above, two were converts from paganism (Martin of Tours and Hilary of Poitiers) and of the baptism of the other three (Athanasius, Evagrius and Damasus) we know nothing. A not unimpressive roll-call, to be sure! And one can add others, such as Ephraem Syrus, Paulinus of Nola, Rufinus of Aquileia, quite possibly Ulfilas, similarly born to Christians but baptized as adult believers.

Augustine's testimony in the *Confessions* to the tenacity of the name of Christ which his tender heart had drunk in with his mother's milk is an eloquent reminder of the seriousness with which one Christian parent took her responsibility towards her catechumen son. Augustine repeatedly declares that no teaching lacking the name of Christ could henceforth win his allegiance. His conversion was but a return to the religion of infancy bound up in his bones.[26]

Statistics, of course, are denied us, and we have no means of knowing how many catechumens from birth were subsequently lost to the Christian faith and never received baptism. By citing this criterion as one measure of the fruitfulness of the system, I am not forgetting the mixture of

---

not consider unbaptized children). 'For the children of Christian families the parents were the catechists in the true sense of the word' (p. 11). The matter merits further investigation. Cf., e.g., Theodoret, *Church History* 4:18:8-9.

[25] Daniélou and Marrou, *The First Six Hundred Years*, p. 303.

[26] *Confs.* 3:4:8, 5:14:25, 6:4:5, 7:5:7.

motives with which baptism was sought. But the deficiencies of a scheme of Christian development which began with catechumenal enrolment from birth must not be judged myopically. Evaluating infant baptism as practised by most Protestant churches in Europe in the later twentieth century by the same touchstone—did it lead on to responsible and committed Christian discipleship?—would issue in a far more damning indictment.

Before moving on to consider a second form of infant dedication current in the later fourth century and beyond, we must face the question whether the infant catechumenate or something akin to it is discernible before the fourth century. It was a feature of the debate between Joachim Jeremias and Kurt Aland that a range of texts that might, or again might not, imply infant baptism were put under the microscope. Two such passages occur in the second-century *Apology* of Aristides, in his description of the practices of the Christian people:

> When a child is born to them they thank God; and if it die in infancy, they thank him exceedingly, because it departed this life sinless...

> And if it happens that one of [the pagans] is converted, he is ashamed before the Christians of the things that he has done, and thanks God, saying, 'In ignorance have I done them.' And he purifies his heart, and his sins are forgiven him.[27]

Jeremias believed that 'thank God' in these paragraphs was an indirect way of referring to baptism.[28] Aland convincingly undermined this interpretation. If the first 'thank God' points to infant baptism, what could 'thank God exceedingly' point to on the baby's early death? And in the second paragraph, baptism is hidden much more obviously under 'he purifies his heart, and his sins are forgiven him'.[29] In a footnote in his response, Jeremias appears to concede the point, insisting only that 'in all the passages, "to give thanks" [εὐχαριστεῖν] evidently indicates not a spontaneous expression of gratitude, but a regular liturgical usage'. But then, on the basis of another passage in Aristides which Aland had first cited and Jeremias now contested, Jeremias kept open the question whether the apologist's 'they thank God' on the birth of a child did not after all imply baptism.[30]

The variety of settings in which 'thanking God' occurs, including 'when a righteous man among them departs from this world' (15:11), strongly suggests a non-baptismal but possible liturgical usage. We have here then a thanksgiving for the birth of a child, rather than the

---

[27] Aristides, *Apology* 15:11, 17:4.
[28] Jeremias, *Infant Baptism*, p. 71.
[29] Kurt Aland, *Did the Early Church Baptize Infants?* (London, 1963), pp. 55-56.
[30] J. Jeremias, *The Origins of Infant Baptism* (London, 1963), p. 48 n. 2.

consecration of the newborn discussed above in a fourth-century context. If the other passage in Aristides should be read as embracing infants in baptism (which perhaps cannot be ruled out), it envisages a different situation, of family or household baptism on conversion, to which the birth of a child to baptised Christians should not be assimilated.[31]

Since in the fourth century and somewhat thereafter, when we know that admission to the catechumenate near birth was common, actual notices of it are infrequent, it should not surprise us if, in the much sparser literature of the pre-Constantinian church, parallels to what we have discerned here in Aristides are similarly elusive. But at least an alternative way of reading some texts is suggested. Jeremias interpreted a catena of references to lifelong, or implicitly lifelong, Christian discipleship in the second and third centuries as reflecting the baptism of the persons in question in early infancy. The best known is Polycarp's noble confession prior to martyrdom: 'For eighty-six years have I served Christ.' Less well known is the testimony of Hierax from Phrygia, martyred with Justin in Rome c.165: 'I have always been, and ever will be, a Christian'.[32]

Aland contested Jeremias' confidence in discerning baptism in all such texts, pointed out that in some of them the span of time begins not from birth but from later childhood or youth, and threw in a parallel text from Clement's letter of c.96, whose chronological implications exposed the shakiness of Jeremias' assumptions.[33] What Aland did not counter-propose was a reading of declarations such as 'I received Christianity from my parents' (by Euelpistos, another fellow-martyr with Justin) consistent with some form of dedication or thanksgiving at birth followed by Christian upbringing leading to later baptism. That is to say, infant baptism should not be regarded as the sole possible starting-gun for a lifetime of Christian faithfulness.

We are not at this stage considering other evidence for the baptising of babies during the period in question, extending roughly from 150 to 250. But we must recognise that no one category of evidence can be considered in isolation from others. In turn this raises the question where amid so much uncertainty we find clarity by which to make sense of obscurity. If only just one of these testimonies had explicitly attested the time of baptism, whether early or later! But again we encounter the strange silence of so many documents about baptism itself. Moreover, responsible researchers are required to be even-handed in adverting to the limitations of our evidence. If little textual precision can be offered in

---

[31] Aland, *Did the Early Church?*, pp. 57-58, Jeremias, *Origins*, pp. 43-48, on *Apology* 15:6. Jeremias views it in terms of family baptism.

[32] Jeremias, *Infant Baptism*, pp. 59-64.

[33] Aland, *Did the Early Church?*, pp. 70-74. Jeremias in *Origins* did not respond to Aland's argument from *1 Clement* 63:3.

favour of some non-baptismal ecclesial welcome of the babies of Christian parents, the same has to be said of actual occurrences of infant baptism. What is being flagged up now is the serious possibility that, in the pre-Nicene centuries, something comparable to what patently obtained for much of the fourth century and into the fifth was observed in the case of at least some children born in Christian families.

One of the leaders of the French-speaking Catholic counter-reform in the sixteenth and seventeenth centuries was François de Sales, who became the bishop of Geneva in exile in 1602. As part of his commendation of Catholic piety to married people, he included Monnica the mother of Augustine among his favourite models of maternal sanctity. He interpreted Augustine's statement that 'right from my mother's womb I was signed with the sign of Christ's cross and seasoned with his salt' (*Confs.* 1:11:17) of Monnica's vowing her child to God before birth. Even while still in the womb, he had 'tasted the salt of God'.[34]

François de Sales' version of Augustine's earliest Christian initiation is not a tenable reading of his *Confessions*. Yet it may serve to mark a transition in our quest for ways in which Christian parental piety marked the birth of children as God-given in a generation that scarcely knew infant baptism. Evidence must now be presented from a different quarter from that of admission to the catechumenate or thanksgiving for birth. The following extracts from the *Life* of an eminent Christian lady of Rome, Melania the Younger, written by her chaplain Gerontius, take us to the heart of the matter. She was 'forcibly united...in marriage' by her parents to Pinian, who declined her plea for them to live together in sexual abstinence until they had two children to inherit their name and worldly goods.

> Indeed, by the will of the Almighty, a daughter was born to them, whom they promptly dedicated to God for the virginal estate...
>
> Although she frequently asked [Pinian] to keep bodily chastity, he would not agree, saying that he wanted to have another child...
>
> Later on, when...she was about to give birth to her second child, the feast of Saint Lawrence arrived. Without taking any rest and having spent the whole night kneeling in her chapel, keeping vigil, at dawn the next day she rose early and went with her mother to the Church of the martyr... And when she returned from the

---

[34] See Pierre Courcelle, *Les Confessions de saint Augustin dans le tradition littéraire. Antécédents et Postérité* (Paris, 1963), p. 384; Clarissa W. Atkinson, '"Your Servant, My Mother": The Figure of Saint Monica in the Ideology of Christian Motherhood', in C.W. Atkinson *et al.* (eds), *Immaculate and Powerful: The Female in Sacred Image and Social Reality* (Boston, MA, 1985), pp. 139-72 at pp. 153-55.

martyr's shrine, she commenced a difficult labor and gave birth prematurely to a child. It was a boy, and after he was baptised, he departed for the Lord...

She took the occasion of her child's death to renounce all her silk clothing. At this time, their daughter who was devoted to virginity also died. Then both Melania and Pinian hastened to fulfill their promises to God.[35]

Gerontius supervised the monasteries Melania founded in Jerusalem for many years after her death at the turn of the year 439-40. He wrote his *Life* about a dozen years later. The two short-lived children were born probably in the early 400s.[36]

Melania's career belongs to the conversion of major sections of the Roman aristocracy to a strongly ascetic Christianity in the latter decades of the fourth and early decades of the fifth centuries. The *Life* is, to be sure, propaganda for asceticism, and not without its textual and historical problems. There is not even certainty how many children Melania bore.[37] Yet our interest is in things baptismal, and the only baptismal practice visible in this account is the baptism of the dying, of the second child who after a difficult and premature birth was baptised before and obviously with a view to his death. Are we to assume that the daughter, who was born earlier but died later, was also baptised before her death? Whatever we make of the text's silence on that point, it is beyond doubt that neither child was baptised routinely after birth, that is, baptised regardless of any imminence of death. The daughter, who alone at birth gave promise of life ahead of her, her parents consecrated (*consecrarunt*; in the Greek version, ἀφιέρωσαν) to virginity. I am inclined to insert 'instead' into this last sentence. That is to say, in this religious milieu, in which in even the most pious families children are not baptised at birth, the dedication of the newborn to virginity serves somewhat as Augustine's initiation into the catechumenate did at Tagaste in AD 354—to mark at the outset of life a parental commitment that the child become a servant of Christ.

'It was not uncommon for pious parents to dedicate their children to a life of virginity from their birth.' Thus Ambrose's biographer summarises the evidence found in the writings of the bishop of Milan and of Jerome.[38] Ambrose's several treatises on virginity display his zeal for this vocation. He urges parents to train their daughters to follow the path of continence. If a husband is sought in the hope of grandchildren, one is

---

[35] Elizabeth A. Clark (ed. and trans.), *The Life of Melania the Younger* 1, 5, 6 (Studies in Women and Religion, 14: New York and Toronto, 1984), pp. 28-30. The Greek text is edited by Denys Gorce, *Vie de Sainte Mélanie* (SC 90; Paris, 1962), pp. 132, 134, 136.

[36] See Clark, *Life*, pp. 28, 85, 140, 196, 197.

[37] Clark, *Life*, p. 197 n. 25.

[38] F. Homes Dudden, *The Life and Times of St. Ambrose* (2 vols; Oxford, 1935), I, p. 150.

surrendering certainty for a prospect that is uncertain. 'Is the girl borne so long in her mother's womb only that she may pass into the power of another? Is care taken to ensure the virgin's gracefulness only that she may more speedily be removed from her parents?' But if parents, like favouring winds, ought to hasten the pursuit of virginity, 'it is more glorious if the fire of tender years, even without being fuelled by its seniors, burst forth of its own accord into the flame of chastity'.[39]

A wealthy Christian mother in Florence named Juliana vowed not only her three daughters to virginity but also her son Lawrence, so named because she believed that she had conceived him with the help of Lawrence the martyr. Ambrose's *Exhortation to Virginity* scripts her model pleading to her children, but chiefly to young Lawrence, to take upon themselves the fulfilment of their parents' vows. She speaks now as a widowed mother to her son.

> Consider who it was helped you to be born. You are the son more of my vows than my labour pains (*dolorum*). Consider the role (*muneri*) to which your father assigned you by calling you by such a name as Lawrence. There we reposed our vows where we derived the name. A successful outcome followed the vows. Render to the martyr what you owe to the martyr. His entreaty won (*impetravit*) you for us; make restitution of what we promised of you by calling you by such a name.

After reminding all her children what they owed to their parents' vows (retelling the story of Jephthah in Judges 11:30-40 to illustrate the power of a parent's vow), she turned again to Lawrence.

> You, my son, whom a true Elkanah [1 Samuel 1:1ff.], that is, a possession of God, gave to me, you my petitioned one, my requested (whence too Samuel got his name); you, I say, the fruit of my entreaties and my vows, how you entered my womb I know not (for I had by then despaired of a male child), you whom my vows, not some hidden rite of intercourse,[40] formed for me; my son, acknowledge, I say, by whom you were gifted to me. He fashioned (*plasmavit*) your face (*ora*), he separated your limbs, he accepted my requests, he to whose temple, to whose obedient service I hallowed you before you were born. Not for parents, not for yourself, but for God were you born. His you began to be before you issued from your mother's womb. We are indeed all his, but you have been specially promised...

---

[39] Ambrose, *Virgins* 1:7:33, 1:12:62 (*PL* 16, cols. 198, 205-6). Ambrose's four treatises on virginity are edited with Italian translation by Franco Gori in the *Bibliotheca Ambrosiana* edition, *Opera* 14/1 and 14/2, *Opere Morali* II/I and II/II (Milan and Rome, 1989). There is an English translation of *Virgins* alone in *NPNF* 2 vol. 10, and of *Virginity* by David Callan (Toronto, 1996).

[40] *quem mihi vota mea, non aliqua solemnis coetus secreta formarunt*. The Italian has: 'che mi sei stato concepito grazie ai miei voti, non per un comune intimo rapporto' (*Opera* 14/2, *Opere Morali* II/II, p. 241). Is Ambrose alluding instead to misplaced confidence in astrology, in 'a particular unobserved sacral conjunction' of the planets?

I am wretched and unworthy, yet like Hannah I promised that you would not withdraw from the face of the Lord all the days and nights of your life.[41]

Not least revealing of this intensely ascetic spirituality is Ambrose's perceptive use of Jesus's blessing of the children, a passage which, although not yet the proof-text for Jesus's approval of infant baptism that it would become, had already been invoked in its support. Ambrose notes in another work, *Virginity*, that in Matthew's Gospel the incident follows immediately on Jesus's commendation of the choice of celibacy for the sake of the kingdom of heaven (Matthew 19:12).

> After this word there are presented for his blessing children (*pueri*), who, innocent of corruption, might at their spotless (*immaculata*) age preserve the gift of purity intact (*integritatis munus*). 'For of such is the kingdom of heaven', who have returned to childlike chastity as though to the nature of infants, in ignorance of corruption...
>
> Do not be surprised at profession (of virginity) among adolescents when you can read of martyrdom among children; for it is written, 'Out of the mouth of infants and babes at the breast you have perfected praise.'...
>
> Do not therefore keep infants away from Christ, for they too have undergone martyrdom for his name: 'For of such is the kingdom of heaven.' The Lord invites them, and do you debar them? For it was of them that the Lord said, 'Allow them to come to me.'... Finally, do not separate especially babies from the love of Christ, for they confessed him in prophetic exultation even while still placed within their mothers' wombs.[42]

In these writings the motif of consecration to virginity at or even before birth overlaps with the training of young children in the ascetic life. The latter is more discussed in the literature than the former.[43] One of the recurrent strains is reprobation of parental discouragement of ascetic zeal in infants and older children, and another is the fulfilment by the latter of vows and pledges of their future consecration made by parents in the context of their birth.

---

[41] Ambrose, *Exhortation to Virginity* 3:15, 8:51-52 (*PL* 16, cols. 340, 351-52).

[42] Ambrose, *Virginity* 6:30, 7:40-41 (*PL* 16, cols. 273, 276-77).

[43] See Heshmat Fawzy Keroloss, 'Virginity in the Early Church: The Meanings and Motives of Sexual Renunciation in the First Four Centuries' (unpubl. dissert., Fordham University, New York, 1996), pp. 312-13, 335; Francisco de B. Vizmanos, *Las Virgenes Cristianas de la Iglesia Primitiva* (Biblioteca de Autores Cristianos, 45; Madrid, 1949), pp. 193-94 (minimal discussion in a work of over 1,300 pages). I have not seen J. Blouet, *Le sanctification des enfants* (Paris, n.d.). Methodius of Olympus (d. c.311) argued that commitment to virginity was appropriate 'from childhood', 'in the first stage of life', *Symposium* 5:3 (*PG* 18, cols. 100-101).

Jerome's letters reveal his familiarity with the dedication of newborn children to virginity in the kind of circles to which Melania the Elder and the Younger belonged in Rome.[44] Writing in AD 413 to Gaudentius who had sought guidance on bringing up his baby daughter Pacatula, Jerome alludes to the practice of some mothers who have 'pledged a daughter to virginity' (*futuram virginem spoponderint*) of dressing her in dull-coloured clothing. Pacatula is now 'a child without teeth and without ideas', but once she is seven she should start memorising the Psalter and the books of Solomon. Jerome writes this letter still in the after-shock of the sack of Rome in 410. Baby Pacatula is 'destined to know tears before laughter and to feel sorrow sooner than joy. Hardly does she make her entrance than she is called on to make her exit.'[45]

Twenty years earlier Jerome wrote to Marcella, another member of a wealthy noble Roman family, in commendation of the life as a virgin of her sister Asella. While still in the womb Asella was blessed, and her father had a dream of her delivery in a bowl of shining glass. Her ceremonial consecration to virginal life took place when she was hardly more than ten years old, 'still wrapped in the coverings (*pannis*) of infancy'. God foreknew the future, comments Jerome, when he sanctified Jeremiah yet unborn, made John to leap in his mother Elizabeth's womb, and set Paul apart as evangelist before the foundation of the world.[46]

Paula, granddaughter of a Christian matron of conspicuous sanctity of the same name, had been born and indeed even conceived to Laeta, Paula senior's daughter-in-law, and Toxotius, through a vow and pledge of her future virginity. Among the playthings of her cradle she was heard to sing 'Alleluia' in her baby-talk.[47] In AD 403 Jerome sent Laeta a letter on bringing up Paula, this child given in answer to her mother's vows. Having gained her by faith, Laeta may hope to win over by the same faith her still unbelieving father. Paula, vowed to Christ before she was conceived, consecrated before she was born, recalls the story of Hannah. Like her, Laeta may be sure that, having returned her first-born to the Lord, she will become the mother of sons. Thus born in answer to a promise, Paula deserves a nurture worthy of her birth, like Samuel in the temple or John the Baptiser in the desert. This child must be instructed as one destined to be the temple of God.

Jerome anticipates Laeta's daunted foreboding at the burden of his detailed counsel—'How shall I, living at Rome surrounded by people, be able to observe all these injunctions?'—by recommending that, once Paula is weaned, she be sent to the monastery in Bethlehem to be brought

---

[44] Grützmacher, *Hieronymus*, III, pp. 250-51.

[45] Jerome, *Epistle* 128:2, 3, 4 (*PL* 22, cols. 1096-9).

[46] Jerome, *Epistle* 24:2 (*PL* 22, col. 427). On Asella, see Vizmanos, *Las Virgenes*, pp. 147, 208, 372-74, 551.

[47] Jerome, *Epistle* 108:26 (*PL* 22, col. 903).

up by her grandmother and namesake and by her aunt Eustochium. 'Give up this most precious of gems, to be placed in Mary's chamber and to rest in the cradle where the infant Jesus cried.' By thus yielding her daughter to be reared among virgins, Laeta should pay back to the full in her offspring what she meantime puts off paying in her own person.[48]

The most interesting passage in this letter from our present perspective belongs to Jerome's reiteration of parental responsibility for children before they reach years of discretion.

> Perhaps you mistakenly reckon that the children of Christian parents, if they have not received baptism, are themselves alone liable for their sin, and that guilt is not also ascribed to those who have declined to give it (i.e. baptism), especially at a time when those who would be receiving it could not object to it. In fact, on the contrary, the salvation of infants is an advantage to adults. To offer your daughter or not lay within your power (although you were in a different situation, since you vowed her before you conceived), but now that she has been offered, you neglect her at your peril.

If it was sacrilege to present for sacrifice an imperfect animal, how much severer punishment awaits the one who 'prepares for the king's embrace a part of her own body and the purity of a spotless soul and then proves negligent?'[49]

Disentangling the different parental offerings in this paragraph is not easy. The offering of Paula that Laeta has made was given before even her conception. What further offering is Laeta being challenged to make? The whole thrust of the letter must point to Paula's strict upbringing as a virgin. In the previous chapter Jerome has told of the sorry end of one Praetextata, aunt of young Eustochium, who dared to deck her out 'after the manner of society', to please her husband but in defiance of the girl and her mother.[50] As we have seen above, Jerome is not confident that Laeta will be able to give Paula's virginal formation the unremitting attention it deserves.

But what then of baptism? It is clearly in this letter something distinct from consecration to virginity, which for Paula had taken place before birth. It seems to be brought in as an analogy of parental responsibility and the cost of not fulfilling it. Jerome's argument rests not so much on the blame attaching to not having children baptised as on the fact that, so long as unbaptised offspring remain minors, parents are automatically responsible for their sins—unforgiven without baptism. Although Jerome's preference for early infant baptism is clear, he nevertheless leaves the choice to the parents. He does not imply that Laeta and

---

[48] Jerome, *Epistle* 107:1-4, 13 (*PL* 22, cols. 868-71, 877).
[49] Jerome, *Epistle* 107:6 (*PL* 22, cols. 873-74).
[50] Jerome, *Epistle* 107:5 (*PL* 22, cols. 872-73).

Toxotius are delaying Paula's baptism, but whether she has been baptised is not certain. For if the case of baptism is introduced for comparison, the burden of this part of the letter is that Laeta should not neglect Paula's strict upbringing as a virgin.

The practice we have been surveying chiefly in the writings of Ambrose and Jerome was common enough in high Roman circles for the poet Prudentius to hail it as one mark of their Christian conversion.

> We see patrician families,
> Noble on both male and female side,
> Vowing their pledged offering,
> The child of most distinguished parents.[51]

Prudentius' long poem on Romanus, a deacon of Palestinian Caesarea martyred at Antioch under Diocletian, portrays also a boy martyr no older than seven. His mother sternly upbraided him when he flinched under the lashes: 'Not such did I pledge (*spopondi*) to God that the fruit of my loins would be; not for this hope of glory did I give you birth, that you should know to bend before death.'[52]

The evidence for dedication of infants at or before birth is not restricted to the church in the West. Theodoret of Cyrrhus, weighty exegete and church historian in the Antiochene tradition who died c.460, recorded his own experience. His parents had been married for many years without having children, for his mother was sterile. Through his father's intervention with the holy man Macedonius, assurance of future birth was given, and it would be 'fitting for the child to be given back to the Giver'. The woman even survived a threatened miscarriage on renewal of her undertaking to consecrate the child to the service of God. Subsequently Macedonius often reminded Theodoret:

> You were born, my child, out of many labours. I spent many nights beseeching God for this alone.... So live a life worthy of these toils. Before you were delivered, you were made an offering by promises.[53]

---

[51] Prudentius, *Peristephanon* II, 521-24 (*On the Martyrs' Crowns*, St. Lawrence; M.P. Cunningham [ed.], *CCSL* 126, p. 275); for a different translation, based partly on a divergent text, M.C. Eagan, *The Poems of Prudentius* (Fathers of the Church, 43; Washington, DC, 1962, p. 125; *PL* 60, col. 330).
[52] *Peristephanon* X, 723-25 (St. Romanus Against the Pagans; *CCSL* 126, p. 355; Eagan, *Poems*, p. 221; *PL* 60, cols. 500-501).
[53] Theodoret, *History of the Monks of Syria* 13:16-18 (*PG* 82, cols. 1408-09). There is a translation by R.M. Price (Cistercian Studies Series, 88; Kalamazoo, MI, 1985), and an edition with notes and French translation by Pierre Canivet and Alice Leroy-Molinghen, *Histoire des Moines de Syrie* (2 vols; *SC* 234, 257; Paris, 1977–79). On Macedonius and Theodoret, see A.J. Festugière, *Antioche païenne et chrétienne:*

Theodoret found himself forced to speak of his birth experiences in one of his letters:

> Even before my conception my parents promised to offer (προσφέρειν) me to God, and from the womb they presented (ἀνέθηκαν) me according to their promises, and provided suitable nurture.[54]

Pierre Canivet is convinced by the vocabulary Theodoret uses that this neo-natal consecration is not to be confused with baptism, but he too easily assumes that Theodoret was baptised soon thereafter.[55]

The Life of Daniel the Stylite moves in a similar world of piety. His pillar was in Anaplus in Persia, where he died in 493. His mother Martha had likewise been sterile and was repeatedly scorned for her barrenness by her husband and other relatives. She betook herself to God in prayer, promising to offer her child, if granted, to him, as Hannah had presented Samuel. Buoyed up by a vision that night, she became pregnant and gave birth to a son, whom for years the parents deferred naming. The name too they wanted to be given by God, as he had been brought into life by God. In due course by a heavenly sign—the presence of a copy of the book of Daniel—the child was named. When he was eleven, he took himself off in single-minded devotion into a monastic community.[56]

In the case of Euthymius (377–473) in Melitene in Lesser Armenia, whose life was written by Cyril of Scythopolis (modern Bethshan; b. c.525), it was to God in his church rather than to the ascetic vocation that his godly parents presented him at birth as they had promised. For after years of barrenness, Dionysia had conceived following sustained prayer and a vision in which God promised to grant her a 'child of encouragement' (*euthumia*), indicating both his name and his future ministry. But it was not until Euthymius' third year that bishop Otreius baptised him and made him a lector.[57] He would become an influential pro-Chalcedonian monastic leader in Palestine.

Libanius, Chrysostome et les moines de Syrie (Bibliothèque des Écoles Françaises d' Athènes et de Rome, 194; Paris, 1959), pp. 283-85; Pierre Canivet, *Le monachisme Syrien selon Théodoret de Cyr* (Théologie Historique, 42; Paris, 1977), pp. 42-44 (but the references to Paulinus of Nola and G.B. De Rossi in p. 43 n. 33 here seem misplaced).

[54] Theodoret, *Epistle* 81, Yvan Azéma (ed.), *Théodoret de Cyr, Correspondance* II (SC 98; Paris, 1964), p. 196.

[55] Canivet, *Le monachisme*, p. 44, with no evidence offered.

[56] *Vita S. Danielis Stylitae* 2-4 (H. Delehaye [ed.], *Analecta Bollandiana* 32 (1913), pp. 121-214 at pp. 122-25; revised version in *PG* 116, cols. 969-1037 at cols. 972-73, in the *Menologion* of the tenth-century Byzantine hagiographer, Symeon Metaphrastes. The *Vita* was composed by one of Daniel's disciples. It is reprinted in H. Delehaye, *Les Saints stylites* (Subsidia Hagiographica, 14; Brussells, 1923).

[57] *Bios...*, Eduard Schwartz (ed.), *Kyrillos von Skythopolis* (Texte und Untersuchungen, 49:2; Leipzig, 1939), pp. 3-84 at pp. 8-10.

There are sufficient attested instances of infant boys being vowed, by their parents or themselves even, to the clerical service of the church for us to regard it as another form of infant dedication in the church of late antiquity. Most evidence relates to the West, where the Second Council of Toledo in AD 527 regulated the treatment of those 'whom the will of their parents assigned from the first years of infancy to office in the clergy'.[58] Of several boy lectors there is no evidence of earlier vows. These range from Felix, martyr at Nola in central Italy perhaps in the early fourth century, whom Paulinus bishop of Nola a century later took as his patron and whom he portrays as serving as a lector from early boyhood (*primis...in annis*),[59] to the Antony later notorious as bishop of Fussala in Augustine's diocese, who had been brought up in the monastery at Hippo.[60]

A papal letter from Zosimus to Hesychius, bishop of Salona in Dalmatia, in 418 lays down that anyone who has volunteered or enrolled (*nomen dederit*) for the ministries of the church from infancy must serve as lector until his twentieth year.[61] Much more interesting for this study is a little noticed statement in a decretal from pope Siricius to Himerius, the bishop of Tarragona, in AD 385. Ruling on various questions relating to ordination, Siricius declares:

> Anyone who has vowed himself to the service of the church from his infancy must be baptised before the years of puberty and join the ministry of the lectors.[62]

If a pledged commitment *Ecclesiae obsequiis* has clerical or ordained service in view, then its separation from later baptism is more remarkable than its parallel with vows of virginity. Almost in the nature of the case, the latter are coloured with a tinge of the exotic and lean towards individualised religion. This glimpse of infant vows to enter the church's

---

[58] Concilium Toletanum II, can. 1, in Gonzalo Martínez Diez and Felix Rodriguez (eds), *La Coleccion Canonica Hispana* (Monumenta Hispaniae Sacra; 4 vols; Madrid, 1966–84), IV, pp. 347-48.

[59] Paulinus, *Carmina* 15:104-08 (*PL* 61, col. 470; P.G. Walsh [trans.], *The Poems of St Paulinus of Nola* (Ancient Christian Writers, 40; New York and Paramus, NJ, 1975), pp. 85-86.

[60] Augustine, *Epistle* 209:3 (*PL* 33, col. 954). Other texts are listed in *PL* 13, col. 1141 n.(e). On boy lectors, see L. Godefroy, 'Lecteur', *Dictionnaire de Théologie Catholique* (15 vols; Paris, 1903–50), IX, cols. 117-25 at cols. 122-3; H. Leclercq, 'Lecteur', *DACL* 8, cols. 2241-69 at 2247-9, and following inscriptions.

[61] Zosimus, *Epistle* 9:3:5 (*PL* 20, col. 672; 56, col. 572; P. Jaffé and W. Wattenbach (eds), *Regesta Pontificum Romanorum* (2 vols; Leipzig, 1885–89), I, p. 50 no. 339.

[62] Siricius, *Epistle* 1:9:13 (*PL* 13, col. 1142; 56, col. 560; Jaffé and Wattenbach, *Regesta*, I, pp. 40-41 no. 255): *Quicumque itaque se Ecclesiae vovit obsequiis a sua infantia, ante pubertatis annos baptizari, et lectorum debet ministerio sociari*. It can, of course, have only males in mind.

clerical hierarchy neither preceded (as a pre-condition of the vow's validity or seriousness!) nor accompanied (ditto) by baptism powerfully confirms how unfamiliar infant baptism must have been at this time in the church at Rome. Siricius' ruling must not, of course, be taken to imply that no such infant-dedicatees had been baptised in their early days, although such a state of affairs would not be inconsistent with what we know of these decades in the West. In turn, the explicitness with which Siricius envisages infants self-vowed to future clerical office from infancy but not receiving baptism until the eve of puberty must increase the likelihood that baptism did not normally accompany the earliest vows of virginity or clerical ministry.

Another unnoticed text in a fragment of Cyril of Alexandria's commentary on John's Gospel, written perhaps 425–28 and certainly no later than 428, similarly distinguishes between infant dedication to the catechumenate and infant baptism:

> When a new-born baby (ἀρτιγενὲς...βρέφος) is brought to receive the chrism of the catechumenate, or (ἤτοι) the chrism of initiation (τελειώσεως) in holy baptism, the person who brings the baby makes the response 'Amen' on his or her behalf.[63]

The incidental nature of this reference, in a discussion of the role of those who make confession on behalf of others, is no less revealing for all the questions it leaves unanswered. Presumably the baby did not receive both chrisms in quick succession, and so what, or who, determined which he or she received? They appear, if not quite as the 'equivalent alternatives' of modern baptismal discussion, at least as parallel rites for the newborn. It is interesting to note the Latin translation in Migne of 'the chrism of the catechumenate (τῆς κατεχήσεως)'—'the chrism *instructionis initiationisque*', of instruction and initiation.[64]

---

[63] Cyril of Alexandria, *Commentary on John*, on John 11:26 (*PG* 74, col. 49; ed. P.E. Pusey, 2 vols, Oxford, 1872, II, p. 276).

[64] In the seventh-century Irish canons attributed to the 'Second Synod of St Patrick', canon 19, 'At What Age they are to be Baptized', states that 'On the eighth day they become catechumens. Later (*Postea*) they are baptized on the festivals of the Lord, that is, Easter, Pentecost and Epiphany' (L. Bieler [ed.], *The Irish Penitentials* [Dublin, 1963], p. 192; John T. McNeill and Helena M. Gamer [trans.], *Medieval Handbooks of Penance* [New York, 1938], p. 84). Whether or not Eoin de Bhaldraithe, to whom I owe this reference, is right in inferring that baptism followed not within the first year but in maturity ('Adult Baptism in the Early Church', *Anabaptism Today* [June, 1997], pp. 10-15 at p. 13), the use of the eighth day for enrolment into the catechumenate, not for baptism, surely echoes earlier practice. It may be compared with a ritual in the Greek euchologion, perhaps of similar date to the Irish canon, when a child is brought by the midwife or nurse to the church doors (but no further) on the eighth day after birth, is blessed by the priest and sealed with the sign of the cross on the forehead, mouth and

This investigation into forms of infant dedication or other recognition of the birth of a child, for example by thanksgiving (cf. Aristides), may seem to have travelled far from baptism. Some, for example, of these pledges to virginity or clerical service were made by the infants themselves, clearly at an age later than that assumed for the baptism of the newborn—but even not then necessarily entailing baptism. So that not every instance noted here can plausibly be regarded as acknowledging the gift of a new life from God and committing parents and baby to his service. Almost certainly further cases remain to be collected, especially in the hagiographical literature, and much has to be clarified. The selectiveness, not to say exotic character, of virginal or clerical consecration of the newborn contrasts with the routineness and potential generality of catechumenal dedication—even if it is in the exceptional Augustine that we observe the latter most plainly. But not all parental vows at or before birth had ascetic or clerical vocations in view.

But we cannot miss the significance that, mostly during the period when all parties agree infant baptism was normally not administered, other, albeit varied, forms of pledging infants to God were being observed. What relationship between these two developments should we envisage, if any? From one angle they seem curiously at odds with each other. The infant vowed to ascetic or clerical life is poles apart from the child whose parents have not baptised him or her out of fear—so the common account has it—of grave sin in later life. The one bespeaks the very seriousness the other dare not espouse. To that extent, these two patterns—of formal catechumenal registration, seen in Augustine, and of

---

breast and receives its name. The prescribed prayer looks forward to its baptism 'at the appropriate time'. At forty days from birth, after the mother has come to the church for thanksgiving, blessing and purification, the child is brought into the church for the first time to commence its life within the church, with baptism still a matter of expectation at the right time. So this fortieth-day ceremony is comparable to admission to the catechumenate. Despite the uncertainties, especially of dating, and the obvious differences, perhaps there is glimpsed here another trace of Irish dependence directly on the Christianity of the Eastern Mediterranean. For the text see now Stefano Parenti and Elena Velkovska (eds), *L'Eucologio Barberini Gr. 336* (Bibliotheca 'Ephemerides Liturgicae', Subsidia 80; Rome, 1995), pp. 96-98 (where other witnesses are listed); earlier, J. Goar, *Euchologion sive Rituale Graecorum...* (Paris, 1647), pp. 321-23. There are translations by Nicholas Bjerring, *The Offices of the Oriental Church* (New York, 1884), pp. 77-79; Isabel F. Hapgood, *Service Book of the Holy Orthodox-Catholic Apostolic (Greco-Russian) Church* (Boston and New York, 1906), pp. 268-70; F.C. Conybeare, *Rituale Armenorum* (Oxford, 1905), pp. 86-88, where the grandmother brings the baby, who is at eight days referred to as a catechumen. I have yet to assimilate the evidence set out in Jaime Sancho Andreu, 'Ritos de la Infancia y la Adolescencia en el Antiguo Rito Hispanico', in Ildebrando Scicolone (ed.), *Psallendum. Miscellanea di Studi in Onore del Prof. Jordi Pinell I Pons, O.S.B.* (Studia Anselmiana, 105, Analecta Liturgica, 15; Rome, 1992), pp. 207-45.

intentionally lifelong vows to the religious or priestly vocation—illustrate the opening up of that fateful gulf in late antiquity in the West between the generality of the Christian *plebs* and the ascetic élite.

But not all parents who enrolled their infants as catechumens did so out of motives arising out of an adequate view of baptism. Indeed as we have noted earlier, many Fathers spoke in lyrical praise of the warm piety of their parents. Nor can registration as catechumen and consecration as virgin always be distinguished, for example, in the case of Basil of Caesarea. In one of his expositions on John's Gospel, Augustine analyses the attitude of the catechumen who shows no interest in baptism but pursues a zealously ascetic life that includes continence. What advantage has baptism to offer when so many of the baptised exhibit lives of mediocre quality?[65] One of the recently discovered Mainz sermons of bishop Augustine on Mark 1:15 ('...Repent...') addresses equally catechumens holding back from baptismal repentance and baptised believers needing to repent of their heedless sinfulness.[66] Which category displayed the higher regard for baptism?

---

[65] Augustine, *Tractatus in Evangelium Iohannis* 4:13 (*PL* 35, cols. 1411-12; *CCSL* 36, pp. 37-38). Cf. likewise Augustine, *Enarrationes in Psalmos* 90:II:6 (*PL* 37, col. 1164; *CCSL* 39, p. 1271).

[66] Augustine, *Sermo Dolbeau* 14 (*Sermo* 352A), Dolbeau (ed.), 'Sermons inédits', pp. 313-20, reprinted in Dolbeau (ed.), *Vingt-six sermons*, pp. 107-14.

CHAPTER 10

The Baptism(s) of Julian the Apostate Revisited

The 'great crisis' that occurred 'in the matter of infant baptism' in the fourth century, as Joachim Jeremias put it in 1958/1960,[1] still awaits satisfactory clarification and explanation. The crisis consisted in Christian parents not having their newborn children baptized. According to Jeremias, this is first attested of Gregory Nazianzen, born c.329–30. Investigation of the case of Julian, later emperor and apostate, should contribute to the larger enquiry, since he was born around May 332 of Christian parents.[2] Surprisingly, given his maximalist assembling and reading of the evidence, Jeremias never mentioned Julian. Scholars who have considered the question of Julian's baptism have frequently betrayed the influence of insecure assumptions about the history of baptism in the patristic era.

In the later nineteenth century a brief debate on whether Julian was baptized at all was sparked off in 1869 by J.F.A. Mücke's outright denial: all the ancient sources were silent, and his not being baptized in early life ran in the family, as the examples of his uncle Constantine and cousin Constantius demonstrated.[3] Friedrich Rode, writing in 1877, was inclined to believe that Julian had been baptized, first because he had been made a lector in the church and secondly because his apostasy would have raised much less hue and cry if he had been only a catechumen.[4] Three years later, Karl Neumann defied all such scepticism and uncertainty, citing Cyril of Alexandria, a later '*fabulosa de Iuliano*

---

[1] Joachim Jeremias, *Infant Baptism in the First Four Centuries* (trans. D. Cairns; London, 1960), p. 87 (cf. *Die Kindertaufe in den ersten vier Jahrhunderten* [Göttingen, 1958], p. 102). Jeremias both exaggerates the crisis, by exaggerating the earlier prevalence of infant baptism, and underestimates its extent and duration.

[2] Jeremias, *Infant Baptism*, pp. 88-89. The same evidence can be read quite differently, as the earliest unambiguous named case in which we know whether a baby of Christian parents was routinely baptized or not. On Julian's birth most follow Frank D. Gillard, 'The Birth Date of Julian the Apostate', *Californian Studies in Classical Antiquity* 4 (1971), pp. 147-51.

[3] J.F.A. Mücke, *Flavius Claudius Julianus: Nach den Quellen*, II. Abth., *Julian's Leben und Schriften* (Gotha, 1869), pp. 70-71.

[4] Friedrich Rode, *Geschichte der Reaction Kaiser Julians gegen die christliche Kirche* (Jena, 1877), pp. 33-34 n. 13.

narratio Syriace scripta' and the fact of Julian's lectorship. '*Neque igitur iam dubitari potest de baptismo Iuliani.*'[5]

Most subsequent writers who touch on the issue (and a notable number do not, from Le Nain de Tillemont in the late seventeenth century to G.W. Bowersock in 1978) simply refer to Neumann or to one or two later authors themselves dependent on Neumann, such as W. Koch in 1927.[6] The main stream of historians during the twentieth century continued to deduce the timing, if not also the fact, of Julian's baptism from his appointment as a lector, and so placed it during his teenage years of quasi-exile at Macellum, an imperial estate near Caesarea in Cappadocia, between approximately 344 and 350.[7]

A partial exception to this consensus was René Braun's essay in 1978: 'Que Julien ait été baptisé, c'est une certitude: sans cela il n'aurait pas été lecteur.' Gregory Nazianzen assumes his baptism, but to locate it during the sojourn at Macellum was no more than conjecture, argues Braun. Sozomen's testimony apparently indicates his infant baptism, at the age of three, for 'le baptême des enfants de parents chrétiens était normal au IVe siècle', and Gregory Nazianzen recommended this age for its

---

[5] Karl J. (Carolus Ioannes) Neumann (ed.), *Ivliani Imperatoris Librorvm Contra Christianos Qvae Svpersvnt* (Leipzig, 1880), pp. 3-5. Strongly inclined to doubt his baptism is Alice Gardner, *Julian Philosopher and Emperor* (New York/London, 1895), pp. 51-52, discounting Christian sources ('their knowledge was imperfect and their hatred intense') but finally conceding in view of Julian's admission to the readership. Her position is misrepresented by Edward J. Martin, *The Emperor Julian* (London, 1919), pp. 27-28, who is persuaded by accounts of Julian's resort to pagan rites to efface all traces of baptism and eucharist. Still unconvinced is Marion Giebel, *Kaiser Julian Apostata* (Düsseldorf/Zürich, 2002), pp. 37-38.

[6] W. Koch, 'Comment l'Empereur Julien tacha de fonder une église païenne', *Revue Belge de Philologie et d'Histoire* 6 (1927), pp. 123-46 at p. 126. Earlier, in his *Kaiser Julian der Abtrünnige: seine Jugend und Kriegshalten bis zum Tode der Kaiser Constantius (331-361). Eine Quellenuntersuchung* (Besonderer Abdruck aus dem XXV Supplementband der *Jahrbücher für classische Philologie*, 1899), pp. 329-488 at p. 357 n. 46, Koch wrote starkly 'Er war getauft worden. Man vergleiche Neumann...' Totally silent on baptism is Joseph Bidez, 'La Jeunesse de l'Empereur Julien', *Bulletin de la Classe des Lettres et des Sciences Morales et Politiques de l'Académie Royale de Belgique* 5th ser., 7 (1921), pp. 127-216, whereas the same author's well-regarded *La Vie de l'Empereur Julien* (Paris, 1930), pp. 28-29, ventures on an imaginative account of Julian's step-by-step experience of catechumenate and baptism, which influenced Robert Browning, *The Emperor Julian* (London, 1975), p. 40.

[7] Otto Seeck (1922), Bidez (1930), A.J. Festugière (1957), Giuseppe Ricciotti (1956, ET 1960), André Piganiol (1972), Robert Browning (1975), Jacques Flamant and Charles Pietri (1995). One may surmise that no little influence was exerted by John Wordsworth's article in William Smith and Henry Wace (eds), *A Dictionary of Christian Biography* (4 vols; London, 1877–87), III, pp. 484-525 at p. 492, which made Julian's admission to the office of reader proof of his baptism in the absence of historical record.

reception.[8] This statement by Braun is an astonishing mixture of sound and unsound, the latter issuing from a misreading of his authority Jeremias at two points. Jeremias not only unmistakeably denied that Gregory's advice to baptize at the age of three, given in 381, had more than short-lived, local influence,[9] but also clearly recognized that the failure of Christian parents to baptize their babies during this period of the fourth century was common enough to constitute the 'great crisis' with which this paper began.

From this review of a scarcely creditable history of scholarly discussion we turn to the original sources, which I will consider in chronological order. Gregory Nazianzen was a contemporary of Julian and his fourth oration against the apostate was delivered in or near 364. He leaves us with no doubt about what he meant to communicate: on gaining the freedom of the imperial throne Julian undid his baptism by a pagan initiation. The language Gregory uses both of the younger Julian and of his baptism (λουτρόν, τελείωσις) makes clear his belief that Julian had received Christian baptism, while providing no clue to the time of this reception.[10]

The church histories of Socrates and Theodoret, both written c.AD 440, alike attest Julian's Christian nurture and enrolment in the readership without even alluding to his baptism.[11] What Socrates implies in stating that 'Julian was a Christian from the outset (ἐξ ἀρχῆς)' is not obvious. He may mean no more than that Julian was a Christian before he became a pagan, rather than be tracing his Christianity to his earliest days. Furthermore, lurking in the background of this enquiry are broader questions about recognition as a 'Christian' in the first half of the fourth century. Whether baptism was always assumed would presumably vary with the persons and circles referring to an individual as a Christian. It is also likely that a later writer might well read more into an earlier reference than it intended at the time. In any case, it would be unwise to place any weight on Socrates' statement in seeking to pin down Julian's baptism.

---

[8] René Braun, 'Julien et le Christianisme', in René Braun and Jean Richer (eds), *L'Empereur Julien: De l'histoire à la legende (331–1715)* (Paris, 1978), pp. 159-88 at p. 162 n. 11.

[9] Jeremias, *Infant Baptism*, p. 96 (*Die Kindertaufe*, p. 114).

[10] Gregory Nazianzen, *Oration* 4:52, J. Bernardi (ed.), *Discours 4–5 Contre Julien* (SC 309; Paris, 1983), pp. 154-57. Alois Kurmann, *Gregor von Nazianz Oration 4 Gegen Julian. Ein Kommentar* (Schweizerische Beiträge zur Altertumswissenschaft, 19; Basel, 1988), pp. 174-81, does not discuss the historical value of Gregory's text.

[11] Socrates, *Ecclesiastical History* 3:1:9-20, G.C. Hansen (ed.), *Kirchengeschichte* (GCS n.f. 1; Berlin, 1995), pp. 188-89; *PG* 67, col. 369; Theodoret, *Ecclesiastical History* 3:1:2, L. Parmentier and F. Scheidweiler (eds), *Kirchengeschichte* (GCS 44; Berlin, 2nd edn, 1954), p. 177; *PG* 82, col. 1085.

The *Against Julian* of Cyril of Alexandria was probably written during 439–41 and so was contemporaneous to the church histories of Socrates and Theodoret. Cyril is more explicit than Gregory Nazianzen on Julian's having attained (ἠξιώθη) holy baptism, which by juxtaposition he links to Julian's proficiency (ἐνήσκητο) in the sacred scriptures.[12] Cyril may imply by having Julian numbered with the believers 'before the time of his reign' that he thought Julian had been baptized in his early adult life rather than as a child, but Cyril scarcely strikes us as furnished with independent and precise knowledge on the matter. He records nothing that he could not have got from Gregory.

Sozomen's *Church History* is of greater but not straightforward interest. Likewise composed in the mid-fifth century, between approximately 443 and 450, it first derivatively (λέγεται) reproduces Gregory Nazianzen on Julian's 'washing off our baptism' by animal blood, ridding himself of the church's initiation (μυήσει).[13] Two dozen lines later Sozomen declares that Julian had been baptized in infancy, which must be the obvious meaning of the Greek: 'born of religiously dutiful parents' ἐκ νέου ἐμυήθη κατὰ τὸν θεσμὸν τῆς ἐκκλησίας.[14] This text has rarely been discussed or even noted by scholars dealing with Julian's baptism, and so has hardly ever challenged the loose consensus that it occurred in the years of Macellum and perhaps not long prior to his assuming the lectorship. The Italian historian, Giuseppe Ricciotti, cites the text only to deny its plain reference to baptism. Julian was indeed baptized at Macellum after having been 'initiated into Sacred Scripture and Christian worship from his infancy'.[15]

How should we evaluate Sozomen's statement? He made 'heavy and completely unacknowledged use' of Socrates' history,[16] so that he may simply have stated explicitly what he understood Socrates to mean by 'Julian was a Christian ἐξ ἀρχῆς'. Certainly no other source has been identified for this paragraph in Sozomen, apart from what Georg Schoo called oral tradition. Schoo suggested tentatively that Sozomen may have reworked Socrates.[17]

---

[12] Cyril, *Against Julian* 1, pref. 3, P. Burguière and P. Evieux (eds), *Contre Julien*, vol. 1 (*SC* 322; Paris, 1985), p. 104; *PG* 76, col. 508.

[13] Sozomon, *Ecclesiastical History* 5:2:2, J. Bidez and G.C. Hansen (eds), *Kirchengeschichte* (*GCS* n.f. 4; Berlin, 2nd edn, 1995), p. 190; *PG* 67, col. 1212.

[14] Sozomon, *Ecclesiastical History* 5:2:7, Bidez and Hansen (eds), *Kirchengeschichte*, p. 191; *PG* 67, col. 1213.

[15] Giuseppe Ricciotti, *Julian the Apostate* (trans. M. Joseph Costelloe; Milwaukee, 1960), p. 13.

[16] Glenn F. Chesnut, *The First Christian Histories* (Macon, GA, 2nd edn, 1986), p. 205.

[17] Georg Schoo, *Die Quellen des Kirchenhistorikers Sozomenos* (Neue Studien zur Geschichte der Theologie und der Kirche, 11; Aalen, 1973 [1911]), pp. 21, 74 and 145.

The vocabulary of Sozomen is wholly consistent with a baptismal meaning. The verb μυέω is well attested in this period of baptizing,[18] and Sozomen used the noun μύησις of baptism in reminting Gregory Nazianzen in the first statement we noted. Ricciotti's paraphrastic rendering is not persuasive, since what Sozomen's text records—ἐκ νέου ἐμυήθη κατὰ τὸν θεσμὸν τῆς ἐκκλησίας—seems distinct from subsequent nurture in the scriptures and formation at the hands of bishops and others. The use of θεσμός fits a specific ordinance such as baptism much better than informal instruction and training, although an element of anachronism lurks in Sozomen's implication that in the first half of the fourth century a 'law of the church' required the baptism of the newborn.

What Ricciotti's reading may unintentionally suggest, but has not hitherto been considered by anyone else, is a non-baptismal interpretation in terms of the newborn's enrolment in the catechumenate, which I have studied elsewhere without benefit of the knowledge of Sozomen's text.[19] Since I cannot (yet) cite any parallel to the use of μυέω of this kind of infant consecration, it must remain unproven. If we must take Sozomen to speak of Julian's infant baptism, we face a fascinating conclusion: this would be the earliest unambiguous and incontrovertible instance of the non-clinical baptism as an infant of a named child of named Christian parents.

Yet improbability hangs over such an outcome. It is to the sole credit of René Braun to have given this text of Sozomen's serious regard in investigating Julian's baptism. But he was quite mistaken in asserting the normality of the baptism of babies of Christian parents in the fourth century, and that in an imperial family also. We cannot depend on this singularly unsupported, unsourced statement by Sozomen to tell us the truth of Julian's baptism.

For the sake of completeness, we must note a third paragraph by Sozomen on the piety of Julian and his brother Gallus at Macellum, where they were admitted to clerical office as readers.[20] It has no

---

Hansen's discussion of sources, Bidez and Hansen (eds), *Kirchengeschichte*, pp. xliv-lxiv, does not touch on this passage.

[18] Cf. G.W.H. Lampe, *A Patristic Greek Lexicon* (Oxford, 1961), s.v.

[19] D.F. Wright, 'Infant Dedication in the Early Church', in S.E. Porter and A.R. Cross (eds), *Baptism, the New Testament and the Church: Historical and Contemporary Studies in Honour of R.E.O. White* (*Journal of the Study of the New Testament*, Supplement Series, 171; Sheffield, 1999), pp. 352-78 (ch. 9 above).

[20] Sozomon, *Ecclesiastical History* 5:2:9-11, Bidez and Hansen (eds), *Kirchengeschichte*, pp. 191-92; *PG* 67, cols. 1213-16.

additional bearing on the baptismal issue. Schoo inclines to identify Gregory Nazianzen's *Oratio* 4 as Sozomen's source in this passage.[21]

Did Julian's elevation to the readership presuppose his baptism? The affirmative answer given by most discussions since Neumann in 1880 has rested partly on a natural assumption and partly on the assertion of Socrates that, while in Alexandria readers might be chosen equally from catechumens as from the faithful, in all other churches only the latter qualified.[22] Neumann thanked Harnack for bringing this information to his notice.[23] Whether we should assume that what Socrates attested c.440 held good a century or so earlier is far from obvious. There is sufficient evidence in the late fourth and early fifth centuries of boys being lectors from kindergarten ages, as also of male offspring vowed to clerical service from birth, and all in contexts where baptism was not routinely given in infancy, to counsel some caution in an area where documentation is not abundant.[24] Nevertheless, the balance of probability rests with Julian's having been baptized before he became a lector.

Where then are we left in respect of Julian's baptism? His own writings reveal nothing of his baptism or his lectorship. Allard noted that, if one did not have other sources, 'on ignorerait même qu'il ait été baptisé'.[25] This silence should not pass unnoticed, given Bowersock's judgement that 'All [Julian's] writings, taken together, provide an insight into character and disposition such as can be had for no other classical figure apart from Cicero.'[26] In this situation perhaps we should not hesitate to accept Gregory Nazianzen's testimony. Gregory and Julian were not only contemporaries but students together for some months in Athens in 355. Gregory unambiguously portrays Julian as a fully initiated Christian, including participation in the eucharist.

If we then ask when the baptism took place, only Sozomen gives an explicit answer, for all its problematic historical value. Julian was initiated as a Christian ἐκ νέου, from babyhood. Sozomen may be basing himself on Socrates, but the only other source to attest Julian's baptism categorically, Cyril of Alexandria, strongly implies by his verb ἠξιώθη that it took place after Julian reached years of responsibility. Cyril's text

---

[21] Schoo, *Quellen*, p. 145, where he should probably refer to Gregory Nazianzen, *Oration* 4:23-24, and not merely to 4:23.

[22] Socrates, *Ecclesiastical History* 5:22:49, Hansen (ed.), *Kirchengeschichte*, p. 301; *PG* 67, cols. 636-37.

[23] Neumann (ed.), *Ivliani Imperatoris*, pp. 4-5.

[24] See briefly, Wright, 'Infant Dedication', pp. 374-75.

[25] Paul Allard, *Julien l'Apostat*, vol. 1 (Paris, 3rd edn, 1906), p. 271, cf. p. 270.

[26] G.W. Bowersock, *Julian the Apostate* (London, 1978), p. 4; cf. p. 1, 'Of the great figures of antiquity few are so abundantly documented and few so legendary as the emperor Julian.'

suggests that temporal link between baptism and lectorship which most historians have retailed.

One way of reconciling these two traditions would be to suppose that Julian was indeed baptized in earliest infancy and then baptized again, presumably as an Arian while under the tutelage of Eusebius of Nicomedia or George of Caesarea. But although some Arians are recorded as rebaptizing, the practice is not attested as early as the 340s, and no shred of evidence even implies it of Julian.

We should perhaps distinguish three rather than two traditions. One, of infant baptism, is recognizably attested only by Sozomen, another, associating the baptism with enrolment as a lector, is clear in Cyril, and a third, the earliest of all by not far short of a century in Gregory Nazianzen, gives no hint as to the time in Julian's life when it was conferred. It is highly plausible that Gregory was the source, direct or indirect, of all the later testimonies. Given the allusive character of Gregory's evidence,[27] due in part, we may surmise, to his dependence on 'those who brag about access to his [Julian's] secret world',[28] and given what we know with confidence of baptismal practice in imperial circles early in Jeremias' 'great crisis', we may rightly wonder whether, after all, we can be sure that Julian ever was baptized.

---

[27] Bernardi at one and the same time stresses Gregory's allusiveness and makes Julian the first Christian emperor as the first to receive baptism other than at the point of death; cf. *Discours* 4–5, p. 18.

[28] Note should be taken of Kurmann's comment, p. 176, on Gregory's attributing his knowledge of Julian's washing away his baptism to οἱ τοῖς ἀπορρήτοις ἐκείνου καλλωπιζόμενοι, 'Es scheint, dass Gregor hinter solchen Formulierungen den Mangel an Information verdecken will'. John A. McGuckin, *St Gregory of Nazianzus: An Intellectual Biography* (Crestwood, NY, 2001), pp. 119-26, cautions against overstating the unhistorical excess of Gregory's two invectives against Julian.

PART B

THE REFORMATION ERA:
SCRIPTURE AND THE APPEAL TO THE FATHERS

Chapter 11

Out, In, Out:
Jesus' Blessing of the Children and Infant Baptism

A common, and perhaps even a characteristic, feature of recent orders of service for the baptizing of infants has been the absence of the pericope of Jesus' blessing of young children in any of its three Synoptic versions—Mark 10.13-16; Matthew 19.13-15; Luke 18.15-17. None of the orders in the Church of England's new *Common Worship* includes it, but it is cited, but not read, in the service of 'Thanksgiving for the Gift of a Child': 'As Jesus took children in his arms and blessed them, so now we ask God's blessing on N'.[1] In the Anglicans' *Alternative Service Book* of 1980, now superseded by *Common Worship*, it was similarly missing from the infant baptismal orders, but found a place within the same grouping of 'Initiation Services' in the 'Thanksgiving' both for a child's birth and for adoption. It was also included in the services for the burial of a child. On every occurrence the Markan text is prescribed.[2] *The Methodist Worship Book* of 1999 not only leaves it out of 'The Baptism of Young Children', but in the 'Thanksgiving for the Birth or Adoption of a Child', placed among a group of 'Pastoral Services', provides Mark 9.36-37 instead.[3]

By contrast *The Methodist Service Book* of 1975 required Mark 10.13-16 to be read in the baptism of infants, just as the same church's *Book of Offices* had in 1936 drawn on the same passage among others in the opening exhortation to the congregation justifying infant baptism.[4] It was present in the order for infant baptism in all versions of the Anglican *Book of Common Prayer* from 1549 to 1928. In the very earliest English Prayer Book, in 1549, its reading belonged to that first part of the service which took place 'at the church door'. As we shall see, this had been its

---

[1] *Common Worship: Service and Prayers for the Church of England* (London, 2000), p. 341.
[2] *The Alternative Service Book 1980* (London, 1980), pp. 215, 220, 319, 330, 944, 948-49. For brief comments see R.C.D. Jasper and P.F. Bradshaw, *A Companion to the Alternative Service Book* (London, 1986), pp. 346, 349-50.
[3] *The Methodist Worship Book* (Peterborough, 1999), p. 400.
[4] *The Methodist Service Book* (Peterborough, 1975), p. A7; *The Book of Offices* (London, 1936), pp. 83-84.

traditional position, but, in accordance with Martin Bucer's recommendation in his *Censura* of Cranmer's first Prayer Book in 1551, from 1552 onwards the whole of the service was placed within the church building at the font.[5] There the Gospel lection remained until the later twentieth century, read as dominical warrant 'of the good will of our heavenly Father towards this Infant' and so removing any doubt 'but that he favourably alloweth this charitable work of ours, in bringing this Infant to his holy Baptism', as the baptizing minister's immediately following exhortation declared to the congregation.[6]

The Roman Catholic Church's 'Rite of Baptism for Children' was revised on the instruction of the Second Vatican Council and promulgated in 1969. The English text in use in the United Kingdom and Ireland, last amended in 1992, lists Mark 10 among the four Gospel passages of which one or two are to be read when baptism takes place apart from the eucharist (the others being in John 3.1-6; Matthew 28.18-20; Mark 1.9-11). When children are baptized within the mass, the lections are taken either from those set for that Sunday or from the lectionary's list of readings for mass with baptism. This list includes Mark 10 among twelve Gospel texts.[7] A revision of the Roman infant baptismal rite is at present under way, with the intention to produce for children a rite of Christian initiation with catechumenate to parallel the highly significant Rite of Christian Initiation of Adults (1972).

Another Church that still finds a place for Jesus' blessing of the children in the latest infant baptism service is the Church of Scotland. In its 1994 'Order for the Sacrament of Holy Baptism for a Child', Luke 18.16-17 appears among eight short biblical passages of which one or more 'may be read'. This authorized (but not prescribed) service directs that Matthew 28.18-20 and Acts 2.38-39 shall first be read. This differential use of biblical lections marks a change from the 1940 *Book of Common Order*, whose rite for infant baptism provided only Mark 10.13-14, 16, followed immediately by 'It is the duty of those who present their children for holy Baptism...' The prayer just before the baptism itself picked up the Gospel reading: 'O Blessed Saviour, who didst take little children into Thine arms and bless them; take this

---

[5] The 1549 and 1552 texts can be seen in several collections, conveniently in J.D.C. Fisher, *Christian Initiation: The Reformation Period* (Alcuin Club Collections, 51; London, 1970), pp. 91, 107. For Bucer's *Censura*, Fisher, *Reformation Period*, pp. 98-99; E.C. Whitaker, *Martin Bucer and the Book of Common Prayer* (Alcuin Club Collections, 55; Great Wakering, 1974), pp. 84-87.

[6] Fisher, *Reformation Period*, pp. 92, 108.

[7] *Rite of Baptism for Children Approved for Use in the Dioceses of England and Wales, Scotland and Ireland* (London/Dublin, 1992), pp. 18, 45, 69, 94, 142.

child...'[8] The prominence of Christ's action and words in this tradition goes back to the Church Service Society's 1867 *Euchologion: or Book of Prayers*, the earliest attempt at a modern service-book for the Church of Scotland. Mark 10.13-16 is read almost at the very beginning of the service, followed by 'Let us not doubt...that the same loving Saviour...will now receive and bless this little one.'[9] This emphasis was taken to excess in the United Free Church's *Book of Common Order* in 1928, immediately before union with the Church of Scotland. The minister's opening address stated, 'The sanction of the ordinance is to be found in the words of our Lord, who spake, saying, " Suffer..." ', namely Mark 10.14-16.[10]

Although the influential continental Reformed orders of the sixteenth century all provided for the reading of this Gospel passage—Strasbourg (from the mid-1520s), Geneva (1542) and Zürich (from 1523)[11]—it was not set down in the more didactic, less liturgical 'Ordoure of Baptisme' which in 1564 the Scottish Church received from John Knox's Genevan usage. It is present only in summary form in a lengthy exposition of the biblical grounds and significance of baptism: 'Also our Saviour Christ admitteth children to his presence, imbrasing and blessinge them. Which testimonies of the Holy Ghoste assure us...'[12] The guidance for the administration of baptism in the Westminster Assembly's *Directory for the Publick Worship of God* (1645) made this summary a little more explicit: 'That the Son of God admitted little children into his presence, embracing and blessing them, saying, *For of such is the kingdome of God.*'[13] It is worth noting that this quotation is from the verse which the

---

[8] *Book of Common Order of the Church of Scotland* (Edinburgh, 1994), pp. 83-84; *Book of Common Order of the Church of Scotland* (London, 1940), pp. 90, 92. The shorter-lived 1979 *Book* never gained the acceptance of 1940. Its baptismal service differed little from the 1940 *Book* in providing for our Synoptic reading and in also picking it up later in a prayer: 'remembering the welcome and the blessing that your Son gave to the little children...', *The Book of Common Order* (Edinburgh, 1979), pp. 47, 52. *The Reformed Book of Common Order* produced by the National Church Association (1977), less fashionable liturgically, was ahead of the competition in omitting the blessing of the children altogether.

[9] *Euchologion: or Book of Prayers* (Edinburgh, 1867), p. 13.

[10] *Book of Common Order* (London, 1928), p. 40.

[11] Fisher, *Reformation Period*, pp. 31, 36, 40, 115, 127, 131. They vary in which Gospel's text they prescribe.

[12] Fisher, *Reformation Period*, p. 120; W.D. Maxwell, *The Liturgical Portions of the Genevan Service Book* (Westminster, 1965 [1931]), p. 106—Knox's 1556 book, *The Liturgy of John Knox* Received by the Church of Scotland in 1564 (Glasgow, 1886), p. 154.

[13] *The Confession of Faith...The Directory for Publick Worship...* (Edinburgh, 1963), p. 150.

1940 *Common Order* omitted from its prescription of Mark 10.13-14, 16. A possible reason for this omission will soon become apparent.

Despite the centuries-long lack of a specific ordering of a baptismal reading of the Synoptic blessing of the children in the Scottish Kirk (parallel, that is, to the prescription in the *Book of Common Prayer*), it was in Scotland in the mid-twentieth century that the hypothesis of a linguistically-grounded connexion between these Synoptic texts and liturgical usage in early Christian baptism received strong endorsement in influential circles of church theology. Joachim Jeremias and Oscar Cullmann in the 1940s and 1950s picked up and elaborated a suggestion of earlier German scholars that the formulation of Mark 10.13-16 and parallels in several places contain indirect references to baptism. This suggests the conclusion that the narrative of the blessing of the children was important for the early church not only on other grounds, but because the church took it as authority for the practice of infant baptism.[14] Cullmann, who leaned heavily on the occurrence of the Greek verb κωλύειν, 'prevent', not only in all three Gospels but also in other references to baptisms in early Christian sources, claimed that 'this story—without being related to Baptism—was fixed in such a way that a baptismal formula of the first century gleams through it'.[15]

It may fairly be said that it was in these decades in the middle of the last century, and in the writings of scholars such as Cullmann and Jeremias, that the quest for historical verification of the apostolic origins of infant baptism reached a maximalist peak. (As a student at Cambridge I remember Professor C.F.D. Moule commenting with a characteristic twinkle in his eye that Jeremias' *Infant Baptism* contained *at least* all the evidence.) The Church of Scotland's Special Commission on Baptism (1954–63) espoused a similar maximalism in reading the biblical and patristic sources, citing both Cullmann and Jeremias and concluding that 'the Evangelists intend us to interpret that blessing [by Jesus] in terms of [the children's] baptism'.[16] It was the thinking and writing of T.F. Torrance that lay behind the extensive reports of the Special Commission. The prominence of (most of) Mark 10.13-16 in the 1940 *Book of Common Order* combined with the influence of Torrance and other Scottish theologians (the books of Cullmann and Jeremias were translated into English by Scottish theologians, not New Testament or patristic scholars) to give the Scottish Kirk a particular attachment to the passage's

---

[14] J. Jeremias, *Infant Baptism in the First Four Centuries* (trans. David Cairns; London, 1960), pp. 54-55, cf. pp. 48-55.

[15] O. Cullmann, *Baptism in the New Testament* (trans. J.K.S. Reid; London, 1950), p. 78, cf. pp. 71-80.

[16] 'Interim Report', in *Reports to the General Assembly of the Church of Scotland 1955* (Edinburgh, 1955), pp. 631-33; Special Commission, *The Biblical Doctrine of Baptism* (Edinburgh, 1958), pp. 48-49.

baptismal interpretation. Had not Calvin spoken of 'this shield against the Anabaptists' in commenting on these verses?[17]

Nevertheless, the revisers of baptismal liturgies in other traditions seem more or less of a common mind as we enter the twenty-first century. The reading of this Synoptic incident in baptizing babies, which has prevailed since the Reformation, is being abandoned in favour of other New Testament passages which speak explicitly of baptism without specific reference to young children—for no such baptismal references are found in the New Testament. If Mark 10.13-16 and its parallels have an appropriate place, it seems to belong, so recent revised service books are telling us, to non-baptismal thanksgiving for a child's birth or adoption. In commenting on this feature in the Anglican *Alternative Service Book*, Jasper and Bradshaw cite in support some words of Ian T. Ramsey in 1971, when he was chairman of the Church of England's Doctrine Commission:

> In the first place Jesus showed a welcoming attitude towards children who had no claim on him, and whose parents, it seems, entered into no obligations. Second, he rebuked his disciples who thought this inappropriate.
>
> Third, he took the opportunity to explain what entry into the Kingdom meant and its preconditions, and finally he blessed them.[18]

We will return briefly at the end to the implications of this departure from a tradition going back to the Reformation. The Reformers were quite capable of starting traditions, in this case partly by an ignorance of the earlier development of orders for baptizing infants—an ignorance for which they were not in the least culpable. Furthermore, the development in question cannot be regarded as the most felicitous in the history of infant baptism. Focusing, then, on the baptismal fortunes of this Gospel pericope in relation to the church's service of paedobaptism casts some light on the contorted evolution of paedobaptism itself.

Despite the arguments of Cullmann, Jeremias and others, there is very little evidence that the early church associated the blessing of little children by Jesus with baptism.[19] This is not merely a matter of a lack of evidence for the reading of one of the three accounts when babies were baptized. Nearly everything we know of baptismal liturgy in the age of the Fathers shows us believer's baptism, so that it would be anachronistic

---

[17] J. Calvin, *Commentaries on a Harmony of the Gospels Matthew, Mark and Luke*, ad loc. (trans. T.H.L. Parker; Edinburgh, 1972), II, p. 252.

[18] Jasper and Bradshaw, *A Companion*, p. 346, citing *Baptism, Thanksgiving and Blessing*, an Anglican Doctrine Commission report of 1971.

[19] Shown in summary fashion by C.E. Pocknee, 'The Gospel Lection in the Rite of Infant Baptism', *Theology* 62 (1959), pp. 496-99 at pp. 496-97.

to draw conclusions from the silence enveloping the use or non-use of Mark 10.13-16 in the baptism of infants. Such information as can be gleaned about the changes made to accommodate young children as the recipients of baptism suggests that they were minimal. When evidence begins to become available for the inclusion of infants in the baptismal rite, first unambiguously in the Hippolytan *Apostolic Tradition* in Rome early in the third century, the only observable change is that the little ones 'who cannot speak for themselves' are baptized first, with parents or other relatives speaking for them.[20] The earliest attestation of how such youngsters were spoken for emerges around the late fourth and early fifth centuries: the parent or other sponsor is asked by the minister about the child 'Does he/she believe?' —precisely so in the third person.[21]

The inclusion of children with minimal dislocation in a rite constructed for persons able to answer the baptismal questions for themselves is clear from the *Apostolic Constitutions*, compiled probably in Syria around AD 400. At the end of its instructions for baptism, which patently presuppose recipients of responsible years, comes the direction, 'Baptize also your infants, for it says, " Let the children come to me and do not prevent them" '.[22] This citation of Luke 18.16 (or possibly Mark 10.14) is the first occasion in patristic literature when this Synoptic passage unambiguously supports the baptizing of babies. The text tells us nothing, however, about the content of the rite, but it is significant in its simple clarity of baptismal reference.

The only other patristic writer before Augustine to reveal a connexion between our Gospel passages and paedobaptism is an opponent of paedobaptism, Tertullian of Carthage, very early in the third century. His treatise on baptism, after counselling its deferment in the case of children, acknowledges that the Lord said (*ait quidem Dominu*s), 'Do not prevent them coming to me', but responds, 'So let them come when they grow up (*adolescunt*), when they learn, when they are taught what they are coming to'.[23] The citation is nearest to Matthew 19.14, but the inferences to be drawn from the passage are far from clear. Tertullian is interpreted more often as opposing established practice than as resisting an innovation.

---

[20] Geoffrey J. Cuming, *Hippolytus: A Text for Students* (Grove Liturgical Studies, 8; Bramcote, 1976), p. 18.

[21] The witnesses are homilies of Asterius (now redated to c.AD 400); see W. Kinzig, *In Search of Asterius* (Göttingen, 1990), and Augustine; J.C. Didier, 'Une Adaptation de la liturgie baptismale au baptême des enfants dans l'église ancienne', *Mélanges de science religieuse* 22 (1965), pp. 79-90.

[22] *Apostolic Constitutions* 6:15:7. M. Metzger (ed.), (*SC* 329; Paris, 1986), II, pp. 344-45. Pocknee, 'The Gospel Lection', p. 497, by a strange confusion credits the work with recording Augustine's initiation into the catechumenate as a baby.

[23] Tertullian, *Baptism* 18:5, ed. Ernest Evans (London, 1964), pp. 38-39, adopting the translation given in his note, p. 105.

Pocknee argues that he places the meaning of *parvuli* at the upper end of its breadth of meaning which encompasses 'any child from a babe in arms to an adolescent'. He furthermore claims that the North African church at the time did not employ any of the three Synoptic narratives as a warrant for infant baptism, since 'otherwise Tertullian's argument is meaningless'.[24] If Pocknee's first point simply highlights Tertullian's virtuosity in controversy, there may be more to the second than at first sight appears, although more often than not the citation of Matthew 19.14 has been assumed to attest precisely the opposite—that it was deployed as justifying the baptism of infants. Pocknee may well be right to the extent that it cannot have been a regular lection in an infant-baptizing rite, for then Tertullian's rejoinder would have had little force. But that some in the Carthaginian Christian community took it to warrant baby-baptism is, I judge, beyond doubt. Tertullian's writings frequently allow us to glimpse informal debates about the interpretation of scripture among local believers.

Yet not everything is straightforward. On another occasion than this essay, Tertullian's famous but frustratingly elusive text deserves more detailed re-examination. At approximately what age, for example, did he think baptism appropriate? Ill-shaped modern discussion is inclined to set only 'adult' over against 'infants', so that the other category Tertullian addresses here, the unmarried, both virgins and widows, may have too quickly encouraged the assumption that delay until adult years is his concern throughout. Perhaps too the Cullmann–Jeremias hypothesis of a κωλύειν-formula ('What hinders baptism...?') merits revisiting in this context, for in the majority of its alleged occurrences, including its earliest patently baptismal one, in Acts 8.36, it has to do with the baptism of believers, not of very young children. As too often in the consideration of the early history of Christian baptism, a preoccupation with paedobaptism's origins may have slanted the enquiry prejudicially. In this instance, starting out on the trail of a supposed 'hindrance-formula' from Mark 10.14 par. may have unhelpfully limited the conceivable options. On the face of it, one of the strangest features of this paragraph in Tertullian's *De baptismo* is his interpreting 'Forbid them not to come to me' in terms not of *parvuli* in any obvious sense of the noun (*pace* Pocknee) but of, let us surmise, young teenagers or older. Did the 'κωλύειν-formula' function at first only with believing respondents? Was it this formula that later suggested a connexion between the Synoptic narrative and the baptism of infants when, *ex hypothesi*, it became more common in the later second century? Are developments of this kind behind Tertullian's puzzling text?

---

[24] Pocknee, 'The Gospel Lection', p. 497.

Many interpreters, to be sure, have no trouble making sense of the passage, and especially of the role of Matthew 19.14. They might be less confident if they were aware how exceptional among the church Fathers is this association between the Gospel pericope to which it belongs and infant baptism. The only other witness is the *Apostolic Constitutions* noticed above. The commonest treatment of the text finds the key in the phrase 'for of such—not " of these" !—is the kingdom of heaven' (Mk 10.14 par.), combined with citation of another of Jesus' sayings which makes childhood a pattern for his disciples. Clement of Alexandria turns to the training of the children in his *Paidagogus* (*Instructor*) 1.5, immediately declaring that 'We are the children'. He quotes John 21.4-5 and Matthew 19.13-14, and then asserts that Matthew 18.3, 'Unless you are converted and become like little children...' is Christ's own explanation of what Matthew 19 means. In terms that might almost seem deliberately to exclude a baptismal reference, he denies that the Lord was 'speaking figuratively of regeneration', but merely 'setting before us, for our imitation, the simplicity that is in children'.[25]

Clement at no point in his works mentions infant baptism. His more illustrious successor in Alexandria, Origen, does so openly, and yet his more extended expositions of the blessing of the children show no inclination to link it with children's baptism. A brief citation of Matthew 19.14 in his commentary on the Song of Songs sets it in the context of the spiritual infancy of 1 Corinthians 3.1-2. A fragment of his commentary on Lamentations depicts 'the little children' of the Matthean text as 'Jews childish in their understanding' whom the disciples of Jesus sought to net as 'fishers of men'.[26] Then in a lengthy section of his commentary on the Gospel itself, the tone is set early on:

> By 'children' we mean those who in Christ are still carnal and infantile, such as Paul the apostle knew the Corinthians to be when he said, 'And I could not speak to you as spiritual...' (1 Corinthians 3.1). Children of this kind both were then and are continually 'offered to Jesus'. A sign of the 'bringing of infants' is the multitude in the church who are infants and sucklings in Christ, 'needing milk, not solid food' (Heb. 5.12).

Paul said the same of suchlike in 1 Corinthians 3.2, and spoke of nursing them as one's own children in 1 Thessalonians 2.7. Origen has ample scope to enlarge on that numerous body of Christians whom he designated 'the simpler souls' (ἁπλούστεροι; in Latin *simpliciores*). They are not to be despised, for did not Jesus not only historically but

---

[25] Clement of Alexandria, *Paidagogus* 1.5, *ANCL* vol. 4, p. 122.
[26] *Commentaire sur le Cantique des Cantiques* (ed. L. Brésard *et al.*; SC 375; Paris, 1991), pp. 324-25 (extant only in Rufinus' Latin); *Origenes Werke* III: *Jeremiahomilien...* (ed. Erich Klostermann; GCS 6; Leipzig, 1901), p. 275, nr. CXIV.

also figuratively become a child in humility and meekness? These childish or childlike ones will be saved as we ourselves become children with children. Origen rings the changes on more than one interpretative framework, but never gets near to a baptismal allusion touching real babies.[27]

Fourth-century interpreters of the blessing narrative are more numerous than pre-Nicene. Hilary of Poitiers' exposition of Matthew's Gospel fastens on the disciples' attempt to prevent the children coming to the Lord. He attributes it to a desire to fulfil a typological design, for these children are the image (*forma*) of the Gentiles who would receive salvation by the hearing of faith (cf. Romans 10.17). Their action therefore did not bespeak unapostolic severity. The gift of the Holy Spirit was indeed to be bestowed on Gentiles by the laying on of hands and prayer, once the work of the law lapsed.[28] Hilary may have in mind the narrative of Acts 8.14-17, but even so is not prompted to refer to baptism. Elsewhere Hilary makes only one brief use of our pericope, in one of his Psalms exegeses when invoking the innocence of these children, for 'of such is the kingdom of heaven'.[29]

Hilary's two works were written in the middle decades of the century. Jerome's commentary on Matthew, written at the end of the century, offers an influential reading of Jesus' words:

> It is significant that he said 'of such', not 'of these', to show that manner of life (*mores*) and not age was what counted, and that a reward was promised to those who had a like innocence and simplicity.

Paul said the same in 1 Corinthians 14.20: 'Brothers, do not be childish (*pueri*) in thought, but infants (*parvuli*) in evil.'[30] Jerome's brief explanation may depend on the commentary on the same Gospel by Apollinarius of Laodicea. Extant only in catena extracts, it likewise cited 1 Corinthians 14.20 in support of 'not "of these" but "of such"', and also other Gospel sayings about becoming like a child (Mark 10.14-15; Matthew 18.4).[31] Jerome's short paragraph in turn constitutes the greater

---

[27] *Origenes Werke* X: *Matthäuserklärung* I (ed. Erich Klostermann; *GCS* 40; Leipzig, 1935), pp. 361-73. A much abridged translation is given by Harold Smith, *Ante-Nicene Exegesis of the Gospels*, IV (Translations of Christian Literature, ser. VI; London, 1928), pp. 224-27.

[28] Hilaire de Poitiers, *Sur Matthieu* II (ed. Jean Doignon; *SC* 258; Paris, 1979), pp. 90-93.

[29] Hilary, *Tractatus super Psalmos* 63[64].12 (ed. A. Zingerle; *CSEL* 22; Vienna, 1891), p. 232.

[30] Jerome, *Comment. in Matheum* III, *ad loc.* (ed. D. Hurst and M. Adriaen; *CCSL* 77; Turnhout, 1969), p. 169.

[31] Joseph Reuss, *Matthäus-Kommentare aus der Griechischen Kirche* (*TU*, 61; Berlin, 1957), pp. 31-32.

part of Bede's expositions of the Markan and Lukan passages.[32] Even in an era when infant baptism was becoming the norm, it did not warrant a mention.

Ambrose's more thoughtful interpretation in his Lukan commentary argues that Jesus cannot have been commending the age of infancy—'weak in physical strength, feeble in wit, immature in wisdom'—over any other age. Otherwise why did Jesus choose adult apostles? 'Therefore not childhood but goodness rivalling a child's simplicity is indicated', as Jesus himself made clear, 'Unless you are converted and become like this child...' (Matthew 18.3). 'So there is in childhood a kind of venerable old age of behaviour, and in old age an innocent childhood', for which he adduces Wisdom 4.8-9. Ambrose continues at length, in praise of 'childlike simplicity'.[33] Nor does any baptismal reference emerge in his two other treatments of the Gospel verses. On Psalm 36.25, 'I was young and I grew old', Matthew 19.14 with 18.3 show that Christ himself taught that 'childhood (*pueritiam*, here perhaps 'boyhood') is strength'. The Latin word is *virtutem*, but in the context, in which Ambrose introduces the 'athlete' of Christ, 'and athletes are called *pueri*', Greek παῖδες, vigour seems intended more than virtue. The precise nuance need not concern the present enquiry overmuch.[34]

Ambrose's third usage introduces a new note in relating Matthew 19.13-15 to the preceding vv. 10-12 on eunuchs. They were followed by the bringing of children for blessing because these were ignorant of corruption and in their spotless age had preserved their natural integrity. 'For of such is the kingdom of heaven—that is, those who have returned to childlike chastity...as though to the condition of infants.'[35] Basil of Caesarea adduces Jesus' acceptance of young children brought to him, together with 2 Timothy 3.15 ('From a child you have known...') and Ephesians 6.4 ('bring up your children in the discipline and instruction of the Lord'), to support his judgment that 'every time, even of the first stage of life, is appropriate for those who come forward for acceptance' into the monastic calling. Basil surrounds this counsel, which appears in different versions of his monastic rules, with safeguards on parental involvement, but how such infant consecration might relate to infant

---

[32] Bede, *Opera* II.3 (ed. D. Hurst; *CCSL* 120; Turnhout, 1960), pp. 325-26, 559.

[33] Ambrose, *Expos. evang. sec. Lucam* 8:57-61, *ad loc.* (ed. M. Adriaen; *CCSL* 14; Tunrhout, 1957), pp. 319-21.

[34] Ambrose, *Explanatio Psalmorum XII* 36.52 (ed. M. Petschenig; *CSEL* 64; Vienna/Leipzig, 1919), pp. 110-11.

[35] Ambrose, *Virginity* 30, in Franco Gori (ed.), *Sant' Ambrogio, Opere morali* II.ii (Milan, 1989), pp. 32-35.

baptism is never clarified.[36] I have elsewhere raised questions which merit further investigation about the different kinds of infant dedication attested in the fourth century and beyond, when infant baptism is very rarely in evidence.[37] Basil's monastic texts illustrate for the first time a more literal reading of the Synoptic incident, but in terms of monastic initiation, not baptism. The treatise on baptism generally accepted as Basil's work three times cites Mark 10.15 ('receive the kingdom of God as a little child...') but always in terms addressed to readers of responsible years. The treatise ends as follows:

> It is necessary and salutary to believe [the Lord] as infants believe their parents and children their teachers, according to the word of our Lord Jesus Christ himself, 'Whoever does not receive the kingdom of God as a little child shall never enter it'.[38]

Basil mentions infant baptism in none of his writings. Despite the subject of this treatise, it is impossible to interpret his citations of Mark 10.15 as implying any suggestion of a paedobaptist interpretation. The first occurrence is preceded by Matthew 18.3 ('...are converted and become like little children...') and that in turn by Matthew 5.20, on the righteousness which exceeds that of scribes and Pharisees.[39] We should not be surprised. Infant baptism seems absent from Basil's consciousness.

Epiphanius of Salamis twice quotes our Synoptic passage in contexts that add nothing fresh to this enquiry. He takes 'children' in a literal sense, but at the same time they are a model for other ages.[40] Gregory of Nyssa cites Matthew 19.14 in his funeral oration on the six-year-old Pulcheria to reassure her father, Theodosius the Great, that she has

---

[36] Basil, *Regulae morales* 19 (*PG* 31, col. 733), *Asceticon magnum*, quaest. 15, 292 (*PG* 31, cols. 952, 1287); *Regula* 7:1-2 (in Rufinus' Latin) (ed. Klaus Zelzer; CSEL 86; Vienna, 1986), pp. 38-39.

[37] D.F. Wright, 'Infant Dedication in the Early Church', in S.E. Porter and A.R. Cross (eds), *Baptism, the New Testament and the Church: Historical and Contemporary Studies in Honour of R.E.O. White* (*Journal for the Study of the New Testament* Supplement Series, 171; Sheffield, 1999), pp. 352-78 (ch. 9 above).

[38] Basil, *Baptism* 2.4.2 (ed. Jeanne Ducatillon; SC 357; Paris, 1989), pp. 226-27. This passage appears to be echoed in the only unattributed (i.e. non-Jerome) section of Bede's exposition of the pericope in Mark and Luke. See n. 32 above. Bede's text likens a child's obedience to the gospel to a pupil's unquestioning acceptance of what his teachers present.

[39] Basil, *Baptism* 1.2.2 (ed. Ducatillon, pp. 110-11); cf. 1:2:19 (pp. 166-67). In his homily on Ps 114.6 LXX [116.6], Basil briefly gives a standard rendering of receiving the kingdom as a child, in terms of humility: *PG* 29, cols. 489-92.

[40] Epiphanius, *Panarion* 64:67:3, 67:5:1-4, in Frank Williams (trans.), *The Panarion... Books II and III* (Nag Hammadi and Manichaean Studies, 36; Leiden, 1994), pp. 196, 312-13.

departed for the presence of the Lord. The Gospel passage was read as the lection for the occasion.[41] Nothing new is added by John Chrysostom's homily on Matthew 19.13-15. Jesus' acceptance of the children was designed to correct his disciples' improper sense of dignity in turning them away. The soul of the young children is pure from all passions. By choice we should practise that freedom which infants possess by nature.[42] This exposition by Chrysostom looms large in the catenae on the Synoptic Gospels from the Greek Fathers published by Cramer.[43] In none of the three Gospels is any reference to baptism discernible.

At this point we may note the collection of Latin homilies on Matthew wrongly attributed to Chrysostom which goes under the name of the *Opus Imperfectum*. Its provenance, authorship and date remain uncertain, although the writer has been viewed as a sixth-century bishop of Arian sympathies.[44] This homilist, like Ambrose earlier, made the connexion with the immediately preceding teaching in Matthew 19 on chastity. Hearing Jesus, people brought to him 'children of the purest chastity'. This sets the tone for the rest of the treatment of our text. 'Of such is the kingdom of heaven, that is, of those chaste by virtue, as children are by age.' So this author retains both a literal and a figurative meaning. The passage 'instructs all parents to offer their sons (*filios*) regularly (*indesinenter*—unceasingly) to the bishops, because in offering them to the bishops, they offer them to Christ. For it is Christ, not the bishop, who lays on hands.' Newborn babies are set *in maligno*, and hence 'must be presented so that prayer may be assiduously made over them'.[45] What the preacher has in mind is not baptism, nor any other one-off rite, but probably the regular presentation of unbaptized children to bishop or priest for sealing with the sign of the cross and other ceremonies.[46]

Cyril of Alexandria's commentary on Luke was delivered in homilies around AD 430. Before devoting most of his attention to being 'babes in wickedness' (1 Corinthians 14.20) but mature in mind, Cyril relates the passage to church practice:

> Infants even to the present time are brought near and blessed by Christ by means of consecrated hands: and the pattern of the act continues even until this day, and descends unto us from the custom of Christ as its fountain. Only the bringing near

---

[41] Gregory of Nyssa, *Opera* IX: *Sermones* I (ed. G. Heil *et al.*; Leiden, 1967), p. 465.

[42] John Chrysostom, *Homilies on Matthew* 62.4, *ad. loc.* (*PG* 57, cols. 600-601).

[43] J.A. Cramer, *Catenae Graecorum Patrum in Novum Testamentum* (Oxford, 1844), I, pp. 154, 374-76, II, p. 134.

[44] See J. van Banning's extensive *Praefatio* in preparation for a new edition (*CCSL* 88; Turnhout, 1988).

[45] Ambrose, *Homily* 32 (*PG* 56, cols. 804-805).

[46] Cf. Wright, 'Infant Dedication', pp. 353-62 (pp. 117-25 above).

of infants takes not place now in an unbecoming or disorderly manner, but with proper order, and sobriety and fear.[47]

To what is Cyril referring? His translator is sure that it is the laying on of hands that immediately followed baptism. Perhaps more likely is a pre-baptismal catechumenal context, as attested in other sources. Again noteworthy is the absence of mention of baptism.

Even Augustine himself, unrivalled champion of paedobaptism, appears not to have utilized this passage to inculcate its necessity with any frequency. The reason may lie in a paragraph in one of his earliest contributions to the debate emerging over the teachings of Pelagius and Caelestius. At issue is why infants are baptized. For Augustine the answer was 'the guilt of original sin', but 'some persons' were advancing Matthew 19.14, 'of such...', as though Jesus commended infancy as meritorious. Augustine doubts that this is the correct meaning, preferring to see tender years as an image of humility. He hastens on to ground infant baptism in a clearer text, Matthew 9.13, 'I came not to call the righteous...' At any rate, Augustine reckoned it a clearer dominical warrant.[48] His extant sermons rarely deal with the Synoptic passage. In one that belongs to the time of the Pelagian controversy, he exhorts parents and others to be diligent in bringing helpless infants to Christ for salvation, with none forbidding. He must have their baptism in mind.[49]

There is no need for the purposes of this paper to pursue further into late antiquity and the early Middle Ages the elusive paedobaptist claims on Jesus' blessing of the children. We may simply note the confirmatory evidence of two later collections. The *Glossa Ordinaria,* the standard biblical commentary of the later Middle Ages, completed by about the mid-twelfth century, on the three Gospel passages assembles no gloss that touches in any way on infant baptism. Nearly all of the *Glossa*'s sources have been reviewed earlier in this paper, so that no interpretative element is there presented which goes beyond the range covered here.[50] The same holds for Thomas Aquinas' patristic *Catena Aurea* on the four Gospels,

---

[47] Translated from the Syriac, R. Payne Smith, *A Commentary...,* II (Oxford, 1859), pp. 561-64. An extract preserved in Greek sums up the more typical figurative explanation: Joseph Reuss, *Lukas-Kommentare aus der Griechischen Kirche* (TU, 130; Berlin, 1984), p. 186.

[48] Augustine, *The Merits and Remission of Sins, and Infant Baptism* 1:19:24.

[49] Augustine, *Sermon* 115.4, in Edmund Hill (trans.), *The Works of Saint Augustine,* III/4. *Sermons 94A–147A* (Brooklyn, NY, 1992), pp. 200-201; cf. 202 nn. 12, 14. *Sermon* 174.9 has a similar anti-Pelagian citation of Mk 10.14. Mt. 19.14 in *Sermon* 353.2 is used to commend humility to newly-baptized believers.

[50] Most conveniently seen in the facsimile reprint of the earliest printed edition (Strasbourg, 1480–81), in K. Froehlich and M.T. Gibson (eds), *Biblia Latina...* (4 vols; Turnhout, 1992), IV, pp. 62, 115, 203.

compiled in the early 1260s. All of his sources on the three Synoptic parallel texts have been considered in this study apart from two: the commentaries of Theophylact, archbishop of Ohrid in Bulgaria (died after 1125), and an unidentified Remig[ius].[51] The former supplies nothing not rehearsed here already, for Theophylact closely followed earlier expositors. The latter, who is most probably Remigius of Auxerre (died c. 908), provides two short extracts on Matthew. The first is of some interest:

> It was also a custom among the ancients that little children be presented to older persons, to be blessed by their hand or mouth. It was according to this custom that little children were offered to the Lord.[52]

It would be worthwhile knowing what Thomas' source was for this extract, since it adds a fresh element to the sum total of patristic (or early medieval) interpretations.

It is not part of this investigation to pursue exegesis of the Synoptic passages in Gospel commentaries of the medieval centuries. We have seen that, apart from two texts, the Fathers failed to associate Jesus' blessing of infants with infant baptism. The exceptions are Tertullian on *Baptism* and the *Apostolic Constitutions*, neither of which in the Latin West seems to have had much influence. Even Augustine did not cite Jesus' words and actions in favour of infant baptism as fulsomely as might have been expected.

The reforms of the baptismal liturgies carried out in the sixteenth century cannot therefore at this point claim patristic precedent. Earlier in this essay note was taken of the place of Mark 10.13-16 par. in early Reformed and Anglican orders. Luther himself from his first German *Taufbüchlein* of 1523 incorporated the Markan passage. Indeed, he adopted the text with a special zeal as the clear example and command of the Lord for infants to be baptized.[53]

If we then ask the derivation of this almost invariable early Protestant usage, the answer lies in the pre-baptismal order for the making of a

---

[51] Thomas Aquinas, *Catena Aurea...* (ed. A. Guarienti; Turin, 1953), I, pp. 283-84, 509, II, p. 247; English translation, *Catena Aurea: Commentary on the Four Gospels* (Oxford, 1843), I/II, pp. 659-62, II, pp. 198-99, III/II, pp. 607-608.

[52] Thomas, *Catena Aurea* I, p. 284; *Commentary* I/II, p. 660. Thomas included a paraphrase in his own *Lectura* on Matthew (ed. R. Cai; Turin, 5th edn, 1951), pp. 241-42. The extract is not found in Remigius' homilies on Matthew in *PL* 131, cols. 865-932, but these seem to be selections from a larger manuscript exposition: cf. *PL* 131, col. 117; L. Scheffczyck, *Lexikon für Theologie und Kirche* (Freiburg, 2nd edn, 1957–67), VIII, cols. 1223-25, at 1224.

[53] Bruno Jordahn, 'Der Taufgottesdienst im Mittelalter bis zur Gegenwart', in K.F. Müller and W. Blankenburg (eds), *Leiturgia: Handbuch des Evangelischen Gottesdienstes*, V: *Der Taufgottesdienst* (Kassel, 1970), pp. 349-640, at pp. 357, 371-72, 420-21.

catechumen which had come to function almost as the preliminary phase of the baptismal occasion as a whole, but carried out not inside the church at the font but outside the church door. This is abundantly attested in the earliest printed baptismal liturgies and throughout the sixteenth century and beyond in the Roman Church.[54] It can be seen in the Sarum baptismal order, which was in widespread use in England on the eve of the Reformation. As part of the *Ordo ad faciendum Catechumenum*, Matthew 19.13-15 was read after two prayers, the first of which was said with the priest's hand on the infant's head, and immediately before the Effeta ceremony (or Ephphatha; cf. Mark 7.13).[55] Only later is the child taken into the church for baptism. The connexions suggest that the Gospel pericope of Jesus' laying hands on children (Matthew and Mark) was enlisted as dominical warrant not for the baptism but, with precise equivalence, for the imposition of hands in their admission as catechumens. This is how scholars generally understand the place of this brief Gospel lection in what had become by the late medieval era a strange recruitment into the infant catechumenate immediately before baptism.[56] It can be tracked further back to the eighth to tenth centuries.[57]

Its earlier history reflects a period when infant candidates were being accommodated within a pattern of initiation designed for responding believers, with baptism at Easter preceded by the Lenten weeks of catechetical preparation. The Gelasian Sacramentary in its various forms presents practice in Rome in the seventh and even sixth century and elsewhere later. The three scrutinies that took place on the third, fourth and fifth Sundays in Lent in this type of baptismal order attracted to themselves, first, it seems, outside of Rome, respectively the three lections Matthew 19.13-14, Mark 10.13-16 and Luke 18.15-16. This development had taken place by the eighth century. Rome itself earlier used only Matthew 11.25-30 for these scrutinies, but this passage also

---

[54] See A. Dold, *Die Konstanzer Ritualientexte in ihrer Entwicklung von 1482–1721* (Liturgiegeschichtliche Quellen, 5–6; Münster in Westf., 1923), pp. 9, 18, 23, 34; H.J. Spital, *Der Taufritus in den deutschen Ritualien von den ersten Drucken bis zur Einführung des Rituale Romanum* (Liturgiegeschichtliche Quellen und Forschungen 47; Münster in Westf., 1968), pp. 89-91; Jordahn, 'Der Taufgottesdienst', pp. 371-72.

[55] J.D.C. Fisher, *Christian Initiation: Baptism in the Medieval West* (Alcuin Club Collections, 47; London, 1965), pp. 5, 164; W. Maskell, *Monumenta Ritualia Ecclesiae Anglicanae*, I (London, 1846), p. 11; Pocknee, 'The Gospel Lection', p. 499.

[56] E.g., Fisher, *Medieval West*, pp. 4-5, following Pocknee, 'The Gospel Lection', pp. 498-99.

[57] C. Lambot, *North Italian Services of the Eleventh Century* (Henry Bradshaw Society, 67; London, 1931), p. 10 (Lk. 18.15-16); G. Kretschmar, 'Die Geschichte des Taufgottesdienstes in der Alten Kirche', in Müller and Blankenburg (eds), *Leiturgia*, V, pp. 1-348, at pp. 306-307, 332.

speaks of babies.⁵⁸ Elsewhere, for example in Milan, only one of the three Synoptic versions was used, normally Matthew 19.13-14(15), with different lections on the two other scrutinies.⁵⁹ The three lections are recorded also in lectionaries, that is, lists of the biblical lections, for Rome and Würzburg in the seventh and eighth centuries.⁶⁰

It seems clear, then, that the Gospel story of the reception and blessing of children by Jesus first came into liturgical focus in the setting of the pre-paschal catechumenate as this was adapted to embrace children. This development can be placed broadly in the sixth century. The inclusion of these Gospel lections was one of the least incongruous aspects of this process of adjustment. At the opposite, dissonant end of the spectrum lay the requirement that infants too, like candidates answering for themselves, should recite the creed and repeat the Lord's Prayer. This was met by the priest placing his hand on their heads and doing the recitations on their behalf.⁶¹

We are reminded that, whatever historical conclusions we reach concerning the early development of the practice of baptizing babies, evidence of liturgical formulation to cater for it scarcely emerges before the end of the patristic era, perhaps not until the sixth century. For some time before this, and certainly for much of the fourth century and well into the fifth, the majority of children born to Christian parents had not been baptized but were enrolled in the catechumenate at birth. The commonest ritual for this purpose was sealing with the sign of the cross, but Augustine, who is the best-known witness to this observance, knew that he had also been seasoned with salt. What we can scarcely trace as yet is the use of laying on of hands, and with it the possible reading of one of our three Gospel passages, for such infant dedications during a century or more that seems almost not to have known infant baptism. Cyril of Alexandria appears to distinguish between the chrism of the

---

⁵⁸ Pocknee, 'The Gospel Lection', p. 498. Fisher, *Medieval West*, pp. 4-5; H.A. Wilson, *The Gelasian Sacramentary* (Oxford, 1894), pp. 34, 38, 42 (without the lections); L.C. Mohlberg, *Liber Sacramentorum Romanae Aecclesiae Ordinis Anni Circuli (Sacramentarium Gelasianum)* (Rerum Ecclesiasticarum Documenta, Series Maior, Fontes IV; Rome, 1960), pp. viii-ix, 36, 39, 53-54 (without the lections).

⁵⁹ A. Dondeyne, 'La Discipline des Scrutins', *Revue d'histoire ecclésiastique* 28 (1932), pp. 5-33, 751-87, at pp. 28-31, 776.

⁶⁰ W.H. Frere, *Studies in Early Roman Liturgy. II. The Roman Gospel-Lectionary* (Alcuin Club Collections, 30; London, 1934), p. 28; Dondeyne, 'La Discipline', p. 773, with further literature.

⁶¹ See Antoine Chavasse, *Le Sacramentaire Gélasien* (Tournai, 1958), pp. 164-66; Dondeyne, 'La Discipline', pp. 774-77; Chavasse, 'L'initiation à Rome dans l'antiquité et le haut moyen-âge', in *Communion solennelle et profession de foi* (Lex Orandi, 14; Paris, 1952), pp. 28-31; H.O. Old, *The Shaping of the Reformed Baptismal Rite in the Sixteenth Century* (Grand Rapids, MI, 1992), pp. 6-9.

catechumenate and the chrism of baptismal initiation for newborn babies.[62] As we have noted, other suitable Gospel verses might equally have served such occasions of infant dedication. There are, then, at least hypothetical possibilities to be borne in mind as a spur to investigation of an obscure phase in the emergence of paedobaptism as the normal baptismal practice.

The fortunes of Mark 10.13-16 par. may be said to have come full circle, or at least be completing full circle. In the early centuries only marginally linked with the baptism of young children, and applied by a few Fathers to one or another non-baptismal form of blessing or dedication, it secured its liturgical place in the awkward assimilation of infants into a catechumenate for responsible believers, in the weeks before Easter. As infants came to monopolize baptism, and it increasingly took place on demand throughout the year, their catechumenal induction collapsed into an immediately pre-baptismal church-door sequence. The Protestant Reformers unified elements of this pre-baptismal observance with baptism itself within the congregational context. No doubt Mark 10.13-16 par. had its own appeal to them as Anabaptists challenged them to furnish their 'Scripture-alone' justification for baptizing babies, but unwittingly they took it over from an originally non-baptismal setting. The tradition they established has been widely questioned and often discarded in the later twentieth century and into the twenty-first. As Pocknee puts it,

> The reading of this lection at the font in connexion with infant baptism has done more than anything else to engulf Christian initiation in false sentimentality and to obscure the true meaning of Holy Baptism.[63]

It belongs more fittingly in a non-baptismal service of thanksgiving or blessing or dedication for a newborn or adopted child. Perhaps the expected Roman recovery of the catechumenate for children will find a place for it. Its removal from services of infant baptism—out again, after being brought in at the Reformation—can only serve the rediscovery of infant baptism as an ordinance or sacrament of the gospel rather than a rite of babyhood.

---

[62] Cyril of Alexandria, *Commentary on John*, on John 11.26 (*PG* 74, col. 49; and P.E. Pusey [ed.], [Oxford, 1872]), II, p. 276.

[63] Pocknee, 'The Gospel Lection', p. 499.

CHAPTER 12

Infant Baptism and the Christian Community in Bucer

The practice of baptizing newborn babies, which was perpetuated by all the branches of the magisterial Reformation, was one of the deepest storm-centres of religious conflict in the sixteenth century, not least in Strasbourg. Inherited from the old church, it had to be purged, in the judgement of the non-Lutheran Reformers at least, of the old church's damaging theological legacy—focused in the Augustinian teaching that infants dying unbaptized were lost—and the more superstitious accretions of popular piety. At the same time, its very continuation without obvious biblical precedent laid the Reformers open to sniping from Catholic opponents who claimed to discern a hypocritical inconsistency with the appeal to *Scriptura sola* (scripture alone).[1] In the life of the reformed churches there was surely no other observance of remotely comparable importance that was maintained with such an embarrassing lack of explicit biblical justification.[2]

To Radicals of every hue, whose variety and prominence created Strasbourg's religious kaleidoscope in the later 1520s and early 1530s, the retention of baby baptism was much more than a gift horse for controversialists. Bucer knew that people like Bernard Rothmann of Münster viewed paedobaptism as 'the seed-bed of the church's desolation and dereliction', responsible for causing 'the knowledge of God to perish from the earth, with scarcely a trace of the true church now

---

[1] In his 1533 treatise on *What Should be Believed about the Baptism of Infants according to the Scriptures of God* (*Quid de Baptismate Infantium...Sentiendum* [Strasbourg, 1533], cited hereafter as *QBI*), Bucer concedes that it does not belong to the *engrapha Christi instituta*, the 'things instituted by Christ that are recorded in Scripture' (sigs. A iii^v-v^r). In his 1530 Gospels commentary he expresses his frustration that the Anabaptists 'read nothing but the Holy Bible' (*Enarrationes*, f. 20r).

[2] See my essay 'George Cassander and the Appeal to the Fathers in the Sixteenth-Century Debates about Infant Baptism', in L. Grane, A. Schindler and M. Wriedt (eds), *Auctoritas Patrum. Beiträge zur Bedeutung der Kirchenväter im 15. und 16. Jahrhundert/Contributions to the Reception of the Church-Fathers in the 15th and 16th Century* (Veröffentlichungen des Instituts für Europäische Geschicthe Mainz, Abteilung Religionsgeschichte, 37; Mainz, 1993) (see ch. 13 below). Cf. H.O. Old, *The Shaping of the Reformed Baptismal Rite in the Sixteenth Century* (Grand Rapids, MI, 1992), pp. 111-44 ('The Defense of Infant Baptism by the Earliest Reformed Theologians').

visible in the world'.³ Yet his own deeply patristic formation made it almost unthinkable to abandon a tradition observed by the universal church without a break—apart from one or two hiccups—since primitive times.⁴ Consensus was a central element in Bucer's appeal to the early Fathers. The notion of a pure patristic consensus which had been the basis of a continuing consensus in subsequent centuries (and offered the best hope for recovering acceptable agreement amid present divisions)⁵ reinforced Bucer's instinctive inclination to stand by the tradition of paedobaptism.

Unequalled Champion of Infant Baptism

These various factors combined with others to make Martin Bucer probably the most dedicated, and certainly the most prolific, champion of paedobaptism among the leading Reformers. He has been called 'the unparalleled master of a theology of infant baptism that placed the sacrament in its proper perspective as an ecclesial herald of Christ's saving presence within the church'.⁶ According to Francois Wendel, 'the baptism of infants found no more convinced apologist than Bucer in the years 1533–34'.⁷ His versatility certainly knew no bounds; Peter Stephens counted 'more than twenty specific grounds for the baptism of infants' advanced in the years 1524–36.⁸ And it is important to note that 'The single permanent element of coercion in the new order [the Strasbourg church ordinance of 1534] was the requirement, aimed at the sects, that all children born to citizens must be baptized as infants.'⁹ Of this settlement Bucer was naturally the chief architect. Babies must be

---

³ *QBI*, sig. E ii^{rv}.

⁴ Cf. *QBI*, sig. C vii^v: 'what the universal church holds, and has always been retained without having been instituted by councils, is most assuredly believed to have been handed down not without apostolic authority'.

⁵ See especially the Preface to the 1536 Gospels commentary, edition of Geneva 1553, ff. *ii^r-iii^v, and D.F. Wright, *Common Places of Martin Bucer* (Courtenay Library of Reformation Classics, 4; Appleford, 1972), pp. 40-41.

⁶ J.G. Lynch, 'Martin Bucer's Theology of Infant Baptism in the Light of the Reformation Paedobaptism Crisis' (dissertation, Institut Catholique, Paris, 1967), p. 244.

⁷ F. Wendel, *L'Église de Strasbourg: sa constitution et son organisation, 1533–1534* (Paris, 1942), p. 37. G. Hammann, *Entre la secte et la cité. Le projet d'église du réformateur Martin Bucer (1491–1551)* (Geneva, 1984), p. 207, speaks of his 'indefectible adherence to paedobaptism'.

⁸ W.P. Stephens, *The Holy Spirit in the Theology of Martin Bucer* (Cambridge, 1970), p. 224 n. 3.

⁹ T.A. Brady, Jr, *Ruling Class, Regime and Reformation at Strasbourg, 1520–1555* (Leiden, 1978), p. 247. For the text see *BDS* V, pp. 31-32, and Wendel, *L'Église de Strasbourg, passim*.

brought for baptism within six weeks of birth, on pain of punishment, including banishment, for parents who refused. And if the Council of the city knew of such refusal, it would instruct the baptism on its own authority.

The strictness of these measures reflects not only the peculiar vigour of the Radicals' protest in Strasbourg—in articulate sophistication more than mere numbers—but also the strength of the conviction that invariable paedobaptism was essential to the preservation of the unified Christian community. When paedobaptism was at issue, that tendency in Bucer's thought which assimilated the religious community to the civil was paramount.[10] This perspective even allowed the justification—with an appeal to Plato—of the baptism of the offspring of godless parents on the grounds that they belong more to the *respublica* ('der gemein und stadt') than to their own parents.[11] Yet although the social function of the rite, as providing the minimum basis for treating the whole population as a single, Christian, community, must be assumed to be a powerfully pervasive consideration, not least in the minds of Strasbourg's magistrates, it does not surface often in Bucer's writings.

A Developing Baptismal Theology

Since the interest of this essay lies in the way Bucer related infant baptism to the church, there is no need to trace the general development of the Reformer's understanding of baptism.[12] But it will be worthwhile reminding ourselves of the remarkable distance his baptismal theology travelled, by comparing his earliest and his final standpoints.

During the 1520s Bucer's discussions of baptism were mostly directed against Catholics. They were marked by a sharp distinction between two baptisms: 'By the baptism of water we are received into the outward church of God, by the baptism of the Spirit into the inward.' It is a matter of hope (*speremus*) that 'those received into the church through baptism

---

[10] See Martin Greschat, 'The Relation between Church and Civil Community in Bucer's Reforming Work', in D.F. Wright (ed.), *Martin Bucer: Reforming Church and Community* (Cambridge, 1994), pp. 17-31.

[11] *Advice from Holy Scripture* (*Bericht auss der Heyligen Geschrift*, 1534), BDS 5, p. 234, cited by Wendel, *L'Église de Strasbourg*, p. 175. In his Romans commentary of 1536 in a similar statement he calls Christ 'their greater parent' (*Metaphrases et Enarrationes...ad Romanos*, p. 331; Wright, *Common Places of Martin Bucer*, p. 307).

[12] See J.M. Usteri, 'Die Stellung der Strassburger Reformatoren Bucer und Capito zur Tauffrage', *Theologische Studien und Kritiken* 57 (1884), pp. 456-525; Lynch, 'Martin Bucer's Theology of Infant Baptism'; K. Heine, 'Die Taufe bei Martin Bucer' (dissertation, Vienna, 1970); Stephens, *Holy Spirit*, pp. 221-37; R. Bornert, *La Réforme protestante du culte à Strasbourg au XVIe siècle* (Leiden, 1981), pp. 339-70; Hammann, *Entre la secte et la cité*, especially pp. 199-211.

are Christ's and will be renewed by his Spirit'—for 'reprobate goats' as well as 'elect sheep' are alike baptized.[13] Of one thing Bucer was certain, that the rite of baptism conveyed no inward reality, and he seems to have believed that the baptism of Christ or the Spirit was rarely, if ever, imparted along with the water ceremony. He put it thus in his Ephesians commentary of 1527:

> Faith and the Spirit are God's gift; he bestows them when he sees fit, not at our word. Certainly those who, as believers already, were baptized by the apostles, had previously been sealed by the Holy Spirit and received faith: what then did baptism or the word of the baptizer confer on them? So too our infants: if they were chosen of God before the foundations of the world were laid, the Lord will grant them the Spirit and faith when he sees fit, but our washing them with water will not for one moment grant them faith or God's Spirit—as some important persons affirm, no less ill-advisedly than irreligiously.[14]

Thus the Bucer of the mid-1520s accommodated infant baptism by minimizing it. On hearing of Carlstadt's rejection of the observance, Bucer and his colleagues told Luther that 'In this controversy we take comfort from the fact that baptism is an external.' Although the baptism solely of adults confessing Christ would comply better with scripture and the church's primitive usage (as well as undermine misplaced confidence in water baptism), 'nevertheless we should not be too reluctant to concede this to the general consensus, that we baptize infants'.[15] Capito and Bucer said much the same to Zwingli and Oecolampadius in the same month, November 1524.[16]

To Bucer in 1526 it was patent from Titus 3.5-6 and Ephesians 5.25-26 that 'purification and regeneration are ascribed to the Spirit and the Word, and in no sense to that weak and beggarly element of the world, water':

> For the apparently regular attribution by Holy Writ of cleansing from sin and renewal of life to baptism is done in such a way as to make it readily obvious to a sound eye that these are achieved by the baptism of Christ who baptizes with the Spirit, and not by the baptism of a human being baptizing with water.[17]

---

[13] *In Ioh.* (1528), *BOL* II, pp. 73, 72.

[14] Cited by Usteri, 'Die Stellung', p. 463 n.2.

[15] *attamen hoc tribuere communi consensui haud ita gravaremur, ut infantes ablueremus*, in *BCor* I, p. 292, no. 83.

[16] *forte non gravatim ferremus parvulos baptizari*, *BCor* I, p. 285, no. 81. See Stephens, *Holy Spirit*, p. 224, for a similarly grudging attitude on Bucer's part.

[17] *Apologia...circa Christi Caenam* (1526), p. 12; Wright, *Common Places of Martin Bucer*, pp. 319-20.

In the 1527 commentary on the Synoptic Gospels Bucer can still declare that, in the liberty won by Christ's blood,

> as now we baptize infants since the advantage of the churches requires it, so too, if it required something different, we would not be at all reluctant to delay baptizing infants, while ever acknowledging that our children are holy and belong to Christ's flock until as adults by their own lives they show it to be otherwise.[18]

By the later 1530s and thereafter, the distinction between the two baptisms, which René Bornert justifiably calls a 'rupture', has disappeared: 'Christ commended baptism as the means whereby participation in himself and heavenly regeneration should be imparted and presented through the church's ministry.'[19] In his *Brief Summary of the Christian Doctrine and Religion Taught at Strasbourg*, called by Wendel 'his theological testament', Bucer wrote as follows in 1548:

> We confess and teach that holy baptism, when given and received according to the Lord's command, is in the case of adults and of young children truly a baptism of regeneration and renewal in the Holy Spirit, whereby those who are baptized have all their sins washed away, are buried into the death of our Lord Jesus Christ, are incorporated into him and put on him for the death of their sins, for a new and godly life and the blessed resurrection, and through him become children and heirs of God.[20]

In England in 1550, in 'On the Significance and Practice of the Sacred Ministry', he rejects interpretations of John 3.5 ('Unless a person is born of water and the Spirit...') which evade the plain sense of *aqua*, water, especially any which would treat it as a metaphor for the Spirit.[21]

Use of *Exhibere*

The advance in Bucer's doctrine of baptism from the mid-1530s is expressed particularly in his use of the Latin verb *exhibere*. With the aid of Irena Backus' marvellous edition of the three recensions of Bucer's

---

[18] *Enarrationes*, f. 62v.

[19] Bornert, *La Réforme*, pp. 341-42; *Metaphrases...ad Romanos* (1536), p. 329; Wright, *Common Places of Martin Bucer*, p. 304.

[20] *A Brief Summary*, sig. C ii^v, ed. F. Wendel, *Martin Bucer: Résumé Sommaire de la Doctrine Chrétienne* (Paris, 1951), pp. 11, 50-52; Wright, *Common Places of Martin Bucer*, p. 84.

[21] *TA*, p. 596. Stephens, *Holy Spirit*, p. 236, seems to me to misread this passage; I have already expressed my view that the distinction between water-baptism and Spirit-baptism vanishes in the later Bucer. According to Bornert, *La Réforme*, pp. 348-51, the distinction is transposed into one 'entre le signe exhibitif et la grâce effective', and eventually into a unification which delivers Bucer from his sacramental dualism.

Johannine commentary, one can detect where *exhibere* was added in 1536 to the 1530 text.[22] Scholars speak of the emergence of 'la notion exhibitive du sacrement',[23] but the ready availability of derivative verbs in French and English has too often obscured the full force of Bucer's usage. It comes out inescapably in his discussion of ceremonies in his 1536 Romans commentary, in a brief sentence which both bears on our concern with infants in particular and reveals how far his baptismal teaching has progressed since a dozen years earlier:

Infantibus exhibuit tantum, parentibus et Ecclesiae iuxta et significavit et exhibuit.

To infants God only imparted [his blessings through the sacrament], to parents and the church he both signified and imparted them.[24]

Bucer is distinguishing between the different ways in which the *intelligentes* and the *non intelligentes*—the comprehending and the uncomprehending—receive sacraments, and illustrates them by circumcision. The point is clear. *Exhibere* cannot mean anything less than 'confer, impart, bestow'. In my translations in *Common Places of Martin Bucer* I rendered it 'present', which may have in its favour that it preserves the two aspects of 'visually portray, depict' and 'give, confer' (somewhat as 'convey' does also). If the significative function of the sacraments is redundant without understanding in the recipients, the same must hold for any stronger function (for what is signified may be absent and future) expressed by 'exhibition' in French or English, i.e. concretely portraying, making present, visibly actualizing, but falling short of real impartation and bestowal.[25] If the role of baptism as signifier is lost on non-understanding babies, this can hardly be different for its 'exhibitive' role. Their only interest consists in their being actually *given* what to others the sacrament also signifies and portrays.

It may well be that Bucer uses *exhibere* with different nuances. It is in any case not to be denied that the baptismal rite does more than signify to the mind; it is essentially for the heirs of Augustine a 'visible word'. But pending more extended investigation,[26] it seems that by 1534, in his most

---

[22] E.g., *In Ioh.* (1530, 1536), *BOL* II, p. 81 lines 10-11, *baptismate significatur et exhibetur* in place of *baptismus significat*; and cf. p. 76 lines 13-14.

[23] J. Courvoisier, *La Notion d'église chez Bucer dans son développement historique* (Paris, 1933), p. 86; cf. Bornert, *La Réforme*, p. 347, 'La théorie de l'exhibition...'

[24] *Metaphrases...ad Romanos*, p. 161. A. Lang, *Der Evangelienkommentar Martin Butzers und die Grundzüge seiner Theologie* (Leipzig, 1900), p. 261, muddies the waters by giving *sacramentum* as the object of *exhibuit* (and of *significavit*?!).

[25] Even Bornert, *La Réforme*, p. 347, blurs the issue by assigning 'la signification et l'exhibition de la réalité de grâce' to the ministerial words and actions, and 'la communication effective du pardon des péchés et de la vie nouvelle' exclusively to God.

[26] See Lang, *Der Evangelienkommentar*, pp. 258-66, for further material.

developed treatise on infant baptism, Bucer was already using 'exhibere' in its fullest sense:

> Our baptism, then, is Christ's baptism, which the church must use, the symbol (*symbolum*) of our acceptance before God. By this symbol for the first time our regeneration and renewal through the Holy Spirit are offered and presented (*exhibetur*) by words and washing in water, out of God's kindness towards us in Christ earlier revealed to us. By it we are first consecrated to and ingrafted into the Father, the Son and the Holy Spirit.[27]

We must not miss what this clarification discloses about Bucer's changing baptismal convictions. It is conveyed by the word 'only' (*tantum*) in the sentence from the commentary on Romans, 'To infants God only imparted...' The wheel has come full circle. Whereas originally Bucer allowed to baptism little more than a purely significative function ('Water baptism is an outward sign of the baptism of Christ'),[28] and was adamant that it actually imparted nothing, now he affirms that for infants the 'only' thing it does is actually impart God's blessings, even when its significative force is futile. Lest it be objected that the subject of *exhibuit* is God and not 'the sacrament', Bucer has said on the previous page that 'the sacraments of God are precisely what they are said to be since they really confer (*re ipsa exhibent*) what they signify—the covenant of the Lord, the cleansing of sins, communion in Christ'.[29] From the mid-1530s Bucer instinctively attributed to the rite itself what a decade earlier he had steadfastly reserved for the baptism of Christ or the Spirit.

Value of Infant Baptism for the Church

In his commentary on John's Gospel, in a passage that survives virtually unaltered through the three editions of 1528, 1530 and 1536, Bucer unfolds the threefold benefit that accrues to the church from paedobaptism.[30] First, the whole people of Christ is reminded that God is the saviour of their children. Students of Bucer are in turn reminded of the key role played in his ripening baptismal understanding by Genesis 17.7, 'where God promised to Abraham that he, God, would be his saviour and the saviour of his seed',[31] and with it Acts 2.39. Bucer reasoned that if offspring were recipients of the promise, then there was every justification for giving them the sign of their inclusion in the covenant of the promise. The advantage of Genesis over Acts was the

---

[27] *QBI*, sigs. A vii^v-viii^r.
[28] *Ground and Basis* (*Grund und Ursach*, 1524), *BDS* 1, pp. 254-55.
[29] *Metaphrases...ad Romanos*, p. 160.
[30] *In Ioh.* (1528–36), *BOL* II, pp. 76-77.
[31] *QBI*, sig. A vi^r.

attestation of this by the circumcision of male babies, but then Bucer could employ an *a fortiori* argument to overcome the New Testament's silence on the baptism of babies: surely the new covenant could not bestow less than the old?[32]

Thus the first benefit listed in the Johannine commentary turns out to have indirect ecclesiological import. If the covenant promises applied equally to the children of the faithful, they must rightly be marked with the sign of membership of God's covenant people. It is worth stressing here that Bucer's arguments to this end lean on the divine promise rather than, and in clear distinction from, divine election.[33] In *What Should be Believed about the Baptism of Infants*, a marginal summary declares that in baptizing babies 'It is the church's task to follow God's promises, not election, not attitude of heart.'[34] The same point is made in the commentary on Romans three years later, in another marginal marker: 'In conferring sacraments, regard is to be had to God's promise, not to election.'[35]

The distinction is significant, for it provided Bucer with one means of living with the tensions between his competing ecclesiological tendencies—inclusivist and exclusivist. At the same time, it betrayed his continuing inclination to minimize the decisiveness of baptism in general and of infant baptism in particular. Although the dominical sacrament was meant to be the initial distinguishing mark of the people of God, Bucer was repeatedly reminded by the Radicals that numerous 'goats' were baptized alongside 'sheep'. Although he could retort that believers' baptism did not exclude them either ('How many did the apostles baptize who nonetheless were never aware of the baptism of the Spirit?'),[36] yet the charge was a much sharper one for paedobaptists to meet. Bucer's answer was to detach from baptism when given to infants much of its significance as the point of demarcation between the church and the world, and to reassign this to subsequent education and discipline and in due course to confirmation. Defenders of infant baptism in most centuries have found it difficult not to do something similar, denying in effect, if not explicitly, that infant baptism was truly or fully or really baptism as the New Testament intended. Bucer cited the precedent of both Abraham's God and Jesus:

---

[32] *QBI*, sigs. B v^v-vi^v. Cf. Hammann, *Entre la secte et la cité*, pp. 206ff.

[33] Here I differ from Lynch, 'Martin Bucer's Theology of Infant Baptism'; Stephens, *Holy Spirit*; and Hammann, *Entre la secte et la cité*.

[34] *QBI*, sig. B ii^v.

[35] *Metaphrases...ad Romanos*, p. 162. Cf. Wendel, *L'Église de Strasbourg*, p. 147, for other references.

[36] *In Ioh.* (1528–36), *BOL* II, p. 92.

God of old wanted to have a people that would be truly his people, and yet he ordered the infants of all to be indiscriminately (*promiscue*) marked with the sign of redemption. Likewise Christ himself made no distinction in blessing all the children offered to him. Accordingly, since God decided thus to offer his grace to his people from infancy and to delay the differentiation which is effected through us until an individual refuses to heed the church's admonition about sin, why do we wish to be wiser and more solicitous for the church's purity than God himself?[37]

The practice of admitting all infants indiscriminately into the church, based on Christ's example, God's promise and the observance enjoined on the patriarchs, could not obstruct the formation of a church of committed believers.[38] Indeed, as we shall see, Bucer believed it greatly facilitated it. Whether he was right is highly doubtful. The attempt to pursue two ecclesiologies at the same time, one comprehensive and the other selective, was probably self-defeating. The requirements of the former must undermine the latter. Bucer's endeavours may here have something to teach the churches of Europe's ex-Christendom, and help them heed the protests against infant baptism of two of the twentieth century's greatest Reformed theologians, Karl Barth and Jürgen Moltmann.

Jesus' blessing of the children has been touched on only incidentally. It was, of course, a major plank in Bucer's defence of paedobaptism. He would not allow that 'such' (*tales*) meant the childlike rather than the very youngest infants.[39] In blessing them Jesus was welcoming them into the kingdom of God, which was the church. He was in fact baptizing them into the church, though without water.[40] He did, however, use 'the sacrament of the laying on of hands', which was thereafter to follow the initial symbol of grace, i.e. baptism.[41] Bucer's prominent contribution to the development of the reformed ceremony of confirmation is well known.[42] What is less familiar is his readiness on occasion to call the imposition of hands a sacrament. He does so in the reply on the sacraments to John a Lasco that he left unfinished at his death. Here he cites Jesus' blessing of the children as 'his administration of this sacrament'.[43] Bucer's references to the action reveal some confusion, but there can be little doubt that the interplay in his mind between what Jesus did to the infants, infant baptism and confirmation (which was integrally

---

[37] *QBI*, sig. B iii^r; cf. similarly *Metaphrases...ad Romanos*, p. 162.
[38] *QBI*, sig. B iii^v.
[39] He noted Luke's use of βρέφη, 'babies', *In Ioh.*, *BOL* II, p. 85.
[40] In *In Ioh.* (1528–36; *BOL* II, p. 74) he argued that Christ did not baptize with water because *Spiritus baptismus* was his prerogative.
[41] *QBI*, sig. B viii^r.
[42] See, e.g., Bornert, *La Réforme*, pp. 360-69.
[43] J.V. Pollett, *Martin Bucer: études sur la correspondence* (2 vols; Paris, 1958–62), I, pp. 294-95.

related to infant baptism) strengthened his conviction that Jesus' blessing was a clear dominical warrant for baptizing babies.

Faith of Church and Parents

The last few paragraphs in this enquiry began with our noting that in his Johannine commentary of 1528–36 Bucer records, as the first of the three benefits accruing to the church from infant baptism, the reminder that God is the saviour of the church's children. The promise was prior, and from it was deduced the propriety of receiving the newborn into the covenant community by the covenantal sign. It was therefore essential for the church to have confidence in the divine promise, and to bring its faith to the baptism of infants. Bucer's accent normally falls on the parents' faith, but occasionally he will say, 'If the parents believe nothing and are hypocrites, the church believes, to which the children belong by fuller right than to their parents.'[44] But this is an infrequent note in Bucer's numerous variations on the theme. There is little anticipation in the Strasbourg Reformer of that questionable shift in recent baptismal discussion which, in the face of tricky issues of pastoral discipline posed by requests for baptism from parents of little or no evident faith, emphasizes the church's rather than the parents' faith.

The second benefit of infant baptism noted by Bucer in his commentary on John relates particularly to the parents or other close relatives. The ceremony impresses on them the need to train in godliness the children they have dedicated to God, and to recognize them not as their own but as God's sons and daughters.[45] Bucer is realistic enough to acknowledge that not all parents will devote to the spiritual nurture of their infants the care that they have promised.[46] Perhaps it is for this reason that he makes relatively little in this context of the Christian family as the basic building-block of the church. Nor does he very often use the image of the family for the church itself, although occasionally he will say that 'we receive babies into the family of Christ through baptism'.[47] In his biblical apologetic for the practice a limited role is played by the alleged implications of the household baptisms in the Acts of the Apostles. More frequent appeal is made to 1 Corinthians 7.14, but again Bucer cannot be said to have developed even on this basis the theory and practice of the Christian family in the interests of paedobaptism.

---

[44] *QBI*, sig. E vii^r.
[45] *In Ioh.*, *BOL* II, p. 77.
[46] *In Ioh.*, *BOL* II, p. 95.
[47] *In Ioh.*, *BOL* II, p. 92; cf. *QBI*, sig. D v^{rv}, and Hammann, *Entre la secte et la cité*, pp. 255-61, on the family as 'lieu ecclésial'.

'Sacrament of Education'

The third fruit of the sacrament belongs especially to the children themselves, who from infancy belong to the company in whose midst worship and the preaching of God's Word flourish.[48] With their milk they drink in a reverence for God. In Courvoisier's happy phrase, Bucer turned infant baptism into a 'sacrament of education'.[49] He rejected the Radicals' facile insistence that the apostles baptized only those solidly instructed in Christ. They

> often baptized people to whom they had spoken about Christ for scarcely an hour... By baptism they admitted them only into a school of piety and an apprenticeship in Christianity (*in scholam pietatis et Christianismi tyrocinium*). They were accustomed to expel them again when it was clearly enough established that teaching them was wasted labour.[50]

This emphasis on the educational process into which baptism initiated children becomes marked in Bucer's writings from the mid-1530s. Gottfried Hammann's exposition helpfully clarifies that for Bucer 'baptism did not install the baptized—infant or adult—in a state, but integrated him into a dynamic body, enrolling him as a candidate in a process of Christian formation and spiritual development'.[51] This emphasis also informed the revision of the Strasbourg baptismal liturgy of 1537, with a direct address to the godparents to assist the parents in the nurture of the child and thus prove themselves 'spiritual fathers and mothers to him'.[52] From another perspective, a scheme of Christian education was necessary if that differentiation between sheep and goats, whose delay an open-door policy of paedobaptism countenanced (as we saw earlier), was to come into sharp focus.

Yet even if this were not achieved, Bucer would still have argued for the value of a residual 'cradle Christianity' fostered by a comprehensive practice of baptizing babies. He comments thus in his exposition of John:

> With their milk they drink in a reverence for God. Hence it happens that, even though not infrequently the leaders and the majority of the population lapse into idolatry, some kind of fear of God and regard for his Word survives in the people. Thus of old the prophets could summon the people back to repentance considerably more easily than if that sort of fear and reverence for the Word had died out among

---

[48] *In Ioh.*, *BOL* II, p. 77.
[49] Courvoisier, *La Notion d'église*, p. 56.
[50] *In Ioh.* (1528–36), *BOL* II, p. 95.
[51] Hammann, *Entre la secte et la cité*, p. 57.
[52] F. Hubert, *Die Strassburger Liturgischen Ordnungen im Zeitalter der Reformation* (Göttingen, 1900), p. 51; J.D.C. Fisher, *Christian Initiation: The Reformation Period* (Alcuin Club Collections, 51; London, 1970), p. 41; Bornert, *La Réforme*, pp. 525-30; Old, *Shaping of the Reformed Baptism Rite*, *passim*.

the people. And it would have died out if God's covenant had not been impressed on them from infancy.

He adds from personal experience:

> And to us too it was especially useful that the whole of our people was from the cradle admitted to the church, whatever its condition (*in qualemcunque ecclesiam*). In this way some belief about Christ and some appreciation of Holy Writ were instilled. These had the effect of opening up a wide window for the recent recovery of the pure gospel, which could not have opened up if no respect for Sacred Scripture had been held by the people.[53]

Only universal paedobaptism provides a safety-net, as it were, to prevent a community's irrecoverable descent into the abyss of godlessness.

The validity of such an assessment for Strasbourg's religious history in the sixteenth century must be left to more expert minds to determine. Its applicability to the infant-baptized ex-Christian masses of Europe at the end of the second millennium cannot perhaps be fairly tested in the absence of some massive surge of theological and spiritual life comparable to the Reformation. But some sage heads reckon that the small dose of religion administered indiscriminately in infant baptism has effectively inoculated generations against catching real Christianity in later life.

Concluding Assessment

Bucer's comment is that of the Reformer whom scholars have characterized as 'homme d'Église' *par excellence*.[54] It embodies, no doubt, his gut conviction that the construction of a true Christian church and society in Strasbourg would be hampered from the outset if any of its population, young or old, stood beyond the claim of God's Word because unbaptized. Yet the ecclesial temper of Bucer's handling of infant baptism is not as strongly marked as might have been expected. Throughout the span of his writings the church has an instrumental role in giving baptism to the newborn, and this was heightened from the time in the middle of the 1530s when he began to speak more decisively of the sacraments as 'channels, vehicles and instruments of the Spirit and grace'.[55] But his commonplace on 'the nature, practice and efficacy of baptism' in his Romans commentary of 1536 is noticeably deficient in its

---

[53] *In Ioh.*, BOL II, p. 77; cf. p. 85: 'We know from experience how useful it is for godliness, and so how pleasing to God, that our children be offered to him from the cradle.'

[54] Courvoisier, *La Notion d'église*, p. 49.

[55] Preface to the *Enarrationes* on the Gospels, 1536 (edition of Geneva, 1553, f. *vi).

ecclesiological dimension,[56] and from time to time his definitions of baptism are similarly inadequate, such as the one thus formally entitled in *What Should be Believed about the Baptism of Infants* which has been given earlier in this chapter (see p. 172 n. 27). My impression is that he does not make prominent use of 1 Corinthians 12.13, 'By one Spirit we were all baptized into one body', although it appears in his listings of proof texts—and it may be a healthily Christocentric bias that makes him say of this verse, at the end of his life, that it attributes to baptism 'incorporation into Christ the Lord, and in that Christ *concorporatio* with all the saints, and through the same Spirit'.[57] Certainly Bucer more instinctively speaks of baptism as incorporation into Christ rather than into his body the church.

Yet at base one senses that Bucer is caught in various binds over infant baptism. At one level the divine promise to believers' children means that they already belong to God's covenant people, and that warrants their baptism into the visible community on earth. This is a standard structural feature of Bucer's apologetic for baptizing babies: the spiritual reality is theirs already, hence they must be given the sign and seal. But because the inscrutability of election means that not all those baptized into Christ are Christ's, a provisional character attaches to one's baptism. Although this was true also of adult baptism, as the disputes with the Radicals made it essential to insist, in fact for sixteenth-century Strasbourg baptism was almost invariably infant baptism. Bucer's own reasoning ascribed specifically to paedobaptism a containing role, the marking of an outer ring, within which another and more decisive line would be drawn, coming into quasi-sacramental focus in confirmation. The clamour of the Radicals in the city and other pressures turned him into an unreserved exponent of baptizing infants, but it provided a boundary that was too accommodating for his dearest aspirations of Christian community.[58]

---

[56] *Metaphrases...ad Romanos*, pp. 320-31; Wright, *Common Places of Martin Bucer*, pp. 285-311.

[57] *On the Significance and Practice of the Sacred Ministry* (1550), TA, pp. 596-97.

[58] See the wider context sketched by H.A. Oberman. '*Europa afflicta*: The Reformation of the Refugees', *Archiv für Reformationsgeschichte* 83 (1992), pp. 91-111.

CHAPTER 13

George Cassander and the Appeal to the Fathers in Sixteenth-Century Debates about Infant Baptism

The subject is an ideal one for a symposium on the church Fathers in the fifteenth and sixteenth centuries. Infant baptism was the weightiest constitutive feature of the old church that the magisterial Reformers perpetuated on the basis of tradition rather than explicit scriptural authority. Luther's preservation of private oral confession, similarly without clear biblical warrant, was of less fundamental significance for the ordering of the reformed church than the continued practice of baptizing the newborn.

The issue remains a live one today, biblically, historically, theologically, ecumenically. Since the sixteenth century, the Anabaptist protest, so despised in its day by Catholics and Protestants alike, has won respectability, ecclesiastically and probably confessionally also. If no consensus yet obtains about the origins of infant baptism, the influential Faith and Order report *Baptism, Eucharist and Ministry* captures the state of the debate with fine precision: 'While the possibility that infant baptism was practised in the apostolic age cannot be excluded, baptism upon personal profession of faith is the most clearly attested pattern in the New Testament documents.'[1]

A growing majority of scholars probably inclines to side with Kurt Aland in his celebrated dialogue with Joachim Jeremias,[2] but Aland's position—that infant baptism was not apostolic and not practised until shortly before the end of the second century but is nevertheless rightly and properly practised today[3]—would have found no supporters in the

---

[1] *Baptism, Eucharist and Ministry* (Faith and Order Paper, 111; Geneva, 1982), p. 4.

[2] For this debate and subsequent contributions, see my articles, 'The Origins of Infant Baptism—Child Believers' Baptism?', *Scottish Journal of Theology* 40 (1987), pp. 1-23, and 'How Controversial Was the Development of Infant Baptism in the Early Church?', in James E. Bradley and Richard A. Muller (eds), *Church, Word and Spirit: Historical and Theological Essays in Honor of Geoffrey W. Bromley* (Grand Rapids, MI, 1987), pp. 45-63 (chs 1 and 2 above).

[3] Kurt Aland, *Did the Early Church Baptize Infants?* (London, 1963), pp. 113-14: 'the practice of infant baptism today can claim that it fulfills in a new time and in a new way what took place in early times in a different manner... [I]t is possible for us to keep on making renewed efforts to realize the demands of the New Testament. According to the

sixteenth century. Too much was at stake for either Catholics or Protestants to opt for this theologically sophisticated stance. Paradoxically, as we will see, Menno Simons could accept that infant baptism began in the time of the apostles without feeling bound for that reason to approve of it—for it was not instituted by the apostles themselves.

By comparison with the Lord's supper, the history of baptismal controversy in the Reformation remains relatively neglected. (The same could indeed be said of the whole span of church history.) For the arguments between Anabaptists and magisterial churchmen, whether in the old church or the new, we lack the equivalent of Walter Köhler's classic survey of the supper-strife.[4] The discussions in the sources are often brief and occasional, as well as widely dispersed. This present essay claims no more than to review some aspects of the debates about the bearing of the patristic evidence on the status of infant baptism.

George Cassander's *Testimonia*

Our starting-point is a work published at Cologne in 1563 by George Cassander (c.1513–66), the irenical Flemish Catholic theologian, entitled *De Baptismo Infantium, Testimonia Veterum Ecclesiasticorum Scriptorum.* Cassander has attracted greatest interest for his persistent efforts to reconcile Catholics and Protestants, but he is badly in need of a critical biography and a comprehensive theological assessment.[5] Little

---

presuppositions that we share, the practice of infant baptism today belongs to that category.'

[4] Walter Köhler, *Zwingli und Luther. Ihr Streit über das Abendmahl nach seinen politischen und religiösen Beziehungen,* I, *Die religiöse und politische Entwicklung bis zum Marburger Religionsgespräch 1529* (Leipzig 1924); II, *Vom Beginn der Marburger Verhandlungen 1529 bis zum Abschluss der Wittenberger Konkordie von 1536* (Gütersloh, 1953).

[5] Cassander is omitted from G. Krause and G. Müller (eds), *Theologische Realenzyklopädie* (Berlin, New York, 1977–), but appears in most of the appropriate encyclopedias; see especially the article by Jules Baudot in F. Cabrol (ed.), *Dictionnaire d'archéologie chrétienne et de liturgie* (15 vols; Paris, 1907–53), II.2 (1925), cols. 2333-40. His works are listed in *Index Aureliensis* VII, pp. 58-63. Among other literature the following may be noted: Ruth Rouse and Stephen C. Neill (eds), *A History of the Ecumenical Movement 1517–1948* (London, 3rd edn, 1986), pp. 38-42; Maria E. Nolte, *Georgius Cassander en zijn oecumenisch striven* (Nijmegen, 1951); Pontien Polman, *L'Élement Historique dans la Controverse religieuse du XVIe-Siècle* (Gembloux, 1932); Joseph Lecler, *Toleration and the Reformation* (New York and London, 1960), I, pp. 270-76; John P. Dolan, *The Influence of Erasmus, Witzel and Cassander in the Church Ordinances and Reform Proposals of the United Duchees of Cleve during the Middle Decades of the 16th Century* (Reformationsgeschichtliche Studien und Texte, 83; Münster, 1957), pp. 87-108; Arthur C. de Schrevel, *Histoire du Seminaire de Bruges* (2 vols;

attention has been paid to Cassander's engagements with Anabaptists, to which his *Testimonia* on infant baptism belongs.[6] It has not been previously noticed, for example, that the text of the *Testimonia* reprinted in Cassander's *Opera Omnia* in 1616 is an expanded version of the 1563 original.[7]

Cassander's collection and discussion may represent the earliest attempt in the sixteenth century at a comprehensive treatment of the evidence to be garnered from the Fathers. He had compiled the collection as part of his recent successful endeavour to convert to a sound mind a prominent Anabaptist (*quidam inter professores et doctores huius erroris eximius*) held in custody *in arce Clivorum*.[8] Now, in response to wider

---

Bruges, 1883-95). The older literature is listed in Hermann Keussen, *Die Matrikel der Universität Köln* II: *1476-1559* (Publikationen der Gesellschaft für Rheinische Geschichtskunde, 8; Bonn, 1919), p. 988.

[6] See, however, Assink Calkoen, *Specimen Historico-theologicum Georgii Cassandri...Narrationem Exhibens* (Amsterdam, 1859), pp. 113-16; H.S. Bender et al. (eds), *The Mennonite Encyclopedia* (4 vols; Scottdale, PA, 1955-59), I, p. 522; George H. Williams, *The Radical Reformation* (London, 1962), pp. 801-802; Karl Rembert, *Die 'Wiedertaufe' im Herzogtum Jülich* (Berlin, 1899), especially pp. 276-77, 476-77, 542-47.

[7] Cassander, *Opera Omnia* (Paris, 1616), pp. 668-99. The 1563 edition also lacks the 'Appendix de Auctoritate Ecclesiarum Apostolicarum ex Tertulliano' (1616, pp. 699-700), as well as his *De Baptismo Infantium, Doctrina Catholicae Ecclesiae, Divinarum Literarum Testimoniis Explicata*, which follows it in the *Opera Omnia* (1616, pp. 701-79) and is often regarded as part of the same work, e.g., by Polman, *L'Élement Historique*, p. 385 n. 2. It was first published quite separately in 1565. The two editions will be cited here as *Testimonia* 1563 and *Testimonia* 1616. I am grateful to the Masters and Fellows of Trinity College Library, Cambridge, for permission to quote from a microfilm of the 1563 edition in the College Library. I am also grateful to Dr Frank Stubbings, Honorary Keeper of Rare Books in Emmanuel College, Library, Cambridge, for supplying me with a photocopy of part of a second 1563 edition of the *Testimonia* (recorded by Herbert M. Adams, *Catalogue of the Books Printed on the Continent of Europe 1501-1600 in Cambridge Libraries* [Cambridge, 1967], I, p. 247 no. 840). In this printing, the text has been re-set from sig. G1^r onwards (as differences of spelling, abbreviation etc. also make clear), and at the end Cassander has added (after recovering from illness, as he says at a note at sig. G6^v) not only errata (which are listed as G6^r in the first printing) but also the interpolations which are identifiable in the 1616 edition, at sigs. G6^v-H1^v. He also now gives the Appendix from Tertullian which appears in 1616 (sigs. H2^r-4^r). The re-set text of sigs. G1^r-6^r already incorporates the additions (two only, but one of them lengthy) relating to this section of the work. In this articles all references are to the original 1563 edition.

[8] *Testimonia* 1563, sigs. B1^r-2^v; *Testimonia* 1616, pp. 673-74: ...*ingenue confessus est, se hunc tantum Ecclesiarum consensum magnificare, seque hac tam concordi veterum Ecclesiasticorum scriptorum consensione plurimum commoveri... Quare impense huiusmodi testimonia sibi exhiberi postulavit, quibus inspectis, et qua pollebat ingenii perspicacitate diligenter exploratis, opinionem suam ex pravo et privato scripturae*

demand, Cassander published it,[9] prefaced with a clarification of the authority of the consensus of the early church conveyed by the testimonies,[10] which in turn are followed by a further discussion of the authority of the universal practice of baptizing infants.[11]

Cassander's witnesses are restricted to Fathers who flourishesd within three hundred years of the death of the last apostle, John, i.e. up to AD 400. (The dates given in the margin are calculated on this basis, which has the curious effect of making them all seem a hundred years earlier.) Cassander largely observes his own limit, but Leo I is included, along with Theodoret of Cyrrhus (only in the 1616 edition) and of course the later Augustine *in extenso*.

The keenest interest attaches to the testimonia of the pre-Nicene era.[12] They are seven in number:

1. *Irenaeus*: Christ came to save all *qui per eum renascuntur in Deum, infantes et parvulos, et pueros, et iuvenes, et seniores.*[13]

2. *Tertullian*: not from *De Baptismo* (which, although best known for its advocacy of the deferment of baptism, reveals that some infants were being

---

intellectu haustam, cum universali hac et perpetua totius Ecclesiae sententia haud difficulter commutavit, usque eo, ut hunc errorem cum nonnullis aliis in aede sacra eiusdem oppidi Clivorum, frequentissima populi concione damnaverit... Haec autem res...occasionem dedit haec vetera testimonia colligendi... The Anabaptist in question is identified by Rembert, *Die 'Wiedertäufer'*, pp. 276-77 (citing Hermann Hamelmann, *Opera Genealogico-Historica, De Westphalia et Saxonia Inferiori...* [Lemgo, 1711], p. 1011), as Johannes Campanus (on whom see Rembert, *Die 'Wiedertäufer'*, pp. 160-302; *Mennonite Encyclopedia* I, pp. 499-500; Christian Hege and Christian Neff [eds], *Mennonitisches Lexikon* [4 vols; Karlsruhe, 1913–67], I, pp. 317-24; Williams, *Radical Reformation*, especially pp. 272-73, 309-11, 457-59), the year 1563 (but Cassander had discussed with Campanus the previous year also) and the place Schloss Angermud, between Duisberg and Kaiserwerth.

Cassander's summary of similar discussions with one Johannes Kremer a Castorp in July 1558 'in arce Dinslachon' (Dinslaken, a few miles north of Duisberg) includes a similarly successful outcome but a less prominent, although not insignificant, role for the appeal to the universal consensus of the early church (*Acta Colloqui..., Opera Omnia*, pp. 1227-34; cf. *Epist.* III, *Opera Omnia*, p. 1085). Better known are Cassander's conversations with Matthias Servaes in Cologne in July 1565 (*Acta Colloqui..., Opera Omnia*, pp. 1234-40; cf. *Epist.* CI, *Opera Omnia*, pp. 1203-04).

[9] *Testimonia* 1563, sig. B3^r; *Testimonia* 1616, p. 674: *Cum autem haec testimonia a nonnullis expeterentur, visum fuit non abs re fore, si in publicum ederentur.*

[10] *Testimonia* 1563, sigs. B4^r-C8^v; *Testimonia* 1616, pp. 675-81.

[11] *Testimonia* 1563, sigs. F2^r-G5^v; *Testimonia* 1616, pp. 692-99.

[12] *Testimonia* 1563, sigs. D1^r-4^r; *Testimonia* 1616, pp. 682-84. The two editions do not differ at this point.

[13] Irenaeus, *Adv. Haer.* 2:22:4; Heinrich Kraft, *Texte zur Geschichte der Taufe, besonders der Kindertaufe in der Alten Kirche* (Kleine Texte, 174; Berlin, 1953), n. 10.

baptized), but from *De Anima*, a passage that stresses only the necessity of baptism for all.[14]

3.-5. *Origen*: three extracts, two from homilies assuming the practice of paedobaptism, finding its justification in the sinfulness of babies and citing Job 14.4-5 (LXX), and a third from the Romans commentary, which also asserts the apostolic origins of the tradition (*Ecclesia ab Apostolis traditionem suscepit, etiam parvulis baptismum dare*).[15]

6. *Dionysius (the Areopagite)*: Cassander's Preface has already explained this position for a passage from the *Ecclesiastical Hierarchy*: *Primus quidem locus debebatur Dionysio, qui si Areopagita ille est, Apostolorum synchronus fuit, utpote Apostoli Pauli discipulus, sed quia de eo inter doctos ambigitur, Origeni illum subieci, iis concedens, qui illum Clemente Alexandrino posteriorem fuisse suspicantur.*[16]

7. *Cyprian*: the famous letter to Fidus, on which Cassander adds a comment by Augustine in a letter to Jerome.[17]

When compared with the list of sources given by Jeremias in his monograph of 1958/1960 (of which Charles Francis D. Moule once said that it provided at least all the evidence), Cassander's collection is limited partly by availability of material but also partly, we must judge, by modesty. He has not cited, for example, the references in the *Martyrdom of Polycarp* and Justin Martyr to those who had been Christians from their early years. The prize witness he could not have known is the *Apostolic Tradition* of Hippolytus.[18] He does not mention the inscriptions,

---

[14] Tertulliam, *De Anima* 39:3–40:1; not in Kraft, who includes selections from *De Baptismo* (and *De Paenitentia*; *Texte zur Geschichte*, no. 13).

[15] *Testimonia* 1563, sig. D2^r; *Testimonia* 1616, p. 682. The texts are: *Comment. in Epist. ad Romanos* 5:9 (Kraft, *Texte zur Geschichte*, no. 12(b)), *In Lucam Homil.* 14 (not in Kraft, perhaps because it adds nothing to the next), *In Leviticum Homil.* 8:3 (Kraft, *Texte zur Geschichte*, no. 12(a)).

[16] *Testimonia* 1563, sig. B3^r; *Testimonia* 1616, p. 674. The passage is *Eccles. Hier.* 7:3:11, not of course in Kraft. Karlfried Froehlich, 'Pseudo-Dionysius and the Reformation of the Sixteenth Century', in Colm Luibheid (trans.), *Pseudo-Dionysius: The Complete Works* (Classics of Western Spirituality; London, 1987), pp. 33-46, especially 45-46.

[17] Cyprian, *Epistle* 64:2,3,5 (Kraft, *Texte zur Geschichte*, no. 19(a)); Augustine, *Epistle* 166:8:23.

[18] Despite his ignorance of the *Apostolic Tradition* and its derivatives, Cassander's reconstruction of the primitive baptismal observance later in his work comes remarkably close to Hippolytus' account in some respects, especially in distinguishing among the categories of candidates between children who could and could not answer for themselves: 'erant et pueri ea aetate, ut ipsi quoque per se acceptam Catechismi doctrinam, hoc est orationem Dominicam, et Symbolum reddere possint.' He has already mentioned the adults 'qui...ipsi pro se respondebant' (*Testimonia* 1563, sig. F6^r; *Testimonia* 1616, p. 694). Hippolytus likewise distinguishes among children in terms of their ability to

but one wonders in any case whether he would have counted them among the *testimonia patrum*.

The post-Nicene witnesses are of course more abundant but they need not detain us at this stage. In the discussion of the *auctoritas* of 'the universal custom of baptizing infants', which follows the *testimonia*, Cassander shows his awareness of other patristic evidence which he has not included in the *testimonia* proper. He knows, for instance, from Tertullian (*De Baptismo* of course) and Gregory Nazianzen that some Fathers counselled the delay of baptism to *aetatem paulo provectiorem, quae mysteria utcunque intelligere et meminisse possit.*[19] Cassander, however, is not thereby disturbed, for two reasons: no-one in the early church rejected paedobaptism as *nefarium*, and even Tertullian and Gregory regarded it as so necessary as to urge the clinical baptism of babies.[20] Some variety of practice in primitive Christianity is allowed for by Cassander. He suggests that at first it may have been only seriously ill children that were baptized, in addition to their converting parents.[21] This is in line with a recent hypothesis that normal paedobaptism developed by extension from the clinical baptism of children.[22] And so Cassander's review is not lacking in sophistication.

Apostolic Institution

But where does the weight of his exposition fall? Is it primarily historical or theological? It is obviously both at the same time. On the one hand it is not theological alone; Cassander does not rest his case on an appeal to the magisterium of the tradition or on the congruity of infant baptism with the theology of the Fathers. Nor is it historical alone, as though primitiveness of origin sufficed. For Cassander, it is important not only that paedobaptism went back to the age of the apostles but was instituted by the apostles themselves.

Cassander's two key witnesses to this effect are Origen and Augustine. We have already noted Cassander's inclusion in his *testimonia* of Origen's assertion in his Romans commentary that the church received the tradition of baptizing infants from the apostles. Two passages from

---

answer for themselves; see Wright, 'The Origins of Infant Baptism', pp. 4-6 (pp. 6-7 above).

[19] *Testimonia* 1563, sig. G2^r; *Testimonia* 1616, p. 697. The texts are Tertullian, *De Baptismo* 18:4-5 (Kraft, *Texte zur Geschichte*, no. 13(b)), and Gregory Nazianzen, *Oratio* 40:28 (Kraft, *Texte zur Geschichte*, no. 24).

[20] *Testimonia* 1563, sig. G2^{rv}; *Testimonia* 1616, p. 697.

[21] *Testimonia* 1563, sig. F5^r; *Testimonia* 1616, p. 694.

[22] Cf. Everett Ferguson, 'Inscriptions and the Origins of Infant Baptism', *Journal of Theological Studies* 30 (1979), pp. 34-46, followed by Wright, 'The Origins of Infant Baptism'.

Augustine making the same point are recorded by Cassander.[23] The African Father repeats it in other places.

Origen and Augustine were the two commonest witnesses cited by the Protestant Reformers also, from the 1520s onwards. In 1525 Oecolampadius appealed to Origen's Romans in *Ein Gespräch etlicher Predicanten zu Basel*,[24] and in the same year Zwingli quoted one of Cassander's Augustinian testimonies in *Von der Taufe, von der Wiedertaufe und von der Kindertaufe*.[25] In his 1528 *Iudicium contra Anabaptistas* Melanchthon appealed to both Origen and Augustine in arguing backwards, according to Pierre Fraenkel, from the Fathers to Scripture.[26]

But Cassander finds it necesssary to be more precise on the apostolic institution of paedobaptism than some Protestants were on some occasions. He knows that Menno Simons, *prudentior et diligentior* than those Radicals who blamed its origin on one of the popes, acknowledged that *iam inde ab Apostolicis temporibus baptismum infantium usurpatum fuisse, ac paulatim invaluisse. Verum huius rei auctores facit Pseudapostolos et falsos doctores.*[27] Cassander thinks it incredible that a practice with such inauspicious beginnings should so soon (*statim*) have pervaded all the churches. In any case, there is no trace of any attack on it in many refutations of false teachers and teachings by the apostles and their successors.[28]

The Reformers were not always as careful as Cassander. Calvin states that *nullus est scriptor tam vetustus qui non eius originem ad*

---

[23] Augustine, *De Baptismo* 4:23 (*Testimonia* 1563, sig. D8^v; *Testimonia* 1616, p. 686), *De Gen. ad Litt.* 10:23 (*Testimonia* 1563, sig. E5^r; *Testimonia* 1616, p. 689).

[24] Noted by Rollin S. Armour, *Anabaptist Baptism: A Representative Study* (Studies in Anabaptist and Mennonite History, 11; Scottdale, PA, 1966), p. 50.

[25] H. Zwingli, in Emil Egli, Georg Finsler et al. (eds), *Huldreich Zwinglis Sämtliche Werke* (Berlin, Leipzig, Zurich, 1905–), IV, pp. 321-22.

[26] Pierre Fraenkel, *Testimonia Patrum. The Function of the Patristic Argument in the Theology of Philip Melanchthon* (Travaux d'Humanisme et Renaissance, 46; Geneva, 1961), p. 186 n. 71, citing the *Iudicium, Corpus Reformatorum* (Halle/Saale, 1835–), I, col. 962.

[27] *Testimonia* 1563, sig. B4^v; *Testimonia* 1616, p. 675. Menno makes the point more than once: in *Verklaringe des Christelycken Doopsels* in *Opera Omnia* (Amsterdam, 1681), fol. 408b, 426b, and in *Een Klare Beantwoordinge over een Schrift Gellii Fabri*, in *Opera Omnia*, fol. 272a (in John C. Wenger (ed.), *The Complete Writings of Menno Simons c. 1496–1561* [trans. Leonard Verduin; Scottdale, PA, 1956], pp. 248, 276, 696). At the second of these texts, Menno reduces the testimony of Origen and Augustine to a beginning in the time of the apostles, although he knows better (so *Een Fundament en Klare Aenwysinge...*, in *Omnia Opera*, fol. 21b; cf. *Complete Writings*, p. 137).

[28] *Testimonia* 1563, sigs. B4^v-5^v; *Testimonia* 1616, p. 675. Menno, of course, believed that very few infants were baptized in the early centuries.

Apostolorum seculum pro certo referat.[29] Similar assertions are to be found in Zwingli and Luther, and in other Reformers too. In most instances, to be sure, there is no reason to doubt that these Reformers believed it to have been instituted by the apostles—or even Christ himself—but their arguments not infrequently stress antiquity rather than precise apostolicity.

Luther cites Augustine's assertion that infant baptism derived from the apostles, but his main argument hinges on the unbroken continuity of the practice for over a thousand years, from the time of the apostles even, rather than on the warrant of apostolic appointment.[30] He sets forth a syllogism: either there has been no church for this long period or baptism has been effective, but it is impossible for there to have been no church for a thousand years or more, so therefore the baptism of infants (for most baptisms have been of infants) has been effective.[31] For this syllogism, institution by apostles is at best dispensable. Indeed, it could be claimed that Luther's appeal to continuity from the beginning functions as a substitute for that incontrovertible assertion of apostolic origins which he knew he could not give.

Tradition and Scripture

There may be significance in the Reformers' reading Origen, Augustine and other Fathers as demonstrating the primitive antiquity rather than the strict apostolicity of paedobaptism. Perhaps it enabled them to cope with the awkward question of non-biblical tradition. In his *Refutation of the Tricks of the Baptists,* Zwingli comments as follows after invoking Origen and Augustine as witnesses that the church received infant baptism from the apostles: *Quo testes non in hoc adduco, ut eis autoritatem tribuam scripturae, sed propter historiae fidem (Origines enim post centum et quinquaginta annos ab ascensione Christi floruit), ne vetustatem baptismi infantium ignoremus simulque possimus adsequi indubitatum esse, quod apostoli citra omnem controversiam infantes baptizaverint.*[32] Zwingli's conclusion—that the apostles themselves baptized infants—cannot conceal his discomfort at having to rely on non-apostolic attestation of apostolic practice.

---

[29] John Calvin, *Institutes* 4:16:8.

[30] Martin Luther, *Von der Wiedertaufe an zwei Pfarrherrn* (1528), in *WA* 26, pp. 159, 166-68 (*LW* 40, pp. 245, 254-57).

[31] Luther, *Tischreden* no. 650 (1533), in *WATR* 1, p. 306 (*LW* 54, p. 113).

[32] Zwingli, *Catabaptistarum Strophas Elenchus* (1527), in Egli *et al.* (eds), *Huldreich Zwinglis Sämtliche Werke*, VI.1, p. 187 (trans. Samuel M. Jackson, *Ulrich Zwingli... Selected Works* [Philadelphia, PA, 1901], p. 251).

The Reformers found themselves permanently impaled on the horns of a dilemma. They deployed a range of arguments based on the Bible in favour of baptizing infants. But none, to my knowledge, claimed that the Bible provided an express warrant for the practice (though Calvin held that the intention of baptism is no less appropriate for children than for adults[33]), and none could avoid resort to patristic testimony to help out. Yet *miserrimum asylum foret*, says Calvin, *si pro defensione paedobaptismi ad nudam Ecclesiae authoritatem suffugere cogeremur.*[34]

So for Calvin, to credit the testimony of Origen and Augustine is not to rely on *nuda Ecclesiae authoritas*. Indeed, it is worth noticing that the *testimonia* of these two Fathers in particular—affirming the apostolic institution of paedobaptism—stand in a class of their own among the patristic evidence commonly cited in the debate. Their force lies not so much in what they attest as the church's observance in their own day (although Origen is early enough for his report not to be insignificant in this respect), as in their claiming the observance to be apostolic. Yet this is not vindicated by their quoting apostolic scripture, because it is not available.

As Martin Bucer admits in an open letter to Bernard Rothmann: *Hoc ergo vobis concedimus, baptisma infantium non esse inter ἔγγραφα Christi instituta, at inter ἄγραφα numerandum certo credimus.*[35] But although Bucer reckons that Rothmann will acknowledge *pleraque Christi ἄγραφα* Bucer can cite nothing remotely as important as infant baptism.

So these two Fathers' *testimonia* belong to an intermediate category: they are neither expositions of scripture—and hence in principle acceptable to the Reformers, like, for example, the doctrine of the Trinity—nor independent post-apostolic traditions. They remain unparalleled, I suggest, in sixteenth-century controversy, in regard to both the fundamental centrality of the observance they sustain and the Reformers' readiness to believe and defend their assertion of the apostolic origin of an unwritten tradition.

The appeal to the Fathers on the baptism of infants was inseparable from the appeal to scripture, which in this case sought to prove, or disprove, the congruity of the practice with the explicit teaching of scripture. Bucer tells Rothmann that *discerniculum [of the ἄγραφα] in eo*

---

[33] Calvin, *Institutes* 4:16:8.
[34] Calvin, *Institutes* 4:8:16.
[35] Martin Bucer, *Quid de Baptismate Infantium...* (Strasbourg, 1533), sigs. Aiiii^v-Av^r; this section Robert Stupperich (ed.), *Die Schriften Bernhard Rothmanns* (Veröffentlichungen der Historischen Kommission für Westfalen, 33, Die Schriften der Münsterischen Täufer und ihrer Gegner I; Münster, 1970), p. 49.

situm est, esse iis, quae scriptura exprimit, consentaneum vel dissentaneum.[36]

Anabaptist Counter-Arguments

But the Radicals also challenged the veracity of Origen's and Augustine's assertions by contesting other aspects of the appeal to the Fathers. In Menno Simons' view, the variety of practice and lack of unanimity among the Fathers counted decisively against the apostolic initiation of paedobaptism. His evidence is of mixed quality. Tertullian's *De Baptismo* was obviously not to be missed, but it is surprising to find Menno alleging, on the authority of *die predicanten van Nordlingen*, that even Cyprian left infant baptism optional (*heeft den Kinder-doop vry gelaten—liberum*).[37] Like other Anabaptists, Menno deduced from numerous passages in patristic writings, especially catechetical addresses and accounts of baptismal liturgy, which placed faith or repentance or instruction or the catechumenate before baptism, that infants could not have been candidates.[38] It was easy enough for Reformers like Bucer, whose versatility in defending infant baptism was second to none, to retort that such reasoning mistakenly inferred the general from the particular.[39] Their counter-argument was already well rehearsed on biblical material and could automatically be extended to the Fathers: the need for adults to come to baptism penitent, believing and instructed did not mean that only adults could come.

But a reply like this, however impeccable its logic, evaded rather than countered the Anabaptist appeal to inconsistency of practice in the early church. In terms of modern discussion, Menno and others were nearer the truth than their Protestant and Catholic opponents, despite their very limited awareness of the widespread deferment of baptism in Christian families in the fourth and fifth centuries. It is arguable that progress in resolving the historical dispute about origins will be possible only with the recognition that the question whether infants were baptized in the early church cannot be satisfactorily answered with a straight yes or no. Differences of category of infants, of circumstances and even of region alone make sense of the evidence.

George Cassander, ardent champion of the Vincentian canon, will hear nothing of such diversity. *Veteres omnes Ecclesiastici et Orthodoxi scriptores uno calamo scripserunt, et uno ore locuti sunt de baptismo*

---

[36] Bucer, *Quid de Baptismate Infantium*..., sigs. Aiiii^v-Av^r.

[37] Simons, *Een Klare Beantwoordinge* (*Opera Omnia*, fol. 271b; *Complete Writings*, p. 695); *Een Fundament* (*Opera Omnia*, fol. 21b; *Complete Writings*, p. 137), and elsewhere. Menno believed Cyprian was a Greek like Origen.

[38] Cf. Armour, *Anabaptist Baptism*, p. 50.

[39] Bucer, *Quid de Baptismate Infantium*, sig. Dviii^v.

parvulorum.⁴⁰ He makes the point repeatedly. His argument is the very reverse of Menno's. The unanimity of *veteres illos omnes Ecclesiarum praefectos et doctores, per universum orbem Christianum*, speaks in favour of their common tradition being apostolic, especially since *plerique Apostolicis temporibus vicini fuerunt*.⁴¹ Cassander uses the strongest language—*absurdissimum, insania*—to dismiss the notion that this common mind on the part of churchmen who otherwise faithfully transmitted the apostles' teaching was no more than a common delusion. And he can cite a Father to provide the clinching principle, Tertullian, who on this occasion is a wholly amenable witness: *quid apud multos unum invenitur, non erratum, sed traditum.*⁴²

Cassander's position is little different from Melanchthon's. When the ancient writers' teachings are clear, *nec est ab illis sine certis et perspicuis scripturae testimoniis dissentiendum.*⁴³ When early tradition is not in dispute, one needs incontrovertible scriptural grounds for abandoning it in preference for novelty.

Infant Baptism and Original Sin

In turn Cassander accuses the Anabaptists of serious disagreement among themselves on whether infants are or can be saved.⁴⁴ He makes much of this issue, not only for its controversial value but also because the universal early consensus on which his argument hinges includes, in addition to the invariable practice, a single shared theological rationale for the practice: *iisdem omnes rationibus et argumentis...utuntur, videlicet infantes originalis peccati contagione vitiatos, peccati et mortis reos teneri, a quo nisi per aquam et spiritum renati purgentur, et sanguine Christi, qui per baptismum efficax est, abluantur, a societate corporis Christi, et ingressu regni caelestis excludi.*⁴⁵ In other words, the Fathers were all good Augustinians! (Cassander is nearer the mark in quoting from John 3.5; no other text was so influential in shaping early Christian thought about baptism.)

When this particular claim is tested against Cassander's catalogue of *testimonia*, it manages to retain some degree of plausibility. Origen in Latin can be read, no doubt unhistorically, as propounding an orthodox western doctrine of original sin, citing as he does Job 14.4-5 (LXX) and

---

⁴⁰ *Testimonia* 1563, sig. B6ᵛ; *Testimonia* 1616, p. 676. Cf. also sig. E7ᵛ/p. 691, sig. F4ᵛ/p. 693.
⁴¹ *Testimonia* 1563, sig. B8ᵛ; *Testimonia* 1616, p. 677.
⁴² *Testimonia* 1563, sig. B5ᵛ-6ʳ; *Testimonia* 1616, pp. 675-76. Cf. sig. F4ᵛ/p. 693. Tertullian, *Prescriptions of Heretics* 28.
⁴³ *Iudicium, CR*, I, col. 962, cited by Fraenkel, *Testimonia Patrum*, p. 186 n. 71.
⁴⁴ *Testimonia* 1563, sigs. B7ʳ-8ʳ, G3ʳᵛ; *Testimonia* 1616, pp. 676-77, 697.
⁴⁵ *Testimonia* 1563, sigs. B6ᵛ-7ʳ; *Testimonia* 1616, p. 676.

Psalm 50(51).7 (LXX), two of Augustine's favourite proof-texts. In fact, Origen is most probably assuming the impurity of newborn pre-existing souls. Tertullian's warning in *De Baptismo* against *innocens aetas* hastening to the font is not among the *testimonia* (although Cassander mentions the work elsewhere in this treatise).

Cassander knew John Chrysosom's homily to the newly-baptized only in Augustine's quotation: *et infantes baptizamus, quamvis peccata non habentes*, which Augustine interpreted as excluding only sins of their own commission, not the stain of original sinfulness.[46] Not only Chrysostom but the Greek Fathers almost to a man never linked infant baptism with original sin. For the rest, the *testimonia* are overwhelmingly derived from Augustine and the Pelagian controversy.

Cassander thus remains happily unaware of the broad consensus of the pre-Nicene Fathers on the sinlessness of infants,[47] and the widespread conviction among the later Greek Fathers that infants were baptized not for the remission of sins at all—whether original or their own—but to receive gifts and graces.[48] Although they lacked the knowledge of the Fathers to support it, those Anabaptists who regarded infants as free from sin (Cassander names Obbe Phillips and Menno Simons[49]) were closer to a patristic consensus than Cassander.

Yet in the end of the day, a consensus of the Fathers eluded all parties to the controversy. It would be harsh to judge them by the canons of modern historical study. Amid much that does not survive serious scrutiny (such as the allegation found among the Anabaptists that paedobaptism had been in effect instituted with the invention of godparents by Hyginus, a short-lived pope who flourished c.140[50]),

---

[46] *Testimonia* 1563, sigs. D5ʳ-6ʳ, G3ʳᵛ; *Testimonia* 1616, pp. 684-85. John Chrysostom, *Baptismal Catecheses* 3:6, Augustine, *Contra Julianum* 1:6:21-22 (Kraft, *Texte zur Geschichte*, no. 26). The *Catecheses* were first published by Antoine Wenger, *Jean Chrysostome. Huit catéchèses baptismales inédites* (SC 50; Paris, 1957); cf. Wright, 'How Controversial', pp. 54-55 (p. 33 above).

[47] Cf. Kurt Aland, *Die Stellung der Kinder in der frühen christlichen Gemeinden und ihre Taufe* (Munich, 1967), pp. 17-21.

[48] Cf. David F. Wright, 'The Meaning and Reference of 'One Baptism for the Remission of Sins' in the Niceno-Constantinopolitan Creed', *Studia Patristica* 19 (1989), pp. 281-85 (see ch. 4 above).

[49] *Testimonia* 1563, sigs. B7ᵛ; *Testimonia* 1616, p. 676.

[50] Cf. Menno Simons, *Verklaringe* (*Opera Omnia*, fol. 411b; *Complete Writings*, p. 253), and elsewhere; Bernhard Rothmann, in a Disputation of 7-8 August 1533, in Stupperich (ed.), *Die Schriften Bernhard Rothmanns*, pp. 113-14. The source of this strange notion is most probably Gratian's *Decretum* III, *De Consecr.* IV. 100 [ed. A. Friedberg, *Corpus Iuris Canonici*, I; Leipzig, 1879], col. 1879). However, the ruling credited there to Pope Hyginus (*In catecumino, et in baptismo, et in confirmatione unus patrinus fieri potest, si necessitas cogit...*) derives from the *Penitential* of Theodore of Canterbury, Bk 2:4:8 (*PL* 99, col. 929 [trans. John T. McNeill and Helena M. Gamer;

Cassander's treatise stands out for its responsible moderation.[51]

Medieval Handbooks of Penance; New York, 1938], p. 202). How it came to be ascribed to Hyginus (in several collections earlier than Gratian's) I have yet to discover.

[51] A cursory comparison with the collection discussed by Balthasar Hubmaier in the second version of his *Der uralten und gar neuen Lehrer Urteil* of 1526 places Cassander in a different league for scholarship. Hubmaier's listing is spattered with gross errors, e.g. his second authority, in 'Anno 137', is one Thonatos, bishop of Carthage, who taught 'das man kein Kindt solt taufen, das nit den glauben bekenet' (Gunnar Westin and Torsten Bergsten (eds), *Balthasar Hubmaier Schriften* [Quellen und Forschungen zur Reformationsgeschichte, 29; Quellen zur Geschichte der Täufer 9; Gütersloh, 1962), pp. 243-49, at p. 244).

CHAPTER 14

1 Corinthians 7.14 in Fathers and Reformers

The fact that modern exegetes find a passage or verse of scripture unusually difficult is sufficient justification for turning to the attempts of earlier centuries to understand it. That 1 Corinthians 7.14 continues to find commentators at sixes and sevens needs no proof here.[1] For me it has long been associated with the enquiry into the origins of infant baptism, not least in the context of the celebrated exchanges on this issue between Joachim Jeremias and Kurt Aland.[2] Aland made much of Jeremias' change of opinion on the implications of the verse between the German and the English editions of *Die Kindertaufe in den ersten vier Jahrhunderten*, although he criticized Jeremias for not pursuing his revised reading to its logical conclusion. The continuing breadth of interpretations of the verse may be illustrated by the contribution of my Edinburgh colleague Professor John O'Neill.[3] In face of wide, if not universal, agreement that the 'sanctification' (ἡγίασται) of the unbelieving husband or wife and the 'holiness' (ἅγιά) of the children do not stem from baptism (for it is self-evident that the former is unbaptized and the structure of the argument requires it of the latter), he insists that in Paul's thought only the baptized are called holy or sanctified. Therefore, he concludes, the perfect tense of ἡγίασται must be read as a future. He finds Theodore of Mopsuestia and Theodoret of Cyrrhus furnishing support for his exegesis. Jeremias had earlier collected some patristic testimonies (including Theodoret) in favour of his reading of the verse.

---

[1] See, e.g., G. Delling, 'Nun aber sind sie heilig', *Gott und die Götter. Festgabe für E. Fascher zum 60. Geburtstag* (Berlin, 1958), pp. 84-93 (reprinted in his *Studien zum Neuen Testament und zum Hellenistischen Judentum: Gesammelte Aufsätze 1950–1968* [ed. F. Hahn *et al.*; Göttingen, 1970], pp. 257-69); E. Best, '1 Corinthians 7:14 and Children in the Church', *Irish Biblical Studies* 12 (1990), pp. 158-66.

[2] Reviewed in David F. Wright, 'The Origins of Infant Baptism—Child Believers' Baptism?', *Scottish Journal of Theology* 40 (1987), pp. 1-23, at pp. 14-18 (see ch. 1 above, pp. 14-17).

[3] John O'Neill, '1 Corinthians 7,14 and Infant Baptism', in A. Vanhoye (ed.), *L'Apôtre Paul. Personnalité, style et conception du ministère* (Bibliotheca Ephemeridum Theologicarum Lovaniensium, 73; Louvain, 1986), pp. 357-61.

Patristic Resources Available

The concern of this paper lies neither with the correct scientific interpretation of 1 Corinthians 7.14 nor with how the early Fathers interpreted it—a task that apparently remains to be done.[4] Nevertheless, it will be useful at the outset to survey the patristic resources that sixteenth-century expositors—I shall be concentrating largely on Protestant writers—drew upon in seeking to make sense of the verse. They turn out to be surprisingly limited—considerably more so than the range available. For example, Augustin Marlorat lists two (supposed) Fathers among his sources for the treatment of 1 Corinthians in his *Novi Testamenti Catholica Expositio Ecclesiastica* (Geneva, 1561), Oecumenius (i.e. Ps.-Oecumenius[5]) and Theophylact, Archbishop of Achrida in Bulgaria in the late eleventh and early twelfth centuries. Marlorat uses neither for 7.14.[6] I have so far found neither cited by name by a Protestant commentator on this verse in the sixteenth century.

The Reformers had, of course, Ambrose's, i.e. Ambrosiaster's Pauline commentary.[7] Chrysostom's homilies were also well known, and four passages from Augustine were also cited, two from *De Sermone Domini in Monte* and two from *De Peccatorum Meritis et Remissione et de Baptismo Parvulorum*.[8] (The last of these also refers to Pelagius' explanation of the verse.) Three of these discussions (the fourth is of marginal significance) were the extracts assembled on this verse in the ninth century in the Augustinian *Collectonea* on the Pauline Epistles by Florus of Lyons,

---

[4] Of the study of patristic texts of 1 Corinthians 7 undertaken by Y. Tissot (see R. Braun, 'Tertullien et l'exégèse de 1 Cor 7', in J. Fontaine *et al.* (eds), *Epektasis. Mélanges patristiques offerts au Cardinal Jean Daniélou* (Paris, 1972), pp. 21-28, at p. 28 n. 47), see the firstfruits in 'Hénogamie et remariage chez Clément d'Alexandrie', in *Revista di Storia e Letteratura Religiosa* 9 (1975), pp. 167-97. In any case, verse 14 requires exceptional treatment within the argument of this chapter.

[5] Cf. M. Geerard (ed.), *Clavis Patrum Graecorum* (5 vols; Turnhout, 1983–87), III, p. 395 no. 7475, cf. no. 7471.

[6] Marlorat uses only sixteenth-century sources: Peter Martyr, Erasmus' *Paraphrases* (which is what the abbreviation 'E' stands for, not for Erasmus Sarcerius as given in Marlorat's list), Calvin and Bullinger, as well as himself ('A', unlisted) and another as yet unidentified brief passage on the Anabaptists ('R', unlisted). See *Novi Testamenti...Ecclesiastica* (s. 1., 7th edn, 1620), pp. 667, 693.

[7] The last four lines of comment *ad loc.* in Conrad Pellican's *In Omnes Apostolicas Epistolas, Pauli, Petri, Iacobi, Ioannis et Iudae...Commenatarii...* (Zürich, 1539) are from Ambrosiaster, slightly altered. The preceding thirteen lines are from the *Paraphrases* of Erasmus, and the first eight in some form from Chrysostom *ad loc.* Pellican has contributed nothing: *Commentarii*, pp. 215-16.

[8] Augustine, *De Sermone...* 1:16:45, 1:22:73 (*PL* 34, cols. 1252, 1266); *De Peccatorum...* 2:25:41–26:42, 3:12:21 (*PL* 44, cols. 175-77, 198-99).

which the sixteenth century knew under the name of Bede.[9] Erasmus' *Annotationes* from 1519 on referred to Augustine's two references to our verse in *De Sermone Domini in Monte*.[10]

The commentary published in the sixteenth century under the name of Primasius of Hadrumetum (d. c. 552) was in fact the bowdlerized version, by Cassiodorus and his pupils, of an anonymous exposition whose author (unknown to Cassiodorus) was Pelagius. On 1 Corinthians 7.14 it incorporates parts of the influential passage from Augustine's *De Sermone Domini in Monte*.[11] Another interpolated form of Pelagius' commentary carries an attribution to Jerome. This was printed by Erasmus in his edition of Jerome.[12] The influence of one or other of these derivatives from Pelagius is undoubtedly discernible in the sixteenth century, even though they are rarely cited by name. It was Pelagius who introduced, in support of the hope that an unbelieving spouse might be won to faith by the demeanour of the believing partner, the citation of 1 Peter 3.1 ('...so that some [husbands], though they do not obey the word, may be won without a word by the behaviour of their wives'). This survives into 'Primasius'-Cassiodorus.[13]

The absentees from this inventory are perhaps neither significant nor surprising. The patristic commentators known to us only from catena fragments were of course inaccessible in the early modern centuries—Cyril of Alexandria, Oecumenius, Origen, Severian of Cabala, Theodore of Mopsuestia and Photius.[14] Theodoret's exegesis makes three

---

[9] See literature cited under *CPL*, pp. 134-35 no. 360. Bede's genuine Augustinian florilegium on Paul remains unpublished, *CPL*, p. 448 no. 1360.

[10] A. Reeve and M.A. Screech (eds), *Erasmus' Annotations on the New Testament: Acts—Romans—I and II Corinthians* (Studies in the History of Christian Thought, 42; Leiden, 1990), p. 463.

[11] *CPL*, p. 200 no. 902; *PL* 68, cols. 521-22. Migne reproduces the edition issued in Paris in 1537 by Jean Gagney. Gagney was himself the compiler of *Divi Pauli Apostoli Epistolae, Brevissimis & Facillimis Scholiis...Illustratae* (Paris, 1538). This does not comment on the main part of 1 Cor. 7.14, but mentions Theodoret and Augustine (35^v). Its explanation of Paul's statement about the children offers two meanings for *sancti—legitimi*, or nurtured into holiness.

[12] Cf. *Opera Omnium...Hieronymi* (9 vols; Basel, 1516), IX, 152^v. The Preface to this volume by Bruno Amerbach raises the question of Jerome's authorship, while recognizing that an ancient MS and the *Glossa* ascribe it to Jerome. See now *CPL*, p. 308 no. 952; *PL* 30, cols. 645-902. Cf. A. Souter, *The Earliest Latin Commentaries on the Epistles of St. Paul* (Oxford, 1927), pp. 207-208.

[13] *PL Supplementum*, I, col. 1201; *PL* 68, cols. 521-22.

[14] Cf. the list in H.J. Sieben, *Exegesis Patrum. Saggio bibliografico sull' esegesi biblica dei Padri della Chiesa* (Sussidi Patristici, 2; Rome, 1983), pp. 189-90; K. Staab, *Pauluskommentare aus der griechischen Kirche* (Münster, 1933), pp. 182, 250, 557-58; J.A. Cramer, *Catenae Graecorum Patrum in Novum Testamentum* vol. V (Oxford, 1844), pp. 132-34.

points, none of which is at all exceptional: first, Paul is not allowing for a believer to enter into marriage with an unbeliever, but speaking only of those married as unbelievers, one of whom subsequently was converted; second, in this context the unbelieving partner ἔχει σωτηρίας ἐλπίδα through the influence of the believer; third, whether or not conversion takes place, their seed μεθέξει τῆς σωτηρίας.[15]

The only patristic witness whose absence is remarkable is Tertullian, who touches on 1 Corinthians 7.14 in at least two of his works. Furthermore, Jerome answers a question from Paulinus of Nola about this verse—how children of baptized believers can be said to be holy without having received the grace of baptism—by referring him to Tertullian. Unfortunately, Jerome seems to have cited the wrong work of Tertullian (*De Monogamia* instead of *Ad Uxorem*), which may help to explain the silence of the sixteenth century.[16]

Texts and Translations

Before proceeding to review a selection of Reformation expositions of 1 Corinthians 7.14, we should look briefly at the text itself and some of its sixteenth-century translations. In later medieval works the Vulgate most commonly reads as follows:

sanctificatus est enim vir infidelis per mulierem fidelem, et sanctificata est mulier infidelis per virum fidelem; alioquin filii vestri immundi essent, nunc autem sancti sunt.

The clarifying addition of *fidelem*, twice (there is a little early support for this), is of no moment, since the meaning in each case is not in doubt. (Wolfgang Musculus is the only commentator who thinks otherwise, as we shall see.) Much more significant is the adoption of *per mulierem/virum* where the Greek has ἐν τῇ γυναικί etc.[17] This version unquestionably

---

[15] *PG* 82, cols. 276-77.

[16] Jerome, *Epistle* 85:2, 5 (*PL* 22, col. 753). See A. d'Alès, 'Tertullien sur I Cor., VII, 14', *Recherches de Science Religieuse* 2 (1911), pp. 54-56, and Braun, 'Tertullien et l'exégèse de 1 Cor 7'. This letter of Jerome was printed in his *Opera Omnia* (Paris, 1533), III, 68ᵛ; in Erasmus' first edition, *Operum Omnium*, vol. IV (Basel, 1516), 89ʳᵛ. Also apparently unused in the sixteenth century was Jerome's application of 1 Corinthians 7.13-14 to more extended family relationships in his *Epistle* 107 to Laeta, encouraging her, on the birth of her daughter Paula, to hope still for the conversion of her father Albinus: *Sanctus et fidelis domus virum sanctificat infidelem. Iam candidatus est fidei, quem filiorum et nepotum credens turba circumdat* (*Ep.* 107:1, *PL* 22, cols. 867-88; *Opera Omnia*, vol. I (Paris, 1534), 19ᵛ; vol. I (Basel, 1516), 25ᵛ).

[17] I have found no instances of the mixed text, *in muliere fideli...per virum fidelem*, adopted in Robert Weber's Stuttgart edition of the Vulgate (except in Pelagius and his derivative, 'Primasius'-Cassiodorus). The Old Latin generally retained *in uxore* etc.; so

undergirds what is probably the dominant interpretation during the pre-Reformation era as a whole, which focuses on the influence of the believing partner on the unbelieving, whose conversion is contemplated with varying degrees of confidence.

Also noteworthy in the Vulgate is the variation in the last part of the verse between *essent* and *sunt* (the Greek has ἐστίν in both places). This variation predates the Vulgate, being found in Augustine and Ambrosiaster, for example. In the latter the reading *essent* clearly facilitates, if it does not require, an interpretation which would exercise long-lasting influence:

> inmundi essent filii eorum, si dimitterent volentes habitare secum et aliis se copularent. essent enim adulteri ac per hoc et filii eorum spurii, ideo inmundi.[18]

Alioquin as understood by Ambrosiaster denotes not, more immediately, the unbelieving partner remaining unsanctified, but the separation of the partners (partly, no doubt, as a consequence of this). That is to say, this exegesis of the last sentence of verse 14 has reference not so much, or not chiefly, to the earlier part of the verse as to verses 12-13. Ambrosiaster's interpretation is clearly recognizable in the *Glossa Ordinaria ad loc.*, and in Gratian's *Decretum* is ascribed to scripture itself.[19]

Finally in the Vulgate's text, *mundi* is a not infrequent variant for *sancti*, being found, for example, in the *Glossa*. I also note, without being able to comment further, that the only change made in Wittenberg's corrected Vulgate of 1529 (apart from the inconsequential dropping of *fidelem*) was *sanctificatur* (twice) for *sanctificatus/a est.*[20]

Erasmus' treatment of this verse is intriguing. His new translation of 1516 was as follows:

Ambrosiaster, Augustine, the Codex Claromontanus (ed. C. Tischendorf; Leipzig, 1852, p. 120), and the Latin Irenaeus (ed. W. Sanday *et al.* Oxford, 1923, p. 134). Cf. P. Sabatier, *Bibliorum Sacrorum Latinae Versiones Antiquae...* (Paris, 1751), vol. III.2, p. 679. For a comprehensive *apparatus* see Tischendorf's *Novum Testamentum Graece* (Leipzig, 8th edn, 1872), vol. II, p. 492 *ad loc.*

[18] H.J. Vogels (ed.), *Commentarius in Epistulas Paulinas*, vol. II (*CSEL* 81), p. 76 *ad loc.*

[19] Gratian, *Decretum*, Pars II, c.xxviii, qu. ii, ed. A. Friedberg, *Corpus Iuris Canonici* (2 vols; Leipzig, 1879), I, col. 1089.

[20] *WADB* 5, p. 654. On this edition, see K. Aland, 'Die Ausgaben der Vulgata des Neuen Testaments von Gutenberg bis zur Clementina', in R. Gryson (ed.), *Philologia Sacra. Biblische und Patristische Studien für Hermann J. Frede und Walter Thiele zu ihrem Siebzigsten Geburtstag*, Bd. II: *Apokryphen, Kirchenväter, Verschiedenes* (Vetus Latina. Aus der Geschichte der Lateinischen Bibel, 24/2; Freiburg, 1993), pp. 654-69, at pp. 662-66.

Sanctificatus est enim *maritus* infidelis, *in uxore*, et sanctificata est *uxor* infidelis, *in marito*, Alioqui filii vestri inmundi *sunt*, nunc autem sancti sunt.

The changes are italicised. But from the second edition of 1519 onwards, Erasmus backtracked, reinstating *per uxorem/maritum* and *essent*. The only new element was *incredulus/a* for *infidelis*. Correspondingly, from 1519 his *Annotationes*, although retaining from 1516 a direct translation of the two Greek phrases—i.e., *in muliere, in viro*—added an endorsement of the Vulgate which reflected his change of mind:

Atque hoc sane loco recte mutavit interpres praepositionem, quod tamen alias aut veretur aut negligit facere.[21]

Furthermore, the vernacular translations largely reflected Erasmus' second thoughts rather than his first. All the English versions I have examined, down to the King James Version of 1611, have 'by',[22] and the French of Olivétan-Calvin likewise renders it 'par'. Similarly Luther in 1522 and still in 1546 has 'durch(s)'.[23] In addition, these various vernacular translations all reflect *essent/sunt* rather than the Greek's ἐστίν/ἐστίν. So much for the recovery of the original languages!

Beyond Luther

I turn now to an examination of a handful of Reformation exegetes, with a special eye on their engagement with their patristic predecessors. Luther comes first, but only so that we may then lay him on one side as utterly unrepresentative, rather like Melchizedek, without ancestry or progeny, in no discernible relationship to what went before and with no discernible influence on what followed. The key for Luther is faith, for all things are pure and holy to faith, and faith knows how to use everything aright, whether good or evil. Faith is so efficacious that living with unbelievers is no obstacle to it. Children are holy not in themselves but to the believing parent's faith—and Luther extends this to cover adult children who are unbaptized.[24] His remarkable emphasis on faith has no obvious interest in

---

[21] Reeve and Screech (eds), *Erasmus' Annotations*, p. 463.
[22] L.A. Weigle (ed.), *The New Testament Octapla* (New York, 1946), pp. 948-49; *The English Hexapla...* (London, 1841), *ad loc.*
[23] *WADB* 7, pp. 104-105.
[24] M. Luther, *Das siebend Capitel S. Pauli zu den Chorinthern Ausgelegt...* (Wittenberg, 1523); *In septimum primae ad Corinthios caput, Exegesis...* (Strasbourg, 1525). For the former, *WA* 12, pp. 121-23; for the latter, *Exegesis*, 27^r-28^v. The dominant note of Luther's interpretation is clearly heard in one of the earliest printed vernacular expositions, by the anti-Philippist Cyriacus Spangenberg (1528–1604) of Mansfeld. In *Die erste Epistel Pauly an die Corinthier. Gepredigt und Auszgelegt...* (Strasbourg, 1569), he cites not only Titus 1.15 but also Romans 8.28 and the examples

its bringing unbelievers to share it but only in its somehow covering and cohabiting with unbelief without loss of faith's own integrity.

Melanchthon's 1523 *Annotationes* on the Epistle do not touch on this verse.[25] His *Commentarius in Epistolas Pauli ad Corinthios* of 1551 may echo Luther at one point (*propter fidem alterius coniugis concubitus sit mundities, et procreati mundi*), but in general it moves much more within the orbit of mainstream sixteenth-century exegesis, while still retaining a marked individual character.[26] His interest is chiefly in the children, whom he takes to be declared not *spurii*, illegitimate, bastards, and hence not to be debarred from God's church in accordance with the Hebrew of Deuteronomy 23.2. Consequently the *consuetudo coniugalis* from which they are born must be pleasing to God. In accord with several other interpreters, Melanchthon in effect transfers the sanctification ascribed by Paul to the unbelieving partner to the marriage itself, and does not answer our question about the sense in which he or she is 'sanctified'. A closely similar handling of the text appeared in Erasmus' *Paraphrases*:

> Itaque maritus quamvis religione profanus, tamen per Christianae consortium, quod ad conjugii negotium attinet, sanctus redditur. Item uxor...sancta puraque redditur, ob legitimum usum matrimonii.[27]

But as we shall see later, Erasmus has more to say about the unbelieving spouse. Lefèvre d'Étaples goes so far as to deny that the unbelieving spouse himself or herself receives any sanctification but only for the purpose of procreation:

> In sanctificatione mulieris fidelis sanctificatur vir infidelis non simpliciter, sed quo ad generationis actum. Et in sanctificatione viri fidelis sanctificatur uxor infidelis non simpliciter: sed quo ad generationis ex viro officium.[28]

---

of Esther's marriage to King Ahasuerus and Constantine's sister's marriage to the godless Licinius to demonstrate the might of faith (xcviii^v, col. 2). I am grateful to the Herzog August Bibliothek, Wolfenbüttel, for providing a microfilm of part of this rare volume (of which there are copies in Strasbourg and Ohio State University, Columbus, OH).

[25] I have seen *Annotationes in Epistolam Pauli ad Romanos unam. Et ad Corinthios duas...* (Strasbourg, 1524); ed. P.F. Barton in R. Stupperich (ed.), *Melanchthons Werke in Auswahl*. vol. IV: *Frühe Exegetische Schriften* (Gütersloh, 1963).

[26] Carolus Gottlieb Bretschneider and Henricus Ernestus Bindseil (eds), *Philippi Melanchthonis Opera*, in *CR* (28 vols; Halle, 1834–60), 15, cols. 1087-88. Spangenberg too refers to Deuteronomy 23.2 (*Die erste Epistel...*, xcix^r, col. 1).

[27] Erasmus, *Paraphrases in Novum Testamentum, ad loc.* (*LB* 7, col. 880). Juán de Valdés, in his commentary, allows that the holiness of one partner affects the other (*la sanctidad del uno haze sancto al otro*) but places the accent on the sanctification making the marriage legitimate (*la sanctificazion pertenezca á hazer lizito el matrimonio*). A non-Christian marriage is illegal, and its offspring illegitimate. I have seen only *La Epistola de San Pablo a los Romanos, i la I. Corintios* (Madrid, London, 1856), pp. 127-28.

This line of exegesis goes back ultimately to Ambrosiaster—see the quotation above on p. 196 (at n. 18), which likewise takes *immundi* to mean *spurii*. Yet Melanchthon recognises its minimal character (*si quis contendat, plus dici*), and proceeds to offer another reading, explaining *sancti* as ingrafted into the church by baptism or by prayer. There may be another echo of Ambrosiaster in his contrasting these two ways of consecrating babies with pagan γενέθλια under the patronage of idols.[29] Not surprisingly, none of the patristic sources goes so far as to interpret the sanctity of the children in terms of baptism or any rite of ecclesial consecration.

We look next at the commentary on the two Corinthian Epistles by Sebastian Meyer of Berne.[30] Although we find here notes very similar to Melanchthon's—*sancti* interpreted as *legitimi, non spurii, tanquam ab immundis ac foeda libidine prognati*, and the same preoccupation with the marriage itself (*Infidelis...sanctificatur quo ad usum coniugii*)—there may be an echo or two of Chrysostom. The latter viewed the apostle's concern in this verse as to dispel the believer's *fear* of being contaminated by conjugal intercourse with an unbeliever. He asserted the superior efficacy of piety over impiety, and pointed out that no warrant is here given to believers to enter into marriages with unbelievers.[31] These three emphases are present in Meyer, although no textual dependence can be claimed. The Reformer appeals to a passage in Augustine's *De Conjugiis Adulterinis* which cites our verse in the course of arguing that 'the Pauline privilege' for a believer to divorce an unbelieving partner, though permissible, is not expedient.[32]

---

[28] Lefèvre d'Étaples, *Epistole divi Pauli apostoli: cum commentaries...* (Paris, [1517]), f. xci^v. He is similarly minimizing about the *sanctitas derivatitia* of the child: *quaedam sanctitas incoata, non consummata, quae si per baptismum consummatur: haec ex sanctitatis fonte proximae et ex spiritu sancto erit sanctitas et tali iam coelum apertum est.*

[29] Ambrosiaster, *quidquid per dicationem idolorum fit, immundum est* (*Commentarius*, vol. II, p. 76); Melanchthon, *pios vehementer abhorruisse ab idolis* (*Commentarius*, CR 15, col. 1088. Hardly any other commentators mention idols here.

[30] Sebastian Meyer, *In utranque epistolam ad Corinthios commentarii* (Frankfurt, 1546), 54^rv.

[31] John Chrysostom, *Homilies on 1 Corinthians* 19:2-3 (*PG* 61, cols. 154-55). The ascendancy of the *sanctitas viri fidelis* over the *immunditiam mulieris infidelis*, and viceversa, is the core of the interpretation given by Francis Titelmann, *Elucidatio in Omnes Epistolas Apostolicas* (Antwerp, 1532), H2^rv. On Titelmann, a Belgian Franciscan, see T.H.L. Parker, *Commentaries on the Epistle to the Romans 1532–1542* (Edinburgh, 1986), pp. 11-14.

[32] Augustine, *De Conjugiis Adulterinis* 1:13-14 (*PL* 40, col. 459).

Wolfgang Musculus

The Pauline commentary of Wolfgang Musculus is full of interest.[33] First, with an explicit reference to John Chrysostom, he spells out the believing spouse's fear: if, as Paul wrote earlier in the letter, the man who is joined to a prostitute becomes one body with her (1 Corinthians 6.16), will not the person bound to an idolater likewise become one body with him or her? But whereas Chrysostom's response assures the fearful that the purity of the believer will prevail over the other's impurity, Musculus appeals to the *virtus nuptiarum* and reduces *sanctitas* to *mundicia coniugalis thori*. Jerome, i.e. the interpolator of Pelagius, provides him with the axiom *ex traditione Dei sanctae sunt nuptiae*,[34] and Ambrose (Ambrosiaster), as we have noted, confirms that the children are *sancti* in the sense of being born of a legitimate marriage.

'The simplest understanding of this passage', Musculus declares,[35] excludes any link with the *sanctitas* which issues from the covenant of God or the Spirit of faith as believers are consecrated into the people of God. The Vulgate's addition of *fideli* to qualify *in uxore* and *in marito* is unacceptable. If anything is to be added, *legitima/o* would suffice. The *sanctificatio*, i.e. *mundicia*, is not to be attributed to the faith of the believing married partner but to the marriage itself, *propter traditionem Dei*. Musculus maintains that the unbeliever remains *impurus* as far as religion is concerned. Otherwise, he says (*Alioqui!*), *molestam pariet disputationem quomodo vir infidelis sanctificatus dici possit*. This is to cut the Gordian knot with a vengeance!

And as if to drive home his radicalism, he applies Paul's counsel also to the believing wife whose husband, although formally a Christian, lives a godless and depraved life. Their cohabitation and intercourse remain

---

[33] Wolfgang Musculus, *In Apostoli Pauli Ambas Epistolas Ad Corinthios Commentarii...*, Editio ultima (Basel, [1611]), pp. 85-86. The text is unchanged from the 1559 and 1566 Basel editions. The 1555 edition listed by H.M. Adams, *Catalogue of Books Printed on the Continent of Europe, 1501–1600, in Cambridge Libraries* (Cambridge, 1967), I, p. 765 no. 2034, is in fact the 1559 first edition; Adams' date belongs to Musculus' 1555 Romans (no. 2029), with which the Corinthians commentary is bound in the Queen's College Library copy.

[34] Ps-Jerome, *PL* 30, col. 737. This is in essence the interpretation given by Claude Guilliaud, *Collatio in Omnes Divi Pauli Apostoli Epistolas* (Lyons, 1542), p. 131: *Tanto honore dignatus est Christus nuptias, ut etiam altero coniugum Christiano, purae & legitimae dicantur*. Parker, *Commentaries on Romans*, p. 81, describes the 1544 edition as 'greatly enlarged', but in the Paris 1550 edition Guilliaud has dropped (108ᵛ) the concluding comment on *Alioqui sunt immundi—id est spurii et illegitimi sunt*. Although he was Sorbonne-trained, accusations of heresy in 1545 forced Guilliaud to revise the work (Parker, *Commentaries on Romans*, pp. 79-82).

[35] Melanchthon twice presents his first interpretation as 'the simplest', *CR*, 15, cols. 1087, 1088.

pure—to the pure wife. Having thus exalted the sanctity of marriage, Musculus has to refute those who cite this verse in attempting to vindicate the sacramental character of marriage.[36] He shows that marriage does not satisfy Augustine's well-known definition of a sacrament.

Turning to the final clauses about children, the Augsburg Reformer continues to surprise us. He prefers a 'simpler' reading than Ambrosiaster's, which we saw related *Alioqui* not to the earlier part of the verse but to the previous verse.[37] The apostle has in mind the sanctity of marriage even between two unbelievers, saying, in effect:

> Unless marriage were holy and clean even between unbelievers, what else would follow than that all the children of unbelievers would be illegitimate and unclean? God forbid! They are *sancti* because born of lawful wedlock.

Musculus' parting shot is a *retractatio*. He acknowledges having at one time 'abused' this verse to debar the error of the Anabaptists who denied baptism to the children of Christians. He had supposed that 'but now they are holy' meant that they belonged to God's people through their believing parent. In the covenant this is undoubtedly valid. But Musculus cannot any longer allow 1 Corinthians 7.14 any place in this discussion, for a reason that should by now not surprise us. He cannot predicate of these children any holiness or purity which is not applicable to unbelieving parents. Note the final exegetical outrage that Musculus has perpetrated: he has reversed the sequence of Paul's reasoning. Instead of concluding the non-Christian parent's sanctity from the assumed sanctity of the children, he has demoted the latter to what he can countenance as the former.[38]

This is a remarkable tour de force of exegesis, which calls for fuller contextualizing than can be offered here. Where had Musculus previously abused the text?[39] Other questions likewise await further investigation.

---

[36] As is done, e.g., by John Eck, *Enchiridion Locorum Communium adversus Lutherum...* (ed. P. Fraenkel; Corpus Catholicorum, 34; Münster, 1979), p. 141 (De Matrimonio): *Sine gratia generare filios, esset plus damnatio quam salvatio. 'Si quis frater...nunc autem sancti sunt' per sacramentum.*

[37] *Ambrosius respicit ad id quod dixit*, ne dimittat eam. *Altera expositio, ad id quod dixit*, sanctificatus est vir infidelis in coniuge.

[38] *Nec de alia agitur sanctitate ac puritate liberorum, quam quae & infidelibus parentibus competit.* J.B. Lightfoot, *Notes on the Epistles of St. Paul* (London, 1904), p. 226, speaks of the 'argumentative ἐπεὶ "since otherwise"...i.e. "since on the contrary supposition it follows that your children are unclean", a thing not to be thought of'.

[39] Musculus' Corinthian commentary was published in 1559. He may be alluding here to his 1555 Romans commentary, where he defends infant baptism against Anabaptist objections appealing to Romans 14.23, 'Whatever is not of faith, is sin.' Faith cannot be present where there is no explicit (*expressum*) word of God (concerning infant baptism) to generate it. Faith does not require such explicitness, says Musculus,

It is instructive to set next to Musculus John Calvin's commentary published in 1546 (although he had first lectured on the Epistle at Strasbourg in 1539).[40] He names none of the expositors with whom he is interacting, and mixes one or two arbitrary elements with some sounder conclusions than Musculus'. The focus is still on the marriage in the first part of the verse. Aware that the *sanctificatio* has been variously understood, he refers it simply to the marriage.

> The godliness of the one avails more to sanctify the marriage than the ungodliness of the other to defile it... As far as the sharing of bed and the whole of life are concerned, the unbeliever is sanctified, lest his uncleanness defile the believer. Yet this sanctification does not benefit the unbelieving partner.

But if the Christian spouse's faith is credited with sanctifying the marriage, does this leave the marriages of the ungodly no better than fornication? Calvin insists that marriage is in itself pure by God's ordination, and distinguishes between its nature and its abuse, which makes it unclean to the ungodly.

He recognizes the last part of the verse as an *argumentum ab effectu*, which moves from the sanctity of the children to the sanctity of the marriage. But he rejects the opinion of some *grammatici* that only *sanctitas civilis*, whereby the children are *legitimi*, is in view. This would not advantage them above unbelievers' children. This passage, *ex intima theologia ductus*, teaches the specially privileged setting apart of the offspring of the godly to be regarded as holy in the church. This requires to be reconciled with the universality of birth in original sin, prompts him to refer readers to his commentary on Romans 10 and 11 for an explanation how believers' children are holy (on Romans 11.16, in fact),

---

> sed satis esse, credere Deum esse in Christo, Deum nostrum et seminis nostri: liberos Christianorum esse sanctos, illorum esse regnum coelorum, participes esse sanguinis et redemptionis Christi, ideoque Christo adferendos...

(edition of Basel, 1600, pp. 252-53).

There is a manuscript in the Berne Burgerbibliothek, MS.h.h.III.59(2), which is ascribed, though not with full certainty, to Musculus (it is not in his hand), entitled 'Von Kindertauff wider die Unruh der Widerteuffern'. (I am indebted to Denise Wittwer Hesse of the Burgerbibliothek for a photocopy. On the MS see E. Bloesch, *Katalog der Handschriften zur Schweizergeschichte der Stadtbibliothek Bern* [Berne, 1895], p. 65.) The treatise includes an explicit citation of 1 Corinthians 7.14 as part of a response to an objection to infant baptism which appealed to Romans 14.23: Wen aber ein Christ der da glaupt die kinder der gläubig sind selig 1 Cor. 7 / vnd dz rÿch der himlen si iren, Matt 19 / vss dem glauben sin kind lasst tauffen / So handelt er nitt on glauben sond(ern) warlich vss sinem glauben... (p. 22). I am grateful to Dr Ernst Koch of Leipzig for help in transcribing this text.

[40] *CO* 49 (*CR* 77), cols. 411-13.

Calvin and Augustine

As so often in Calvin's exegetical corpus, it is almost impossible to identify textual dependence on earlier expositors. Yet the salient features of his relation to the patristic traditions are clear. He follows the tendency set by Ambrosiaster to affirm sanctity of the mixed marriage, not of the unbelieving partner in it. Yet he rejects Ambrosiaster's and others' restriction of the children's 'sanctity' to legitimacy. His final paragraphs probably suggest the long reach of Augustine's somewhat embarrassed grappling with this verse in *De Peccatorum Meritis et Remissione*.

In the much-cited passage in *De Sermone Domini in Monte*, written in the mid-390s, Augustine's interest seizes on an application of 1 Corinthians 7.14 which we have not so far found in any of our Reformation exegetes:

> I believe that it had already occurred (*provenerat*) that some wives had come to faith through their believing husbands, and some husbands through their believing wives... Consequently, the children were now Christian, having been sanctified at the instigation of one of the parents (*auctore uno ex parentibus*) or with the consent of both. This would not happen if the marriage was dissolved when one became a believer, and if the spouse's unbelief was not borne with so far as to afford an opportunity for him or her to come to faith.[41]

What Augustine means by *Iam...erant parvuli christiani, qui...sanctificati erant* is not further clarified.

When he got to grips with the verse almost two decades later, in the early years of the Pelagian dispute, he had to counter its citation in support of the denial of original sin in infants and hence of their need for baptism to deal with it. Sanctification, he establishes, may be of various kinds. The sanctification of catechumens, for example, does not avail for their salvation unless they are baptized.

> *Ac per hoc et illa sanctificatio, cuiuscumque modi sit, quam in filiis fidelium esse dixit apostolus, ad istam de baptismo et de peccati origine vel remissione quaestionem omnino non pertinet.*

To vindicate this position, he argues from the situation of the 'sanctified' unbeliever of the first part of the verse. No one would be so unprincipled, *quodlibet in his verbis intelligat*, as to suppose that a non-Christian husband needs no baptism because his wife is a Christian, and that he

---

[41] Augustine, *De Sermone Domini in Monte* 1:16:45 (*PL* 34, col. 1252, but note the correct reading *si* [not *nisi*] *uno credente*, as in *CCSL* 35, p. 52, ed. A. Mutzenbecher).

already possesses remission of sins because *sanctificatus dictus est in uxore*.[42] The nature of the *sanctificatio* enjoyed by the unbelieving husband or wife and by the children is kept deliberately obscure by Augustine at this point.

He comes back to Paul's statement near the end of book 3. His insistence on the necessity of baptism remains unqualified, but he now offers alternative interpretations. First, as he has set forth elsewhere (presumably in *De Sermone Domini in Monte*) and as Pelagius himself has expounded the passage, sometimes wives had won their husbands to Christ and vice-versa and 'the Christian will of even a single parent had prevailed to make their children Christian'. This last phrase (*parvulorum ad quos faciendos christianos*) appears to resolve the uncertainty we noted above about the reference to the children in *De Sermone Domini in Monte*. The parallelism holds: the children had been sanctified by being brought to baptism and faith.

The second option marks a more significant advance:

> *aut si, quod magis verba apostoli videntur sonare et quodam modo cogere, aliqua illic intelligenda est sanctificatio,*

whether because the husband or wife refrained from intercourse during menstruation, or

> *propter aliam quamlibet, quae ibi aperte posita non est, ex ipsa necessitudine coniugiorum atque filiorum sanctitatis asperginem.*[43]

It is, I suggest, this context of discussion in Augustine that Calvin's commentary rather distantly echoes. Both feel the need to assert, as Calvin puts it, 'the universal propagation of both sin and condemnation in the seed of Adam'. But his divergent understanding of baptism enables Calvin to give more substantial content to the holiness of believers' children. By the blessing of the covenant, the *naturae maledictio* is destroyed for them, and they are consecrated to God through grace. Because this is true of them, they must be baptized.[44] By the same token, we can readily comprehend why Calvin cannot afford to ascribe the

---

[42] Augustine, *De Peccatorum Meritis et Remissione* 2:25:41–26:42 (*PL* 44, cols. 175-77).

[43] Augustine, *De Peccatorum Meritis et Remissione* 3:12:21 (*PL* 44, cols. 198-99).

[44] *CO* 49 (*CR* 77), cols. 412-13. Spangenberg (*Die erste Epistel...*, xcix^r, col. 2) attacks Pelagius, the Anabaptists and Calvin for holding that the offspring of Christians are holy before baptism and without baptism. Against this 'gross error' he cites John 3.6, 1.12-13, Ephesians 2.3 and John 3.5. For Spangenberg, the holiness of the children of 1 Corinthians 7:14 is external only, and all the emphasis falls on the goodness of the mixed marriage. For the holiness that counts before God the children must be baptized (xcix^r, col. 1).

sanctification effected through the believer to his or her married partner, but only to the marriage itself.

Sanctification as Converting Influence

One interpretation of the first part of 1 Corinthians 7.14 is shared by virtually all the patristic authorities whose influence was felt in the sixteenth century. This view interprets the sanctification that is wrought in or through the Christian wife or husband as an influence that makes for the other partner's conversion. As we have noted, Augustine is careful to respect the tense of the Greek ἡγίασται, referring to instances that had presumably already occurred. Pelagius, citing 1 Peter 3.1, likewise says that 'it has often happened that a husband was won (*lucri fieret*) through his wife'.[45] This is preserved in both Pseudo-Primasius[46] (the Cassiodoran expurgated Pelagius), where it precedes the similar sentiment from Augustine's *De Sermone Domini in Monte*, and Pseudo-Jerome (the interpolated Pelagius).[47] John Chrysostom's homily uses the present tense throughout: 'the purity of the believing husband overcomes the impurity of the unbelieving wife... Hence there is hope that the lost partner may be saved through the marriage... What harm is there, tell me, both when the requirements of piety remain unimpaired and when there are good hopes about the unbeliever?... The wife is to lead her man to desire the truth.'[48]

Ambrosiaster's comment is more elusive:

Habere illos [i.e. the unbelieving partners] *beneficium bonae voluntatis ostendit* [i.e. Paul], *qua (quia) horrorem nominis Christi non habent, et ad tuitionem hospitii pertinet, in quo signum fit crucis, quo mors victa est; sanctificatio enim est.*[49]

Some of Ambrosiaster's wording is picked up in Erasmus' *Paraphrases*, which mediated to the sixteenth century an influential and attractive expression of this sense of sanctification. The baptized wife *non admiscetur Ethnico, sed obsequitur marito: nec amat impium, sed tolerat futurum pium*. The husband who does not yet profess Christ gives grounds for 'this hope about himself', since *in uxore non horret Dei cultum*. He is not wholly a pagan, but to some degree already a Christian, since he compliantly lives with a wife who professes the name of Christ, and *crucis signum communi lectulo praefixum videt aequis oculis*.[50]

---

[45] *PL Supplementum* I, col. 1201.
[46] *PL* 68, cols. 521-22.
[47] *PL* 30, cols. 736-37.
[48] *PG* 61, cols. 154-55.
[49] *CSEL* 81, p. 76.
[50] *LB* 7, cols. 880-81.

In addition to the evident dependence on Ambrosiaster, Erasmus may here be echoing Chrysostom's reiterated note of hope, and even Augustine's mention of tolerance, although this last element with one or two others is also found in Pseudo-Oecumenius.[51] But this interpretation of our verse became very common in the medieval centuries. It is found, for example, in Haimo of Auxerre in the ninth century,[52] Bruno of Chartreux in the eleventh,[53] Hervé of Bourgdieu (Pseudo-Anselm)[54] and Peter Lombard[55] in the twelfth, Thomas Aquinas in the thirteenth,[56] Nicolas of Lyra in the fourteenth,[57] and Dionysius the Carthusian in the fifteenth.[58] And on the way it lodged in the *Glossa Ordinaria*.[59] Here, as often in other commentaries, it is not the only interpretation offered, but it is invariably the first in order.

We will accordingly round off this review of sixteenth-century Protestant exegesis of 1 Corinthians 7.14 by looking at some Reformers who consider this interpretation in terms of a converting influence. Zwingli provides two meanings for *sanctificatus est*, first, attracted to faith by the demeanour of the Christian wife, and second, reckoned among the family and people of God, although *infidelis*. (Zwingli also notes that in the New Testament, but not the Old, *mulier viro aequatur*[60].) The Zürich Reformer had cited our verse in his first defence of infant baptism in the letter to Strasbourg of December 1524.[61] Since the children even of one

---

[51] Pseudo-Oecumenius, *Commentaria in Epistolas Pauli, ad loc.* (*PG* 118, col. 729). This is in turn clearly dependent on Chrysostom.

[52] *PL* 117, col. 545, partly echoing Augustine. Cf. B. Smalley, *The Study of the Bible in the Middle Ages* (Oxford, 1942), pp. 39-40.

[53] *PL* 153, cols. 157-58; Smalley, *Study*, p. 48.

[54] *PL* 181, col. 878—very largely Augustine; Smalley, *Study*, p. 79 n. 2.

[55] *PL* 191, col. 1392—Augustine again. He also uses Ambrosiaster and Haimo *ad loc.*

[56] Thomas Aquinas, *In Omnes D. Pauli Apostoli Epistolas Commentarii*, Editio Nova (Liège [?Leodii], 1867), vol. I, pp. 377-78.

[57] Nicholas of Lyra, *Postilla super epistolis beati Pauli Apostoli* (Mantua, 1478), e5v: sanctificatus est enim, *id est conversus ad fidem*, vir infidelis per mulierem fidelem, *ipsum ad hoc inducentem. hoc enim frequenter fiebat in primitiva ecclesia.*

[58] Dionysius the Carthusian, *In Omnes Beati Pauli Epistolas Commentaria* (Cologne, 1533), xlv; *Opera Omnia*, 42 vols in 44 (Montreuil, Tournai, Parkminster, 1896–1935), XIII, pp. 153-54.

[59] *Biblia Latina cum Glossa Ordinaria* (Strasbourg, c. 1480), reprint ed. M.T. Gibson and K. Froehlich (Turnhout, 1992), vol. IV, p. 317.

[60] Zwingli, *Opera Omnia* (Zürich, 1581), vol. IV: *...In Plerosque Novi Testamenti...Annotationes*, p. 464. The *Annotatiunculae per Leonem Iudae...Conceptae* were first published at Zürich in 1528. I have not seen this edition.

[61] E. Egli *et al.* (eds), *Huldreich Zwinglis Sämtliche Werke* (Berlin, Leipzig, Zurich, 1905–), VIII, pp. 272-73 no. 355. Those familiar with latter-day debates about the New Testament basis for infant baptism are likely to be surprised at the limited use made of 1 Corinthians 7.14 in this context in the sixteenth century. The reason for this must lie in

Christian parent are *sancti*, that is, *fideles*, what can prevent their receiving baptism? For the parents he prefers the conversion interpretation.

Bullinger follows a different tack.⁶² Correctly discerning the sequence of Paul's thought (*ignotius demonstrat per notius, nempe per illud quod erat indubitatum apud omnes*), he makes the children's status as *sancti* rest both on their being children of promise in terms of Genesis 17.7 and on their being born of a mixed marriage in which one partner's uncleanness is sanctified by the other's faith. He concedes nothing more to the unbeliever's *sanctificatus* (which he carefully distinguishes from *sanctus*) than the neutralizing, as it were, of the impediment of impiety. He quotes Erasmus' *Paraphrases*, unacknowledged, but none of the Fathers that I can recognize.

The Lutheran Erasmus Sarcerius (1501–59), superintendent and chaplain to Count William of Nassau, weighs up the sense of *sanctificari pro converti*, but decides instead that the apostle uses the word *politice..., pro servari ab ignominia et dedecore*. Likewise *sancti* is applied to the children *politice*, of their legitimate birth from a legitimate marriage.⁶³

---

the verse's embarrassing parallelism between the believing and the unbelieving spouse and the infant. Hence it is not listed among the *rationes e divinis litteris ductae* in George Cassander's *De Baptismo Infantium, Testimonia Veterum Ecclesiasticorum Scriptorum* (Cologne, 1563), in *Opera Omnia* (Paris, 1616), pp. 679-80 (cf. my article 'George Cassander and the Appeal to the Fathers in Sixteenth-Century Debates about Infant Baptism', in L. Grane, A. Schindler and M. Wriedt (eds), *Auctoritas Patrum. Contributions on the Reception of the Church Fathers in the 15th and 16th Century* (Veröffentlichungen des Instituts für Europäische Geschichte Mainz, Abteilung Religionsgeschichte, 37; Mainz, 1993), pp. 259-69 (see ch. 13 above).

Particularly remarkable is the absence of reference to the verse in discussions of the fate of children dying without the benefit of baptism, as, e.g., Luther's 1542 *consolatio*, *Ein Trost den Weibern, welchen es ungerade gegangen ist mit Kindergebären* (WA 53, pp. 202-208), Bugenhagen's exposition of Psalm 29 (30) with which Luther's work was printed (G. Geisenhof, *Bibliotheca Bugenhagiana* [Leipzig, 1908], pp. 360-63 nos. 307-10) and Bugenhagen's later and longer treatise *Von den ungeborn kindern und von den kindern die wir nicht teuffen können...* (Wittenberg, 1551; Geisenhof, *Bibliotheca*, pp. 432-39 nos. 389-95). I am grateful to my research student, Dr Charlotte Methuen, for securing a copy of this Bugenhagen treatise. Exceptionally, Spangenberg does raise this question in his preaching on 1 Corinthians 7.14 but refers to his discussion of it elsewhere in his 'Brautpredigten', which I have not yet been able to follow up (*Die erste Epistel...*, xcix^v, col. 1).

⁶² Heinrich Bullinger, *Commentarii in Omnes Pauli Apostoli Epistolas...* (Zürich, 1582), pp. 128-29; first edition, *In priorem D. Pauli ad Corinthios Epistolam Commentarius* (Zürich, 1534), 79^v-81^r. This text remains unaltered.

⁶³ Erasmus Sarcerius, *In D. Pauli Epistolas ad Corinthios Meditationes* (Strasbourg, 1544), 183^v. This item is missing from M.U. Chrisman, *Bibliography of Strasbourg Imprints, 1480–1599* (New Haven, CT, and London, 1982).

Peter Martyr Vermigli

Finally we come to the most extensive sixteenth-century discussion of this verse, in Peter Martyr Vermigli's commentary.[64] It is also the discussion which engages at greatest length with the Fathers, especially Augustine. He first cites Augustine, Jerome, Cyprian and Ambrose as witnesses that Christians must not marry unbelievers, so that Paul is here speaking only of marriages in which one partner has subsequently come to faith.[65]

In what sense, then, is the unbeliever sanctified *per fidelem* (which Martyr also glosses as *a fideli*)? He notices Augustine's appeal to past conversions of one partner through the other, in his *De Sermone Domini in Monte*, but finds this inadequate, because it does not address the removal of contamination. By this I take it that Martyr has in mind mixed marriages wherein conversion does not take place but which must also be covered by this sanctification. He moves on, then, to the *aspergo sanctitatis* which, in *De Peccatorum Meritis et Remissione*, Augustine presented as extending to spouses or children from the believer in the family. Martyr applies this in two different senses.

In the case of the husband (and presumably, *mutatis mutandis*, the wife), Martyr understands it as *facilitatem et gradum quodammodo ad Christianismum*. In terms reminiscent of Erasmus in particular, he regards the unbeliever's readiness to bear with a wife committed to Christ and thus to have some *commercium* with Christians, as a sign that he is not far from the kingdom. As Jerome said in *Against Jovinian*, the unbeliever who is willing to live with a believer is already *candidatum fidei*.[66] In the context this is indeed Jerome's paraphrase of 1 Corinthians 7.14, and Martyr alone in the sixteenth century seems to know of it.[67] He agrees with Augustine that this *aspergo sanctitatis* does not make the unbelieving partner a Christian, but disagrees with him about children, who need no faith to be Christians or receive remission of sins.[68] At the end of the day, what most concerns Peter Martyr is the avoidance of *contaminatio* from the pagan spouse. Before turning more closely to the second part of our verse, he assesses, with the help of Augustine and Chrysostom, other problems and scruples attending mixed marriages. In a

---

[64] Peter Martyr Vermigli, *In Selectissimam D. Pauli Priorem ad Corinthios...Commentarii Doctissimi*, Editio secunda.... (Zürich, 1572). For 1 Cor. 7.14, there is no variation from the first edition of Zürich, 1551.

[65] Martyr, *In Selectissimam...*, 90^rv.

[66] Jerome, *Against Jovinian* 1:10 (*PL* 23, cols. 233-34). Jerome used the same phrase in *Epistle* 85:5 when he recommended Tertullian's explanation to Paulinus (see n. 16 above): *sanctos dici fidelium filios quod quasi candidati sint fidei*.

[67] Martyr, *In Selectissimam...*, 90^v.

[68] Martyr, *In Selectissimam...*, 91^r, engaging also with Augustine, *De Peccatorum Meritis* 2:26:45, whence he derives his illustration of the sanctification of *cibi*.

number of summarizing remarks, as his exposition continues, Martyr keeps returning to the sanctification of the marriage.

Three possibilities are advanced for the meaning of the *sanctitas* of the children. The first discerns in it the enjoyment of a good and godly education, which they would lack if their parents were divorced and they were assigned to the unbelieving parent. He attributes the gist of this interpretation to Augustine's exposition of the Sermon on the Mount, but quotes him rather loosely.[69] In any case, it is an inadequate basis for establishing the *sanctificatio* of a mixed Christian–pagan marriage, which is Paul's purpose here. Augustine's son, Adeodatus, had a godly upbringing and was baptized but these could not rescue or sanctify the unlawful liaison from which he was born.[70]

The second option is also found wanting. To suppose merely *puritatem et sanctitatem civilem*, whereby the children are *legitimi*, would accord to the Corinthian Christians' marriages nothing more than pagans enjoyed. Martyr's commentary seems here to depend on Calvin's, in rejecting Ambrosiaster's influential exegesis. So, like many Protestant expositors, and in terms still close to Calvin, Martyr sees in the children's *sanctitas* their belonging to the church of Christ by virtue of election, not by mere physical birth. Yet since election is inaccessible to us, we baptize them on the grounds of birth from one believing parent, for election very often, but not invariably, coincides with birth.[71]

A lengthy ensuing discussion of issues raised for Martyr by this conclusion takes him away from 1 Corinthians. He twice dissents from Augustine, on parents' faith availing for babies and on the perdition of babies dying unbaptized. Because he insists that baptism seals rather than imparts, he can ascribe to these *sancti* infants the *radix fidei* through the possession of the Spirit.[72]

Concluding Comments

It is not part of my remit to determine how 1 Corinthians 7.14 should be interpreted today. But for what it is worth, a recent summary lists six possible solutions, and regards as most persuasive the view that sanctification is what makes the marriage relationship pure, thus removing grounds for dissolution. This purity is perceived more in ethical than

---

[69] Martyr, *Inquit enim: Eorum filii ad Christum adducuntur, illique in Baptismo consecrantur* (Martyr, *In Selectissimam...*, 92^r). But as we saw above, Augustine speaks only of the children 'being Christians'.

[70] Martyr, *In Selectissimam...*, 91^v-92^r.

[71] Martyr, *In Selectissimam...*, 92^r.

[72] Martyr, *In Selectissimam...*, 92^v-95^r.

ritual or legal terms.[73] This reading undoubtedly takes the context in the first section of the chapter (verses 1-16) with full seriousness, even if others may also satisfy this criterion. One contrary indication is Paul's predication of sanctification not of the marriage but of a partner in the marriage, followed by a correlative affirmation similarly about persons—the children of such a marriage.

When the Dominican Lancelotto Politi (Ambrosius Catharinus, 1484-1553) essayed the exegesis of this verse in his commentary on the New Testament Epistles, he began as follows:

> I will not relate the fabrications of others, since (to tell the truth frankly) I have not read one which I could assent to. So I will present what by the grace of God (so long as it is true) I have arrived at by my own meditation.[74]

Little did he know that on this verse, by the mid-sixteenth century, there was nothing new under the sun. His explanation, although expressed in his own terms, follows familiar lines, stressing that, by virtue of the believing partner in a marriage, the other partner is regarded as sanctified and their children reckoned (*respici*) as holy and pure. But theirs is not *actualis munditia*, which comes with the receiving of grace, but rather 'a kind of preliminary candidacy for grace, so to speak' (*quaedam...ad gratiam praecedens, ut ita dicam, candidatio*).[75]

Politi's qualifications in this last quotation (*quaedam...ut ita dicam*), together with his imprecision concerning the character of the sanctity involved, remind us of the difficulties that this text posed to sixteenth-century interpeters. Unlike the Fathers, they encountered little in their social and pastoral context that resonated with the issues agitating Paul. I have found no evidence, for example, of an application to the problems of mixed Catholic–Protestant marriages, nor indeed to the wider discussions of the Christian standing of marriage in the light of the Reformers' rejection of the superiority of virginity and celibacy and of the old church's ban on divorce.[76] Several exegetes, as we have seen, do their best to make sense of the verse in the setting of primitive Christianity's minority existence amid Graeco-Roman paganism. The

---

[73] S.E. Porter, 'Holiness, Sanctification', in G.F. Hawthorne *et al.* (eds), *Dictionary of Paul and His Letters* (Downers Grove, IL, and Leicester, 1993), pp. 400-401. See also B.S. Rosner, *Paul, Scripture and Ethics: A Study of 1 Corinthians 5–7* (Arbeiten zur Geschichte des Antiken Judentums und des Christentums, 22; Leiden, 1994), pp. 168-71.

[74] Lancelotto Politi, *Commentaria...in Omnes Divi Pauli, et Alias Septem Canonicas Epistolas...* (Venice, 1551), p. 173.

[75] Politi, *Commentaria...*, p. 174.

[76] One exception is Cyriacus Spangenberg, who uses the occasion of our verse to condemn the papists' error in treating idolatry as grounds for divorce by virtue of its being spiritual adultery (*Die erste Epistel...*, xcix^r, col. 1).

most difficult element, no less for modern exegetes than ancient and sixteenth-century, resides in the parallelism between unbelieving wife or husband and the children.

CHAPTER 15

The Donatists in the Sixteenth Century

In an age of schism attention was bound to be paid to the most prominent schism of the early centuries in the West. Furthermore, Augustine ensured that the sixteenth century knew all about Donatism. His anti-Donatist writings filled a good-sized volume, and it was in them that the African Father significantly developed the Latin theological tradition's understanding of the church and sacraments—and in them too that he spelt out the first considered Christian justification of the coercion of religious dissidents. Anyone seeking patristic guidance on any of these topics could scarcely avoid encountering the Donatists.

But, if sixteenth-century churchmen were well informed about Donatism by Augustine, directly or indirectly (for example, by the medium of standard compilations such as Gratian's *Decretum* or Peter Lombard's *Sentences*),[1] until mid-century they were largely ignorant of the refutation of the Donatists by Augustine's predecessor, Optatus of Milevis. The first printing of Optatus' *Contra Parmenianum Donatistam* took place at Mainz in 1549,[2] but it remained unknown to Calvin. When François Baudouin produced a new edition in 1563, this one-time secretary of the Genevan Reformer, now his bitter critic, equipped it with a long preface addressed to Calvin, which was another salvo in the literary warfare between them in the last years of Calvin's life.[3] Baudouin also used a manuscript of the *Gesta* of the decisive Carthage conference between Catholics and Donatists of 411 to write a history of the

---

[1] For their clever use of Augustine's anti-Donatist arguments in support of their case for the repeatability of penance, see Marcia L. Colish, *Peter Lombard* (2 vols; Brill's Studies in Intellectual History, 41; Leiden, 1994), I, pp. 585, 600-602.

[2] Edited by Johannes Cochlaeus (Dobneck), *Optati Milevitani Quondam Episcopi, Libri sex, De schismate Donatistarum, contra Parmenianum Donatistam....* (Mainz, 1549). This edition was used by the Magdeburg Centuriators, *Quarta Centuria Ecclesiasticae Historiae...* (Basel, 1560), cols. 1098-1102 and elsewhere.

[3] On this 'battle in print' see briefly Wulfert de Greef, *The Writings of John Calvin* (Grand Rapids, MI, and Leicester, 1993), pp. 207-208. Baudouin's edition was published by Claude Fremy at Paris. His Preface (which was omitted in his second edition of 1569) is given in *PL* 11, cols. 1108-30.

encounter. It was published after his death together with the first, quite inadequate, edition of the *Gesta* in 1588.[4]

Since no Donatist writings were available to sixteenth-century readers (the situation is hardly better today), Augustine's characterization of the African counter-church ruled the roost. In reality, any individual or group who could be made to fit Augustine's criticisms could be labelled 'Donatist'. As far as I am aware, no-one appropriated the designation for himself, as though it were a badge of honour, yet there was no shortage of controversialists ready to stigmatize others with one or more of the errors of the Donatists.

Leonard Verduin's intriguing apologia for the free-church principle entitled *The Reformers and Their Stepchildren*[5] takes its chapter titles from the derogatory names the latter were called by the former. Verduin starts with 'Donatisten', for a chapter devoted wholly to the Radicals' opposition to 'Christian sacralism' or 'Constantinianism'. This rejection of the alliance of church and state is not, I would judge, the most prominent ground for the Reformers' assimilation of the Radicals to the Donatists, but it is common enough. Wolfgang Musculus made a free German version of Augustine's *Epistle* 185, *De correctione Donatistarum*, at the behest of Martin Bucer, who supplied it with a preface and an appendix and published it in 1535 as *Vom Ampt der oberkait in sachen der religion und Gotsdiensts*.[6] One of Bucer's objectives was to expose as false a reading of Augustine's letter advanced by Sebastian Franck and others that made Augustine an advocate of tolerance towards Donatists and Circumcellions. This interpretation of

---

[4] Edited by Jean (Papire) Masson, *Gesta collationis Chartagini habitae...* (Paris, 1588). Baudouin's Historia is reprinted in *PL* 11, cols. 1439-1506. See Serge Lancel, *Actes de la Conférence de Carthage en 411*, Tome I (*SC* 194; Paris, 1972), pp. 367-68, 373; Pontien Polman, *L'Élément historique dans la controverse religieuse du XVI*[e] *siècle* (Gembloux, 1932), pp. 481-83. Dr James S. Alexander of St Mary's College, St Andrews, has written a paper on 'John Calvin, François Baudouin and the Acts of the Carthage Colloquy' (1955).

[5] Grand Rapids, 1964, and Exeter, 1966.

[6] Bucer's Foreword and Afterword are edited by Walter Delius in *BDS* 6:2, pp. 17-38; see pp. 24-25 in particular. A review of the listing of sixteenth-century printings of Augustine's works in *Index Aureliensis: Catalogus Librorum Sedecimo Saeculo Impressorum* (Baden-Baden, 1965–), Part I, vol. 2 (1966), pp. 396-445, shows hardly any other editions of any of his anti-Donatist writings separate from *Opera Omnia*. This contrasts markedly with, for example, the anti-Pelagian works. Luchesius Smits, *Saint Augustin dans l'oeuvre de Jean Calvin*, vol. 1 (Assen, 1957), p. 181, comments on the paucity—only forty-six in all—of Calvin's citations of and references to the anti-Donatist works (cf. pp. 157-60), but a good many more uses of letters on Donatism must be added (cf. pp. 179-80). See also Remko J. Mooi, *Het Kerk- en Dogmahistorisch Element in de Werken van Johannes Calvijn* (Wageningen, 1965), especially pp. 245-55.

Epistle 185 goes back at least as far as Erasmus, who has it in mind more than once when he cites Augustine's authority for a policy that never punishes heretics without hearing them, *etiam cum reverentia*, and without instruction, and even then never touches their person.[7]

More typical of the magisterial Reformers' identification of the Radicals with the Donatists is this comment by Urbanus Rhegius:

> The Donatists murder human souls, make them go to eternal death, and then they complain when humans punish them with temporal death. A Christian magistrate must make it his first concern to keep the Christian religion pure.[8]

The mentality discernible in these words helps explain the misattribution, to 'Donatists' of both eras, of the total rejection of civil power in human society. Their denial that the sword had any place in matters of religion, and in the hands of the saints, could easily seem to fall not far short of its wholesale abandonment.[9]

Much more pervasive in the campaign to tar the Radicals with the Donatist brush is their common quest for a pure church and consequent separation from the ungodly. Urbanus Rhegius' polemical response to the leading Münster Anabaptist, Bernhard Knipperdolling, which was published with a preface by Luther in 1535, was entitled *Widerlegung der Münsterischen newen Valentinianer und Donatisten Bekentnis*.

> There Bernhard resorts to a truly Donatist trick. They condemned and abandoned the whole of Christendom because of some evil false Christians... Thus they are genuine Donatists and Novatianists... The fact that there are wicked rogues among us is not our concern; we have not told them to drink and gourmandize, to be immoral and covetous... We do not want to tear the net because it has some foul fish in it, as the hyper-holy Anabaptist Bernhard has done at Münster. He betrays himself in this and exposes his heart as having the very Anabaptist devil in him that blinded the Donatists... Bernhard is a new Donatist who has objected to people living immorally and has sought to erect at Münster a completely unspotted holy church... I would certainly prefer to be a flagrant publican or open sinner in the

---

[7] E.g., *Letters* 1033, to Albert of Brandenburg, 19 October 1519 (P.S. Allen [ed.], *Opus Epistolarum Des. Erasmi Roterodami* [12 vols; Oxford, 1906–58], IV, p. 102 [hereafter Allen]), and 1167, to Lorenzo Campegio, 6 December 1520 (Allen, IV, p. 407); *Supputatio Errorum in Censuris Beddae*, in *LB* 9, col. 582.

[8] Translated by Verduin, *Reformers*, p. 50, from Günther Franz *et al.* (eds), *Urkundliche Quellen zur hessischen Reformationsgeschichte*, Bd. 4: *Widertäuferakten, 1527-1626* (Marburg, 1951), p. 112: 'Die Donatisten erwurgen die seelen, sie bringen inen den ewigen tod, und sie clagen sich, das man sie mit zeitlichen tod strafft. Derhalb soll ainer christlichen oberkeit nichs ernstlichers anligen vor allen dingen, dann die christlich religion rein und mit gsunder lehr erhalten.' This justification by Rhegius in June 1536 of the coercion of dissidents makes considerable use of Augustine's anti-Donatist arguments, especially *Letter* 93 and *Compelle intrare*.

[9] Cf. Verduin, *Reformers*, pp. 48-49.

Christian church than the holiest Pharisee in Bishop Bernhard's heretical dive (Spelunck).[10]

The same complaint is an element in Melanchthon's *Loci*, in the section on the church headed *Contra Donatistas*:

> Nam et nostra aetate Anabaptistae renovant errores Donatistarum, et impii abiiciunt ministeria, et...iactitant se constituere Ecclesiam, in qua nulli sint mali.[11]

Such an identification of the purist separatism of Donatists and Anabaptists is also almost a refrain in Calvin, for example on Psalm 26.5, 'I abhor the assembly of evildoers, and refuse to sit with the wicked':

> Many go seriously astray in this way, imagining when they see evil mixed with good that they will be infected with pollution unless they immediately withdraw from the whole congregation. This scrupulosity drove the Donatists of old, and earlier still the Cathari and the Novatianists, into disastrous schisms. In our own day too, the Anabaptists...have segregated themselves.[12]

Calvin perceived a parallelism between the infallibilist ecclesiology of the old church and the perfectionist ecclesiology of the old and new puritans.[13] The Magdeburg church historians even found in Augustine's

---

[10] From the edition in *Der Ander Teil der Bücher D. Mart. Luth...*. (Wittenberg, 1551), f. 422^{rv}. Luther's Preface is in *WA* 38, pp. 338-40. Much more of Rhegius' attack is directed at the Münsterites' Valentinian character (cf. Robert Stupperich, 'Melanchthon und die Täufer', *Kerygma und Dogma* 3 [1957], pp. 150-70, at p. 167). My translation is indebted to Verduin, *Reformers*, pp. 113-14. Rhegius' work has been edited by Robert Stupperich in *Schriften von evangelischer Seite gegen die Täufer* (Veröffentlichungen der Historischen Kommission für Westfalen, 32; Münster, 1983); for its place in Rhegius' developing appeal to the Fathers, see Scott H. Hendrix, 'Validating the Reformation: The Use of the Church Fathers by Urbanus Rhegius', in Walter Brandmüller *et al.* (eds), *Ecclesia Militans. Studien zur Konzilien- und Reformationsgeschichte*, Bd. II (Paderborn, 1988), pp. 281-305, at pp. 297-298.

[11] *CR* 21, col. 841. See also Pamela Biel, 'Bullinger Against the Donatists: St Augustine to the Defence of the Zurich Reformed Church', *Journal of Religious History* 16 (1991), pp. 237-46.

[12] *OC* 31, col. 266; cf. col. 143 on Psalm 15.1. In his *Preface* to the Book of Revelation (1530, 1546), Luther identified the fourth evil angel (cf. Rev. 7.1-2, 8.12) with Novatian and his Cathari and the Donatists in their pretensions to purity: *WADB* 7, pp. 410-13.

[13] Calvin, *Institutes* 4:8:12, in *OS* 5, pp. 144-45. Cf. Thomas Rogers, *The Catholic Doctrine of the Church of England: An Exposition of the Thirty-Nine Articles* (ed. John J.S. Perowne; Parker Society; Cambridge, 1854), pp. 178-79: 'the papists...maintain that in faith and doctrine the church...never erreth, never hath erred and never can err; ...these which say, the church cannot err for manners. Such were the Donatists, and are the Anabaptists...' Cf. p. 134.

Contra litteras Petiliani a statement that made the Donatists claim to be not only themselves *iustos...sed etiam iustificatores hominum*.[14] This illustrates the remarkable ingenuity shown by some sixteenth-century writers in ferreting out from Augustine's anti-Donatist corpus errors in Donatism beyond the territory familiar to a modern student of the movement.[15]

Greater interest by far attaches to the various contemporary counterparts discerned by sixteenth-century churchmen to the Donatists' rejection of sacraments performed by unworthy ministers. This is of course but another perspective on ecclesiological perfectionism, but it looms large enough to merit treatment in its own right. It is this error that brings condemnation on Donatists and all suchlike in article VIII of the Augsburg Confession. The previous year at the Marburg Colloquy, discussion of the same point must have confirmed Luther's suspicions of Zwingli's theological instability. When Luther asserted that whenever the words 'This is my body' are said, the body of Christ is present regardless of who says them, Zwingli quivered: Luther must 'be careful, for in this way the papacy will be brought in'. Luther would not be careful.

> Even if Peter came and would celebrate the mass, I would not know whether he believes... God establishes the sacrament upon his word and not upon our holiness, as the Anabaptists and Donatists do... We cannot prohibit a bad priest from celebrating the sacrament.

Zwingli could. 'It would be an absurdity if the ungodly could do this [i.e. cause the body of Christ to be present].' But for Luther this is the only path to security.

> According to God's word the godly and the ungodly act as ministers. Matthew 23, which deals with the Pharisees, proves this. Judas was a traitor, and yet he held the apostolic office. Augustine says in opposition to the Donatists that the ministry

---

[14] *Quarta Centuria*, col. 378, citing Augustine, *Contra litt. Petil.* 2:14:35 (*PL* 43, col. 269). The point is repeated by Rogers, *Catholic Doctrine*, p. 135. The Magdeburg *Quinta Centuria*, col. 628, bases on Augustine's *Letters* 93 and 185 the charge that the Donatists claim to possess the power to justify; the one baptized by them is justified by them. Cf. Augustine, *Letter* 185:9:37 (*PL* 33, col. 809).

[15] Thus the Magdeburg history credits the Donatists with believing in freedom of the will: *Quarta Centuria*, col. 378, and col. 628, citing Augustine's quotation of Gaudentius' letter in *Contra Gaudentium* 1:19:20 (corrected reference; *PL* 43, cols. 715-16), where the Donatist bishop appeals to Ecclus. 15.14.

must not be entrusted solely to the virtuous because the basis of our belief is the word of God.[16]

The same emphasis recurs repeatedly in magisterial Reformation critiques of Anabaptist radicalism, for example, through the successive editions of Melanchthon's *Loci Communes* from 1535 onwards.[17] And the same proof-text is invariably present—in the Augsburg Confession, at Marburg, in the *Loci*—Matthew 23.2-3:

> The teachers of the law and the Pharisees sit in Moses' seat. So you must obey them, says Jesus, and do everything they tell you. But do not do what they do, for they do not practise what they preach.

But these verses were no less useful to Roman Catholic controversialists, who found the most worrying modern reviviscence of Donatism not in Anabaptism but in Lutheranism, or in Protestantism more generally. Why did Arius stray from the true faith?, asked Ambrosius Catharinus in his 1520 *Apologia pro Veritate Catholicae et Apostolicae Fidei ac Doctrinae adversus Impia ac valde Pestifera Martini Lutheri Dogmata*. Because he hated distinctions, just as Martin does.

> Novatianists, Pelagians, Donatists and the rest of the troop of heretics in general, whom you imitate in this matter to a tee (*ad regulam*), hated distinctions... So listen to a distinction that is not novel, not deduced or adduced by human initiative, but the sound and inviolable judgment of the Holy Spirit and the teacher and Lord of all... 'Do what they say, but do not do what they do.'[18]

A distinction of this kind, argued Catharinus, would have enabled Luther to see the fallacy of charging his Catholic critics with lapsing into the ancient error of the Donatists—for whom a bad bishop was no bishop—by virtue of their application of the Petrine texts to the papacy. For according to the implications that Luther believed were inescapably inherent in this interpretation, a pope who failed to strengthen the brethren (Luke 22.32) would not be a successor of Peter, nor would a pope who deviated from Peter's heaven-revealed faith and confession (Matthew 16.16-19). Luther coined a verb or two to snare Eck, by this sophistic counter-exegesis, in the Donatist trap:

---

[16] *LW* 38, pp. 27-28; *WA* 30:3, pp. 125-27. Cf. *Concerning Rebaptism, LW* 40, pp. 250-51, *WA* 26, p. 163.

[17] *CR* 21, cols. 509, 840.

[18] Josef Schweizer (ed.), *Corpus Catholicorum* 27 (Münster, 1956), p. 28.

Et Eccius iterum Donatissabit ac Pighardissabit, papam non esse qui mare non calcat, id est affectibus mundanis non imperat, quia Petrum non refert nec sequitur.[19]

But the Donatist card could be played to similar effect from the opposite side of the table. Jaroslav Pelikan gives a particularly judicious summary, which deserves to be quoted at length.

> Above all, [Catholic writers] were intent on defending the Catholic doctrine of the priesthood against 'the insanity of the Donatists' [Latomus]. To apply Matthew 16:18 to Peter as an individual, not to the papacy, was a repetition of the Donatist heresy that 'ecclesiastical authority does not reside in wicked ministers' [Cajetan], which was a failure to distinguish the sacraments of the church, even those confected by such ministers, from the 'false sacraments that are in the temples of idols' [Driedo]. Against this 'same old defence of the heretics' and Donatists, they taught that 'the church is holy, even though the wicked also are present in it..., not on the basis of a holiness of life or a probity of morals, but from the dignity of the office' of the priesthood and the sacraments [Cochlaeus]. Such a statement could find almost verbatim parallels in the confessions of the Lutheran and Reformed churches [Augsburg, Second Helvetic], which likewise quoted the familiar admonition of Christ to obey the Pharisees who sat in the seat of Moses as evidence that God made use of the ministry of evil men. That same passage became the Roman Catholic proof text in response to the complaint that clergy were living in sin as well as in support of the idea that the authority of Peter was not affected by his fall.[20]

As Eck put it, broadening the scope of the Donatist precedent,

Quod dixit Luther, dixerunt omnes haeretici. Ideo Augustinus invehitur contra Donatistas, qui universalem ecclesiam coartare volebant ad angulum paucorum haereticorum.[21]

---

[19] Luther, *Contra malignum I. Eccii iudicium...defensio* (1519), WA 2, p. 643, and cf. pp. 632-33, 635, 653; *Resolutio...super propositione XIII. de potestate papae* (1519), WA 2, pp. 193-94. In his *Apologia* Ambrosius Catharinus refutes this last passage from Luther's *Resolutio* (ed. Schweizer), pp. 149ff. He also disputes (pp. 272-73) Luther's assertion, in *Ad dialogum Sylvestri Prieratis...responsio* (1518), that we cannot fulfil God's commands in this life, *sicut S. Augustinus locupletissime contra Donatistas et Pelagianos testatur* (WA 1, p. 649). In this linking of Donatist and Pelagian we should not discern an anticipation of the insights of modern Augustinian scholarship. As this paper illustrates elsewhere, the pairing or grouping of heretical labels was common practice (cf. Luther's *Resolutiones disputationum de indulgentiarum virtute*, WA 1, p. 620: by the darkness of human opinion and reason 'prope facti sumus Pelagiani sensu et Donatistae opere').

[20] Jaroslav Pelikan, *Reformation of Church and Dogma (1300–1700)* (The Christian Tradition, 4; Chicago and London, 1983), p. 273.

[21] J. Eck, *Enchiridion locorum communium* I (ed. Pierre Fraenkel; Corpus Catholicorum, 34; 1979, p. 34). Cf. Pierre Fraenkel, *Testimonia Patrum: The Function*

It was a comfort to Catholic apologists to discern the parallel between Donatists and Lutherans: both companies were too tiny to be the true catholic church. And if Lutherans claimed to be abandoning only corruption in the church, so likewise had the Donatists.

So who were the Donatists in the sixteenth century? Both Protestants and Catholics traced the pedigree of modern-day heresies, collapsing them into ancient errors, but when magisterial Reformers descried neo-Donatism in Anabaptist Radicals, Catholic apologists exposed it in the mainstream Reformation itself. And the fresh availability of Optatus' refutation of Donatism replenished their ammunition, for Optatus had rested his case not solely on *successio doctrinae* (which each party in the fourth and fifth centuries recognized the other to have preserved) but also on *successio personarum*. Baudouin turned the fire of Optatus on Calvin, Beza later addressed the issue directly in *De veris et visibilibus Ecclesiae Catholicae Notis*, and the Magdeburg historians' interpretation of Optatus was challenged.[22]

This polyvalence of the anti-Donatist case particularly embarrassed, and even divided, the Reformers. Joachim Westphal cited Augustine's undermining of the Donatist reliance on ministerial purity against Calvin's position on the *manducatio impiorum* in the Supper. Calvin in response pleaded Augustine's distinction developed against the Donatists between receiving the sacrament and enjoying the benefit thereof. The focus shifts from the ministers of the sacraments to their recipients.

> *Imo totus in hoc est contra Donatistas Augustinus, ut doceat quae bona sunt, male utentium vitio naturam non mutare, ne ideo baptismus censeatur nullus esse, quia incredulis propter abusum non prodest.*[23]

Reformation leaders found themselves awkwardly in the middle, under fire from both flanks. They were attacked by Catholic teachers for their neo-Donatist abandonment of the unity of the church on the grounds of its alleged corruption, yet most of them refused, in true Augustinian

---

of the Patristic Argument in the Theology of Philip Melanchthon (Travaux d'Humanisme et Renaissance, 46; Geneva, 1961), p. 166 n. 14. But already in his expositions of the Psalms in 1519–21, Luther made anti-papal capital out of verses like Psalm 19.4 (*In omnem terram exivit sonus eorum*) and 22.28 ('All the ends of the earth will...turn to the Lord'), following Augustine's example against the Donatists: they are rightly directed *in nostros novos dontatistas, qui negant, in India et Perside et Asia esse fideles* (WA 5, p. 547), *...in Romanam tyrannidem et sectas eius, qui non sinunt esse in toto orbe Christianos, nisi captivi serviant illi* (WA 5, p. 666).

[22] For details see Polman, *Élément historique*, pp. 481-83, 156-57.

[23] Calvin, *Last Admonition to Westphal*, OC 9, cols. 159-60; cf. *Institutes* 4:17:34 (*OS* 5, p. 396). The reference is to Westphal's citation in his *Collectanea Sententiarum D. Aurelii Augustini ep. Hipponensis de Coena Domini...* (Regensburg, 1555), from Augustine, *Contra Cresconium Grammaticum* 1:25:30 (*PL* 43, cols. 461-62).

fashion, to doubt the validity of their own ordination at the hands of the old church. George Williams notes the 'strong disposition within the Radical Reformation to question the legitimacy of any ordination deriving from the *ancien régime*', and in certain quarters to repudiate also a reformed call and ordination.[24] Luther's understanding of ordination, and of the relation between it and corrupt priestly consecration, undoubtedly underwent some development. 'Luther cannot deny that through the ministry of the papists and their baptism the evangelicals have come into the fellowship of the true Church.'[25] What Augustine's rebuttal of Donatism provided was justification of this stance coupled with denial of any credit to the church of the papacy, for God is the true minister of the sacraments.

The Scottish Reformation started off on a more radical note. In debate with Quintin Kennedy, abbot of Crossraguel in Ayrshire in 1562, John Knox based his own authority on an extraordinary call of God. All true ministers received their ministerial warrant direct from God, for because of the corruption of the papal hierarchy, God had suspended the usual order of calling and commissioning ministers. The *First Book of Discipline* of 1560 specifically debarred the laying on of hands and the very term 'ordination' was discountenanced.[26] This was at worst semi-Donatist, for re-ordination was obviously excluded, although early Scottish Protestantism was made of sterner stuff than to panic at the sniff of Donatism.

The validity of baptism was also at issue. Calvin referred to the Donatists' practice of measuring the force and value of the sacraments by the worth of the minister.

> Such today are our Catabaptists, who deny that we have been duly baptized because we were baptized by impious and idolatrous men under the papal government. They therefore passionately urge rebaptism.[27]

The discussion clearly assumes that the unacceptability of infant baptism *per se* was not the sole impulse behind the practice of rebaptizing. Verduin argues that

---

[24] G.H. Williams, *The Radical Reformation* (Sixteenth Century Essays and Studies, 15; Kirksville, MO, 3rd edn, 1992), p. 1081. In the first edition (London, 1962, p. 687) Williams spoke of the clergy of the magisterial Reformation refusing, on 'anti-Donatist' principle, to question their authorization from the old church.

[25] John M. Headley, *Luther's View of Church History* (New Haven, CT, and London, 1963), pp. 219, and 216-220 in general.

[26] John Knox, *Works* (ed. David Laing; 6 vols; Edinburgh, 1846–64), VI, pp. 191-92; James K. Cameron (ed.), *First Book of Discipline* (Edinburgh, 1972), p. 102. Discussion in Richard L. Greaves, *Theology and Revolution in the Scottish Reformation* (Grand Rapids, MI, 1980), pp. 72-75.

[27] Calvin, *Institutes* 4:15:16 (*OS* 5, pp. 296-97).

early Anabaptism was not so much a matter of anti-paedobaptism as of a matter of anti-Constantinianism... [R]ebaptism did not necessarily go hand in hand with a rejection of paedobaptism... What was opposed...was not so much paedobaptism as such but 'christening'. The outright rejection of infant baptism came when it became apparent that the Reformation was heading in a neo-Constantinian direction. Not until the Reformers began to embrace the old institution of 'christening' did the Anabaptists by way of reaction make a clean sweep of the board.

According to this interpretation, outright Radical opposition to infant baptism came only when the Reformers 'became' its fanatical proponents.[28]

The intrinsic inseparability of infant baptism and state church needs no underlining. Karl Barth believed that the former belonged inherently to the era of the latter,[29] and the threat that the abandonment of paedobaptism represented to the *civitas-ecclesia* or *ecclesia-civitas* was vividly perceived from Zwingli onwards.[30] Yet the Anabaptists' grounds for rejecting it were irrelevant in the light of their actual practice of rebaptizing. Their opponents insisted on styling them 'Anabaptistae' or 'Catabaptistae' precisely in order to place them unambiguously under the provisions of the imperial mandate issued at the Diet of Speyer on 23 April 1529:[31]

> Whereas it is ordered and provided in *common* [i.e. canon] *law* that no man, having once been baptized according to Christian order, shall let himself be baptized again or for the second time, nor shall he baptize any such, and especially is it forbidden in the *imperial law* to do such on pain of death; ...this old sect of anabaptism, condemned and forbidden many centuries ago, day by day makes greater inroads and is getting the upper hand... We therefore renew the previous imperial law, ...that...every anabaptist and rebaptized man and woman of the age of reason shall be condemned and brought from natural life into death by fire, sword, and the like.[32]

This mandate renewed the earlier imperial mandate of 4 January 1528, which likewise subjected the Anabaptists to the sanctions of the Theodosian and Justinianic codes. It had evoked a protesting pamphlet by Johann Brenz of Hall, published in late summer 1528, which rejected the mandate's identification of modern Anabaptists with ancient Donatists and hence, for this and other considerations, denounced their punishment

---

[28] Verduin, *Reformers*, pp. 196-98 (emphasis original).
[29] K. Barth, *Church Dogmatics* IV/4. *The Christian Life (Fragment)* (Edinburgh, 1960), p. 168.
[30] Cf. Franklin H. Littell, *The Origins of Protestant Sectarianism* (New York, 1964), pp. 70ff.
[31] Littell, *Origins*, p. xv.
[32] Williams, *Radical Reformation*, p. 359.

by the sword.³³ The general argument, 'so commonly employed by the earlier Luther, that heresy, being spiritual, cannot be touched by the sword of the magistrate',³⁴ need not detain us. Since the Anabaptists refuse to take an oath to the civil government, they deserve civil penalty, but no more than the deprivation of civil rights.

Brenz's reasons for disputing the application of the Theodosian statute to the Anabaptists are of variable quality. The text of the statute specifies only those caught in the act of rebaptizing, and only in the act of rebaptizing ministers of the church.³⁵ Furthermore, the known character of Theodosius and his official to whom the law was addressed requires us to believe that it 'contemplated nothing imprudent or ungodly... We may surely infer that this law contemplated in addition to mere rebaptism other circumstances which are not named.' Although the original context of the decree is unknown (hence the debates among the jurists), comparison with adjacent enactments in the codes reveals that execution for 'the misuse of one sacrament' would be an utterly disproportionate punishment. If rebaptism is so serious, why are pope and priest not condemned for baptizing again in church after an emergency baptism at home? And if Anabaptists err, they do so in company with the 'learned and godly martyr' Cyprian. Brenz's conclusion is simple:

> All of these considerations indicate that the imperial law which condemned the Anabaptists to death had reference not to mere rebaptism, but to some associated civil offense which is not mentioned. Otherwise so Christian an emperor would have overstepped all humanity and justice.³⁶

---

³³ Johann Brenz, *Ob ein weltliche Oberkeyt mit Götlichem vnd billichem rechten möge die Widerteuffer durch fewr oder schwert vom leben zu dem tode richten lassen* (Hagenau, 1528). It was incorporated in its entirety (from an earlier Latin translation) in Sebastian Castellio's *De Haereticis, an sint persequendi...* (Magdeburg, 1554; facsimile reprint, ed. Sape van der Woude; Geneva, 1954), which also appeared the same year in French and German versions (see Walter Köhler, *Bibliographia Brentiana* [Berlin, 1904], nos. 29, 261-64). Quotations given here are from Roland H. Bainton's translation, *Concerning Heretics Whether they are to be persecuted... An anonymous work attributed to Sebastian Castellio...* (New York, 1935). The 1528 text is critically edited by Martin Brecht et al., *Johannes Brenz Werke: Frühschriften*, Teil 2 (Tübingen, 1974), pp. 472-98.

³⁴ Bainton, *Concerning Heretics*, p. 53.

³⁵ The text available to Brenz read 'ministris' instead of 'mysteriis'; Bainton, *Concerning Heretics*, p. 164 n. 24.

³⁶ Bainton, *Concerning Heretics*, p. 168 (Brecht et al. (eds), *Johannes Brenz Werke*, p. 496); and for earlier quotations and summaries, pp. 164-167 (Brecht et al. [eds], *Joahnnes Brenz Werke*, pp. 492-95).

But if, *per impossibile*, the law did stigmatize rebaptism pure and simple, the blame lies with the bloodthirsty bishops who were common enough at the time!

Brenz was a lone voice, not so much in rejecting the imperial mandate and arguing against the death penalty for heresy,[37] as in refuting the assimilation of Anabaptists to Donatists.[38] Even Brenz's attitudes would later harden,[39] and in any case his protest in 1528 did not avail to head off the 1529 mandate and the Anabaptists' sufferings. And even in their persecution they reminded Luther of the Donatists, as these extracts from sermons on John's Gospel from the early 1530s reveal.

> I am directing these words against the Anabaptists, who inflict sufferings on themselves, who forsake all and then boast of being martyrs... But do not choose your own affliction. Neither you nor anyone else has been ordered to incur damages to life and limb voluntarily...
>
> In times past St Augustine had his troubles with the Donatists. They, too, were of that ilk, seducers who invited the bigwigs to kill them and make them martyrs. And if no one else laid hands on them, they threw themselves from bridges, jumped from houses, and broke their necks, appealing to the words, 'He who loves life more than Me is not worthy of Me.' ...
>
> The monks are practically as bad as the Donatists. Although they do not go to the extremes of killing themselves they are nonetheless of the devil's household; for they claim: 'If you want to be perfect, go and sell all. Forsake father and mother, wife and child.' ...
>
> Years ago under the papacy, servants deserted the service of their masters, and wives ran from the household of their husbands and from submission to them, went on

---

[37] See Williams, *Radical Reformation*, pp. 300-301, for Ambrose Blaurer and the Memmingen Resolutions of March 1531.

[38] Thomas Cranmer, who was no mean student of the Fathers, must be cleared of seeming so completely to collapse the distance between the Donatists and Anabaptists as to ascribe to the former also the denial of infant baptism. See *A Confutation of Unwritten Verities in Miscellaneous Writings and Letters of Thomas Cranmer* (ed. John E. Cox; Parker Society; Cambridge, 1846), pp. 59-60. Although it is accepted that an unknown editor compiled the treatise from materials in Cranmer's *MS Commonplace Books* (now British Library Royal 7.B.XI and XII), this instance shows the extent of his incompetence. There is no basis for his confusion in the MSS, on which see Paul Ayris and David Selwyn (eds.), *Thomas Cranmer Churchman and Scholar* (Woodbridge, 1993), pp. 286, 312-15.

[39] H.S. Bender *et al.* (eds), *The Mennonite Encyclopedia* (4 vols; Scottdale, PA, 1955–59), I, p. 420.

pilgrimages, and became monks and nuns. Those were real Donatists. The Anabaptists are reviving this practice.[40]

Or again from the Table-Talk:

> *Ego credo anabaptistas...esse incendiarios, quia se ipsos interficiunt et nihil fatentur et credunt se fieri martyres, ut Donatistae, qui praecipitabant se in aquas...ut occiderentur et fierent martyres.*[41]

These quotations illustrate not only Luther's gifted imagination, but also the versatility of the image of the despised Donatists. They were fair game to all, and no one in the sixteenth century would plead their cause.[42]

In reality, Donatism's fortunes in the sixteenth century belonged to the disputes over who owned Augustine. George Williams comments that

> It is an anomaly of the Reformation era that precisely the Protestants—who in the most important respects (except for their theological devotion to Augustine) were much more like the 'nationalist,' 'puritan,' and often bellicose schismatics of North Africa than were the pacifistic Anabaptists—turned out to be almost as zealous as the Catholics in applying the anti-Donatist laws against the Radical Reformation.[43]

But such a massive exception deserves better than to be enclosed in brackets. Yet Williams suggests something beyond what he intends. It was precisely because the Protestants could be made to look so much like the Donatists that they had to affix the label so polemically on others. They did so with no little success. It is perhaps no coincidence that the

---

[40] *LW* 23, pp. 202-205; *WA* 33, pp. 320-24.

[41] *WATR* 5, p. 19 no. 5231 (September 1540).

[42] When Luther resumed hostilities with Erasmus in the 1530s (cf. Martin Brecht, *Martin Luther: The Preservation of the Church 1532–1546* [Minneapolis, MO, 1993], pp. 78-84) and his letter on Erasmus to Nicholas Amsdorf of March 1534 was immediately published, John Choler urged Erasmus to reply: *Non satis est et quod te bilinguem impostorem,... ethnicum et Epicurum vocet, Anabaptistam, Sacramentarium, Arrianum, Donatistam, hereticum ter maximum...clara voce appellat...?* (*Letter* no. 2936, Allen, X, p. 388). Luther had not been so precise: by implication he had blamed Erasmus for sowing the weed seeds from which these rank heresies grew (*Letter* no. 2093, *WABr* 7, p. 37). Erasmus' *Purgatio adversus Epistolam non sobriam Martini Lutheri* mocks the suggestion that a handful of ambiguous statements of his can have engendered *in ecclesia tot sectarum formae* (ed. Cornelis Augustijn, in *Opera Omnia Desiderii Erasmi Roterodami* [ed. Hans Trapman *et al.*; Amsterdam, 1969–], IX:1, pp. 478-80).

[43] Williams, *Radical Reformation*, p. 361.

rehabilitation of the heirs of the Anabaptist protest has had to wait almost as long as the rehabilitation of the 'Donatist church'.[44]

---

[44] The title of William H.C. Frend's still central history, *The Donatist Church* (Oxford, 1952). Cf. the comments of Robert Markus: 'It is the Catholic Church of Optatus and Augustine, between Constantine and the disappearance of Roman rule in 430, that constitutes the anomaly in African Christianity... If there was a religious "movement" in late Roman Africa, it is that of Catholicism. The problem is not to trace the roots of Donatism, but rather to assess the factors which assisted the advance of Catholicism in the face of the indigenous Christianity of Africa' ('Christianity and Dissent in Roman North Africa: Changing Perspectives in Recent Work', in Derek Baker [ed.], *Schism, Heresy and Religious Protest* [Studies in Church History, 9; Cambridge, 1972], pp. 35, 30).

CHAPTER 16

Development and Coherence in Calvin's *Institutes*: The Case of Baptism (*Institutes* 4:15–4:16)

In the later twentieth century scholars became increasingly hesitant to use the epithet 'systematic' in characterizing John Calvin's chief work, the *Institutes of the Christian Religion* (to use its traditional English-translation title), or even John Calvin himself as a theologian. The position may be changing again in the light of Richard Muller's judicious consideration of this and related issues in *The Unaccommodated Calvin* (New York, 2000). Nevertheless, students of Calvin remain less certain than their predecessors of earlier generations about his masterful unification of the masses of material gathered up in the final 1559 edition and about its very high degree of internal coherence.[1]

This essay examines a conveniently circumscribed section of the *Institutes* (1559) as a test case in assessing Calvin's effectiveness in harmonising expositions drawn in very large part from two different earlier editions. Book 4:15 derives mainly from the first edition of 1536, preserving even its title, *De Baptismo*, from that location, except that then it introduced a sub-division of a single chapter on the sacraments rather than a separate chapter.[2] Although the additions it has acquired by the time of 1559 are numerous, so that no one section of Book 4:15 lacks some expansion, five (4, 12 and 20-22) are entirely post-1536 in origin and the half of section 19 which was in 1536 has been fetched from the concluding general pages of the chapter on the sacraments, nevertheless the shape of the 1536 treatment is easily recognizable in 1559.[3] Most of

---

[1] Cf. François Wendel, *Calvin: The Origins and Development of his Religious Thought* (trans. Philip Mairet; London, 1963), pp. 120-21: 'Apart from these various additions, it must be said that he modified his text very little... [T]his edition of 1559 stands out among its predecessors by its greater coherence. Never did the author succeed so well in mastering the enormous material he had to organize.'

[2] For 1536: *OS* 1, pp. 127-36; Calvin, *Institutes of the Christian Religion, 1536 Edition* (trans. Ford Lewis Battles [London, 1986], pp. 94-102, 277-79 [hereafter Battles 1536]). All translations in this paper are my mine, albeit indebted in part to Battles.

[3] For 1559 see *OS* 5, pp. 285-303; Calvin, *Institutes of the Christian Religion* (ed John T. McNeill, trans. Ford Lewis Battles; 2 vols; London, 1961), II, pp. 1303-23 (hereafter McNeill-Battles).

the additions are not worth recording in this present enquiry. The 1543 edition has furnished a fresh definition of baptism at the outset of chapter 15. At the end of section 2 the significance of water for spiritual cleansing is expanded, mostly from 1539. Section 4 on repentance and the error of penance comes largely from 1543 but also partly from 1550 and 1559. About half of section 6 on baptism in Christ was first present in the 1539 version. A sizeable addition in sections 7-8 rejects the view of Augustine and other ancients affirming a difference between John's baptism and Christian baptism, deriving very largely from 1539. The new section 12, from 1543, is concerned wholly with Paul's inner struggle set out in Romans 7. Half of section 18 comes from 1539, expanding Calvin's awkward attempt to demonstrate that no rebaptism was involved in Paul's dealing with the Ephesian disciples in Acts 19. The first half of section 19 was added only in the final edition, as an indictment of sundry post-apostolic accretions to the rite of baptism. The last three sections, 20-22, reject emergency baptism by laymen and baptism by women. A major part of them was introduced only in 1559, but the 1543 edition and exceptionally the 1545 Latin edition also contributed to them.[4]

Despite these varied enlargements and other more minor ones, the framework of the original 1536 text is still plainly discernible and its salient emphases have survived intact in Book 4:15 of the ultimate edition. What every edition after 1536 lacks of its treatment of baptism is the long final paragraph (numbered section 23 in Ford Lewis Battles' English translation of the 1536 text) in which Calvin reconciles the practice of infant baptism with his preceding account of the nature and meaning of the sacrament.[5] From 1539 onwards all editions would contain what became the greater part of Book 4:16 in 1559, which could thus be viewed as an extensive elaboration of the discarded conclusion to the 1536 discussion of baptism. Yet Calvin's division of his material on baptism in 1559 is in some ways less felicitous than the unitary section in the first edition, where all, including a brief consideration of infants as proper subjects of baptism, is subsumed under a single sub-heading of 'On Baptism'. From 1539 to 1550, the (slightly amputated) section from 1536 (which eventually was developed into 4:15 in 1559) was extended by an apologia for infant baptism, which in 1559 became a separate chapter entitled 'Infant Baptism Accords Very Well with Christ's Institution and with the Nature of the Sign'.[6] The arrangement is

---

[4] These additions and other alterations can be tracked with skilful care through the edition and translation recorded in the previous note.

[5] *OS* 1, pp. 135-36; Battles 1536, pp. 101-102.

[6] McNeill-Battles' translation of *optime* as 'best' is tendentious and probably misleading. Both comparative and superlative forms in later Latin often carry simply emphatic force. If Calvin really meant 'best', implying 'better than baptism preceded by

puzzling in the light of the fact that in the life of the churches known to Calvin in France, Geneva and elsewhere almost all of the recipients of baptism were very young children. Yet in 1559 he could expound the essence of baptism with only marginal references to infants.

The first mention of infants in Book 4:15 (1539–1559) occurs in the discussion of original sin in 4:15:10. 'Even infants as well bear their own condemnation with them from their mother's womb... Indeed, their whole nature is like a seed of sin and so cannot fail to be odious and abominable to God.' There immediately follows a statement which is left ambiguous in the McNeill-Battles translation. 'Through baptism, believers are assured that this condemnation has been removed and withdrawn from them.'[7] The Latin *a se*, 'from them', can refer only to the subject of the sentence, 'believers', and not to the infants who were the subject of the preceding couple of sentences. The two other mentions of infants are found near the end of Book 4:15 (where they provide a useful anticipation of 4:16), in the context of Calvin's rejection of emergency baptism and its necessary concomitant, administration by laymen and laywomen. Twice he denies the need for baptism in haste at the point of death because God has declared that the offspring of believers are adopted as his before they are born. Deprivation of baptism does not bar them from the kingdom of heaven, and if they survive to be baptized, they are baptized because they already belong to the body of Christ.[8] These mentions of infant baptism are clear enough in their own terms, but they appear rather surprisingly near the end of a chapter whose train of thought has scarcely prepared the reader to think of very young children as appropriate subjects of baptism. That this surprise is not solely the product of a modern critical mind is evident from the fact that Calvin's own introduction to the original conclusion of the 1536 part-chapter on baptism (which did not survive into later editions) read as follows:

> But because from what has been said—that the use of the sacrament consists in two aspects, first, that we be instructed in the Lord's promises, and secondly, that we profess our faith before men—doubt could arise why the children of Christians are baptized while still infants who seem incapable of being taught anything by however many lessons or of having an inwardly conceived faith to which they

---

faith', this would greatly aggravate the charge of incoherence between these two chapters.

[7] *OS* 1, p. 131, Battles 1536, p. 97; *OS* 5, p. 292, McNeill-Battles II, pp. 1311.

[8] *OS* 5, pp. 301-303; McNeill-Battles II, pp. 1321-23. A mistranslation in McNeill-Battles may be noted here, about a fifth from the end of 4:15:22, where *Accedit postea sacramentum sigilli instar* should be rendered 'The sacrament is added afterwards like a seal.'

might give outward testimony, we shall briefly explain the reason for paedobaptism.[9]

From 1539 onwards this task of vindicating the giving of baptism to unteachable and unbelieving infants was fulfilled by what became Book 4:16 in the final *Institutes*.[10] The textual history of 4:16 was much more straightforward than that of 4:15. With the exception of the long refutation of Servetus in section 31, and about half-a-dozen sentences elsewhere, only one of which will merit a mention in due course, the whole of 4:16 was introduced into the 1539 edition. The response to Servetus was inserted in the 1559 edition, as we might expect, after the confrontation between the two of them in 1553.

We can now proceed to a comparison of the two chapters in the last version of the *Institutes*. As we have seen, Book 4:15 presents an exposition of baptism which hardly ever takes cognisance of the baptism of infants. In addition to the mentions noted above, it is presumably implicit in 4:15:17, where Calvin replies to people who questioned the value of Calvin's own, or perhaps everyman's, baptism during the several years after its reception when its word of promise was not accepted in faith. The identity of these questioners is not obvious, although the strangeness of Calvin's rejoinder suggests that they were Anabaptists. For Calvin seems to assume their premise that baptism was devoid of benefit so long as faith was lacking. Hence he responds in terms not of the infant of Christian parents who is within God's promise from before birth but of a responsible person 'blind and unbelieving who for a long time failed to grasp the promise given in baptism'. During that time baptism 'benefited us not a whit' (*non profuisse nobis hilum*). The divine promise remained in force, but it was up to believers to embrace it in faith, for 'God will assuredly provide what was promised (i.e. remission of sins) to all believers.'[11] At work here there seems an understanding of infant baptism which is congruent with the overall thrust of Book 4:15 but scarcely with the case spelt out in 4:16.

In line with the puzzling reticence just noticed is the silence on circumcision in 4:15:9, where the 'Prototype of baptism in the Old Covenant' (McNeill-Battles' heading) is the baptism in the Exodus cloud and sea of 1 Corinthians 10.2. And in the next section, as we saw in part above, Calvin subsumes the newborn within the reach of original sin but immediately goes on to speak not of baptismal forgiveness for such

---

[9] *OS* 1, p. 135; Battles 1536, p. 101.
[10] *OS* 5, pp. 303-41; McNeill-Battles II, pp. 1342-59.
[11] *OS* 5, pp. 297-98; McNeill-Battles II, p. 1317. Again a minor correction in the translation: just below the middle read 'provide the promised [remission]' for 'fulfil the promise'.

infants but of believers' assurance of the lifting of condemnation for their own guilt (4:15:10).

In reality, these features are not surprising in the light of the burden of Book 4:15 as a whole. It repeatedly so emphasizes faith that it might almost have been written with solely believers' baptism in view. It begins (from 1543 onwards) by defining baptism as a sign of initiation into the community of the church and the ranks of God's children, but then continues, as in 1536 and thereafter, with the twofold purpose of baptism: 'first, to serve our faith before him and secondly, to serve our confession before other people'. From this point in section 1 to the end of section 12 Calvin sets out the three things that baptism brings (*affert*) to our faith. It confirms that our sins are completely remitted, for God 'wills that all who have believed be baptized for the remission of sins', with a reference in 1536 to Matthew 28.[19] and Acts 2.[38, 41]. The primary thing in baptism is that we receive it with the promise that 'Those who have believed and been baptized will be saved' (Mark 16.16). The second gift conferred by baptism is our mortification in Christ and our rising to new life in him (Romans 6.3-11), which is 'truly experienced by those who receive baptism with the required faith' (4:15:5). The third benefit is the attestation of our union with Christ and hence our share in all the blessings he bestows. The faith then to which baptism conveys good things is the faith of the recipients of baptism, who become beneficiaries of threefold blessing themselves. So although infants too are encompassed with original sin, it is believers who are assured that they themselves have had this condemnation lifted from them (4:15:10). In Romans 8.1 Paul teaches that those implanted in Christ and his body through baptism are absolved of condemnation 'so long as they persevere in faith in Christ' (4:15:12).[12]

The same prominence for faith is maintained throughout Book 4:15. Since the second purpose of baptism is that it serves our confession before others, it is 'the mark (*nota*) whereby we openly profess our desire to be reckoned with the people of God' (4:15:13). This public confessional function of baptism is spelt out emphatically in section 13. Calvin moves on next to the proper conferring and receiving of the sacrament. Since it is given 'to arouse, nourish and strengthen our faith', we must take it from the very hand of its author in the confidence that he inwardly fulfils through it everything it outwardly symbolizes (4:15:14). Calvin explicitly disavows any intention to disjoin its reality and truth from the external sign, yet 'from this sacrament, as from all others, we obtain nothing but what we receive by faith'.[13]

---

[12] *OS* 5, pp. 285-86, 288, 289, 292, 294; McNeill-Battles II, pp. 1303-304, 1307, 1311, 1313.

[13] *OS* 5, pp. 294-95, 296; McNeill-Battles II, pp. 1313-14, 1315.

Insofar as it is a symbol of our confession we ought to bear witness by it to our confidence in God's mercy and to our purity in the forgiveness of sins, which has been won for us through Jesus Christ, and to our entry into the church of God in order to live unitedly with all believers in a single harmony of faith and love. (4:15:15)[14]

This backcloth explains the sharpness of the question addressed in section 17, where Calvin responds with some earnestness to the probing query 'what faith of ours followed baptism for some years'. The questioners' aim was to expose the baptism as invalid, since baptism 'is not sanctified to us except when the word of promise is accepted by faith'.[15] The very same backcloth was itself illumined beyond any uncertainty by Calvin's own question in the 1536 edition's concluding paragraph on baptism: why were children baptized when they had no faith to be instructed in the Lord's promises or to be publicly professed?[16]

The dominant emphases of Book 4:15 find their explanation in the 1536 edition from which it mostly derives. Although at a few places others' errors may be in view, the main target is undoubtedly the sacramental theology and practice of the Roman Church. Zwingli's minimalism, and perhaps that of the Anabaptists also, is apparently in Calvin's mind when he dissents from regarding baptism as 'nothing more than a badge or mark' (*tesseram et notam*; 4:15:1).[17] The conclusion in 1536 was obviously directed against Anabaptist rejection of infant baptism, although, as we have seen, the logic of the preceding bulk of the section makes the raising of the question why then infants were baptized inescapable. Elsewhere the 'Catabaptists' are explicitly faulted for rebaptizing those earlier baptized by immoral or godless ministers (4:15:16, 1559), and the desire to undermine the Anabaptist case may lie behind Calvin's strange exegesis of Acts 19.1-6 (4:15:18). Yet the brevity of the attention paid to infant baptism in the 1536 treatment rules out Anabaptism as his chief concern, while several elements plainly identify the old church as the opposition: the misconception, responsible for multiple abuses, that baptism cleansed only from past sins, the extravagant claim that baptism delivered entirely from original sin, the 'theatrical pomp' and 'outlandish defilements' which cluttered up a simple rite, and above all the pervasive stress on the necessity of faith. This last led Calvin in 1536 to declare somewhat hazardously ('if this argument fails us') that 'none are saved except by faith, whether children or adults, and baptism

---

[14] *OS* 5, p. 296; McNeill-Battles II, p. 1315.
[15] *OS* 5, p. 297; McNeill-Battles II, p. 1317.
[16] *OS* 1, p. 135; Battles 1536, p. 101.
[17] *OS* 5, pp. 285-86; McNeill-Battles II, p. 1304.

rightly belongs to infants because they have faith in common with adults'.[18]

The polemic against Roman errors had become more accentuated by the last edition of 1559, with extended treatment of penance and liturgical accretions, for example, and added sections debarring clinical baptism, especially by women. These serve only to throw into clearer relief the ubiquitous highlighting of faith throughout Book 4:15. The argument with the Anabaptists was developed separately, in what ended up as Book 4:16, almost entirely introduced in 1539, as we have noted. It is to this that we must now turn.

The first feature that merits notice is Calvin's calling this chapter an 'appendix' added to curb the ravings of the Anabaptists, which carries surprising implications. Would Calvin have given no direct treatment of infant baptism without the need to refute the Radicals? Does he believe that Book 4:15 has adequately dealt with baptism including paedobaptism—apart, that is, from responding to Anabaptist clamour? The introduction of 4:16 as an 'appendix' does not help readers wishing to know how the relationship between the two chapters is to be understood.

Calvin deems it necessary *de novo* to enquire into the *vis* and *natura* of baptism, which he finds in its indicating the purging of sins and the mortification of the flesh, which consists in sharing in Christ's death, through which in turn believers (*fideles*) are reborn. Everything in scripture concerning baptism can be referred to this *summa*, except that baptism is also a symbol (or badge, *tessera*, 1539-1554) attesting our religion before the world (4:16:2).[19] This differs from the definition given early in 4:15 only in that the elements of the *summa* were there presented under the head of serving our faith before God.

Calvin immediately embarks upon the parallels between baptism and circumcision, which, together with the continuity of the Abrahamic covenant, occupy much of sections 3-6 and 10-16.[20] He introduces Jesus' blessing of the children, and argues that, if it is objected that it was not baptism, his 'receiving, embracing, laying on of hands and prayer, by which Christ present in person makes it clear both that they are his and are sanctified by him', was surely far greater than baptism (4:16:7). To reason from the silence of the New Testament makes no more sense on baptism for infants than on women's presence at the Lord's supper. However, the statement that 'When we attend to the purpose for which

---

[18] *OS* 1, p. 136; Battles 1536, p. 101.

[19] *OS* 5, p. 306; McNeill-Battles II, p. 1325.

[20] A banal mistranslation in McNeill-Battles, II, p. 1328, has to be indicated, about three-quarters into 4:16:5. Instead of 'the word "baptism" is applied to infants', read 'the word of baptism is intended for infants', that is, the promise of the covenant, the substance of baptism.

[baptism] was instituted, we see plainly that it belongs no less to infants than to older persons' is left unpacked at this point (4:16:8). The benefit of infant baptism to parents is confirmation of God's promise that he will be the God of their seed also. As for the infants themselves, they do receive some benefit (*Nonnihil...emolumenti*—'a modicum'?): by being engrafted into the church they are 'that much more commended' (*aliquanto commendatiores*) to the other members, and as they grow up, knowledge of their having received this early symbol of adoption will sharpen their zeal for godliness (4:16:9). In an *ad hominem* rejoinder to the Anabaptists Calvin insists on the prior regeneration of elect infants—and hence their fitness for baptism on Anabaptist premises—who die young (4:16:17).[21]

Eventually, in sections 19ff, Calvin comes to the crucial issue of faith, and at times almost appears as if answering questions raised by his own arguments in Book 4:15. Faith may indeed come from hearing (Romans 10.17), but this is not God's invariable rule; the Spirit may illumine apart from preaching. What is at risk if 'infants are said to receive now part of that grace whose full bounty they will shortly hereafter enjoy?' Then, in a couple of sentences expanded by Calvin in 1550 and again in 1559 but still reflecting his wrestling with the issue, he muses:

> So, if he pleases, why should the Lord not in the present enlighten with a faint glimmer those whom he will later illumine with the full brilliance of his light, *especially if he has not stripped them of ignorance before snatching them from the prison of the flesh*? I have no wish rashly to assert that they are endowed with the same faith as we experience in ourselves, **or have at all a knowledge similar to faith**—a question I prefer to leave unresolved. (4:16:19)[22]

The italics indicate the addition in 1559, the bold the one in 1550, where I translate *notitiam fidei similem* differently from McNeill-Battles' 'the same knowledge of faith'.

Circumcision too was a sign of repentance and faith, so that any attack on infant baptism for its supposed lack of these also impugns circumcision (4:16:20). In fact, as circumcision again shows, the sequence of understanding followed by sign which obtains in adults need not hold for infants. Infants are 'baptized unto future repentance and faith...and the seed of each is hidden in them by the secret operation of the Spirit' (4:16:20). For their baptism, 'nothing more of present efficacy is requisite than the confirmation and sanctioning of the covenant made with them by the Lord' (4:16:21). Biblical verses apparently putting repentance and faith before baptism do not apply to infants, who 'must be assigned to another category (*catalogum*)', for 'There are found

---

[21] *OS* 5, pp. 311, 312, 313, 321; McNeill-Battles II, pp. 1330, 1331, 1332, 1340.
[22] *OS* 5, p. 323; McNeill-Battles II, p. 1342.

many statements in Scripture whose interpretation depends on their context' (4:16:23). Abraham and Isaac exemplify the difference in sequence (4:16:24). The 'law and rule of baptism' must not be derived from Matthew 28.19 and Mark 16.16 as though it was first instituted then, since Jesus had from the outset taught his disciples to baptize. Mark 16.16 has nothing to do with infants (4:16:27-8). As for the parallel alleged between baptism and the Lord's supper, whereas self-examination is prescribed before the latter, in scripture 'the Lord makes no choice of ages' as far as baptism is concerned (4:16:30).[23]

It remains to pinpoint more precisely the *prima facie* discrepancy between chapters 4:15 and 4:16, but first we should chart the clear water between 4:16 and the discarded last paragraph of the 1536 sub-chapter on baptism. In the latter, of course, Calvin quite explicitly faced up to his original two-part purpose of baptism in setting out to vindicate the baptizing of babies. He first proposes, as in 4:16:19 (1539–1559), the propriety of God's giving a foretaste of blessedness to those who will enjoy it in full hereafter. He then emphatically insists on the universal application of Mark 16.16, dissenting unambiguously from the reading which he would endorse from 1539, that it applied only to those of age to respond to the gospel.

> But I assert to the contrary, that this is a general statement, so often inculcated and repeated in Scripture that it cannot be evaded by so trivial a solution... The principle remains fixed, that none are saved except by faith, whether children or adults.[24]

Thus Calvin is led, like Luther before him, to credit infants also with faith. His meaning is not that 'faith always begins from the mother's womb', but rather that 'all God's elect enter eternal life through faith, at whatever age they are removed from this prison of corruption'. If, however this reasoning proves defective, Calvin says he falls back on Jesus' blessing of the children, circumcision and 1 Corinthians 7.14.[25]

It is also on the use of scripture that Book 4:15 and 4:16 markedly diverge. It would be an exaggeration that the former chapter builds its case from the New Testament and the latter from the Old, but this is not far from the truth. A number of baptismal texts come up for consideration in 4:16 only to be declared irrelevant to the discussion of infant baptism: Matthew 28.19, Mark 16.16, Acts 2.37-38 (although 2:39 is welcomed as evidence for the covenantal promise), 8.37, Romans 6.4, Galatians 3.27 and 1 Peter 3.21. The problem would be lesser if Calvin had not cited some of these verses in establishing his fundamental

---

[23] *OS* 5, pp. 324, 326, 328, 335; McNeill-Battles II, pp. 1343, 1345, 1346, 1352.
[24] *OS* 1, pp. 135-36; Battles 1536, p. 101.
[25] *OS* 1, 136; Battles 1536, p. 102.

understanding of baptism in 4:15, where, for example, at the very outset 'the primary point' of baptism is its acceptance with the promise of Mark 16.16, 'He who believes and is baptized will be saved.' The difficulty is by no means confined to one or two isolated texts, but pervasive throughout these chapters. The only traditionally baptismal texts which Calvin retains for infant baptism in 4:16 are Jesus' blessing of the children, 1 Corinthians 7.14, 12.13, Colossians 2.11-12 and Titus 3.5.

No less problematic for the coherence of Calvin's account of baptism in the *Institutes* is his basic emphasis on faith for its reception and the enjoyment of its benefits. In Book 4:15 the requirement of faith is built into the essential structure of baptism. The provision of a new opening definition in 1543—'Baptism is the sign of initiation...'—does not compromise Calvin's affirmation that its twofold end is to serve our faith before God and our confession before our fellow human beings. Baptism 'brings (*affert*) three things to our faith' and from it, as from all other sacraments, 'we gain nothing except what we receive in faith'. How universally Calvin understood this insistence is evident in 1536 in his attributing faith to infants also. Such a stress is scarcely to be squared with the manner in which he defends the baptizing of the newborn in Book 4:16.

This incoherence prompts many questions. How can Calvin have been so unaware of what seems so obvious to modern readers? In adding the 1539 defence of paedobaptism to his 1536 exposition of the meaning of baptism, he can hardly have failed to re-read the latter, for he made several additions to the 1536 text for the 1539 edition. It is true that in 4:16:1 from 1539 on, Calvin declared that he will 'endeavour so to compose this discussion that by explaining the mystery of baptism *clarius* it will carry considerable weight (*non parum...momenti*)'. The force of *clarius* is probably not strictly comparative. If it is, it would have to imply 'more clearly than what is now Book 4:15'. Much more likely is a meaning akin to 'particularly clearly'.[26] It is scarcely plausible to seek an explanation of this apparent incoherence in Calvin's working methods in the series of revisions of the *Institutes*.

What we see in effect in this one compilation by Calvin is a close parallel to what we observe in successive separate writings by Luther. For example, in a work of 1521 in response to the papal bull of excommunication the previous year, *Defence and Explanation of All the Articles*, that is, the articles condemned in the bull, he is far more emphatic than Calvin in 1536 on the absolute necessity of faith in the recipient of baptism, which led him almost irresistibly into that notion of

---

[26] *OS* 5, p. 304; McNeill-Battles II, p. 1324. The translation in the latter omits a brief phrase in the Latin at this point. See also the long editorial note on the composition of 4:16 (1539) in *OS* 5, pp. 303-304.

the faith of infants which Calvin had come to share, as we have seen, by 1536 and which he had not conclusively rejected even in 1559. Luther himself was singing to a different song-sheet by 1528, the year of his major attack on the Anabaptists in *Concerning Rebaptism*. By then, he is still arguing that no-one can prove that infants do not have faith, but the extraordinarily strong insistence of 1521 on faith is heavily muted. The development in Luther's thought and writing, occasioned of course by his shifting his aim from the old church to the Anabaptist Radicals, finds a parallel in Calvin, except that attacks on both fronts over a shorter span of years are bound together within the covers of one work. This circumstance has the effect not only of making the movement in his teaching that much more obvious, but also of rendering it less plausible, if not downright impossible, for his interpreters to argue that since his early anti-Catholic treatise his mind had matured and come to soften its bold outlines.

Another reading of the situation merits an airing which views Calvin in a much more favourable light. In the impressive exhibition held in the Grossmünster in Zürich in 2004 to mark the quincentenary of the birth of Heinrich Bullinger, the printed commentary at one point stated that the Reformers recognized only one form of baptism in the Bible, that of infant baptism. Well, one can understand how that impression has gained currency. The English *Book of Common Prayer* contained no service for the baptism of those of riper years until shortly before the 1662 revision, and then only grudgingly. Similarly, the Scottish *Forme of Prayers*, often known as Knox's Liturgy, took no cognisance of other than infant baptism. Yet the impression is absurd as far as Calvin's *Institutes* are concerned—as though Book 4:15 were kept solely in order to undergird 4:16. In reality, as we have seen, it appears to undermine it more than undergird it. The truth may be somewhat different, that the scrupulously biblical Calvin knew that faith-baptism was the norm and that infant baptism, if he was to adhere to a proper biblical perspective, had to be approached only from that angle and not in its own independent terms. Despite the near-universality of infant-baptismal practice, it is then Book 4:15 which contains the heart of the matter and remains appropriately titled 'On Baptism'. Infant baptism had to be justified, to be sure, but not by abandoning the foundations—biblical and, at that time, Lutheran foundations—laid in 1536, as Luther had been inclined to do in confronting the Anabaptists. Although the weight of attention in the Reformed tradition which looks to Calvin as one of its most productive fountain-heads has undoubtedly leant more preponderantly on Book 4:16's defence of paedobaptism, this has not done justice to Calvin himself—unless, that is, he is to be faulted for maintaining 4:15 in place as his basic statement on baptism, which must take precedence over 4:16.

If Calvin is to be read in this way, he turns out to be a remarkably modern theologian of Christian baptism. Only since the later twentieth century has a consensus been building among major infant-baptizing confessions acknowledging that in an important and proper sense—one which does not disqualify infant baptism—faith-baptism is the normative expression of baptism, and constitutes the starting of reflection on the baptism of the newborn. This far-reaching shift in baptismal thinking, already clearly foreshadowed in the Faith and Order text of the World Council of Churches, *Baptism, Eucharist and Ministry* (1982), and inspired powerfully by a revisiting of the New Testament sources of Christian initiation, is already well integrated into liturgical theology and revised rites of baptism within the Roman Catholic and Anglican communions, and its influence is being felt elsewhere also, even within churches in the Reformed family, as is evident in the new statement on baptism and the revised baptismal section of the Act anent the Sacraments approved by the General Assembly of the Church of Scotland in 2003.[27] The redirection in baptismal understanding that this represented may be gauged from the fact that until the very last years of the twentieth century this church had never in all its history made legislative provision for the baptism of other than infants. The extraordinarily extensive labours of a Special Commission on Baptism during 1953–63 had issued in a new Act (1963) which at no point envisaged any subjects of baptism except the newborn. In the experience of the Church of Scotland the turn taken in respect of baptism in the early years of the twenty-first century was a return to the New Testament but also in effect to a major emphasis of Calvin's *Institutes*.

This interpretation of the two chapters on baptism in the *Institutes* may prove unduly generous. The alternative would be to censure Calvin for an egregious instance of maladroit composition. There is an inherent attraction in hailing Calvin as the unwitting trailblazer well in advance of the most promising development in centuries towards bridging the baptismal divide.

---

[27] *General Assembly 2003* (Edinburgh, 2003), sect. 13, pp. 1-17.

CHAPTER 17

Baptism at the Westminster Assembly

Introduction: Baptism's Neglect

The choice of subject may surprise readers. Baptism did not provoke any of the Westminster Assembly's momentous debates—although, as will be seen, it did give rise to some lengthy and divisive discussions. Nor can the Westminster divines be said to have made any remarkable contribution to the church's understanding or practice of baptism.

Yet a reaction of surprise that baptism should enjoy a paper of its own in a conference commemorating the Westminster Assembly may have more to do with a wider neglect or devaluation of baptism, at least when compared with the Lord's supper. Modern ecumenical conversations have paid it little attention—and the section on baptism in the landmark Faith and Order statement *Baptism, Eucharist and Ministry* (Geneva, 1982) has been judged the least accomplished of the three. We have no history of Christian baptism nor a comprehensive account of baptism in the Reformation. The magisterial Reformers' differences from the old church on baptism were relatively slight, and both joined in scornful dismissal of the Radical Anabaptists' protest. Compared with the mass and the inner-Protestant 'supper-strife', baptism was very small beer. One has only to reflect on the massively contrasting weight of preoccupation displayed over the proper minister of baptism on the one hand and of the Lord's supper on the other.

Whether this relative depreciation of baptism faithfully reflects the witness of the New Testament is a large question for another occasion. Let me simply affirm my judgment that it would be far truer to the apostolic testimony to portray the church as a baptismal community than as a eucharistic community, as it is commonly called today. The conviction grows on me that the devaluing of baptism, in much of British evangelical church life, for example, cannot be understood in detachment from the predominance of infant baptism and its largescale failure—its failure, that is, in such a high proportion of cases measured on any realistic assessment, actually to initiate people into the church. Inevitably, if paedobaptism is so often ineffective, it cannot sustain grandiose theological pretensions. Inevitably, the focus shifts to some later occasion of confirmation or admission to communion or to full membership.

Inevitably, reductionist treatment is meted out to the New Testament presentations of baptism, to make them fit our experience of the administration of infant baptism on the ground.

Such contemporary concerns may help to sharpen our investigation of baptismal deliberations at the Westminster Assembly. After all, the Westminster documents have to a major degree shaped baptismal understanding and practice in the Reformed churches in the West. And the very fact that our instinctive initial reaction at the pairing of baptism and Westminster suggests that its approach to the sacrament has been assimilated among our churches without much controversy may point up the special value of bringing to it the harder questions of the present—the kind of questions, for example, that the dissolution of Christendom in the western world poses to the practice of baptizing infants. For, as Karl Barth well recognized, Christendom and paedobaptism go together.[1]

The Westminster Documents and Minutes

Four of the Westminster documents deal with baptism: the Confession of Faith, the Directory for Public Worship, and the Larger and Shorter Catechisms. The minutes of the Assembly record next to nothing of the discussions on the contents of the Catechisms, and, as far as baptism is concerned, very little of those on the Confession. The only extended minutes of baptismal debate relate to the Directory for Public Worship.

Not that the extant minutes are a high-quality record. This is the verdict of the late Robert Paul:

> [T]hese manuscript 'Minutes' are something of a misnomer, since they appear to be little more than the hasty notes of a scribe, probably written in preparation for a fuller account to appear at some later date. The speeches are often cryptic to the point of being almost meaningless, there are frustrating gaps in the text where the scribe had possibly intended to insert summaries of the speeches to be obtained from the notes of the speakers themselves, and the whole is written in an execrable seventeenth century hand of extraordinary abstruseness and complexity.[2]

---

[1] Cf. K. Barth, *The Teaching of the Church Regarding Baptism* (trans. E.A. Payne; London, 1948), pp. 52-54; 'Am I wrong in thinking that the really operative extraneous ground for infant-baptism, even with the Reformers, and ever and again quite plainly since, has been this: one did not want then in any case or at any price to deny the existence of the evangelical Church in the Constantinian *corpus christianum*—and today one does not want to renounce the present form of the national church (*Volkskirche*)?' (p. 52).

[2] Robert S. Paul, *The Assembly of the Lord: Politics and Religion in the Westminster Assembly and the 'Grand Debate'* (Edinburgh, 1985), pp. 72-73. See also his Appendix IV, 'Interpreting the "Minutes"', pp. 562-64. Among the oddities of the manuscript is the

Fortunately, not least for the purposes of this paper, the Library of New College, Edinburgh, holds an invaluable manuscript transcript in highly legible copper-plate script of the original manuscript minutes (which are in Dr Williams's Library, London). The transcript was made in the late 1860s and early 1870s under the auspices of a Church of Scotland committee.[3] The published copy of part of the minutes, edited by Alexander F. Mitchell and John Struthers in 1874, presents this

---

misspelling of names. George Gillespie, one of the Scottish commissioners, commonly appears as 'Gelaspi'.

[3] On these matters see Paul, *Assembly of the Lord*, p. 73, with notes. In June 1867 the Church of Scotland's General Assembly appointed a committee to obtain a transcript of the manuscript minutes held in Dr Williams's Library, London (*Principal Acts of the General Assembly of the Church of Scotland...1867*, p. 60). This committee, convened until his death by Professor Alexander F. Mitchell and then from 1899 by Thomas Leishman, until it was discontinued by the 1904 Assembly, arranged for the completion of the transcript (on the difficulties of this task see *Principal Acts...1868*, pp. 63-65, and subsequent annual reports to the Assembly), which it presented to the 1875 Assembly which deposited it in the General Assembly Library (*Principal Acts...1875*, p. 85). The committee also secured the publication of most of volume III of the minutes, in 1874 (see next note), and in 1892 also of Alexander F. Mitchell and James Christie (eds), *The Records of the Commissions of the General Assemblies of the Church of Scotland holden in Edinburgh in the Years 1646 and 1647* (Scottish History Society, 11; Edinburgh, 1892); see *Principal Acts...1890*, p. 82; *1892*, p. 78, but failed despite years of effort to find adequate funds for the publication of the rest of the Westminster Assembly's minutes (*Principal Acts...1881*, p. 64; *1904*, p. 68). This task of publication from the original manuscripts *de novo* is well on its way to achievement under the editorship of Dr Chad Van Dixhoorn in Cambridge. Further investigation is called for to clarify some of the General Assembly reports on the progress of the project (e.g. *Principal Acts...1870*, p. 75; *1871*, p. 69; *1872*, p. 76; *1887*, p. 68).

The transcript secured by Mitchell's committee was largely, if not wholly (see next note), the work of Edward Maunde Thompson, of the Manuscripts Department of the British Museum. On Thompson (1840–1929), later Principal Librarian of the British Museum 1888–1902 (with title of Director from 1898), see *Dictionary of National Biography 1922–1930* (London, 1937), pp. 834-36, although this tribute by F.G. Kenyon does not mention Thompson's transcript of the Westminster Assembly's minutes. On the Church of Scotland's General Assembly Library see briefly John Howard, 'New College Library', in David F. Wright and Gary D. Badcock (eds), *Disruption to Diversity: Edinburgh Divinity 1846–1996* (Edinburgh, 1996), pp. 187-202, at pp. 192-93. The transcript appears in the printed *Catalogue of Books, Pamphlets and Manuscripts in the Library of the General Assembly of the Church of Scotland* (Edinburgh, 1907), p. 441: 'Minutes of the sessions of the Assembly of Divines at Westminster, August 4, 1643—March 25, 1652. 3 vols. in 5. folio.' In the preparation of this paper I have been wholly dependant on the New College transcript, which, following Paul, *Assembly of the Lord*, I cite as 'TMs.', and not on the original manuscript. In manuscript the minutes extend from 4 April 1643 to 24 April 1652.

transcript.[4] This volume covers the Assembly's proceedings from November 1644 to March 1649 and hence does not include the debates on the Directory for Public Worship and contains little about baptism.

The minutes can be supplemented, and sometimes corrected, from the accounts of participants, especially the *Journals* of the noted Hebraist, John Lightfoot, covering July 1643 to December 1644, and the *Notes* of George Gillespie of debates from February 1644 to January 1645, together with the briefer general comments in Robert Baillie's *Letters and Journals*.[5] Both Lightfoot and Gillespie are of value in supplying some of the deficiencies of the minutes in relation to the sessions on baptism.

---

[4] *Minutes of the Sessions of the Westminster Assembly of Divines, While Engaged in Preparing their Directory for Church Government, Confession of Faith and Catechisms (November 1644 to March 1649), From Transcripts of the Originals Procured by a Committee of the General Assembly of the Church of Scotland*, Edited for the Committee by Alex. F. Mitchell and John Struthers (Edinburgh, 1874, reprinted, Edmonton, Alberta, 1991), cited hereafter as 'Mitchell and Struthers'. On Mitchell, see briefly Nigel M. de S. Cameron *et al.* (eds), *Dictionary of Scottish Church History and Theology* (Edinburgh, 1993), p. 594, and on Struthers, *Fasti Ecclesiae Scoticanae* (2nd edn, 1915), I, p. 391. Only further research will clear up some uncertainty over Struthers' contribution to the transcripts published by Mitchell and Struthers. According to the General Assembly record, E.M. Thompson (see previous note) transcribed volume II, and Struthers an important part of volume III (*Principal Acts...1868*, p. 64; the Assembly Acts give no more detail). Mitchell and Struthers, p. ix, state that the transcripts of volume III were made by Thompson and Struthers, but also that 'the Minutes throughout stand in [their published] text as, after repeated and careful revision, it was fixed by Mr. Thompson'. Furthermore, the five folio volumes of the transcript in New College Library appear to be all in a single hand. Paul, *Assembly of the Lord*, p. 73, with n. 5, if anything compounds the confusion. It may well be that the transcript we now have is wholly Thompson's production.

It should be noted that where Mitchell and Struthers insert an ellipsis (...) in their text, it does not indicate omission of material in the minutes but merely gaps in the transcript itself, nearly always immediately evident from parts of lines or several lines at a time left blank. Here the transcript faithfully reproduced the original: see Paul, *Assembly of the Lord*, p. 73, cited above. Mitchell and Struthers might have obviated any misunderstanding of their practice had they been fully consistent, but, e.g., cf. p. 180, 'Her   '; p. 182, 'Debate of   '. The present essay uses ellipsis (...) to indicate only my omission of material from the source. I have modernized the spelling of the manuscript minutes only in giving 'that' for 'yt' and 'and' for the copula.

[5] John Lightfoot, *The Journal of the Proceedings of the Assembly of Divines, from January 1, 1643, to December 31, 1644...* (ed. John Rogers Pitman; *The Whole Works...* (13 vols; London, 1822–25), XIII; London, 1824), cited as 'Lightfoot'; George Gillespie, *Notes of Debates and Proceedings of the Assembly of Divines and Other Commissions at Westminster, February 1644 to January 1645*, ed. David Meek (Edinburgh, 1846), cited as 'Gillespie'; *The Letters and Journals of Robert Baillie, A.M., Principal of the University of Glasgow, M.DC.XXXVII–M.DC.LXII* (ed. David Laing; 3 vols; Edinburgh, 1841–42), cited as 'Baillie'.

The Confession of Faith and the Grace of Baptism

The Second Committee appointed to work on the Confession of Faith, whose assigned subjects included the sacraments, brought its report on baptism to the full Assembly on 29 December 1645.[6] Debate is recorded as having taken place on nine days in January, possibly ten, and again on 11 September 1646, with the chapters on the sacraments (27) and on baptism (28) winning final approval on 10 November 1646.[7] But apart from some tantalizingly brief indications (for example, a small group was instructed on 11 September to consider 'what children are to be baptized'),[8] the minutes record nothing of the debates except on 5 January, one of several days on which 'the grace of God in baptism' (so 9 January) was on the table.

The Assembly on 5 January began with a phrase which was presumably in the Second Committee's draft but did not survive into the Confession itself, 'the grace of God bestowed sometimes before'. Let us recall the statement in the Confession as approved:

> The efficacy of baptism is not tied to that moment of time when it is administered; yet notwithstanding, by the right use of this ordinance, the grace promised is not only offered, but really exhibited and conferred by the Holy Ghost, to such (whether of age or infants) as that grace belongeth unto, according to the counsel of God's own will, in his appointed time. (28:6)

We can only presume (for we have no way of knowing) that it was a draft something like this which elicited some disagreement on 5 January 1646, between Jeremiah Whitaker and a more prominent member of the company, Herbert Palmer, who was the first divine to be nominated by Parliament to the Assembly and later on one of its assessors (roughly, deputy chair) and the Master of Queen's College, Cambridge. Whitaker declared

> That it doth confer grace I do not find, but our divines do hold it. When they oppose the Papists, they say it is more than a sign and a seal. Chamier saith the grace that is signified is exhibited, so it is in the French Confession; it doth *efficaciter donare*.[9]

---

[6] Mitchell and Struthers, pp. 164, 173. For the composition of the Second Committee see Paul, *Assembly of the Lord*, pp. 555-56.

[7] Mitchell and Struthers, pp. 173-82, 280, 299. The uncertainty concerns 19 January 1646: '*Ordered*—Report of that Committee concerning Baptism (be taken) be made on Wednesday morning' (p. 180).

[8] Mitchell and Struthers, p. 280; cf. p. 175, 'Debate of Baptism. Debate about dedication to God' (2 January), 'Debate upon Baptism; "the grace of God bestowed sometimes before"' (5 January).

[9] Mitchell and Struthers, p. 175.

Whitaker takes his stand on Scripture:

> That which the Scripture ascribes to baptism we are to ascribe. Baptism is an ordinance to effect these ends... Baptism saves, 1. Accompanied with the sign and thing signified, it is a saving ordinance. For without grace none of these things can be.[10]

Palmer's response is not easy to follow with entire clarity. He asserts that 'What the Scripture speaks of efficacy of baptism, it speaks of those that are grown up. We must suppose the person to be baptized to be a believer.'[11] He certainly denies that the sacrament is a naked sign—'there is no nakedness in a seal'—but he apparently envisages baptism as conferring its gifts on those who already enjoy grace. He seems to reject the notion that baptism imparts the grace of conversion; 'he that is without the first grace hath nothing to make him in a capacity of receiving; he is dead'.[12] But Whitaker is not satisfied: Palmer has not answered the scriptures he quoted. 'The Scripture speaks more about conferring than it doth either of signing and sealing.'[13]

Such is our intriguingly brief glimpse of a debate that must have engaged weighty theological considerations. On my reading of the minutes, the draft before the Assembly at this point did not contain the language now present—'not only offered, but really exhibited and conferred'—but the text is not lucid enough to allow certainty on this question. Whitaker not only advances the word 'exhibited' but also evinces awareness of its Latin original—'*in conjuncta exhibitione*, Ursin[us]'. The verb was widely used in Reformation disputes on the Lord's supper, especially by Martin Bucer, but its currency in this context goes back at least to Aquinas.[14] Its pairing with 'conferred' reveals its meaning, which is stronger than 'exhibit' in modern English. The word 'convey' comes near to the double reference of *exhibere*, as does 'present' itself.

---

[10] Mitchell and Struthers, p. 175.
[11] Mitchell and Struthers, p. 176.
[12] Mitchell and Struthers, p. 176 with n. 1.
[13] Mitchell and Struthers, p. 176.
[14] Mitchell and Struthers, p. 176. On *exhibere*, cf. D.F. Wright, 'Infant Baptism and the Christian Community in Bucer', in D.F. Wright (ed.), *Martin Bucer: Reforming Church and Community* (Cambridge, 1994), pp. 95-106, at pp. 99-100 (see ch. 12 above, pp. 171-72); W.I.P. Hazlett, 'Les entretiens entre Melanchthon et Bucer en 1534: réalités politiques et clarification théologique', in M. de Kroon and M. Lienhard (eds), *Horizons Européens de la Réforme en Alsace...Mélanges offerts à Jean Rott...* (Strasbourg, 1980), pp. 207-25, at p. 223 n. 40.

Baptismal Regeneration

What then about the efficacy of baptism according to the Westminster Confession? Its central affirmation seems clear: 'the grace promised is not only offered, but really exhibited and conferred by the Holy Ghost' (28:6). It is true that a variety of qualifications to this assertion are entered in the chapter on baptism: efficacy is not tied to the moment of administration (28:6), grace and salvation are not so inseparably annexed to baptism that no person can be regenerated or saved without it (28:5) or that all the baptized are undoubtedly regenerated (28:5). But these qualifications serve in fact only to highlight the clarity of the core declaration, which is set forth as follows in the preceding chapter on sacraments in general:

> neither doth the efficacy of a sacrament depend upon the piety or intention of him that doth administer it, but upon the work of the Spirit, and the word of institution; which contains...a promise of benefit to worthy receivers (27:3).

The Westminster divines viewed baptism as the instrument and occasion of regeneration by the Spirit, of the remission of sins, of ingrafting into Christ (cf. 28:1). The Confession teaches baptismal regeneration. We should note also that while the Catechisms use the language only of 'sign and seal',[15] the Directory for Public Worship has the following passage in the model prayer before the act of baptizing:

> That the Lord...would join the inward baptism of his Spirit with the outward baptism of water; make this baptism to the infant a seal of adoption...and all other promises of the covenant of grace: That the child may be planted into the likeness of the death and resurrection of Christ.[16]

But if the Assembly unambiguously ascribes this instrumental efficacy to baptism, it is not automatically enjoyed by all recipients: it contains 'a promise of benefit to worthy receivers' (27:3), who from one point of view are 'those that do actually profess faith in and obedience unto Christ, but also the infants of one or both believing parents' (28:4), and

---

[15] Larger Catechism A. 165: 'Baptism is a sacrament of the New Testament, wherein Christ hath ordained the washing with water...to be a sign and seal of ingrafting into himself, of remission of sins...'; Shorter Catechism A. 95: '...a sacrament, wherein the washing...doth signify and seal...'

[16] The words 'join the inward baptism...with the outward' did not win immediate acceptance from the Assembly on 19 July 1644, according to TMs. II, pp. 261-63. Whitaker declared the child to be as capable of the working of the Spirit in baptism as afterwards, Stephen Marshall was sure that, as a sign, baptism fulfilled all three functions of a sign, viz., to signify, to seal (*obsignare*) and to exhibit, and Palmer affirmed that, since God baptizes through ministerial instruments, 'if he doe it he doth it inwardly as well as outwardly' (p. 263).

from another, 'such (whether of age or infants) as that grace belongeth unto, according to the counsel of God's own will, in his appointed time' (28:6). But it would surely be a perverse interpretation of the Confession's chapter on baptism if we allowed this last allusion to the hidden counsel of God to emasculate its vigorous primary affirmation.

Profession of Faith

I have been struck, in re-reading the Confession and Directory for Public Worship and scrutinizing records of the debates, at the Assembly's relatively muted concern with faith as a prerequisite for baptism to have effect. The key stipulation is, of course, present: baptism is for 'those that do actually profess faith in and obedience unto Christ, but also the infants of one or both believing parents' (28:4). Westminster provides no support for a tendency observable in recent years for the requirement of sincere and credible Christian faith on the part of at least one parent to be transposed into an emphasis on the faith of the receiving congregation. While heightened congregational involvement is to be welcomed, this shift is motivated to some measure by a desire to accommodate the baptism of children whose parent or parents cannot with any honesty be acknowledged as believers or church members. Increasingly, indeed, granny is the one pressing for the baptism. From other angles also infant baptism is becoming a more tangled pastoral issue as the norms of marriage and family disintegrate.

In the light of these present-day concerns, it is instructive to note the absence from the Directory for Public Worship of any provision for the parent(s) to be called upon to profess their faith afresh at the baptism, or to undertake any vows or commitments in relation to the child. The question was one which occupied the assembled divines on two occasions, in July 1644 (12 and 15 July) and again on 9-11 October later that year. For the second debate we have invaluable reports by Lightfoot and Gillespie. The latter records that the Assembly voted by 28 to 16 to include a parental profession of faith, in the form of affirmative answers to credal questions.[17] The deletion of such a section from the Directory was the work of the English Parliament in early 1645.[18] What the Commons and Lords dropped was the following paragraph:

> It is recommended to the parent, to make a profession of his faith, by answering these and the like questions:
>
> Dost thou believe in God the Father, Son and Holy Ghost?

---

[17] Gillespie, p. 91.

[18] *Journals of the House of Commons* (51 vols; London, 1803), IV, p. 70; *Journals of the House of Lords* (123 vols; London, 1890–91), VII, p. 264.

Dost thou hold thyself bound to observe all that Christ hath commanded thee, and wilt thou endeavour so to do?

Dost thou desire to have this child baptised into the faith and profession of Jesus Christ?

All that Parliament added by way of compensation was the phrase 'requiring his [the parent's] solemn promise for the performance of his duty'.[19]

The minutes together with the reports of Lightfoot and Gillespie enable one to follow with reasonable confidence a quite surprising range of arguments batted to and fro on the desirability of recommending such a profession.[20] The Scots, with Alexander Henderson to the fore, 'did urge it mightily, because of the use of it in all reformed churches'.[21] Citing Calvin's exegesis of 1 Peter 3.21, Henderson reckoned a profession in the form of questions and answers 'as ancient as the baptizing of infants and taken from that practise used in baptizing of adults'. It added to the solemnity of the occasion.[22] For others like Thomas Wilson and Philip Nye, the usage of the Reformed churches and Scotland was inadequate ground, if it did not satisfy the criteria of scripture or prudence. 'We may pray reformed churches may be reformed more than they are.'[23] The Scots were clearly not of one mind, for Samuel Rutherford opposed it as lacking warrant in scripture, and he wanted nothing in the Directory that could not command full uniformity.[24] George Walker reminded his colleagues that they were constructing a directory, not 'an obligatory'.[25]

---

[19] For the text, *Journals of the House of Lords* VII, p. 264 (5 March 1645) and Gillespie, p. 91; and TMs. II, p. 493, in part only. See A.F. Mitchell, *The Westminster Assembly: Its History and Standards* (London, 1883; reprinted, Edmonton, Alberta, 1992), pp. 218-19. The omitted paragraph would have appeared immediately after 'if he be negligent', i.e. where the inserted phrase is now placed. Lightfoot, pp. 314-15, includes an earlier form of the questions proposed to the Assembly by its committee:

1 Do you believe all the articles of faith contained in Scripture?
2 That all men and this child are born in sin?
3 That the blood and Spirit washeth away sin?
4 Will you have, therefore, this child baptized?

This came forward for discussion on 9 October 1644, according to Lightfoot. The manuscript minutes contain neither this set of questions nor the form that later failed to secure Parliament's approval.

[20] TMs. II, pp. 251-53 (12 and 15 July), pp. 479-93 (9-11 October 1644); Lightfoot, pp. 314-16 (9-11 October); Gillespie, pp. 88-91 (9-11 October).

[21] Lightfoot, p. 315.

[22] TMs. II, pp. 489, 481; Gillespie, p. 91.

[23] TMs. II, pp. 483-84.

[24] Gillespie, p. 90; TMs. II, pp. 481, 486.

Taking a stand on the Bible proved no easy matter. No parental profession had been required in circumcision, Stephen Marshall pointed out, and Thomas Valentine concurred.[26] For Samuel Gibson the conversion of the Philippian jailor was decisive; neither he nor his family were baptized until he made a profession of his faith.[27] William Bridge was unmoved by this precedent, for it would place members of the church on a par with non-members.[28] Strong support was raised by Edmund Calamy, for whom 'the parents' profession is the ground of the admission of the child',[29] which unnerved William Bridge, lest this argued that the federal holiness of the parent was not the ground of baptizing his offspring.[30] More than one divine was worried that the requirement of a profession would look like a concession to the Anabaptists. As Bridge put it,

> This confession must be either in regard of the child, and that holds out the necessity of actual confession in baptism, as the Anabaptists hold; if in regard of the parent, then it is a wrong to the parent.[31]

The questions and answers at baptism were indeed very ancient, conceded Charles Herle, who followed William Twisse as prolocutor in the chair of the Assembly, 'but in those times the Anabaptists ware not risen in the world'.[32]

Fear of seeming to appease 'the Anabaptists' surfaced on other occasions in the baptismal debates, as we shall see, for 'Anabaptism' was no merely historical threat. Robert Baillie's letters from the Assembly years sound the alarm at 'the great increase and insolencie, in diverse places, of the Antinomian and Anabaptisticall conventicles'.[33] Such apprehension in relation to a parental profession of faith added a further complication to the difficult task of reaching a consensus when the criteria—scriptural warrant, antiquity, uniformity as a feasible goal, etc.—were inadequate. Jeremiah Burroughes of Stepney thought it ironic that 'this explicate profession' should be urged by those who regarded the church covenant as a human intervention, for it was equally so.[34]

---

[25] TMs. II, p. 487.
[26] TMs. II, p. 481; Gillespie, p. 91.
[27] TMs. II, p. 483; Gillespie, p. 90.
[28] TMs. II, p. 485.
[29] TMs. II, p. 485.
[30] TMs. II, p. 480.
[31] Gillespie, p. 90.
[32] TMs. II, p. 480; Gillespie, p. 89.
[33] Baillie II, p. 215; cf. pp. 218, 224.
[34] TMs. II, p. 480.

The silence of the Directory on the need for a profession of faith—after, that is, Parliament had dispensed with it—contrasts starkly with the first attested adaptation of the early church's baptismal liturgy to accommodate children who could not answer for themselves. When a child was brought forward, parents were asked by the minister 'Does he/she believe?', in this direct third-person form.[35] The procedure could not have attested more unambiguously that infants were being included in a rite devised for faith-professing candidates. The outcome of the Westminster Assembly's tortuous deliberations reflected many centuries of practice, undisturbed by the mainstream Reformation, in which infant baptism, not faith-baptism, had been *de facto* the norm.

In Public or in Private?

Two other issues likewise kept the assembled divines busy for days during consideration of the Directory's draft section on baptism. One was whether dipping, i.e. immersion, should be mentioned, and if so in what terms, and the other was what emerged eventually in the Directory as the stipulation that baptism was not to be

> administered in private places, or privately, but in the place of publick worship and in the face of the congregation, where the people may most conveniently see and hear; and not in the places where fonts, in the time of Popery, were unfitly and superstitiously placed.

'Here', records John Lightfoot, 'began we to enter into the ocean of many vast disputes'.[36] They spent all of 11 July 1644, on it, and returned to it on 9 October, when the location of the font was on the table. The Scots, as Gillespie tells us, claimed that there was 'no place so fit for seeing and hearing of the people as the pulpit...the pulpit is chosen for the fittest place'.[37] Not surprisingly they did not prevail, but Scottish practice reflected their plea, with basins affixed to the outside of the pulpit and bairns held up aloft by parents to ministers to sprinkle with baptismal dew from above.[38] The height of the pulpit determined how hazardous the elevation was.[39]

---

[35] Cf. J.C. Didier, 'Une adaptation de la liturgie baptismale au baptême des enfants dans l'Eglise ancienne', *Mélanges de science religieuse* 22 (1965), pp. 79-90.

[36] Lightfoot, p. 297.

[37] Gillespie, p. 89; Lightfoot, p. 315.

[38] See the present writer's article, 'Baptism', in Cameron (ed.), *Dictionary*, p. 57 (ch. 21 below).

[39] Paedobaptism in other forms has occasionally afforded an unwitting recollection of the etymological and symbolic links between baptism and death by immersion in water. According to the *Financial Times* of 2 March 1996, President Boris Yeltsin was nearly drowned by a tipsy priest when being baptized in a Siberian village as a child. I recall a

The prior question—in private, or only in public?—implicated weighty considerations of theological import. Robert Baillie's letter expresses his relief.

> We have carryed, with much greater ease than we expected, the publickness of baptisme. The abuse was great over all this land. In the greatest parosch in London, scarce one child in a-year was brought to the church for baptisme. Also we have carried the parents presenting of his child, and not their midwives, as was their universall custome.[40]

Edmund Calamy made the same point more sharply: 'great abuse in the city [of London: he was vicar of St Mary's, Aldermanbury], in 2 or 3 yeares none baptized in the church'.[41] For centuries in the medieval West the majority of babies may well have been baptized by midwives or other lay persons. The custom rested, of course, on the Augustinian premise of the necessity of baptism for eternal salvation. The Westminster Confession and the Directory for Public Worship trod delicately in eschewing this notion with its abusive consequences but without relaxing the reins irresponsibly. Thus the Directory:

> [O]utward baptism is not so necessary, that, through the want thereof, the infant is in danger of damnation, or the parents guilty, if they do contemn or neglect the ordinance of Christ, when and where it may be had.

And so 'to propound the case of sickness' as justification for private baptism 'is to go too near the tenet of the absolute necessity', as Thomas Wilson put it.[42]

The argument between public and private baptism again reveals the company of divines searching in vain for decisive scriptural guidance. Was not circumcision done in private houses? Gillespie was not convinced, and in any case 'circumcision and baptism differ, because of the wound and plastering it'. No blood on the synagogue floor![43] 'All the nation was baptized, when they were to come out of Egypt; but this could

---

story that used to go the rounds of the Anglican theological colleges. What should a vicar do if he accidentally dropped a baby into a deep stone font? Replace the lid on the font and turn in the Prayer Book to the service for Burial at Sea! Karl Barth commented scornfully on the loss in dramatic vividness as complete immersion yielded to affusion which itself was reduced from a real wetting to a sprinkling and eventually to the 'mere moistening with as little water as possible' of 'the innocuous form of present-day baptism'; Barth, *The Teaching of the Church Regarding Baptism*, pp. 9-11.

[40] Baillie II, pp. 204-205.
[41] TMs. II, p. 244.
[42] Lightfoot, p. 297; TMs. II, pp. 244-45.
[43] Lightfoot, p. 297; TMs. II, p. 245.

not be done in a congregation', retorted John Lightfoot.[44] Stephen Marshall could cite 'reasons a man may give many why in the publique congregation, but noe instance of it in the new testament'.[45] Lazarus Seaman added that it provided 'noe instance...in a private place by any ordinary minister either'.[46] The quest for precise scriptural precedent threatened at such junctures to issue in absurd minimalism.

A more substantive aspect of this question was the child's relationship to the church. Calamy is credited with asserting that 'Baptisme properly is noe church ordinance/Baptized and then added to the church', but Samuel Rutherford retorted: 'It is admission to the church; *ergo*, it must be in the face of the church.'[47] It was left to Seaman to supply another word of sanity: 'If the church go to the child, when the child go to church, this is not to be thought private baptism.'[48] Amid the ebb and flow of conflicting opinions, in which one reluctantly admires the ingenuity of the assembled minds more than their sweet reasonableness, it is astonishing to find on this issue no forthright appeal to the principle of holding Word and sacrament together. One might have expected it to clinch the argument, so that baptism could only properly take place when and where the Word was ministered. The divines too easily lost sight of the theological wood amid varied individual trees of New Testament baptisms.

Debate over Dipping

At times when one eavesdrops on the Assembly's deliberations, one can only marvel at the providence that produced such a majestic outcome from such an astonishing pot-pourri of discussion. This is nowhere more keenly felt than in the protracted altercations over whether the Directory should mention dipping. Herein, says Lightfoot, 'fell we upon a large and long discourse',[49] on which they spent at least three days, 21 July and 7-8 August 1644, according to the minutes. Lightfoot was absent on 7 August. In the end, the Directory kept silent. To baptize the child,

> which, for the manner of doing of it, is not only lawful but sufficient, and most expedient to be, by pouring or sprinkling of the water on the face of the child, without adding any other ceremony.

---

[44] Lightfoot, p. 298.
[45] TMs. II, p. 245.
[46] TMs. II, p. 249.
[47] Lightfoot, p. 297; TMs. II, p. 244.
[48] Lightfoot, p. 297; TMs. II, p. 245.
[49] Lightfoot, p. 299.

As Lightfoot commented, 'it was thought fit and most safe to let it alone'.[50] Later the Confession would be explicit, 'Dipping of the person into the water is not necessary' (28:3), but the course of reasoning that led to this change of mind is hidden from us.

On 7 August the company voted and split down the middle: 24 were for keeping a mention of dipping, 25 were against. And this was after a re-count: 'it was voted so indifferently that we were glad to count names twice', wrote Lightfoot. 'And there grew a great heat upon it: and when we had done all, we concluded upon nothing in it.'[51] The arguments were truly wondrous in their variety and virtuosity:

if dipping is needed to depict burial, 'what must answer dying?' (Francis Woodcock);[52]

if we say dipping is necessary, 'we shall further anabaptisme' (John Ley, and John Lightfoot);[53]

what was the 'proper native signification' of the Greek verb *baptizo*? (Gillespie);[54]

how could 5000 be dipped in a day? (George Walker);[55]

what happened in Jewish proselyte baptism, which was followed by John the Baptist and the disciples of Jesus? (Thomas Coleman and Lightfoot gave different answers);[56]

Lightfoot was in his element citing the rabbinic commentators;

others reported what was the practice in Muscovy and Spain, or registered that 'those that incline most to popery are all for sprinkling';[57]

the Hebrew host 'baptized into Moses' were not immersed (John Arrowsmith);[58]

---

[50] Lightfoot, p. 301.
[51] Lightfoot, p. 300.
[52] TMs. II, p. 265.
[53] TMs. II, pp. 265, 275.
[54] TMs. II, p. 267.
[55] TMs. II, p. 266.
[56] TMs. II, p. 271 (Coleman: proselytes went in up to their necks and dipped themselves all over), p. 272 (Lightfoot: sprinkling attested by Rabbi Solomon).
[57] TMs. II, pp. 270, 276.
[58] TMs. II, p. 266. John Macleod in his *Scottish Theology in Relation to Church History since the Reformation* (Edinburgh, 2nd edn, 1946), pp. 253-54, relates Neil Macmichael's exposition of 1 Corinthians 10.1-5:

1. The Israelites were baptised, both adults and infants; for the Apostle declares it.
2. They were not immersed, a fact which Moses and other inspired writers testify. 3.

the meaning of Hebrew words was ventilated and Latin terms flew to and fro.

And early on Lazarus Seaman posed one of the Assembly's dilemmas: we must follow the mind and institution of Christ, but if that turns out to be dipping, we will be hard put to it to persuade parents to have their children baptized.[59]

1 Corinthians 7.14: Holiness, Federal or Real?

With some relief, we turn to some contested exegesis. In one of his letters from Westminster Robert Baillie wrote home as follows:

> We have ended our Directorie for baptisme. Thomas Goodwin one day was exceedinglie confounded: He has undertaken a publicke lecture against the Anabaptists: it was said, under pretence of refuting them, he betrayed our cause to them: that of the Corinthians, our chief ground for the baptisme of infants, 'Your children are holy', he exponed of a reall holiness, and preached down our ordinare and necessar distinction of reall and federall holiness. Being posed hereupon, he could no wayes cleare himselfe, and no man took his part.[60]

The Directory ended up with the statement that the children of believers 'are Christians, and federally holy before baptism, and therefore are they baptized'. John Lightfoot was unfortunately absent from the Assembly on 16 July 1644, when the meaning and implications of 1 Corinthians 7.14 were rehearsed at length and in depth. We may judge it one of the company's better days. The minutes are ample but not clear at every point.

Goodwin kept up his end from first to last.

> It is such a holynesse as if they dy they should be saved/whether a holynesse of election or regeneration I know not; but I thinke it is they have the holy ghost.[61]

Lazarus Seaman spelt out the alarm that others showed: 'all agree that this holynesse is the ground of baptisme...except he can make out this, the baptizing of infants is gone as toutching his judgment'.[62] Goodwin in

---

The Egyptians who pursued them were immersed. 4. The Israelites had baptism without immersion, and the Egyptians immersion without baptism. 5. The baptism of Israelites was salvation, and the immersion of the Egyptians drowning.

I owe this reference to Donald Macleod, 'The Free Church College 1900–1970', in Wright and Badcock (eds), *Disruption to Diversity*, pp. 221-37, at pp. 231-32.

[59] TMs. II, p. 265.
[60] Baillie II, p. 218.
[61] TMs. II, p. 256.
[62] TMs. II, p. 258; cf. p. 256: Goodwin's interpretation removes the 'common and ordinary' ground of infant baptism and lays new ground.

effect denied any distinction between real and federal holiness: the holiness predicated of the children of a single Christian parent by Paul is the same as that of 'I will be your God and you shall be my people. Therefore be holy.' If 1 Corinthians 7.14 speaks of any other holiness, then baptism is the seal of some other holiness than the holiness of salvation.[63]

But saving holiness is what infallibly saves, commented Stephen Marshall anxiously.[64] As Rutherford put it, 'wher ther is reall and inherent holynesse ther must be a seeing of god, and being in the state of salvation'. But 'the Lord hath election and reprobation amongst Infants noe lesse than those of age'.[65] This emerged as the main objection to Goodwin's interpretation, which was alleged to imply that all such infants would indubitably be saved (so Marshall) and that the decrees of election and reprobation could not stand (Rutherford).[66]

So argument ensued on the difference between an indefinite proposition and a universal proposition. Goodwin's case rested on the former: 'an indefinite faith founded upon an indefinite promise'.[67] Herbert Palmer could not concur: Paul's answer to the 'inconvenience' to a child from one parent's infidelity must be 'a universal proposition and *de fide* we are bound to believe it *de omnibus et singulis*'.[68] To be sure, Goodwin did not entertain every notion that some divines read into his position. He denied that he was speaking of a holiness received by the child by traduction from the parent, as Richard Vines had supposed ('and so they shall be borne regenerate and really holy'),[69] but only of a holiness by way of designation.[70] Calamy came back at Goodwin: 'he judges of the reall holynesse of the infant by the reall holynesse of the parent'. But this is how we all proceed, rejoined Goodwin; it is the children of believers that we baptize.[71]

---

[63] TMs. II, p. 275: 'that which you call federall holynesse and that which I call reall doe both coincidere in this'.
[64] TMs. II, p. 257.
[65] TMs. II, p. 256.
[66] TMs. II, pp. 256, 257.
[67] TMs. II, p. 258: the 'terminus' of human judgment is to be the infant's salvation, but the minister is not to have an infallible judgment of it, but 'such a judgment as answers the promise'. But at p. 260, if the minute is reliable, Goodwin apparently accepted that the verse in some sense embodied 'a universal proposition': 'if the children are by a warrant from the apostle acounted holy soe as to be brought into the bosome of the church/then the unbeliever must needs be sanctified to the believers bed'.
[68] TMs. II, p. 260.
[69] TMs. II, p. 258.
[70] TMs. II, p. 259.
[71] TMs. II, p. 261.

The combined learning and piety of the Westminster theologians did not resolve the exegesis of 1 Corinthians 7.14. The verse had inevitably engaged the attention of previous generations of expositors, and had found the early Fathers and the Reformers of the sixteenth century espousing a variety of theories that, if not universally comprehensive, was at least indefinite.[72] But whereas earlier exegetes had been especially preoccupied with avoiding the attribution to the children of a holiness which they could not comfortably credit also of the unbelieving partner, the dominant concerns of the divines at Westminster led in other directions. The irony lay in their very captivity to this verse in the first instance, for at least one thing can be incontrovertibly deduced from it—that the children in question who are declared 'holy' had not been baptized, nor, if the parallel with the unbelieving spouse extends this far, is their imminent baptism implied. This is, I think, the only place in the New Testament where children are in view of whom we know for certain whether they have or have not been baptized. They have not—but are said to be already 'holy'.

Infant Baptism and Federal Theology

The sentence that eventually appeared in the Directory for Public Worship—'they are Christians, and federally holy before baptism'—appears to owe the inclusion of 'federally' to Goodwin's opposition. If the minutes can be trusted, the wording before the Assembly at the outset of this discussion was 'they are Christians and holy...'[73] This is not the only statement in the Westminster documents' deliverances on baptism that ventures explicitly into the special language of covenant theology. This latter species of theology is in no way my territory, but I raise a question for others to ponder and adjudicate upon. It was a comment by Sinclair Ferguson on the renewed interest displayed in the sixteenth and seventeenth centuries in the Bible's teaching on the covenant that set me thinking.

> [I]t was given fresh impetus by the Anabaptist accusation that the mainstream Reformers had thoughtlessly acquiesced in the 'unbiblical' practice of infant baptism. In response the Reformers argued that God had made one covenant with men with Jesus Christ at its heart, administered in two dispensations, the 'old' and the 'new'. Since the children of believers received the initiatory sacrament of this

---

[72] See my '1 Corinthians 7:14 in Fathers and Reformers', ch. 14 above.
[73] TMs. II, p. 255, at the beginning of session 254 on the morning of 16 July 1644.

covenant in the restricted administration of the 'old covenant', they must also receive the initiatory sacrament of baptism in the 'new covenant'.[74]

Was it the case, as this statement suggests, not only that covenant theology afforded a strong defence of baptizing infants, but also that the imperative to defend the baptizing of infants enhanced the attractiveness of doing theology covenantally? I find the implication—or is it my inference?—intriguing. There is no doubt in my mind that infant baptism was the single most substantive constitutive element of the church that the Reformers perpetuated from the old church without explicit biblical authorisation. In vindicating it they displayed immense versatility, but it was no easy task. Does the pressing necessity of doing so help to explain the shift towards the federalization of theology? Can it be shown that the apologia for paedobaptism was a significant organizing centre in the structural elaboration of covenant theology?

Concluding Assessment

It is no part of the purpose of this paper to enter into critical engagement with Westminster's presentation of Christian baptism in the light of more recent theological viewpoints. It should probably be faulted, for example, for not relating church baptism to Christ's own baptism, or perhaps to his whole work of identification with us understood as his baptism for us.[75] More serious would be a demonstration of internal inconsistency, such as that hinted at by George S. Hendry in reporting hypothetically a contention that 'even the definition of the sacrament given in the Confession implies conditions which cannot be literally fulfilled in the case of infants'.[76] He gives no more detail than this, but we might well ask whether baptism can be 'unto [the party baptized] a sign and seal of the covenant of grace...and of his giving up unto God through Jesus Christ, to walk in newness of life' (28:1) if the party is incapable of discerning the signification of walking in newness of life. But that may be too harsh a judgment. If it is guilty of deep-seated inconsistency, the Westminster Confession would be in good company, according to Karl Barth, who

---

[74] Sinclair B. Ferguson, 'The Teaching of the Confession', in Alasdair I.C. Heron (ed.), *The Westminster Confession in the Church Today* (Edinburgh, 1982), pp. 28-39, at p. 37.

[75] Cf. George S. Hendry, *The Westminster Confession for Today: A Contemporary Interpretation* (London, 1960), p. 225: 'The sacrament of baptism rests ultimately on Christ's own baptism, in which he became "ingrafted" into us, to bring us the benefits of the covenant of grace (Matt. 3:13-15), and which he consummated by his death (Mark 10:38; Luke 12:50).'

[76] Hendry, *The Westminster Confession for Today*, p. 226.

finds serious incoherence between John Calvin's treatment of baptism in general and defence of infant baptism in particular.

> One may read the 15th and 16th chapters in Book IV of the *Institutio* one after the other and convince oneself whether the great Calvin was sure of his subject and where he obviously was not sure, but visibly nervous, in a hopelessly confused train of thought, abusing where he ought to inform and when he wants to convince, seeking a way in the fog, which can lead him to no goal, because he has none.[77]

Barth here points up the continuing dilemma of church and theology in seeking to defend infant baptism from a Bible—or at least a New Testament—which knows only the baptism of converts.

Yet there can be no respectable future for paedobaptism which does not treat it fully as Christian baptism. In these terms, its hopes lie in being made more central and fundamental to Christian education and nurture. One of the gravest scandals attending the practice of infant baptism is that too often baptized children growing up are unaware of their baptismal identity. From time to time young adults coming forward for full membership turn out to be unsure whether they were baptized as babies. One major answer to this ignorance is the 'improvement' of baptism inculcated explicitly by the Larger Catechism (Q/A 167), and indirectly by the Directory for Public Worship, both in the home and in Sunday school and Bible class. According to the New Testament, baptism, not conversion, is the locus of our acquiring Christian identity. As the Directory puts it, in baptism children are 'received into the bosom of the visible church, distinguished from the world, and them that are without, and united with believers'.[78]

'Distinguished from the world': in the early church there was no doubt about this. But it has been one of the sad features of the story of infant baptism, not least to the present day in the declining churches of post-Christendom, that it has so often served to obscure that distinction. Perhaps a revisiting of Westminster may help us to recover it.

---

[77] Barth, *The Teaching of the Church Regarding Baptism*, p. 49; cf. p. 48, where he accuses Calvin in *Institutes* 4:16 of forgetting what he wrote in 4:15. See my 'Development and Coherence in Calvin's *Institutes*: The Case of Baptism (*Institutes* 4:15–4:16)' (ch. 16 above).

[78] Cf. Confession 27:1, on sacraments in general: 'instituted...to put a visible difference between those that belong unto the church and the rest of the world'.

PART C

TOWARDS A MODERN CONSENSUS

CHAPTER 18

The Baptismal Community

For whatever reason the last few years have witnessed a resurgence of interest in the success of the early church. To describe the history of Christianity up to Constantine as a success story may sound triumphalist, but it seems to merit this recognition. The 'Jesus movement' grew to about five percent of the population of the Roman Empire in less than three centuries. By some very broad-brush calculations it has recently been estimated that such expansion required growth, on average, of 40 per cent per decade, or 3.42 per cent every year. This is the finding of the sociologist Rodney Stark, whose little book *The Rise of Christianity*[1] has stimulated fresh debate about 'How the Obscure, Marginal Jesus Movement Became the Dominant Religious Force in the Western World in a Few Centuries', as his paperback publisher subtitled his work, without his knowledge.[2] *Newsweek* went one step further, calling the book an account of 'how the west was won for Jesus'.[3]

No less interesting from a present-day standpoint are the circumstances in which Christianity made its way in the Mediterranean world. For most of the period before Constantine Christians were liable to persecution, and many died for their faith as martyrs. Though pluralism and inclusiveness in religion were the order of the day, Christians maintained an exclusive stance and counted adherents of all other religions as fair game for evangelism. No philosophy or cult was off limits and the older view that Greco-Roman paganism was withering away by the first century is no longer a consensus among scholars. The mores of Roman imperial society tolerated a fair degree of sexual license, not wholly unbridled but permissive enough, so long as certain traditional norms were observed.

---

[1] Rodney Stark, *The Rise of Christianity: A Sociologist Reconsiders History* (Princeton, NJ, 1996).

[2] See Stark, *Rise of Christianity*, pp. 6-7 of the paperback edition, published in San Francisco in 1997. See also Rodney Stark, 'E Contrario', *Journal of Early Christian Studies* 6 (1998), p. 262. Most of that issue is devoted to responses to Stark's book. For a survey of recent discussion see Danny Praet, 'Explaining the Christianization of the Roman Empire: Older Theories and Recent Developments', *Sacris Erudiri* 33 (1992-93), pp. 7-119.

[3] 'The Low to the Mighty', *Newsweek* 9 April 1996, p. 62.

Christianity, however, steadfastly refused to smooth its path to success by accommodating to the prevailing attitude toward immorality.

As one reflects on the context within which the church of the early Fathers attained sufficient strength (not solely in numerical terms) to attract the interest and then the favour of a Roman emperor, it is difficult not to observe uncanny parallels to the situation facing Christians in much of western society today. The difference, of course, and it is a massive one, is that today's religiously and culturally pluralist society, so inclusively tolerant and sexually besotted, has emerged out of Christendom. No return to the innocence of pre-Constantinian pre-Christendom is possible. Yet believers today can learn from earlier generations without drowning in nostalgia or painting the past in the hues of utopian idealism.

This lecture highlights certain features in the formation of the early Christians, in what was the decisive 'making' of them. The subject addresses how Jesus' followers in the first three centuries came to be the kind of people capable not only of surviving but also of multiplying in an alien environment.

Baptism as a Touchstone in the New Testament

For some time now it has been fashionable, especially in ecumenical circles, to describe the church as a eucharistic community. However, in the light of the New Testament it is more accurate to view it as a baptismal community. That may be no more congenial to some evangelical Christians today than the eucharistic characterization, especially to members of infant-baptizing churches. For whatever else one can say about the prevalence of infant baptism for most of Christian history, among biblical Christians it has been attended by a far-reaching baptismal reductionism. When most of a congregation has experienced baptism as unwitting babies, it goes against the grain to regard baptism as a major defining feature of its common Christian identity.

It is an instructive exercise to assemble the New Testament's scattered mentions of baptism and to note how often it functions as a criterion, a touchstone, an agreed point of reference. The marks of Christian unity in the Holy Spirit include 'one baptism', but not 'one eucharist' (Ephesians 4.5). Not many today would challenge divisive groups lining up between this or that stellar preacher, 'Were you baptized in the name of...Paul?' (1 Corinthians 1.13). The Great Commission commands the making of disciples by baptizing and teaching (Matthew 28.19-20). On the Day of Pentecost those cut to the heart by Peter's preaching were told to 'repent and be baptized every one of you...so that your sins may be forgiven; and you will receive the gift of the Holy Spirit' (Acts 2.38). When Paul wrote against antinomianism ('Are we to continue in sin so that grace may increase?' Romans 6.1), it is remarkable that he cited the significance of the baptismal experience (vv. 1-4). And the New Testament's language about baptism is very often realist rather than symbolical.

In the congregations of patristic Christianity an unbaptized Christian was an anomaly, if not an impossibility. Catechumens, undergoing a thorough preparation for baptism, might be called Christians (so the question was answered when it was raised), but if they died unbaptized, except in martyrdom, it was assumed they would not enjoy salvation and eternal life. Martyrdom was universally seen as blood-baptism, substituting for water baptism not yet received. It is worth noting that the earliest known building adapted for permanent use as a church, at Dura-Europos on the Euphrates River, around AD 240, included a small room set apart as a baptistry.

Baptismal Screening

More significant by far was the extraordinary care with which the gate of baptism was guarded. In contrast to most church practice today, primitive Christianity apparently made baptism accessible only to the most serious and committed candidates. It seems as if the early church was more concerned to weed out and deter than to attract and welcome. Most of the patristic evidence shows that the church disallowed the prompt baptizing of converts, in contrast to the practice in the Book of Acts. The reasons for change must include the recruitment of largely Gentile rather than Jewish believers.

The most informative source by far is the *Apostolic Tradition*, attributed to Hippolytus of Rome, normally dated around 215.[4] This text, however, is problematic, for it is reconstructed from later, derivative documents. Furthermore debate has not settled whether all the writings attributed to Hippolytus belong to him. More recent attention has shifted to the different strands or layers of material in the reconstituted text. A commentary published in the Hermeneia series by Paul Bradshaw and colleagues argues for the composite character of the work, incorporating traditions later than the early third century. This should not be surprising in a church-order text. Like the *Didache*, the earliest writing in this genre, church-order manuals customarily claim earlier, preferably apostolic, origins for later developments in teaching and practice. However, Bradshaw and his fellow commentators conclude that the baptismal section in the *Apostolic Tradition* is no later than the time of Hippolytus in the early third century, and probably earlier.

---

[4] Geoffrey J. Cuming (ed.), *Hippolytus: A Text for Students* (Bramcote, 1976). See now Paul F. Bradshaw *et al.* (eds), *The Apostolic Tradition* (Hermeneia; Minneapolis, MN, 2002).

What, then, does the *Apostolic Tradition* prescribe for those desiring to be baptized? First, applicants and enquirers were sifted.

> Those who come forward for the first time to hear the word shall first be brought to the teachers before all the people arrive, and shall be questioned about their reason for coming to the faith. And those who have brought them shall bear witness about them, whether they are capable of hearing the word. They shall be questioned about their state of life; has he a wife? Is he the slave of a believer? Does his master allow him? Let him hear the word. If his master does not bear witness about him that he is a good man, he shall be rejected.[5]

Instruction follows on how these inquirers were to conduct their lives. 'If any man is not living with a wife, he shall be instructed not to fornicate, but to take a wife lawfully or remain as he is. If anyone is possessed by a demon, he shall not hear the word of teaching until he is pure.'[6]

The questioning moved on to the petitioners' occupations. Brothel-keepers were to cease or be rejected, and sculptors and painters must likewise give up making idols. A number of other rulings are similarly unsurprising, even though one wonders whether the church was in fact attracting such a variety of enquirers—people involved in any way in gladiatorial contests, prostitutes, astrologers, cutters of the fringes of clothing, and makers of phylacteries.[7]

Those who taught children were encouraged to give it up, but they could be accepted if they were no good at anything else.[8] A soldier under authority was to be rejected unless he promised never to kill, even if ordered to, and not to take the military oath. And if a Christian wanted to become a soldier, he could not be baptized. An official who wielded the power of the sword or a city councillor must lay down his office if he wanted to be baptized. In a differentiated ruling that reflects social distinctions, a man's concubine—his mistress or partner—could become a catechumen if she were his slave, had reared her children, and had remained faithful to him alone. But the male in such a liaison must make the woman his lawful wife or be rejected.[9]

The rigour of this screening process is closely paralleled by the treatise on *Idolatry*, by Tertullian of Carthage, written a few years earlier.[10] He was even more inclined to exclude those whose qualifications were

---

[5] Cuming (ed.), *Hippolytus*, p. 15.

[6] Cuming (ed.), *Hippolytus*, p. 15.

[7] Cuming (ed.), *Hippolytus*, pp. 15-16.

[8] Cuming (ed.), *Hippolytus*, pp. 15-16: 'He who teaches children had best cease; but if he has no craft, let him have permission.'

[9] Cuming (ed.), *Hippolytus*, pp. 15-16.

[10] Tertullian, *Idolatry*, trans. Stanley L. Greenslade, in *Early Latin Theology* (Library of Christian Classics; London, 1956).

questionable. Underlying this fencing of the baptismal waters at the first hurdle was the urgency of breaking the bondage of the old order of idolatry,[11] which Tertullian found subtly pervasive throughout so much of daily life. The building up of the baptismal community in a potentially hostile society called for careful application of demanding standards.

Remaking Pagans into Christians

According to the *Apostolic Tradition*, 'catechumens shall continue to hear the word for three years', immediately conceding that progress, not lapse of time, is what matters.[12] It is not known, however, how many catechumens had to wait three years. Clement of Alexandria prescribed the same period, and another source said that some might have to remain catechumens for five years.[13] If persecution loomed, the catechumens would often be baptized speedily, not because to die in martyrdom unbaptized was to forfeit salvation but because it was believed that the gift of the Spirit received through baptism would strengthen them to stand fast under pressure and prevent them from lapsing. Though there was some adjustment to one's circumstances, the catechumenal process was thorough and serious. The controlling purpose was 'to re-form pagan people, to resocialize them, to deconstruct their old world, and reconstruct a new one, so that they would emerge as Christian people who would be at home in communities of freedom'.[14]

This would be accomplished by catechumens hearing the word both from teachers or catechists, such as Justin Martyr at Rome or Clement and Origen at Alexandria, and in homilies in congregational worship. The catechumens were allowed to remain in these services up to the ministering of the Lord's supper. Their withdrawal at that point ensured that while still unbaptized they would know nothing of the sacred mysteries of the supper and of baptism itself. Some evidence, particularly from Origen's ministry as a presbyter in Caesarea, indicates non-eucharistic assemblies for daily instruction during the week, when catechumens were a recognizable element in the audience.[15]

The re-formation of pagans as Christian men and women required both doctrinal and ethical teaching. Kreider calls the latter the 'folkways' of the community, and he stresses the importance of inculturating

---

[11] Alan Kreider, *Worship and Evangelism in Pre-Christendom* (Cambridge, 1995), p. 21.

[12] Cuming (ed.), *Hippolytus*, p. 16.

[13] Clement of Alexandria, *Stromata* 2:18, in *ANCL* 12, p. 56. Canon 73 of the Council of Elvira (c. 305) stated that a convert who had been a informer must remain a catechumen for five years.

[14] Kreider, *Worship and Evangelism*, p. 23.

[15] Kreider, *Worship and Evangelism*, pp. 22-23 n. 1.

incomers in the history of the people of God.[16] A delightful little work by Augustine, *Instructing the Untaught*, begins, after establishing that his hearers are sitting comfortably, with a broad sweep of sacred history from Genesis through to the present situation of the church. Such an inculcation of the 'big picture' might have much to commend it today in an age of postmodern fragmentation and concentration on the immediate and individual existence.

During their catechumenate, applicants for Christian baptism were not to pray with the faithful. They were to pray only on their own. Nor were they to give the kiss of peace, 'for their kiss is not yet holy'.[17]

When at last the time for baptism approached—generally in the third century this was at Easter time—those who had persevered were again examined: Had they lived as befitted Christians-to-be? Had they honoured the widows, visited the sick, performed good deeds? When their sponsors attested that they had, they were set apart, perhaps by a special recognition as the *electi* or *competentes*, chosen or designated for baptism. Now they would 'hear the gospel', which probably indicates a phase of concentrated teaching on the Rule of Faith (later, in the fourth century, on the creed). During this period they received a daily laying on of hands by the bishop in exorcism.[18] Even at this advanced stage the lurking presence of an alien power might be exposed by exorcizing and the candidate rejected. How was the demonic indwelling identified? Presumably by some uncontrolled bodily agitation as the bishop's hands were laid on the applicant's head.

Being Baptized, Body and Soul

The baptismal ceremonies involved bodily experiences: having a bath on Thursday, fasting on Friday, and on Saturday another and more climactic laying on of hands by the bishop to 'exorcize all alien spirits, that they may flee out of them and never return into them', followed by his breathing or blowing into their faces, and his signing or sealing their foreheads, ears, and noses with the sign of the cross.[19] Saturday night was spent wholly in vigil with the candidates being further read to and instructed. They were allowed to have nothing with them, except what they would offer during the eucharist.[20]

---

[16] Kreider, *Worship and Evangelism*, pp. 24-25.
[17] Cuming (ed.), *Hippolytus*, pp. 16-17.
[18] Cuming (ed.), *Hippolytus*, p. 20.
[19] Margaret R. Miles, 'Christian Baptism in the Fourth Century: The Conversion of the Body', in *Carnal Knowing: Female Nakedness and Religious Meaning in the Christian West* (Tunbridge Wells, 1992), pp. 24-25, 197-206.
[20] Cuming (ed.), *Hippolytus*, pp. 17-18.

When a cock crowed on Easter Sunday morning, the water was prepared and prayed over. The bishop used a designated 'oil of exorcism' to anoint each person after he or she had said, 'I renounce you, Satan, and all your service and all your works.' Deacons and presbyters had roles to play as well as the bishop. The candidates were baptized naked, in three categories, the children first, then the men, and then the women. The women had to loosen their hair and take off all their jewelry. 'Let no-one take any alien object down into the water.' Of the little ones, those who could speak for themselves should do so, and for the others parents or someone from their families would speak for them.[21]

A deacon went down into the water with each candidate, and the baptizer asked each one the three creedal questions one at a time, with the recipient responding 'I believe' to each one, followed each time by baptism itself (immersion or affusion?) with the deacon's hand on the head of the one being baptized. The first and third questions were brief, but the second was more extended. 'Do you believe in Christ Jesus, the Son of God, who was born from the Holy Spirit from the Virgin Mary and was crucified under Pontius Pilate and died, and rose again on the third day alive from the dead, and ascended into heaven and sits at the right hand of the Father, and will come to judge the living and the dead?'[22]

Emerging from the water, the newly baptized were anointed with the 'oil of thanksgiving' by the presbyter, and they dried themselves and put on their clothes. Then at last they could 'enter the church'. The bishop prayed over them, anointed them again with the 'oil of thanksgiving', signed them on the forehead, and kissed them. Then, and not until then, 'they shall pray together with all the people...and they shall give the kiss of peace.'[23] The text of the *Apostolic Tradition* proceeds without a break into their first communion service.

By the late second century, in general though not necessarily in every detail, this is the way Christians were baptized. The elaborateness of the occasion had obviously not emerged overnight, even though the development cannot be traced point by point. The whole experience was powerfully meaningful. As Miles puts it, the actions 'realize—make real—in a person's body the strong experience that, together with the religious community's interpretation of that experience, produced a counter-cultural religious self'.[24] That was what was needed in the Roman world at the time, and it helps explain the prominence of exorcisms in

---

[21] Cuming (ed.), *Hippolytus*, p. 18.

[22] Cuming (ed.), *Hippolytus*, p. 19. No Greek text of this section is extant; by different prepositions a Latin version distinguishes Jesus' birth from (*de*) the Spirit and from (*ex*) Mary.

[23] Cuming (ed.), *Hippolytus*, pp. 19-21.

[24] Miles, 'Christian Baptism', p. 24.

what Willimon has called a 'detoxification' exercise.[25] It is not difficult to visualize such a baptismal experience, extending from the initial serious inquiry about becoming a Christian through to the full incorporation into the community—holy kiss and all—and participation in the Lord's supper, as definitively marking, shaping, *making* the baptized believers.

What about Infants?

Can infant baptism possibly carry this rich freight of meaning? The history of infant baptism, at least in the Protestant traditions since the Reformation, illustrates that the greatest challenges its practitioners and defenders face is simply how to treat it as (full and proper) Christian baptism in the New Testament sense.

As already noted, infants too young to speak for themselves were baptized according to the Hippolytan rite. This is not the occasion to discuss the early history of infant baptism, but it is worth pointing out that the inclusion of babies seems to have involved no special adjustment of the observance beyond what is minimally evident in the *Apostolic Tradition*. There is, for example, nothing in this text to lead its readers to suppose that the baptized children did not take part in the Lord's supper that immediately followed the baptism. The first detailed evidence of how infants were specially accommodated in the act of baptism itself emerged around AD 400. The baptizing minister asked the parent or other presenting person about the child, 'Does he (or she) believe?' That is, the baby went through the whole service exactly as did adults or older children able to answer for themselves—except that their believing was attested on their behalf by someone else who responded to the three questions posed in the third person, with the response, 'He (or she) believes.'

Creativeness of Baptism

The baptism of believers, then, was strongly formative in the experience of pre-Constantinian Christianity. It became a fertile source of creative developments in the early churches. Baptism was described in a rich variety of imagery that spoke of the decisiveness of its experience: death and life, burial and resurrection; birth and new birth; darkness and light; unclothing, nakedness, reclothing (putting off, putting on); crossing over from Egypt through the waters of the Red Sea to the Promised Land; from the seventh day (the Sabbath) to the eighth day (the Lord's day); and so forth. So much of the dominant biblical images of salvation could

---

[25] William Willimon, quoted in Kreider, *Worship and Evangelism*, p. 26.

be anchored in baptism, as seen in early Christian paintings, such as the catacomb frescoes.

The catechumenate was directed toward the act of baptism. As an intensive period of instruction and purification leading up to baptism at Easter, the catechumenate contributed to the formation of Lent. More importantly, in the fourth and fifth centuries the catechetical process resulted in major series of addresses by Cyril of Jerusalem, John Chrysostom, Theodore of Mopsuestia, Ambrose, Augustine, and others. Many of the most significant patristic expositions of essential Christian beliefs clustered around baptism.

Eventually those beliefs found fixed verbal expression in the Apostles' Creed, and earlier in the looser Rule of Faith. Baptismal profession was the occasion for the development of creeds, first in question-and-answer form. The creed of the Council of Nicaea in 325 differed from all earlier creeds in not being a baptismal creed. Interestingly the Apostles' Creed has retained its place in baptismal services today in many churches. The later Nicene Creed (381) became connected with the observance of communion.

Also noteworthy is the bond between baptism and the blood-baptism of martyrdom, graphically evident in the *Passion of Perpetua*. The lines connecting baptism with death begin, of course, with Jesus' own words about his forthcoming passion as a baptism (Mark 10.39), and continued through the centre of New Testament baptism, according to Romans 6.1-4. The widespread practice of the baptism of the dying children of believers is another link.

The weight placed on baptism as the cleansing of all past sin meant that serious postbaptismal sins were to be dealt with by other means. Here lay the origins of one of baptism's less happy progeny, the penitential discipline of medieval Christendom. But the heyday of penance and associated practices (to whose harsh elaboration the Celtic churches made a signal contribution) came only with the rise of infant baptism as the norm.

The baptismal making of the early Christians may seem to belong to a lost age. But the recovery of the catechumenate by the Roman Catholic Church and of discipling by a number of evangelical communities suggests that one may well benefit from revisiting the baptismal doctrine and practice of the first Christian centuries. As Tertullian wrote, 'People are not born Christians, they have to be made into Christians.'[26]

---

[26] Tertullian, *Apology* 18, in *ANCL* 11, p. 88.

CHAPTER 19

One Baptism or Two?
Reflections on the History of Christian Baptism[1]

I have no doubt that some of my audience have undergone two baptisms—two water baptisms, that is. They may not now regard their first one as a baptism, but such a nicety need not detain us at this stage. (After all, it was certainly baptism in the mind of all those involved at the time who were capable of judging, and would be so reckoned by the great consensus of Christian people down the centuries.)

I am also confident that many of my listeners can immediately think of churches which they instinctively regard as outstanding when measured by recognized yardsticks, but most of whose baptisms are not in their view Christian baptisms. These congregations' main form of baptism is not that of my presumed hearers, and so much the worse for that, since the latter's is alone true Christian baptism.

One baptism or two? Is the state of affairs I have conjured up a matter of great concern to evangelical Christians today? It is my conviction that it should be, and if this lecture achieves anything, I hope it will at least provoke some to reflect afresh on 'the waters that divide', as Donald Bridge and David Phypers entitle their helpful introduction to 'the baptism debate'.[2] For this split among us is a blatant affront to a cherished axiom of the Reformation—the perspicuity of the scriptures. How can they be so clear to the reading of faith if they speak to us in such contradictory terms on baptism? I doubt if any other disagreement poses so sharp a challenge to this pristine protestant conviction. It is high irony that this principle should have been so powerfully articulated in the very context in which this gulf first opened up. Medieval anticipations of the sixteenth-century breach between magisterial and Anabaptist Reformers were of negligible significance.

It is also surprising that the ecumenical movement, which has occupied so many of the energies of the churches in the twentieth century, should have been so slow to grasp this particular nettle. It is only in the last ten

---

[1] The Laing Lecture for 1987, London Bible College.
[2] Donald Bridge and David Phypers, *The Water that Divides: The Baptism Debate* (Leicester, 1977; 2nd edn, *The Water that Divides: A Survey of the Doctrine of Baptism* [Fearn, Ross-shire, 1998]).

years or so that it has featured high on the agenda of the Faith and Order arm of the World Council of Churches. Its earlier, long-lasting preoccupation with the interrelated issues of ministry and eucharist has contributed, I suggest, to an ecumenical undervaluing of baptism, which finds a parallel in evangelical Christianity. Both main traditions have for too long given inadequate recognition to the constitutive and practical significance of baptism in New Testament Christianity. When ecumenical theologians tell us that the church is a eucharistic community, I respond that they would be far truer to the New Testament to call it a baptismal community. When they set before us the goal of intercommunion, I want to place a higher premium on interbaptism. It is my judgement—or perhaps I should say my impression (the subject would make a good research topic)—that in the New Testament baptism is more often made the ground of exhortation, admonition and instruction than the Lord's supper. This is what I mean by the constitutive and practical significance of baptism for the apostolic churches. It is seen most obviously in Romans 6.1-4, where Paul exposes the absurdity of continuing to sin so that grace might increase by reminding his Roman readers of what happened to them in baptism. A similar style of reasoning on the basis of baptism is found elsewhere, most remarkably at 1 Corinthians 15.29, where Paul grounds belief in the resurrection of the dead in the obscure practice of baptism 'for the dead'.

We have still to recover the importance of baptism as a point of reference and departure in our applied theology. How many of us, faced with Paul's problem in Romans 6, would have dealt with it in terms of the baptismal character of the Christian, as he did? How many of us have learned to repel the assaults of Satan as Luther did, by declaring '*Baptizatus sum*' ('I have been baptized', or perhaps 'I am a baptized person'—to bring out the force of the perfect tense)? (Did not Jesus act in very much the same way according to the Gospels, when, in the face of Satanic testing, he determined to be true to his baptismal calling?). The emphasis in some modern theology on baptism as the ordination of all God's people picks up another strand in Luther, namely his insistence that all Christians are priests by virtue of their baptism, but this is an applied theological use of baptism which may not have obvious New Testament warrant.

Baptism and Christian Unity

What is crystal-clear in the Pauline letters is the correlation between baptism and Christian unity. Here are four illustrations of this theme: (1) 1 Corinthians 12.13—although we are many separate individuals, 'we were all baptized by one Spirit into one body, whether Jews or Greeks, slaves or free'; (2) Galatians 3.27, where the argument is quite similar—'all of you who were baptized into Christ have been clothed with Christ. There is neither Jew nor Greek, slave nor free, male nor female, for you are all one in Christ Jesus'; (3) 1 Corinthians 1.13—'Were you baptized into the name of Paul?' Their baptism into the single name of Christ renders their party divisions outrageously incongruous; (4) (and here we rejoin the title of this lecture) Ephesians 4.5, where, in a notably triadic or trinitarian passage, Paul lists among the realities that constitute our oneness in the Spirit 'one Lord, one faith, one baptism'.

This last text requires more extended consideration. There are two things it does not mean. First, it is not a knock-down argument (or an argument of any kind) against second baptism. The oneness it affirms is not that of temporal oneness (though one could compile a long list of distinguished theologians who have used it as a conclusive proof-text to this end). Second, the baptism of which Paul speaks is very simply the ordinance or rite or sacrament that was administered to new believers and initiated them into the church of Christ. That is to say, this 'one baptism' is not Christ's one baptism on our behalf in his atoning life, death and resurrection. This intepretation was advocated by J.A.T. Robinson[3] and has enjoyed the support in recent years of some theologians, particularly in the neo-orthodox tradition. (A letter that T.F. Torrance once wrote to *The Scotsman*[4] on the occasion of some baptismal controversy in the Church of Scotland distinguished between 'a rite of initiation [in water] and the actual baptism [in blood] with which Christ was baptized on our behalf'. Although he proceeded to ground 'the mere rite' in Christ's baptism, this exegesis has damaging consequences for the way we think about and practise baptism, as well as losing contact with the context in Ephesians 4.)

Paul's undoubted meaning here is simply that the baptism we undergo is common to us all, as is the 'one Lord'. Baptism is a unifying factor because each of us severally passes through it into the one body of Christ. This (in my view indubitable) reading of the text may have implications for the repetition of baptism, and is quite compatible with more than one explanation of the relation between Christ's baptism and ours, but it does not say anything as such about either subject.

Having clarified the meaning of Ephesians 4.5, we must not pass without allowing God's word in Paul's words to address its challenge to us. Are you able as a college community to make this confession your own and to declare that you are all united by a common baptism? 'One

---

[3] J.A.T. Robinson, 'The One Baptism as a Category of New Testament Soteriology', *Scottish Journal of Theology* 6 (1953), pp. 257-74, reprinted in his *Twelve New Testament Studies* (Studies in Biblical Theology, 34; London, 1962), pp. 158-75. For conclusive refutation see W.E. Moore, 'One Baptism', *New Testament Studies* 10 (1963–64), pp. 504-16.

[4] 15 June 1977.

Lord' —yes; 'one faith' —yes; but 'one baptism'? We come back to the questions with which we began. Are 'the waters that divide' so deep and broad that we cannot link hands in fellowship from one side to the other?

In his commentary on Ephesians, Bishop B.F. Westcott comments that we might have expected to find in this list in chapter 4 the phrase 'one bread' or some similar mention of the eucharist.[5] We know from 1 Corinthians 10.17 that Paul was capable of arguing from the 'one loaf' of the supper to our oneness in Christ's body, but he did not do so here. The various quasi-credal or confessional formulae discernible in the New Testament, chiefly in the Epistles, never, unless I am mistaken, refer to the Lord's supper. Baptismal allusions, on the other hand, are identifiable in several of them.[6] This should not surprise us, for the occasion of baptism was perhaps the most significant context for the confession of the faith in the early church. This was not a matter of testifying to one's own experience, as happens at too many Baptist baptisms today, but of making one's own the common confession of the believing community of which one was becoming, in baptism, a member.

The Nicene Creed

Of the early formal and fixed creeds of the church the one which enjoys the widest acceptance among the different Christian traditions is the Nicene Creed, or, more accurately, the Niceno-Constantinopolitan Creed, for it derives not from the Council of Nicaea of 325 but from the second ecumenical council at Constantinople in 381. Its date of origin is important for the interpretation of its clause about baptism, 'We acknowledge one baptism for the remission of sins.' Not only in the New Testament but also in the most authoritative creed of the Christian church we encounter an affirmation of 'one baptism'. What does the phrase denote in the Nicene Creed?

This is not a question that allows of a prompt and confident answer, for it has yet to receive the extended scholarly discussion it deserves. My response, based upon research in the relevant patristic sources, is not yet as assured as I would like it to be. It is certainly paradoxical, for I conclude that the Nicene acknowledgement of 'one baptism for the remission of sins' already implies some parting of the waters. Its baptism is the baptism of believers, or at least of those who have sins to be remitted, and does not embrace infant baptism, or, as we should call it for clarity's sake, 'baby baptism'. This is not because baby baptism had not entered the practice of the eastern church by the later fourth century. It

---

[5] B.F. Westcott, *St Paul's Epistle to the Ephesians* (London, 1906), pp. 58-59.

[6] Cf., e.g., Rom. 10.9, 1 Tim. 6.13-14. Cf. J.N.D. Kelly, *Early Christian Creeds* (London, 3rd edn, 1972), pp. 15ff.

certainly had, although how commonly it was observed is difficult to say. But in so far as the fourth-century Greek Fathers touch explicitly on the question, they seem to have believed that babies were not sinners or sinful and hence, if baptized, were not baptized 'for the remission of sins'.

A lecture does not lend itself to a detailed presentation of the evidence that justifies such an interpretation.[7] A few indications must suffice on this occasion. John Chrysostom's enormous corpus of homilies and other works contains less than a handful of references to paedobaptism, but one of his baptismal catcheses speaks directly to this question.[8] He enumerates ten gifts of baptism, for it is a mistake to think that it confers only the remission of sins. 'It is on this account that we baptize even infants, although they have no sins, that they may be given the further gifts of sanctification, righteousness, adoption as sons', etc. The only other source whose evidence is directly to the point is a poem by Gregory Nazianzen, one of the Cappadocian trio whose reconstructive theological work lies behind the creed of 381. He refers to baptism as a seal of God—for infants only a seal, but for adults a remedy as well as a seal.[9] The same writer's oration on baptism appears to bear out the implication of this poetic allusion, that infants have no need of baptismal healing or medicine. Babies in danger of death must be baptized without delay, he advises, 'for it is better that they should be unconsciously sanctified than depart this life unsealed and uninitiated'. Others should wait until they are at least about three years old, 'when they may be able to listen and to answer something about the sacrament...' Even then they come to the font only to be fortified 'because of the sudden assaults of danger that befall us', 'for of sins of ignorance owing to their tender years they have no account to give'.[10]

The eastern Fathers of the fourth century seem generally to have viewed the benefits of baptism for babies as twofold—the bestowal of gifts such as eternal life, and strengthening against the hazards of earthly existence. I have found no evidence to suggest that any of them could have applied the baptismal clause of the Nicene Creed to baby baptism. However unfamiliar we may be with the baptismal theology of these Greek Fathers, their reasons for baptizing babies were broadly those advanced by the Pelagians in their controversy with Augustine in the fifth century in the West. Although infant baptism is attested in the church

---

[7] Cf. my essay, 'How Controversial Was the Development of Infant Baptism in the Early Church?', in J.E. Bradley and R.A. Muller, *Church, Word and Spirit: Historical and Theological Essays in Honor of Geoffrey W. Bromiley* (Grand Rapids, MI, 1987), pp. 45-63 (see ch. 2 above).

[8] John Chrysostom, *Baptismal Catecheses* 3:6 (trans. P.W. Harkins, *St John Chrysostom: Baptismal Instructions* [Westminster, MD, 1963]), p. 57.

[9] Gregory Nazianzen, *Carmina Dogmatica* 9:91-92 (*PG* 37, cols. 463-64).

[10] Gregory Nazianzen, *Oration* 40:28, cf. 40:17.

from the late second century onwards, if not earlier, it was very much a rite in search of a theology until Augustine supplied it in his doctrine of original sin.

What, then, is the reference of 'one baptism for the remission of sins'? The context of this statement is the early church's bewildering hang-up over the problem of post-baptismal sin. The clause may be paraphrased as follows: in so far as baptism is given for the remissions of sins, a person may receive it only once. There may be, indeed there are, other means for the remission of sins after baptism, but baptism itself cannot be repeated for this purpose. Texts in support of this interpretation are to be found in Cyril of Jerusalem's *Catechetical Lectures* and in Chrysostom's *Baptismal Catecheses*.[11] Cyril's explanation is particularly interesting. If it were possible to receive baptism a second or third time, 'it might be said, " Though I fail once, I shall go right next time".' If you fail once, 'there is no setting things right, for there is " one Lord, one faith, one baptism" (!). None but heretics are rebaptized, since their former baptism was not baptism.' Chrysostom's explanation agrees with Cyril's: 'Since the old contract of debt is destroyed, let us be alert to prevent any second contract. For there is no second cross, nor a second remission by the bath of regeneration. There is remission, but not a second remission by baptism.'

So the baptismal clause in this fundamental creed turns out to have a very restricted reference. Its 'one baptism' is not the 'one baptism' of Ephesians 4. It affirms not the common, single baptism that unites all the baptized, but the unrepeatability of the baptismal remission of sins. In these terms, it cannot easily encompass baby baptism, which a consensus in the East in the fourth century refused to link with the forgiveness of sins. (One can visualize an indirect relevance of the Nicene statement to paedobaptism. Even if it is accepted that babies are not baptized for the remission of sins, the creed presumably excludes the possibility of those baptized as babies being subsequently baptized again for the remission of [post-baptismal] sin).

Rebaptism

Another important issue in the early church to which the Nicene Creed says nothing is the rebaptism within the Catholic Church of those already baptized in heresy or schism. Cyril of Jerusalem, as we have just seen, explicitly debars such an assertion of 'one baptism' from excluding the rebaptism of heretics. Given the prominence of rebaptism controversies in the western church, particularly from the mid-third century for almost another two hundred years, it is remarkable that hardly any of the local

---

[11] Cyril, *Procatechesis* 7; Chrysostom, *Baptismal Catecheses* 3:23, 63:4.

creeds in use in the West include an affirmation of 'one baptism'.[12] More specifically, it never featured in any creed in the North African church of Cyprian and Augustine, which was a hotbed of disputes over rebaptism. Although one can easily enough conceive how the Nicene clause could be cited to the disadvantage of the rebaptizing Donatist, it originally had nothing to do with this western quarrel. Moreover, it is important to insist upon the irrelevance of the Nicene Creed to the questions of schismatic baptism faced by the North African Fathers. The history of baptismal practice and discussion is littered with the inappropriate application of texts and formulae (such as the assertions of 'one baptism' in Ephesians 4 and the Nicene Creed), without regard to their original meaning. Cyprian rebaptized schismatics, and the Donatists rebaptized Catholics, not because these schismatics and Catholics had committed serious post-baptismal sin but because the schismatic or Catholic baptism they had received was, in the judgement of the rebaptizers (Cyprian and the Donatists) no baptism at all. The latter regarded themselves, of course, as dispensing not rebaptism but (first) baptism *de novo*. We must further remember that such rebaptismal policy had nothing whatever to do with the form or manner of administration of the false baptisms. Their rejection by the baptizers was a straightforward corollary of their refusal to recognize anything from God—grace, Spirit, salvation, forgiveness—outside their own true church which was the Catholic Church for Cyprian, and the Donatist Church for the Donatists.

Cyprian's practice, which the Donatists later followed, was controversial in his own day and was abandoned by the Catholic Church within half a century. Augustine spelt out an influential theology of baptism that justified this abandonment and the church's recognition of the validity, within strict limits, of baptism administered outside the church. The Augustinian position became the norm in western Christianity, so that rebaptism *on the grounds argued by Cyprian and his successors* has not been common since the patristic era. Even during the centuries when the Roman Church accorded no churchly status whatever to Protestant bodies, it did not normally rebaptize converts from Protestantism, although it often hedged its bets by the use of conditional baptism ('If you have not been baptized, I baptize you...').

But from time to time church history throws up instances of the administration of rebaptism based on a rejection of the church character of the communion in which baptism was first received. How frequently this has happened, I cannot say: the subject requires further research. Some Waldensians practised rebaptism on these 'Cyprianic' grounds. According to the Fourth Lateran Council the Greek church had

---

[12] The evidence can be seen in A. Hahn, *Bibliothek der Symbole und Glaubensregeln der Alten Kirche* (Breslau, 1897).

rebaptized Catholics (canon 4). Some nineteenth-century Anglicans refused to accept baptisms that had not been dispensed by an episcopally ordained minister. The more conservative sectors of American Presbyterianism on several occasions in the nineteenth century debated whether Roman Catholic baptism was valid, if the Roman Church could not be recognized as a true church of Christ. Other practices of rebaptism on similar, Cyprianic, grounds could almost certainly be catalogued.

Anabaptism

It has been suggested[13] that some cases of rebaptism by sixteenth-century Anabaptists fall into this category. Some Anabaptists, it is argued, rejected Catholic or mainstream Protestant baptism not because it was infant baptism and therefore not Christian baptism at all, but because they rejected root and branch the Constantinian captivity of the state church, whether Roman Catholic or magisterial Protestant. It has even been claimed that some of them practised Anabaptist paedobaptism—that is, the second and only true baptism they administered was infant baptism. The subject has not yet been sufficiently researched for this account of Anabaptist practice to be accorded great significance.[14] But is a salutary reminder that between the Anabaptists and the magisterial Reformers yawned a far deeper gulf than separates many today who cannot join hands across 'the waters that divide'. It is a sound instinct when discussing this sixteenth-century split not to speak about baptism first of all, and perhaps not to speak about it too much at all.[15]

Nevertheless, baptism is our legitimate talking-point on this occasion. Mainstream Anabaptism, taking its stand on its repristination of New Testament Christianity, could not countenance infant baptism and hence practised ana- or rebaptism. For this Anabaptists suffered, being branded frequently as 'Donatists' and subjected to the sanctions of the anti-Donatist legislation of the early Christian Roman emperors, especially Justinian.[16] The injustice of this treatment has not been adequately acknowledged and repented of by the churches that have inherited the legacy of the magisterial Reformers. Something comparable to the mutual rescinding in 1965 by Pope John VI and Patriarch Athenagoras

---

[13] L. Verduin, *The Reformers and Their Stepchildren* (Grand Rapids, MI, 1964), pp. 195-97.

[14] Verduin's evidence from Luther does not stand closer scrutiny, as correspondence with Dr Euan Cameron of Newcastle University has helped me realize. But the records of very early Anabaptism in the Wassenberg district are clear enough.

[15] This was brought home to me when a Mennonite scholar submitted for a theological dictionary article on 'Anabaptist Theology' which made no mention of baptism at all.

[16] Cf. Verduin, *Reformers and Their Stepchildren*, ch. 1; G.H. Williams, *The Radical Reformation* (London, 1962), pp. xxiii, 239-40.

of Constantinople of the ancient sentences of excommunication of their respective sees would be a splendid gesture. For the iniquity of the punitive measures inflicted on the Anabaptists in the sixteenth century lay not so much in the use of the sword (which was merely par for the course in that age) but in trapping the Anabaptists under legislation directed against Donatists. Both groups rebaptized, but for quite different reasons. The Donatists had no scruples over baby baptism, but rejected Catholic baptism, whether of babies or of adult converts. The mass of the Anabaptists failed to find paedobaptism in the New Testament, and hence administered only believers' baptism. The theologians among the establishment Protestants should not have tolerated the labelling of the Anabaptists as 'Donatists'. We find here another example of the tendency in the history of baptism for significant distinctions to be collapsed into simple catch-all constants, such as 'one baptism' or 'rebaptism'.

Modern Debate: Lima

The modern baptismal divide corresponds in broad terms to that of the sixteenth century, but there is at least one major difference. We appear to have so downgraded the importance of baptism that it has become possible for some of us, at any rate, to disallow a denomination's baptismal practice without calling into question its character as 'church'. For example, the congregations of the Baptist Union of Scotland seem able to regard 95% of the baptisms administered in the Church of Scotland as not Christian baptism without casting aspersions on the Kirk's right to be called a Church of Christ (unless I am being over-generous to Scottish Baptists). But it is *prima facie* an anomalous standpoint to adopt, especially if one holds, with the Reformers of every stripe, that the ministry of the gospel sacraments is an indispensable mark of the church. Such an attitude could not conceivably have gained currency until after the sixteenth century. It suggests an awkward dilemma for the stricter sort of Baptists to this day, for a church that is not a baptismal community is, by New Testament standards, a very odd entity indeed.

The second half of the twentieth century is witnessing some unprecedented developments on the baptismal scene. In 1982 was published the so-called Lima report, *Baptism, Eucharist and Ministry* (*BEM* for short).[17] This is a product of the Faith and Order Commission within the World Council of Churches, and reached its final form at a conference in Lima in which Catholics and Eastern Orthodox were full participants along with Lutherans, Reformed, Baptists, Anglicans and

---

[17] *Baptism, Eucharist and Ministry* (Faith and Order paper, 111; Geneva, 1982). Cf. my *Baptism, Eucharist and Ministry (the 'Lima Report'): An Evangelical Assessment* (Rutherford Forum Papers, 3; Edinburgh, 1984) (see ch. 22 below).

others. It comprises text and commentary. Although the main text does not represent in every respect a consensus of belief, it is an agreed statement, in that it embodies agreement on how each of the three topics is to be understood, including points of continuing difference.

This is a report of enormous importance. It has already become within most of the churches the standard starting-point for ecumenical reflection on baptism, eucharist and ministry. In a nutshell, its approach to the divergence in baptismal practice suggests that there may not be much difference between infant baptism followed by Christian nurture within the believing community issuing in personal confession of faith, and the nurture of a child within the congregation, perhaps after thanksgiving for its birth and the parents' commitment to their Christian responsibility, leading to baptism on personal confession of faith.[18] Two key sentences which appear in the commentary are these: 'The differences between infant and believers' baptism become less sharp when it is recognized that both forms of baptism embody God's own initiative in Christ and express a response of faith made within the believing community... A rediscovery of the continuing character of Christian nurture may facilitate the mutual acceptance of different initiation practices.'[19]

There is nothing breathtakingly new in *BEM*'s consideration of baptism, except that, on the basis of agreement among official representatives of Baptists as well as the majority of paedobaptist churches, it claims to offer a path to interbaptism—the mutual recognition of the two dominant forms of baptism. Much might be said about *BEM*,[20] which is a text we dare not ignore. I commend it for study, for one reason in particular. If, with our evangelical commitment to the supreme authority and the clarity of scripture, we have been unable to find a route through the baptismal impasse (a bridge across the baptismal gulf), ought we not to start thinking about a biblical frame of reference in which we can agree to accept and live with both baptismal traditions? It is at least worth considering.

'Equivalent Alternatives'

What the Lima report proposes in theological terms is already a reality in some churches, namely, the observance of both infant and believers' baptism as 'equivalent alternatives' (this being almost a technical phrase by now) in the normal course of congregational life. The United Reformed Church in England and Scotland and the Church of North India are the two bodies following this procedure best known to me, but

---

[18] Cf. *BEM*, 'Baptism', para. 12.
[19] *BEM*, 'Baptism', commentary (12).
[20] For my brief evaluation see my *Baptism, Eucharist and Ministry* (ch. 22 below).

some independent congregations mostly south of the border are also 'double-practice' churches. Others have moved some way to this position by openly and formally authorizing the non-observance of their norm of paedobaptism—and hence allowing with approval the non-baptism as babies of the offspring of Christian parents. The French Reformed Church and one of the main American Presbyterian Churches have adopted this policy, which has even to a limited extent been at least condoned by one or two bishops in the Church of England.

Each of these two groups of churches is in its way highly significant. The United Reformed Church and the Church of North India are the result of church unions in which both Baptists and paedobaptists were involved. It will be very interesting to observe how baptismal practice develops in such churches. Will believers' baptism slowly make baby baptism less and less common? I have so far been unable to find out anything about trends in the Church of North India, nor has any clear change yet been identified in the United Reformed Church. One would expect that, in so far as each individual congregation will have to come into these united churches out of either a Baptist or a paedobaptist tradition, with no prior experience of an 'equivalent alternatives' baptismal ministry, cross-fertilization will proceed slowly, except perhaps where congregations originally of different traditions become a single congregation within the united church.

The other category of churches that have officially countenanced a departure from invariable paedobaptism as the norm, is even more interesting. The reasons behind their revised policy are no doubt of different kinds: recognition of the greater reluctance of even some Christian parents today to decide for their children; accommodation to the unceasing and perhaps increasing questioning of infant baptism on both historical and theological grounds (after all, the two most influential Reformed theologians of this century have forcefully rejected infant baptism, Karl Barth and Jürgen Moltmann); respect for a new atmosphere of ecumenical baptismal debate; even perhaps an attempt to come to terms with the difficulties of administering a consistent paedobaptist discipline as the age of Christendom and the Christian society no longer provides viable models for remnant or gathered churches.

The *BEM* approach, exemplified in the fully-fledged 'double-practice' churches, appears to accept that there is no realistic hope of reaching agreement on one form of baptism. One could, however, put a different complexion on their expectations—namely, that agreement, if it is to come at all, will emerge only from allowing the two baptisms to cohabit within one family. I find it intriguing that one of the chief architects of the *BEM* construction, Geoffrey Wainwright, who is a Methodist, is on

Polarization

One short-term or medium-term result of ecumenical encounter on baptism has in fact been increased polarization.[22] (This experience has many parallels in ecumenical engagement.) Baptists have rightly challenged paedobaptists whether they really regard infant baptism as full, complete baptism. If they do, why do they place so much stress on confirmation or admission to communicant membership? Are we not members of Christ's body by virtue of baptism, and ought not baptism to admit to the Lord's table? *BEM* itself points up the incongruity of interposing some other ecclesiastical rite between baby baptism and entry to the Lord's supper.[23] It is an index of the unbiblical imbalance some of our evangelical churches have fallen into on baptism that this later ceremony is accorded greater significance than baptism itself. It is not unknown, even in our blue-riband evangelical congregations, to have a teenage convert baptized prior to a service, in the presence of the elders alone, before he or she proceeds into the congregation to be admitted to communicant status on a par with others who had the good fortune to have been baptized in infancy. If we administer baptism to babies, we have no warrant to treat it as less than the full dominical ordinance or sacrament.

This polarization may retard progress. Baptists may be more likely to adjust to a 'double-practice' policy when paedobaptists accept that baby baptism is incomplete until something like confirmation (i.e., a formal, public personal profession of faith) has taken place. Baptists might be readier to 'buy' paedobaptism on these terms—baptism by instalments, as it were. I very much hope that this will not be the case. It is surely far healthier to acknowledge that we have inherited two different patterns of baptism, and to accept the other's practice without being able to endorse it, than to fudge the issue in this way,

Origins

I also refuse to abandon the historical enquiry into the beginnings of Christian baptism. I cannot resign myself to the view that everything has been said that can be said and that, short of the discovery of new evidence

---

[21] G. Wainwright, *Christian Initiation* (London, 1969), pp. 80-83.

[22] Cf. G. Warner, 'Baptism from Accra to Lima', in M. Thurian (ed.), *Ecumenical Perspectives on Baptism, Eucharist and Ministry* (Faith and Order Paper, 116; Geneva, 1983), p. 27.

[23] *BEM*, 'Baptism', commentary (14) (b).

(such as Paul's lost third letter to Timothy on how to baptize babies), no headway will be made on baptismal origins. There is no time now to open up this aspect of our subject. I have recently argued elsewhere that a surprising amount of the evidence in the earliest centuries is patient of the interpretation that quite young children were baptized on their own profession.[24] It is intriguing that the very first attestation of infant baptism as the normal practice (in Hippolytus' *Apostolic Tradition*, c. 215) is in the form of an instruction how to baptize first those who can answer for themselves and then those who cannot. At what age would children in a newly converted family be able to answer for themselves? We have already cited the recommendation of Gregory Nazianzen that infants should preferably not be baptized until they were about three years of age when they could listen and 'answer something about the sacrament'. It is evidence like this that makes me protest vehemently at talk of 'adult baptism'. We should all take our bearings from the earliest differentiation between those too young to answer for themselves and those, perhaps of quite young, *infant* years, who could. (This distinction also, by the way, provides a ready approach to the baptism of handicapped persons who might not be able to answer for themselves.)

Among other evidence I advance in the study referred to is that inferred from epitaph inscriptions from the third and fourth centuries of young children who were baptized just prior to death. An American scholar, Everett Ferguson of Abilene in Texas, has argued that paedobaptism began from the clinical baptism of very young children.[25] That is to say, baby baptism was perhaps at first given only to dying babies, while others were baptized as and when they could answer for themselves.

The debate about origins was not exhausted by the celebrated exchange between the German scholars Joachim Jeremias and Kurt Aland some twenty years ago.[26] On balance Aland probably had the better of that controversy; it is unlikely that in the first few decades of the church babies were baptized. But it is also true that baby baptism, when it did develop, seems to have been accepted with little or no protest. Tertullian objected (as he did to a good deal else), but on the basis of a baptismal theology and a view of the 'innocence' of infants neither of which many today could share. Those who hold that only professing believers were baptized in the New Testament congregations cannot comfortably dismiss the fact of the development of infant baptism within a century or so. The

---

[24] Cf. my 'The Origins of Infant Baptism—Child Believers' Baptism?', *Scottish Journal of Theology* 39 (1987), pp. 1-23 (ch. 1 above).

[25] E. Ferguson, 'Inscriptions and the Origins of Infant Baptism', *Journal of Theological Studies* n.s. 30 (1979), pp. 34-46.

[26] For the bibliographical details see my study 'The Origins of Infant Baptism', p. 2 n. 4 (see above p. 2 n. 4).

situation may have required that degree of historical distance from apostolic Christianity's polemical attitude to circumcision in the conflict with the Judaizers for Christians to have perceived a proper parallelism with the Old Testament's covenantal seal.

'Believers' Baptism'

So let us not abandon the question how baptism began. At the same time there is a second issue we should take up together across 'the waters that divide'. When paedobaptist churches baptize persons of mature years on profession of faith are they administering believers' baptism? To put it another way: can we reach an agreed theological understanding about our respective baptisms *of those who answer for themselves*? This may seem a non-issue, but I assure you that it is a substantial one. In the course of recent discussions between representatives of the Church of Scotland and the Baptist Union of Scotland it has become apparent that some in the Church of Scotland deny that it ever practises believers' baptism. The phrase 'believers' baptism' seems to carry with it a theology of baptism that they reject. It would be helpful if both sides could find an agreed, new way of describing the baptismal practice in question. 'The baptism of those who can answer for themselves' is too much of a mouthful, but it avoids the unhappy sound of 'believers' baptism' in some Reformed ears. But the challenge to reach agreement in this quarter goes deeper than words. Again *BEM* is a good starting-point, with its pregnant sentence, 'Baptism is both God's gift and our human response to that gift'.[27] It is perhaps the gravest consequence of the division that has separated our two baptisms that each practice has attracted to itself a one-sided theology. Paedobaptists have allowed the passivity of the baby in baptism to become the supreme paradigm of the reception of divine grace, so that baptism of those who have brought themselves at least physically to the font has to be hedged around lest it fail to express the priority of grace over faith. Baptists, on the other hand, have made personally articulated faith so constitutive of baptism that it has become a testimony to their own religious experience rather than to the grace of God. How many of those who have been baptized as believers were taught to think of what was happening to you in terms of Romans 6—or even of Acts 2.38—'Repent and be baptized, every one of you, in the name of Jesus Christ, so that your sins may be forgiven. And you will receive the gift of the Holy Spirit'? (There is indeed scriptural warrant for confessing 'baptism for the remission of sins' along with the Nicene Creed.) Baptists and paedobaptists urgently need to talk together, not first and foremost

---

[27] *BEM*, 'Baptism', para. 8.

about what they do differently but what they, *prima facie*, do alike—namely, baptize professing converts.

Rebaptism Today

But probably the most sensitive issue in this field is the one with which I began and to which in conclusion I return—rebaptism. *BEM* declares, 'Baptism is an unrepeatable act. Any practice which might be interpreted as " re-baptism" must be avoided.'[28] This is a curious use of language. If baptism is strictly unrepeatable, i.e., incapable of being repeated, why should it be necessary to warn against repeating it? Perhaps a second baptism never, in the courts of theologians if not of heaven, repeats a first baptism but merely cancels it out altogether. Is *BEM* asserting that 're-baptism' never happens, but that we ought to be extremely careful not to let it appear that it is happening? We should probably discern in this statement in *BEM* unhappiness with the practice of conditional baptism on the opposite pole of the baptismal spectrum.

It remains to be seen whether in the 'double-practice' churches the pastoral pressure for rebaptism increases or decreases. It is, of course, absolutely fundamental to the 'double-practice' position that a person may receive only one form of baptism. But in these churches for the first time some who have been baptized as babies will be exposed to the administration of baptism on believing profession as one of the church's two norms. It is quite conceivable that in this context requests for rebaptism will grow in number.[29]

Two particular points about this question should be stressed. First, we must all do our utmost to sympathize with the deep-seated dismay, even revulsion, felt in the traditional paedobaptist churches at this practice, It is sometimes more instinctive than articulately rational, but it arises from a sense that from its beginnings the church has unambiguously affirmed 'one baptism'. Behind this conviction lies too often an uncritical lumping together of the very different kinds of rebaptism encountered in church history, which I have attempted to disentangle from each other in this lecture. But although they differ, they have all been rejected by the vast majority of the Christian world. The church in its history has manifested for the most part a profound antipathy to repeating baptism.

In the second place, those who belong ecclesiastically to the mainstream tradition must come to terms with the fact that one kind of demand for rebaptism currently abroad among the churches lacks

---

[28] *BEM*, 'Baptism', para. 13.

[29] However, recent correspondence with Principal Martin Cressey of Westminster College, Cambridge, has disclosed that the pressure for rebaptism in congregations of the United Reformed Church is not related to the URC's 'double-practice' order, but arises especially from charismatic experience (see below).

historical precedent and is animated by the utmost seriousness about baptism. The rebaptism that ensues when someone ceases to believe that infant baptism is the genuine article is nothing new; it was what the Anabaptists did in the sixteenth century. Unprecedented, however, is the desire for rebaptism on the part of those who, while not rejecting infant baptism in principle, have come to the position of being unable to accept that their own baptism satisfied the requirements of true Christian baptism. It is important to notice immediately that this conviction may be reached not only about one's baptism as a baby but also about one's prior baptism as, allegedly, a believer. We can all visualize baptisms whose circumstances raise the sharpest doubts in our minds about their meaningfulness to anyone involved, apart perhaps from the baptizing minister.

This is sensitive territory, and must be trodden warily, if not delicately. One may have not a little sympathy with the attitude I have summarized, but disquiet at the same time. On the one hand, the case has not been won by the rigorists, like Colin Buchanan, in some of the Grove Booklets, whose arguments seem to amount to saying 'a baptism is a baptism is a baptism', and cannot ultimately escape from an *ex opere operato* stance about the reality (but not necessarily the efficacy) of every formally valid baptism.[30] The uncompromising opponents of rebaptism need to give greater consideration to the earthly or human pole of the baptismal event. If *BEM* is correct in saying that 'Baptism is both God's gift and our human response to that gift', does baptism exist if there is no human response? Or is the human response constituted merely by the (passive) receiving of baptism? To put it another way, in the language of initiation, is a beginning which has no continuation and leads nowhere a real beginning at all? Do we not gravely devalue Christian baptism if we insist that every baptismal rite, however perfunctorily and unfruitfully and unbelievingly received, must bear the full weight of the great New Testament theology of baptismal incorporation in Christ?

On the other hand, counter arguments lie ready to hand. It is disturbing that behind such a pursuit of rebaptism there often lurks an unhealthy preoccupation with giving expression to one's own experience rather than humbly recognizing the marvel of God's electing grace, when he set his love upon us in Christ before the world began, and of all he accomplished for us in Christ without our knowledge and before our hearts ever consciously opened to his love. Moreover, in the pastoral context, the lines must be exceedingly difficult to draw, although in the last resort we must not let this 'thin end of the wedge' argument prove decisive.

---

[30] Cf. C. Buchanan's *One Baptism Once* (Grove Booklets on Ministry and Worship, 61; Bramcote, 1978), p. 61.

But we must surely stand firm in resisting requests for a second baptism from those who do not repudiate their first. This would be brazen rebaptism. It often smacks of a safety-first policy ('you can never be too sure...') that is profoundly un-Protestant. You can indeed have too much of a good thing. To grant rebaptism to those who want to feel that they really have done the right thing by the New Testament, beyond the shadow of a doubt, would be a more blatant depreciation of their first baptism than anything we have considered so far. I would therefore support a point that was made in the report on recent discussions between Scottish Baptists and Church of Scotland representatives. They advised Baptist ministers considering requests for a second baptism to point out to the persons concerned that they were in effect denying their first baptism.[31] Objection was taken to this recommendation by some in the Church of Scotland, who were aghast that such a possibility should be even canvassed in a report to which their representatives were party, but I believe it was soundly based.

Much more could be said, and no doubt will be said. May it be said not to score party points off each other, but in an endeavour to recover the baptismal grounding of Christian life and church life to which the New Testament bears ample witness. It has long been my conviction, not least as a result of reading in the great Reformers, that evangelical Christians have not faced up to the heavily realistic ways of talking about baptism used by the New Testament writers.

If more remains to be said, let it also be marked by a readiness to re-examine cherished traditions on all sides. *BEM* addresses sharp questions to practitioners of each of the two main inherited patterns of baptism. In particular, let those who deny the genuineness of baby baptism, yet acknowledge the genuineness of the churches that practise it, ask themselves whether they are not implicated in a deep inconsistency. Above all, let us not acquiesce in our difficulties in giving reality to 'one baptism', whether it is the baptism common to all Christians of Ephesians 4 or the Nicene Creed's once-for-all baptismal response to the gifts of God in the gospel.

---

[31] Cf. *Reports to the General Assembly 1986* [of the Church of Scotland] (Edinburgh, 1986), p. 311 (para. 62).

CHAPTER 20

Scripture and Evangelical Diversity with Special Reference to the Baptismal Divide

The Challenge

The issue is this: is the credibility of our evangelical confession of scripture as God's word undermined or dissolved by our diversity understood in a strong sense as our disagreements about the teaching of scripture? The relationship between our common conviction of the God-given authority of scripture and our divergent interpretations and applications of it could be examined from many angles. The social and cultural historian, for example, would highlight the currents of thought and life that have fostered or fathered different readings of the Bible in successive eras and in disparate contexts. But our concern in this paper is fundamentally a theological or doctrinal one. It will take seriously both the shared commitment to follow where scripture leads that characterizes the evangelical community and the integrity of our doctrinal diversity as constituted by sincere but discrepant appropriations of scripture.

We could of course profitably focus largely on what supposedly unites us: are we really of one mind about the nature and status of scripture? Can our protestations of concordant minds survive the deafening clamour of our discordant voices? Since I believe that in good measure they have so survived within the Tyndale Fellowship for half a century, I want to direct our attention elsewhere, although it will be impossible to avoid noticing some of the shafts of light that our transparent differences cast on our variant perspectives on the Bible.

Without an agreed starting-point, our conflicting evangelical conclusions would be much less of a problem. No one is disconcerted when travellers taking their bearings from different lodestars reach different destinations. Within the Tyndale Fellowship the common ground is expressed in the Doctrinal Basis of the wider Fellowship (IVF/UCCF) of which we are part, wherein we commit ourselves to believing in

> The divine inspiration and infallibility of Holy Scripture, as originally given, and its supreme authority in all matters of faith and conduct.

But for the purposes of this present discussion it would not greatly matter if our unifying platform were a much older statement, such as the Thirty-nine Articles or the Westminster Confession, or a more recent one, like the Lausanne Covenant. Given our united stance on this umbilical point, why the scandal of our grievous dissensions?

Let us spell out more closely the challenges that our disagreements pose to our professed agreement about scripture. In a word, they place in the dock the adequacy of 'scripture alone', that is, its ability to lead God's people by the Spirit to a right understanding without the help of a *magisterium*, an authoritative teaching office, whether this be ecclesial (papacy, council, body of tradition) or confessional (Calvin's *Institutes* or the Lutheran *Book of Concord*) or professional (the guild of biblical scholars). Do not our failures to agree the teaching of scripture expose as fanciful our cherished devotion to the vernacular accessibility of the Bible to all who would read, in the conviction that it will infallibly lead them into all truth? What price the perspicuity of scripture if we cannot reach accord on the subjects of baptism? or on one of the variety of ecclesiologies on offer in the ecumenical supermarket? or on the destiny of unbelievers, heretics and apostates? or on the role of God's electing love in determining the population of the eternal kingdom? or on the ordination of women to whatever we ordain men?

Perspicuity

Such questions range over a broad spectrum of underlying issues, a number of which we need not address in this paper. But let us not make our task unnecessarily intractable, in a kind of theological masochism. We hold no brief for an untrammelled privatization of the Bible. I doubt if the Reformers' conviction of its perspicuity ever implied its normal spiritual capacity to teach the solitary reader, working unaided from scratch, the doctrines of, say, the Apostles' Creed. The clarity and certainty (or definiteness) of scripture, as Zwingli termed it, was thought to function more in a responsive mode. It denoted the verifiability of the Reformation gospel in the pages of the Bible by literate citizens at last able, thanks to translation and printing, to check for themselves. (The Bereans of Acts 17.11 were indeed a noble model.) The doctrine of perspicuity was part of early Protestantism's appeal to the Christian populace of Europe over the heads of the representatives of the old church, who demanded that discussion of such controverted themes be left in the theologically safe hands of the curia and the universities. The Bible's transparency came into its own in the public disputations—town-wide Bible studies, in effect—which so often issued in a community's quasi-democratic vote henceforth to live by the Reformation gospel. Teaching and preaching almost invariably preceded adjudication by popular resort to the open Bible. And basic to the whole enterprise was the Reformers' recovery of the plain or 'literal' sense of the scriptures, over against the spiritualizing or allegorizing of much of the earlier tradition.

Thus William Tyndale's *Pathway into the Holy Scripture* sets forth the heads of evangelical doctrine before concluding in the following terms:

> These things, I say, to know, is to have all the scripture unlocked and opened before thee; so that if thou wilt go in, and read, thou canst not but understand. And in these things to be ignorant, is to have all the scripture locked up; so that the more thou readest it, the blinder thou art, and the more tangled art thou therein, and canst nowhere through... And therefore, because we be never taught the profession of our baptism, we remain always unlearned... And now, because the lay and unlearned people are taught these first principles of our profession, therefore they read the scripture, and understand and delight therein.[1]

Even in the Westminster Confession's very different affirmation, the qualifications are significant:

> All things in scripture are not alike plain in themselves, nor alike clear unto all; yet those things which are necessary to be known, believed, and observed, for salvation, are so clearly propounded and opened in some place of scripture or other, that not only the learned, but the unlearned, in a due use of the ordinary means, may attain unto a sufficient understanding of them (I:7).

The limitation here set for the scope of perspicuity—'those things...necessary to be known, believed, and observed, for salvation' may be worth pondering in the context of diversity.

Diversity Regnant

First, however, we must move back from the problem of evangelical diversity to the givenness of diversity in the Christian revelation. The point scarcely needs labouring. If the Bible in some sense has a single divine author, in an inescapably obvious sense it is the work of many varied human authors. An earlier age may have tended to assume that the

---

[1] William Tyndale, *Doctrinal Treatises and Introductions to Different Portions of the Holy Scriptures* (ed. H. Walter; Parker Society; Cambridge, 1848), pp. 27-28; also in *The Work of William Tyndale* (ed. G.E. Duffield; Courtenay Library of Reformation Classics, 1; Appleford, 1964), pp. 23-24. Cf. similarly his Prologue to the Exposition of 1 John: 'If our hearts were taught the appointment made between God and us in Christ's blood, when we were baptized, we had the key to open the scripture, and light to see and perceive the true menaing of it, and the scripture should be easy to understand' (*Expositions and Notes on Sundry Portions of the Holy Scriptures* [ed. H. Walter; Parker Society; Cambridge, 1849], p. 141; *The Work of William Tyndale*, p. 175).

unity prevailed over the diversity. The Westminster Confession, for example, bypasses the human authors when it affirms that

> it pleased the Lord, at sundry times, and in divers manners, to reveal himself, and to declare...his will unto his church; and afterwards, ...to commit the same wholly unto writing (I:1).

Yet some appreciation of the distinctive characteristics of, say, the Old Testament prophetic books and the four Gospels has rarely been wholly absent in the church's life, even if both Augustine and Calvin expended energy on harmonies of the Synoptics and Calvin also on a harmony of Exodus–Deuteronomy. Although the plurality, as much as the diversity, of the four Gospels was felt to be theologically difficult in the earliest centuries,[2] from Irenaeus' time onwards the four creatures of Revelation 4.7 (cf. Ezekiel 1.10, 10.14) were recruited to identify, and justify, the Gospels' fourfold witness. Even if much popular Christian piety, not solely in the evangelical mould, deploys the Bible in an undifferentiated fashion and harmonizes instinctively, there can be no excuse for this collapsing of the pluriformity of scripture when it ascends to the pulpit.

Today, however, diversity rules. Its superiority to unity and uniformity runs deep in the assumptions of our culture. Theologically, it is increasingly warranted by a more eastern than western doctrine of the Trinity, with differentiation enjoying primacy over oneness. In the study of the Bible the results are only too familiar. Not only is 'Biblical Theology' long dead and buried, and 'the theology of the Old Testament' a discipline in danger of demise, but one may not be on safe ground in talking even of 'the theology of Paul' for why should Paul have been more successful than other writers in maintaining consistency (if indeed this mattered to him) over several years addressing varied situations and readerships? Those who deplore these atomistic drives should not be blind to the floods of new light that a precise focus on topics such as the theology of Luke (the evangelist, not the Gospel) continues to pour on holy scripture.

Evangelical diversity of the late twentieth century owes not a little to the magnification of diversity in recent academic theology. The radical Sojourners-type evangelicalism of Mennonite and similar inspiration leans heavily on the Jesus of the Synoptic Gospels, while charismatic evangelicalism majors on Acts and traditionally neglected areas of the Paulines. Both may be contrasted with the older mainstream for whom

---

[2] O. Cullmann, 'The Plurality of the Gospels as a Theological Problem in Antiquity', in his *The Early Church* (ed. A.J.B. Higgins; London, 1956), pp. 37-54; H. Merkel, *Die Pluralität der Evangelien als theologisches und exegetisches Problem in der Alten Kirche* (Traditio Christiana, 3; Berne, 1978).

Paul is the purest gospel, and within Paul, Romans. The polarization between kingdom ethics and creation ethics pits modern against ancient.

So even though conservative biblical scholarship remains resistant to contemporary pressures to fragment the Bible for purposes of critical study (and in this Fellowship we have set ourselves the goal of re-invigorating Biblical Theology[3]), nevertheless the high profile enjoyed by the diversity of scripture has interacted in some interesting ways with inherited patterns of pre-critical diversity—for example, between paedobaptism and credobaptism, or between different ecclesiastical polities.

Diversity and Devaluation

One outcome has been a relativizing of differences. Not only would very few now concur either with Calvin in identifying four orders of ministry as given by the Lord to his church, or with the Anglican Ordinal to which it was 'evident unto all men diligently reading holy Scripture and ancient Authors' that the orders of bishop, priest and deacon existed from the apostles' time, but most would acknowledge that scripture prescribes no one pattern of ministerial leadership. No more does it lay down a single framework for acts of worship and certainly not one that forgets 1 Corinthians 14.26. Without surrendering the conviction that our own church's doctrinal distinctives and ways of ordering its corporate life are agreeable to scripture, we now have ampler warrant for granting the same recognition to others also. Ecumenism has become both easier and more difficult: easier, because churches have grown less inclined to advance exclusive claims, e.g., for episcopacy or for infant baptism, but more difficult, because the issue rests increasingly on pragmatic considerations or the lightweight appeal of the pooling of insights, even when they are biblical ones.[4]

So there are dangers in a greater readiness to let the diversity of the biblical testimony provide a covering, as it were, for the divergences of church beliefs and practices. It may make us more vulnerable, or more captive, to tradition rather than scripture. If our way of doing things is at best only partly biblical, the same is true of everyone else's way also. More seriously, the relativism bred by increasing acquiescence in

---

[3] Cf. Dan Beeby, 'Scripture: From Rumour to Recovery', in *Gospel and Culture* Newsletter 17 (Summer, 1993), pp. 1-6.

[4] Cf. Ernst Käsemann's conclusion in his celebrated essay 'The Canon of the New Testament and the Unity of the Church', in his *Essays on New Testament Themes* (London, 1964), pp. 95-107, at p. 103: 'the New Testament canon does not, as such, constitute the foundation of the unity of the Church. On the contrary, as such (that is, in its accessibility to the historian) it provides the basis for the multiplicity of the confessions.'

diversity may foster indifferentism, or at least the devaluation of subjects on which agreement eludes us. One reason for the neglect, and hence weakness, of ecclesiology among evangelicals, at least in a movement like IVF/UCCF, is an understandable reluctance to tackle an issue that cannot fail to prove divisive in an interdenominational context. We cannot afford to give it a high profile, and perhaps it does not deserve a high profile. If we cannot reach a common mind on it, it cannot be too important. Such, I suggest, has been the fate of the doctrine of the church among evangelicals.

More damagingly still, a compliant condoning of diversity, with the supposed blessing of scripture's diverse presentations, may insidiously make common cause with a subjectivism or individualism that are destructive of the objective truthfulness of scripture. It ceases to be public truth, accessible and ascertainable by agreed canons and criteria, and is instead privatized. When the unity of the biblical witness recedes behind its pluralism, it becomes that much easier to argue that my private reading of it, *coram Deo* of course, has validity. As Roy Clements has put it in an unpublished paper, 'Thus the Bible becomes a kind of Zen text, from which everybody gets their own spiritual buzz without being concerned to know whether it is the same buzz as anybody else.'[5]

It is time to move from general considerations to the particular case of baptism. The baptismal divide is not new; indeed, the sixteenth century viewed it in altogether starker colours than we moderns are used to. The moderating of passions owes something to the greater modesty shown by both sides in appealing to scripture, but it remains irreducibly a disagreement about the teaching of scripture, even if that disagreement pivots not so much on proof-texts as on the proper relation between the two Testaments.

It is surely also a classic instance of apparently intractable division nurturing indifferentism. I well remember, during conversations between the Church of Scotland and the Baptist Union of Scotland, a senior representative of the Kirk, a cleric of impeccable ecumenical credentials, concluding that, if the Lord had allowed his church to be so divided for so long about baptism, he could not have meant it to be too important. (A consistent application of this criterion might dissolve the ecumenical movement altogether or resolve all its problems at a stroke!) Evangelicals, whose defining characteristics, according to David Bebbington, include conversionism,[6] have instinctively viewed their paedobaptism as something less than full New Testament baptism (a minimizing tendency welcomed by credobaptists), while evangelical Baptists have too often

---

[5] Roy Clements, 'An Overview of Evangelicalism Today', delivered at the UCCF Triennial Consultation, Swanwick, on 7 May 1994.

[6] David Bebbington, *Evangelicalism in Modern Britain: A History from the 1730s to the 1980s* (London, 1989), pp. 5-10.

operated with a diluted or desiccated baptismal theology. For the purposes of this discussion I will assume the commonly held differentiation between the two forms of baptismal administration, without considering more penetrating questions, such as how far either of them corresponds to the so-called converts' baptism of much of the New Testament.

It is my conviction that the New Testament does not allow us to regard baptism as a second-order issue, let alone an *adiaphoron*. Whether we call it a sacrament or an ordinance, we agree that it belongs to that very small category of acts that Jesus explicitly instructed his followers to perpetuate. Most ecclesiologies in the Reformation tradition make its proper administration essential to the being of the church. (Baptists who have been conscientiously unable to recognize paedobaptism as Christian baptism should have had great difficulty in discerning the church in paedobaptist communions, as their sixteenth-century forebears certainly did.) Our embarrassing disagreement about baptism has undoubtedly contributed to our widespread failure to make our baptismal experience and character the ground of exhortation, admonition and instruction as frequently as the New Testament does. Credobaptists may justifiably claim that paedobaptism renders this impossible, but I wonder if their own performance is much more creditable. Faced with confusion surrounding the ritual reality, we take refuge in spiritualizing—even with passages like Romans 6.1-4, with a banal tautology as the outcome.[7]

Ecumenical progress in recent decades in both the Old World and the New has produced united churches in which both baptismal practices have equal status. The United Reformed Church in Britain and the Church of North India, to name two examples, offer both, strictly as alternatives. Hence there can be no question of allowing rebaptism of those baptized as babies, or of pressurizing parents who choose not to have their infants baptized. This kind of way forward is hinted at in the influential Faith and Order document *Baptism, Eucharist and Ministry*.[8] What many will be tempted to sniff at as merely another brand of ecumenical fudge has recently received cautious endorsement from George Beasley-Murray, announcing his conversion to the recognition of the legitimacy of infant baptism on the part of credobaptists.[9] It is not too

---

[7] See my Laing Lecture, 'One Baptism or Two? Reflections on the History of Christian Baptism', *Vox Evangelica* 18 (1988), pp. 7-23, at pp. 7-8 (see ch. 19 above, p. 270).

[8] *Baptism, Eucharist and Ministry* (Faith and Order Paper, 11; Geneva, 1982), pp. 4-5 'Baptism' 12, with Commentary): 'The differences between infant and believers' baptism becomes less sharp when it is recognized that both forms of baptism embody God's own initiative in Christ and express a response of faith made within the believing community.'

[9] George R. Beasley-Murray, 'The Problem of Infant Baptism: An Exercise in Possibilities', in Faculty of Baptist Theological Seminary, Rüschlikon (ed.), *Festschrift*

difficult to envisage other possible perspectives on this route round, or perhaps through, the impasse over baptism. When larger challenges, such as the balance of continuity and discontinuity between old and new covenants, remain unresolved, provisional action of this kind may be all that is feasible and may be justified not despite their remaining unresolved but because of it.

Let us approach the question from another angle: are we right to assume that Christ the King and Head of the church intended it to observe only one baptismal practice? Adherents of both positions have traditionally answered in the affirmative. The occasional administration of baptism to adult converts on their own profession of faith by paedobaptist churches does not conflict with this answer, and in no sense makes them dual-practice churches in terms of the ecumenical accommodation noted above, for it does not concede the propriety of not baptizing children born within the church community.[10] But it reminds us that the two baptismal stances are not neatly balanced alternatives, wholly exclusive each of the other. While Baptists have hitherto refused to recognize paedobaptism as baptism, and hence have baptized all candidates *de novo*, paedobaptist churches have usually accepted believers' baptism as authentic Christian baptism.

'One Baptism'

The nub of the issue is this: how should we understand our baptismal diversity in the light of the Pauline affirmation of 'one baptism'?

> There is one body and one Spirit, just as you were called to the one hope that belongs to your call, one Lord, one faith, one baptism, one God and Father of us all, who is above all and through all and in all (Eph. 4.4-6, RSV).

Günther Wagner (International Theological Studies: Contributions of Baptist Scholars, 1; Berne, 1994), pp. 1-14.

[10] Some paedobaptist theologians, such as T.F. Torrance, would deny that such cases represent 'believers' baptism'. Such an attitude is sustained by the biblically wholly unwarrantable assumption that infant baptism is the theologically normative baptism. This was the implicit, and sometimes almost explicit, assumption of the Church of Scotland's Special Commission on Baptism of 1953-62, whose voluminous reports are distilled in *The Biblical Doctrine of Baptism* (Edinburgh, 1958), and *The Doctrine of Baptism* (Edinburgh, 1966); T.F. Torrance was convenor of the Commission. In the early church, the reality is almost the reverse. In the first extant text which comes near to depicting infant baptism as a routine (rather than, say, clinically emergency) practice, Hippolytus' *Apostolic Tradition* early in the third century, the inclusion of very young children is discernible solely in the instruction that parents or someone else from the family should speak for those little ones who cannot answer for themselves. The whole of the rest of the complex ceremony envisages responsibly participant candidates.

These verses merit considered attention. Of this list of unifying realities, which constitute the basis on which Paul may exhort the Ephesians to maintain unity in practice, baptism is the most visible and concrete.[11] 'One body' in the context probably has a reference wider than the single community of the Christians at Ephesus. One might speculate on some other occasion about the implications of the non-inclusion of 'one supper of the Lord'.

Notice what exalted company 'one baptism' keeps—the Trinity and the constitutive spiritual qualities of faith and hope. ('One love' is also absent!) Although the definition of 'one body' has not escaped entanglement with the Babel of divided churches, or perhaps better, an internally divided church, 'one baptism' remains the most contentious of these given unities. According to credobaptists, the common baptism to be shared in and acknowledged by all does not encompass paedobaptism. As we noted earlier, champions of a baptism for believers only have perhaps rarely faced up to the implication of their position, namely, that most Christians for most of church history have been unbaptized. One suspects that living with this conclusion has been made tolerable only by devaluing baptism altogether.

A Single Theology of Baptism

Does this mean, then, that modern ecumenical rapprochement entails the recognition of two baptisms, since no church union appears to have involved the abandonment of one of the two versions of baptism? Not if each of the two patterns can be understood in terms of a single theology, the obvious elements of which would include: baptism's dominical status, its grounding in the once-for-all saving work of Christ, its incorporation of the baptized in the body of Christ through the Spirit, and its expression of a response of faith to the gospel of Christ's redemption as it is appropriated for the baptized. I hope that such a summary embodies sufficient common ground for this present discussion to continue. I commend to you Beasley-Murray's similar listing of those 'elements of

---

[11] For a conclusive refutation of the hypothesis that 'one baptism' means Christ's one baptism on behalf of all in his atoning incarnation, crucifixion and exaltation (argued by, e.g., J.A.T. Robinson, 'The One Baptism as a Category of New Testament Soteriology', *Scottish Journal of Theology* 6 [1953], pp. 257-74, reprinted in his *Twelve New Testament Studies* [Studies in Biblical Theology, 34; London, 1962], pp. 158-75), see W.E. Moore, 'One Baptism', *New Testament Studies* 10 (1963–64), pp. 504-16. See also my study 'The Meaning and Reference of "One Baptism for the Remission of Sins" in the Niceno-Constantinopolitan Creed', *Studia Patristica* 19 (1989), pp. 281-85 (see ch. 4 above).

faith...cherished alike by churches which practice infant baptism and those which practice believer's baptism only'.[12]

It is also worth noting at this point the more general considerations behind his re-thinking exercise.[13] Since there is no single theology of baptism accepted by all Baptists, Baptists cannot insist on a Baptist interpretation of believers' baptism before recognizing its authenticity when administered in non-Baptist denominations. One thing this means, I take it (Beasley-Murray does not spell it out), is that the validity of baptism on profession of faith cannot be made conditional on the acceptance, by candidate, minister or congregation, that such profession is essential for every administration of baptism. Similarly, he argues, the currency of obnoxious interpretations of paedobaptism does not exclude the possibility of another interpretation of it being found acceptable to credobaptists. He proceeds to find this, to his own measured satisfaction, along two lines of thought—a view of infant baptism which sees it as attesting the beginnings of the work of grace in the baptized, and a reconsideration of the relation of believers' children to Christ's salvation which appeals to 1 Corinthians 7.14.[14]

We need not become preoccupied with the specifics of this argument, since we are reflecting on baptism for the sake of illustration rather than definition. I will, however, add one point of substance. Since all paedobaptist churches also baptize some non-infants, who seek baptism on their own initiative and answer for themselves (i.e., responsibly, in a literal sense), these churches cannot afford to incorporate in their theology of baptism any elements that are applicable only to babies. So the helpless and unresponsive passivity of babies should not be made theologically integral to baptism; still less should traces of Adamic perversity be discerned in a frightened baby's squawking and squealing at the font. Baptism administered to tiny babies may be an admirable testimony to 'the priority of grace over faith' (a quasi-liturgical phrase in some Church of Scotland usage), but if true of the baptismal experience at all, it is surely no less true of a believer's baptism. Of ourselves we do not believe, nor do we baptize ourselves, but that does not require that none comes to baptism unless carried in another's arms. An obvious point, perhaps, but a telling illustration of the tendency for infant baptism to become the theological, as well as the practical, norm.

What makes baptism so helpful an example in considering evangelical (and wider) diversity is its inescapably visible expression of our

---

[12] Beasley-Murray, 'Problem of Infant Baptism', p. 8.

[13] Beasley-Murray, 'Problem of Infant Baptism', pp. 6-7.

[14] Beasley-Murray, 'Problem of Infant Baptism', p. 9. See my paper '1 Corinthians 7:14 in Fathers and Reformers', in D.C. Steinmetz (ed.), *Die Patristik in der Bibelexegese des 16. Jahrhunderts* (Wolfenbütteler Forschungen Band 85; Wiesbaden, 1999), pp. 93-113 (see ch. 14 above).

differences. Often the situation is the very reverse: we use the same words, we perform the same or closely similar actions, but freight them with a varying weight of meaning. In the case of the Lord's supper, we may well feel that the different nuances of the three Synoptic accounts of the Last Supper, together with 1 Corinthians 11 and perhaps John 6 also, justify some diversity in interpretations of the observance. But not all readings of the supper pass muster, nor can divergences from the common core of actions, such as the continued withholding of the cup from communicants in many Catholic churches.

Even when we confess 'one Spirit, ...one Lord, ...one God and Father of us all', the common formula will undoubtedly conceal significant variations of belief. Is he the 'one Spirit' of charismatic immediacy, bestowing gifts, inspiring prophetic utterance and empowering all God's people, or is the 'one Spirit' thirled more to the authoritative exposition of the written word and the faithful's reverent attendance thereupon and obedience thereto? Although in this instance the differerces soon become evident, the intercessory prayer and evangelistic preaching of the Westminster Calvinist and the Wesleyan Arminian may not be recognisably discordant, especially if they owe vastly more to scripture than to Westminster or Wesley. Words are elusive quantities, as the fathers of Nicaea discovered when they resorted to *homoousios*, and as twentieth-century drafters or refiners of doctrinal bases have perhaps been too slow to acknowledge. Has a written confession ever kept a church from falling into heterodoxy?

The attractiveness of recent attempts to bridge 'the waters that divide' is that they penetrate behind divergent practice and dare to claim that both administrations of baptism can be embraced within one theological framework with little remainder. The one baptizes believers' babies and nurtures them within the community of faith until they profess the faith responsibly for themselves. The other dedicates or gives thank for believers' babies and nurtures them within the community of faith until in baptism they respond to the gospel in their own profession. For both categories of baptismal subjects the prospective perspective is critical, both from the early acknowledgement of a child as God's gift to be reared in and to faith, and from the later time of responsible decision, which is not so much an arrival as a fresh point of departure.

In this example of evangelical diversity, then, can we continue to do different things while believing, not precisely the same, at least broadly compatible things about them, within a bipolar framework of Christian nurture that binds together two significant moments in spiritual development? This proposal is arguably not a whit inferior to the dominant mode in which we do or say the same thing while believing different things as we do so.

Dangerous Diversity

Some will judge that the diversity of our baptismal observances is well toward the soft end on a scale of intractability. I would demur (but not fervently) if only because of my conviction that our apparently irreconcilable disagreement has ministered to a general depreciation of baptism, as explained earlier. The deepening paganization of society may assist the recovery of the New Testament's weighting of baptism. I would not for a moment deny that immensely graver challenges threaten to open up such deep chasms of diversity that institutional unity will experience insupportable strains. Is Jesus Christ the only Saviour of sinful humanity, or is it conceivable that the 'one God and Father of us all' of Ephesians 4 will be sundered from the 'one Lord', 'one Spirit, one faith, one hope' of Ephesians 4, let alone from its 'one body, one baptism'? Is the homosexual life-style as acceptable to God as the heterosexual, within precisely the same norms? Recent argumentation in favour of this enormous paradigm shift has sought to justify it in terms of the Trinity's differentiation-in-unity, and to base the rejection of discrimination against homosexuality on acceptance of diversity, not on our common humanity, in Adam and in Christ.[15]

These two pressure points, so vastly disparate in themselves, are nevertheless alike reinforced by the powerful all-inclusiveness abroad in the secular liberal establishment, which magnifies diversity, whether religious, cultural or sexual. Christian liberalism, it seems, lacks the courageous clarity to resist joining the celebration, and evangelicalism is not immune to the temptations that afflict a minority perceived as intolerant, exclusive and mean-minded. We will need to be alert to the forces of the contemporary intellectual glorification of diversity combining with the thrust of current hermeneutics to shatter scripture into a thousand pieces. In this context, our evangelical diversities are reduced to their proper proportions, although we dare not suppose that they are invulnerable to the distortions and exaggerations of the spirit of the age. Freedom of self-expression, individuality and non-conformity are unquestioned virtues; adherence to external norms, regard for the traditional and uniformity enjoy little esteem.

It behoves us, therefore, to be respectful of biblical limits to diversity. The sequence of magnificent unities set forth in Ephesians 4 could bear extended reflection, not least in the light of Paul's response to the intolerable diversity of the Christians at Corinth. Their allegiance to human leaders, or even in a partisan sense to Christ himself, was incompatible with their 'one baptism' (whether in the name of Christ or

---

[15] Cf. P.B. Jung and R.F. Smith, *Heterosexism: An Ethical Challenge* (Albany, NY, 1993), pp. 187-88; M. Williams, 'Quest for an Evangelical Ethics', *Anvil* 11 (1994), pp. 27-28.

of the Trinity), itself grounded in the 'one crucifixion' of Christ for all (1 Corinthians 1.12-13). This approach to managing, and curbing, diversity is not altogether different from a Reformation perspective that insists on *solus Christus* and *sola fide* and *sola gratia*, as well as *sola scriptura*. But instead of highlighting the 'sole' which excludes all others, so that, for example, salvation can be received solely by faith trusting in God's gratuitous mercy, and not by meritorious performance or heredity or nationality, Ephesians 4 directs us to the unifying realities in which our diversities may find common ground, as I have sought to do with baptism.

Discerning Our Unity

At stake in the phenomenon of evangelical diversity in the face of the perspicuity of the one scripture is not so much the need to discriminate between the acceptable and the unacceptable (where, in Reformation terms, the fourfold *solus/a* comes into play), as the ability to discern our unity, rooted in commitment to the one word of God written, behind and through our differences. A certain obligation weighs with me to take seriously the divergent view of a brother or sister who shares my professed fidelity to the scriptural revelation. Such an attitude is mandated by several considerations, ranging from our common fallibility 'in Adam', the virtue of docility, the diversity of the mode of the biblical witness, our lack (in God's wise providence) of an authoritative inspired interpretation of scripture, the ecclesial setting of the unfolding of its meaning for God's people, and the hermeneutical significance of the entirely trustworthy truthfulness of scripture. James Packer has somewhere drawn helpful attention to this last point. Just as the conviction that marriage is ordained of God for lifelong permanence fires the tenacity to work through, and even live with, discord and distress in one's marriage, so a belief in scripture's infallibility never lets us off the hook of grappling not only with the problematic phenomenon of the text but also with our puzzling failures to agree on what it teaches. The dynamic sense of 'infallible' — incapable of failing us, sure not to deceive, bound to lead us aright — commits us to an unceasing endeavour to reach a common mind on scripture's teaching.

An interesting comparison may be drawn between the opening verses of Hebrews and the first chapter of the Westminster Confession, partly quoted above. Hebrews contrasts the many and various ways of God's earlier speech through the prophets with his having now spoken by his Son. The exalted presentation of this one Son that follows in the first two chapters shows the sovereign character of this revelation 'in the last days'. The Confession, on the other hand, applies part of Hebrews 1.1 ('at sundry times, and in divers manners') to the whole span of God's pre-scriptural revelation (making no distinction between the prophets and the divine Son), and goes on to declare 'those former ways of God's revealing his will unto his people being now ceased', not since Christ the Son has come but since God has committed his whole revelation to writing. An intriguing instance of diversity of theological framework! What the Confession misses, by its creative use of Hebrews, is the central finality of Christ in God's revelation, but what neither of them tells us is that, though distributed diversity of divine utterance is a thing of the past (as both in different ways affirm), we have no unitary access to God's definitive Word, whether the focus is on his Son or his scripture.

If we may be allowed to combine apostolic scripture and latter-day confession, together they remind us of what our specialized concentrations on separate parts or strands or layers of the Bible frequently forget. ('I am a Paul man; don't ask me about Hebrews'; 'my field is Acts; ask someone else about John'; 'I'm for Q; let others rally round Mark.') Well, Christ is not divided, though we have many presentations of Christ. But though they be many, they together constitute one word of God, like the many members of the one body of Christ. It is our insistent task ever to be striving to apprehend the one Christ in the one scripture. This will mean not only, in terms of Article 20 of the Church of England, that the Church (*nota bene*!) may not 'so expound one place of Scripture that it be repugnant to another', but that we perpetually ask ourselves and our fellow-labourers whether our subtly differentiated expositions are true to the unities of Ephesians 4. Are our varying ecclesiologies recognizably expressive of 'one body', our Christologies of 'one Lord', our pneumatologies and charismatologies of 'one Spirit'? Criteria of consistency, complementarity, compatibility and the like will be important, but it will also be necessary to give further thought to the nature of the unity of faith that is intended to bind us together.

I assume that this unity is not to be conceived of in mathematical terms, as though different evangelical convictions about, say, women's ministry, were fractions of the truth which when added together made up a complete whole. Is the unity found along developmental lines, with one interpretation to some measure subsuming or capping another, and to that extent superseding it? Or is it best regarded as the unity of different perspectives on a single reality? None will be perfect or comprehensive, but their partiality will not be such that they can be fitted together like the discrete segments of a pie-chart. They will be complementary to each other not because there is no overlapping between them but because they all merit recognition as valid (but never impeccable or exhaustive) apprehensions of the 'one body' or the 'one baptism', etc.

My own experience, and perhaps yours also, would bear out the point at issue here. I operate with a certain body of functional theology which has (so I dare to believe) a leading influence on my routine thoughts and decisions. It has its strengths and weaknesses, its one-sided pre-occupations and its surprising silences and lacunae (e.g., its blissful innocence of the millennial varieties of evangelicalism which might otherwise have served as a searching test-bed for this consideration of evangelical diversity). But when I hear or read others expounding a theme or an emphasis that have no place in my working theology, more often than not I instinctively recognize their truthfulness and importance. Yet rarely do such experiences lead to my rejigging my functional theology to incorporate what I have neglected or never known of. Some marginal adjustment may occur, but for the most part I am happy to let others be the guardians of, say, the eucharistic dimension of the church's being or the significance of the inclusion or exclusion of *Filioque*.

Not even the pope, with all his advisers and consultants, can hold the whole corpus of theology in his mind. As individuals we are diverse, and the communities and communions we comprise are diverse. Important ingredients of our diversity are our limitations as human beings—of time and space, of economic status, of intellect and industry, etc.—and as fallen creatures. A certain modesty is appropriate on these and other counts, especially when those with whom we do not see eye-to-eye share the same allegiance to scripture.

Charismatic and Reformed: Some Concluding Reflections

Let me finally attempt to apply some of these general reflections to an influential divide in recent British evangelicalism which is often located between Reformed and charismatic (where 'Reformed' has, I think, a broader reference than the tradition issuing from the Swiss-Genevan Reformation). It is in reality not so easily mapped. It is surely in good part cultural: classical and pop, or trad and mod, or broadsheet and tabloid. But then again it parallels in important respects the magisterial-radical breach in the sixteenth-century Reformation. In some cases it may embody different psychologies: cerebral and emotional, rational and affective, even spiritual and embodied, for it is one of the paradoxes of this divide that those who make most of the Holy Spirit insist most on visible, even physical evidences of his working.

How does this manifestation of diversity stand up to the scrutiny of Ephesians 4.4-6 or the Reformation's fourfold *solus/a*? Early critiques like that of F.D. Bruner[16] discerned in the stress laid on Spirit-baptism a Galatian-type threat to *sola gratia*, and we might add to 'one baptism'. More recently, claims for revelations and prophecies can appear to infringe on *sola scriptura*. But it is difficult to conclude that responsible

---

[16] F.D. Bruner, *A Theology of the Holy Spirit: The Pentecostal Experience and the New Testament Witness* (Grand Rapids, MI, 1970).

charismatic varieties of the Christian faith fall foul of Ephesians 4. The restriction of supernatural phenomena to the apostolic era alone itself seems a post-biblical or extra-biblical straitjacket.

The last paragraphs have scarcely scratched the surface, but it is no part of my purpose to enter into the substance of this debate. While I do not minimize the detrimental effects of this manifestation of diversity, and would myself regard the charismatic metamorphosis of considerable tracts of English evangelicalism as more bane than blessing, the divide contains within itself, on my reading, significant intrusions of culture, tradition, temperament and taste. As an instance of evangelical diversity I do not view it as anywhere near as threatening to our common confession of scripture as the baptismal breach. It will need to survive, as the baptismal split has done, centuries of biblical and theological scrutiny before its challenge looms equally large. Long before then it will surely in part have proved amenable to the wisdom we may now be learning as we seek to bridge 'the waters that divide'.[17]

---

[17] A useful starter is R.S. Fyall's booklet *Charismatic and Reformed* (Edinburgh, 1992).

CHAPTER 21

Baptism in Scotland

Article from Nigel M. de S. Cameron *et al.* (eds), *Dictionary of Scottish Church History and Theology* (Edinburgh, 1993), pp. 56-58.

Celtic Period

Bede identifies the administration of baptism as one of the three issues on which c. 600 Augustine of Canterbury demanded that the British (i.e. Celtic) bishops conform to universal (Roman) practice.[1] How the Celtic observance differed has never been conclusively determined: possibilities include single immersion, not triple; omission of confirmation or chrism as the 'completion' of baptism (although Patrick mentions both); most likely, their administration by presbyters or even deacons—in which case Celtic custom remained more primitive than the later reservation of confirmation–chrism for bishops.[2] A century later Celtic baptism might still be of questionable validity.[3] An account of Kentigern's death indicates he baptized not at Easter but at Epiphany—which in the East originally marked Christ's baptism.[4]

Adomnán's *Life of Columba* records a typical variety of subjects for baptism: two old men as new believers, one of them on his death-bed (1:33, 3:14), an infant brought by parents (2:10), and two households, one clearly including children (2:32, 3:14). It has been suggested that the Celtic church used clinical baptism in place of extreme unction. Immersion was probably practised as well as affusion. But apart from Bede's enigmatic note, there is no reason to believe that medieval Scotland's baptismal belief and practice were at all peculiar.

---

[1] Bede, *Ecclesiastical History* 2:2.

[2] F.E. Warren, *The Liturgy and Ritual of the Celtic Church* (Woodbridge, 2nd edn, 1987), pp. 64-67; H. Williams, *Christianity in Early Britain* (Oxford, 1912), pp. 473-75; C. Thomas, *Christianity in Roman Britain to AD 500* (London, 1981), pp. 202-27, 'Baptism and Baptisteries'.

[3] Theodore of Canterbury, *Penitential* 2:19.

[4] D. McRoberts, 'The Death of St Kentigern of Glasgow', *Innes Review* 24 (1973), pp. 43-50.

Reformation

Nor in the sixteenth century did baptism prove as contentious as in most countries where the Reformation took root and Protestantism prevailed. The Reformation radicals' rejection of infant baptism touched Scotland only marginally, and there was only a 'late and slow growth of Baptist churches on Scottish soil'. To this day Baptists remain a small, albeit vigorous, body. For these and other reasons the established church has developed a more rigid attitude to baptism than most Reformed churches, and has appeared ecumenically out of step.

The essentials of the new Reformation understanding may be gathered from the *First Book of Discipline*, the Scots Confession (SC) and the *Book of Common Order* (1564). Anabaptist errors are condemned but not specified (SC 23). Baptism and the Lord's supper are treated together as 'the two chief sacraments...alone...instituted by the Lord Jesus' and straitly denied, in the manner of Calvin or Bucer, to be merely 'naked and bare signs'. They distinguish God's covenant people from outsiders and 'seal in their hearts the assurance of his promise, and of that most blessed conjunction, union and society, which the chosen have with their Head, Jesus Christ'. The language is sharply realist: 'by baptism we are engrafted into Christ Jesus, to be made partakers of his righteousness, by which our sins are covered and remitted' (SC 21).

Because sacraments are 'seales and visible confirmations of the spirituall promises contained in the Word', they must be 'annexed' to the true preaching of the gospel.[5] The requirement that baptism be administered only at the time of preaching, whether Sunday or weekday, did not preclude variable practice. Sermon and sacraments should take place before noon, but afternoon baptisms were allowed when travel was involved.[6] The noise factor might advance baptism before the sermon; the post-baptismal celebration was already a problem.

The normal expectation was that baptism should take place on the next preaching day after birth. This reflected the Calvinist insistence that it be administered 'in the face of the congregation' and also the rejection of the notion that babies dying unbaptized were consigned to hell or limbo and hence needed emergency baptism. The 1618 General Assembly at Perth allowed private baptism in emergency, but the Presbyterians never conceded this and the 1638 Glasgow Assembly banned it. The Scots Confession (22) restricted baptismal administration to 'lawful ministers', which meant those appointed to preach and 'lawfully called by some Kirk'. The *Second Book of Discipline* endorsed this.[7] Concern was repeatedly expressed at baptism by unqualified persons—priests (perhaps

---

[5] J.K. Cameron (ed.), *The First Book of Discipline* (Edinburgh, 1972), p. 90.

[6] Cameron (ed.), *First Book of Discipline*, pp. 181-82.

[7] J. Kirk (ed.), *The Second Book of Discipline* (Edinburgh, 1980), pp. 184-85.

still using the Latin, Sarum, rite); readers (often ex-priests), although they were briefly authorized to baptize between 1572 and 1576; doctors;[8] laymen (the 1583 Assembly even declared that baptism by a layman was not baptism); and, of course, women (SC 22). The medieval church had sanctioned lay baptism *in extremis*.[9] The Church of Scotland still insists that only the ordained may baptize, but the reason—the rejection of quasi-magical notions about baptism—is often forgotten.

The Scots Confession declared Rome's sacraments to be 'so adulterated...with their own additions that no part of Christ's original act remains in its original simplicity' (SC 22). Yet the Reformed church did not reject the validity of Roman baptism,[10] although sundry accretions were purged and fonts mostly went out of use. Many were smashed because of their idolatrous carvings, others left unused at the church door. The *First Book of Discipline* specifies that each church must have 'a basen for baptizing',[11] which was commonly bracketed to the pulpit.[12] Baptism was normally administered from the pulpit, with the child held up by parent or sponsor, not taken into his arms by the minister as the *Book of Common Prayer* provided.

After Westminster

The Westminster Assembly's *Directory of Public Worship* (1645) laid down the lines of baptismal practice and understanding that Scottish Presbyterianism would follow in the main. It assumed (unlike the other Westminster documents) that only infants would be baptized. Some of the *Directory*'s most basic provisions—only by a minister; 'in the face of the congregation'; a role for sponsors (not godparents) only in the father's 'necessary absence'—were to be frequently breached. Baptism in private houses became surprisingly common in the nineteenth century, and misconceptions still constrained unordained people to baptize ill babies on the spot. The old church's response to the first Protestant baptisms had been to doubt their validity and order conditional re-baptism under pain of parental excommunication (council of 1559).[13] After the re-establishment of Presbyterianism in 1690, the nonconforming

---

[8] Kirk (ed.), *Second Book of Discipline*, p. 189.

[9] D. Patrick, *Statutes of the Scottish Church 1225–1559* (Edinburgh, 1907), pp. 30-32, 62, 186-87.

[10] T. Thomson (ed.), *The Booke of the Universall Kirk of Scotland. Acts and Proceedings of the General Assemblies of the Kirk of Scotland, 1560–1618* (3 vols; Edinburgh, 1839–45), I, p. 75.

[11] Cameron (ed.), *First Book of Discipline*, p. 203.

[12] G. Hay, *The Architecture of the Scottish Post-Reformation Churches 1560–1843* (Oxford, 1957), pp. 22, 185, 188-90.

[13] Patrick, *Statutes*, pp. 186-87.

Episcopalians adopted various measures towards Presbyterian baptisms. Some rejected them altogether and, in a most uncatholic fashion, gave second baptism. Others re-baptized conditionally, while yet others treated Presbyterian sacraments (as Augustine had the Donatists') as valid but 'useless' unless the baptized joined their ranks. The extent of re-baptizing in Scotland, as elsewhere, has almost certainly been underestimated.

Although a sect of 'Waderdowpers' (Waterdippers) was recorded in Edinburgh in 1624, Baptist practice became clearly noticeable only in the 1650s when Cromwell's occupying armies during the Commonwealth included Baptists.[14] Some Kirk ministers even abandoned paedobaptism, but in 1672 toleration ended and the law required the baptism of all children within thirty days of birth. A permanent Baptist presence came only in the mid-eighteenth century. When the Haldane brothers, Robert and James, converted to believers' baptism early in the nineteenth century, for a time they followed a dual practice, baptizing both infants and believers in the embryonic Congregationalist movement, but it proved divisive and was short-lived.[15]

Presbyterian baptismal theology in Scotland has had little cause to take serious note of the case for believers' baptism. Despite the wide impact of his general theology, even Karl Barth's rejection of infant baptism created little disturbance. As a consequence, baptism has rarely been high on theological agenda, and differences have not run deep until relatively recent years.

Church of Scotland Special Commission

The most extensive Scottish investigation of baptism came from the Church of Scotland Special Commission on Baptism set up under T.F. Torrance's convenership in 1953, 'to carry out a fresh examination of the Doctrine of Baptism, and...to stimulate and guide such a study throughout the Church as may lead to theological agreement and uniform practice'.[16] Glasgow Presbytery had overtured the Assembly in dissatisfaction at diversity of administration and belief.[17] The Commission hoped to report in 1956,[18] but its work was finally wound up only in

---

[14] Cf. W.I. Hoy, 'The Entry of Sects into Scotland', in D. Shaw (ed.), *Reformation and Revolution* (Edinburgh, 1967), pp. 178-211.

[15] See D.W. Bebbington (ed.), *The Baptists in Scotland: A History* (Glasgow, 1988), *passim*.

[16] *Principal Acts of the General Assembly of the Church of Scotland 1953* (Edinburgh, 1953), p. 372.

[17] *Assembly Papers of the Church of Scotland* (Edinburgh, 1954), p. 44.

[18] *Reports to the General Assembly of the Church of Scotland 1954* (Edinburgh, 1954), pp. 591-92.

1963. Its lengthy reports appeared in *Reports to the General Assembly of the Church of Scotland*: on New Testament doctrine (*1955*, pp. 609-62); the Fathers (*1956*, pp. 605-46); medieval, Reformation and Anglican teaching (*1957*, pp. 647-706); the Church of Scotland with particular attention to John Knox, Robert Bruce, Robert Rollock and Robert Boyd, John Forbes (1593–1648) and the Westminster tradition (*1958*, pp. 685-763); and the Church of Scotland since 1843, and Church of Scotland assessment of Baptist teaching (*1959*, pp. 629-62).

In 1960 (*1960*, pp. 677-92) the Commission presented a draft on 'The Doctrine of Baptism' and 'A Form of Instruction about Baptism'. 'The Doctrine' was revised in 1961 (*1961*, pp. 715-31, but an overture sent down under the Barrier Act proposing that it be recognized as 'an authoritative interpretation of the Biblical and Reformed doctrine of Baptism as contained in the primary and subordinate standards of the Church' (*1962*, pp. 709-23; *1963*, pp. 773-83) was frustrated. The Assembly merely noted its acceptance by a majority of Presbyteries as a valid statement of biblical and Reformed doctrine and commended it to general consideration.[19] *The Doctrine of Baptism* was published in 1966, and earlier *The Biblical Doctrine of Baptism* (1958).

However, the Commission's proposals for tidying up the administration of infant baptism did become church law. In 1933 and in 1951 the Assembly had spelled out the conditions parents had to meet. The 1963 provisions (which envisaged solely infant baptism) required that one parent be a member of the Church of Scotland or a permanent adherent or desirous of becoming a member. But the Commission failed to bring about uniformity of practice. Indiscipline has continued, and in 1990 the General Assembly re-opened the question whether one parent need normally be a member.

The Commission's labours, resting largely on T.F. Torrance's work, suffered from a density of expression. Its argument relied on some questionable linguistic analysis and focused on the theologically questionable notion that 'baptism' refers primarily to 'the one, all-inclusive, vicarious baptism of Christ for all men'. This basic conception, which could distinguish between 'the water rite' and 'the real baptism—Christ's', issued in a doctrine of sophisticated elusiveness which not surprisingly—since it sat loose to historical and contemporary baptismal realities—proved unequal to the demands of pastoral confusion and disorder.

---

[19] *Principal Acts of the General Assembly of the Church of Scotland 1963* (Edinburgh, 1963), p. 462.

Ecumenical Dimensions

The ecumenical movement has been slow to give baptism the attention it deserves. In 1984 the Church of Scotland and the Baptist Union of Scotland appointed a group to study a report, *Baptists and Reformed in Dialogue*,[20] that issued from conversations between the World Alliance of Reformed Churches and the Baptist World Alliance.[21] The group's findings[22] were largely ground-clearing, but even so the General Assembly faulted them for inadequately representing the Kirk's tradition,[23] although it consented to continuing exchanges.[24]

Though the Church of Scotland has agreed,[25] in response to *Baptism, Eucharist and Ministry*, that in any future reunion infant and believers' baptism should be 'equivalent alternatives'[26] in a so-called 'double-practice' arrangement (as implemented by several Reformed churches), this commitment has scarcely affected its approach to domestic difficulties, whether doubts about the biblical warrant for infant baptism or requests for faith-baptism after conversion or charismatic experience later in life. In 1976, in a case of an elder's second baptism brought by Hamilton Presbytery,[27] and in the 1983 Panel of Doctrine's review in the light of recent problems,[28] reaffirmation was the order of the day. The influence of the Special Commission is recognizable, for example in the assumption that infant baptism is the theological norm and in the particular interpretation of 'one baptism' in Ephesians 4.5 and the Nicene Creed.

---

[20] *Baptists and Reformed in Dialogue* (Studies from the World Alliance of Reformed Churches, 4; Geneva, 1984).

[21] For the broader context of these conversations see T.W. Moyes, 'Scottish Baptist Relations with the Church of Scotland in the Twentieth Century', *Baptist Quarterly* 33 (1989), pp. 174-85.

[22] *Reports to the General Assembly of the Church of Scotland 1986* (Edinburgh, 1986), pp. 279, 306-17.

[23] *Principal Acts of the General Assembly of the Church of Scotland 1986* (Edinburgh, 1986), p. 19.

[24] *Principal Acts of the General Assembly of the Church of Scotland 1987* (Edinburgh, 1987), p. 21; cf. *Reports to the General Assembly of the Church of Scotland 1987* (Edinburgh, 1987), pp. 380-89.

[25] *Principal Acts of the General Assembly of the Church of Scotland 1985* (Edinburgh, 1985), p. 28.

[26] *Baptism, Eucharist and Ministry* (Faith and Order Paper, 111; Geneva, 1982), 'Baptism', commentary (12).

[27] *Assembly Papers of the Church of Scotland 1976* (Edinburgh, 1976), pp. 31-33; *Principal Acts of the General Assembly of the Church of Scotland 1976* (Edinburgh, 1976), p. 103.

[28] *Reports to the General Assembly of the Church of Scotland 1983* (Edinburgh, 1983), pp. 152-63.

Only with a fresh and landmark report from the Panel of Doctrine to the General Assembly of 2003, and the consequent re-writing of the Church's regulations on baptism, did the Church of Scotland formally take on board approaches to the doctrine and practice of baptism integral to baptismal renewal among churches worldwide.[29]

The Scottish churches' sole ecumenical achievement on baptism is the adoption of a common baptismal certificate—apart from the incorporation of most of the Churches of Christ into the United Reformed Church, which resulted in some 'double-practice' URC congregations in Scotland. Further erosion of inherited divisions is likely. The sharp reduction in recent decades in infant baptisms in the Church of Scotland and other churches has been accompanied by a slow increase in baptisms on profession of faith. The Church of Scotland now administers more believers' baptisms than Scottish Baptists, while the latter on rare occasions baptize, as believers, children of seven or so. The Church of Scotland in particular wrestles with the relationship of baptism to church membership, and whether baptized children should be admitted to the Lord's supper. While some churchmen hanker after the indiscriminate general baptism of earlier ages, believers' baptism is likely to come increasingly to the fore, both ecumenically and with the rapid recession of Christendom, in Scotland as elsewhere in the West—for infant baptism came into its own only in the era of Christendom after Constantine.

---

[29] *The Church of Scotland General Assembly 2003* (Edinburgh, 2003), sect. 13, pp. 1-17.

CHAPTER 22

Baptism, Eucharist and Ministry (the 'Lima Report'): An Evangelical Assessment

Introduction

Baptism, Eucharist and Ministry (*BEM* for short) is a report produced in 1982 by the Faith and Order Commission of the World Council of Churches (WCC).[1] It reached its final form at a conference in Lima in Peru, and hence is often referred to as the Lima document or text. It is presented as 'the fruit of a 50-year process of study stretching back to the first Faith and Order Conference at Lausanne in 1927' (p. viii).

BEM claims to demonstrate 'a remarkable degree of agreement'. 'That theologians of such widely different traditions should be able to speak so harmoniously about baptism, eucharist and ministry is unprecedented in the modern ecumenical movement' (p. ix). The Faith and Order discussions involved representatives not only of the major denominational churches belonging to the WCC, including Anglica/Episcopalian, Lutheran, Reformed or Presbyterian, Baptist and Orthodox, but also of other bodies, especially the Roman Catholic Church, that are not members. The Faith and Order Commission has been called 'the most comprehensive theological and ecclesiastical forum in Christendom', and the Lima meeting 'the nearest thing to an Ecumenical Council since Nicaea II in 787'![2] We must take seriously the fact that *BEM* embodies agreement between a very wide range of churchmen on three issues that have for long periods sharply separated church from church.

Questions to be Answered

The report has been commended to the broadest possible consideration among the churches, who are asked to involve 'the whole people of God at all levels of church-life' in the process of receiving and evaluating it. It

---

[1] *Baptism, Eucharist and Ministry* (Faith and Order Paper, 111; Geneva, 1982).

[2] By, respectively, Nikos Nissiotis, the moderator of the Commission, and J.K.S. Reid, a Church of Scotland representative at Lima. See the latter's pamphlet *Lima 1982: A Report* (Church of Scotland Inter-Church Relations Committee; Edinburgh, 1982), p. 1.

is a safe forecast that, within two or three years of its publication, *BEM* will have been discussed more widely than any other doctrinal statement in modern times. It will soon constitute a standard point of departure for all inter-church consultations on ministry and the sacraments. It has already become the focus of a growing body of theological writing, sufficiently voluminous to warrant a six-monthly bibliographical survey.[3] No other report of the twentieth century will exercise such a pervasive influence on thinking about these subjects in the churches.

In assessing *BEM*, the churches have been asked by the Faith and Order Commission to comment on four specific questions:

— the extent to which your church can recognize in this text the faith of the Church through the ages;

— the consequences your church can draw from this text for its relations and dialogues with other churches, particularly with those churches which also recognize the text as an expression of the apostolic faith;

— the guidance your church can take from this text for its worship, educational, ethical, and spiritual life and witness;

— the suggestions your church can make for the ongoing work of Faith and Order as it relates the material of this text on Baptism, Eucharist and Ministry to its long-range research project 'Towards the Common Expression of the Apostolic Faith Today'.[4]

It is not the intention here to attempt a precise response to these questions, but rather to offer a more basic biblical and theological assessment which might help church bodies and groups, official and unofficial, to formulate an informed response. But some comment is called for on the first of the above questions, if only to declare it unanswerable!

'The faith of the Church through the ages' is an exceedingly elusive phenomenon. The divisions that have marked much of Christian history—between Latin West and Orthodox East, between Protestants and Romans, between Lutherans and Reformed, between establishment Protestants and Anabaptists, between Anglicans and Methodists...—make it difficult to speak other than of the faith (or faiths) of the *churches.* Since at least the sixteenth century, the churches of the West have had no single faith on any of these subjects.

So what might the question mean? Perhaps it is asking whether the basic convictions of all the separate churches are recognizable in this single statement—whether it succeeds in giving unified expression, on

---

[3] The Board for Mission and Unity of the Church of England's General Synod updates its *'BEM' Bibliography* every six months.

[4] *BEM*, p. x.

ministry, let us say, to the faiths of papal, episcopal, presbyterian and congregational churches. But even if this is how the question is to be construed, it scarcely becomes any more answerable. Twentieth-century Presbyterians, for example, are in no position to answer for sixteenth-century Rome or seventeenth-century Anglicanism or eighteenth-century Methodists, any more than they can for 'the Church' of all the centuries. How could an infant-baptizing church in the present day decide whether *BEM* does justice to the faith of the Anabaptists of the Reformation on believers' baptism? The most that could be expected of any one contemporary church is that it should answer for 'the faith of *its own tradition in* the Church through the ages'.

Perhaps, however, the question implies that behind the disagreements of the churches over the centuries there lurks a common faith on each of these thorny issues, which *BEM* claims to have unearthed and formulated. This might suggest, for example, that, although some traditions have held the Lord's supper while others have celebrated the Mass, they have all shared certain fundamental beliefs about the observance (called 'the eucharist' by *BEM*) which are here spelt out. This might be described as a 'highest common factor' approach to ecumenical agreement, but the 'highest' turns out to be disappointingly low. To continue with our example, while all churches will agree that this observance was instituted by Christ, they have not historically ('through the ages') agreed even on the central point that both bread and wine should be received by all the participants.

In fact, this first question put to the churches by Faith and Order raises two further questions, which may be stated with much greater clarity. First, what is the right path to ecumenical concord? In terms of the two possible interpretations discussed in the preceding paragraphs, is it to fuse together in some all-embracing whole the beliefs of all the separate church traditions, so that in the resulting amalgam each tradition can acknowledge its own convictions, whatever else the amalgam may contain, or is it to pare away the idiosyncrasies of each distinctive tradition until one arrives at a common core, underlying and overlaid by the accretions that differentiate the traditions from each other?

An evangelical evaluation would find each of these approaches wanting. It would note that the *BEM* text is part of Faith and Order's long-term project 'Towards the Common Expression of the Apostolic Faith Today'. The second further question provoked by the enquiry about 'the faith of the Church through the ages' is whether this is the proper starting-point or standard of reference for reaching 'an expression of the apostolic faith today'. It seems to imply without further investigation that 'the Church through the ages' has preserved the faith of the apostles. It begs the question of apostolic scripture and ecclesiastical tradition. As we shall see, although *BEM* provides encouraging evidence of a stronger biblical commitment in ecumenical theology, at some points it remains disturbingly captive to non-apostolic tradition. It must be the responsibility of evangelical Christians to subject *BEM* to a stringently scriptural critique.

Text and Commentary

The three statements are each divided into numbered paragraphs. References will be given to these and not to page numbers. Each of the statements is quite separate from the others. Nothing (other than the covers!) holds them together. The doctrine of the church which must undergird any doctrine of sacraments and ministry is accessible, if at all, solely to the eye of the detective. There is scarcely any cross-referencing between the three sections. Consequently they may validly be assessed independently. In the comments that follow it will be argued that the sections on baptism and eucharist, although broadly parallel in structure, differ markedly in theological flavour.

Alongside several of the paragraphs of the main text are added commentary paragraphs. While the former demonstrate 'the major areas of theological convergence', the latter 'either indicate historical differences that have been overcome or identify disputed issues still in need of further research and reconciliation' (p. ix). This implies that the commentaries do not enjoy the status of the text itself. It may also imply that what is said in them has been less carefully researched than what is said in the text. It is certainly the case that the commentaries, especially in the ministry section, contain some quite tendentious and even patently erroneous statements.

Baptism

Divergence of baptismal practice has proved one of the hardest nuts for the ecumenical movement to crack. Very few church unions have brought together the believer-baptizing (credobaptist) and the infant-baptizing (paedobaptist); although one such is the United Reformed Church in Britain, which has congregations in Scotland. In Commentary 12 but not in the main text, *BEM* holds out the example of such churches, which 'regard as equivalent alternatives for entry into the Church both a pattern whereby baptism in infancy is followed by later profession of faith and a pattern whereby believers' baptism follows upon a presentation and blessing in infancy', as worthy of wider consideration. It is surely the only viable goal if credobaptist and paedobaptist are to enter a united church.

Not surprisingly, *BEM* does not attempt to decide between the two forms of baptism. It suggests rather that both may be embraced within a single framework of understanding 'when it is recognized that both forms of baptism embody God's own initiative in Christ and express a response of faith made within the believing community' ('Baptism', Commentary 12). In a finely balanced statement baptism is declared to be 'both God's gift and our human response to that gift' ('Baptism', 8). This merits long and careful reflexion. If believers-baptists have tended to make baptism too much an occasion of public response, in the Church of Scotland in recent years, at least since the report of the Special Commission on Baptism in 1961, the opposite exaggeration has been abroad, partly because infant baptism has been taken as the norm, not only in practice but also theologically. The strength of *BEM* is to give balanced recognition to both the divine initiative ('The Holy Spirit is at work in the lives of people before, in and after their baptism', 'Baptism', 5) and the human reception and response—'The necessity of faith for the reception of the salvation embodied and set forth in baptism is acknowledged by all churches' ('Baptism', 8), 'The personal faith of the recipient of baptism and faithful participation in the life of the Church are essential for the full fruit of baptism ('Baptism', Commentary 12).

It is not *BEM*'s aim to argue the case for infant baptism. It merely asserts that, 'While the possibility that infant baptism was also practised in the apostolic age cannot be excluded, baptism upon personal profession of faith is the most clearly attested pattern in the New Testament documents' ('Baptism', 11). A leading Anglican evangelical expert in this field, Colin Buchanan, has criticized *BEM* for letting 'the foundations of infant baptism go by default'.[5] There is some force to this stricture; some reference to relevant Old Testament material would have been worthwhile. But the sentence quoted above is a fair statement of the situation. It remains an open question whether infants were baptized in the earliest decades of the church. The real case for paedobaptism is a (biblical-) theological one, not a (biblical-) historical one.

Paedobaptists would have a greater chance of a meeting of minds with credobaptists if this were taken more seriously. In other respects, also, the *Baptism* part of the Lima report is to be welcomed for its biblical character. For example, 'one Lord, one faith, one baptism, one God and Father of us all' (Eph. 4.4-6) is cited correctly in connexion with 'our common baptism ('Baptism', (6)), not invoked improperly as a self-evident proof-text against re-baptism, as happened in recent debates in the Church of Scotland. At the same time, the nervousness surrounding this question is reflected in one of the few careless statements in this

---

[5] Colin Buchanan, *ARCIC and Lima on Baptism and Eucharist* (Grove Worship Series, 86; Bramcote, 1983), p. 6. At the same time he recognizes 'the widespread reaction against infant baptism' (p. 8). See n. 13 below.

section of *BEM*: 'Any practice which which might be interpreted as "re-baptism" must be avoided' ('Baptism', 13)—'interpreted by whom?'[6]

BEM on baptism is sufficiently biblical to question 'how a further and separate rite can be interposed between baptism and admission to communion' ('Baptism', Commentary, 14(b)). In so far as it allows for laying-on-of-hands or chrismation (anointing), it seems to envisage them solely as elements of the occasion of baptism itself ('Baptism', 14, 19). There is some New Testament evidence that may support this view. What is clear is that a separate later rite of confirmation or admission to communion is no more than a church-made observance, and ought not to be regarded as on a par with, or even more important than, infant baptism. Although *BEM* takes no stance on the admission of children to communion, it is right to suggest that 'Those churches which baptize children but refuse them a share in the eucharist before such a rite may wish to ponder whether they have fully appreciated and accepted the consequences of baptism' ('Baptism', Commentary, 14).

BEM's account of 'The Meaning of Baptism' ('Baptism', 2-7) is largely an uncontroversial presentation in terms of the different images used in the New Testament—participation in Christ's death and resurrection ('Baptism', 3), conversion, pardon and cleansing ('Baptism', 4), the gift of the Spirit ('Baptism', 5), incorporation into Christ's body ('Baptism', 6), the sign of the kingdom ('Baptism', 7). Ample scriptural references are given in these paragraphs. Nevertheless, acute questions have been raised about their affirmations, which appear to speak both of meaning and of efficacy, as though every baptism invariably conferred the benefits spelt out here. The response of the Baptist Union of Scotland to *BEM* makes this point very forcibly,[7] and Colin Buchanan draws attention to the ambiguity: 'There has to be a *credibility* to our statements on baptism, and the high-sounding and marvellous claims of [this section] can only be sustained by hedging their unqualified appearance with some qualifications about the conditions under which baptism is truly efficacious.'[8] In fact he believes that these qualifications are provided in the following paragraphs on 'Baptism and Faith' ('Baptism', 8-10), from which we have quoted above. 'Personal commitment is

---

[6] Buchanan, *ARCIC and Lima*, p. 7 n. 1, suggests for those who 'have already received infant baptism, and yet long for the attractiveness of the plunge' an 'opportunity for renewal of baptismal vows (even, if desired, with water—even submersion in water)'. This sounds to me very much like re-baptism. It is at least open to being interpreted as such. Similarly in some parts of the Church of Scotland admission to communicant status (confirmation) has functioned virtually as a dry re-baptism. The whole issue has yet to receive full examination.

[7] Max Thurian (ed.), *Churches Respond to BEM*, vol. III (Faith and Order Paper, 135; Geneva, 1987), pp. 230-45, at p. 234.

[8] Buchanan, *ARCIC and Lima*, p. 5.

necessary for responsible membership in the body of Christ... Baptism is related not only to momentary experience, but to life-long growth into Christ... As they grow in the Christian life of faith, baptized believers demonstrate that humanity can be regenerated and liberated' ('Baptism', 8-10). When the statements on 'The Meaning of Baptism' are taken within the context of the *Baptism* section as a whole, they cannot be read as favouring any notion of the automatic conferral of new life, whether on infants or believers.

At the same time, as the Scottish Baptist Union comments, the report provides no basis for answering questions such as 'If faith is necessary for the...wholeness of baptism where does that leave infant baptism in and of itself where such faith does not follow?'[9] It is important to affirm in response that this is a question which evangelical paedobaptists take with utmost seriousness. Faith and Order discussions consequent upon *BEM* must also face it squarely.

A note about the use of sacramental language may be in place at this point. Modern evangelical theology has often spoken of baptism (and also communion) as *symbolizing* new life in Christ. It has preferred to speak in terms of signification or even representation rather than of baptism actually effecting what it signifies. Although the Lima document refers to baptism several times as a sign ('of new life through Jesus Christ' ['Baptism', 2]; 'of our common discipleship' ['Baptism', 6]; 'of the kingdom of God and of the life of the world to come' ['Baptism', 7]), it commonly uses realist language, as though baptism confers what it signifies. Such a way of speaking about the Christian sacraments is more in line with the usage of the New Testament (cf. Acts 2.38, 1 Peter 3.21, Romans 6.3) and of the Reformers than is our more recent evangelical tradition. It should not be taken to imply baptism's automatic efficacy. Rather it indicates that when baptism is administered in accordance with the command and intention of Christ (a requirement which, in the case of infant baptism, includes 'only to the children of believers'), we should have no doubt that God's promises are indeed fulfilled.

Finally we must ask whether *BEM* is likely to promote the mutual recognition of baptism between paedobaptists and credobaptists. For Scotland the prospects are not hopeful. The Baptist Union's response identifies their problem with infant baptism as not its indiscriminate administration but its lack of biblical warrant, although at one point they say, 'We are not convinced that infant baptism cannot be excluded. According to our reading of the New Testament we think it was excluded'.[10] This at least leaves room for common biblical study on the problem.

---

[9] Thurian (ed.), *Churches Respond*, vol. III, p. 234.
[10] Thurian (ed.), *Churches Respond*, vol. III, pp. 234, 233.

The position which *BEM* seems to be feeling towards can be expressed thus: there is not a great deal of difference between the practice of infant baptism followed by Christian nurture leading to personal profession of faith, and the practice of infant dedication followed by Christian nurture leading to baptism on profession of faith.[11] While *BEM* does not articulate such an understanding in so many words, it implies it in Commentary 12, which has been partly quoted above. 'A rediscovery of the continuing character of Christian nurture may facilitate the mutual acceptance of different initiation practices.'

In order to encourage movement towards this kind of understanding, *BEM* urges practitioners of both patterns of baptism to reconsider aspects of their practice. To paedobaptists it warns against 'apparently indiscriminate' administration ('Baptism', 16, Commentary 21(b)). Greater realism would have deleted 'apparently' and spoken also of a misguided generosity in baptismal administration.

Paedobaptists have perhaps still to take seriously to heart that malpractice at this level prejudices a central aspect of baptismal theology—the necessity of faith—as applied to infant baptism. Infant-baptists are also urged to give greater importance to the post-baptismal nurture of children ('Baptism', 16).

Credobaptists, on the other hand, are asked to give more visible expression to 'the fact that children are placed under the protection of God's grace' ('Baptism', 16). The comments of the Baptist Union of Scotland on this point are disappointing.[12] They fail to give adequate regard to what remains the deepest objection that can be raised against the baptism of believers only—viz., the uncertainty in which the young children of believers are left. Do they, or do they not, belong to the Lord and to his body, the household of faith? It is on this front that any sequel to *BEM* must focus its attention.

Credobaptists could also have justifiably been challenged by Lima to reconsider their theology of baptism. Within the Church of Scotland serious evaluation of the case for believers' baptism has tended to baulk and refuse early on in the course and to be thrown, perhaps rather over-sensitively, by a presentation of baptism as the candidate's public witness. As the comments of the Scottish Baptist Union acknowledge, 'We have been in danger of letting our people treat [baptism] more as a confessional device than an act full of much richer symbolic meaning.'[13]

---

[11] Cf. R.G. Wilburn, 'The One Baptism and the Many Baptisms', *Theology Today* 22 (1965–66), pp. 59-83, at p. 81.

[12] Thurian (ed.), *Churches Respond*, vol. III, p. 235.

[13] Thurian (ed.), *Churches Respond*, vol. III, p. 236. The Methodist Geoffrey Wainwright, *Christian Initiation* (London, 1969), pp. 82-83, has argued that 'at bottom the Baptist pattern offers the best possibility of a unified initiation complex in which the

Nothing would advance mutual understanding more than an unambiguous recognition by credobaptists of baptism as embodying God's own initiative in Christ.

Controversial disciplinary cases within the Church of Scotland in recent years have hindered ecumenical rapprochement over baptism. In particular they have made the paedobaptist Kirk more inflexible at a time when other paedobaptist churches have been learning to live with, and even encourage, greater flexibility in practice. 'It *is* fully possible for those who believe in infant baptism not to insist on giving it in every instance, and Anglican parishes, for instance often include families where parents have chosen *not* to bring their children to baptism in infancy.'[14] The Church of Scotland, however, has experienced no 'baptismal reform movement'. Elsewhere, in France, Switzerland and the USA, for example, Reformed churches have made regular provision for the deferral of baptism. The Kirk's response to *BEM* should include a declaration of a readiness to allow, with approval, deferral of the baptism of children of believers, at the latter's request, as an interim step towards the mutual recognition of different baptismal practices.

Movement along these lines in Scotland would need to be reciprocated. *BEM* implies that the Baptists in the Faith and Order Commission went along with its acceptance of both forms of baptism. Colin Buchanan's question is very much to the point: 'Is it possible that the Faith and Order conversations include rather ecumenically and flexibly minded Baptists [wets?!], who are not quite as representative of the general run of Baptists on this point as the optimism of the report suggests?'[15]

Nevertheless Scottish Baptists, in response to Lima, have acknowledged their 'need to listen again to the arguments that would justify infant baptism on the basis of the biblical record', and 'to decide quite definitely how [they] regard infant baptism—as a denial of Apostolic faith and practice, as an historical aberration, as an inadequate though justifiable alternative to believers' baptism'.[16] The readiness to go on asking such questions should encourage paedobaptists to face up to equally searching questions themselves.

Eucharist

The *Eucharist* section of *BEM,* although in structure broadly parallel to *Baptism,* is noticeably longer. More significantly, it displays less evidence of the disciplined control of theology by the word of God in scripture,

---

divine and the human roles in the work of salvation are suitably expressed', and has suggested modifications to enable it to become the ecumenical pattern of the future.

[14] Buchanan, *ARCIC and Lima,* p. 6.
[15] Buchanan, *ARCIC and Lima,* p. 7.
[16] Thurian (ed.), *Churches Respond,* vol. III, p. 236.

and consequently greater signs of being the prey of confessional ecclesiastical interests. It also tends to overstate the role of the eucharist within the whole economy of the Christian faith. It could be accused of pan-eucharisticism.

The designation 'eucharist' is not in common use in Protestantism, and some recognition of this fact ought to have been included in *BEM*. The report occasionally uses other names, such as 'the Lord's Supper' ('Eucharist', 28, 30), and no doctrinal significance should be read into its dominant use of 'eucharist'. This term has a long history in the churches, and has become the standard title of the supper in technical discussion. As we shall see, this part of *BEM* shows a particular proclivity for technical language.

'The Meaning of the Eucharist' is presented under five headings: Thanksgiving to the Father, Anamnesis or Memorial of Christ, Invocation of the Spirit, Communion of the Faithful, Meal of the Kingdom. The second and third of these require special discussion, but we must note that, although the order may seem strange (the last two should surely come before the third), most of these sections couple some biblically-based material with a tendency to exaggerate the importance of the sacrament. For example, under 'The Eucharist as Communion of the Faithful' we are told that 'It is in the eucharist that the community of God's people is fully manifested. Eucharistic celebrations always have to do with the whole Church, and the whole Church is involved in each local eucharistic celebration' ('Eucharist', 19). At one level this is patently untrue for all those churches who do not admit to communion baptized infants who are acknowledged to be members of Christ and his church. At another level it seems unnecessary theological bombast, and in fact is more appropriately predicated of baptism, where it is not said in *BEM*.[17]

The same section declares that 'The eucharist embraces all aspects of life' ('Eucharist', 20), and 'eucharistic liturgy is near to the concrete and particular situations of men and women' ('Eucharist', 21). Not only is the latter no more than a half-truth or a pious aspiration, but if *BEM*'s detailed prescriptions for the celebration of the eucharist are followed ('Eucharist', 27—twenty-one elements are listed!), it is even less likely to become the communion meal of Christian people in places of residence, work and recreation, i.e., the *real* 'concrete and particular situations of men and women'. The alert reader will easily collect other overblown statements about what eucharist is and does. Their tenour is bound to seem strange against the background of the experience of churches like the Church of Scotland which, in most congregations, observe the

---

[17] The *Ministry* section of *BEM* several times refers to the congregation as 'the (local) eucharistic community' ('Eucharist', 20, 24, 27, 30). This bears precious little relation to reality for many churches, not least the Church of Scotland, and is open to the same criticism.

communion less than once a month and perhaps only a handful of times a year. If all of *BEM*'s highflown rhetoric about the eucharist were true, the Kirk could hardly have survived as Christ's church at all!

The report naturally recommends that the eucharist take place at least every Sunday ('Eucharist', 31). What it does not explore is the relation between frequency of observance and the importance assigned to the ordinance. The weekly Lord's supper of the Brethren and many Baptist churches does not mean that they assign it a higher value than does the quarterly practice of the Church of Scotland. Indeed, if the criterion is the full manifestation of God's people in the eucharist (see above), then the Kirk's quarterly communion comes nearer to the ideal than either the Anglicans' traditional 8 a.m. celebration for the zealous remnant or the Roman Catholics' frequent masses at hourly intervals.

If frequency is of great significance, then the circumstances of many 'union-and-readjustment' congregations in the Church of Scotland and the Church of England must lead us to question the 'clerical captivity' of the eucharist. *Weekly frequency for some congregations will require that others than ordained ministers be authorized to preside.* BEM does not broach this issue, merely reporting that 'In most churches, [Christ's] presidency is signified by an ordained minister' ('Eucharist', 29). If we took the New Testament more seriously, it would scarcely be a question of the first order.

BEM's account of the meaning of the eucharist is set out in a Trinitarian pattern, with the second part its character as *anamnesis* or memorial of Christ. 'The biblical idea of memorial as applied to the eucharist refers to [the] present efficacy of God's work [in Christ] when it is celebrated by God's people in a liturgy' ('Eucharist', 5). Behind this and similar statements lies the kind of understanding of biblical terms for 'remember, memory' which was developed partly in the now-discredited 'biblical theology' movement and partly in the liturgical movement represented by scholars like Gregory Dix. It sought to assert that *anamnesis* denoted more our reminding God than our own remembering, more the making present of the past than the remembrance or commemoration of it, and hence the actualization of the sacrifice of the cross in the sacrament itself. Although biblical scholars would no longer endorse such an interpretation without major qualifications, its influence lingers on. As Colin Buchanan comments, Lima gives 'an odd air of purporting to say something terribly important on this front', although in the event, in his judgement, *anamnesis* is not loaded with offensive doctrinal constructions in *BEM*.[18]

---

[18] Buchanan, *ARCIC and Lima*, p. 14. He detects 'a slowly growing doubt' among theologians about *anamnesis* as 'a good wooden horse for importing, into the scriptures and into the liturgy, ideas of eucharistic sacrifice which derive from the Middle Ages or the nineteenth century or the wit of contemporary man' (p. 13).

I find the whole section on *anamnesis* (why not use a good honest English word instead?) somewhat exaggerated, with unacceptable implications at some points:

1. The report relates *anamnesis* and intercession in such a way as to suggest that both are linked in a single address to God ('Eucharist', 8-9).[19]

2. Commentary 8 declares that 'It is in the light of the significance of the eucharist as intercession that references to the eucharist in Catholic theology as "propitiatory sacrifice" may be understood. The understanding is that there is only one expiation, that of the unique sacrifice of the cross, made actual in the eucharist and presented before the Father in the intercession of Christ and of the Church for all humanity.' Although this is not part of the main text, its appearance is disturbing. Such a salvage operation for a notion that embodies one of the worst ecclesiastical perversions of the Lord's supper should have no place in a report seeking 'Common Expression of the Apostolic Faith Today'.

3. 'Christ's mode of presence in the eucharist is unique' ('Eucharist', 13). Wherein this uniqueness consists is not further clarified in the main text of *BEM*, but the parallel Commentary paragraph records the churches' different understandings of the relation between the real presence of Christ in the eucharist and the bread and wine, without endorsing any particular understanding.[20] In fact the uniqueness of the mode of Christ's presence has no substance without the affirmation of one or other of these understandings, and ought to have been relegated to the Commentary where they are noted.

The third limb of the trinitarian meaning of the eucharist deals with the invocation of the Spirit, again presented in transliterated Greek as *epiklesis*. 'The whole action of the eucharist has an "epikletic" character because it depends upon the work of the Holy Spirit' ('Eucharist', 16). This is an odd statement, which is intelligible only as a half-unsuccessful attempt to break out of the confines of Catholic and Orthodox tradition. The question requires careful examination.

All Christians agree that the Holy Spirit is 'the One who makes the historical words of Jesus present and alive'. Therefore 'the Church prays

---

[19] Cf. 'Eucharist', Commentary 14, 'The eucharist is...a prayer addressed to the Father'.

[20] Almost accidentally, para. 32 says that 'Some churches stress that Christ's presence *in the consecrated elements* continues after the celebration' (my italics). The intended emphasis is probably on 'continues...', but in fact this is the only place in the report where Christ's presence *in* the eucharistic bread and wine is spoken of so precisely. The concern of the paragraph is with reservation (see below), and this unparalleled manner of relating Christ's presence to the bread and wine should not have been allowed to slip in almost casually in this way.

to the Father for the gift of the Holy Spirit in order that the eucharistic event may be a reality' ('Eucharist', 14). This is true of all the corporate acts of God's people, for example, preaching, prayer for the sick, evangelism and baptism. The church's whole life is dependent upon the Spirit.

But this does not lead us to talk about its *epikletic* character, because this would be to give priority to the secondary (prayer for the Spirit) over the primary (the gift of the Spirit). Rather we should speak of its spiritual or Pentecostal or pneumatic or pneumatological or charismatic character.

The Commentary to paragraph 14 reveals why the report majors on *epiklesis*. It comes out of traditions that relate the invocation of the Spirit to 'a special moment of consecration'. This is one of those occasions on which we have to resort to the Commentary to find out why something is in the text itself.

This interpretation is borne out by Commentary 15, which returns to 'the mystery of the real and unique presence of Christ in the eucharist. Some are content merely to affirm this presence without seeking to explain it. Others consider it necessary to assert a change wrought by the Holy Spirit and Christ's words, in consequence of which there is no longer just ordinary bread and wine but the body and blood of Christ.' Though less than explicit, this is sufficiently eloquent to give the game away.

The main text of paragraph 15 states that 'It is in virtue of the living word of Christ and by the power of the Holy Spirit that the bread and wine become the sacramental signs of Christ's body and blood'. Evangelical Christians have not been accustomed to using the language of 'becoming' in connection with the communion, but a moment's thought should indicate its appropriateness. By whatever words we relate the bread and wine to Christ's body and blood, all are agreed that *something* is true of the bread and wine of the eucharist which is not true of other bread and wine. At some point this particular bread and wine become something that they were not before, whether symbols or vehicles (a term used by Protestant Reformers) or embodiments of Christ's body and blood. So talk of 'becoming' is in general quite in place, although particular assertions about it may be found objectionable.

In order to arrive at a balanced evaluation of the *Eucharist* section of *BEM*, we must note certain welcome features:

1. There is no suggestion that a valid celebration of the eucharist depends upon the participation of a priest or minister possessing a special kind of ordination or standing in any episcopal or apostolic succession.

2. Conspicuous by their absence are terms like 'transubstantiation' and modern equivalents or substitutes such as 'transignification'. At the same time, as we have seen, the Commentary at more than one place is in effect talking about this Catholic doctrine.

3. No obvious reference to 'eucharistic sacrifice' appears in the report itself, as distinct from the Commentary. Paragraph 4, after speaking of the supper as the church's great 'sacrifice of praise', goes on to mention that 'the bread and wine, fruits of the earth and of human labour, are presented to the Father in faith and thanksgiving'. As it stands, this is not objectionable, but neither is it necessary. Thanksgiving, which is the theme of this part of the report, is easily enough made without presentation to the Father. (The reference to 'fruits of the earth and of human labour' falls into the error, here relatively harmless, of 'incidentalism', that is, failing to discern the difference between the substantial and the peripheral or accidental.)

4. In various ways the Lima text provides a more biblical account of communion than Reformed Christians have come to expect from ecumenical discussions involving Catholics, whether Roman, Orthodox or Anglican. There is a healthy emphasis on the communion as community meal. (By the way, no insistence on communion in both kinds is included. Is this now *invariable* Catholic practice? It would be a gross example of ecumenical selectivity if acceptance of *BEM* could co-exist with anything other than a full eating and drinking by all the participants.) The work of Christ, incarnate, crucified, risen and glorified, is set at the heart of the church's eucharistic worship. It is asserted that 'The celebration of the eucharist properly includes the proclamation of the Word' ('Eucharist', 12; cf. 27, and 3: 'The eucharist...always includes both word and sacrament'. Not only in its use of capitals does the report reveal some ambiguity about the place of preaching. Is it not part *of the sacrament*?)

It is therefore all the more regrettable that at the points noted above this second section of *BEM* should betray the heavy hand of Catholic and Orthodox preoccupations. Worst of all, perhaps, is an attempt, very near the end, to find room for the reservation of the elements, where, perhaps by careless drafting, it is by implication acceptable that some churches do not 'place the main emphasis on the act of celebration itself and on the consumption of the elements in the act of communion' ('Eucharist', 32).

Evangelicals will want to place on the agenda of Faith and Order some of the issues *BEM* does not tackle, not least the question of lay presidency. Indeed, this may be but one aspect of a biblically warranted concern to move in the opposite direction to *BEM*. Whereas this report, with its *anamnesis* and *epiklesis* and its long list of standard elements for the observance of the eucharist, seems to be moving towards a more complex, tradition-laden ecclesiasticization of the sacrament, evangelical churchmen will aspire after a greater biblical simplicity. In the circumstances in which many churches find themselves in the later twentieth century, if the Lord's supper is to become the weekly grace-meal of the Christian community, it will need to be released from many of the encumbrances of earlier, 'Christian' centuries.

Ministry

When approaching ecumenical statements on ministry, Presbyterian antennae are pre-sensitized to detect any insinuation of bishops, especially when produced, from the New Testament, magically, like rabbits out of a hat. A preoccupation with what *BEM* has to say about bishops, however understandable, would be unfortunate if it allowed us to ignore other concerns of the *Ministry* section, concerns that are of greater contemporary relevance, at least to the needs of the Church of Scotland, as well as biblically more pressing.

'The Calling of the Whole People of God' rightly comes in the van of this part of *BEM*. The doctrine of the church is prior to the doctrine of ministry. Before ever ordained ministry is mentioned, 'All members are called to discover, with the help of the community, the gifts they have received and to use them for the building up of the Church and for the service of the world to which the Church is sent' ('Ministry', 5). All this is well said. In seeking to overcome their differences about ordained ministry, 'the churches need to work from the perspective of the calling of the whole people of God' ('Ministry', 6). It is questionable whether Lima has succeeded in carrying through these fundamental insights of the opening paragraphs, but if the foundation is solidly laid, the superstructure can be remodelled subsequently.

In moving on to discuss 'The Church and the Ordained Ministry', the report stresses the interrelatedness of ordained and lay ministries. 'The ordained ministry has no existence apart from the community. Ordained ministers can fulfil their calling only in and for the community. They cannot dispense with the recognition, the support and the encouragement of the community' ('Ministry', 12). What is missing here is an awareness of the community's responsibility for (ordained and lay) ministry, which is firmly spelt out by John Tiller, the General Secretary of the Church of England's Advisory Council for the Church's Ministry. One of the two 'basic ideas' undergirding his proposals is that 'The local Church, as the Body of Christ in a particular place, should be responsible for undertaking the ministry of the Gospel in its own area'.[21]

Because it presents the ordained ministry as signifying 'the otherness of God's initiative' ('Ministry', 42; cf. 12) and the church's 'fundamental dependence on Jesus Christ' ('Ministry', 8; cf. 12), *BEM* will perpetuate the notion that ordained ministers come, like God and Christ, from outside the congregation, and will do little to encourage that

---

[21] John Tiller, *A Strategy for the Church's Ministry* (London, 1983), p. 48.

congregational assumption of responsibility for ministry (in other than financial terms!) which is so sorely needed in the Church of Scotland. It is a subtle but perilous step between recognizing that 'from the beginning, there were differentiated roles in the community' and that 'the Church has never been without persons holding specific authority and responsibility' ('Ministry', 9), and elevating the ordained ministry into something *sui generis*, not merely special among the ministries of the community as a whole but constitutive of it and hence of them (cf. 'Ministry', 8). That fateful step is taken by *BEM* in these paragraphs on 'The Church and the Ordained Ministry'.[22] Of the congregation's role in ordination, the report says only that 'By receiving the new minister..., [it] acknowledges the minister's gifts and commits itself to be open towards these gifts' ('Ministry', 44).

Hence it is not surprising that the rest of the *Ministry* section concentrates almost entirely on ordained persons. If our basic objectives are biblically determined, it is precisely this virtual identification between ministry and ordained personnel that has to be exposed and overthrown. Few tasks are more urgent for the contemporary church.

Three particular points illustrate what happens when the orientation is skewed in this way. Part of the responsibility of the ordained ministry is said to be 'celebrating the sacraments' ('Ministry', 13). Not at all! Celebrating the sacraments is the privilege and joy of God's people as a whole, and must not be usurped by the clergy alone. Secondly, we are also told that 'It is especially in the eucharistic celebration that the ordained ministry is the visible focus of the deep and all-embracing communion between Christ and the members of his body' ('Ministry', 14). This is even more offensive. Presidency—yes; but to ascribe to the ordained president such a role is millennia away from the New Testament, where bread and wine have this function and where presidency at the eucharist is never a matter of explicit concern (as Commentary 14 recognizes). Thirdly, *BEM* endeavours to justify the continued use of 'priest' to designate ordained ministers, again arrogating to an individual what belongs in the New Testament only to Christ and to the church as a whole ('Ministry', 17).[23] The Commentary 17 attests the unambiguous

---

[22] The report may be inconsistent on this crucial question. It is difficult to square para. 8 ('The ministry of such [ordained] persons...is constitutive for the life and witness of the Church') with Commentary (13), which asserts that the ordained ministry's tasks are not exclusive to it. 'Any member of the body may share in proclaiming and teaching the Word of God, may contribute to the sacramental life of the body.'

[23] Cf. Tiller, *Strategy*, p. 68. 'The most appropriate term to describe the whole ministry of the laity is "priestly service"'; E. Schweizer, *Church Order in the New Testament* (Studies in Biblical Theology, 32; London, 1961), p. 176: 'All the New Testament witnesses are sure of one decisive fact: official priesthood, which exists to conciliate and mediate between God and the community, is found in Judaism and

New Testament usage, but the force of tradition and custom prevented Faith and Order acting upon what biblical scholars have been saying for generations—indeed, ever since the Reformation.[24]

When the report comes to discuss the particular forms of the ordained ministry, it unequivocally declares that 'the New Testament does not describe a single pattern of ministry which might serve as a blueprint or continuing norm for all future ministry in Church' ('Ministry', 19; cf. 22, Commentary 11). At the same time, no recognition is given of the fact that in the New Testament and other early Christian writings 'presbyter' and 'bishop' are virtually interchangeable terms. This is obviously pertinent to the significance to be attached to the role of the bishop when the later differentiation of usage developed. The New Testament provides no basis for regarding bishops as a distinct 'order' from presbyters.

What *BEM* offers is a commendation to non-episcopal churches of episcopacy not as in any sense a theological necessity, nor as a guarantee of the church's unity or continuity in the apostolic tradition, but as a particularly appropriate sign and safeguard of these realities (cf. 'Ministry', 38). 'Churches without the episcopal succession...are asked to realize that the continuity with the Church of the apostles finds profound expression in the successive laying on of hands by bishops and that, though they may not lack the continuity of the apostolic tradition, this sign will strengthen and deepen that continuity' ('Ministry', 53(b)). At the same time episcopal churches are called to recognize 'both the apostolic content of the ordained ministry which exists in churches which have not maintained such succession and also the existence in these churches of a ministry of *episkopé* in various forms' ('Ministry', 53(a)).

Lima's advocacy of episcopacy to churches like the Church of Scotland is thus remarkably light on theology. If the ministry of *episkopé* is judged to be essential for the unity of the body ('Ministry', 23), it is a 'fact that the reality and function of the episcopal ministry have been preserved in many...churches [which have not retained the form of historic episcopate], with or without the title " bishop" ' ('Ministry', 37; cf. 24). The episcopal succession is commended chiefly because it serves, symbolizes and guards 'the continuity of the apostolic faith and communion' ('Ministry', 36), and in particular within that continuity provides for 'the orderly transmission of the ordained ministry' ('Ministry', 35; cf. 29).

---

paganism; but since Jesus Christ there has been only one such office—that of Jesus himself. It is shared by the whole Church, and never by one church member as distinct from others.'

[24] Commentary 17 is not strictly accurate in saying that 'In the early Church the terms "priesthood" and "priest" came to be used to designate the ordained ministry and minister *as presiding at the eucharist*' (my italics). They are often used without that specific reference in patristic texts.

This continuity in the apostolic tradition is understood in an historical sense. Commentary 36 even ascribes to Clement of Rome, who flourished in the late first century, an interest in 'the means whereby the *historical* continuity of Christ's presence is ensured in the Church thanks to the apostolic succession'.[25] Not only is this a quite erroneous interpretation of Clement, but it is also theologically repugnant, if not nonsensical. Whatever can 'the historical continuity of Christ's presence in the Church' mean? In any case, the churches of the Reformation are likely to place much less weight on historical continuity than on *fidelity* to the faith of the apostles. After all, episcopacy does not have a very impressive track record as an agent of the historical continuity of the apostolic tradition, nor in the present day has its performance in safeguarding the apostolic faith been at all noteworthy.[26]

Faith and Order's difficulty is in finding secure grounds for asking non-episcopal churches to think seriously about episcopacy. It would be wiser to stick to the undeniable—that the threefold pattern of ministry became universal at an early stage in the church's history (cf. 'Ministry', 22), has survived unbroken in the orthodox East, and was universal in the West until the Reformation, and that union with the major episcopal churches in the present is inconceivable without the adoption of episcopacy by the other churches. The weight of the argument would then rest on two points: the primitive origin of episcopacy and its wide extension in space and time (with no claim for its performance in safeguarding the apostolic faith), and the importance assigned to reunion as a goal for the churches.

On these two points evangelical churchmen will be found to espouse a range of varying viewpoints, as no doubt too will churchmen of other theological persuasions. What evangelicals are unlikely to respond to with any enthusiasm is the proposition that episcopal succession is 'a sign of the apostolicity of the life of the whole Church' ('Ministry', 38), for it

---

[25] Clement's interest in succession from the apostles operates on a much humbler level, that of ensuring that properly appointed presbyter-bishops are not deposed without cause. The same Commentary paragraph also misconstrues Clement's younger contemporary, Ignatius of Antioch, who shows no awareness of 'apostolic succession'. In Ignatius' letters, the bishop is correlated to God the Father, and the deacons to Christ, while the presbyters parallel the apostles. A phrase like 'the *actual* manifestation in the Spirit of the apostolic community' again verges on the unintelligible.

[26] *BEM* makes no allusion to that role of the bishop which some in the Church of Scotland find attractive, in the pastoral care of the clergy. This proposal raises a further question: if bishops minister to other ordained ministers, who ministers to bishops? And so on... The more pivotal a particular form of ministry becomes, e.g., of bishops in relation to clergy as suggested, the less safely can that form of ministry itself be left uncared for and unlimited. The history of the papacy furnishes ample illustration of this point.

too obviously flies in the face of the history they treasure from the Reformation onwards. It may be significant that when the Lima document speaks about apostolic tradition in the church it never once mentions the apostolic scriptures ('Ministry', 34). Others have noted that the whole report contains not a single positive recognition of the witness of the Reformation.[27]

At an earlier stage in the *Ministry* section, *BEM* declares that 'The ordained ministry should be exercised in a personal, collegial and communal way' ('Ministry', 26). The unpacking of this statement in the rest of the paragraph would lead most Presbyterians to identify these three dimensions naturally with 'the minister', the Kirk Session and the congregation—if, that is, the ordained eldership may count as 'a college of ordained ministers'. Parallels are not hard to seek in other denominations. A Baptist church, for example, will have a college of deacons as well as the regular church meeting of members. The Commentary (26) gives a different interpretation, for it suggests that such 'an appreciation of these three dimensions' lay behind the affirmation of the Lausanne Faith and Order Conference in 1927 that episcopal, presbyteral and congregational elements must all have 'an appropriate place in the order of life of a reunited Church'. Despite the Commentary, the text of *BEM* at this point seems to have the congregation in view, although the report's use of 'community' is sometimes ambiguous.

The following paragraph puts the application to the congregation beyond doubt. 'At the level of the local...community there is need for an ordained minister acting within a collegial body. Strong emphasis should be placed on *the active participation of all members in the life and decision-making of the community*' ('Ministry', 27, my italics). If there is a word from the Lord for the Church of Scotland in the *Ministry* section of *BEM*, it is surely this. Most of the Kirk makes *no* provision for the active participation of the membership in the decision-making of the community, except episodically, when a minister has to be elected, and perhaps perfunctorily at the annual congregational meeting. Is the Church of Scotland capable of facing up to this challenge from Faith and Order? It is arguable that the Church's ability to respond effectively to the task of re-evangelizing Scotland, whether within or without church union, will depend far more on changes at this level than on restructuring at the top.

---

[27] *BEM*, 'Ministry', 19, merely says that 'At some points of crisis in the history of the Church, the continuing functions of ministry were in some places and communities distributed according to structures other than the predominant threefold pattern',

CHAPTER 23

The Lima Report:
Baptism and *Eucharist* Compared

By any standards the World Council of Churches' (WCC) Faith and Order Report on *Baptism, Eucharist and Ministry* (*BEM* for short) is a noteworthy document. Finally approved at a conference in Lima early in 1982, it harvests the fruits of over half a century's inter-confessional study since the first Faith and Order Congress at Lausanne in 1927. Full participation by Roman Catholics and members of some other churches not belonging to the WCC has provoked the claim that Lima saw 'the most comprehensive theological and ecclesiastical forum in Christendom', at least since the Second Council of Nicaea in 787.

The Report is presented as attesting 'a remarkable degree of agreement' on three of the most contentious issues of faith and order and with the aim of becoming 'part of a faithful and sufficient reflection of the common Christian Tradition on essential elements of Christian communion' (p. ix). It is commended for the widest possible discussion among the churches. My local information suggests that no ecumenical document has ever received such widespread attention. *BEM* requests each church to indicate the consequences it can draw from its study of the text for 'its relations and dialogues with other Churches, particularly with those Churches which also recognize the text as an expression of the apostolic faith' (p. x).

BEM consists of three separate statements, each comprising a main text which 'demonstrates the major areas of theological convergence', and parallel comments on some paragraphs which 'either indicate historical differences that have been overcome or identify disputed issues still in need of further research and reconciliation' (p. ix). These three sections are not integrated with each other. There is no cross-reference between them. Unlike the reports of ARCIC, which appeared at intervals between 1971 and 1982, no attempt has been made to unify the three statements within a single theologically cohesive framework. This is particularly apparent with *Baptism* and *Eucharist*. Although these two sections are arranged in parallel, with each containing chapters on institution, meaning and celebration (*Baptism* has two others: 'Baptism and Faith' and 'Baptismal Practice'), some surprising differences are discernible between theirs. In what follows references are to the numbered paragraphs of each section.

The first contrast is that *Eucharist* is far more explicitly sacramental than *Baptism*. In *Baptism*, it is only incidentally that the reader learns that baptism is a sacrament at all. It is spoken of as a sacrament only once in the text, in the very last sentence ('Baptism', 23).

Otherwise the word occurs solely in 'Baptism', Commentary 13, in an unobtrusively routine manner. The first assertion about 'the meaning of baptism' is that 'baptism is the sign of new life through Jesus Christ ('Baptism', 2). Similar uses of 'sign' recur. 'Baptism is a sign and seal of our common discipleship' ('Baptism', 6). 'It is a sign of the Kingdom of God and of the life of the world to come' ('Baptism', 7). Indeed there is a certain freedom in the use of the word 'sign'. 'Christians differ in their understanding as to where [in baptism] the sign of the gift of the Spirit is to be found' ('Baptism', 14). 'Mutual recognition of baptism is acknowledged as an important sign and means of expressing the baptismal unity given in Christ' ('Baptism', 15). Nowhere is baptism expounded in explicitly sacramental terms.

Eucharist, by contrast, begins its account of 'the meaning of the Eucharist' with the affirmation that 'The Eucharist is essentially the sacrament of the gift which God makes to us in Christ through the power of the Holy Spirit' ('Eucharist', 2). Indeed, in the preceding paragraph on the institution it has already twice been spoken of as a 'sacramental meal' ('Eucharist', 1). Thereafter, use of the term is frequent. The eucharist is declared to be 'the sacrament of the unique sacrifice of Christ' ('Eucharist', 8) and 'the sacrament of the body and blood of Christ, the sacrament of his real presence' ('Eucharist', 13), 'the bread and the wine become the sacramental signs of Christ's body and blood' ('Eucharist', 15), and God's people share in this its 'new sacramental meal' ('Eucharist', 31). (Some confusion is caused by the assertion 'the Eucharist...always includes *both word and* sacrament' ['Eucharist', 3, my italics]. It is, it seems, both sacrament and more than sacrament.)

The noteworthy feature in this first contrast is the reticence amounting almost to silence about the sacramental character of baptism. Perhaps this is simply an accidental quirk of drafting with no further significance. It may, however, be linked to a further identifiable difference.

Secondly, *Baptism* keeps closer to the New Testament than *Eucharist*. Not only do we find Ephesians 4.4-6 ('one Lord, one faith, one baptism, one God and Father of us all') correctly used as a witness to 'our common baptism' ('Baptism', 6) (rather than abused as so often as a knock-down proof text against re-baptism), but infant baptism is introduced with a historically proper reserve: 'While the possibility that infant baptism was also practised in the apostolic age *cannot be excluded*, baptism upon personal profession of faith is the most clearly attested pattern in the New Testament documents' ('Baptism', 11, my italics). Moreover baptism as 'incorporation into the body of Christ' is taken with sufficient seriousness to cast doubt upon any 'further and separate rite...interposed between baptism and admission to communion' ('Baptism', Commentary 14(b)). Although anointing or chrismation and laying on of hands are referred to more than once ('Baptism', 14, Commentary 14(a), 19), the Report is clearly thinking of them as constituent parts of the single baptismal rite, and not as subsequent quasi-sacramental observances.

The extent to which *Baptism* is more disciplined by scripture than *Eucharist* is most easily demonstrated by noting some of the contents of the latter. The end of 'Eucharist' 13 contains a clear allusion to 1 Corinthians 11.29 ('discern the body') in a sense which would surely not command the assent of most contemporary exegetes: 'All agree that to discern the body and blood of Christ [in the eucharist], faith is required.' Also included is a whole section on the 'epikletic' character of the eucharist ('Eucharist', 14-18) for which no New Testament support is adduced, and another section on its 'anamnetic' character (if we may take a leaf out of *BEM*'s own book in adopting this form) which affirms a fulsome account of the 'biblical idea of memorial as applied to the Eucharist' with next to no biblical basis ('Eucharist', 5-13). In general *Eucharist* is less generously supplied with biblical references than Baptism. Moreover, 'The Meaning of the Eucharist' ('Eucharist', 2-26) seems to be deliberately structured on a trinitarian pattern. No such dogmatic shape is imposed on 'The Meaning of Baptism' ('Baptism', 2-7), which is organized around the salient New Testament images for baptism.

Thirdly, *Baptism* is more modest in its claims for baptism than *Eucharist* is for the eucharist. The middle section of *BEM* suffers from what one can call pan-eucharisticism. It succumbs to the temptation to oversell its subject. For example, the Report affirms that 'it is in the Eucharist that the community of God's people is fully manifested' ('Eucharist', 19). But can this bald assertion hold true for the majority of churches in which children do not take part in the Lord's supper, by no means all of them credobaptist (believers-baptist) churches, whose refusal to baptize infants may reflect ambivalence about their place within the people of God? Again, 'eucharistic liturgy is near to the concrete and particular situations of men and women' ('Eucharist', 21). Does this affirm much more than a half-truth? Would it not be much truer if the eucharist were released from its clerical captivity to be shared more freely in homes, places of work etc.—the *real* 'concrete and particular situations of men and women'? 'The world...is present in the whole Eucharistic celebration' ('Eucharist', 23); but surely only in firstfruit, pledge or earnest, or in token, or in the concern of God's people. 'The very celebration of the Eucharist is an instance of the Church's participation in God's mission to the world' ('Eucharist', 25); but surely in most cases much less obviously than is a service of the word with unbelievers and outsiders fully welcomed without let or hindrance? Is it only the eucharist that 'brings into the present age a new reality which transforms Christians into the image of Christ' ('Eucharist', 26)? Does it really advance enlightened understanding to affirm that 'the Eucharist embraces all aspects of life' ('Eucharist', 20)? Finally, can it be credibly claimed that 'Christ's mode of presence in the Eucharist is unique' ('Eucharist', 13), independently of any insistence on a particular interpretation of the manner of that presence? The main text bases this assertion on the truth—which none will contest—of the words of Jesus: 'This is my body...my blood.' 'Eucharist', Commentary 13 recognizes differences in understanding Christ's presence in the supper. If all accept his real presence, this by no means implies a unique mode.

Indeed this strain of theological overkill leaves one wondering how churches, like the Church of England's sister national church north of the border, which for centuries have existed with communion no more often than once a quarter, have survived at all as churches or succeeded at all in mission to the world. By comparison *Baptism* is marked by an admirable restraint. In expounding the meaning of baptism, it confines itself in the main to paraphrase of biblical statements. Only once does it permit itself a more expansive utterance: 'Through the gifts of faith, hope and love, baptism *has a dynamic which* embraces the whole of life, extends to all nations, and anticipates the day when every tongue will confess...' ('Baptism', 7). *Eucharist*, one feels, would have omitted the words in italics.

Fourthly, *Baptism* is less prescriptive than *Eucharist*. This difference can be seen at a glance by comparing *Baptism* 20 and *Eucharist* 27, the two paragraphs which specify the basic elements expected in the celebration of each observance. *Baptism* lists six elements, *Eucharist* no fewer than twenty-one—including acts of praise at the beginning and at the end, preparation of the bread and wine, and 'the Amen of the whole community'. No doubt baptism has often been a shorter, less complex observance than the eucharist (although this would not hold for such an influential text from the primitive church as Hippolytus' *Apostolic Tradition*), but it is nevertheless surprising to find *Baptism* adopting a minimalist approach and *Eucharist* a maximalist one. This comment is not merely a statistical one. It points to the extent to which the communal meal of the early Christians has been a prey to the liturgical accretions of the centuries, and leads us on to the next contrast.

Fifthly, *Baptism* is less encumbered by the legacy of ecclesiastical tradition than *Eucharist*. *Baptism* grapples of course with the deep age-long divide in baptismal practice between paedobaptists and credobaptists, but does so in a sensitive manner which suggests how the gulf may be bridged within one overarching theological interpretation, even if not always within a single ecclesiastical communion. 'Baptism is both God's gift and our human response to that gift' ('Baptism', 8): a simple assertion holding together emphases too often sundered by theologies patterned one-sidedly on either paedobaptism or credobaptism. Furthermore, 'both forms of baptism embody God's own initiative in Christ and express a response of faith made within the believing community' ('Baptism', Commentary 12). As infant baptism is followed by nurture towards personal profession of faith, so believers' baptism is the fruit of nurture within the household of faith. If this approach succeeds, it does so by not sitting too close to the obsessions of the past, and by addressing sharp questioning challenges to both traditional positions.

Eucharist, on the other hand, is ever threatened with being overwhelmed by traditional preoccupations. A good example is paragraph 32 on reservation of the elements. 'Some Churches stress that Christ's presence in the consecrated elements continues after the celebration.' This already relates Christ's presence to the bread and wine ('*in* the consecrated elements') in a more precise way than has hitherto appeared in either text or commentary. It should not have been allowed to slip in here in this casual fashion. Other churches, the text continues, 'place the main emphasis on the act of celebration and on the consumption of the elements in the act of communion'. What measure of control by a sound eucharistic theology can *BEM* be credited with when it endeavours to accommodate the views of 'some Churches' that fail to 'place the main emphasis on the act of celebration'? Is it really adequate simply to exhort each church to 'respect the practices and piety of the others' on reservation? Is this not a theological cop-out, a surrender to traditional custom? Commentary 8 proposes a similar salvage operation for Catholic theology's 'propitiatory sacrifice'. While welcoming the substantial convergence on major issues, one would have hoped for greater theological courage in overcoming the past on others, in a document which comes out of a quest for the apostolic faith.

A more substantial matter is that of the *epiklesis* of the Spirit to which the Report devotes five paragraphs ('Eucharist', 14-18), two with commentary. The importance of the general role of the Spirit in the eucharist as in all communal acts of God's people should have been more clearly disentangled from age-old preoccupations with the moment of consecration. It is doubtful whether, without the latter, affirmation of the eucharist's special 'epikletic' character would really be warranted. This becomes clear in the following statement: 'The whole action of the Eucharist has an "epikletic" character because it depends upon the work of the Holy Spirit' ('Eucharist', 16), which tries to affirm the primary (the activity of the Spirit) in terms of the secondary (invocation). Why not speak more directly of the 'spiritual' or 'pneumatic' or 'pentecostal' or 'charismatic' character of the eucharist? It is noteworthy that *Baptism* can affirm the importance of the invocation of the Spirit for the celebration of baptism without getting caught up in technical 'epikletics' ('Baptism', 20).

To identify such differences between the baptismal and eucharistic sections of *BEM* is not of course to determine one's evaluation of them. Some may argue, for example, that *Baptism*'s preference for 'sign' rather than 'sacrament' is theologically neither here nor there, or that *Baptism* is somewhat lightweight theologically or biblically. Perhaps it should be faulted for not saying more about Christ's one baptism for sinners, or for not grasping more firmly the nettle of paedobaptism by considering relevant Old Testament material. Some students of *BEM* are likely to find *Eucharist* sophisticated and *Baptism* indecisive.

More to the point for present purposes is the question *why* such differences exist between the two sections. Perhaps an examination of earlier drafts might throw light on the matter, but it must be remembered that the vast majority of readers of *BEM* will look at nothing beyond the Report itself. It must be valid to assess the text of *BEM* on its own merits without further background inquiry. Even if separate working parties drafted the two sections, one assumes that their final form emerged from the scrutiny of a single body under the Faith and Order Commission.

Perhaps an explanation for the differences is to be sought, at least in part, in the contrasting positions of the two sacraments among the churches. Baptism presents a fundamental divergence of practice. One of the two standard patterns, believers' baptism, has normally been held to rule out the other pattern, infant baptism, in principle. Although some theological divergence may be found to underlie the divergence in practice, this need not be the case, if only because all paedobaptist churches administer some believers' baptisms, however infrequently. No church can afford to have a theology of baptism that excludes the baptism of believing converts. It is radical divergence in baptismal order rather than baptismal faith that constitutes such an unparalleled challenge to ecumenical advance. (It is surely quite conceivable that major divides will be bridged on central issues such as eucharist, ministry, authority and primacy before some credobaptist churches can be brought to recognize infant baptism.) Awareness of this circumstance may have marvellously clarified the minds of Faith and Order participants, kept them nose-down to simplicities and essentials and produced a statement marked by a commendable degree of realism.

From another angle, less is at stake with baptism than with eucharist. In no church does its administration theologically require an ordained person, let alone an ordained person with particular qualifications of priesthood or succession. Even if in practice baptism is nearly always administered by ordained clergy, it is not by definition a clerical preserve. To that extent it may be held not to matter so much, professionally speaking. The eucharist raises problems of a different kind. The divisions on this front lie much more in theology than practice. In the Lima Report there is no parallel in *Eucharist* to the paragraphs on 'Baptismal Practice'. It could be argued that the outward actions in the eucharist do not significantly vary between ecclesiastical traditions, but at the level of interpretation a great deal is at stake. *Eucharist*'s greater theoretical expansiveness may find its roots in the need to reconcile divergent understandings rather than divergent practices. The theological divide includes the question of who may preside at the eucharist. In eucharist, unlike baptism, the traditionally indispensable role of priestly officials is at issue. This question scarcely rears its head in *Eucharist* but features prominently in the *Ministry* section of *BEM*. (The inflation of *Eucharist* compared with *Baptism* is in fact further reinforced by *Ministry*, where baptism rates only a brief mention.) Such considerations, involving the professional importance of certain kinds of Christian ministers, may well have encouraged a more tenacious traditionalism in *Eucharist*. According to 'Ministry' Commentary 17, even the continued use of 'priest' as a title for Christian ministers depends on their eucharistic role. It is perhaps a further merit of *Baptism* that it has succeeded in avoiding this entanglement with *Ministry* that *Eucharist* has suffered. Progress may be possible on *Baptism* alone, but it is doubtful whether *Eucharist* can make headway except in tandem with *Ministry*.

Whatever the explanation for the differences this article claims to identify, one may ask whether the balance is right. Is eucharist in fact that much more important than baptism? Would one get that impression from reading the New Testament? Perhaps *BEM* cites a greater amount of New Testament material on baptism than eucharist simply because baptism loomed larger than eucharist in the New Testament churches. Issues of church life and Christian discipleship are in the New Testament more frequently and substantially handled in terms of baptism than of eucharist. In itself this is a remarkable fact, given the once-for-all character of baptism and the repeated observance of eucharist. The *Ministry* part of *BEM* four times refers to the congregation as 'the eucharistic community' ('Ministry', 20, 24, 27, 30). It is arguable that 'baptismal community' would be a designation more faithful to the self-awareness of the apostolic churches. For many denominations it must be a more adequate description of the congregation, for 'eucharistic community' omits baptized children not yet admitted to the Lord's table. Interbaptism thus deserves greater prominence in ecumenical discussion. It should at least be allowed to question whether it does not provide the best approach to intercommunion.

Chapter 24

Habitats of Infant Baptism

No factor is responsible for as much damage in the natural world as the loss or degradation of the habitats of flora and fauna. The effects of direct human intrusion, in hunting, poaching and overfishing, for example, are all too familiar to us. The same goes for atmospheric pollution, with its more indirect consequences. Less obvious often is the deterioration or destruction of habitats through changes such as the draining of marshland, the eradication of hedgerows, deforestation, innovations in agricultural techniques and the introduction, accidental or deliberate, of competing species.

Conservationists consequently devote great energies to safeguarding, rescuing, reinstating and improving habitats at risk. Nothing conduces so much to the flourishing of a plant or a mammal as its enjoyment of a healthy and adequate habitat. Conversely, the success of a rescue operation based on a breeding programme in captivity may in the long term depend on the restoration of a lost habitat in the wild.

The image of the habitat lends itself to a consideration of the setting or settings within which the baptism of infants most naturally belongs. Such an enquiry is suggested not least by the varied ecological history of the observance. Some of the habitats in which it has from time to time been naturalized have distorted or stunted its identity or viability. It may never have been an endangered species, but perhaps it might not be so widely rejected in some of the fastest growing sectors of world Christianity—the Pentecostal and Baptist, in particular—if it had been more frequently observed growing to its proper dimensions in its native environment.

Family and Parents

Infants do not bring themselves to baptism. That is almost invariably the responsibility of parents whose own Christian faith claims baptism for their newborn. Within the Reformed tradition to a distinctive degree, a set of convictions about the place of the believing family in the gathering of the people of God in accord with his covenant promise has furnished a standard warrant for conferring the sign of the new covenant on babies. We may therefore regard the Christian family as an essential habitat—the essential micro-habitat—of infant baptism. From this it follows that if the

Christian identity of the family or the integrity of the family itself is insecure, infant baptism will not thrive as it ought.

Ministers have long been used to baptizing the children of parents only one of whom is a believer—or at least is willing publicly to undertake to bring the child up 'in the nurture and admonition of the Lord'. Much more recent is the complex of pastoral problems presented by the swelling tides eroding the normative unit of the two-married-parents family in much of the western world. Should baptism be expected to bear fruit in the lives of infants of cohabiting unmarried parents? That is to say, is it appropriately given when the context which the Christian tradition has invariably held to be the God-assigned habitat for childbearing—the one-flesh union of marriage—is not operative?

The rapid growth of a massive aversion to marriage in large areas of decaying Christendom in the West has left the family an increasingly elusive entity. Government-led social policy cannot abandon the health of the family as an ideal, yet frequently is found defending it with a studious silence, or perhaps ambivalence, about marriage. It may even flinch from provoking charges of discrimination against single parents by suggesting that children fare best in a stable home made by two parents, even if they are unmarried. That infant baptism has suffered from this multi-factorial disturbance of its age-old family habitat is undoubted. The steep decline in the number of babies being brought for baptism (so steep in some Church of Scotland parishes that infant baptism has become so gravely endangered as to be almost extinct) has not a little to do with a sense that 'christening' is not for the unmarried mother or for partners living together but uncommitted to each other beyond the visible future. A confusion of popular instincts and traditional sentiments interacts with diverse pastoral policies of congregations and pastors. The outcomes are bound to vary enormously, yet rare will be the local church untouched by the huge waves of disaffection for marriage sweeping across society.

Must infant baptism continue to decline *pari passu* with the decline of the familial habitat? Reflection on the image of the habitat may suggest guidelines for responding to some of the dilemmas thrown up by changing social patterns. What if the overriding consideration in deciding whether baptism should be encouraged or conferred were the identification of a parental habitat in which the tender plant of baptism is most likely to take root and bear the promised fruit—that is, a life within the community of Christian faith? Such an approach might well lead to a responsible child-centred baptismal policy in preference to a formalistic insistence on the standing of the parents. The loving and firmly believing single mother is likely to offer a healthier habitat for her baby's baptism to flourish than married parents whose indifference to their child's Christian upbringing has been overborne only by grandparental pressure.

Habitat-focused questions along these lines encourage a forward-looking perspective on infant baptism, rather than a preoccupation with a baby's antecedents. They foster a proper concern with the future of the baptized child and with the realization of the potential of baptism, with a corresponding lessening of emphasis on the parents' (or parent's) status and the status of the newly baptized.

In fact, the rethinking of infant baptism that the changing face of parenting necessarily requires may contribute constructively to its liberation from its false domestication. Critics within and without the churches fault reactionary defences of the nuclear family on a number of grounds. One aspect of the historical ecology of paedobaptism in such a traditional context has been its reduction to an event in the life of the family, to the detriment of its locus in gospel and church. Its micro-habitat in the family circle has smothered it, so to speak, so that it scarcely seems to belong any longer to the local body of Christ as a sacrament of the gospel. The baptism may still take place in the congregation's normal Sunday worship, but its reception is preponderantly conditioned by accompaniments of family tradition, from the precious christening robe to the party for relatives from far and near. The familial reductionism of baby-baptism is even more marked if the minister is persuaded to administer it in a private gathering in home or hotel, or if parents and child travel back for it to the grandparents' congregation, in preference to the congregation in which the child's baptism must be 'improved' (as our forefathers used to say) week in, week out.

Part of the problem can be traced to many a church's bankruptcy of practice and imagination when it comes to celebrating baptism of its members' newborn. Why not a church party afterwards, instead of (or at least before) a family do? Does the congregation offer guidance on the selection of godparents where these have a role, or should it itself designate instead a suitable person to serve as a kind of baptismal guardian? New Testament baptismal vocabulary abounds with the imagery of clothing. Even if the renewed interest in immersion at paedobaptism is not taken on board—with the possibility of unclothing and reclothing in white, according to early church custom—baptism at any age is not a proper occasion for candidates (meaning etymologically 'those clothed in white') to be decked out in finery or fashion. Theologically this is wholly incongruous.

Confining infant baptism solely or predominantly to the habitat of the family—essential as that habitat must be—produces a stunted plant devoid of growth potential. Or perhaps more appropriately, baptism is thereby hybridized, into a celebration of birth (rather than of new birth in Christ), whose future extrapolation looks forward to other milestones in the child's development with not even a nominal counterpart in the church-grounded pilgrim's progress. The task of clawing back infant baptism from the choking luxuriance of familial custom must struggle against generations of assumption and practice. Paradoxical though it must seem, the task may benefit opportunistically from the demise of the hegemony of the two-married-parents family that the new millennium portends. The inherited shape of family life crumbles on all sides. As far as baptism is concerned, the disintegration may allow (we dare not put it higher than this) some recovery of its essentially ecclesial character. The church is the critical habitat for the vitality of infant baptism—and the family or parental context has significance only within the larger habitat.

Secularization and family decay are interrelated in complex ways. The latter will not provide the fortuitous opportunity hinted at in the previous paragraph if the former is given free rein with baptism. Traditionalism reinforced by secularism will denature baptism, transmuting it into a naming ceremony or a welcome-to-baby celebration or a commitment to responsible parenthood or some other innocent or worthy role—but all bereft of its core identity as incorporation into Christ. As fewer and fewer parents show any interest in this Christian baptism for their offspring, ministers experience the subtle temptation to tailor some lesser baptism to suit sub-Christian tastes. What is incontrovertibly already happening with weddings and funerals (popular songs instead of hymns, readings from any book but the Bible, prayers in theistic terms at best) will surely dumb down baptism too. This secular familial captivity of infant baptism will be resisted only if the indispensable habitat of responsible parenthood is not allowed to take complete possession of the plant. The baptism of newborn children is viable as familial event only when rooted in an unmistakeably ecclesial habitat.

The Local Community

Ministers of the word and sacraments of the gospel rightly sense a threat to their responsibility when tenacious family forces bid to determine how the baptism of its latest progeny shall be conducted. Even more threatening can be the pressure of the wider community's expectations. For baptism is uniquely a point at which popular attitudes to the church or 'religion' impinge upon ministerial roles. This is likely to be most true in countries with an established or officially national church, but probably obtains to some degree wherever a paedobaptist church has long had a paramount presence within its neighbourhood. In such a situation the custom of baptizing newborn babies commonly gathers around itself a body of widely-held understandings, hopes and fears. Often they will reflect the wisdom of popular religion (in part what an earlier generation called superstition), which may stand at some remove from the teaching of catechism, creed and confession. It finds expression, for example, in calling infant baptism 'christening' and in visceral convictions that without it the new life is somehow vulnerable or at risk, at least of missing out on some of the health, wealth and happiness that are otherwise everyone's birthright. Most readers will already have in mind local traditions that retail the potential deficit sooner or later of the baby that is not properly 'done', as the saying goes.

The vigour of this broader communal take on infant baptism often makes itself felt in the congregation's baptismal ministry through the conduit of the family—not always the parents, or solely the parents—of a newborn baby. In a paedobaptist context, there are solid biblical and theological grounds for reckoning seriously with the family, even if its quest for baptism for its newest member is driven by a somewhat debased notion of what it is all about. Part of the difficulty of dealing with such a situation rests precisely on the fact that the request reflects a generalized populist view of baby-baptism and that the church's response to the request is likely to be fed back in interaction with it. How infant baptism is handled easily becomes a test case for relations between the church and its feeder community. An unrestrictive provision of baptism on request will help to lubricate smooth church-community harmony, while a more restrictive approach may issue in a clash between inconsistent understandings of baptism, souring relations with more than one family.

Is the wider catchment area of a church one of the habitats in which infant baptism is meant to grow successfully? Among the complicating factors that frustrate a simple answer is the recognition that behind the dissonance between the church's view of baptism—as expressed, for example, in its order of service for baptism—and communal views lies normally a hangover from an earlier age when the majority of the population had their children baptized more or less as a matter of routine. To state the issue thus is not to pass judgement but simply to facilitate understanding. When the civil and the ecclesial communities were virtually coterminous, baptism functioned almost as a mark of belonging to both. Few in the Reformed tradition today would defend the practice of general or indiscriminate baptism, regardless of the parents' overt attachment to the life of the congregation. Most of us find the Swedish experience, in which still some 90% of babies are baptized in the Lutheran church but well below 5% of the population attend worship, more bemusing than enviable.

From the perspective of this paper, what happens to infant baptism when it is earthed not so much in the community of faith as in the wider community in which it is set? A case for an open baptism policy—allowing baptism for the children of parents with little or no church connexion—is sometimes advanced precisely in the interests of a sense of community solidarity which extends even to a feeling that this is 'our church'. Even though 'we' do not belong to it, in some way it belong to 'us'. Such a case may be made along the following lines for the special circumstances of a parish marked by multiple social deprivation—in UK terms, an 'urban priority area' or UPA. In such a world, lone-parent families require all the support a church fellowship can provide, and children at risk from neglect or abuse need the affirmation of childhood that infant baptism expresses. In the bleakness that blights life in many a UPA, every opportunity to celebrate something good and beautiful should be welcomed. In this setting, infant baptism witnesses signally to Jesus' special concern for the marginalized and despised. The last thing that parents struggling to survive against a host of pressures should have to face is rejection by the church—for rejection is how refusal or reluctance to baptize their babies will be received.

An argument of this kind carries considerable emotive force. Nor is there any reason why a parallel case should not be formulated for the distinctive circumstances of a parish community much higher up the socio-economic scale. Yet it is difficult to escape the impression that when infant baptism is cultivated within this communal habitat, its identity as the sacrament of incorporation into Christ in his body is gravely imperilled. In reality, baptism is being made to serve any number of purposes which, however laudable in themselves, are not integral to its distinctive role. Planting infant baptism in this habitat, which is found near the margins of the worshipping congregation, fosters its adulteration. The testing demands of relating church to community are not to be met by the abuse of baptism. It is perhaps a sobering measure of the widespread lack of consensus about the rationale for infant baptism that it has proved so pliable to service such diverse ends.

Consider, for example, the notion that baptism is an affirmation of babyhood or childhood—which might seek support from some of the sayings of Jesus about children. The sacraments of the gospel, however, are not age-specific. That baptism has a defining connexion with babyhood—rather than with teenage or adult years—could be concluded only by ignoring the New Testament's witness to baptism. There, if infants are included at all, they are embraced invisibly in baptisms that are determined by the conversion and faith of their parents. That is to say, if baptism bears a special message about young children, it is one that relates to the offspring of believing parents, not to children generically, by virtue of their tender years alone.

One could pursue a fresh line of enquiry at this point, investigating what happens to baptism when the habitat in which it is naturalized is that of babyhood. Fixing baptism in this setting is entirely understandable, for paedobaptism has been the common form of the sacrament for most of the church throughout most of its history. Yet although it has in practice been the norm from some time after Augustine until the present, to assume therefrom that infant reception is integral to baptism may quickly end up with two baptisms, not one (cf. Ephesians 4.4). Treating the passivity of the babe in arms at the font as illustrative of God's—or the parents'—role understands infant baptism in terms that cannot be applied to believers' baptism. Baptism is always done to us, not by us, but the command 'Be baptized' (Acts 2.38) implies no less intentional an act than 'Take and eat'. The same caveat holds for the claim that infant baptism demonstrates 'the priority of grace over faith'—where the faith in view is the future faith of the child.

Even more questionable are illustrations that fetch the meaning of baptism from natal or antenatal experience. The baby in the womb surrounded by protecting and nourishing water is made to speak of the child held within the life-giving waters of God's love. Or baptism may be likened to the breaking of the mother's waters and the child's emergence from the confines of the womb to the new wide world of God's kingdom. Resort to such images may appear harmless enough, but they only too easily so shape conceptions of baptism that faith- or conversion-baptism becomes the problematic exception instead of the norm—as it undoubtedly was in the early centuries. The difficulty can be traced back to siting baptism in the habitat of babyhood instead of the believing family in the worshipping congregation.

The dominical appointment of baptism gives us no authority to turn it into a thanksgiving for birth or a celebration of babyhood—or for that matter into a custom hallowed by communal tradition whose observance is justified in terms of pre-evangelism, building bridges with the unchurched, social cohesiveness, the welfare needs of vulnerable children, the nurture of a sputtering spark of parental faith, or many another such commendable objective. We have no biblical warrant for baptizing except where we can believe that all are being baptized by the one Spirit into the one body of Christ (cf. 1 Corinthians 12.13), and are so baptized into Christ as to die with him to sin and rise with him to newness of life (cf. Romans 6.2-4), to be no less than clothed with him (cf. Galatians 3.27).

The Congregation

One resort of those who seek to defend the baptism of children whose parents cannot credibly be received as believing Christians is to shift the locus of faith in the baptismal service to the congregation. The shift may be invoked sometimes in terms of a quasi-parental or adoptive role for the congregation in cases of a parent or parents felt to be inadequate in more than the spiritual care of the child. At work here is a wider tendency, observable also in changing attitudes towards confirmation or admission to the Lord's supper. In an age when teenagers and young adults shy away from any kind of life-commitment and frequently lack the decisiveness to make a public profession of faith, the spotlight focuses instead on the faith of the receiving congregation. The persons being confirmed or admitted are viewed not so much as enlisting to be Christ's faithful soldiers and servants unto their lives' ends but rather as setting out on a journey in the first faltering steps of faith.

Much might be said about this broader tendency to soft-pedal the call to pledge oneself openly and irrevocably to Christ, but our subject is infant baptism. Placing baptism centrally in the local congregation is to plant it in its native habitat, apart from which it cannot truly thrive. It has been a healthy Reformed insistence that baptism be administered in the face of the congregation. It is there with unequalled appropriateness that the essential ecclesial lineaments of baptism are evident. Only there does the people of Christ recognizably welcome a new member in his name. And beyond doubt the congregation's role is that of participants, not spectators, for which role faith is indispensable. Furthermore, this is a faith that believes for the parents and the child, that the promises of God in Christ in the covenant of grace are fulfilled for them here and now, no less than it believes for the congregation in its vocation of welcome and integration of the baptized, and for each member severally in reaffirming afresh his or her own baptismal pledge.

But it is a false step to imagine that the corporate faith of the church can do duty, vicariously as it were, for the parents' absent or uncertain faith. Neglecting the vital habitat of the believing family cannot be compensated for by overtaxing the habitat of the believing congregation. Both are essential for the flourishing of baptism, the former within the latter, neither one without the other. Unless the conditions exist for the healthy growth of the seed of the Spirit in the baptized in that environment where the new person is reared and trained, there can be little hope that the church can provide that habitat on its own. Most baptismal theology in the Reformed tradition would recognize no normal grounds for believing that it is meant to do so—for believing, that is, in the propriety of baptizing the child of unbelieving parents in the confidence that the congregation's faith and nurture of the child will suffice.

What emerges at this point is the essential correlation between the habitat of the Christian family or parent(s) and the habitat of the Christian congregation. The health of one safeguards the other. Together they contribute to the proper planting and successful growth of infant baptism. In particular they together serve to protect the integrity of baptism as an apostolic ordinance. For example, if baptism is viewed as part of the children's programme of a church, its necessary rootedness in the soil of parental faith may well be played down in favour of its value as the church's contact with a new child in the community as early as may be in the child's life. Something very similar happens when infant baptism in dubious cases or worse is justified in terms of the evangelistic opportunity it offers when many non-church folk are present on this special occasion.

This way of squaring the ministerial conscience has been not uncommon in both the Church of England and the Church of Scotland on the part of those uncomfortable with their church's lax (as they see it) baptismal discipline.

But baptism is intended to be neither an instrument of congregational outreach nor a slot within the church's ministry to children—although when allowed to be itself, it may well be of value to both. The indispensability of baptism may also need defending when some other activity of the church minimises it. In recent years within the Church of Scotland, pressure from the Christian Education department to promote the admission of children to the Lord's table led to a move to extend admission even to unbaptized children who attended the Sunday school. Had it succeeded it would have sanctioned action somewhat similar to a possibility discussed above, in which the congregation's faith would stand as surety in the baptism of children whose parent or parents could not responsibly speak for them at the font—but were concerned enough to send them to Sunday school. On the other hand, there is some evidence of an increasing tendency for parents who are active church members to decline baptism for their infants—and some Reformed churches in different parts of the world have recognized this choice as a proper baptismal option.

It is surely a critical test of a satisfactory baptismal theology that it can encompass both infant and believers' baptism within a single understanding. As I see it, baptism as the sign of the covenant is appropriately given by Christ's ministers whenever there are grounds for believing that God is calling persons into his covenant people which is the body of Christ. These grounds are of two kinds: for those able to speak for themselves, it is their faith, professed (cf. Acts 8.12, [37], 11.16-17, 16.31-33, etc.); for those not so able, it is their birth to parents whose faith enables them to speak on their children's behalf.

In the church of the early Fathers, these two patterns were held more closely together than is generally apparent today. This happened partly in the baptism of children jointly with their parents following the latter's conversion. It happened also in the manner in which the earliest known adaptation of the baptismal liturgy to cater for infants preserved the requirement of faith professed. Just as candidates of sufficient years answered 'I believe' to the credal questions, so the baptizing ministers asked of parents sponsoring those too young to answer for themselves 'Does he/she believe?'

The family of faith and the congregation of faith—these then are the two key habitats for infant baptism's flourishing. Like concentric circles, the smaller habitat and the larger mutually enrich each other. As the child develops, nurtured as a plant is within a habitat that provides the right conditions of sturdy growth and escapes degradation and pollution, so he or she progressively spreads out and takes his or her rightful and independent place within the congregation. The movement from dependence on parental faith to self-owned faith in the worshipping community may be a seamless one, especially if the mini-habitat is firmly integrated in the macro-habitat and each strengthens the other.

Nor must the wider community be forgotten, for this is the church's primary field of service and witness, and baptism is like the door into the church. If the two essential markers in a baptismal ecology are faith and the church, it is an ecology that is open to the world beyond these, for baptism is a sacrament of the gospel. It is no less true of it than of the eucharist that in it God's people proclaim the Lord's death and resurrection until he comes. Baptism best serves the town or neighbourhood when it is true to its evangelical, that is, its kerygmatic nature, not when it is dispensed according to communal expectations or the requirements of the church's social welfare programme.

We probably should not expect sacraments of the gospel to thrive in an ecclesial context where the gospel itself is stunted or impoverished. Sacraments testify to the gospel in a secondary sense also, that the form and style of their presentation disclose the gospel by which a particular pastor or congregation lives. A test that I would like to see applied to all ordinands in their final church assessment is simply this: do they show credible evidence of having a gospel to live by and die for? Not of course an idiosyncratic gospel of their own devising but the apostolic gospel of Christ which they have so made their own that with Paul they can truly call it 'my gospel' (cf. Romans 2.16, 16.25, 2 Timothy 2.8). Where the gospel of God's grace in Jesus Christ is robustly nurtured in church ministry, there the sacraments of that gospel may be expected to thrive in their native soil.

CHAPTER 25

Children, Covenant and the Church

This lecture starts with a story, the history in outline of the use of the Gospel account of Jesus' blessing of the children in Mark 10.13-16 par.[1] A widespread feature of recent orders of service for infant baptism has been the omission of this pericope altogether, as in the Church of England's *Common Worship* (2000; and earlier in the *Alternative Service Book*, 1980) and the *Methodist Worship Book* (1999), or its drastic demotion in prominence, as in the Church of Scotland's *Common Order* of 1994. This contrasts markedly with an earlier generation of such service books, represented by the 1928 *Book of Common Order* of the (Scottish) United Free Church, where infant baptism begins with 'The sanction of the ordinance is to be found in the words of our Lord, who spake, saying, "Suffer..."' (Mark 10.14-16). The Gospel passage now commonly appears in services of Thanksgiving for, or Blessing of a Child

This recent consensus, which declines to see in Jesus' blessing of the children any connection with the baptism of children, in fact reflects the mind of the early church Fathers almost to a man. It was the sixteenth-century Protestant Reformers who brought the account into the baptism of infants, probably not fully understanding what they were doing but finding it a useful shield against Anabaptist protests. Its apologetic value in favour of paedobaptism reached a peak in the mid-twentieth century when, in writers like Joachim Jeremias, Oscar Cullmann and T.F. Torrance, by way of the so-called κωλύειν-formula it furnished even liturgical evidence of apostolic practice. As the Church of Scotland's Special Commission on Baptism put it, 'the Evangelists intend us to interpret that blessing [by Jesus] in terms of [the children's] baptism'.[2]

This late-twentieth-century departure from the Reformation tradition belongs to the recovery of infant baptism as an ordinance or sacrament of the gospel, rather than a rite of babyhood. It is also one instance of the

---

[1] For documentation see David F. Wright, 'Out, In, Out: Jesus' Blessing of the Children and Infant Baptism', in S.E. Porter and A.R. Cross (eds), *Dimensions of Baptism: Biblical and Theological Studies* (*Journal for the Study of the New Testament*, Supplement Series, 234; Sheffield, 2002), pp. 188-206 (see ch. 11 above).

[2] 'Interim Report', in *Report to the General Assembly of the Church of Scotland 1955* (Edinburgh, 1955), pp. 631-33; Special Commission, *The Biblical Doctrine of Baptism* (Edinburgh, 1958), pp. 48-49.

continuing reassessment of the biblical and historical evidence for infant baptism. The latter's connection with the subject of this lecture scarcely needs explication. Among evangelicals, especially of a Reformed hue, the most standard argument for paedobaptism has been covenantal. The continuity between Israel and the church within the one Abrahamic covenant renewed in Jesus Christ finds particular expression in the parallel between circumcision and infant baptism. As the Westminster Confession of Faith states it:

> Sacraments are holy signs and seals of the covenant of grace... The sacraments of the Old Testament, in regard of the spiritual things thereby signified and exhibited, were, for substance, the same with those of the New (par. 27).

The practice of baptizing the newborn is the most obvious and common way in which testimony is given to the conviction that children of believing parents 'are heirs of the covenant of grace', in the words of an earlier *Book of Common Order*.[3]

The binding of infants to the covenant in baptism undoubtedly gathers strong *prima facie* support from the essential evangelical insistence on grounding theology on both Testaments together. Yet the tradition has rarely escaped damaging ambivalence. In the first place, do the infant-baptized become (or are they recognized as already being) members of the church, of the covenant people of God? Communions which both baptize babies and several years later admit to communicant membership are often in the toils at this point. The impression is sometimes given in my own church that baptism designates membership of the body of Christ for infants but not of the Church of Scotland. For that they must wait until their teens or later, and very few do so. Secondly, does baptism, or more accurately the Holy Spirit through baptism, effect anything for babies or merely mark them out as future recipients? Does baptism, for example, confer specific covenantal blessings on babies, such as new birth or remission of sin, specifically original sin, as Augustine influentially argued?

Behind such questions lies a much more important one: can the New Testament's presentation of Christian baptism, which I take in decidedly realist terms, be applied to baby-baptism? The issue is less pressing if baptism, whatever its subjects, is understood only in symbolic terms, but I must insist that this approach does scant justice to the New Testament texts. As a general method of construing baptism it most certainly owes something, and perhaps a very great deal, to the demands of encompassing infants as its commonest recipients.

---

[3] *Book of Common Order of the Church of Scotland* (London, 1940), p. 89.

The phrase 'Christian initiation complete in baptism', associated in the Church of England with Colin Buchanan and others,[4] is intended to deny that baptism administered to infants needs 'completion' by some later rite incorporating personal profession of faith. The assertion evokes decades of debate over the relation between baptism and (episcopal) confirmation. The diminishing importance assigned to confirmation is in part the result, as well as a major cause, of the admission of baptized children to the Lord's supper—an action which at one time attested powerfully to the conviction 'Christian initiation complete in baptism'. A somewhat different, yet not irreconcilable, path to infant communion has followed the rediscovery of the early Christian pattern of initiation set out in the Hippolytan *Apostolic Tradition*, in which admission to the supper follows immediately upon baptism, even for the infant newly-baptized, so it seems. In this setting initiation for none of the baptized is complete without their sharing in the other dominical ordinance of the covenant community.

It may be the case that most evangelical ministers or churches have not endorsed the admission of young children to the communion table. It surely merits more serious consideration than it commonly receives. In its favour is the weighty argument that it takes the baptism of infants genuinely as baptism, as making them truly members of Christ's people. Thus it has the virtue of putting both ordinances of the new covenant on an equal basis, dissolving the anomaly that the infant-baptized have been welcomed into the Christian community but are debarred for years from its communal meal celebration. It should be noted in addition that the change in practice relates also, again partly as cause and partly as effect, to a re-evaluation of the Lord's supper itself, more as food for the journey of growing up in Christ, rather than as the privilege of those who have 'arrived'. We are seeing, I suggest, a continuation of the desacralization of much that the Reformers carried over without radical questioning from the old church. Finally we must take account of the fact that in the early church infant communion is recorded almost as early as infant baptism is indisputably attested, in the mid-third century in Cyprian of Carthage. It is apparently assumed a generation or so earlier in the *Apostolic Tradition* ascribed to Hippolytus.

When we seek the wisdom of scripture on my subject, the Old Testament proves more obviously helpful than the New Testament. Therein, however, lies a good part of the problem. At this stage it will be useful to unpack the problem at some length.

---

[4] Cf. E.C. Whitaker, *Sacramental Initiation Complete in Baptism* (Bramcote, 1975). It was also the position adopted by the influential international Anglican consultation at Toronto in 1991: D.R. Holeton (ed.), *Christian Initiation in the Anglican Communion* (Bramcote, 1991).

We are in a circle, whether vicious or virtuous, compounded as much of tradition as of scripture, with the 'tradition' element deriving in large measure from the Reformation—which makes it unpalatable or uncomfortable to question. Let me spell this out more fully. We are mostly products of a western Christianity or Christendom in which infant baptism has been virtually universal for some millennium and half, since around 500. The grounds for infant baptism espoused in the evangelical community are in the main those espoused by the Reformers, and especially the parallel with circumcision within the context of a covenantal framework for salvation-history. Few of us accept the Augustinian theology of original guilt as eternally fatal in infants dying unbaptized, a theology which lay behind the universality of infant baptism from the early medieval era onwards. Augustine did not need to defend the practice of baptizing babies, and made limited reference to the precedent of circumcision.

The sixteenth-century Reformers, on the other hand, were confronted with the urgency of justifying the rite in the face of Anabaptist protests which took *sola Scriptura* more strictly than did the likes of Luther, Calvin and company. Covenantal parallelism proved the most sophisticated and durable of their apologiae, which in turn made the assumption of universal paedobaptism (made legally binding in some Reformation strongholds, such as Geneva) a factor in the rise of covenantal theology to prominence in the later sixteenth and the seventeenth centuries.[5] Although covenantal continuity is not, I suppose, the only respectable biblical-theological matrix for infant baptism, I judge that it remains the most satisfying approach for most evangelical apologists. The Church of Scotland's Panel on Doctrine in 2003 based its justification heavily on the household paradigm without enlisting a covenantal framework for this—and was criticized in the General Assembly for doing inadequate justice to the covenantal argument.[6]

Against this summary sketch of the circle, vicious or virtuous, in which, so I would argue, much of the paedobaptist evangelical constituency is now placed, we must focus in on a couple of segments of the circle, and first on the analogy with circumcision. Here is one writer's estimate:

---

[5] Cf. the judgment of John W. Riggs, *Baptism in the Reformed Tradition: A Historical and Practical Theology* (Columbia Studies in Reformed Theology; Louisville, KY, 2002), p. 122: 'From a historical perspective, the Reformed use of covenant to interpret Christian baptism first arose, almost always, when arguing for infant baptism. In other words, its origin was not in theological or exegetical reflection on baptism as such but as a specific response to the challenge to a long-held practice of infant baptism.'

[6] Church of Scotland, *Reports to the General Assembly 2003* (Edinburgh, 2003), sect. 13, pp. 1-17, especially sect. 13, pp. 12-15.

> The very centre of Calvin's theology of infant baptism rests upon the view that there exists an anagogic relationship between circumcision in the Old Testament and infant baptism in the New Testament.[7]

And the context of that relationship is, for Calvin, the one covenant of grace. Yet how securely is this relationship grounded in the New Testament? Overall there is not much evidence that the parallel commended itself to Christian writers before about 200—although thorough research on early Christian attitudes to circumcision remains to be done. For most of the first two or three centuries the common Christian stance towards circumcision was polemical. It was frequently linked with the sabbath as elements of the Jewish order superseded by the coming of the Messiah Jesus. This was a most unpropitious climate in which to advance circumcision as a typical anticipation of infant baptism, or of baptism as a whole. Remember that all the explicit New Testament patterns of baptism present faith-baptism or conversion-baptism.

By the time of Cyprian in the mid-third century, the analogy with circumcision is clearly established, to the extent that his *Letter* 64 responds to a bishop uncertain whether it was permissible to baptize a baby before the eighth day indicated by the precedent of circumcision. But we have already noted Augustine's relatively low use of the link, and Augustine is by a massive distance the most expansive patristic writer on infant baptism. A dossier of patristic sources without Augustine would be thin indeed.

There is, of course, Colossians 2.11-12. My reading of this discerns no direct connection between circumcision and baptism but rather each related separately to Christ's death. It is arguable that circumcision is spiritualized as Christ's death in Colossians and in Galatians, just as elsewhere it is spiritualized as rebirth. I was struck by the NRSV translation of these verses:

> In him also you were circumcised with a spiritual circumcision, by putting off the body of the flesh in the circumcision of Christ; when you were buried with him in baptism, you were also raised with him through faith in the power of God, who raised him from the dead.

The fact that it is so singular a text does not aid exegesis. The juxtaposition of baptism and circumcision and the density of the verses would make the development of an interpretation paralleling the two understandable, but this seems not to have happened until around 400. A review of the patristic evidence concludes that it

---

[7] Egil Grislis, 'Calvin's Doctrine of Baptism', *Church History* 3 (1962), pp. 46-65, at p. 51.

does not suggest that the analogy between circumcision and baptism gave rise to the practice of infant baptism, nor that Colossians 2:11-12 were initially understood to imply infant baptism. It suggests rather that this analogy was not used as an argument for infant baptism until after the practice has arisen on other grounds.[8]

The invocation of circumcision with its covenantal context was generally not an original feature in Reformers' baptismal teaching. It emerges in general terms when, having nailed their colours to the mast of *sola Scriptura*, they had to row back from an initial emphasis on the necessity of faith for the beneficial reception of baptism. This repositioning occurred when the opposition against whom this emphasis was directed, the old Roman Church, was supplanted by the new foe of Anabaptism. We should not underestimate the seriousness of the challenge posed by Anabaptist radicals. More than one of the magisterial Reformers had to overcome early doubts about infant baptism, independently of Anabaptist protests. It can be seriously argued that the baptism of babies was the single most significant constitutive element of church order that the Reformers preserved without explicit biblical warrant.

It is instructive to track the movement of baptismal thought in Luther and in Calvin as they confronted first one and then a different set of opponents. In 1521 Luther produced a *Defence and Explanation of All the Articles Which were Unjustly Condemned by the Roman Bull*—the bull of excommunication, 'Exsurge Domine', of 15 June 1520. The first Article Luther defends is his denial that 'the sacraments give grace to all who do not put an obstacle in the way' and his assertion that the worthy reception of the sacraments also requires 'genuine repentance for sin' and 'a firm faith within the heart'. When he comes to baptism, Luther first quotes Mark 16.16, 'He who believes and is baptised will be saved'. There follows a series of apparently unqualified statements.

[Christ] puts faith before baptism for where there is no faith, baptism does no good.

[W]ithout faith, no sacrament is of any use, indeed it is altogether deadly and pernicious.

---

[8] See J.P.T. Hunt, 'Colossians 2:11-12, the Circumcision/Baptism Analogy, and Infant Baptism', *Tyndale Bulletin* 41 (1990), pp. 227-44, at p. 244. This valuable article, which includes a survey of selected patristic sources, is based on the author's unpublished Durham University MA thesis, 'The History of the Interpretation of Colossians 2:11-12 up to the Council of Chalcedon, with particular reference to the Uses of these Verses as an Argument for Infant Baptism' (1988). His conclusion that 'It was not until the mid-fourth century that Colossians 2:11-12 were used explicitly in connection with infant baptism' (p. 241) requires revision since the source he has in view, Asterius, has more recently been dated later, c.400.

> [T]here must be an unwavering, unshaken faith in the heart which receives the promise and sign and does not doubt that what God promises and signifies is indeed so.

> [I]t is better, if faith is not present, to stay far away from these words and signs which are the sacraments of God.

> For this reason, he who is baptised must hold these words [of Mark 16.16] to be true and must believe that he will certainly be saved if he is baptised as these words say and the sign signifies.[9]

Luther does not forget infants altogether:

> [E]very day...wherever in the whole world baptism is administered, the question is put to the child, or the sponsors in his stead, whether he believes, and on the basis of this faith and confession, the sacrament of baptism is administered.[10]

But apart from this one reference, the whole article reads as if it concerned believers' baptism.

Then came the Zwickau prophets to Wittenberg in December 1521. Luther sent a revealing letter to Melanchthon on 13 January 1522. The prophets were citing Mark 16.16 and arguing that, since children could not believe in their own person, they were not to be baptized. Luther advances two responses, *fides infantium* and *fides aliena*. Without the latter, he reflects, 'there is nothing else to be debated, and baptism of small children simply has to be rejected'.[11]

Luther has no difficulty citing scripture in support of 'extrinsic faith', that is, faith exercised by someone else on my behalf. Such faith

> belongs to me personally but is really also someone else's faith... Christ never rejected a single person who was brought to him through someone else's faith... The testimonies and examples of the whole Scripture are on the side of extrinsic faith, that is...personal faith, which attains faith, and whatever is desired for someone else.[12]

As for children's lack of faith, how will the prophets prove it? 'Perhaps by the fact that children do not speak and express their faith.' But we are silent during sleep and do not stop being believers. 'Can't God in the same way keep faith in small children during the whole time of their infancy, as if it were a continuous sleep?' But does the church believe that 'faith is infused into infants'? There is no scripture passage which would

---

[9] George W. Forell (ed. and trans.), *Career of the Reformer* II, *LW* 32, pp. 12-16.
[10] Forell, *LW* 32, p. 14.
[11] Gottfried G. Krodel (ed. and trans.), *Letters* I, *LW* 48, p. 368.
[12] Krodel, *LW* 48, p. 369.

force the church to believe this. The church has the authority not to baptize infants at all. 'Baptism is free and not compulsory like circumcision.' Perhaps Augustine and the subsequent church have erred on this point—for it is 'a special miracle of God that the article that infants are to be baptised is the only one which has never been denied, not even by heretics'. The letter reads like Luther's conversation with himself. He comes back to Mark 16.16; opponents who cite it cannot prove from it that children do not believe.[13]

By the time of his most extensive treatment of the subject, *Concerning Rebaptism* in 1528, Luther insists that the onus is on the Anabaptists to prove the negative, that children cannot have faith. He is content to show from scripture that they may have faith.[14]

> There are Scripture passages that tell us that children may and can believe, though they do not speak or understand. So, Psalm 72 [106.37-38], describes how the Jews offered their sons and daughters to idols, shedding innocent blood. If, as the text says, it was innocent blood, then the children have to be considered pure and holy—this they could not be without spirit and faith. Likewise the innocent children whom Herod had murdered were not over two years of age [Matthew 2.16]. Admittedly they could not speak or understand. Yet they were holy and blessed. Christ himself says in Matthew 18 [19.14], 'The kingdom of heaven belongs to children.' And St John was a child in his mother's womb [Luke 1.41] but, as I believe, could have faith.
>
> Yes, you say, but John was an exception. This is not proof that all baptized children have faith. I answer, wait a minute, I am not yet at the point of proving that children believe. I am giving proof that your foundation for rebaptism is uncertain and false inasmuch as you cannot prove that there may not be faith in children.[15]

Furthermore, Jesus commands us to bring the children to him. In Matthew 19 [v.14] he embraces them, kisses them, and says that theirs is the kingdom of heaven. The misled spirits like to fend this off by saying, Christ is not speaking of children, but of the humble. This, however, is a false note, for the text clearly says that they brought to him children, not the humble. And Christ does not say to let the humble come to him, but the children, and he reprimanded the disciples not because they kept the humble, but the children away. He embraced and blessed the children, not the humble, when he said, 'Of such is the kingdom of heaven.' So also Matthew 18 [v.10], 'Their angels behold the face of my Father', is to be understood as referring to such children, for he teaches us that we should

---

[13] Krodel, *LW* 48, pp. 367-71.
[14] Conrad Bergendoff (ed. and trans.), *Church and Ministry* II, *LW* 40, pp. 241-42.
[15] Bergendoff, *LW* 40, p. 242.

also be like these children. Were not these children holy, he would indeed have given us a poor ideal with which to compare ourselves.[16]

By 1528 and *Concerning Rebaptism*, Luther's earlier vacillation of mind has passed and he trots out a series of vigorous claims and arguments. He repeats what he had written elsewhere, that 'the most certain form of baptism is child baptism', for an adult might deceive on coming forward and a child cannot. If God has not commanded the baptism of children, nor 'has he specifically commanded the baptism of adults, nor of men or of women, so we had better not baptise anybody'.[17] In this work Luther also develops his distinctive argument that faith is so uncertain a quality ('Always something is lacking in faith') that none should base their baptism on it but only on the command of God. So an adult wanting to be baptized should say:

> I want to be baptised because it is God's command that I should be, and on the strength of this command I dare to be baptised. In time my faith may become what it may. If I am baptised on his bidding I know for certain that I am baptised. Were I to be baptised on my own faith, I might tomorrow find myself unbaptised, if faith failed me, or I became worried that I might not yesterday have had the faith rightly.[18]

And one who had been baptized as a child might say:

> I thank God and am happy that I was baptised as a child, for thus I have done what God commanded. Whether I have believed or not, I have followed the command of God and been baptised and my baptism was correct and certain. God grant that whether my faith today be certain or uncertain, or I think that I believe and am certain, nothing is lacking in baptism.[19]

Luther has come a long way since he argued that there had to be 'an unwavering, unshaken faith in the heart' to receive the promise and sign of baptism. In the course of *Concerning Rebaptism* we scarcely notice the following statement among such a varied case:

> If they now believe that through the covenant of circumcision God accepts both boys and girls and is their God, why should he not also accept our children through the covenant of baptism?[20]

---

[16] Bergendoff, *LW* 40, p. 243.
[17] Bergendoff, *LW* 40, pp. 244, 245.
[18] Bergendoff, *LW* 40, p. 253.
[19] Bergendoff, *LW* 40, p. 253.
[20] Bergendoff, *LW* 40, p. 244.

Calvin's movement of faith is comparable to Luther's, with this difference, that while the shift in Luther's thinking is observed in separate writings over a spread of years, in Calvin's case it is discernible in the different editions of one work, the *Institutes*. What in the final 1559 edition is Book 4:15 is derived mostly from the first 1536 version directed chiefly against the Catholic Church, whereas Book 4:16 comes from the 1539 edition and was originally aimed at the Anabaptists. As a number of scholars have recognized, Book 4:15 defines baptism in such terms that it might almost have been written of believers' baptism only. There is only one explicit reference to the baptism of infants (4:15:22), and at a couple of other places where the argument seems to invite mention of it, it is absent (4:15:9, 4:15:10). At the outset the chapter declares that baptism was given for two ends, 'first, to serve our faith before him, secondly, to serve our confession before men'.[21] The rest of the chapter unpacks this initial statement.

[The Lord] wills that all who believe be baptised for the remission of sins [Matthew 28.19; Acts 2.38].

[T]he chief point of baptism is to receive baptism with this promise, 'He who believes and is baptised will be saved' [Mark 16.16] (4:15:1).

Peter...adds that this baptism is not a removal of filth from the flesh but a good conscience before God [1 Peter 3.21], which is from faith (4:15:2).

[T]hose who receive baptism with right faith truly feel the effective working of Christ's death in the mortification of their flesh, together with the working of his resurrection in the vivification of the Spirit [Romans 6.8] (4:15:5).

[O]ur faith receives from baptism the advantage of its sure testimony to us...John first baptised, so later did the apostles, 'with a baptism of repentance unto forgiveness of sins' [Matthew 3.6, 11; Luke 3.16; John 3.23; 4.1; Acts 2.38, 41] (4:15:6).

[T]hose whom the Lord has once received into grace, engrafts into the communion of his Christ, and adopts into the society of the church through baptism—so long as they persevere in faith in Christ...are absolved of guilt and condemnation (4:15:12).

[Baptism] is the mark by which we publicly profess that we wish to be reckoned God's people; by which we testify that we agree in worshipping the same God; ...by which finally we openly affirm our faith (4:15:13).

---

[21] *Institutes of the Christian Religion* 4:15:1 (ed. John T. McNeill; trans. Ford Lewis Battles; Library of Christian Classics; 2 vols; London, 1961), II, p. 1304. All quotations are from this translation.

> [Baptism] is given for the arousing, nourishing, and confirming of our faith (4:15:14).

> [F]rom this sacrament, as from all others, we obtain only as much as we receive in faith (4:15:15).[22]

Near the beginning of Book 4:16, which from the very first embarks on an assault against Anabaptist rejection of paedobaptism, Calvin gives a fresh account of the 'force and nature' of baptism.

> Scripture declares that baptism first points to the cleansing of our sins, which we obtain from Christ's blood; then to the mortification of our flesh, which rests upon participation in his death and through which believers are reborn into newness of life and into the fellowship of Christ. All that is taught in the Scriptures concerning baptism can be referred to this summary, except that baptism is also a symbol for bearing witness to our religion before men (4:16:2).[23]

The *Institutes* continues immediately with a section on baptism and circumcision. There is no difference, argues Calvin, between the two 'in the inner mystery, by which the whole force and character of the sacraments has been weighed'—he means God's fatherly favour, the forgiveness of sins, eternal life, regeneration—but only in the 'very slight factor' of the outward ceremony (4:16:4).[24] Hence,

> If the covenant still remains firm and steadfast, it applies no less today to the children of Christians than under the Old Testament it pertained to the infants of the Jews (4:16:5).[25]

After devoting a brief section to Jesus' blessing of the children, Calvin turns to a lengthy rebuttal of Anabaptist objections against the baptism-circumcision parallel (4:16:10-16). He next asserts that infants are quite capable of being regenerated, as Christ's own infancy demonstrates. Without regeneration, dying infants must surely perish.

To the further objection that infants were incapable of hearing preaching and hence of faith, the Reformer advances various counter-

---

[22] *Institutes*, II, pp. 1304, 1305, 1307, 1308, 1313, 1313-14, 1314, 1315.

[23] *Institutes*, II, p. 1325.

[24] *Institutes*, II, p. 1327.

[25] *Institutes*, II, p. 1328. A little further on in this section Battles' translation reads 'since the word "baptism" is applied to infants', but inaccurately. The Latin *baptismi verbum* denotes what Calvin has just called 'the inner mystery' of baptism declared in the word of the sacrament. This is evident when Calvin proceeds immediately to talk of the sign, i.e. outward baptism, as 'the appendage of the word'. Henry Beveridge's translation has 'the word of baptism is destined for infants'(2 vols; London, 1949, II, p. 532). The French of the 1560 *Institution* reads 'la parolle du Baptesme s'adresse aux petits enfans' (ed. Jean-Daniel Benoit; 5 vols; Paris, 1957–63, IV, p. 343).

arguments. God can use other means than preaching to grant illumination. What danger is there

> if infants be said to receive now some part of that grace which in a little while they shall enjoy to the full? (4:16:19).[26]

In a passage whose complex construction over three editions reflects Calvin's continuing struggle with this question, he expostulates,

> [W]hy may the Lord not shine with a tiny spark at the present time on those whom he will illumine in the future with the full splendour of his light—especially if he has not removed their ignorance before taking them from the prison of the flesh? I would not rashly affirm that they are endowed with the same faith as we experience in ourselves, or have entirely the same knowledge of faith—this I prefer to leave undetermined (4:16:19).[27]

In another variation on the same theme:

> infants are baptised into future repentance and faith, and even though these have not yet been formed in them, the seed of both lies hidden within them by the secret working of the Spirit (4:16:20).[28]

More than one issue of coherence is raised by Book 4:16 of the *Institutes*. One which will not be pursued here is the coherence of 4:16 within itself. On the one hand Calvin insists on the regeneration of elect baptized infants, but on the other hand asserts that,

> In infant baptism nothing more of present effectiveness must be required than to confirm and ratify the covenant made with them by the Lord. The remaining significance of this sacrament will afterward follow at such time as God himself foresees (4:16:21).[29]

More serious is the charge of incoherence between 4:15 and 4:16, in the light of the marked emphasis in the former on baptism's purpose as serving faith and public confession. The disjunction between the two chapters is sharply evident in the use of scripture: 4:15 mostly cites the New Testament, 4:16 the Old. Part of Calvin's argument in the latter denies that New Testament statements which require faith and repentance before baptism apply to infants. Running through 4:16 is the principle that considerations advanced against the baptism of baby children would

---

[26] *Institutes*, II, p. 1342.
[27] *Institutes*, II, p. 1342.
[28] *Institutes*, II, p. 1343.
[29] *Institutes*, II, p. 1345. For fuller documentation on Calvin, see ch. 16 above.

count equally against circumcision—and are thereby automatically disqualified.

The heirs of Calvin have largely focused on Book 4:16 because it is there that he provides his apologia for infant baptism, and for churches in the Reformation tradition baptism has continued to be overwhelmingly infant baptism. But it says a great deal for Calvin's fidelity to scripture that 4:15 retains its place into the final edition of the *Institutes*, even though the impression is given that there is one theology of baptism and another of infant baptism. Too much of the later tradition has either lost sight of the former or simply collapsed it into the latter and hence worked with a doctrine of baptism that to all intents and purposes has been a doctrine of infant baptism alone. This has happened despite Calvin and despite the influential Westminster Confession of Faith, whose chapter on baptism preserves a commendable balance.

> Not only those that do actually profess faith in and obedience unto Christ, but also the infants of one or both believing parents are to be baptised (par. 28:4).

If such a statement had been borne in mind, it would have been impossible to equate baptism with infant baptism *simpliciter* or to approach baptism through infant baptism. Yet in the Church of Scotland the Special Commission on Baptism under Professor T.F. Torrance, surely the most extended and paper-productive investigation of baptism in the whole history of the Christian church, issued in a revised Act on baptism in 1963 which envisaged solely infant baptism. When in 2000 the Kirk sought to consolidate its various legislative enactments on the sacraments into a single Act, it was discovered that never since the Reformation had it made any provision in the law of the Church for baptism on profession of faith.

There is no need to spell out the difficulties which such an approach lands one in. (There is the New Testament, for example!) Among evangelicals, it has been directly and indirectly responsible for a massive baptismal reductionism. Infant baptism has been practised, of course, but with little confidence in talking of it in the baptismal tones of the New Testament. Countless hordes of babies have been baptized without ever coming into living membership of the covenant community of Christ. In Scotland, and I feel sure in England also, the population includes far more unchurched baptized people than the membership of the national church.

Significant changes in theological reflection on baptism have been afoot for some years, not least in paedobaptist communions, with the still emerging consensus that if there is a baptismal norm it is faith-baptism. This holds true for Roman Catholicism, Anglicanism, some Reformed churches, including the Church of Scotland as of May 2003, and more broadly in ecumenical circles in the wake of *Baptism, Eucharist and*

Ministry (1982). This consensus does not entail the abandonment of infant baptism but rather that, in terms of the reception of baptism, baptismal theology starts with baptism on profession of faith and provides for the baptism of non-respondent babies within this framework.

This major sea-change in the churches' attitudes to baptism points forward to a position not generally held since the age of the Fathers—as far as the Latin West is concerned, the era before Augustine of Hippo. When we look closely at the Reformation, we can still recognize a foreshadowing of this nascent consensus in the movement of baptismal teaching in Luther and Calvin sketched above. The post-Reformation succession built one-sidedly on the anti-Anabaptist slant that finally determined the Reformers' writings, but particularly in Calvin, the sequence in the *Institutes* of Book 4:15 followed by 4:16 in outline embodies the kind of way into understanding baptism, inspired by the New Testament, which informs much contemporary baptismal thought and revision of baptismal orders of service.

This also links up with early Christian liturgical practice. If we grant that some infants were baptized from at least the late second century, the dominant pattern in teaching and rite remained baptism on profession of faith. The first known liturgical adjustment to cope with the baptism of infants is attested around 400. The questions were addressed not to the child but to parent or sponsor in the form 'Does he/she believe?', with the response 'He/She believes'. There is hardly any theology of specifically infant baptism before Augustine. Vast reaches of preaching and catechesis on baptism, in John Chrysostom, for example, hardly ever mention infant recipients.

Biblical Christians should welcome this movement for change within baptismal thinking, even though it is bound to have the effect of relativizing the claims of infant baptism. Such a correction was long overdue. The case for infant baptism has for centuries suffered from overkill, from exaggerated biblical deductions and maximalized historical enquiries. I never tire of citing C.F.D. Moule's oral comment on Joachim Jeremias' *Infant Baptism in the First Four Centuries*, 'It contains at least all the evidence.'

This paper's return to our theme of covenant is also overdue. The covenant people of God is a community of faith. It is as such that the Abrahamic covenant finds its fulfilment in the new covenant of Christ, as Paul argues in Galatians 3.6-29, especially verses 7, 9, 14, 26, 29. That is why circumcision cannot serve simply as a model for Christian baptism. Second-century Christian writers saw in circumcision a mark of Jewish ethnicity. So if children belong to the new covenant people of Christians, they do not do so on special non-faith terms, of birth or nationality—and certainly not of innocence. (The late Alan Stibbs used to say that what had killed the gospel at the font was baby-worship.) There is no double-entry scheme on offer. The millennium-old experience of Christendom was recruitment largely from birth, on the basis of physical kinship.

The question, then, is whether children belong to the covenant community. To that I would answer in the affirmative, on a presumption of inclusiveness, whether or not it is thought appropriate to baptize them.[30] Whether by baptism, by dedication or by thanksgiving and blessing, we welcome the children of the faithful as the gift of God and we are right to treat them as new members of God's people, not as no better than little pagans or unbelievers.

This presumption of covenantal inclusiveness comports well with several features in the New Testament.

> i. Children are addressed in some of the Epistles as though part of the community of Christians in Colossae, Ephesus and elsewhere. What assumptions does their presence imply?
>
> ii. The household baptisms of Acts indicate an inclusiveness extending beyond the modern nuclear family, presumably encompassing slaves also.
>
> iii. The descendants to whom the promise extends in Acts 2.39, 'to you and your descendants' (as in the promises to Noah, Genesis 9.9, to Abraham, Genesis 13.15, 17.7-8, Galatians 3.16, and to David, Psalms 18.50, 89.34-37, 132.11-12), began life as children of their parents.
>
> iv. Jesus welcomed children, took them in his arms, laid his hands on their heads and blessed them. Mark twice in successive chapters has Jesus taking children in his arms, with a cuddle or a hug, I imagine (9.36-37; 10.14-16). Who were 'these little ones who believe in me, Jesus' (Mark 9.42, Matthew 18.6), whose angels in heaven, according to Matthew 18.10, always behold the face of Jesus' Father in heaven?

If this presumption of the inclusion of children within the covenant people is sound we may make it a basis for the reconsideration of certain features of church life.

> i. The decision to allow children to join in the Lord's supper was driven, at least in the Church of Scotland, by the realization that children, most of them baptized, were welcomed into the church at the outset but were then largely out of the church, in Sunday School or Bible Class, for years, after which their full inclusion was expected but often did not happen. At least where baptism is thought appropriate to mark their inclusion, their exclusion from the other covenant ordinance is difficult to defend.

---

[30] My own position, for what it is worth, views infant baptism as an *adiaphoron*, a matter on which Christians may differ without breaking fellowship. In my judgement, it is untenable to *demand* infant baptism on the basis of scripture, but at the same time its advocates have sufficient biblical arrows in their quiver not to face dogmatic rejection. Baptism itself, of course, is emphatically not an *adiaphoron*. No baptism, no Christian.

ii. If infant baptism is practised, it should be made an important reference-point for instruction and formation. Children should grow up knowing that they belong to Christ and his church as enacted in baptism. They should be brought up believing this, and on the basis of my argument in this paper this need not be restricted to baptized infants alone.

iii. The question arises of the inclusion of children within the normal diet of worship. This was one of the principles of the influential long ministry of the late William Still in Gilcomston South Church, Aberdeen, without for a moment involving the reduction of the level of worship to that of a children's service.

iv. Even more controversially, and at first sight paradoxically, we should seriously consider the refocusing of energies away from special children's ministries towards adult ministries. If only in more of our churches the immense time, imagination and enterprise expended on children's ministries were paralleled in ministries to adults, especially men. Our strategy has often appeared to seek to reach parents through children, but a recent statistic revealed the huge disparity between the effect of the conversion of a child and of a mother, and even more so of a father, on other members of a family.[31]

v. More tentatively, I raise the question of our listening to and learning from children, of children ministering to the rest of us. The Church of Scotland has recently experimented with children's forums, and invited representatives to attend the General Assembly of 2002 and to speak.[32] (Annual youth assemblies send delegates to be present and participate throughout each General Assembly.) That children might be involved in decision-making may seem far-fetched, but if we listen to children at home, perhaps we should do so in church. We are increasingly accustomed to forms of feedback on adults' and teenagers' experience of the church, and it would be a short step to extend this to children.

Concluding Reflections

The wide-ranging exercise which this article has attempted can be viewed in part as a process of disentanglement from aspects of the complex legacy of the Reformation, which has reached us, again in part, as Christendom, entailing a heavy element of continuity from the pre-Reformation western church. Within this context, infant baptism has been a mixed blessing. It has unambiguously marked children as heirs of the promises of the covenant, but often with major disagreement among us

---

[31] According to research in America, if a child is the first person to become a Christian, there is a 3.5% probability that the rest of the family will follow; if the mother is the first, 17%; if the father, 93%. Reported in *Evangelicals Now* 18.5 (May, 2003), p. 28. It must be said that 3.5% is not negligible.

[32] *Reports to the General Assembly 2003*, sect. 29, pp. 4-5.

on when they enter into their inheritance. In fact, very many of the infant-baptized, probably a good majority, never enter into that inheritance, if we judge by standard criteria. If we believe that baptism is a dominical ordinance, to whomsoever it is given, hard questions about tolerable levels of ineffectiveness seem inescapable.

What is proposed here concentrates on a less specific inclusiveness focused on children growing up within the heart of our churches, or within the fold of the covenant community, if that language is preferable, as 'little ones who believe in Jesus', mini-believers or believers-in-the-making. The boundaries of such inclusiveness will almost by definition be open, porous, permeable. Whether all will be members of the church, of the covenant people, need not be pressed.

In many churches the concept of membership has been becoming more problematic. We are undoubtedly moving into an era that is characterized by looser patterns of belonging, before and after believing, and children are surely very much to the point. This may prove bothersome to some evangelicals. We tend to be precisionists, to want to have things tied down and buttoned up, insistent on people conforming, meeting conditions. Calvin got a bloody nose when he attempted in his first years in Geneva to get all the citizens individually to state where they stood on the Reformation. This issue is not irrelevant to the question of the presence of children at the supper. If you bring the Sunday School in as a group, what about any unbaptized children among them?

If we baulk at the possibility of unbaptized children at the communion table—as I do—let us be sure that we know why we do. Attitudes towards the sacrament of the supper in some quarters still reek of the hypersacralism of the late medieval church. There is surely gross incongruity between the scrupulous care with which we fence the table and the freedom with which we dispense the other sacrament instituted by Christ, on the grounds, for example, that it presents an evangelistic opportunity. Yet in the Scottish tradition it is communion, not baptism, that has been known as a converting ordinance. Discrepant views of the two sacraments of the gospel continue to distort pastoral policy.

The vision granted to the prophet Zechariah of the Jerusalem to which the Lord has returned to dwell in, the Jerusalem now called the faithful city, the holy mountain, includes the following picture:

> Once again men and women of ripe old age will sit in the streets of Jerusalem, each with cane in hand because of his age. The city streets will be filled with boys and girls playing there (Zechariah 8.4-5).

Is this a sight of the new heavenly Jerusalem to come? Do the streets of our city of God on its earthly pilgrimage ring with the playing of boys and girls? The presence of children may demand of us less of a prim-

and-proper solicitude lest they disturb the peace of our Sunday morning expositions.

CHAPTER 26

Recovering Baptism for a New Age of Mission

The 1995 General Assembly of the Church of Scotland was asked by one of its education committees to authorize the admission of unbaptized children to the Lord's supper in certain circumstances. Two or three years earlier the Assembly had agreed that

> where a Kirk Session is satisfied that baptized children are being nurtured within the life and worship of the church and love the Lord and respond in faith to the invitation 'take, eat,' it may admit such children to the Lord's table, after pastorally overseeing the response of faith of such children to see when it is right for them to come to the Lord's Table.[1]

When this provision was under debate, questions were raised about invidious division among the children of the congregation, some of whom, in the Sunday school in particular, might not have been baptized. It was chiefly discrimination of this kind—some, baptized, being taken and others, unbaptized, being left—that the 1995 request was intended to obviate. Why, it was argued, should children be excluded as second-class citizens on a technicality, merely because they happened not to have been baptized?

The rejection of the suggestion afforded cold comfort. It was difficult to conceive how it could ever have surfaced in the Church of Scotland, no less, which not only nurtures a sizable *amour-propre* as far as theology is concerned (not without good cause, it should be said) but sponsored barely a generation ago probably the most extended investigation of baptism that topic has ever received from a church. The Special Commission on Baptism beavered away for a decade, 1953–63, under Professor T.F. Torrance's convenership, reported at length in minute print to the General Assembly year after year, and published *The Biblical Doctrine of Baptism* (1958) and *The Doctrine of Baptism* (1966).[2] It was as fulsome in its theology of baptism as it was exhaustive in its research.

---

[1] *The Church of Scotland General Assembly 1992* (Edinburgh, 1992), I, p. 553; II, p. 33.

[2] For details see the article 'Baptism' by the present writer in Nigel M. de S. Cameron *et al.* (eds), *Dictionary of Scottish Church History and Theology* (Edinburgh, 1993), pp. 56-58 (ch. 21 above).

Nevertheless, three decades later, a child's lack of baptism is regarded in some circles in the same church as incidental, unfortunate perhaps, but not to be allowed to debar the child from the Lord's table.

Readers of this volume of essays in honour of one of the most powerful evangelical theologians of the twentieth century may be shaking their heads knowingly and muttering, 'Well, what do you expect? The Kirk's not what it was, theologically.' One does not need to be a James Packer to expose the nakedness of the proposal: if unbaptized children, why not unbaptized teenagers and adults?—to say nothing of a raft of other more substantial objections. But if we are of one mind in showing it the door, how healthy is the theology of Christian baptism among the evangelical churches today? It may not be only a few Church of Scotland bureaucrats who have relegated baptism to the status of a doctrinal Cinderella. But neglecting or ill-treating baptism may have more serious consequences than losing one's theological respectability: it may damage the church's mission at a time in western society when primary mission rises ever higher on all the churches' agenda. If theology finds its ultimate *raison d'être* in the vitality of the people of God, as James Packer has so splendidly exemplified, belittling or ignoring baptism must prejudice its missionary integrity For baptism is above all the sacrament or ordinance of the church's missionary advance.

On a number of measures, baptism comes off a poor second to holy communion. Only very recently has it begun to attract major attention in ecumenical contexts. Not a few commentators have judged the section on baptism in the influential Faith and Order report *Baptism, Eucharist and Ministry* (Faith and Order Paper, 111; Geneva, 1982) lacking in sophistication compared with the other two. The history of Christian baptism largely remains to be written, both for formative eras like the patristic age and the Reformation and from an overall perspective. Solid dogmatic treatises on baptism are scarcely two a penny in the publishers' catalogues. In terms of church order, the question who may administer baptism hardly rates a mention alongside who may preside at the eucharist. What an irony that so much ink—or blood—should have been spilt over the latter, and so little concern evinced over who may rightly admit people to the church in baptism.

The Church as Baptismal Community

It has become a commonplace in recent ecumenical discussion to describe the church as a eucharist community. It would be far truer to the New Testament to describe it as a baptismal community. To make this point is not merely to correct an ecumenical imbalance; it is to challenge evangelical indifference, for the New Testament's (and for that matter, the Reformation's) baptismal language is much more realist than modern evangelical piety has generally allowed. Without attempting a close exegetical study, it may nevertheless be worth reminding ourselves of a string of New Testament declarations.

> Jesus came to them and said, 'All authority in heaven and on earth has been given to me. Therefore go and make disciples of all nations, baptizing them in the name of the Father and of the Son and of the Holy Spirit.' (Matthew 28:18-19)

> 'Brothers, what shall we do?' Peter replied, 'Repent and be baptized, every one of you, in the name of Jesus Christ for the forgiveness of your sins. And you will receive the gift of the Holy Spirit.' (Acts 2.37-38)

> We were all baptized by one Spirit into one body...and we were all given the one Spirit to drink. (1 Corinthians 12.13)

> You are all sons of God through faith in Christ Jesus, for all of you who were baptized into Christ have clothed yourselves with Christ. (Galatians 3.26-27)

> There is one body and one Spirit just as you were called to one hope when you were called—one Lord, one faith, one baptism; one God and Father of all, who is over all and through all and in all. (Ephesians 4.4-6)

> This water [around Noah's ark] symbolizes baptism that now saves you also—not the removal of dirt from the body but the pledge of a good conscience toward God. It saves you by the resurrection of Jesus Christ. (1 Pet. 3.21)

Note the absence from Ephesians 4 of 'one eucharist'! I omit, as likely to be contentious, John 3.5, 'Jesus answered, "I tell you the truth, no one can enter the kingdom of God unless he is born of water and the Spirit"', even though no biblical text was cited as often as this with reference to baptism in the early Fathers. Peter's summons in his Pentecost address may be taken as standing for the special interest in baptism shown throughout the Acts of the Apostles. The Ethiopian's question, 'Look, here is water. Why shouldn't I be baptized?' (Acts 8.36) must reveal part of the burden of Philip's witness to him. What Paul heard from Ananias, 'And now what are you waiting for? Get up, be baptized and wash your sins away, calling on his name' (Acts 22.16), helps to explain the boldness of Paul's baptismal teaching.

The centrality of baptism to the experience of the New Testament churches is evident also in the way it is cited to correct abuses of one kind or another. To the divided parties of Corinth it was enough to say 'Is Christ divided? Was Paul crucified for you? Were you baptized into the name of Paul?' (1 Corinthians 1.13). How many pastors today would instinctively tackle the gross misunderstanding of 'going on sinning so that grace might increase' as Paul did?

> We died to sin; how can we live in it any longer? Or don't you know that all of us who were baptized into Christ Jesus were baptized into his death? We were therefore buried with him through baptism into death in order that, just as Christ was raised from the dead through the glory of the Father, we too may live a new life. (Romans 6.2-4)

Colossians 2.12-13 shows how readily Paul invoked the burial imagery of baptism:

> ...having been buried with him in baptism and raised with him through your faith in the power of God, who raised him from the dead. When you were dead in your sins and in the uncircumcision of your sinful nature, God made you alive with Christ.

How many among us would think of describing the Israelites of the exodus as 'baptized into Moses in the cloud and in the sea' (1 Corinthians 10.2)? Or include 'instruction about baptisms' (Hebrews 6.2 — whatever the plural might denote) among the basics of the faith?

Low Baptismal Consciousness

The apostolic churches evince a baptismal consciousness rarely to be glimpsed in evangelical churches today. This is particularly the case in infant-baptizing communions. It would not be uncommon in the Church of Scotland, for example, for older teenagers or young adults coming forward for what until recently could be called admission to the Lord's table to be unaware whether they had been baptized or not ('I must ask my parents'). But apart from such uncertainty, baptism occupies a fairly marginal niche in the teaching programmes and hence the corporate mind of many an orthodox congregation. A different story might have to be told of believer-baptizers, but I would expect considerable variation, with conversion in many instances eclipsing baptism as the moment constitutive of Christian identity. On a nondenominational canvas, a problem typically encountered in mass evangelism — 'she has become a Christian/been converted, and now she has to find a church to join' — is a quintessentially modern one, which would have been almost incomprehensible to the church of most earlier centuries. That is to say, the notion that one could 'become a Christian' prior to and apart from being 'baptized by the one Spirit into the one body' is one that the church of the Fathers and the Reformers would have found bizarre.

Why is it that the baptismal consciousness of so much church life in the West burns so low? Why is it that so few Christians who would otherwise identify cordially with the broad witness of the Reformation would think of defying devilish assaults on the soul as Luther did — with the words 'I have been baptized'? The answers are no doubt to be sought in several different directions, not all of which need detain us here. They would include an understandable but exaggerated reaction against sacramentalist fundamentalism, which views participation in baptism as the be-all and end-all of church membership—a reaction still responsible for the ignoring or spiritualizing of biblical references to baptism in too much biblical exposition from evangelical pulpits. Coupled with this, one must cite the practice of indiscriminate baby baptism that still prevails in some European countries, especially where Lutheranism is the state church, and is still widely influential elsewhere, though more patchily than earlier in the twentieth century. Where baptism is so easily given and received, with so little effect, it cannot—so many biblical Christians would reason—amount to very much. Some would even claim that it is not better than nothing but actually worse than nothing! In broad terms this conviction inspires the work of the Movement for the Reform of Infant Baptism (MORIB),[3] whose newsletters reflect the analysis that indiscriminate infant baptism has created massive obstacles to the evangelization of England. On this reckoning it has, alas, been only too effective; its injection of a minimal dose of the virus of Christianity has successfully inoculated generations of English men and women against catching the real thing in later life. This diagnosis of the root causes of pervasive spiritual indifference may be losing its plausibility with the passing of the years, but its validity cannot be wholly discounted.

Baptism and De-Christianization

There may even be factors in the de-Christianizing religious situation in the West which threaten to breathe new life into a turning-the-blind-eye generosity in baptismal administration. Interest in the institutional church seeps away at an alarming rate. As fewer and fewer people express any need for it, those who do are likely to be greeted with unquestioningly open arms. In this age of accountability, ministers will be increasingly tempted to notch up every chance of demonstrating that there is still a demand for what they have to offer, even if their services—in marrying and burying as well as baptizing—are increasingly demanded on sub-Christian or non-Christian terms. Where the consumer is king, it will surely prove harder for clergy to remain ministers of Christ's word and sacraments in servicing the expectations of ever more minimally Christian folk-religion. Already granny, rather than the child's parents, is the real promoter of many an infant baptism, and already pastors are grappling routinely with requests for baby baptism from cohabiting unmarried parents or from a single parent with the other one nowhere in sight.

The last paragraphs of course no more than draw attention to some of the implications for baptism of the messiness that complicates the life and

---

[3] Its president is Bishop Colin Buchanan, and it is now known as Baptismal Integrity.

ministry of Christ's church as the society within which it is set slides into an ex-Christian ethos. It is messy because it is a slide rather than an abrupt leap, and the carryover from the Christian past, in memory, instinct and conscience, lives on with varying degrees of vitality. It is messy no doubt for other reasons also, such as inconsistent or unprincipled church practice in earlier years which has now come home to roost. And we may be tempted to welcome the sharper lines of the harsh new environment of hostility, scorn and indifference toward Christianity simply because the messiness may diminish. This would be cold comfort, to be sure, but it holds out for baptism clear hopes of a recovery of its intrinsic connection with the Christian mission.

We should not imagine, however, that as the church increasingly finds itself, in Europe at least, in a primary mission field, this recovery of baptism will be straightforward. For inclusiveness is a prominent element in the religious psyche of the ex-Christian West, and baptism always marks boundaries. It is the rite whereby persons are included in the family of Christ, but only by drawing lines between church and non-church, between Christian and non-Christian. A baptismal ministry which seeks to be faithful to the New Testament's presentation of baptism cannot fail to run athwart the inclusivist spirit of the age. In a number of ways the pre-Constantinian experience of the church becomes more and more pertinent at the end of the second millennium. Not least is this the case for baptism.

Now the baptismal experience of the church of the early Fathers was very largely of believer's baptism, or perhaps better conversion-baptism. Historical study is steadily consolidating the conclusion that infant baptism did not really come into its own, as the common practice, until after Augustine, perhaps in the sixth century. This is not to deny that some babies were baptized from at least the middle of the second century (grounds for confidence before this are lacking),[4] but rather to confirm historically what Karl Barth claimed, that infant baptism belongs to Christendom. Its flourishing took place in the context of that long phase of western religious history marked by the coterminousness of the Christian and the civil communities. Christendom began in the era of the Christian Roman Empire after Constantine and has continued in Europe, and in less formalized ways in the regions of the world colonized from Europe, until the latter twentieth century. Even where establishment or national recognition of one particular church survives (in England and Scotland, for example), the reality rings increasingly hollow. For the first time for over a millennium and a half, Christians in western, or at least European, society now live in a post-Christendom world. To that extent, pre-Constantinian Christianity must come into its own again.

---

[4] See the early chapters in this book.

Infant Baptism and New Testament Baptism

From several quarters infant baptism is likely to encounter growing criticism. In addition to factors already mentioned, such as the deeper historical uncertainty attending claims for the practice of normative paedobaptism from apostolic times and the disintegration of civil communities united by a shared Christian identity attested in universal baptism of babies, others lie nearer the biblical and theological knuckle. One reason for the muffling of the New Testament's clarion baptismal notes is the sheer embarrassment most evangelicals incur when attempting to make them ring true of baby baptism, or of young children baptized as babies. At this point I should perhaps make it plain that my purpose in this essay is not to reject the biblical and theological credentials of infant baptism, as I hope the following remarks will confirm. To attempt to do so in a volume dedicated to honouring Jim Packer would be discourtesy indeed. My concern is rather to persuade us to face up to the connections between the prevalence of paedobaptism, not least in Reformed Christianity, and the strange silence on baptism in the church. One cause of this silence, I would submit, is our gross discomfort in treating both forms of baptism—of infants and of believers (or in the very earliest distinction between them, in Hippolytus' *Apostolic Tradition* early in the third century, of those who cannot and those who can answer for themselves) —as 'one baptism'.

Of course we would testily repel any suggestion that we believed in two baptisms, and no doubt our baptismal orders of service employ some New Testament baptismal affirmations when babies are being baptized. But when we are free of such liturgical constraints, we display our true colours. The children of the church family do not grow up being taught that in baptism they died to sin and rose in Christ to newness of life. They do not learn of their identity as those who in baptism have put on Christ, or who were baptized by the Spirit into the body of Christ.[5] Moreover, because we have become accustomed to aiming off, as it were, in accommodating what the New Testament says about baptism to our infant baptism, even when we do baptize believing converts we lack the crispness of apostolic conviction that in baptism they pass from the bondage of

---

[5] Galatians 3.27 ('all of you who were baptized into Christ have been clothed with Christ') was an embarrassment to Augustine in controversy with the Donatists, as he tried to sustain his position that the baptism they received in schism was real, but wholly unbeneficial so long as they remained outside the Catholic Church. Armed with texts like Galatians 3.27, the Donatists impaled him on the horn of a dilemma: either deny that our baptism is real baptism or concede that, if real, it must bestow the Spirit, clothe with Christ, etc. For Augustine's response see David F. Wright, 'Donatist Theologoumena in Augustine? Baptism, Reviviscence of Sins and Unworthy Ministers', in *Congresso Internazionale su S. Agostino nel XVI Centenario della Conversione. Atti II* (Studia Ephemerides 'Augustinianum', 25; Rome, 1987), pp. 213-24 (see ch. 8 above).

Egypt to the freedom of the Promised Land—an Old Testament type that the New Testament encourages us to apply to baptism.

By now some readers will be indignantly protesting that I do their ministry and their church practice an injustice. The broad brush, however, is the only implement I can use in this wide-ranging portrayal of baptismal neglect. In the nature of the case, it can be only impressionistic as a generalization, but I could cite sufficient particular instances to make me believe that it will sound the ring of truth for many. The difficulty we experience in treating baby baptism as New Testament baptism, pure and simple, accounts, at least in part, for our uneasiness in the face of what a document like *Baptism, Eucharist and Ministry* says about baptism. A common evangelical response faults it for using verbs in the indicative mood rather than in the optative or in some other form expressing the ideal instead of the assumed reality. We would prefer such texts to convey the message that it ought to be true that all who have been baptized have been clothed with Christ, instead of assuming it to be true *simpliciter*. And we may wish to insert 'or will be clothed with Christ', for the overconfident sacramentalism we detect in *Baptism, Eucharist and Ministry* unnerves us most of all when it purports to speak without qualification of paedobaptism.

Analyzing such ecumenical statements is, no doubt, a specialist skill in which few of us have been trained; my comments here barely scratch the surface. My point is this: we bridle at their language not always or solely for the reasons of high theological principle we verbalize, but because, in our almost single-minded preoccupation with babies as the recipients of baptism, we have become past masters at a kind of baptismal reductionism. We balk at the indicatives of *Baptism, Eucharist and Ministry* when it is the indicatives of the New Testament that truly bother us. We have got used to handling the latter, but we see no good cause to extend similar considerations to documents emanating from twentieth-century Geneva.

Note again the case that is being advanced here. As a result of thinking of baptism almost exclusively in terms of baby baptism—of making the latter not only the norm in practice but also the theological norm—we have subjected the New Testament's witness to baptism to a compliant reductionism. We have shrunk the apostolic testimony to what we can comfortably believe about paedobaptism.[6] Integral to these convictions is

---

[6] The extent to which we have been unaware of the shift that has taken place is illustrated by appeals to the passivity of the child in baptism as theologically virtuous—and even sometimes (heaven forfend!) to the child's squalling as expressive of fallen nature's hostility to grace! The same reasoning would lead to the dosing of unwitting babies with the bread and wine of the supper. While it is true that baptism is not self-administered, nor is the supper. 'Take and eat' is on par with 'Be baptized' in respect of the recipient's initiative, as Karl Barth recognized.

the awareness that infant baptism is only too often a failure. Far from being an initiation, a beginning, it rapidly turns out to be a dead end. One indubitable fact about Britain at the end of the twentieth century ought to have given the churches a sobering pause for thought long ago. I refer to the millions of infant-baptized persons who are now by any meaningful measure de-churched. The fault, to be sure, does not lie solely with the churches' baptismal policies, but they cannot escape a heavy weight of blame. It is difficult not to conclude that the baptismal practices of the mainstream churches of the Reformation in modern Britain in recent decades have been a colossal failure. Evangelicals in the main are as ready as any to recognize the failure. Endeavours such as MORIB/Baptismal Integrity are attempting to address it. But it is a thousand pities that too salient a feature of the evangelical response has been the downgrading of the significance of baptism. If so frequently the baptism of a baby leads not to his or her incorporation into the living community of faith but simply nowhere, what is so wonderful about baptism?

In practice, the centre of gravity shifts to conversion, profession of faith, confirmation, admission to communion. Confirmation, that fruitful seedbed of confusion, is treated as compensating for baby baptism's inadequacies, although what is being confirmed—the baptized person, the baptismal vows or promises, or baptism itself—and by whom—God the Holy Spirit, the minister or the candidate—has never met with a consensus. Although there are some grounds for viewing admission to communion or confirmation as gathering up a feature or features of a primitive baptismal rite that got sundered from baptism itself, the modern observance is little more than a deposit of ecclesiastical tradition—by comparison, that is, with the dominical status of baptism. It is a matter of grief, therefore, when confirmation is viewed as 'completing' baptism, or otherwise eclipses it in importance. The credibility of confirmation must be tested by the preeminence it gives to baptism. When adult believers are being baptized, there should be no need for confirmation or admission at all. When a group of candidates is presented for confirmation and one of them has not been baptized, any action should be avoided that appears to rate the baptism as a mere preliminary requirement—such as holding it in advance in the vestry or hall in the presence of the elders alone, or reducing it to the barest minimum in order to arrive as soon as possible at the real business of the service. Thus does human tradition make void the word of God (cf. Mark 7.13).

The Reformers' Problems

It is again cold comfort to realize that the cluster of problems highlighted in this essay is largely the legacy of the sixteenth-century Reformers.

Their appeal to the supremacy of scripture—not so much scripture alone as scripture supreme over all other loci of authority—left them at first hesitant and latterly resourcefully versatile in vindicating the baptism of babies. It was, one may judge, by far the most significant constitutive feature of Protestant church life that they perpetuated without explicit scriptural warrant. The devising of a new rite of confirmation was probably their most lasting attempt to secure what they concluded was unattainable on the basis of infant baptism alone. A key figure in the development of evangelical confirmation was Martin Bucer, the Reformer of Strasbourg and later England. It emerged out of his struggles to establish in Strasbourg a viable programme of Christian discipline to ensure the formation of an authentically Christian community. In the process he came

> to detach from baptism when given to infants much of its significance as the point of demarcation between the church and the world, and to reassign this to subsequent education and discipline and in due course to confirmation...
>
> [He] ascribed specifically to paedobaptism a containing role, the marking of an outer ring, within which another and more decisive line would be drawn, coming into quasi-sacramental focus in confirmation.[7]

Several of the magisterial Reformers, while insisting on the strictest universality of infant baptism, experimented in other ways in their quest for a genuine fellowship of committed believers, an *ecclesiola* within the *ecclesia* of the broad people's church identified by paedobaptism.[8] These endeavours to some degree acknowledge the attractiveness of the Anabaptists' vision of a covenanted community, but as stalwart champions of the ideal of late-medieval Christendom, the mainstream Reformers recoiled instinctively from the Radical Reformers' abandonment of one of Christendom's key foundations, universal infant baptism, in pursuit of that vision.

The obligation to have one's children baptized, on pain of legal sanctions, is a thing of the past, yet it has left a mark on expectations and aspirations that can still sometimes be discerned at the turn of the millennia. The case for unrestricted administration of baby baptism is still occasionally made in all good faith. More common is the minister preju-

---

[7] David F. Wright, 'Infant Baptism and the Christian Community in Bucer', in David F. Wright (ed.), *Martin Bucer: Reforming Church and Community* (Cambridge, 1994), pp. 95-106, at pp. 101, 106 (see ch. 12 above, pp. 173, 178). See also Amy Nelson Burnett, *The Yoke of Christ: Martin Bucer and Christian Discipline* (Sixteenth Century Essays and Studies, 24; Kirksville, MO, 1994).

[8] David F. Wright, 'Sixteenth-Century Reformed Perspectives on the Minority Church', in John H. Leith (ed.), *Calvin Studies VII: Papers Presented at a Colloquium...January 28-29, 1994* (Davidson, NC, 1995), pp. 15-29.

diced in favour of acceding to every request for baptism, even in defiance of his denomination's stipulated conditions. Yet to recognize that our contemporary problems have their roots in the Reformation does not excuse our fecklessness in confronting them in the present. On the contrary, such a recognition should liberate us to grapple with them all the more vigorously, especially if we judge that in their unbudging allegiance to paedobaptism the Reformers were less critical of Christendom than they might have been. They were after all not only for the most part honourable men but also fallible human beings.

Shifting Convictions

So where do we go from here? By now some personal confession is overdue. I have hitherto defended, and still can and do defend, the biblical and theological credentials of baby baptism in time-honoured Reformed fashion. Nevertheless, the conviction has been growing on me for some years that the practice of baby baptism in mainstream Protestantism (including Anglicanism) in Britain in recent decades has been fraught with immense harm to the church of Jesus Christ. The reasoning that undergirds this unwelcome conviction has been spelled out in the earlier sections of this essay, if not comprehensively, at least at sufficient length to enable readers to seize the gist of it. The conviction is unwelcome not only because I regard the standard Reformed justification of paedobaptism to be as sound as ever (see further below) but also because of the challenge it poses to my more general conviction that healthy theology and healthy practice go together. How can the biblical-theological basis for infant baptism be so secure if administering it faithfully creates so much agonizing for conscientious ministers of the gospel? And if squaring the circle in order to reconcile the high promise of baptism with its high failure rate leads to the minimizing of the significance of baptism that I have laboured to demonstrate above? In my book, the toughest charge that paedobaptism has to answer is its responsibility, not alone but heavy enough, for disabling evangelical churchmen (but not the Reformers, it must be said) from believing and teaching the New Testament's witness to baptism at anywhere near its face value.

I am now inclined to regard infant baptism as consistent with scripture but not required by it, much like episcopacy, or presbytery for that matter. What cannot be claimed for it on credible biblical grounds is that it is normative baptism, whether theologically or practically. That distinction must rest with believers' baptism or conversion-baptism. Placing the theological rationale for baby baptism somewhat lower down the scale of *credenda* should enable us to tackle its discontents with greater freedom of movement. After all, it appears in none of the creeds of the universal church; I have argued elsewhere that the Nicene Creed's 'one baptism for the remission of sins' cannot originally have encompassed the baptism of infants.[9]

Future Prospects

Once again, where do we go from here? We may expect infant baptism in part to wither on the vine, along with the dregs of Christendom. Already requests for it inspired by residual folk-Christianity are decreasing. In an age of growing sensitivity to children's rights, it is also likely that in more of the committed Christian families in our congregations parents will opt not to have their babies baptized—and if my argument is heeded, we will not strive officiously to persuade them otherwise. They will resort instead to the increasing availability of services of dedication or thanksgiving or blessing for the birth of a child. We may expect such services, even when not centrally provided by a particular denomination (as is the case still in the Church of Scotland),[10] to be more and more the resort of ministers concerned to avoid both abusing baptism and turning away empty-handed those seeking baptism for their children on unacceptable grounds. Services to mark the birth of a child come in various shapes and sizes.[11] It is critical that while they may function as alternatives to baptism, they must not become substitutes for it—infant baptism in all but water, as it were. They dare not leave the impression that a person, whether parent or child, has settled his or her account with the living God. To that extent, they should remain purposefully open-ended—open to the subsequent hearing of the gospel and the response of faith in baptism.

A growing number of churches now formally operate a dual-practice administration of baptism. In many cases this has come about from the union of churches of divergent baptismal order, as in the United Reformed Church in Great Britain. Other churches have simply given formal recognition of the acceptability of the parental choice not to have their offspring baptized as persons unable to answer for themselves. Yet other churches which have in no way qualified their expectation that children born to members will be baptized—again the Church of Scotland is an example—are nevertheless likely to feel the influence of this increasing flexibility in baptismal practice.

---

[9] David F. Wright, 'The Meaning and Reference of "One Baptism for the Remission of Sins" in the Niceno-Constantinopolitan Creed', *Studia Patristica* 19 (1989), pp. 281-85 (see ch. 4 above).

[10] See Graeme Dunphy, *Celebrating Child-Birth in the Church: Baptism or Dedication?* (Edinburgh, 1991). See now *A Welcome to a Child: Four Orders for Thanksgiving and Blessing* (Edinburgh, 2006).

[11] See the helpful discussion by Philip Tovey, '"Can We Have the Baby Done?" Infant Initiation and Pre-baptismal Rites', *Anvil* 12 (1995), pp. 137-44.

It enjoys the endorsement of no less than *Baptism, Eucharist and Ministry*, which must rank as the most widely studied document of the ecumenical movement. While it does not go so far as to recommend adoption of the dual-practice system, it points forcefully to the emerging consensus that sees much less difference than our forefathers did between infant baptism followed by nurture leading to personal profession of faith and infant dedication followed by nurture leading to baptismal profession of faith.

Evangelical Disagreement

This is an appropriate point at which to cite an important reason for evangelicals' devaluation of baptism which has so far been merely alluded to: namely, our deep-seated disagreement about it. A similar fate has befallen another bone of evangelical contention—ecclesiology; better to leave it buried than have it dug up and noisily scrapped over. Yet our failure to agree about the proper subjects of baptism represents a serious challenge to cherished evangelical convictions about the perspicuity of scripture,[12] as well as leaving believers-baptists free to practise what paedobaptists regard as rebaptism.[13] Welcome evidence of some meeting of minds, not least in a recent article by George Beasley-Murray,[14] will strengthen the developing flexibility surveyed above. But flexibility must not be allowed to foster indifference to baptism.

The shift in my own thinking toward viewing the baptism of babies as something akin to an *adiaphoron* has been promoted by a deepening conviction of the centrality of baptism to the church's mission of the gospel. Baptism is, when all is said and done, one of the only two specific observances which the churches of the Reformation believe that Christ the Lord commanded his followers to perpetuate.

Saving Infant Baptism

This paper is not a call for the abandonment of infant baptism—although I have often thought that a moratorium on baptizing babies for, say, ten years would enable it to be resumed on a much sounder basis. But rather

---

[12] Cf. my 'Scripture and Evangelical Diversity with Special Reference to the Baptismal Divide', Philip E. Satterthwaite and David F. Wright (eds), *A Pathway into the Holy Scripture* (Grand Rapids, MI, 1994), pp. 257-75 (see ch. 20 above).

[13] See my 'One Baptism or Two? Reflections on the History of Christian Baptism', *Vox Evangelica* 18 (1988), pp. 7-23 (see ch. 19 above).

[14] George R. Beasley-Murray, 'The Problem of Infant Baptism: An Exercise in Possibilities', in Faculty of Baptist Theological Seminary, Rüschlikon (ed.), *Festschrift Günther Wagner* (International Theological Studies: Contributions of Baptist Scholars, 1; Berne, 1994), pp. 1-14.

than indulging such daydreams, let me evince my *bona fides* by spelling out the terms that would alone to my mind justify the continuation of the practice.

1. A principled discipline of administration, so that only those parents who are regularly worshipping church members would expect to have their infants baptized. Easier said than done, I know; hence what follows next.

2. The adoption of a service or services to mark the birth of a child, to enable ministers to escape from the straitjacket of an all-or-nothing choice. I have no doubt at all that theologically and liturgically respectable orders are already on hand, and biblical precedents are not hard to seek.

3. The unambiguous owning of baby baptism as New Testament baptism—period. I see no defensible future for a paedobaptism which cannot bear the full weight of the New Testament's baptismal witness. If this creates problems for tidy theological systems, so be it; better to be faithful to scripture than to the *magisterium* of any of our dogmatic theologies.

4. The nurture of baptized children as members of the church and the people of God. I view early admission to the Lord's table as entirely consistent with such a stance. By one Spirit they have been baptized into the one body of Christ; their full belonging is not a matter of hope or prospect, but of present enjoyment.

5. The making of baptism an explicit and frequent reference-point in Christian education from the earliest stages. The baptized must grow up knowing that they are in Christ by baptism, that in baptism they died and rose again with Christ, and that through baptism they are his for ever. This fifth point is really an aspect of the previous one, but is to the best of my knowledge neglected enough to merit highlighting separately. It has many different facets, according to the different facets of New Testament baptism. For example, in terms of Galatians 3.27-28, baptized children should grow up knowing that baptism is the great leveler; in baptism individuals of all kinds are received on the common basis of grace alone.

6. A cluster of lesser practical requirements that would make baptism unambiguously a congregational occasion rather than a family one, and also heighten the dramatic vividness of the rite. If there has to be a party, make it a church one; the baptism shall always take place in the home church at the time of a main Sunday service; the local minister shall baptize (even if the baby's aunt or granddad is a minister); imaginative efforts will be made to enhance the solemnity and awesomeness of the observance (why not immersion, like the Orthodox?); all billing and cooing over the baby will be banned (it was the late Alan Stibbs, with whom Jim Packer must have shared many a platform, who averred that baby worship had killed the gospel at the font).

7. The notes of the gospel to be sounded loud and clear, so that all present will be left in no doubt that baptism is a sacrament of the gospel. If infant baptism deserves to be saved from the ruins of Christendom, it will only be by returning it to baptism's New Testament configurations—ecclesial, kerygmatic, mystagogic, Christological. Then infant baptism will truly be an apostolic focus for the church's apostolic mission.

CHAPTER 27

Christian Baptism: Where Do We Go From Here?

The question assumes that we know where we are, where 'here' is. We need to make sure that this is really the case. As I respond to the invitation to turn from historian of church and theology into a didactic and prophetic role, I want to make clear, with all the modesty I can muster, that 'here' is to be found at the end of a careful reading of *What has Infant Baptism done to Baptism? An Enquiry at the End of Christendom* (Milton Keynes, 2005). To put it in other words, the departure point for this exercise is the strange history of infant baptism sketched in that book, which inevitably involves parts of the history of believers' baptism.

Although written by someone who still endorses the acceptability of infant baptism (but with an enthusiasm considerably more muted than a generation ago), the book's hopefulness for a more consensual future for Christian baptism rests on the widespread and still spreading recognition, especially on the part of churches that for most of their history have baptized very few persons other than infants, that it is both valid and important to regard faith-baptism, that is, the baptism of individuals responding in their own person to questions about their faith in Jesus Christ, as the norm, in an appropriately qualified sense, of Christian baptism, both in theology and in practice. You are not 'here' unless you have come to terms with this remarkable development of the later twentieth and early twenty-first centuries, which is truly one of the greatest facts of the modern era about baptism. Coming to terms with it entails recognizing that it does not require the rejection of infant baptism, although it is likely to issue in more modest appreciations of that practice in the light of historical and theological re-evaluation.

One of the directions in which we should move—and here I address fellow paedobaptists—will lead us to abandon over-argued efforts to prove that infants were baptized in the churches of the New Testament. That in fact they were cannot (so I judge) be ruled out, but the case falls far short of proof, and advocates of baptizing babies are on safer territory in relying on biblical-theological rather than historical grounds. The historical question is not even clarified if the investigation is extended to the writings of the Apostolic Fathers, traditionally viewed as the earliest group of post-New Testament texts. I have recently argued that:

> the Apostolic Fathers of themselves barely sustain a picture even of obscurity concerning infant baptism. So far are they from dispersing the shadows of the New Testament that, if one started from the Apostolic Fathers and not the New Testament, one could scarcely claim that the baptizing of infants was even obscurely in view.[1]

At the same time, advocates of exclusive believers' baptism should abandon efforts to trace a thin red line of unbroken continuity of the principled practice of baptizing only believers from the apostolic era to the emergence of Anabaptism in the sixteenth century. They must bring themselves to accept how minimal and rare were challenges to infant baptism during that long period of more than a millennium. To guard against misconceptions that still enjoy some currency, the Donatist Christians of early North Africa baptized the newborn just like the mainstream Catholic Christians of the region. When they re-baptized members of the Catholic church who joined them, this had nothing to do with rejection of infant baptism. When Catholic families became Donatists, all alike, from the youngest to the oldest, were re-baptized.

The way forward, then, must encompass the blocking off of historical excursions which promise false security, in the shared knowledge that the true history of baptism of itself favours dogmatism on neither side of the traditional divide. Although infant baptism held almost unchallenged sway for so many centuries, its universal prevalence cannot be read back into the first century, while at the same time the central liturgical form of services of infant baptism for the best part of two millennia, before and after the Reformation, indirectly disclosed the extraordinarily persistent influence of faith-baptism as the normative pattern.

More important for further progress toward greater rapprochement on baptism will be a serious revisiting of the New Testament witness. Readers of *Evangelical Quarterly*[2] may be surprised to learn that renewed biblical study has lain behind some of the significant milestones in recent work on baptism, including the World Council of Churches' Faith and Order document on *Baptism, Eucharist and Ministry* (1982) and the post-Vatican II reconsideration in the Roman Catholic Church leading to the *Rite of Christian Initiation of Adults* (from 1972). What is needed now is a programme of Bible study involving participants who start from

---

[1] David F. Wright, 'The Apostolic Fathers and Infant Baptism: Any Advance on the Obscurity of the New Testament?', in A.F. Gregory and C.M. Tuckett (eds), *Trajectories through the New Testament and the Apostolic Fathers* (Oxford, 2005), p. 133 (see ch. 3 above, p. 54).

[2] This article first appeared in *Evangelical Quarterly* 78 (2006), pp. 163-69.

different baptismal positions, and not least among those Christians who profess to accord a greater authority to scripture than they comfortably associate with the World Council of Churches and the Roman Catholic Church. Such a programme might start by listing all the occurrences of the noun 'baptism' and the verb 'baptize' in the New Testament, with the initial aim of determining how many of them refer to the actual water-rite of baptism. Some will be obviously metaphorical, such as Jesus' looking forward to his death as a baptism (Mark 10.38-39, Luke 12.50), others less obviously so, including Paul's portrayal of the Israelites as baptized into Moses (1 Corinthians 10.2). There may emerge another category of references about which agreement may not be readily forthcoming: does John the Baptizer's declaration that the one who is to come will baptize with the Holy Spirit (Mark 1.8 par.) contain a reference of any kind to the (future) rite of Christian baptism? Or again was the Corinthians' being 'baptized by one Spirit into one body' (1 Corinthians 12.13) an experience that happened through ordinary baptism? This last verse may suggest another discrete category, of places where what is spoken of as baptism is a gift or experience of the Spirit distinguishable from water-baptism but symbolized or sealed or even embodied by it.

My purpose at this stage is not to influence the outcome of this exercise, except to stress that the first objective is to ascertain everything said in the New Testament about Christian baptism as an action involving at the very least a baptizer, one or more persons being baptized and water. Yet I do feel bound to sound a cautionary note, lest New Testament statements apparently made about baptism in a straightforward sense be ruled out of account on *a priori* grounds, such as a preformed conviction that we cannot take at face value declarations such as 1 Peter 3.21, 'baptism now saves you'. This biblical study should ask how many of the texts in question contain explicit guidance that they are to be taken in a symbolic sense only.

What is proposed here is a very basic exercise, bracketing off issues such as the subjects of baptism, that is, the persons baptized or to be baptized. It is all-important that it be undertaken in groups embracing different prior convictions on the bones of traditional baptismal contention. Once this ground-laying work has been done, the conversation might well proceed to ask two questions of the verses and passages about Christian baptism in the New Testament: first, what do they affirm about what God does or has done in or through or as a result of baptism? Secondly, what do they affirm about what human beings do or receive or experience in or through or as a result of baptism? These are admittedly weightier questions, whose answers contribute significantly to the shaping of our doctrine of baptism. Let me again plead that they be addressed without regard to the identity of the subjects of these baptisms, whether they be adults answering for themselves, babies in arms, adults who may have no right to speak in their own name (household slaves?) or children somewhere in between—unless, that is, any New Testament verse is found making different affirmations about different subjects of baptism.

My hope would be that an open-minded Bible study along these lines, shared in by Christians who take the New Testament with the utmost seriousness but who have previously occupied divergent positions around 'the waters that divide', would prove an instructive and even revealing experience, and would lay a healthy basis for a promising discussion capable of fruitful engagement with inherited differences. If this seems utopian, a fanciful lurch into unreality, then we should remind ourselves that the last half-century or so has in fact witnessed a greater meeting of Christian minds on baptism than ever before in the history of the church. *Baptism, Eucharist and Ministry* is one measure of this, as is the considerable number of churches in many different parts of the world which now officially recognize both infant baptism and believers' baptism as 'equivalent alternatives'. These 'dual-practice' churches offer to the Christian parents of newborn children the choice between seeking baptism for them as infants or waiting for them to seek it for themselves in later years. Further testimony to this wide-ranging recent rapprochement on baptism is to be found in those paedobaptist churches which have revised their orders of service for baptism to make it clear that the correct starting-point is what, for shorthand convenience, we continue to call believers' baptism—rather than infant baptism itself!

So let us not be unhopeful about the prospects for a growing level and extent of agreement on matters baptismal—which may, of course, stop some way short of endorsement of a 'dual-practice' regime, let alone conversion from one to another of the traditional conflicting positions on the subjects of baptism. Discord on this last issue is by no means the only, and perhaps not even the most substantial, challenge to be faced in the quest for a biblical baptismal consensus. I am much more interested in the different baptismal traditions each recovering in their own terms the centrality of baptism to the existence and identity of their several churches than in their coming to an agreement on practice. After all, that agreement might conceivably be bought at the cost of a continued depreciation of baptism itself, which might be the worst of all possible worlds. For myself, I have more in common with an exclusive believers-baptist who treats baptism as seriously as the New Testament than with a paedobaptist minimizer of its significance.

But what if we fail to surmount age-old disagreements? What if advocates of believers' baptism remain conscientiously unable to regard infant baptism as valid Christian baptism and continue to treat those who once received it as unbaptized? What if many paedobaptists try in vain to discern in the believers' baptisms they have observed anything more than a high-profile act of personal testimony, or are baffled beyond words when members, perhaps even office-bearers, of Baptist churches remain unbaptized for years or even decades?

There are, no doubt, several ways of responding to such an impasse. The most damaging, in my judgement, is disengagement in the resigned recognition that these issues are intractable, followed by slipping into the conclusion that, given inveterate disputes between parties who each seek to be taught by scripture, baptism cannot be a matter of primary importance. I defy anyone to conduct the basic scrutiny of the baptismal references in the New Testament recommended above and emerge with the conclusion that baptism was a second-order issue in the apostolic churches. There are on the contrary strong grounds for viewing them as baptismal churches, that is, not only churches which converts entered through baptism but churches which could be repeatedly recalled to their distinctive identity by reference to their baptism. The greatest tragedy of our familiar baptismal divisions is that we allow them to lull us into a gravely unbiblical devaluation of baptism itself. Our disagreements may be of secondary importance, our unreconciled diversity of practice likewise (especially when it comes down to the mode of baptism — sprinkling, immersion, affusion), but it would be a severe affront to New Testament teaching to reckon baptism itself as anything less than fundamental to the church of Jesus Christ.

Consequently it is a solemn matter for one church or body of Christians to decide that it will not recognize another's baptisms, for this is tantamount to questioning the very character as 'church' of that other body. Given the standard identification of a true church of Christ in the lineage of the Reformation by reference to requisite marks, of which one is the ministry of baptism and the Lord's supper, it is hard to see how a company of people lacking baptism, according to the estimate of another church, could qualify for acceptance as a church. In reality, the assessment is rarely driven to this drastic verdict. Few Baptist churches in the UK, I would guess, go so far as to unchurch the paedobaptist Church of England or Church of Scotland. In any case since both these churches also baptize some persons each year on profession of faith (for no infant-baptizing church recognizes or practises solely the baptism of the newborn), the issue is more complicated. Nor is it confined to a contemporary dimension, for hardline believers-baptists may by the force of their own doctrinal logic be consigning vast reaches of the millennium before the Reformation to churchlessness, when infant baptism prevailed almost entirely unchallenged. Martin Luther liked to tease his Anabaptist opponents in the sixteenth century: did they really believe that there had been no baptisms for a thousand years, and hence no church of Jesus Christ? This is more than a clever debating point. It powerfully illustrates how deeply these baptismal controversies cut into the foundations of the Christian church in history.

In tracking where we go from here, we run up against crucial questions about how we evaluate major disagreements of this kind. Can we assign our actual disagreements any theological significance—other than to slang off our opponents as blinded to the truth of scripture by the devil? At what point may we justifiably conclude that scripture itself may not be clear enough to prescribe a single resolution? This would *prima facie* conflict with the Reformers' cherished notion of the clarity or perspicuity of scripture, but only on the proper recipients of baptism, not on its cardinal importance as such. Several of the Reformers worked with the category of *adiaphora* (plural), literally matters of indifference, referring to practices neither commanded nor condemned by scripture and hence tolerant of variety so long as the true doctrine of the gospel is safeguarded. When as an elder of the Church of Scotland I have been formally asked whether I 'acknowledge the Presbyterian government of this Church to be agreeable to the Word of God', I have never regarded my affirmative answer as a judgement that no other form of church government is similarly agreeable. Indeed, I might be strongly of the view (some of the time!) that Presbyterian polity is decidedly preferable to other ones, without believing it to be mandated by scripture. Could there be a parallel here to baptism? I am happy to acknowledge infant baptism to be agreeable to the word of God, without being able to regard it as prescribed by it. Its observance is therefore an *adiaphoron* (singular), a matter on which Christians should be able to tolerate variety in practice and to disagree without breach of fellowship. Integral to this position is a recognition of the Christian seriousness of my brother or sister who either wants to insist on infant baptism (so that having babies baptized would be a clear duty of both parents and the church leadership) or is unable to countenance the practice at all.

Why might this route merit a sympathetic theological hearing? First, I suggest, because of the impasse so often reached when Christians genuinely attempt to cross-question the New Testament for an answer. Is it faithless to conclude that there is no new light to shine forth from New Testament scripture on this question? Believing in the unity, entire truthfulness and clarity of scripture does indeed commit us to an ever-fresh lifelong searching of it until we are brought to a common and more perfect mind on its teaching, but it is certainly arguable that tireless revisiting of the issue of the subjects of baptism may have blinded Christians, especially in the evangelical constituency, to the hugely more obvious message of the fundamental place of baptism in the ordering of the new Christian community.

There is a second reason why we might be justified in favouring on baptism what came to be called in some ecumenical circles 'reconciled diversity'. It is surely the case that lack of agreement on who may be baptized rests essentially not on divergent readings of certain New Testament verses—1 Corinthians 7.14, the household baptisms in Acts, Jesus' blessings of children, for example—but on a far deeper fault-line among students of the Bible, one which runs through the relationship between the two Testaments. Proponents of the baptism of babies characteristically rely heavily on the unity or continuity between Israel and the church, often but not invariably focused on the doctrine of God's single covenant with his chosen people. This is an apologetic for infant baptism which has deeper and wider roots than simply a parallel with circumcision, appealing, for example, to the importance of the family as a building block of the people of God. By contrast, the case for believers' baptism has typically been based on the New Testament alone—which is, after all, the only part of the Bible where we encounter Christian baptism. The first Anabaptists' rejection of infant baptism was but one aspect of their wholesale rejection of a comprehensive ordering of church, state and society which found most of its biblical warrants in the economy of Israel rather than in the marginalized minority congregations of the New Testament.

Unresolved disagreements on how to relate the Old Testament to the New are fraught with massive geopolitical implications in the twenty-first century. By comparison baptismal disputes may seem very small beer, although they provide a window into one of the biggest basic issues dividing especially but not solely biblical or evangelical Christians in our time—divisions which the massive growth of the Pentecostal and charismatic church families has made more prominent. In respect of baptism in this context a degree of rapprochement has been long overdue, from both sides. The mainstream Reformers bequeathed a defence of paedobaptism which even in its ablest exponents leaned quite disproportionately on the Old Testament. Believers-baptists are right to demand that the heirs of the Reformers owe them an apologia for infant baptism which unashamedly owns the full-orbed New Testament witness to Christian baptism. In turn devotees of exclusive believers' baptism face sharp questions about the apparent irrelevance of the Abrahamic covenant and the viability of a schema of almost total discontinuity between God's ways of gathering his people in the Old and New dispensations.

But for our purposes as we look for the way forward from here, the major question is whether all progress towards a greater consensus on baptism must be halted until we can together work our way satisfactorily through this much vaster problem. I am convinced that the salience of baptism in New Testament Christianity does not allow us to follow this sequence of engagement. By the same token, the rediscovery of that salience should instruct us not to wait: dare we go on ignoring the plain import of the New Testament's presentation of baptism while we continue debating in time-honoured fashion whether or not infants were included in baptism in the New Testament, aware all the time that beneath this question lurks a far more massive one which we scarcely know how to tackle together? Such considerations lead me to sympathize with moving forward by embracing divergent stances on baptism rather than giving priority to overcoming the divergence. The priority must belong to granting baptism the decisive place it has in apostolic Christianity. Who knows whether by putting first things first, secondary issues may also begin to appear in a fresh light?

Scripture Index

Genesis
9.9   358
13.15   358
17.7   172, 207
17.7-8   358

Exodus
33.3   48

Numbers
19   49

Deuteronomy
23.2   198

Judges
11.30-40   129

1 Samuel
1.1ff   129

Job
14.4 (LXX)   31, 50
14.4-5 (LXX)   183, 189

Psalms
1–15   33
15.1   215
18.50   358
19.4   219
22.28   219
26.5   215
29(30)   207
36.25   158
50(51).7 (LXX)   190
51.5 (50.7, LXX)   31
89.34-37   358
106.37-38   351
114.6 (116.6, LXX)   159
132.11-12   358

Ezekiel
1.10   288
10.14   288
18.4   41

Zechariah
8.4-5   360

Wisdom of Solomon
4.8-9   158

Matthew
2.16   351
3.6   353
3.11   353, 379
3.13-15   255
3.14   24, 52
5.20   159
9.13   161
11.25-30   163
16.16-19   217
16.18   218
18.3   19, 52, 156, 158, 159
18.4   157
18.6   358
18.10   52, 351
18.23-25   108
19   156, 160, 202
19.10-12   158
19.12   130
19.13-14   156, 163, 164
19.13-15   19, 23, 51, 149-65, 344
19.14   154, 155, 156, 158, 159, 161, 351
21.14-17   21
23.30-35   xxxii
23.37   xxxii
28.18-19   364
28.18-20   xxxv, 150
28.19   52, 230, 234, 353
28.19-20   260

Mark
1.8   379
1.9-11   150
1.15   138
7.13   163, 370

9.36   51
9.36-37   149, 358
9.42   358
10.13-14   150, 152
10.13-16   19, 23, 51, 149-65, 344
10.14   21, 24, 154, 155, 156, 161
10.14-15   157
10.14-16   151, 344, 358
10.15   159
10.16   150, 152
10.38   255
10.38-39   50, 379
10.39   267
16.16   52, 230, 234, 235, 349, 350, 351, 353

Luke
1.41   351
2.22   31, 32
3.16   353, 379
12.50   50, 255, 379
18.15-16   163
18.15-17   19, 23, 51, 149-65, 344
18.16   154, 155, 156
18.16-17   150
22.32   217

John
1.12-13   204
3.1-6   150
3.23   353
3.3-5   52
3.5   12, 19, 27, 40, 50, 52, 170, 189, 204, 364
3.6   204
4.1   353
6   295
9.21   78
11.16   136
11.26   165
20.23   110
21.4-5   156

Acts
1.5　52
2.37-38　234, 364
2.38　230, 260, 281, 314, 340, 353
2.38-39　xxxiv, 150
2.39　xxvi, xxxii, 21, 51, 172, 234, 358
2.41　230, 353
8.12　342
8.14-17　157
8.36　24, 52, 155, 364
8.37　234, 342
8.38　52
10.47　24, 52
11.14　51
11.16-17　342
11.17　24, 52
16.15　51
16.31-33　342
16.33　51
17.11　286
18.7　51
19　227
19.1-6　231
19.3-4　52
21.21　16, 18, 51
22.16　364

Romans
2.16　343
5.12　75
5.18-19　75
6　269, 281
6.1　261
6.1-4　261, 267, 269, 291
6.2-4　340, 365
6.3　95, 314
6.3-4　48, 52
6.3-11　230
6.4　234
6.8　353
7　227
8.1　230
8.18　197
9.10-29　73
10–11　202
10.9　271
10.10　40
10.17　157, 233
11.16　202
11.28　xxxii

14.23　201, 202
16.25　343

1 Corinthians
1.13　260, 270, 364
1.13-16　52
1.16　51
3.1　156
3.1-2　156
3.2　156
5–7　210
6.16　200
7　195
7.1-16　210
7.12-13　196
7.13-14　195
7.14　xxv, xxxiv, 13, 14, 15, 16, 37, 41, 51, 175, 192-211, 234, 235, 252-54, 294, 383
10.1-5　251-52
10.2　52, 365, 379
10.17　271
11　295
12.12-13　297
12.13　52, 178, 235, 269, 340, 364, 379
14.20　157, 160
14.26　289
15.29　13, 269

Galatians
3.6-29　357
3.7　359
3.8　xxxii
3.9　357
3.14　357
3.16　358
3.26　357
3.26-27　364
3.27　52, 107, 113, 234, 269, 340, 368
3.27-28　375
3.29　xxxiv, 357
5.2　18

Ephesians
2.3　204

4　270, 273, 274, 284, 296, 297, 298, 300, 364
4.4　58, 339
4.4-6　52, 292, 299, 312, 328, 364
4.5　260, 270
5.25-26　169
6.4　158

Colossians
2.11　16, 18
2.11-12　xxv, 18, 19, 51, 53, 235, 348, 349, 365

1 Thessalonians
2.7　156

1 Timothy
6.13-14　271

2 Timothy
2.8　343
3.15　158

Titus
1.15　197
3.5　52, 235
3.5-6　169

Hebrews
1.1　297
5.12　156
6.2　365

1 Peter
3.1　194, 205
3.20-21　52
3.21　234, 246, 314, 353, 364, 379

1 John
1.8　31

Revelation
4.7　2887.1-2　215
8.12　215

Name Index

Abraham xxxii, xxxiv, 49, 77, 173, 232, 234
Adam 25, 30, 32, 36, 38, 39, 40, 74, 75, 76, 82, 86, 204, 296, 297
Adams, H.M. 181, 200
Adeodatus 65, 71, 94, 95, 209
Adomnán 301
Adriaen, M. 157, 158
Aelias 120
Agaësse, P. 76
Ahasuerus 198
Aland, K. 4, 5, 6, 7, 8, 9, 10, 11, 12, 13, 14, 16, 17, 18, 19, 20, 22, 24, 28, 32, 45, 46, 62, 83, 123, 125, 126, 179, 190, 192, 196, 280
Albert of Brandenburg 214
Albinus 195
Alès, A. d' 195
Alexander, D.C. 72, 95
Alexander, J.S. 213
Allard, P. 144
Allen, P.S. 214
Alypius 71, 94, 95, 96, 100
Ambrose of Milan 37, 65, 66, 69, 71, 124, 128, 129, 130, 132, 158, 160, 193, 200, 208, 267
Ambrosiaster 193, 196, 199, 200, 201, 203, 205, 206, 209
Amerbach, B. 194
Amphilochius 59
Amsdorf, N. 224
André-Delastre, Louise 91, 103
Andresen, C. 55
Andreu, J.S. 137
Angenendt, A. 87
Antony (of Egypt) 61
Antony (of Fussala) 135
Apollinarius of Laodicea 157
Aquinas, T., see Thomas
Argyle, A.W. 24
Aristides 11, 46, 125, 126, 137
Armour, R.S. 185, 188
Arrowsmith, J. 251
Asella 131
Asterius the Sophist xxiii, 33, 57, 59, 62
Athanasius 61, 66, 124

Athenagoras, Patriarch of Constantinople 275
Atkinson, Clarissa W. 92, 127
Attwater, D. 91
Auf der Maur, H.J. 3, 7
Augustijn, C. 224
Augustine xxiii, xxvii, 7, 31, 33-43, 62-88, 89-104, 105-15, 117, 118, 119, 121, 122, 124, 127, 135, 137, 138, 154, 161, 162, 164, 171, 182-88, 190, 193, 194, 196, 199, 201, 203-205, 206, 208, 209, 212-16, 218, 219, 220, 223, 224, 225, 227, 264, 267, 273, 274, 288, 304, 347, 348, 351, 357, 367, 368
Augustine of Canterbury 301
Ayris, P. 223
Azéma, Y. 134

Backus, Irena 170
Badcock, G.D. 240, 252
Baillet, A. 91
Baillie, R. 241, 247, 249, 252
Bainton, R.H. 222
Baker, D. 225
Bannerman, J. xxxviii-xxxix, xl
Banning, J. van 160
Barnabas 47, 48, 49, 53
Barnes, T.D. 120
Barth, G. 5, 15
Barth, K. xxvi, xxvii, xxviii, 3, 4, 5, 6, 10, 17, 20, 21, 22, 86, 174, 221, 239, 249, 255, 256, 278, 304, 367, 369
Barton, P.F. 198
Basil the Great (of Caesarea) 34, 59, 63, 65, 120, 121, 124, 138, 158, 159
Batiffol, P. 106
Battles, F.L. 226, 227, 228, 229, 230, 231, 232, 233, 234, 235, 353, 354
Baudot, J.L. 90, 180
Baudouin, F. 212, 213, 219
Bavaud, G. 105, 106, 108
Baxter, R. xxxiii
Beasley-Murray, G.R. 13, 15, 24, 291, 293, 294, 374
Bebbington, D.W. 290, 304
Bede 158, 159, 194, 301

Beeby, D. 289
Beinert, W. 55
Bender, H.S. 181, 223
Benoît, A. 47
Benoit, J-D. 354
Bergendoff, C. 351, 352
Bergsten. T. 191
Bernardi, J. 141, 145
Berrouard, M.F. 79
Best, E. 192
Beveridge, H. 354
Beza, T. xxxii, 219
Bhaldraithe, E. de 136
Bidez, J. 140, 142, 143
Biel, Pamela 215
Bieler, L. 136
Bindseil, H.E. 198
Bjerring, N. 137
Blankenburg, W. 55, 162, 163
Blaurer, A. 223
Bloesch, E. 202
Blouet, J. 130
Boniface, bishop of Cataquas 79, 80
Bonner, G. 38, 81, 82, 83, 85
Bornert, R. 168, 170, 171, 174, 176
Boston, T. xxxiii-xxxv
Bougaud, L.-V.E. 91, 92, 101
Bouissou, G. 93
Bourke, V.J. 94
Bowersock, G.W. 140, 144
Bowles, O. xxxiii, xxxiv
Boyd, R. 305
Bradley, J.E. 82, 179, 272
Bradshaw, P.F. xxiii, 45, 78, 149, 153, 261
Brady, Jr, T.A. 167
Brandmüller, W. 215
Braun, R. 140, 141, 143, 193, 195
Brecht, M. 222, 224
Brenz, J. 221, 222, 223
Brésard, L. 156
Bretschneider, C.G. 198
Bridge, D. 268
Bridge, W. 247
Bright, W. 59
Brix, L. 92
Bromiley, G.W. 22, 40
Brown, P. 74, 88, 95, 98
Browning, R. 140
Bruce, R. 305
Bruner, F.D. 299
Bruno of Chartreux 206

Bucer, M. 150, 166-78, 187, 188, 213, 243, 302, 371
Buchanan, C. 283, 312, 313, 316, 318, 346, 366
Bugenhagen, J. 207
Bullinger, H. 193, 207, 236
Burguière, P. 142
Burleigh, J.H.S. 73
Burnaby, J. 56
Burnett, Amy N. 371
Burnish, R.F.G. 55
Burroughes, J. 247
Butler, A. 91, 101

Cabrol, F. 180
Caelestius 35, 37, 38, 81, 161
Caesarius 65
Cai, R. 162
Cajetan, T. 218
Calamy, E. 247, 249, 250, 253
Calkoen, A. 181
Callan, D. 129
Calvin, J. xxx, xxxi, xxxii, xxxiii, xxxiv, xxxvi, 153, 185, 186-87, 193, 197, 202, 203-205, 209, 212, 213, 215, 219, 220, 226-37, 246, 256, 286, 288, 289, 302, 347, 348, 349, 353-57, 360
Cameron, A. 120
Cameron, E. 275
Cameron, J.K. 220, 302, 303
Cameron, N.M. de S. xxxv, 241, 301, 362
Campanus, J. 182
Campegio, L. 214
Canivet, P. 133, 134
Capito, W.F. 169
Carlstadt, A. 169
Cassander, G. 166, 179-91, 207
Cassian, J. 65, 124
Cassiodorus 194
Castellio, S. 222
Catharinus, A. (L. Politi) 210, 217
Celsus 9
Chadwick, H. 69, 70, 72, 91, 93, 94, 97, 98, 100
Chalmers, T. xxxv
Chamier, D. 242
Chaussin, L. 90
Chavasse, A. 164
Chesnut, G.F. 142
Chiarini, G. 89
Choler, J. 224

Chrisman, M.U. 207
Christie, J. 240
Cicero 144
Clark, Elizabeth A. 66, 128
Clark, Gillian 64, 65, 103
Clement of Alexandria 156, 193, 263
Clement of Rome 51, 325
Clements, R. 290
Clerck, P. de 87
Cochlaeus, J. (Dobneck) 212, 218
Coleman, T. 251
Colish, Marcia L. 212
Constantine xxvi, 66, 139, 198, 225
Constantius 139
Conybeare, F.C. 137
Costelloe, M.J. 142
Cote, W.N. xxix
Courcelle, P. 102, 127
Courvoisier, J. 171, 176, 177
Cox, J.E. 223
Cramer, J.A. 160, 194
Cramer, P. 67, 70, 73, 80, 84, 85, 87
Cranmer, T. 223
Crespin, R. 98, 106, 109, 110
Cressey, M. 282
Cristiani, L. 92, 101
Cristiani, M. 89
Cromwell, O. 304
Cross, A.R. 46, 51, 53, 143, 159, 344
Cross, F.L. 50, 57
Crouzel, H. 61
Cullmann, O. 19, 23, 24, 52, 152, 153, 155, 288, 344
Cuming, G.J. 154, 261, 262, 263, 264
Cunningham, W. xxxv-xl
Cunningham, M.P. 133
Cyprian of Carthage 18, 24, 29, 30, 31, 36, 62, 63, 109, 111, 114, 183, 188, 208, 222, 274, 346, 348
Cyril of Alexandria 136, 139, 142, 144, 145, 160, 161, 164, 165, 194
Cyril of Jerusalem 27, 56, 57, 58, 59, 267, 273
Cyril of Scythopolis 134

Damasus 124
Daniel 134
Daniel the Stylite 134
Daniélou, J. 117, 124
Dardanus 77
David, King xxxv, 358
Davies, J.G. xxix
De Rossi, G.B. 134

Delaroche, B. 73, 79
Delehaye, H. 134
Delius, W. 213
Delling, G. 192
Deogratias 74
Devreesse, R. 59
Didier, J.C. 7, 14, 29, 33, 35, 36, 37, 40, 62, 64, 71, 79, 83, 154, 248
Diez, G.M. 135
Dinocrates 64, 65
Diocletian 133
Dionysia 134
Dionysius the Areopagite, see Pseudo-Dionysius
Dionysius the Carthusian 206
Dix, G. 318
Dodd, A. 163
Doignon, J. 157
Dolan, J.P. 180
Dolbeau, F. 76, 122, 138
Dölger, F.J. 65, 122, 123
Donatus 191
Dondeyne, A. 164
Döpp, S. 45
Dossetti, G.L. 56
Doutreleau, I. 10
Draper, J.A. 47
Driedo 218
Ducatillon, Jeanne 159
Dudden, F.H. 128
Duffield, G.E. 287
Dujarier, M. 123
Dunphy, G. 373
Dutton, Marsha L. 101

Eagan, M.C. 133
Eck, J. 201, 217, 218
Egli, E. 185, 186, 206
Elizabeth (mother of John the Baptist) 131
Elkanah 129
Empie, P.C. 55
Ennodius 65
Ephraem Syrus 65, 69, 124
Epiphanius of Salamis 57, 159
Erasmus, D. 193, 194, 195, 196, 197, 198, 205, 206, 207, 208, 214, 224
Esau 74
Eudoxia 120
Euelpistos 126
Eusebius of Caesarea 61
Eusebius of Nicomedia 145
Eustochium 132

Euthymius 134
Evagrius 124
Evans, E. 25, 27, 154
Evans, R.F. 36, 38
Evieux, P. 142
Evodius, bishop of Uzalis 71, 94, 96, 119

Fairweather, E.R. 73
Felix, bishop of Thibiuca 61
Felix, martyr at Nola 135
Ferguson, E. 12, 13, 23, 53, 62, 184, 280
Ferguson, S.B. 254
Festugière, A.J. 133, 140
Fidus, bishop 29, 30, 183
Finaert, G. 114
Finn, T.M. 84
Finsler, G. 185
Fisher, J.D.C. 150, 151, 163, 164, 176
Flamant, J. 140
Fleteren, F.V. 101
Floëri, F. 106, 107
Florus of Lyons 193
Forbes, A.P. 55
Forbes, Frances A. 90, 101
Forbes, J. 305
Forell, G.W. 350
Fraenkel, P. 185, 189, 201, 218
Franck, S. 213
François de Sales, bishop of Geneva 127
Franz, G. 214
Fremy, C. 212
Frend, W.H.C. 90, 98, 225
Frere, W.H. 164
Friedberg, A. 190, 196
Froehlich, K. 161, 183, 206
Fyall, R.S. 300

Gagney, J. 194
Gallus 143
Gamer, Helena M. 136, 190
Gardner, Alice 140
Gaudentius 131, 216
Gavigan, J.J. 92, 97
Gebhardt, E. 57
Geerard, M. 193
Geerlings, W. 45
Geisenhof, G. 207
Gennadius 66
George of Caesarea 145
Gerontius 66, 127, 128

Gibb, J. 93
Gibson, M.T. 161, 206
Giebel, M. 140
Gillard, F.D. 139
Gillespie, G. 240, 241, 245, 246, 247, 248, 249, 251
Giry, F. 90, 101
Goar, J. 137
Godefroy, L. 135
Goodwin, T. 252, 253, 254
Gorce, D. 128
Gorgonia 65
Gori, F. 129, 158
Grane, L. 77, 166, 207
Gratian 190, 191, 196, 212
Greaves, R.L. 220
Greef, W. de 212
Greenslade, S.L. 262
Grégoire, H. 120
Gregory Nazianzen 21, 34, 35, 38, 42, 56, 57, 63-66, 70, 119, 120, 124, 139-44, 146, 184, 272, 280
Gregory of Nyssa 35, 57, 63, 65, 124, 159, 160
Gregory, A.F. 378
Greschat, M. 168
Grislis, E. 348
Grossi, V. 79
Grützmacher, G. 119, 131
Gryson, R. 196
Guarienti, A. 162
Guilliaud, C. 200

Hadrian 11
Hahn, A. 59, 274
Hahn, F. 192
Haimo of Auxerre 206
Haldane, J. 304
Haldane, R. 304
Hamelmann, H. 182
Hammann, G. 167, 168, 173, 175, 176
Hammerich, H. 84
Hannah 130, 131, 134
Hansen, G.C. 141, 142, 143, 144
Hapgood, Isabel F. 137
Harkins, P.W. 33, 56, 58, 272
Harnack, A. von 144
Harting-Corre, Alice L. 85
Hartke, W. 97, 102
Hawthorne, G.F. 210
Hay, G. 303
Hazeland, Mrs E.A. 92
Hazlett, W.I.P. 243

Headley, J.M. 220
Hege, C. 182
Heil, G. 160
Heine, K. 168
Heliodorus 65
Henderson, A. 246
Hendrix, S.H. 215
Hendry, G.S. 255
Herbert, Mary E. 90, 101
Héring, J. 52
Herle, C. 247
Hermas 46, 48, 49, 50, 52
Herod 351
Hervé of Bourgdieu (Pseudo-Anselm) 206
Hesse, Denise W. 202
Hesychius, bishop of Salona 135
Hierax of Phrygia 126
Higgins, A.J.B. 288
Hilary of Poitiers 124, 157
Hill, E. 161
Hill, G.F. 120
Himerius, bishop of Tarragona 135
Hippolytus xxiii, 6, 7, 9, 10, 11, 20, 21, 28, 47, 62, 65, 78, 86, 154, 183, 261, 262, 263, 264, 265, 266, 280, 292, 330, 346, 368
Holeton, D.R. 346
Holl, K. 57
Hombert, P.-M. 75, 76, 79
Howard, J. 240
Hoy, W.I. 304
Hubert, F. 176
Hubmaier, B. 191
Hulbert, H. 3
Hunt, J.P.T. 349
Hurst, D. 157, 158
Hyginus, bishop of Rome 190, 191

Ignatius of Antioch 46, 48, 49, 50, 51, 52, 53, 325
Innocent, bishop of Rome 38
Irenaeus 9, 10, 13, 20, 182, 196
Isaac 49, 234

Jackson, S.M. 186
Jacob 49, 74
Jaeger, W. 57
Jaffé, P. 135
Jasper, J.C.D. 149, 153
Jefford, C.N. 47
Jentsch, W. 123
Jephthah 129

Jeremiah 131
Jeremias, J. xxvi, 4, 5, 6, 7, 8, 9, 10, 11, 12, 14, 15, 16, 18, 19, 20, 21, 22, 23, 24, 32, 33, 34, 44, 45, 46, 47, 51, 52, 53, 62, 65, 66, 83, 84, 116, 121, 125, 126, 139, 141, 152, 153, 155, 179, 183, 192, 280, 344, 357
Jerome 36, 37, 39, 64, 65, 66, 67, 69, 119, 122, 124, 128, 131, 132, 133, 157, 159, 183, 194, 195, 200, 208
Job 32
John Chrysostom 27, 28, 33, 34, 38, 56, 57, 58, 59, 63, 65, 66, 67, 69, 82, 117, 121, 122, 124, 160, 190, 193, 199, 200, 205, 206, 267, 272, 273, 357
John the Baptist 50, 131, 351, 379
John VI, Pope 275
John, Apostle 182
Johnson, M.E. 45, 78
Jordahn, B. 162
Judas Iscariot 216
Julian 79, 98
Julian of Eclanum 33, 34, 79, 82
Julian the Apostate 98, 139-45
Juliana 129
Jung, P.B. 296
Jungmann, J.A. 123
Justin Martyr 8, 9, 10, 12, 13, 19, 20, 126, 183, 263
Justinian 275

Käsemann, E. 289
Kasper, W. 3
Kelly, H.A. 87
Kelly, J.N.D. 25, 31, 55, 119, 271
Kempen-van Dijk, P.M.A. van 90
Kennedy, Q. 220
Kentigern 301
Kenyon, F.G. 240
Keross, H.F. 130
Keussen, H. 181
Kinzig, W. 33, 154
Kirk, J. 302, 303
Klaus, B. 14, 28
Kleinheyer, B. 3, 7
Klostermann, E. 156, 157
Knipperdolling, B. 214, 215
Knox, J. xxx, xxxi, 151, 220, 236, 305
Koch, E. 202
Koch, W. 140

Köhler, W. 180, 222
König, H. 45
Kotila, Heikki 90
Kraft, H. 6, 7, 10, 11, 12, 18, 19, 21, 33, 35, 36, 182, 183, 184, 190
Krause, G. 180
Kreider, A. 99, 263, 264
Kremer, J. 182
Kretschmar, G. 55, 163
Krodel, G.G. 350, 351
Kroon, M. de 243
Kugener, M.-A. 120
Kurmann, A. 141, 145
Kyle, R.G. xxxi

Laeta 66, 131, 132, 133
Laing, D. xxx, xxxi, 220
Laistner, M.L.W. 117
Lambot, C. 163
Lamirande, E. 117
Lampe, G.W.H. 143
Lancel, S. 79, 213
Lang, A. 171
Lasco, J. a. 174
Latte, R. De 71, 79, 86
Latomus 218
Laurentin, A. 123
Lawless, G. 71, 72, 95
Lawrence 129
Lecler, J. 180
Leclerq, H. xxix, 89, 92, 135
Lefèvre d'Étaples, J. 198, 199
Lehmann, K. 55
Leishman, T. 240
Leith, J.H. 371
Le Nain de Tillemont, L.-S.140
Leo I 182
Lepelley, C. 72
Leroy-Molinghen, Alice 133
Ley, J. 250
Licinius 198
Lienhard, M. 243
Lightfoot, J. 241, 245, 246, 248, 249, 250, 251, 252
Lightfoot, J.B. 201
Ligier, L. 3
Lindello, J. xxx
Lippold, A. 120
Littell, F.H. 221
Louis the Pious xxix
Luibheid, C. 183
Luther, M. xxxvi, 162, 169, 179, 186, 197, 198, 207, 214, 215-20, 222, 223, 224, 234, 235, 236, 269, 347, 349-53, 357, 381
Lynch, J.G. 167, 168, 173
Lynch, J.H. 78, 79

Macedonius 133
Macleod, D. xxxv, 252
Macleod, J. 251
Macmichael, N. 251
MacMullen, R. 120
Macrina 65
Madec, G. 86, 89
Mairet, P. 226
Mandouze, A. 71, 79, 89, 94, 95, 97, 100, 102, 103
Mani 39
Marcella 131
Marcellina 65
Marie de Gonzagne, M. 94
Mark, deacon to Porphyry 120
Markus, R. 225
Marlorat, A. 193
Marrou, H. 117, 124
Marshall, S. 244, 247, 250, 253
Martha (mother of Daniel the Stylite) 134
Martin of Tours 65, 124
Martin, E.J. 140
Martin, S. 90
Martindale, J.R. 77
Mary (mother of Jesus) 50, 132, 265
Maskell, W. 163
Masson, J. 213
Maxwell, W.D. xxxi, 151
McCauley, L.P. 119, 120
McGuckin, J.A. 145
M'Millan, S. xxxiii
McNeill, J.T. 136, 190, 226, 227, 228, 229-35, 353
McRoberts, D. 301
Meehan, D.M. 119
Meek, D. 241
Meer, F. van der 103, 117, 118
Melanchthon, P. 185, 189, 198, 199, 200, 215, 217, 243, 350
Melania the Elder 131
Melania the Younger 66, 127, 128, 131
Melchizedek 197
Merkel, H. 288
Methodius of Olympus 130
Methuen, Charlotte 207
Metzger, M. 154
Meyer, S. 199

Michel, A. 106
Migne. J.-P. 194
Miles, Margaret R. 264, 265
Milinski, W. 3
Mitchell, A.F. 240, 241, 242, 243, 246
Mitchell, N. 47
Moffat, R. xxx
Mohlberg, L.C. 164
Molte, Maria E. 180
Moltmann, J. 174, 278
Monnica 66, 68, 69, 70, 71, 72, 89-104, 118, 122, 127
Montgomery, W. 93
Mooi, R.J. 213
Moore, W.E. 270, 293
Morrison, A. 95
Moses 217, 218, 251, 365
Moule, C.F.D. 84, 152, 183, 357
Moule, H.C.G. 92
Moyes, T.W. 306
Mücke, J.F.A. 139
Müller, G. 180
Müller, K.F. 55, 162, 163
Muller, R.A. 82, 179, 226, 272
Murray, I.H. xxx
Murphy, T.A. 55
Musculus, W. 195, 200-203, 213
Mutzenbecher, A. 203

Nagel, E. 8, 25, 63, 83
Navigius 94, 95
Nebridius 71, 94
Neff, C. 182
Neill, S.C. 180
Neumann, K.J. 139, 140, 144
Neunhauser, B. 7, 55
Nicholas of Lyra 206
Nissiotis, N. 308
Noah 358, 364
Nonna 119
Nye, P. 246

O'Donnell, J.J. 69, 71, 72, 89, 92, 93, 95, 96, 97, 98, 99, 100, 101, 117
O'Ferrall, Margaret M. 89, 90, 91, 98
O'Meara, J.J. 90, 92
O'Neill, J.C. 13, 192
Oberman, H.A. 178
Oecolampadius xxxii, 169
Oecumenius 194
Old, H.O. 164, 166, 176
Olivétan, P.R. 197
Optatus of Milevis 63, 212, 219

Origen 9, 31-33, 35, 36, 61, 62, 156, 183, 184, 185, 186, 187, 188, 189, 190, 194, 263
Ortiz, I. 55
Osiek, Carolyn 47, 49
Otreius 134
Outler, A.C. 94, 98

Pacatula 64, 131
Packer, J.I. 297, 363, 368, 375
Palmer, H. 242, 243, 244, 253
Pannenberg, W. 55
Parenti, S. 137
Parker, T.H.L. 153, 199, 200
Parmentier, L. 141
Paton, W.R. 120
Patricius 68, 71, 89, 95, 97, 100, 101, 103, 118
Patrick 301
Patrick, D. 303
Paul, Apostle 13, 14, 15, 16, 17, 18, 53, 131, 156, 183, 192, 194, 195, 198, 200, 201, 204, 205, 207, 209, 210, 227, 230, 253, 260, 269, 270, 271, 280, 288, 289, 293, 296, 298, 364, 365, 379
Paul, R.S. 239, 241
Paula (senior) 131
Paula 66, 131, 132, 133, 195
Paulinus of Nola 37, 65, 69, 124, 134, 135, 195, 208
Payne, E.A. 239
Peeters, P. 120
Pelagius 7, 35, 37, 38, 73, 79, 81, 88, 161, 193, 194, 195, 200, 204, 205, 218
Pelikan, J. 29, 218
Pellican, C. 193
Perels, O. 4
Perowne, J.J.S. 215
Perpetua 17, 61, 64, 65, 267
Peter, Apostle xxxv, 216, 217, 218, 260, 353, 364
Peter Lombard 206, 212
Petschenig, M. 158
Philip 364
Phillips, L.E. 78
Phillips, O. 190
Photius 194
Phypers, D. 268
Pietri, C. 140
Piganiol, A. 140
Pilkington, J.G. 94

Pinian 66, 127, 128
Pitman, J.R. 241
Pizzolato, L.F. 89, 100, 103
Pocknee, C.E. 153, 154, 155, 163, 164, 165
Politi, L., see Catharinus A.
Pollett, J.V. 174
Polman, P. 180, 181, 213, 219
Polycarp 9, 45, 46, 48, 49, 54, 61, 126
Polycrates 9, 61
Pontius Pilate 265
Poque, Suzanne 123
Porphyry 120
Porter, S.E. 46, 51, 53, 143, 159, 210, 344
Possidius 101, 102, 118
Pourrat, P. 106
Praet, D. 259
Price, R.M. 133
Prierias, S. 218
Primasius of Hadrumetum 194
Protogenes 123
Prudentius 132
Pseudo-Dionysius 183
Pseudo-Jerome 200, 205
Pseudo-Oecumenius 193, 206
Pseudo-Primasius 205
Pulcheria 159
Pusey, E.B. 94
Pusey, P.E. 136, 165

Rabbi Solomon 251
Raffson, C. 90
Ramsey, I.T. 153
Rebillard, E. 86
Reeve, A. 194, 197
Reid, J.K.S. 152, 308
Rembert, K. 181, 182
Remigius of Auxerre 162
Reuss, J. 157, 161
Rhegius, U. 214, 215
Ricciotti, G. 140, 142, 143
Richard, M. 57, 59
Richer, J. 141
Riggs, J.W. 347
Rist, J.M. 68, 71, 72, 74, 82, 92, 93, 95
Ritter, A.M. 55
Robinson, J.A.T. 270, 293
Rode, F. 139
Rodriguez, F. 135
Rogers, C.F. xxix
Rogers, T. 215, 216

Rollock, R. 305
Romanus 133
Rordorf, W. 47
Rosner, B.S. 210
Rothmann, B. 166, 187, 190
Rouse, Ruth 180
Rousseau, A. 10
Rufinus of Aquileia 65, 69, 124, 159
Rufinus the Syrian 37, 38
Rutherford, S. xxxi-xxxiv, 246, 250, 253

Sabatier, P. 196
Samuel 34, 120, 129, 131, 134
Sanday, W. 196
Sarcerius, E. 193, 207
Satan 269
Satterthwaite, P.E. 374
Satyrus 65
Scheffczyck, L. 162
Scheidweiler, F. 141
Schindler, A. 76, 77, 164, 207
Schnaubelt, J.C. 101
Schoedel, W.R. 50
Schoo, G. 142, 144
Schrevel, A.C. de 180
Schroeder, H.J. xxvii
Schwartz, E. 134
Schweizer, E. 323
Schweizer, J. 217, 218
Scicolone, I. 137
Screech, M.A. 194, 197
Seaman, L. 250, 252
Seeck, O. 140
Seitz, C. 55
Selwyn, D. 223
Servaes, M. 182
Servetus, M. 229
Severian of Cabala 194
Shaw, B.D. 90
Sheed, F.J. 94
Sherren, W. 90, 101
Sieben, H.J. 194
Simon Magus 112
Simon, M. 19
Simonetti, M. 89
Simons, Menno 180, 185, 188, 189, 190
Simplicianus of Milan 73, 74, 121
Siricius, bishop of Rome 36, 135, 136
Skutella, M. 93, 95
Smalley, B. 206
Smith, C.C. xxix

Smith, H. 157
Smith, R.F. 296
Smith, R.P. 161
Smith, W. 92, 140
Smits, L. 213
Socrates 141, 142, 144
Solignac, A. 76
Solomon 64
Souter, A. 194
Sozomen 140, 143, 144, 145
Spangenberg, C. 197, 204, 207, 210
Spark, Muriel 100
Spital, H.J. 163
Staab, K. 194
Stark, R. 259
Steinmetz, D.C. 294
Stephen 119
Stephens, W.P. 167, 168, 169, 170, 173
Stephenson, A.A. 57
Stibbs, A. 357
Still, W. 359
Strobel, A. 4, 9, 11, 14, 15, 20, 21
Struthers, J. 240, 241, 242, 243
Stubbings, F. 181
Stupperich, R. 187, 190, 198, 215
Suicer, J.C. 55
Symeon Metaphrastes 134

Taylor, J.H. 76
Tertullian 7, 8, 10, 12, 19, 23, 24, 25, 26, 27, 28, 30, 31, 42, 63, 155, 162, 181, 183, 184, 188, 189, 190, 193, 195, 208, 262, 263, 267, 280
TeSelle, E. 37, 38, 42, 82, 85
Theodore of Canterbury 301
Theodore of Mopsuestia 58, 59, 124, 192, 194, 267
Theodoret of Cyrrhus 123, 124, 133, 134, 141, 142, 182, 192, 194
Theodosius II 120
Theophylact, archbishop of Ohrid 162, 193
Thomas Aquinas 161, 162, 206, 243
Thomas, C. 301
Thompson, E.M. 240, 241
Thomson, T. 303
Thurian, M. 279, 313, 314, 315, 316
Thurston, H. 91
Tiller, J. 322, 323
Timothy 46, 280
Tischendorf, C. 196
Tissot, Y. 193

Titelmann, F. 199
Tonneau, R. 59
Torrance, T.F. 44, 152, 270, 292, 304, 305, 344, 356, 362
Tovey, P. 373
Toxotius 131, 133
Trapé, A. 90, 100
Trapman, H. 224
Tréhorel, E. 93
Tryckare, T. xxx
Tuckett, C.M. 378
Twisse, W. 247
Tyndale, W. 287

Ulfilas 65, 124
Ursinus 243
Usteri, J.M. 168, 169

Valdés, J. de 198
Valentine, T. 247
Van Dixhoorn, C. 240
Vanhoye, A. 192
Veer, A.C. de 115
Velkovska, Elena 137
Verduin, L. 23, 185, 213, 214, 215, 221, 275
Verecundus 71, 94
Vermigli, P.M. 193, 208-209
Victorinus 71, 96
Vincentius Victor 77
Vines, R. 253
Vizmanos, F. de B. 130
Vogels, H.J. 196

Wace, H. 92, 140
Wainwright, G. 278, 279, 315
Walahfrid 85
Walker G. 246, 251
Walker, J. xxxiii
Wall, W. 50
Walsh, P.G. 135
Walter of Arrouaise 91
Walter, H. 287
Warfield, B.B. 85
Warner, G. 279
Warren, F.E. 301
Waszink, J.H. 14, 25
Wattenbach, W. 135
Weber, R. 195
Weigle, L.A. 197
Weischer, B.M. 57
Wendel, F. 167, 168, 170, 173, 226
Wenger, A. 33, 56, 58, 121, 190

Wenger, J.C. 185
Wesley, J. 295
Westcott, B.F. 271
Westin, G. 191
Westphal, J. 219
Whitaker, E.C. 150, 346
Whitaker, J. 242, 243, 244
White, R.E.O. 116
Wiedemann, T. 64
Wilburn, R.G. 315
William of Nassau, Count 207
Williams, F. 159
Williams, G.H. xxiii, 181, 182, 220, 223, 224, 275
Williams, H. 301
Williams, M. 296
Williams, N.P. xxvii, 25, 31, 32, 34, 35, 37, 38, 42, 57
Willimon, W. 266
Willis, G.G. 105, 106, 111, 114
Wilson, H.A. 164
Wilson, T. 246, 249
Wissowa, G. 97
Wood, D. 64
Wood, Susan K. 55

Woodcock, F. 250
Wordsworth, J. 140
Woude, S. van der 222
Wriedt, M. 77, 166, 207
Wright, D.F. xxxv, xl, 44, 46, 51, 62, 64, 68, 69, 71, 77, 78, 81, 82, 84, 88, 98, 99, 143, 144, 159, 160, 166, 167, 168, 169, 170, 173, 178, 179, 184, 190, 192, 207, 240, 243, 252, 254, 256, 272, 276, 277, 280, 291, 293, 344, 362, 368, 371, 373, 374, 377, 378

Yarnold, E.J. 86
Yeltsin, B. 248

Zanchi, G. xxxiii
Zechariah 360
Zelzer, K. 159
Zeno of Verona 63
Zingerle, A. 157
Zosimus 135
Zumkeller, A. 95
Zwingli, H. xxxii, xxxvi, 169, 185, 186, 206, 216, 221, 231, 286

Subject Index

Aberdeen 359
Abrahamic covenant 232, 345, 357, 383
adiaphoron/adiaphora 291, 358, 374, 382
adolescents 130, 155
adoption xxiv, 33, 56, 81, 233, 244, 272
adultery 97
adults 4, 10, 30, 35, 37, 57, 66, 68, 74, 75, 81, 85, 155, 176, 231, 233, 234, 251, 276, 352, 363, 365, 379
Africa 36, 39, 72, 78, 94
   African Christianity 225
   African church 213
Alexandria 31, 144, 156, 263
almsgiving 28
American Presbyterian Churches 278
Anabaptism 217, 221, 231, 247, 251, 275-76, 302, 347, 349, 354, 378
   anti-Anabaptism 357
Anabaptists xxxiii, 23, 77, 153, 165, 179, 180, 181, 188, 189, 190, 193, 201, 214, 215, 219, 220, 221, 222, 223, 224, 225, 231, 232, 233, 236, 238, 247, 252, 254, 268, 275-76, 283, 309, 310, 344, 351, 353, 371, 381, 383
anamnesis 317, 318, 319, 321, 329
Anaplus, Persia 134
Anglicanism xxviii, 237, 249, 289, 305, 310, 318, 356, 372
   Anglican orders 162
Anglicans 149, 275, 276, 308, 309, 316, 321, 346
antinomianism 247, 260
Antioch 63, 133
Antiochene tradition 133
apostasy 139
Apostles' Creed 267, 286
Apostolic Fathers 44-54
ARCIC 327
Arians xxiii, 33, 145
Arminians 295
asceticism 128, 130, 134, 138
Asia 45
Asia Minor 8, 9, 10, 20
atonement 19, 270

propitiation 319, 331
Augsburg Confession 217, 218
Augustinianism 37

babies xxviii, 4, 7, 9, 12, 13, 18, 27, 28, 32, 33, 34, 35, 39, 42, 43, 47, 49, 57, 62, 77, 82, 97, 104, 120, 125, 127, 137, 141, 143, 153, 154, 164, 165, 166, 173, 183, 209, 249, 260, 266, 272, 278, 279, 281, 283, 291, 294, 334, 335, 337, 338, 340, 345, 347, 348, 355, 357, 369, 373, 379, 382
babyhood 9, 34, 144, 165, 339, 340
baptism
   administration of baptism 41, 301, 323, 332, 366, 373
   administration of baptism by laymen and women 227, 228
   adult baptism xxix, xxxvii, xxxviii, xxxix, 39, 43, 56, 65, 78, 83, 84, 87, 100, 178
   efficacy of adult baptism xxxviii, xxxix
   age of baptism xxxiii, 6, 8, 9, 10, 21, 25, 35, 36, 51, 61-67, 79, 92, 98, 100, 136, 141, 144, 155, 234, 242, 245, 272, 280
   agents of baptism 107
   baby baptism xxv, xxvi, xxviii, xxx, xxxiii, 4, 9, 10, 19, 20, 22, 23, 24, 25, 26, 27, 28, 29, 30, 32, 35, 63, 67, 116, 153, 155, 166, 173, 176, 177, 234, 271, 272, 273, 276, 278, 279, 280, 284, 291, 295, 335, 338, 366, 368, 369, 370, 371, 372, 374, 375, 377, 383, 345
   baptism for the dead 13, 269
   baptism of blood 27, 261, 267, 270
   baptismal candidates 81
   baptismal clothes xxix
   baptismal community 238, 260, 263, 269, 276, 333, 363-65
   baptismal consciousness 365-66
   baptismal controversies 270, 382
   baptismal formula 152
   baptismal incorporation 19

baptismal initiation 165
baptismal liturgies 20, 47, 61, 79, 151, 153, 162, 163, 176, 248, 332, 373
baptismal neglect 369
baptismal preparation 86
baptismal questions/interrogations 7, 13, 21, 40, 79, 81, 266
baptismal reception 25
baptismal reductionism 88, 260, 356, 369, 370
baptismal reform movement 316
baptismal regeneration xxiv, xxxvi, 244
baptismal ritual 39
baptismal scrutinies 163, 164
baptismal theology 6, 280, 291, 315
baptismal vows 370
baptisms (Heb. 6.2) 365
bath 52
bath of regeneration 58, 273
baptistery xxviii, xxix, xxx, 36, 261
   font, the xxviii, xxix, 71, 77, 90, 150, 165, 190, 248, 281, 303, 357, 375
   baptismal pools xxix
believers' baptism xxx, xxxvii, xl, 4, 5, 7, 10, 11, 20, 35, 63, 71, 100, 230, 268, 271, 277, 278, 281-82, 291, 292, 293, 294, 301, 304, 306, 307, 311, 315, 316, 332, 340, 342, 350, 353, 365, 367, 372, 377, 378, 380, 383
Catabaptists, see Anabaptists
child baptism xxx, 3-21, 42, 68, 132, 352
child believers' baptism 6, 9, 16, 21, 280
Christ's baptism 6, 172, 255, 301
christening 221, 336, 337
common baptism 270, 293, 312
conditional baptism 275, 282
confession of faith 28, 40, 78, 230, 231, 235, 337, 271, 277, 355
confessional formulae 271
conversion-baptism 6, 15, 21, 68, 71, 72, 78, 256, 261, 291, 340, 348, 367, 372
credobaptism 4, 6, 13, 25, 27, 289, 365
cult act of baptism 96

death-bed baptism xxvi, 14, 62, 65, 66, 68, 69, 71, 73, 74, 103, 280, 301
   delay of baptism xxvi, 7, 8, 23, 26, 34, 36, 42, 63, 65, 66, 67, 70, 83, 84, 86, 100, 116, 155, 170, 182, 184, 316
devaluation of baptism 269, 381
Donatist baptism 113, 114
early baptismal rites 7
emergency baptism 8, 12, 13, 20, 21, 27, 28, 34, 62, 222, 227, 228, 302
equivalent alternatives (common baptism) 136, 277-79, 306
ex opere operato 283
efficacy xxx, 109, 113, 115, 242, 243, 244, 283, 313, 314
external baptism 168, 169
faith-baptism xl, 5, 21, 78, 85, 236, 237, 248, 306, 340, 348, 356, 377, 378
false baptism 274
household baptism(s) xxv, 5, 11, 17, 18, 20, 21, 44, 47, 51, 126, 175, 331, 358, 383
imagery xxviii, 266, 365
indiscriminate baptism 174, 338
infant baptism, paedobaptism (see also baby baptism) xxiii, xxv-xxix, xxxi, xxxiii-xl, 3-21, 22, 23, 24, 26-40, 42, 43, 44, 46, 48, 51, 52, 54, 56, 57, 61, 62, 63, 65, 66, 67-87, 98, 100, 121, 125, 126, 127, 130, 136, 137, 142, 143, 149, 150, 152, 153, 154, 155, 156, 158, 159, 161-70, 172, 173, 174, 175, 176, 177, 178, 179, 180, 181, 182, 184, 186-91, 192, 201, 202, 206, 220, 223, 227, 228, 229, 231, 232, 233, 234, 235, 236, 237, 239, 246, 248, 252, 254, 255, 256, 260, 266, 267, 271, 272, 275, 277, 278, 279, 280, 283, 289, 294, 301, 302, 304, 305, 306, 307, 312, 313, 314, 315, 316, 328, 329, 332, 334-49, 351, 353, 355, 356, 357, 358, 359, 360, 362, 365, 366, 367, 368-78, 380, 382, 383
   necessity of infant baptism xxvii, 84, 85

Subject Index

origins of infant baptism 3-21, 152, 179, 186
inscriptions 11, 12, 13, 20, 23, 35, 62, 65, 66, 80, 83, 183-84, 280
interbaptism 269, 333
internal baptism 168, 169
John's baptism 227, 251
lay administration of baptism 249, 303
minister of baptism 107, 238
mode of baptism
    affusion xxviii-xxix, 249, 265, 381
    dipping 248, 250, 251, 252
    immersion xxviii, xxix, 248, 251, 252, 265, 301, 313, 336, 375, 381
    triple immersion 301
    sprinkling xxix, 249, 250, 251, 381
mutual recognition of baptism 314, 316, 328
nakedness 86, 265, 266
    reclothing 266
necessity of baptism 35, 41, 48, 50, 183, 204, 249
one baptism 27, 35, 38, 39, 52, 55-60, 81, 82, 260, 268, 269-84, 292, 293, 296, 299, 305, 312, 328, 332, 364, 373
origins of baptism 3, 7, 21, 44, 51, 61, 279-81
outward ceremony 354
participation in Christ' death and resurrection 313
post-baptismal remission 26
post-baptismal sin(s) 26, 58, 89, 100, 267, 273,
pre-baptismal instruction 47
premature baptism 26
primitive Christian baptism 11, 15, 183
prison baptism 61
private baptism 249, 250, 303
proselyte baptism 5, 6, 10, 11, 15, 16, 17, 18, 20, 251
    proselytes 6
realism/realist language 332, 363
rebaptism 25, 58, 145, 220, 222, 223, 227, 231, 273, 274, 275, 276, 282-84, 291, 304, 313, 328, 351, 374, 378
rebaptizers 274

remedy 57
renewal of baptismal vows 313
schismatic baptism 59, 113, 274
second baptism 25, 26, 27, 58, 59, 270, 273, 284, 304
Spirit-baptism 168, 169, 170, 172, 173, 244
spiritualizing 19
subjects of baptism 5, 10, 21, 43, 47, 48, 115, 227, 286, 374, 379, 380, 382
two baptisms 281, 339
unbaptized Christians 17
unbaptized 85, 261, 263 360, 362, 363, 381
union with Christ 230
validity of baptism 220
visible word 171
water-baptism 168, 169, 170, 261, 268
Baptism, Eucharist and Ministry (BEM) xxiii, 20, 44, 237-38, 276-84, 291, 308-33, 356-57, 369, 380
Baptists 271, 276, 278, 279, 281, 284, 292, 294, 302, 304, 308, 316, 318, 326, 334, 381
    Baptist Union of Scotland 3, 22, 276, 281, 284, 290, 306, 307, 313, 314, 315
    Baptist World Alliance 306
    Scottish Baptists 276, 307, 316
Bethlehem 131
Biblical Theology 288, 289
blessing 116, 137, 149-65
    see also dedication, thanksgiving
Brethren, the 318
Bulgaria 193
burial xxviii, 266

Caesarea 31, 32, 33, 63, 133, 263
Calvinism 286
Calvinists 295
Capuchin missionaries xxx
Carthage 8, 30, 70, 74
    Carthaginian church 8, 155
Cassiciacum 94
Catabaptists, see Anabaptists
catacombs, the 267
Catauas 79
catechesis 9, 86, 120, 123, 163, 188, 267, 272, 357
    catechism(s) 239, 256, 337
    catechists 124

instruction 10, 136, 262, 263, 267
catechumenate 46, 66, 86, 118, 122, 123, 124, 125, 127, 136, 137, 143, 150, 161, 163, 164, 165, 263, 264, 267
pre-baptismal schooling xxx
catechumens 28, 65, 69, 71, 77, 102, 103, 108, 109, 118, 120, 121, 122, 123, 124, 136, 137, 138, 144, 163, 203, 261, 263
Cathari 215
Catholic Christianity 70
   Catholic Church 23, 58, 102, 106, 107, 108, 109, 110, 114, 115, 118, 273, 274, 368
   Catholic tradition 31
   Catholicism 70, 92, 98
   Catholics 77, 78, 111
   universal church 112
Celtic Christianity 267, 301
   charismatic movement 282, 288, 295, 298, 299, 300, 306, 383
chastity 127, 129, 160
children xxvi, xxvii, xxx, xxxi, xxxii, xxxiii, xxxv, 4, 5, 6, 10, 13, 14, 15, 16, 17, 27, 29, 36, 37, 40, 41, 42, 46, 47, 49, 50, 57, 59, 62, 63, 65, 67, 71, 73, 79, 80, 85, 86, 98, 116-22, 125, 126, 127, 130, 132, 133, 137, 149, 150, 152, 154, 157, 158, 160, 162-65, 170, 175, 176, 178, 183, 184, 187, 192-211, 228, 231, 234, 245-50, 252, 253, 254, 256, 262, 265, 267, 277, 280, 292, 294, 301, 313, 314, 315, 316, 335, 337, 340, 341, 342, 344-61, 357, 362, 363, 368, 371, 373, 375, 380
childhood 9, 11, 156, 158, 339
newborn child xxvii
chrism 136, 164, 301
chrismation 265, 313, 329
Christendom xxvi, 88, 214, 239, 267, 278, 307, 327, 335, 347, 358, 359, 367, 371, 373, 376
post-Christendom xxxiii, 256
pre-Christendom 260
Christian emperors 65, 124, 145
church and state 213
Church of England 149, 153, 277, 278, 298, 309, 318, 322, 330, 342, 344, 346, 381
Church of North India 277, 278, 291

Church of Scotland xxiv, xxv, xxix, xxxi, xxxiii, 3, 4, 5, 10, 17, 22, 44, 150, 151, 152, 237, 240, 276, 277, 281, 284, 290, 292, 294, 303, 304, 305, 306, 307, 308, 312, 313, 315, 316, 317, 318, 323, 324, 326, 330, 335, 342, 345, 347, 356, 358, 359, 362, 363, 365, 373, 381, 382
Church Service Society 151
Cicumcellions 213
circumcision xl, 6, 15, 16, 18, 19, 21, 29-31, 34, 41, 47, 53, 62, 77, 171, 173, 232, 233, 247, 249, 281, 347, 348, 349, 351, 352, 354, 356, 357, 383
spiritual circumcision 30
cleansing 69, 107, 169, 227, 267, 313, 315, 354
clerical ministry 135, 136, 137, 138, 144
clothing xxix, 111, 113, 131, 336
Cologne 180, 182
common baptismal certificate xxix
Commonwealth period 304
concupiscence 41
condemnation 37, 230, 353
confessions 237
confirmation 43, 174, 178, 238, 279, 301, 313, 340, 346, 370, 371
congregational churches 310
Congregationalism 304
consecration 34, 46, 105, 113, 137, 172
Constantinianism 213
anti-Constantinianism 221
Constantinian revolution xxvi
neo-Constantinianism 221
Constantinople 55
contamination 208
contract 273
conventicles 247
conversion xxxix, 9, 15, 17, 67, 68, 71, 72, 77, 80, 84, 89, 92, 94, 98, 120, 124, 126, 128, 133, 205, 207, 208, 243, 247, 256, 291, 306, 313, 339, 342, 359
adult converts 6
conversionism 290
converts 81, 88, 282,
Corinth 45
Corinthian Church 15, 19
Council of Carthage 418, xxvii, 62
Council of Chalcedon 349

Council of Constantinople 56, 271
Council of Elvira 66
Council of Nicaea 271, 295
Council of Trent xxvii
covenant xxxi, xxxii, xxxviii, 53,
    172, 173, 175, 178, 200, 201, 203,
    204, 232, 233, 234, 244, 247, 255,
    281, 302, 334, 341, 342, 344-61,
    345, 347, 348, 349, 352, 357, 358,
    383
  covenant community 346, 356, 358,
    360
  covenant people of God 5
  covenant theology 254, 255
  covenantal sign 175
Covenanting Puritans xxxii
creationism 39, 74, 75
credobaptists 290, 293, 294, 311, 312,
    314, 315, 316, 329, 330, 331, 332,
    381, 383
creeds 27, 57, 59, 271, 273, 337
  creedal questions 265

damnation 36, 38
death 13, 37, 42, 50, 51, 66, 74, 75,
    82, 95, 96 99, 104, 113, 121, 124,
    125, 128, 228, 248, 266, 267
death and resurrection xxviii, 343
death of Christ 19
de-Christianization 366-67
dedication 46, 116-38
demons 33, 57, 111, 262
Diet of Speyer 221
Dinslachon (Dinslaken) 182
disciples 9, 364
discipleship 45, 46, 49, 125, 126, 314,
    328, 333
divine promises 229, 231, 232, 233,
    234, 235, 244, 253, 302, 350 353
Docetism 50, 107, 108, 112, 113, 114,
    212, 213, 216, 219, 224, 275
Donatism 23, 76, 77, 78, 92, 98, 105-
    15, 212-25, 274, 275, 276, 304,
    368, 378
double/dual practice 304, 306, 307
  double/dual practice churches 282,
    278, 279, 292, 373, 374, 380
Duisberg 182
Dura-Europos 261
dying children 12

East, the 29, 33, 34, 35, 36, 37, 38,
    57, 82, 273, 309, 325

Easter 6, 18, 84, 86, 136, 163, 264,
    265, 267, 301
Eastern churches 33, 112, 271
  eastern tradition 35
ecclesiological perfectionism 216
ecclesiology xxxii, 107, 173, 174,
    178, 215, 216, 286, 290, 291, 311,
    344-61, 374
  church as the body of Christ 51
  community of faith 357, 370
  community of souls 40
  exclusivist ecclesiology 173
  inclusivist ecclesiology 173
  incorporation into Christ xxiv, 170,
    178, 266, 283, 293, 313, 329,
    339
  infallibilist ecclesiology 215
  invisible church xxxii, xxxiv
  visible church xxxii, xxxiv, xxxvi,
    85
ecumenism 4, 238, 268, 269, 278, 279,
    286, 289, 290, 292, 306, 307, 308,
    311, 316, 356, 363, 369, 374, 382
Edinburgh 304
Effeta ceremony (Ephphatha)163
election 42, 74, 173, 178, 209, 233,
    234, 252, 253, 283
  elect xxxii, 169, 355
England 367
epiklesis 319, 320, 321, 329, 331, 332
Epiphany 136, 301
episcopacy 31, 289, 324, 325, 372
  apostolic succession 325
  episcopal churches 310
  episcopal succession 324
  monepiscopacy 4
Episcopalians 304, 308
eucharist (communion/Lord's supper)
    xxxvi, xxxvii, xxxviii, 18, 92, 140,
    144, 180, 232, 234, 238, 263, 264,
    265, 266, 267, 269, 271, 277, 279,
    295, 302, 307, 308, 310, 311, 313,
    314, 316-22, 327-33, 340, 342,
    346, 360, 362, 363, 365, 369, 375,
    381
  admission to communion 313
  eucharistic community 238, 260,
    269, 317, 333, 363
  eucharistic controversy 216
  eucharistic liturgy 329
  eucharistic theology 299
  infant communion 346
  Mass, the 310

memorial 317, 318, 329
one eucharist 260, 364
pan-eucharisticism 317, 329
paschal celebration 86
real presence in the eucharist 328, 331
reservation of the elements 321
transubstantiation 320
evangelicalism xxiv, xxxv, xxxviii, xxxix, 238, 260, 267, 269, 277, 279, 285-300, 310, 314, 347, 363, 364, 366, 369, 370, 382, 383
evangelical piety 364
evangelical theology 314
evangelicals 320, 321, 325, 345, 356, 360, 374
evangelical paedobaptists 314, 347
evangelism 259, 320, 365
evil 74, 87
excommunication xxxi, 276, 349
exodus 86
exorcism 84, 87, 264, 266
exsufflation 39

faith 27, 41, 48, 51, 74, 77, 78, 80, 95, 110, 122, 169, 175, 197, 198, 201, 202, 203, 204, 208, 229, 230, 231, 233, 235, 236, 244, 245, 246, 253, 262, 281, 293, 294, 295, 314, 327, 330, 331, 332, 339, 340, 341, 342, 343, 349, 350, 351, 352, 353, 354, 355, 356, 364, 373
corporate faith 341
extrinsic faith 350
necessity of faith 235, 312
Faith and Order 269, 276, 291, 308, 309, 310, 314, 316, 321, 324, 325, 326, 327, 332, 363, 378
family/families 21, 46, 192-211, 337
fasting 10
federal holiness 247, 252, 253, 254, 255
fidelis 12, 40, 62, 80, 105, 232
Florence 129
foreknowledge 75
forgiveness xxiv, 30, 32, 37, 40, 49, 64, 108, 111, 112, 113, 125, 229, 231, 260, 264, 273, 274, 281, 354
fornication 97
Fourth Lateran Council 274
France 228, 316
Franks xxix

Free Church of Scotland xxviii, xxxv, xxxix
free will 74
French Confession 242
French Reformed Church 278
Fussala 135

gathered churches 278
Gaul 9, 10, 20
Gaza 120
Geneva xxx, xxxi, 151, 212, 228, 360, 369
Gentile converts 18, 20
gift of the Spirit 28
glosses 161
godparents 176, 190, 303
grace xxxviii, 28, 30, 31, 42, 74, 77, 85, 93, 94, 95, 105, 106, 107, 108, 110, 111, 114, 174, 195, 204, 233, 242, 245, 255, 260, 274, 281, 283, 294, 315, 340, 341, 342, 345, 348, 355, 364, 369, 375
Great Commission xxxviii
guilt 37, 39

Hamilton, Scotland 306
heaven 85
hell 85
heresy 33, 38 57, 58, 59, 115, 222, 223, 224
heretics xxxii, 217, 273, 286, 351
heterodoxy 59, 295
hindrance formula (κωλύειν) 19, 23, 24, 51, 152, 155, 344
Hippo 73, 74, 79, 135
historical evidence 5, 6
historical questions 22
holiness 14, 15, 16, 17, 192, 197, 201, 204, 252, 253, 254, 352
Holy Spirit 27, 34, 40, 50, 78, 80, 107, 109, 110, 111, 112, 114, 169, 170, 172, 178, 217, 233, 244, 246, 260, 265, 269, 281, 292, 293, 295, 296, 298, 299, 312, 313, 319, 320, 328, 331, 332, 340, 345, 353, 355, 364, 365, 368, 370, 375, 379
pneumatology 298, 320
household(s) 46, 47, 70, 91, 95, 97, 102
hypersacralism 360

idolaters xxxi
immorality 231

impenitent 111
incidentalism 321
individualism 290
infants xxxii-xxxvii, 4, 5, 7, 10, 13, 28, 36, 37, 38, 40, 41, 42, 47, 48, 51, 52, 56, 57, 61, 62, 73, 75, 77, 81, 83, 85, 88, 97, 101, 117, 121, 126, 130, 135, 137, 138, 150, 155, 160, 161, 162, 167, 171, 172, 176, 182, 188, 189, 190, 203, 207, 227, 228, 230, 232, 233, 234, 236, 242, 244, 245, 248, 249, 251, 252, 272, 280, 301, 312, 317, 347, 350, 354, 355, 356, 368, 371
    infancy 46, 69, 100, 116, 120, 131, 135, 136, 142, 144, 145, 174, 176, 177, 311, 316
    infant blessing 165, 311, 344
    infant catechumenate 125
    infant consecration 143
    infant dedication 116-38, 159, 164, 165, 295, 315, 358
    infant faith 234, 235, 236, 238, 351
    infant mortality xxxix
    infant presentation 311
    infant salvation 84
    infant thanksgiving 295, 358
infantes 9
ingrafted/ingrafting into Christ xxxi, 172, 244, 255, 302, 353
initiation 136, 142, 149, 150, 165, 230, 235, 237, 255, 270, 277, 283, 315, 346
    pagan initiation 141
innocence 14, 25, 26, 30, 31, 35, 280
innovation 38
inspiration of scripture 285
    infallibility of scripture 285, 297
    literal sense of scripture 287
    perspicuity of scripture 268, 277, 374
    trustworthiness of scripture 297
    typology 157
instrument(s) 244
intercommunion 269, 333
Irish canons 136
Israel 5, 19
Italy xxix, 119
IVF/UCCF 285, 290

Jeremias–Aland debate 4, 5, 22
Jerusalem 57, 128
Jerusalem Church 16

Jesus' blessing of the children xxvi, xxvii, 5, 19, 20, 21, 23, 51, 52, 130, 149-65, 174, 175, 232, 234, 235, 344, 351, 354, 358, 382
Jewish Christians 18
Jewish law/law of Moses 18, 19
Jewish Passover 18
Jews, the xxxiii, 15
Judaism 15
judgement 85, 87
justification 212
Justinian code, the 221, 275

Kaiserwerth 182
King James Version 197
kingdom of God/heaven 37, 38, 40, 49, 77, 130, 156, 159, 160, 228, 286, 313, 314, 328, 340, 351
kiss of peace 264, 265
Kuruman, Botswana xxx
κωλύειν, see hindrance formula

lapsing 263
Last Supper 18, 295
Lausanne 308, 326, 327
Lausanne Covenant 286
lay ministries 322
laying on of hands 19, 163, 164, 174, 220, 232, 264, 313, 329
lectionaries 150
lections 160, 163, 164, 165
lector/lectorship 140, 142, 144, 145
Lent 86, 163, 267
lex orandi lex credendi 29, 32
Lima, Peru 308, 327
limbo 85
liturgy xxv, 7, 46, 188, 236, 318, 357, 368
    liturgical theology 237
Lord's Prayer, the 164
Lord's supper, see eucharist
love 231
Lutheranism 217, 218, 236, 286, 338, 366
Lutherans xxxvi, 219, 276, 308, 309

Macellum, Cappadocia 140, 142, 143
Magdeburg 215, 216, 219
magisterial Reformation 23, 217, 220
magisterial Reformers 77, 166, 179, 180, 219, 238, 275, 349, 371
magisterium 286
Manichaeism 39, 70, 100

Marburg Colloquy 216, 217
marriage 192-211, 245
  mixed marriage(s) 14, 15, 16, 17, 41, 192-211, 335
martyr(s) 61, 128, 129, 133, 135, 223, 259
martyrdom 9, 17, 27, 31, 46, 77, 86, 126, 130, 261, 263, 267
Melitene, Lesser Armenia 134
membership 95, 238, 271, 307, 345, 360, 366
  communicant membership 279, 345
Mennonites 275, 288
mercy 109, 231
Methodism 149, 344
Methodists 278, 309, 310
midwives 136, 249
Milan 37, 71, 72, 95, 102, 117, 118, 121, 164
milk and honey 48, 49
  milk 176
ministry 269, 277, 308, 309, 311, 322-26, 332, 333
  ministers 110, 114, 115
  ordained ministry/ministries 322, 323, 326
  ordination 220, 269
monasticism 158, 159
  monasteries 131, 135
  monastic initiation 159
Montanism 26
mortification 230, 232, 353, 354
Movement for the Reform of Infant Baptism/Baptismal Integrity 366, 370
Münster 166, 214
Muslims xxxiv
mystagogy 86, 376
mystery, the/mysteries 34, 235, 354, 263

neo-orthodoxy 270
neophytes 58
Nepal xxx
new birth xxiv, 99, 266
New College, Edinburgh xxxiii, xxxv, xxxviii, xxxix
new covenant 357
new Israel 5
Nicene Creed 27, 35, 55-60, 267, 271, 272, 273, 274, 281, 284, 306, 373
Niceno-Constantinopolitan Creed 55, 59, 81-82, 271, 272

Nola, Italy 135
nominal Christians 118
non-episcopal churches 324, 325
North Africa 7, 20, 23, 59, 63, 65, 378
  North African church 7-8, 112, 155, 274
notae 230
Novatianists 214, 215, 217
nurses 136

oaths 222, 262
obedience 244, 356
oikos-formula 20
oil 265
oral confession 179
ordinance(s) xxiv, xxxvii, 165, 167, 242, 243, 249, 250, 270, 279, 291, 341, 344, 346, 358, 360, 363
original guilt xxvii, 37, 68, 161, 347
original sin xxvii, 25, 28, 29, 30, 31-33, 34, 36, 37, 39, 40, 41, 42, 50, 68, 81, 82, 84, 85, 87, 161, 189-91, 202, 203, 228, 230, 273, 345
Orthodox Church xxviii, 276, 308, 321, 375
Ostia 72, 92, 95

pacifism 224
paedobaptists 4, 13, 42, 43, 173, 277, 278, 279, 281, 282, 291, 294, 311, 314, 315, 316, 330, 331, 337, 356, 377, 380, 381
paganism 140, 210, 259
pagans xxiii, xxxiii, 8, 12, 123, 263
Palestine 134
papal churches 310
  papacy xxx
  papists xxxii
pardon 313
parents xxx-xxxv, 6, 7, 15, 16, 17, 18, 21, 34, 40, 41, 42, 47, 65, 70, 74, 79, 80, 85, 97, 98, 100, 102, 116, 117, 118, 123, 124, 126, 127, 129, 132, 133, 135, 137, 141, 143, 164, 168, 171, 175, 176, 203, 204, 207, 209, 229, 244, 245, 247, 249, 252, 253, 277, 278, 291, 301, 303, 305, 335, 336, 337, 338, 339, 340, 341, 342, 343, 345, 356, 373, 375, 380
parvuli 6, 7, 8, 9, 21, 31, 155, 157, 182, 183, 189
passover 86

Subject Index

Pelagian controversy 29, 37, 74, 79, 82, 83, 112, 161, 190, 203, 272
Pelagianism 23, 37, 38, 83, 88, 101, 218
  anti-Pelagianism xxvii, 37, 38, 43, 81, 83, 84, 87
Pelagians 35, 36, 38, 39, 40, 42, 79, 82, 86, 217
penance 26, 227, 267
penitential system, the 86
  penitential discipline 8, 267
penitents 48
Pentecost 84, 86, 136
Pentecostalism 334, 383
perdition 37, 209
persecution 6, 259
perseverance 230, 353
Perth 302
pluralism 259, 260
postmodernism 264
prayer 28, 232
preaching 176, 233, 260, 302, 321, 355
predestination 74, 85
premature death 33
Presbyterianism xxviii, xxx, xxxviii, 275, 303, 304, 310, 382
Presbyterians 302, 308, 310, 326
priests 269
profession of faith xxxix, 3, 245, 246, 247, 248, 267, 282, 292, 294, 295, 307, 311, 312, 315, 340, 346, 353, 356, 357, 381
promise xxx
Protestantism 86, 125, 165, 217, 266, 275, 284, 286, 302, 303, 317, 371, 372
Protestants xxv, xxvii, xxxvi, xxxvii, 27, 162, 179, 180, 185, 188, 193, 209, 210, 224, 238, 276, 309, 320, 344
providence 85
puberty 135, 136
puer/pueri 9, 98, 99, 100, 118, 130, 157, 158
purification 137, 169, 267
purity 130, 231

Queen's College, Cambridge 242

Radical Reformation 224

Radical Reformers 166, 168, 173, 176, 178, 188, 213, 214, 219, 220, 221, 232, 236, 238, 302, 349
Reformation xxvi, xxvii, xxviii, 87, 153, 165, 177, 180, 195, 196, 221, 224, 238, 248, 266, 268, 286, 291, 297, 299, 302, 305, 310, 324, 325, 326, 344, 347, 356, 357, 359, 360, 363, 365, 370, 372, 374, 378, 381
Reformed tradition xxiv, xxviii, xxxii, xxxviii, 151, 162, 236, 237, 299, 305, 334, 341, 347, 338, 368
Reformed theology 22, 281, 341, 372
Reformed Christians 276, 321
Reformed churches 166, 218, 239, 246, 302, 303, 306, 308, 309, 316, 342, 356
Reformed evangelicals 345
Reformers xxvi, xxvii, xxxvi, xxxvii, xxxviii, 153, 165, 166, 167, 185, 186, 187, 236, 239, 254, 255, 276, 278, 284, 286, 287, 314, 320, 346, 347, 349, 354, 365, 370, 382, 383
regeneration xxxix, 169, 170, 172, 233, 244, 252, 253, 314, 354, 355
remission of sins 25, 27, 31, 32, 35, 37, 39, 49, 55-60, 72, 74, 82, 100, 106, 107, 108, 109, 110, 111, 112, 113, 114, 190, 204, 208, 229, 230, 244, 271, 272, 273, 345, 353, 373
renewal 170, 172
repentance 26, 28, 48, 57, 77, 227, 233, 260, 349, 353, 355, 364
representation 314
reprobation 253
resurrection of the dead 266, 269
reviviscence of sins 78, 105-15
righteousness 33, 56, 77, 159, 272, 302
rite(s) 270
ritual cleansing 17
Roman Catholic Church xxxvi, 150, 225, 231, 237, 267, 274, 349, 353, 378, 379
  anti-Catholicism 236
  Catholic Counter Reformation 127
Roman Catholicism xxvii, xxix, 232, 303, 320, 356
Roman Catholics xxxii, 166, 168, 179, 180, 188, 210, 212, 217, 218, 219, 274, 275, 276, 295, 308, 309, 310, 321, 327, 378

Roman Empire 19
Rome 8, 9, 10, 11, 13, 20, 36, 38, 65, 70, 95, 127, 131, 136, 154, 163, 164, 263
Roman Church 163
Roman practice 6, 7
Rule of Faith 264, 267

sabbath 19
sacralism 213
sacrament of education 176
sacrament(s) xxxii, xxxvi, xxxvii, xxxviii, 13, 18, 34, 38, 40, 53, 57, 73, 77, 80, 81, 87, 90, 105, 106, 107, 109, 110, 113, 114, 115, 119, 122, 150, 165, 167, 170, 171, 172, 173, 174, 176, 178, 201, 216, 218, 219, 220, 222, 226, 227, 228, 230, 235, 239, 242, 244, 250, 254, 255, 256, 270, 272, 276, 279, 280, 291, 302, 304, 309, 311, 314, 318, 320, 321, 323, 328, 332, 337, 338, 343, 344, 345, 349, 350, 354, 355, 356, 360, 363, 366, 369, 376
Salona, Dalmatia 135
salt 117, 118, 164
salvation 35, 37, 40, 48, 50, 52, 74, 75, 77, 85, 99, 110, 111, 112, 132, 161, 203, 235, 243, 244, 252, 253, 261, 263, 266, 274, 287, 294, 297, 312, 353, 364, 379
    eternal death 214
    eternal life xxiv, 36, 37, 40, 234, 261, 272, 354
    eternal salvation 112, 249
    rebirth 41, 95, 96, 232, 348
    redemption 19, 174
sanctification 34, 56, 81, 105, 113, 120, 192-211, 231, 232, 253, 272
Sarum rite 303
Satan 269
Sbeitla (ancient Sufetula, Tunisia) xxviii
schism(s) 58, 59, 78, 105, 106, 108, 109, 111, 112, 113, 114, 115, 215, 368
schismatics 105, 106, 107, 109, 111, 112, 113, 114, 224, 274
Schloss Angermud 182
Scotland 245, 301-307, 311, 367
Scots Confession xxxi, 302, 303
Scottish Church 151, 152
Scottish Presbyterianism 303

Scottish Protestantism 220
Scottish Reformation, the 220
seal/sealing 13, 35, 52, 57, 120, 121, 122, 123, 136, 203, 209, 243, 244, 253, 255, 264, 272, 281, 302, 328, 345, 379
Second Council of Nicaea 308, 327
Second Council of Toledo 135
Second Helvetic Confession 218
Second Synod of St Patrick 136
Second Vatican Council 150
secularism 337
service of thanksgiving 165
sexual abstinence 127
sign of the cross 117, 121, 122, 127, 136, 164
sign(s) 230, 243, 244, 255, 302, 313, 314, 328, 332, 342, 345, 350
signification 314
signing 117, 264, 265
sin(s) 27, 28, 29, 30, 31, 32, 33, 34, 37, 38, 41, 64, 69, 72, 76, 82, 85, 90, 106, 107, 110, 111, 112, 113, 114, 132, 137, 170, 174, 190, 201, 204, 232, 246, 267, 267, 269, 272, 349, 364
    pre-cosmic sin 32
    sinlessness 14
    transmission of sin 36, 38, 39, 40
slaves 11, 49, 91, 92
Smyrna 48, 49, 50, 51
sola gratia 166, 297, 299
sola scriptura 286, 297, 299, 347, 349
solidarity 40
solus Christus 297
soul 31, 32, 36, 39, 41, 49, 61, 70, 72, 74, 75, 80, 87, 107, 156, 160, 214
spirituality xxxii
sponsors xxxi, xxxiv, 8, 26, 40, 78, 79, 264, 303, 350
state church 221, 366
St Gallen xxix
St George's Anglican Church, Tunis xxviii
Strasbourg 151, 166, 167, 168, 175, 177, 178, 202, 206, 371
subjectivism 290
Sunday School 358, 360
superstition 337
Switzerland 316
symbol(s) 172, 231, 232, 233, 320, 354
    vehicles 320

Subject Index 407

symbolism 48, 62, 65, 86, 230, 248, 261, 315, 345, 364, 379
  water-symbolism 65
Syria 154

Tagaste 68, 91, 92, 98, 100, 128
teenagers 9, 363, 365
thanksgiving for birth 127, 137, 149, 277, see also blessing, dedication
Theodosian code 221, 222
Thirty-nine Articles 286
tradition 32, 39, 184
traducianism 74, 75
transignification 320
Trinity 187, 245, 288, 293, 296, 297
Turks xxxii
Tyndale Fellowship 285, 289

United Free Church 151, 344
United Reformed Church 277, 278, 282, 291, 307, 311, 373
unmarried women 8
unmarried, the (single) 26
USA 316
Uzalis 119

Valentinianism 215
Vikings xxix
Vincentian canon 188
virginity 66, 128, 129, 130, 131, 132, 135, 136, 137
virgins 8, 26, 85, 132, 133, 138, 155
vivification 353
Vulgate 195, 196, 200

Waderdowpers (Waterdippers) 304
Waldensians 274
washing 26, 52, 56, 58, 142, 145, 170, 172, 244, 364

Wassenberg 275
water 47, 48, 50, 52, 57, 65, 75, 96, 170, 174, 227, 244, 248, 249, 250, 251, 263, 265, 266, 270, 271, 305, 313, 373, 379
West, the xxvi, xxvii, xxviii, 29, 31, 36, 37, 38, 42, 57, 58, 67, 68, 82, 83, 133, 135, 136, 138, 162, 212, 239, 249, 272, 274, 307, 309, 335, 357, 367
western Christianity 273, 274
  western tradition 36
Westminster Assembly xxiv, xxxiii, 151, 238-56, 303
Westminster Confession of Faith xxiv-xl, 244, 247, 249, 255, 286, 287, 288, 297, 298, 345, 356
Westminster Larger Catechism xxxv, xxxvi
Westminster Shorter Catechism xxxv, xxxvi, xxxix
Westminster tradition 305
widows 8, 26, 49, 155, 264
witness 231
women, see baptism, administration of baptism by laymen and women
World Alliance of Reformed Churches 306
World Council of Churches 237, 269, 276, 308, 327, 378, 379
Würzburg 164

years of discretion 132
youths 45

Zürich 151, 206, 236
Zwickau prophets 350

Studies in Christian History and Thought
(All titles uniform with this volume)
Dates in bold are of projected publication

David Bebbington
Holiness in Nineteenth-Century England
David Bebbington stresses the relationship of movements of spirituality to changes in their cultural setting, especially the legacies of the Enlightenment and Romanticism. He shows that these broad shifts in ideological mood had a profound effect on the ways in which piety was conceptualized and practised. Holiness was intimately bound up with the spirit of the age.
2000 / 0-85364-981-2 / viii + 98pp

J. William Black
Reformation Pastors
Richard Baxter and the Ideal of the Reformed Pastor
This work examines Richard Baxter's *Gildas Salvianus, The Reformed Pastor* (1656) and explores each aspect of his pastoral strategy in light of his own concern for 'reformation' and in the broader context of Edwardian, Elizabethan and early Stuart pastoral ideals and practice.
2003 / 1-84227-190-3 / xxii + 308pp

James Bruce
Prophecy, Miracles, Angels, *and* Heavenly Light?
The Eschatology, Pneumatology and Missiology of Adomnán's Life of Columba
This book surveys approaches to the marvellous in hagiography, providing the first critique of Plummer's hypothesis of Irish saga origin. It then analyses the uniquely systematized phenomena in the *Life of Columba* from Adomnán's seventh-century theological perspective, identifying the coming of the eschatological Kingdom as the key to understanding.
2004 / 1-84227-227-6 / xviii + 286pp

Colin J. Bulley
The Priesthood of Some Believers
Developments from the General to the Special Priesthood in the Christian Literature of the First Three Centuries
The first in-depth treatment of early Christian texts on the priesthood of all believers shows that the developing priesthood of the ordained related closely to the division between laity and clergy and had deleterious effects on the practice of the general priesthood.
2000 / 1-84227-034-6 / xii + 336pp

Anthony R. Cross (ed.)
Ecumenism and History
Studies in Honour of John H.Y. Briggs
This collection of essays examines the inter-relationships between the two fields in which Professor Briggs has contributed so much: history—particularly Baptist and Nonconformist—and the ecumenical movement. With contributions from colleagues and former research students from Britain, Europe and North America, *Ecumenism and History* provides wide-ranging studies in important aspects of Christian history, theology and ecumenical studies.
2002 / 1-84227-135-0 / xx + 362pp

Maggi Dawn
Confessions of an Inquiring Spirit
Form as Constitutive of Meaning in S.T. Coleridge's Theological Writing
This study of Coleridge's *Confessions* focuses on its confessional, epistolary and fragmentary form, suggesting that attention to these features significantly affects its interpretation. Bringing a close study of these three literary forms, the author suggests ways in which they nuance the text with particular understandings of the Trinity, and of a kenotic christology. Some parallels are drawn between Romantic and postmodern dilemmas concerning the authority of the biblical text.
2006 / 1-84227-255-1 / approx. 224 pp

Ruth Gouldbourne
The Flesh and the Feminine
Gender and Theology in the Writings of Caspar Schwenckfeld
Caspar Schwenckfeld and his movement exemplify one of the radical communities of the sixteenth century. Challenging theological and liturgical norms, they also found themselves challenging social and particularly gender assumptions. In this book, the issues of the relationship between radical theology and the understanding of gender are considered.
2005 / 1-84227-048-6 / approx. 304pp

Crawford Gribben
Puritan Millennialism
Literature and Theology, 1550–1682
Puritan Millennialism surveys the growth, impact and eventual decline of puritan millennialism throughout England, Scotland and Ireland, arguing that it was much more diverse than has frequently been suggested. This Paternoster edition is revised and extended from the original 2000 text.
2007 / 1-84227-372-8 / approx. 320pp

Galen K. Johnson
Prisoner of Conscience
John Bunyan on Self, Community and Christian Faith
This is an interdisciplinary study of John Bunyan's understanding of conscience across his autobiographical, theological and fictional writings, investigating whether conscience always deserves fidelity, and how Bunyan's view of conscience affects his relationship both to modern Western individualism and historic Christianity.
2003 / 1-84227-223-3 / xvi + 236pp

R.T. Kendall
Calvin and English Calvinism to 1649
The author's thesis is that those who formed the Westminster Confession of Faith, which is regarded as Calvinism, in fact departed from John Calvin on two points: (1) the extent of the atonement and (2) the ground of assurance of salvation.
1997 / 0-85364-827-1 / xii + 264pp

Timothy Larsen
Friends of Religious Equality
Nonconformist Politics in Mid-Victorian England
During the middle decades of the nineteenth century the English Nonconformist community developed a coherent political philosophy of its own, of which a central tenet was the principle of religious equality (in contrast to the stereotype of Evangelical Dissenters). The Dissenting community fought for the civil rights of Roman Catholics, non-Christians and even atheists on an issue of principle which had its flowering in the enthusiastic and undivided support which Nonconformity gave to the campaign for Jewish emancipation. This reissued study examines the political efforts and ideas of English Nonconformists during the period, covering the whole range of national issues raised, from state education to the Crimean War. It offers a case study of a theologically conservative group defending religious pluralism in the civic sphere, showing that the concept of religious equality was a grand vision at the centre of the political philosophy of the Dissenters.
2007 / 1-84227-402-3 / x + 300pp

Byung-Ho Moon
Christ the Mediator of the Law
Calvin's Christological Understanding of the Law as the Rule of Living and Life-Giving

This book explores the coherence between Christology and soteriology in Calvin's theology of the law, examining its intellectual origins and his position on the concept and extent of Christ's mediation of the law. A comparative study between Calvin and contemporary Reformers—Luther, Bucer, Melancthon and Bullinger—and his opponent Michael Servetus is made for the purpose of pointing out the unique feature of Calvin's Christological understanding of the law.

2005 / 1-84227-318-3 / approx. 370pp

John Eifion Morgan-Wynne
Holy Spirit and Religious Experience in Christian Writings, c.AD 90–200

This study examines how far Christians in the third to fifth generations (c.AD 90–200) attributed their sense of encounter with the divine presence, their sense of illumination in the truth or guidance in decision-making, and their sense of ethical empowerment to the activity of the Holy Spirit in their lives.

2005 / 1-84227-319-1 / approx. 350pp

James I. Packer
The Redemption and Restoration of Man in the Thought of Richard Baxter

James I. Packer provides a full and sympathetic exposition of Richard Baxter's doctrine of humanity, created and fallen; its redemption by Christ Jesus; and its restoration in the image of God through the obedience of faith by the power of the Holy Spirit.

2002 / 1-84227-147-4 / 432pp

Andrew Partington,
Church and State
The Contribution of the Church of England Bishops to the House of Lords during the Thatcher Years

In *Church and State*, Andrew Partington argues that the contribution of the Church of England bishops to the House of Lords during the Thatcher years was overwhelmingly critical of the government; failed to have a significant influence in the public realm; was inefficient, being undertaken by a minority of those eligible to sit on the Bench of Bishops; and was insufficiently moral and spiritual in its content to be distinctive. On the basis of this, and the likely reduction of the number of places available for Church of England bishops in a fully reformed Second Chamber, the author argues for an evolution in the Church of England's approach to the service of its bishops in the House of Lords. He proposes the Church of England works to overcome the genuine obstacles which hinder busy diocesan bishops from contributing to the debates of the House of Lords and to its life more informally.

2005 / 1-84227-334-5 / approx. 324pp

Michael Pasquarello III
God's Ploughman
Hugh Latimer: A 'Preaching Life' (1490–1555)

This construction of a 'preaching life' situates Hugh Latimer within the larger religious, political and intellectual world of late medieval England. Neither biography, intellectual history, nor analysis of discrete sermon texts, this book is a work of homiletic history which draws from the details of Latimer's milieu to construct an interpretive framework for the preaching performances that formed the core of his identity as a religious reformer. Its goal is to illumine the practical wisdom embodied in the content, form and style of Latimer's preaching, and to recapture a sense of its overarching purpose, movement, and transforming force during the reform of sixteenth-century England.

2006 / 1-84227-336-1 / approx. 250pp

Alan P.F. Sell
Enlightenment, Ecumenism, Evangel
Theological Themes and Thinkers 1550–2000

This book consists of papers in which such interlocking topics as the Enlightenment, the problem of authority, the development of doctrine, spirituality, ecumenism, theological method and the heart of the gospel are discussed. Issues of significance to the church at large are explored with special reference to writers from the Reformed and Dissenting traditions.

2005 / 1-84227-330-2 / xviii + 422pp

Alan P.F. Sell
Hinterland Theology
Some Reformed and Dissenting Adjustments
Many books have been written on theology's 'giants' and significant trends, but what of those lesser-known writers who adjusted to them? In this book some hinterland theologians of the British Reformed and Dissenting traditions, who followed in the wake of toleration, the Evangelical Revival, the rise of modern biblical criticism and Karl Barth, are allowed to have their say. They include Thomas Ridgley, Ralph Wardlaw, T.V. Tymms and N.H.G. Robinson.
2006 / 1-84227-331-0 / approx. 350pp

Alan P.F. Sell and Anthony R. Cross (eds)
Protestant Nonconformity in the Twentieth Century
In this collection of essays scholars representative of a number of Nonconformist traditions reflect thematically on Nonconformists' life and witness during the twentieth century. Among the subjects reviewed are biblical studies, theology, worship, evangelism and spirituality, and ecumenism. Over and above its immediate interest, this collection provides a marker to future scholars and others wishing to know how some of their forebears assessed Nonconformity's contribution to a variety of fields during the century leading up to Christianity's third millennium.
2003 / 1-84227-221-7 / x + 398pp

Mark Smith
Religion in Industrial Society
Oldham and Saddleworth 1740–1865
This book analyses the way British churches sought to meet the challenge of industrialization and urbanization during the period 1740–1865. Working from a case-study of Oldham and Saddleworth, Mark Smith challenges the received view that the Anglican Church in the eighteenth century was characterized by complacency and inertia, and reveals Anglicanism's vigorous and creative response to the new conditions. He reassesses the significance of the centrally directed church reforms of the mid-nineteenth century, and emphasizes the importance of local energy and enthusiasm. Charting the growth of denominational pluralism in Oldham and Saddleworth, Dr Smith compares the strengths and weaknesses of the various Anglican and Nonconformist approaches to promoting church growth. He also demonstrates the extent to which all the churches participated in a common culture shaped by the influence of evangelicalism, and shows that active co-operation between the churches rather than denominational conflict dominated. This revised and updated edition of Dr Smith's challenging and original study makes an important contribution both to the social history of religion and to urban studies.
2006 / 1-84227-335-3 / approx. 300pp

Martin Sutherland
Peace, Toleration and Decay
The Ecclesiology of Later Stuart Dissent
This fresh analysis brings to light the complexity and fragility of the later Stuart Nonconformist consensus. Recent findings on wider seventeenth-century thought are incorporated into a new picture of the dynamics of Dissent and the roots of evangelicalism.
2003 / 1-84227-152-0 / xxii + 216pp

G. Michael Thomas
The Extent of the Atonement
A Dilemma for Reformed Theology from Calvin to the Consensus
A study of the way Reformed theology addressed the question, 'Did Christ die for all, or for the elect only?', commencing with John Calvin, and including debates with Lutheranism, the Synod of Dort and the teaching of Moïse Amyraut.
1997 / 0-85364-828-X / x + 278pp

David M. Thompson
Baptism, Church and Society in Britain from the Evangelical Revival to *Baptism, Eucharist and Ministry*
The theology and practice of baptism have not received the attention they deserve. How important is faith? What does baptismal regeneration mean? Is baptism a bond of unity between Christians? This book discusses the theology of baptism and popular belief and practice in England and Wales from the Evangelical Revival to the publication of the World Council of Churches' consensus statement on *Baptism, Eucharist and Ministry* (1982).
2005 / 1-84227-393-0 / approx. 224pp

Mark D. Thompson
A Sure Ground on Which to Stand
The Relation of Authority and Interpretive Method of Luther's Approach to Scripture
The best interpreter of Luther is Luther himself. Unfortunately many modern studies have superimposed contemporary agendas upon this sixteenth-century Reformer's writings. This fresh study examines Luther's own words to find an explanation for his robust confidence in the Scriptures, a confidence that generated the famous 'stand' at Worms in 1521.
2004 / 1-84227-145-8 / xvi + 322pp

Carl R. Trueman and R.S. Clark (eds)
Protestant Scholasticism
Essays in Reassessment

Traditionally Protestant theology, between Luther's early reforming career and the dawn of the Enlightenment, has been seen in terms of decline and fall into the wastelands of rationalism and scholastic speculation. In this volume a number of scholars question such an interpretation. The editors argue that the development of post-Reformation Protestantism can only be understood when a proper historical model of doctrinal change is adopted. This historical concern underlies the subsequent studies of theologians such as Calvin, Beza, Olevian, Baxter, and the two Turrentini. The result is a significantly different reading of the development of Protestant Orthodoxy, one which both challenges the older scholarly interpretations and clichés about the relationship of Protestantism to, among other things, scholasticism and rationalism, and which demonstrates the fruitfulness of the new, historical approach.

1999 / 0-85364-853-0 / xx + 344pp

Shawn D. Wright
Our Sovereign Refuge
The Pastoral Theology of Theodore Beza

Our Sovereign Refuge is a study of the pastoral theology of the Protestant reformer who inherited the mantle of leadership in the Reformed church from John Calvin. Countering a common view of Beza as supremely a 'scholastic' theologian who deviated from Calvin's biblical focus, Wright uncovers a new portrait. He was not a cold and rigid academic theologian obsessed with probing the eternal decrees of God. Rather, by placing him in his pastoral context and by noting his concerns in his pastoral and biblical treatises, Wright shows that Beza was fundamentally a committed Christian who was troubled by the vicissitudes of life in the second half of the sixteenth century. He believed that the biblical truth of the supreme sovereignty of God alone could support Christians on their earthly pilgrimage to heaven. This pastoral and personal portrait forms the heart of Wright's argument.

2004 / 1-84227-252-7 / xviii + 308pp

Paternoster
9 Holdom Avenue,
Bletchley,
Milton Keynes MK1 1QR,
United Kingdom
Web: www.authenticmedia.co.uk/paternoster

www.ingramcontent.com/pod-product-compliance
Lightning Source LLC
Chambersburg PA
CBHW071434300426
44114CB00013B/1426